AF901365

# Money on the Silk Road

The evidence from Eastern Central Asia to c. AD 800

For Tao, Simon and Nina

Helen Wang

# Money on the Silk Road

## The evidence from Eastern Central Asia to *c.* AD 800

With a catalogue of the coins collected by Sir Aurel Stein

THE BRITISH MUSEUM PRESS

First published in 2004 by The British Museum Press
A division of The British Museum Company Ltd
46 Bloomsbury Street, London WC1B 3QQ

A catalogue record for this book is available from the British Library

ISBN 0 7141 1806 0

Design by Esterson Associates
Printed in England by Cambridge University Press

# Contents

# Tables

# Maps

# Plates

# Acknowledgements

In 1991, shortly after I started working in the Department of Coins and Medals at the British Museum, my colleagues Andrew Burnett and Joe Cribb suggested that I should work on the coins collected by Sir Aurel Stein, and encouraged me to develop that work as a PhD thesis. Michael Crawford was instrumental in the initial introductions to University College London, and Georgina Herrmann and Richard Reece, at the Institute of Archaeology, UCL, kindly agreed to be supervisors. At this stage, I had a little knowledge of Eastern Central Asia, but was a beginner in terms of numismatics. For a long time, their collective faith in me was far greater than my own confidence in the potential of the collection and my ability to do anything with it. I would like to thank them for their continued support, and hope their faith has been rewarded.

This book is essentially a revised version of the thesis, and I would like to thank Nina Shandloff, John Banks, Janet Larkin, Stephen Dodds, Kirstin Munro, Richard Abdy, John Falconer, Rachel Roberts, Andrew White and Elvina Noel for their help in the process of transforming the thesis into a book.

In terms of the financing of this project, my thanks go to Neil Kreitman, who initially funded my post at the British Museum. I am also grateful to Professor and Mrs Ikuo Hirayama, and to the International Numismatic Commission, for providing funds which enabled me to attend the Silk Road Numismatic Conference in Lanzhou in 1994, to travel on to Xinjiang and, crucially, to meet with Chinese scholars in the field. I am particularly grateful to three Chinese scholars whom I met in 1994: Jiang Qixiang of the Xinjiang Institute of Archaeology, who sadly passed away in June 2002; Kang Liushuo of the Lanzhou Numismatic Society and Huang Zhigang, editor of *Xinjiang Qianbi*, as they have generously supplied copies of specialist publications, journals and articles which are otherwise impossible to obtain in the UK.

There is no formal training available for understanding Chinese coins, and I am therefore especially grateful to those who work in the field and who have shared their knowledge and expertise with me. The late Yevgeny Zeymal and Nina Ivotchkina, both of the Hermitage Museum, were particularly kind to an absolute beginner. François Thierry of the Cabinet des Médailles, Bibliothèque Nationale, has been hospitable and helpful in equal measure, and on many occasions entrusted me with manuscript copies of his work long before they were published. Jonathan Skaff shared his work on Sasanian coins found in Xinjiang. Zhou Weirong, Wang Dan and other friends at the China Numismatic Society have also helped by supplying publications and assisting in other practical matters. My greatest thanks though are for my friends and colleagues in Coins and Medals: for Joe Cribb, who has taught by his own example how important it is to 'look at the coins', an activity that can be as rewarding as it is exasperating; and for Elizabeth Errington, Vesta Curtis and Mary Hinton, who have witnessed both the exasperation and the delight.

For the contemporary documentary evidence I have relied heavily on the published catalogues with transcriptions and translations. I cannot read Kharoshthi, Tocharian B, Khotanese or Tibetan, and have been overwhelmed by the kindness and interest of those scholars who can read these very rich sources. I would like to thank Harry Falk and Richard Salomon for their comments on the Kharoshthi chapter; Ursula Sims-Williams, Oktor Skjærvø and Hiroshi Kumamoto for their help on the Khotanese chapter; Takeuchi Tsuguhito and Sam van Schaik for their help on the Tibetan chapter; and Wang Tao for his comments on the Chinese chapters. Their contribution has been invaluable. The errors, of course, are mine.

My family and friends have helped in so many ways, not least with childcare and pleasurable distractions: my parents and siblings, my in-laws, Laura and Jay Rivkin, and Siam Kee Yeoh. Above all else, this book is dedicated to Tao, and to our children, Simon and Nina, with love.

# Introduction

Money on the Silk Road is a complex subject and requires a multi-disciplinary approach. The first striking difficulty is the paucity of direct historical references to money, especially before the seventh century. Very little is known about money in the various kingdoms in Eastern Central Asia before the arrival of the Chinese. Even during the Western Han period (206 BC – AD 24), when the Chinese gained substantial ground in the region and records were made about it, the picture is still by no means clear. The Chinese historical references concerning Eastern Central Asia during the Western Han period present intelligence gathered on the various kingdoms: whether the peoples were settled, semi-settled or nomadic, and the natural produce and manufactured products of those kingdoms. The *Shiji* and the *Hanshu* introduce 51 kingdoms, of which 26 had over a thousand men able to take up arms, yet the only references to coins are to those issued in Jibin (probably Kashmir), Wuyishanli (probably Herat) and Anxi (probably Parthia). In Jibin 'they use gold and silver to make coins, with a mounted rider on the obverse and a human head on the reverse'; in Wuyishanli 'the obverse of the coin is exclusively that of a human head, with a mounted rider on the reverse'; in Anxi 'they use silver to make coin, the obverse being decorated exclusively with the king's face and the reverse with that of his consort' (*Hanshu*, juan 96A; Hulsewé 1979: 106, 115, 117). To the Chinese, these were all foreign coins. The overwhelming lack of information about coins elsewhere in Eastern Central Asia in the historical texts suggests several possibilities: that most of the states did not use coins; that the reporters did not see or hear about coins there; that the coins in common use were Chinese and therefore did not stand out as being different or worth reporting; or that the references to the foreign coins were later insertions, as Hulsewé (1979: 27) suggested, the results of travellers' tales among the rich in the capital.

Archaeological evidence has, however, provided a much richer source to explore, in the form of coins and in the contemporary documentary evidence found through archaeology yet largely ignored in previous surveys of money in Eastern Central Asia. With regard to the different aspects of money and its use, this study opens up a number of possibilities for a new understanding of money on the Silk Road.

### The coins

The impact of Chinese coins in Eastern Central Asia cannot be underestimated. For the period before AD 800, the history of Eastern Central Asia basically alternated between Chinese and non-Chinese control of the region, and to a large extent this is reflected in the coin evidence. The majority of Chinese coin-types are of the periods when there was strong Chinese authority, and even after the Chinese had withdrawn there is strong evidence of local production of Chinese-style coins.

There is no evidence for the use of any coins in Eastern Central Asia earlier than the arrival of the Chinese coins. It is important then to consider how Chinese coins arrived in the region. The most viable approach was through the Hexi corridor (Gansu), an area of such strategic importance that whoever controlled the Hexi corridor also controlled land communications between China and Central Asia. Indeed, it is believed that the Qin were able to create the first centralized state in China at least in part as a result of their control of trade with Central Asia through the Wei and Tao valleys (Eberhard 1977; Frank 1992). During the Qin dynasty (221–207 BC) large-scale building of fortifications (collectively known as the Great Wall) was undertaken in eastern Gansu, at massive human, material and financial expense. Excavations of large quantities of Qin banliang coins in Qingyang, Pingliang, Tianshui and Longnan, and the find of several thousand Qin banliang coins at Dingxi further reflect the importance of eastern Gansu as a stronghold of the Qin. Western Gansu was split among non-Chinese peoples whose economy depended on livestock as well as agriculture. As a whole, Gansu escaped the wars further east, and at the beginning of the Han dynasty in 206 BC had a stable foundation on which to develop economically. Early Han banliang coins have been found throughout Gansu, for example at Yongdeng, Wuwei, Jiayuguan, Tongwei, Linxia, Jiuquan, Dunhuang, Tianshui, Pingliang and Qingyang. A stone mould for casting banliang coins has also been unearthed at Dingxi, clear evidence that banliang coins were being made locally in Gansu during the early Western Han period (GSQBXH 1989).

Archaeologists have uncovered even larger numbers of Han dynasty wuzhu coins throughout Gansu: for example, hundreds of thousands of wuzhu coins have been found at Wuwei, Huixian and Wenxian. Bronze moulds for casting wuzhu coins have been unearthed at Lintao and Qingyang, providing further evidence that wuzhu coins were being produced in Gansu. However, there is little evidence for local coin production in Eastern Central Asia at this time. After the Chinese military victory over Ferghana in 101 BC, many of the smaller kingdoms[1] in Eastern Central Asia sent envoys to the Chinese court to establish tribute arrangements. As the frequency of communications increased, more Chinese outposts were set up and farming colonies were established to ensure adequate food supplies for Chinese troops, visiting envoys and merchants, and chains of watch-towers and beacons were built to mark and guard the routes. The Xiongnu were the main rivals to the Chinese expansion, and Chinese attacks on the Xiongnu continued until the Xiongnu finally submitted to the Chinese in 60 BC (*Hanshu*, juan 96A; Yü Ying-shih 1986: 411; Hulsewé 1979: 73, 78). Eastern Central Asia came under Chinese control and was known to the Chinese as 'the Western Regions'. A protectorate was established with its headquarters at Wulei (near modern-day Luntai), at the approximate centre of Eastern Central Asia. The post of Protector-General (*duhu*) was installed, to take orders directly from the Han central government. High-level posts were introduced under his charge, and they and all the leaders of the various kingdoms who acknowledged Han rule received a seal of authority. It seems that the existence of the Protector-General served to confirm rather than invalidate the authority of the local leaders and their officials who had received Han titles, seals and ribbons of office (Loewe, in Hulsewé 1979: 64). However, the picture of the currency situation in Eastern Central Asia during the Western Han period is still not clear. Some Western Han banliang and wuzhu coins have been found in the region, but the majority have been found alongside wuzhu coins of the Eastern Han period (AD 25–220). It is not unreasonable to suppose that most of the Western Han coins found in Eastern Central Asia arrived with Eastern Han coins. The only possible exceptions are the Western Han coins found at Loulan, which are associated with military supplies, and perhaps also the Western Han coins found at Jiaohe. These were garrison towns of the Chinese troops.

It is possible to look at the Eastern Han coins found in Eastern Central Asia with a little more confidence. Large quantities of Eastern Han wuzhu and clipped wuzhu coins have been found in the region. There is also textual evidence of local metalworking: *Hanshu* juan 96A and 96B record that many kingdoms in the Western Regions were able to make their own iron weapons (Hulsewé 1979). Wuzhu coins have been found near metalworking sites, but as yet no moulds have been found. It is therefore significant that the major hoards of wuzhu coins have been found in the two regions which are known to have produced coins locally: Khotan and Kucha. In the first century AD the kings of Khotan began to issue their own coins. These were the bilingual Sino-Kharoshthi coins, with an inscription on one side in the Kharoshthi script, and a Chinese inscription on the other side. They are found almost exclusively in the Khotan region. Meanwhile the distribution of Kushan coins in Eastern Central Asia is also limited to the Khotan region, with just one exception found at Loulan, at the eastern end of the southern route. The bilingual inscriptions and comparative weights indicate a marriage of the Kushan and Chinese coin systems, which in turn supports the role of Khotan as a land-equivalent of a port of trade. Whilst the coins produced in Khotan combined both Western and Chinese coin traditions, those produced in Qiuci (modern-day Kucha) followed mostly the Chinese tradition. Production of Chinese-style coins at Qiuci appears to have been prompted by the need to maintain the coinage in Eastern Central Asia following the Chinese withdrawal from the region in the early second century, and the collapse of the Eastern Han dynasty in AD 220. Following this, the three strongest economic regions in central China emerged as the Three Kingdoms of Wei, Wu and Shu. Chinese political influence in Eastern Central Asia declined, but Gansu remained under the Wei kingdom, the strongest of the Three Kingdoms. During the early years of Wei rule no coins were issued, and grain and textiles were used as money (Peng Xinwei 1965: 240–6). Later, the wuzhu system was restored but central China fragmented further, and in much of northern China no new coins were issued, and grain and textiles were used in exchange.

In Eastern Central Asia after the Han dynasty, however, coin production appears to have taken place on a very large scale in Qiuci, and the Chinese-style coins from this region are known as 'Qiuci coins'. Exact dates for these coins are difficult to determine, but it is likely they were produced during the Wei, Jin and Southern and Northern Dynasties period, in other words in the period between the collapse of the Han dynasty and the re-establishment of Chinese authority in Eastern Central Asia during the seventh century. As they are found at sites with coins of the Tang dynasty, it can be assumed that they remained in circulation until the seventh or eighth century. The most likely scenario for the development of the Qiuci coins is that small Chinese coins arrived in the Qiuci kingdom, probably as the result of close links with Gansu following the collapse of the Han dynasty. After Qiuci had broken free from Xiongnu control in the second century, the kingdom continued to grow in strength. The territory of Qiuci between the second and seventh centuries is recorded as measuring over 190 km north–south and some 320 km east–west. It was an important Buddhist centre, as well as a trading centre.

In addition to the local manufacture of coins in Khotan and Qiuci, there is also evidence for the use of gold and silver coins in Eastern Central Asia. Although early reports of Chinese missions to the West tell of gifts of gold and describe the gold and silver coins in use to the west of the Pamirs, the earliest physical evidence of gold and silver coins in Eastern Central Asia are the gold Byzantine solidi and silver Sasanian drachms and their respective imitations. These are found almost exclusively in the Turfan region. A glance at the archaeological evidence indicates that only a handful of gold coins (mostly imitations) are known and these have come from tombs at the Astana cemetery. This observation has prompted a number of scholars to insist that they had a special purpose as part of the burial assemblage. But, as Jiang Boqin (1994) and Skaff (1998) have demonstrated, the silver Sasanian coins and derivatives served as the main currency in circulation at Gaochang. Over a thousand silver coins are known, and these have been found in tombs at Astana and also at the Gaochang city site. Another remarkable find was the large hoard of 947 Sasanian and Arab–Sasanian coins found with 13 gold bars in a rock crevice near Wuqia, in north-western Xinjiang, indicating one of the routes by which gold and silver were brought into the region, probably by Central Asian merchants. It is known that the Gaochang kingdom enjoyed close relations with the Western Turks, and that Sogdians acted as intermediaries between Byzantium and the Western Turks. A likely scenario therefore would be that Sogdians took gold to the Western Turks, and the Western Turks took the gold on to Gaochang. Most of the Sasanian coins found in Eastern Central Asia fall into two distinct groups: those of the fourth century and those of the late sixth and early seventh centuries. This contrasts with the dates of Sasanian coins found in central China, where 80 per cent are issues of the late fifth century. These three distinct periods reflect the great outputs of Sasanian coinage in ancient Iran, during the reigns of Shapur II (309–79), Piruz (459–84) and Khusrow II (590–628). It is probable that the Sasanian coins may have arrived in Eastern Central Asia and China by different routes at different periods, probably owing to different stimuli.

It appears that the coins of the fourth century and late sixth to early seventh century may have followed a route through to Qiuci and Gaochang. However, coins of the fifth and sixth centuries appear to have followed another route from Bactria to Wakhan, across the Pamirs, Tashkurgan, Yarkand, Khotan, Shanshan, then eastwards either via Dunhuang, or through the Qaidam Basin to the Koko Nor lake, then via Lanzhou into central China. Sasanian coins arrived in China also by maritime routes in the late fifth century (Xu Pingfang 1995).

At the beginning of the seventh century, there appears to have been some impetus among the states on the northern route, particularly Qiuci and Gaochang, to issue bilingual or commemorative coins, namely the Qiuci script coins and the Gaochang jili coins. While the inspiration for the new style of inscriptions on the new coins may have come from Chinese and/or Sasanian coins, the coins themselves followed the familiar Chinese-style coins. The new coins do not appear to have been made in great quantity, yet they reflect the momentous political changes that were happening both to the east and to the west, and the desire by these states to issue not just new coins but coins that would reflect their independent political authority. This should be seen in the light of the reunification of China under the Sui dynasty (589–618), and the re-establishment in 610 by the Sui government of the Yiwu (Hami), Shanshan and Qiemo prefectures, and the installation of a Commandant of the Western Regions (*Xiyu xiaowei*) to represent the Sui court and manage military and administrative affairs in Eastern Central Asia. The development of communications with this region was considered important enough for the court to order the official Pei Ju (d. 627) to go to Zhangye to supervise trading with the Western Regions in the markets there, and to persuade the leaders of the Western Regions to come to pay tribute at the Sui court: 'The prefectures and commanderies through which the foreign merchants passed were wearied by their welcoming and sending off, the expense for which ran into hundreds of millions' (*Suishi*, juan 67, Pei Ju zhuan; quoted in Peng 1965: 274, n3; Kaplan 1993: 232).

The paper contracts from Gaochang reveal a sudden shift *c.*700 from Sasanian silver coins to Chinese bronze coins, which marks the arrival of sufficient Tang dynasty Kaiyuan tongbao coins into Eastern Central Asia, about eighty years after they were first issued in central China (621), and sixty years after the Chinese took control of Gaochang (640). The abrupt change in coinage can be seen as the result of a political development. The impact of the Kaiyuan tongbao, like the wuzhu, coinage was far-reaching. Supply of coins, or at least master specimens from which local issues might be cast, appears to have been good. Qianyuan zhongbao coins were issued in central China from the beginning of the An Lushan rebellion in 758. In the 760s the Tibetans dominated the Hexi corridor, severed communications between central China and Eastern Central Asia, and isolated the Chinese protectorates at Anxi and Beiting for almost twenty years. Yet the Anxi mint was able to produce local issues of Chinese Kaiyuan and Qianyuan coins, and, independently of central China, to create coins for the Dali and Jianzhong reign periods. The distribution of these coins, like the wuzhu, indicates that they were widely circulated in Eastern Central Asia.

### The documents

It is fortunate that large quantities of contemporary documentary evidence have survived in Eastern Central Asia. They have provided proof to support and sometimes to correct the results of our investigation of the coin evidence. Many of the documents that have survived are contracts. These record the exchange of different types of goods, and as such serve as the documentation of an exchange. Furthermore, as records of loans, advance payments, notation of arrears and general accounts, these documents highlight the element of time that was often involved in making payments or in settling accounts. They also indicate that the hierarchies of different forms of money were not constant, resulting in different hierarchies of money in different regions at different times.

At the Juyan sites in Inner Mongolia, Han dynasty documents reveal that official salaries at the borders were reckoned monthly, and that salary payments were sometimes in coin and sometimes in textiles. On a small number of documents the sources of the coins and textiles from central China are indicated. However, the latter documents all refer to arrears of salary payments, and the sources are the storehouses in the capital city and prefectures. From these examples it is clear that the Han government was prepared to transport coins and textiles over very long distances when local sources were insufficient. The special attention paid to these temporary supplements (their origins were recorded at every stage) indicates that their supply was exceptional rather than regular. The origins of coins and textiles for regular salary payments were not usually recorded. This suggests that in normal circumstances there were probably sufficient reserves of coins and textiles to meet the salary payments, perhaps because coins were already available locally or because the Chinese made coins wherever they went. However, a number of documents indicate that salaries were not paid strictly every month; some show accumulated pay over several months; and others show payments partially reduced on account of a previous advancement. Clearly, there were not always sufficient reserves to pay all salaries monthly. The documentary evidence from Juyan reveals that coins were not the only form of money at this Chinese settlement, and that grain and textiles also played an important role. Officials at the border were paid in coins or in textiles. In the latter case, the quality and dimensions of the textiles were specified, and, in documents relating to salary payments, the equivalent value of the textiles was given in coin. One fragment from Dunhuang reveals that in the late first or early second century one roll of plain silk had a value of 600 coins, which was equivalent to one month's salary for an official at the rank of captain (*hou*). If this calculation can be seen as a convention, it would confirm that plain silk was reckoned by weight at 24 coins per *liang*, and by length at 150 coins per *zhang*, and that these were the standard equivalents, adjustable by means of premiums or discounts.

Although the coin evidence suggests that Chinese coins were widely distributed throughout Eastern Central Asia, the documentary evidence from Niya offers unique evidence concerning money and economic life in one kingdom of Eastern Central Asia where Chinese coins were known but were not widely used. Niya lay between the important centres at Loulan and Khotan, both of which have yielded large quantities of

Chinese coins, suggesting they were indeed in general use there. Yet the Kharoshthi documents from Niya suggest very limited use of Chinese coins at this site, moreover that the people who used Chinese coins were those who had contact with outsiders. More precisely, it suggests that Chinese coins were used for trading with Chinese people. At this time Niya was an independent polity with its own king and government, and day-to-day affairs were not subject to a Chinese administration. Although it lay between important sites on the southern route, and there was frequent communication with Khotan and Loulan both by the people of Niya and other travellers passing through on that route, it would appear that Chinese coins were known and used in Niya in addition to other more established local media of exchange. In the Kharoshthi documents, the value of goods was often expressed in *muli*. While the nature of *muli* itself has yet to be confirmed, it appears to have been a general measure of value, and unit of account. But, although the value was expressed in *muli*, the payments were often made in other forms. The Kharoshthi documents indicate that the indigenous population engaged regularly in exchange of goods, such as textiles and grain. Indeed, the secular documents from Niya concern court rulings on disputes, contracts of sale, records of loans, tax collection, hire and rent. There are sufficient examples of these activities to confirm patterns of exchange of carpets, textiles, grain and animals, and to determine a hierarchy (albeit a hazy one) of items used in payments. Grain was an important medium of exchange, and was used to buy camels. Camels were the most common form of payment for slaves. Horses, camels, carpets, corn and wine were used to purchase land. Horses, cows, carpets and textiles were used in payments of fines and penalties. Taxes were paid in kind, and collected centrally.

Most of the documents from the Turfan region have come from the cemeteries at Astana and Kara-khoja, both associated with the Gaochang kingdom. Many of these have been published. Chinese historians have pieced together over ten thousand fragments from the tombs to form 1,600 documents, of which 250 are contracts. The contracts deal with the purchase of land, houses, slaves, loans of grain, textiles and coins, rent of land and hiring of labour. More importantly, they allow us to track the different forms of money used at different times in the region. From the third to the sixth century, silk and carpets were the main forms of money. After the establishment of the Gaochang kingdom in 502, textiles continued as the main forms of money, although the types of textiles changed from silk and carpets to silk and cloth (cotton or linen). In the mid sixth century a change occurred, and silver coins and/or grain replaced textiles and carpets. There appears to have been a hierarchy, with silver coins preferred for transactions of a superior nature. After the Chinese takeover in 640 several changes took place. Silver coins remained the superior form of money, but silk largely replaced grain as the secondary form. Labour was paid for in silver coin; purchases in silver coins and/or silk, and loans were made mostly in silver coins and silk. After the eighth century, locally made Chinese coins again became dominant.

The fact that most of the gold coins from the Turfan area were found in tombs is significant. Gold coins were seldom specified in the fifth-century tomb inventories; and the change in terminology from weight to coin reflects a change in the status of Byzantine coins in local use in the Gaochang kingdom in the sixth and seventh centuries. Gold coins are conspicuously absent from the contracts, which would further support their special rather than general use.

The Khotanese documents confirm that in the seventh and eighth centuries Chinese or Chinese-style coins were the major form of money in the region. The large quantities of coins recorded in the documents also indicates that the coins were counted in 'strings' of one thousand coins as well as individually. However, coins were not the only form of money here; payments were also made particularly in textiles as at Niya and Gaochang, as well as in grain, livestock and other local produce. The transactions recorded in the Khotanese documents relate to the indigenous population of Khotan; people of Chinese and Sogdian origin are clearly identified as being different. The contemporary Chinese and bilingual Khotanese–Chinese documents from the Khotan region are fewer in number, yet confirm the results drawn from the Khotanese documents. It would appear that Chinese, or Chinese-style, coins were widely used here, but side by side with other local traditions. It is also worth noting that some sort of vouchers were issued in Khotan, possibly indicating the use of credit notes, and perhaps a prototype of paper money.

Again, the documents in Tocharian B, although fewer in number, confirm the use of large quantities of Chinese or Chinese-style coins north of the Tarim Basin in the seventh and eighth centuries. They also highlight the role of the monastery as a centre of economic life, and the mechanisms by which the monasteries functioned.

The Tibetan documents of the eighth century reveal that Chinese, or Chinese-style, coins and grain were the main forms of money during the Tibetan occupation, that coins were used in the purchase of people and livestock, and that grain was used in the purchase of land and property, loans and hiring of labour. The documents suggest a far greater use of coins than was previously suspected, a result that is supported by the Khotanese documents. Furthermore the documents indicate that the unit of one thousand coins was used and that it corresponded with the Tibetan *srang* of *dmar*, which the documents prove was equivalent to 1,000 coins or 1 *liang* [Chinese weight] of silver. There is also evidence for early forms of money drafts, bills and tickets in the Tibetan documents. These, like the Khotanese vouchers, may have parallels with the Tang dynasty remittance system known as 'flying cash' (*feiqian*), which was the precursor of paper money in central China.

The documentary evidence examined in this study has revealed a general pattern showing that although coins were often regarded as the major form of money, they were not the only forms of money, and that there was significant use of textiles, grain and other media of exchange, far greater than in central China. Tax was usually paid in coin or local produce, especially in the form of textiles, carpets, grain and animals. The recurrence of carpets as media of exchange in documents from different regions at different times suggests that these were probably well-established forms of money in Eastern Central Asia; it is likely that they coexisted with coins and that they may have had deep cultural associations in traditions of payment and exchange. Loans, both in coin and in kind, were extremely common, and for various purposes: sometimes to finance travel for trade, sometimes just to tide a family over until the next harvest. Repayment was usually specified in the same form of payment as the loan.[2]

We should also emphasize the role of silk in this context. Silk was produced locally in Eastern Central Asia; it was also imported from central China. Many of the documents found in Eastern Central Asia record the use of silk and other textiles as money, and it is true that the dry climate of the region has preserved numerous examples of textiles at sites and in tombs: various types of silk, cotton, wool, felt, linen and hemp. However, as textiles, and indeed grain, also have a practical function, it would be extremely difficult, and possibly misleading, to attempt to identify the surviving specimens as money-textiles or textiles, and grain-money or grain, unless both the archaeological context and the textual evidence indicated this might be feasible. None the less, the continued use of various kinds of carpets as media of exchange indicates that these were well-established forms of money in Eastern Central Asia.

As a general rule, I have tried to let the coin and documentary evidence speak for itself rather than imposing my own thoughts from the beginning. This is the first attempt on my part to look at money on the Silk Road in such a multi-disciplinary way. In consulting such an extensive range of source materials, this study has drawn little from the very rich sources in the Chinese historical texts, such as the Tang dynasty chronicles. This is intentional, with the aim of keeping the whole study manageable and focused. There are several advantages to such an approach. It was important to be able to accommodate the different types of materials in a simple and flexible way and at the same time to offer a way to confirm or correct the historical records. The results are encouraging.

In the contemporary documents my approach has been to examine the direct evidence for money, with consideration of the linguistic implications. But, I do not read Kharoshthi, Tocharian B, Khotanese or Tibetan, and obviously will have missed out some of the evidence. In many cases I have opened up questions, which a more in-depth study may help to answer.

Finally, why does this study end *c.*AD 800? In the eighth century the Tang dynasty temporarily lost control of the Western Regions. After this, the history of the Silk Road entered a new phase, and other influences, including the arrival of Islam, brought new changes. However, the evidence in the Tibetan documents of the early ninth century was so interesting and so relevant that I felt this material could not be omitted.

## Notes

1. The word 'kingdom' is used for convenience to represent the Chinese term *guo*. The 'kingdoms' were, however, more similar to chiefdoms in the historical sense.
2. The practice of repaying double the loan is not unique to Eastern Central Asia. Hudson (2000: 135–6) notes that in ancient Mesopotamia, Greece and Rome repayments and penalties were calculated as double the original loan. Furthermore, he points out that charging interest is different from imposing a penalty for the late payment of an obligation (e.g. a proportion of one's harvest as tax). In ancient Mesopotamia, Greece and Rome interest rates were usually administered by law and remained constant over time (Hudson 2000: 143). The interest rate was the smallest unit fraction of the local measurement system: in Mesopotamia it was one-sixtieth per month, in Greece one-tenth per month and in Rome one-twelfth per month. Hudson (2000: 136) observed that 'this system did not respond fluidly to market supply and demand'.

Part 1

# Background, sources and the approach

# 1 The Silk Road and the archaeology of Eastern Central Asia

## The Silk Road: fact and fiction

In April 1994, over two thousand years after the Han court had sent its first envoy, Zhang Qian, to make contact with the West,[1] a Chinese government delegation set out for the Commonwealth of Independent States, which had been formed by eleven former Soviet republics in 1991. The delegation's aim was 'to restore the tradition of the Silk Road' (Wang 1996). But what did this mean?

The term 'Silk Road' was coined in the nineteenth century by the German scholar Baron von Richthofen (1878: 454) to describe the land communications and trading networks between the ancient empires of East and West. It is a highly evocative term, conjuring up a rosy image of long-distance trade in luxury goods. Silk is China's most famous invention and export commodity, and represents luxury, beauty and strength. It has very positive associations. The most basic function of a road is to link one place to another, in real terms or as metaphor. In this way, the word 'road' conveniently skirts the more complex issues of political authority, military frontiers and religious, ethnic and cultural diversity. Indeed, the abstract concept of the 'Silk Road' is so universally accessible that it has been translated word-for-word into almost all languages. Following the enormous political changes of the late twentieth century, including China's 'open-door policy', the collapse of communism in Eastern Europe and the dissolution of the former Soviet Union, the 'Silk Road' has become a positive and potent symbol for peaceful international co-operation, and commercial and cultural communication.

By linking the major archaeological sites and historic centres between China and the Mediterranean on a map, it is possible to trace out a so-called 'Silk Road'. However, the history of the 'Silk Road' is a vast and complex subject, and requires the broadest interdisciplinary approach. It is against this background of many different cultures, traditions, languages and scripts, not to mention the physical geography of this vast area, that the hope for genuine and effective co-operation legitimizes the use of the symbolic term 'Silk Road'.

## The many names for this region

The Chinese name Xinjiang ['New Borderlands'] is the shortened form of the Xinjiang Uighur Autonomous Region of the People's Republic of China, the political name for the region since 1955. The region has been known variously in the West as Sinkiang, Sin-kiang, Turkestan, Turkistan, Chinese or Eastern Turkestan (to distinguish it from Russian Turkestan), Inner Asia, Innermost Asia, Serindia, Central Asia, Chinese Central Asia, Eastern Central Asia, High Asia, the Gobi, Chinese Tartary, and Kashgaria (Dabbs 1963). The terms are used specifically or indiscriminately, and the choice of name is often determined by the desire to emphasize the remoteness of the region, the mystery of the ancient world or the Chinese, Turkic or other political and cultural influences in the region. Even the archaeological explorer Sir Aurel Stein used a variety of names as the titles of his publications in preference to 'Xinjiang province', the political name for the region from 1884 to 1955: *Ancient Khotan* (1907), *Desert Cathay* (1912), *Serindia* (1921),[2] *Chinese Turkestan* (1923), *Innermost Asia* (1928), *Ancient Central Asia* (1933).

Such titles reveal the complexity of a region in which many boundaries have changed through history, and which has been home to an ethnically and culturally diverse population. The broader terms 'Inner Asia' and 'Central Asia' are currently used in the West and include Xinjiang. In 1978 UNESCO adopted the term 'Central Asia', defining it as the 'territories lying at present within the boundaries of Afghanistan, the Western part of China, northern India, north-eastern Iran, Mongolia, Pakistan and the [now former] Central Asian Republics of the USSR' (Dani and Masson 1978). In academic circles, the term 'Inner Asia' is preferred; for example, in 1979 the Asian Studies Research Institute at Indiana University was renamed the Research Institute for Inner Asian Studies. In 1990 the Cambridge University Press published *The Cambridge History of Inner Asia* (edited by Denis Sinor); and at the School of Oriental and African Studies, University of London, the Circle of Inner Asian Art and Archaeology was founded in 1995. There is inevitably some overlap in the use of the two terms, as in the case of Joseph Fletcher, Professor of Chinese and Central Asian History, Harvard University, who wrote the chapter 'Ch'ing Inner Asia' in *The Cambridge History of China, vol. 10, Late Ch'ing 1800–1911* (1978), and the 'Central and Inner Asia Register' compiled by The Cambridge Committee for Central and Inner Asia.

Chinese scholars usually refer to this area by its official name, the Xinjiang Uighur Autonomous Region, or Xinjiang for short, or by its traditional name *Xiyu* ['the Western Regions'], found in the Chinese dynastic histories.

In this book, I have used Xinjiang when referring to the region in modern times. When referring to historical times I have used the term Eastern Central Asia with the specific intention of conveying a more precise geographic location without the political and cultural associations inherent in the many other names for this region.

## The geography

Xinjiang lies in the northwestern corner of China, sharing its borders with Mongolia, Kazakhstan, Kyrgyzstan, Tajikistan, Afghanistan and the disputed territories of Jammu and Kashmir (Map 1). To the east lie the Chinese provinces of Qinghai and Gansu, and to the south lies Tibet. Xinjiang is China's largest political unit and covers approximately 1.6 million sq km, one-sixth of the land area of China, and larger than France and Spain combined. It can be divided into five physiographic regions: the Northern Highlands, the Dzungarian Basin, the Tianshan Mountains, the Tarim Basin and the Kunlun Mountains.

The Northern Highlands, bordering on Mongolia, include the Altai Mountains (average height 1,400 m), which slope gently on the Xinjiang side. The Dzungarian Basin covers some 700,000 sq km, and is bordered by the Altai Mountains to the northeast, the Tianshan Mountains to the south and the Alatao Mountains to the northwest. It is open to the east and west, allowing the passage of moist air currents from the west, which bring rainfall in the Dzungarian Basin. A ring of oases lie at the foothills of the mountains, around the steppeland and the desert in the centre of the Basin. The Ertix River rises in the southern slopes of the Altai Mountains and flows northwards to Siberia and the Arctic. The larger Yili River flows west from the western Tianshan Mountains to Lake Balkhash. It is the largest river in Xinjiang, and the Yili Valley is the most fertile river valley in Xinjiang.

The Tianshan Mountains run 1,600 km east to west through the region, thereby dividing the region into northern and southern Xinjiang. The Tianshan Mountains are snow-covered and rise to over 7,000 m. South of the Tianshan Mountains is the Tarim Basin.

The Tarim Basin covers an area of 350,000 sq km. There are mountains on three sides of the Tarim Basin: the Tianshan in the north, the Pamirs in the west, and the Kunlun in the south. The barren Taklamakan Desert, covering some 337,600 sq km, almost fills the Tarim Basin. The Tarim and Kongque Rivers are the main watercourses in the Tarim Basin, and both feed into the Lop Nor salt lake. Many smaller rivers in southern Xinjiang dwindle and disappear in the desert. The low rainfall means that the rivers are the main water resource in Xinjiang. The rivers to the north of the Taklamakan Desert run east to west, allowing a barrier of vegetation to form against the encroaching desert, whilst the rivers south of the desert run south to north and offer little protection from the desert.

The Kunlun Mountains, known as 'the backbone of Asia', rise over 7,300 m above sea level. Dry and bare, they form an almost impenetrable barrier separating Xinjiang from the Tibetan plateau. There are passes at the western and eastern ends of the Kunlun, for example in Jammu and Kashmir, and at Ku'ergan in Xinjiang. The A'erqin Mountains at the eastern end of the range reach into the Chinese province of Qinghai and merge with the Zoulangshan Mountains in Gansu (*TNEB* 1998: 213–15).

### The history

The history of Eastern Central Asia cannot be seen in isolation. The many states of the region lay at the periphery of much larger political entities, such as the Kushan and Han empires and Xiongnu tribal confederacy, and were heavily influenced by them. The early history of the region is known from the Chinese dynastic histories, from Sima Qian's *Shiji*, which was largely based on Zhang Qian's account of the region, and from chapters dedicated to the Western Regions (e.g. *Hanshu* juan 96A; 96B, *Zhoushu* juan 50) and from relevant sections in the general annals and biographies of statesmen, for example *Hanshu* juan 61 on Zhang Qian and Li Guangli (Deng Yanlin 1958; Wilkinson 2000; XJ-History 1987). *Hanshu* juan 96A and 96B were probably compiled from reports filed by 'local administrators, who were required to submit to the (Chinese) Protector-General's office reports which included factual information such as population figures, for the purposes of organizing taxation and liability for military service' (Hulsewé 1979).

The Chinese accounts of Eastern Central Asia are concise, and, inevitably, from a Chinese perspective. As Brough (1965) and di Cosmo (1994) have pointed out, there are cases of inaccuracy and Chinese prejudice, particularly against nomadic peoples, and there is, of course, greater detail in those histories which relate to periods when the region was under Chinese political authority. However, they are the only early historical accounts relevant to the region, and such discussion, especially when combined with archaeological evidence, is helpful in confirming which parts of the text are reliable and which are not. In addition to the Chinese histories there remain the important records by Buddhist monks of their travels through the region from China to India and back: for example, Fa Xian (*c*.337–*c*.422) and Xuan Zang (602–64), whose books have been an invaluable source for studying the history of the Silk Road (Needham 1954: 207–11; Needham 1959: 522–5).

From the seventh century onwards, it is possible to compare the Chinese histories with other historical traditions for a more comprehensive picture of events in the region, as Beckwith's (1987) history of the Tibetan empire in Central Asia has shown. In an earlier publication (1977) he outlined the case for an early medieval *florissance* in Eurasia (600–840) based upon the following important political developments: (1) the rise of the Muslim Caliphate, succeeding the Sasanian empire, to become the major political, economic and cultural force in southwestern Europe and North Africa; (2) the unification and expansion of the Tibetan empire as the major power in central Eurasia; (3) the reunification of China under the Tang dynasty, which became the economic and cultural centre of eastern Eurasia; (4) the creation of the Turkic steppe empire uniting northeastern Eurasia, playing a major role in East–West communications; (5) the development of the Frankish kingdom into the economic, cultural and political centre of Europe; and (6) the transformation of the Eastern Roman empire into the Greek Byzantine empire. The repercussions of these international political developments were felt also in Eastern Central Asia.

General histories of Eastern Central Asia are constantly being revised and refined as new information comes to light from a variety of different sources: archaeology, numismatics, contemporary documentary evidence, from both inside and outside the region (Frank 1992; Adshead 1993; Yu Taishan 1996; Zhang Guangda and Rong Xinjiang 1998).

### The archaeology

Despite the long tradition in China of collecting and studying antiquities, it is only in the past century that the field of modern archaeology has been established. The first sustained modern archaeological fieldwork in China is generally accredited to the Swedish geologist Johan G. Andersson (1874–1960), for his excavation of Zhoukoudian and neolithic sites in north China in the 1910s and 1920s. However, this postdates Sir Aurel Stein's first archaeological expedition to Eastern Central Asia (1900–1) by twenty years or more. Stein's name is absent from most Western archaeological dictionaries and textbooks (e.g. Renfrew and Bahn 1991). Those reference books which do include him tend to focus on his later work in Iran and

Baluchistan and completely ignore his achievements in Eastern Central Asia (Bray and Trump 1982). Why has Stein been ignored? Falkenhausen's (1993) discussion of the development of archaeology in China dismisses the work of Stein and his contemporaries as 'pre-World War I expeditions sent from several European countries into Xinjiang and Tibet – treasure-hunting endeavours which, in spite of their undeniable contributions to scholarship, can hardly be considered as archaeological fieldwork in a strict sense'. This is a damning statement, no doubt influenced by current trends in Western archaeology and the Chinese resentment towards Stein and his contemporaries, commonly regarded as foreign devils who plundered antiquities from China (Hopkirk 1980).

However, for an understanding of archaeology in Eastern Central Asia, the activities and achievements of Sir Aurel Stein and other early explorers should not be ignored. It is more constructive to view them in the context of their own times. The history of archaeology in Eastern Central Asia in fact reflects the fascinating picture of the history of archaeology in China. It can therefore be arranged briefly in four phases, beginning with (1) archaeological exploration by Sir Aurel Stein and his contemporaries in the late nineteenth and early twentieth centuries; (2) archaeological work by joint Chinese and foreign teams in the 1920s to 1930s; (3) Chinese-only teams after the 1950s; (4) joint Chinese and foreign teams since the 1980s.

***Phase 1***

This phase is characterized by the work of Europeans, Japanese and Americans, most notably Sir Aurel Stein (1862–1943) of Britain, Sven Hedin (1865–1952) of Sweden, Paul Pelliot (1878–1943) of France, Albert von le Coq (1860–1930) and Albert Grünwedel (1856–1935) of Germany, Langdon Warner (1881–1955) of the USA and Count Otani (1876–1948) of Japan (Dabbs 1963; Hopkirk 1980). The materials they collected in Eastern Central Asia are now housed in various museum and library collections around the world. The Stein collections, for example, are housed in the British Museum, British Library, Victoria and Albert Museum, Royal Geographical Society, the Ashmolean Museum and Bodleian Library, Oxford, the National Museum of India and the Library of the Hungarian Academy of Sciences (Wang 1999; Falconer et al. 2002). The Hedin collections are in the National Museum of Ethnography, Stockholm;[3] the Pelliot collections are in the Bibliothèque Nationale and the Musée Guimet, Paris; the collections of von le Coq and Grünwedel are in the Staatsbibliothek Preussischer Kulturbesitz and Museum für Indische Kunst, Berlin; Langdon Warner's collections are at Harvard University; and the Otani collections are in the Central Museum of Korea, Seoul, in Ryukoku University Library, Japan, and in the Lushun Museum, Dalian, China (Rong Xinjiang 1996).

Reports of their work enjoyed wide circulation both in the general press and in academic publications. In the nineteenth and early twentieth century there was tremendous interest in China's past and its part in world history. This was stated explicitly in the first issue of the *Journal of the Shanghai Literary and Scientific Society*, June 1858, produced by westerners living in China, and affiliated to the Royal Asiatic Society of Great Britain and Ireland:

> The object aimed at is essentially to bring to light and accumulate facts which may aid in the onward progress of Christian civilization; and it is well known that there are questions of historical interest and philosophical theories in the West, which only await the revelations which this [Chinese] empire, and this alone, can furnish, to supply these lacunae which sometimes leave a doubt regarding the most plausible hypotheses.

For several decades, archaeology in Eastern Central Asia was dominated by foreigners. By the 1920s, growing nationalism in China, encouraged by the Nationalist Anti-Foreign Campaign, combined with fervent protest by Chinese intellectuals, brought an end to solely foreign archaeological exploration in Eastern Central Asia. Henceforth, the Chinese would insist on joint archaeological projects, with appropriate Chinese representation. As Hedin (1943: 16) understood well,

> [It] had borne in upon the learned Chinese world the fact that their native soil contained a wealth of palaeontological, archaeological and other objects of inestimable scientific value; and . . . they asserted . . . that they themselves had more right to reap these harvests than representatives of foreign nations. At the same time they raised the equally natural claim that relics of China's geological and human history should not be taken from their rightful owners, but should hereinafter belong to China and be preserved in Chinese museums.

As Hedin felt at the time, the Chinese press was not so liberal; it preferred that no foreigners at all should be tolerated in China (Hedin 1943: 15–16). The 'learned Chinese world' included such prestigious institutions as the National University of Peking, the Tsing-Hua Library, the National Museum of Chinese History, the Central Observatory, Peking Library and The Art Museum, and, as the joint expedition demonstrated, these bodies were willing to co-operate with foreign archaeologists and the results were fruitful.

***Phase 2***

The most successful of the joint Western–Chinese archaeological projects was the 1927–1935 Sino-Swedish Expedition, which Hedin had negotiated. It is interesting to examine some of the details. There were three proposed aims to the expedition: (1) Deutsche Lufthansa was to finance German air experts and Swedish and Chinese scientists in the establishment of an air route between Berlin and Peking/Shanghai; (2) the Swedish government was to finance a team of mainly Swedish personnel on various scientific investigations; and (3) a feasibility study would investigate, by motor car, the possibility of laying two roads between central China and Xinjiang. Archaeology was just one part of the programme.

The negotiations were not easy and were fraught with cultural subtleties. The first part of the expedition had initially proposed a team of five Swedes, one Dane, eleven Germans and ten Chinese, yet the total number of Chinese personnel varied from day to day. The Chinese complained of racism in the use of the term 'expedition' and wished it to be replaced by 'mission', on the (even more racist) grounds that 'expeditions' were carried out only among blacks and savages, and not in a country with such an ancient culture as China. Although Deutsche Lufthansa had agreed to fund much of the first part, Chinese opposition demanded that the 'mission' should be regarded as a purely Chinese initiative in which a number of Europeans had been granted permission to participate. At one stage in the negotiations, Hedin wrote in the draft contract: 'No archaeological excavation is to be undertaken by the mission except on such a small scale as will not in a serious way hinder the movements of the mission, and the material thus collected requires no special equipment for transportation'. A colleague had him tone it down and agree to 'large scale excavations so long as they do not hinder the movements of a mission'. Eventually, it was agreed that there were to be two leaders, one Chinese and one Swede, and that all the archaeological collections were to be taken to Peking, though after further negotiation it was agreed that duplicates should be given to the Swedes as a goodwill gesture. When it came to signing the contract, Hedin admitted to remarking coldly: 'This is a Peace of Versailles that you want to impose on me'. None the less, just a few pages later in the report of the expedition he volunteered: 'As far as I myself am concerned, I never had occasion to regret my acceptance of the conditions laid down by the Chinese' (Hedin 1943).

One of the Chinese specialists on Hedin's mission was the young scholar Huang Wenbi [Huang Wen-pi] (1893–1958), who had trained in Chinese philosophy at the prestigious Peking University and had been kept on to teach there. Huang was also a member of the University's Archaeological Association, established in 1924. This is more important than it might at first appear, since there was no formal archaeological training in China at that time.

Over sixty years later, the Sino-Swedish Expedition is viewed favourably in China. In October 1992 an international symposium was held in Xinjiang to follow up the results of 'The Sino-Swedish Expedition to the Northwestern Provinces of China 1927–1935 under the auspices of Dr Sven Hedin'. The symposium also marked the centenary of Huang Wenbi's birth, and, to coincide with this double celebration, Huang's reports, collected articles and his diary of the 1927–30 epedition were published in China (Ma Dazheng et al. 1994).

***Phase 3***

The Sino-Swedish Expedition in 1927 marked the formal beginnings of Huang Wenbi's remarkable career in archaeology. Huang went on to make a further three solely Chinese expeditions to Xinjiang in 1933, 1943 and 1957, and became the most important Chinese archaeologist working on Eastern Central Asia during this period. Most of the material he collected is now housed in the National Museum of Chinese History, Beijing.

Archaeological work in China is divided into two periods: before and after the founding of the People's Republic of China in 1949. Before 1949, the first major centre of archaeological research in China was the Institute of History and Philology, in Nanjing, founded in 1928, which concentrated on excavations at the ancient Shang capital at Yinxu, in central China, and neolithic sites in Shandong, and paid little attention to the archaeology of Eastern Central Asia. However, in the 1940s the Chinese archaeologist Xia Nai conducted several important excavations in Gansu, which changed the traditional views that Chinese neolithic cultures derived from the West.

After 1949 archaeology came to be organized under the State Bureau of Cultural Relics (*Guojia wenwuju*), itself a government ministry, and an archaeological framework was established gradually across the country. It is now usually the case that each province and region has its own department of cultural relics. The prestigious Peking University established its archaeology programme in 1953, which it ran from within the History Department. In 1983, archaeology was made independent of the History Department at Peking University to form China's first university archaeology department. Archaeology is considered in the Soviet model as part of the social sciences. Consequently, the highest-ranking archaeological institution in China, the Institute of Archaeology (*Kaogu yanjiusuo*), founded in 1950 originally within the Chinese Academy of Sciences, was transferred in 1971 to the Chinese Academy of Social Sciences (*Zhongguo shehui kexue yuan*) (Falkenhausen 1993: 840; Wang Tao 1997). The current archaeological framework within Xinjiang is discussed below.

For many years the Xinjiang Museum (*Xinjiang bowuguan*) was the sole organization responsible for archaeological work in the region. The Xinjiang Institute of Cultural Relics and Archaeology (*Xinjiang wenwu kaogu yanjiusuo*), based in Urumqi, was founded in 1987, and is currently the only organization allowed to conduct archaeological excavations in the region. For a while the Institute was brought under the aegis of the Xinjiang Academy of Sciences, but this created a number of difficulties. Although the Institute is concerned with archaeology and antiquities, these are officially the responsibility of the State Bureau of Cultural Relics, whereas responsibility for the Academy lies with the Bureau of Education. To solve these difficulties, the Institute now comes under the Xinjiang Cultural Office (*Xinjiang weiwu'er zizhiqu wenwu ju*), itself under the Xinjiang government. In the 1990s the Institute had a staff of over fifty people, working in five sections: archaeological, scientific, curatorial, exhibitions and research. In order to deal with the backlog of reports and to provide an outlet for publishing recent finds and reports, the quarterly periodical *Xinjiang Wenwu* [Cultural Relics of Xinjiang] was established in 1985. Another topical periodical, *Xiyu yanjiu* [The Western Region Studies] was established by the Xinjiang Academy of Social Sciences (*Xinjiang shehui kexueyuan*) in 1991.

These changes mean that two organizations have have been involved in archaeological work in Xinjiang: the Xinjiang Institute of Cultural Relics and Archaeology, and the Xinjiang Museum. The Institute of Archaeology at the Chinese Academy of Social Sciences in Beijing has also sent out teams to work in Xinjiang.

The Xinjiang Museum was established in 1953, and in the late 1950s young history graduates from Beijing and Shanghai were given jobs at the Museum. Many of them have spent their working lives first at the Museum and later at the Institute. Key figures in Xinjiang archaeology, they are now reaching retirement age.[4] In 1990 the Chinese government issued new directives concerning museum and archaeological work, effectively limiting the museums to exhibition work. As a consequence, finds made between 1949 and 1987 are housed in the Xinjiang Museum, and most finds from 1987 onwards are in the Xinjiang Institute of Cultural Relics and Archaeology. Other collections include those of local museums, for example at Turfan and Khotan, and at the Cultural Relics Offices.

The county-level Cultural Relics Offices that are spread throughout the region are part of the archaeological framework and are subordinate to the Xinjiang Uighur Autonomous Region Cultural Department and Bureau of Cultural Relics. They are responsible for maintaining existing sites and for taking in new finds as they appear. Staff at the Cultural Relics Offices do not undertake excavations themselves, but report directly to the Bureau of Cultural Relics in Urumqi, which then liaises with the Xinjiang Institute and Xinjiang Museum to decide whether further action should be taken. The Cultural Relics Offices may consist of only a couple of employees and a strongroom for storing any finds before they are taken to Urumqi, for examination at the Xinjiang Institute or exhibition at the Xinjiang Museum. The Xinjiang Institute of Cultural Relics and Archaeology is reponsible for keeping up to date with the smaller local finds housed at the Cultural Relics Offices.

In July 1998 an important announcement was made concerning changes in policies governing archaeological research and conservation in Xinjiang. These positive changes include construction projects for the preservation of sites; the modernization and creation of new museums; major archaeological research projects, including completion of old site reports; the establishment of a Xinjiang Grottoes Institute; advanced professional training; and exhibitions overseas.[5]

Much of the work that was undertaken during the early years of Chinese archaeology was intended to test the validity of Chinese historical texts (Falkenhausen 1993). This is, however, more difficult to do in Xinjiang. Xinjiang is a region of enormous ethnic, cultural and religious diversity, and archaeology has had a political and social role to play: in establishing the history of the different ethnic groups, at the same time as confirming the historical right of the Han Chinese to govern the region; as a way of 'strengthening unity' and maintaining social stability among the diverse population; and of documenting the arrival and development of Islam in Xinjiang. Another important approach has been of a comparative nature, looking at the mutual influences of Xinjiang and central China,[6] and increasingly, of Xinjiang, China and the rest of the world.

Prior to 1949 there were no museums in Xinjiang, nor was there any Chinese summary of archaeological sites in Xinjiang. In 1953 and 1957 the Chinese government ordered archaeological surveys of sites in Xinjiang, and in 1956 staff from the Institute of Archaeology of the Chinese Academy of Social Sciences, in Beijing, went to conduct excavations in the region, training a group of people from different ethnic backgrounds in order to form a working team of archaeologists. Once the basic archaeological structure was in place, they undertook further surveys and excavation of key sites in the oases skirting the Taklamakan Desert, in the Tarim Basin, in the reaches of the Yili River and on the grasslands north of the Tianshan Mountains. The archaeological work covered neolithic cultures, ancient political, economic and cultural connections, and trade routes. The key subjects were human remains, bronzes and ironware, ceramics, textiles, coins, documents, glass, ancient irrigation techniques, Buddhism and the Silk Road (Map 2). Many of these are also significant for understanding archaeology in central China (Yue Feng and Meng Fanren 1997).

There has been archaeological work at sites throughout Xinjiang, with the excavation of over five hundred tombs at Astana and Kara-khoja, near Turfan, and of tombs in Khotan, Kashgar, Korla and Aksu. Survey work and excavations have been conducted at Loulan and near the Kongque River. In northern Xinjiang there have been excavations of tombs at Yili, Hami, Changji and in the Altai region, and palaeolithic surveys have been made in the Altai region and at Ererqisihu.

***Phase 4***

On 22 February 1991 the State Bureau of Cultural Relics promulgated Regulations for Foreign Particpation in Archaeological Work in China, 'potentially the most important development in Chinese archaeology since 1949 . . . For the first time, Chinese and foreign archaeologists have an approved bureaucratic framework for engaging in bilateral excavations' (Olsen 1992: 1; ZWJ 1992: 20–1). One of the first proposals to be approved under these new regulations was the Sino-French project to excavate the sites at Karadong and by the Keriya River in southern Xinjiang. The project, consisting of personnel from the Xinjiang Institute of Cultural Relics and Archaeology and the Équipe Archéologie de l'Asie Centrale (of UMR Archéologies et sciences de l'antiquité, Centre National de la Recherche Scientifique, Paris), made regular excavations between 1991 and 1996 (Debaine-Francfort and Idriss 2001).[7] Sino-Japanese teams have also been very active at Loulan and Niya (Zhong-Ri 1996, 1999).

Other important initiatives have included issues of conservation, such as the International Conference on the Conservation of Grotto Sites: Conservation of Ancient Sites on the Silk Road, organised by the Getty Conservation Institute (California), the Dunhuang Academy (Gansu) and the National Institute of Cultural Property (*Zhongguo wenwu yanjiusuo*) (Beijing), in October 1993.

The major conservation project at the ancient ruins of Jiaohe, near Turfan, also included excavation and site-mapping. This was a four-year project launched by the Chinese government, UNESCO and the Japan Trust Fund for the Preservation of World Cultural Heritage in 1992 'to protect and restore in a planned way' the ruins at Jiaohe. Fieldwork at the site was completed in 1994, a conference was held in 1995 and the project was completed in 1996 (Jie Yaohua 1999).

In addition to joint excavation and conservation projects, there is also growing international co-operation on projects which aim to bring together material from particular sites, thereby making existing collections more accessible, for more comprehensive research. These projects do not include excavation *per se*, but focus on existing collections and specialist knowledge, and will be of enormous benefit to future archaeological fieldwork and interpretation. A notable example is The Silk Road Project: Re-uniting Turfan's Scattered Treasures, a three-year project (1996–8) funded by the Henry Luce Foundation, which aimed to bring together Chinese and American scholars working in the fields of archaeology, history, art history and religious studies, and to compile a Chinese–English database of all the most important publications and finds from Turfan (Hansen 1997, 1998a). The International Dunhuang Project at the British Library is a collaborative project between institutions worldwide to digitize and make freely available on the internet all their holdings of Central Asian manuscripts. A current aim of the project is to have sixty thousand images from the Stein collections, linked with those from other collections, on the IDP website by 2005.[8] Perhaps the most ambitious of all the current projects is the Mellon International Dunhuang Archive, funded by the Andrew

F. Mellon Foundation, based in New York, to reconnect virtually, by digital imaging, the wall paintings in the cave temples at Dunhuang with the paintings, manuscripts and textiles from the site, now dispersed in various museum and library collections worldwide (Russell-Smith 2002).[9]

### Silk Road numismatics in China

The earliest surviving catalogue of Chinese coins is the 1603 edition of Hong Zun's *Quanzhi* compiled in the twelfth century, which borrowed from earlier texts such as the *Qianpu* by Gu Xuan (d. 549) (Wang Guichen 2000; Tu Yanzhi 2000; Yang Weisheng 2000; Zou Zhiliang 2000). Although there is a long history of numismatics in China, the primary aim of a Chinese numismatist was to build up a full range of coins throughout the ages. Meagre attention was paid to interpreting the coins beyond their initial identification; greater importance was attached to the previous owner of a piece than to its geographic origins. Even today there is no formal training available in numismatics in China.

In 1982 the China Numismatic Society (*Zhongguo qianbi xuehui*) was established to promote numismatics within China (Dai Zhiqiang and Zhou Weirong 1997). With the agreement of the State Bureau of Cultural Relics, the society was set up under the aegis of the People's Bank of China. There are obvious advantages to this arrangement, including access to funds, archival material, modern equipment and a long-established communications network both within China and overseas. The society immediately started a quarterly journal, 'China Numismatics' (*Zhongguo Qianbi*), with international distribution. Local numismatic societies were encouraged, many of which produced journals, though sometimes with limited readership.[10] The China Numismatic Museum, housed at the Beijing headquarters of the People's Bank of China, was opened in 1982 (ZQBXH 1992: 71–8) and major redevelopments were completed in time for the Museum to host the ICOMON conference in autumn 2002 (ICOMON 2003).

In 1989, the China Numismatic Society established the Silk Road Coins Research Team, in which eleven provinces or regions participate, with the guidance of the Society in Beijing, to study the coins found on the Northern (grasslands of Xinjiang and Inner Mongolia), Middle (Xinjiang, Gansu Corridor to Xi'an) and Southern (Sichuan and Yunnan) Silk Roads. The numismatists who attended the XI International Numismatic Congress meeting in Brussels in 1991 were members of this team, and the provincial catalogues of coins published in China are also the products of this teamwork. These include *Xinjiang Numismatics*, edited by Dong Qingxuan and Jiang Qixiang (1991), and *Sichou zhilu huobi*, edited by Zhang Zhongshan (1999). Six major meetings on Silk Road coins have been held, and three major surveys have taken place: a survey taking several months in Inner Mongolia, over 4,000 km covered in Yunnan and Sichuan, and over 6,000 km in Gansu and Xinjiang. These surveys are important ways of establishing the contents of local collections, including those in the Cultural Relics Offices. If a local Cultural Relics Office decides that a find is important it will contact colleagues in the provincial capital, who will decide on further action. If no contact has been made, or if the provincial Cultural Relics authorities have not passed on information to the provincial numismatic society, usually based at the provincial bank of the People's Bank of China, then this information remains obscure. Some coins find their way directly into private collections. Many interesting small coin finds are seen first by private collectors; these may be the result of chance finds or unofficial digging at sites. Valuable finds often disappear quickly to Urumqi or more prosperous collectors elsewhere. The promotion of numismatics and coin-collecting has, unfortunately, also had the negative effect of stimulating production of very high quality forgeries.

Despite the obvious advantages of the arrangements with the People's Bank of China, the major disadvantage is that specialists based at universities or archaeological institutions have not always been able to participate or offer papers for publication in conference proceedings, owing to lack of time or funds (Wang 1995). However, the situation has improved in recent years.

In China, the most important collections of coins from Eastern Central Asia are to be found in the National Museum of Chinese History, Beijing; the China Numismatic Museum, Beijing; the Xinjiang Museum, Urumqi; and the Gansu Provincial Museum, Gansu. The Shanghai Museum also has a significant collection of Central Asian coins, donated by Du Weisheng (1992).

### Notes

1. By 177 BC the Xiongnu had overcome most of the states in Eastern Central Asia, and were able to draw on the resources of the region. These resources were significant, and the region became known as 'the right arm of the Xiongnu'. Zhang Qian's mission, in 138 BC, was to seek military alliance with enemies of the Xiongnu, and cut off its 'right arm'; see Yü Ying-shih 1987.
2. 'The term "Serindia" adopted (in the form Sérinde) by valued French fellow-scholars, is excellently suited for the designation of this region, well-defined by nature as well as by historical relationship' (Stein 1921: viii).
3. For details of the Sven Hedin Foundation, created in 1952 in accordance with Hedin's will, see www.ethnografiska.se/hedinweb/htmsidor/organi.htm, accessed 29 April 2002.
4. They include Mu Shunying and Wang Binghua (both former Directors of the Institute), Wang Mingzhe (Deputy Director of the Institute) and Jiang Qixiang (Researcher, at the grade of Professor, in numismatics).
5. See *Zhongguo wenwu bao* [Chinese Cultural Relics News] 52 (cumulative 617), 5 July 1998. The changes in the policies governing archaeological research in Xinjiang are discussed in http://www.lehigh.edu/~immfl/ecn/mair.html, accessed 3 February 2000.
6. Keightley (1983: xxiv): 'the origins of the Chinese civilization will not be fully understood until the Neolithic and Bronze Age context of the Eurasian steppe as a whole is clarified'. This clearly has implications for the political interpretation of the origins of Chinese civilization. The comparative study of materials is a direct response to the new Chinese school of archaeology, as proposed by the doyen of Chinese archaeology, Su Bingqi. He argued that Chinese civilization was a synthesis of local cultures, challenging the traditional thinking whereby Chinese civilization developed in one location and then diffused outwards. See Wang Tao (1997); Xiang Da (1983: 175–81).
7. The results of this project were displayed in the exhibition *Keriya, mémoires d'un fleuve* at the Espace Electra, Paris, 2001.
8. See http://idp.bl.uk, accessed 16 April 2002.
9. See www.mellonorg/artstor20%announcement.html, accessed 29 October 2001.
10. In January 1997 regional numismatic journals were ordered to cease publication indefinitely. Personal communication from Sheng Guanxi, Editor of *Zhoushan Qianbi*.

# 2 Money on the Silk Road

In focusing on the monetary systems of Eastern Central Asia to c.AD 800, this study covers a period of over nine hundred years in a vast geographical area, with a very diverse ethnic population of different cultures and traditions. It is important to consider first the nature of money, its forms and functions, in a way that is appropriate to these parameters. As the evidence from archaeological sites in Eastern Central Asia indicates that coins of the Chinese tradition were a significant form of money in this period, this chapter also makes special reference to the history of Chinese money.

### Definition of money

Definitions involve meanings and contexts. Taking the statements 'I have money / I do not have money' as a base, it is clear that the etymologies of the equivalent words for 'money' in different languages reflect different monetary experiences which are specific to the cultural origins of the word. For example, the English word 'money' derives from the Latin *moneta*, the name of the goddess in whose temple at Rome money was coined (*OED* 1971: 1836). Its equivalent in Chinese, *qian* 錢, derives from 'a farming tool used in ancient times' (Xu Shen, c.55–c.149). Neither etymology is appropriate to the other, nor immediately relevant to paper money, credit cards, shell money, feather money, cloth money or any other forms of money. Furthermore, neither etymology indicates its function.

Much of the discourse on the definition and nature of money has been inspired by detailed research or first-hand experience in specialist disciplines, such as numismatics, ancient history, anthropology, economics, finance and banking (Smith 1776; Marx 1867; Simnel 1907; Polanyi et al. 1957; Dalton 1976; Melitz 1974; Grierson 1975; Crockett 1979; Burnett 1991; Howgego 1995; Williams 1997). The perspective of the discussant is crucial to the outcome; a modern Western perspective of money applied inappropriately to a traditional non-Western money system will inevitably lead to distorted interpretations. It is for this reason that much of the most illuminating work about money has come from anthropologists. For example, by living among the Lele people in the Kasia District of the Belgian Congo (now the Democratic Republic of Congo) between 1949 and 1953, Mary Douglas (1958) was able to observe the Lele tradition of using cloth money, and how it accommodated other forms of money. The Belgian colonial authorities issued coins and paper money denominated in Belgian Congo francs and centimes. Taxes were payable in the Belgian Congo currency, but in reality were often paid in cloth money at an official exchange rate of 10 francs per cloth. Within the Lele community itself, the Belgian Congo currency was used only as a substitute for payments in cloth, and even then its value had to be translated into cloths. Other objects which were used in high-value payments, such as camwood, salt, copper bars, goats and, before the 1930s, slaves, were also valued in cloths. Some of the young Lele were employed by the colonists, and received their wages in European coins and paper money. By earning colonial francs and transferring them into the cloth system at the official exchange rate, the young Lele were able to acquire more cloth than the older generations, which eventually led to disruption in the traditional cloth system. Douglas's observations identified several different money-objects in use among the Lele, and described the different ways in which these money-objects were used.

Coins are not the only form of money. Furthermore, as Douglas (1958) has shown, a community in which coins are available does not necessarily exclude other forms of money, nor is the coinage in such a community necessarily the dominant form of money.

Since the forms and uses of money vary according to different cultural and chronological contexts, a universal definition of money, whilst desirable, often seems unattainable. However, Joe Cribb (1986) tries to encompass different aspects of monetary experience in different cultural communities throughout the historical period. He defined money as 'any object (or record of that object) which is regularly used to make payments according to a law which guarantees its value and ensures its acceptability', and determined that every object used as money must be payable, measurable and acceptable. Wicks (1992) expanded Cribb's definition of money to 'a convention established in relation to payments which dictates that particular objects with agreed measures of value are recognised as the regular means of discharging the obligation to pay', and expanded the three criteria to 'a physical money-object (or record of that object); an explicit measure of value, which may or may not be identical with the money-object; and a time-related element, regular use'. The two functions of money are to serve in payment, and to serve in the fulfilment of an obligation, whether of a commercial, fiscal, administrative, religious or social nature. In this way, all payments are transactions involving payer(s) and recipient(s).

Cribb's definition does not exclude other useful observations about money. Payment and obligation can have different implications: the fulfilment of a payment is usually quantitative, the fulfilment of an obligation is usually qualitative (Polanyi 1977: 102–6). The quantitative and qualitative elements meet in the 'agreed measure of value'. The distinction made by economic anthropologists between 'general purpose money' and 'special purpose money', the latter used only in specific contexts, is also helpful (Parry and Bloch 1989).

### Coinage: problems and approach

Coins are man-made, usually have the sole function of serving as money, and are durable. Other money-objects may also be man-made, but they may have other non-monetary functions, and especially in the case of organic forms of money, such as textiles, feathers and grain, are often perishable. It is therefore far easier to identify coins as money in an archaeological context than most other money-objects.

Coins are the most familiar form of general purpose money. They are usually small, regular measures of metal with a distinguishing mark of some kind to represent the authority under which they are issued or under which they circulate. Authorities choose to issue coins because they believe there will be some benefit to the state. The act of issuing coinage can be seen as an assertion of political authority and the right to rule, as a means of improving or maintaining social and economic stability, and as a means of financial gain. For coinage to function smoothly, the issuing authority must control it. Coinage is a convention: 'its value is conventionally fixed by the authority of the state with the agreement of the public, it can only function if the value of the coinage, as fixed by the state, is accepted by those who use it; otherwise, market forces will tend to discount overvalued coins towards their individual bullion values' (Burnett 1991). In extreme circumstances the official coinage may be rejected by the public, as in Ceauşescu's Romania, where Kent cigarettes became a more respected currency than the coins issued by the state (Weatherford 1997).

Early names for coins often describe their physical attributes, and have proved remarkably persistent over time, distance and culture. For example, the *dinar* derives, via Syriac, from the *solidus* of the Roman Empire, known as the *denarious aureus* meaning 'gold coin' (Grierson 1975). The English term *cash* meaning 'ready money' is also commonly used to describe all Chinese cast copper alloy coins with a square hole in the centre. It derives from the pidgin English word *cash* meaning a small base-metal coin, derived from the Portuguese *caixa*, from the Indian *karsha* meaning 'small copper coin' (Cribb 1987). In the European cultural sphere, money terms such as 'pound', 'stipend' and 'expense' share the Latin root *pendere* meaning 'to hang', as in a balance. Equivalents such as *libra*, *lire* and *livre* share the Latin root *libra* meaning 'to hang freely' (Grierson 1975). In a similar way, in the East Asian cultural sphere, financial terms often share the same written element *bei* 貝 meaning 'cowrie-shell', an early form of money in China: for example *mai* 買 meaning 'to buy', *mai* 賣 meaning 'to sell', *dai* 貸 meaning 'loan', and *fu* 賦 meaning 'tax'. The comparatively recent coin-names *yuan* (China), *yen* (Japan) and *won* (Korea) share the same original meaning of 'round', and were terms for the European-style silver dollar coins that circulated in East Asia between the seventeenth and the twentieth century (Cribb 1987: 113).

The pressing question then is how to interpret the coin evidence. For finds of Greek and Roman coins, there is already a great variety of guidance and expertise available, in the form of specialist coin catalogues (e.g. the British Museum Catalogues), conventions for recording coin finds and coin hoards (e.g. the Royal Numismatic Society's series *Coin Hoards*) and lists of finds and hoards with an impressive degree of consistency (e.g. the *Sylloge Nummorum Graecorum*). This framework, built by specialists with substantial experience, means that there is some predictability with regard to, say, finds of Roman coins in Britain, and the confidence to engage in statistics and theoretical studies in the world of Roman coins (e.g. Reece 1987; Casey and Reece 1988; Lockyear 1997).

This is not the case for all series of coins, and certainly not the case for Chinese coins. The traditional approach to numismatics in China, whereby scholar-collectors sought to collect rare specimens or a full run of Chinese coins through the ages, with a greater interest in pedigree than provenance, has developed only recently into a more dynamic discipline (see Chapter 1). New catalogues are being produced, for example, the ambitious sixteen-volume Daxi series [*Zhongguo lidai huobi daxi*, 'Great series on Chinese money'] and the more compact *Zhongguo guqianpu* (Liu Jucheng 1989). Whilst these are often improvements on previous catalogues, such as the widely used *Lidai guqian tushuo* (Ding Fubao 1973), they do not match the precision or consistency of the catalogues, lists and sylloges available for Greek and Roman numismatics. In part, this reflects the young age of the subject, and the current state of knowledge and expertise, but to a large extent it reflects also the unique nature of Chinese coins, and the difficulty in interpreting finds and hoards of them.

From the first Chinese scientific archaeological reports, published in archaeological journals such as *Wenwu*, *Kaogu*, *Kaogu yu wenwu* and *Kaogu xuebao*, it is clear that coins are seen as a useful means of dating of a site. But even this most basic assumption is problematic.

The first major problem is the 'wuzhu' coin. This was the major coin-type in China for over seven hundred years (118 BC–AD 621), and occasionally turned up in strings of coins even in the late nineteenth century. There are few systematic studies of this coin-type, and identification of wuzhu coins is rudimentary and inconsistent: it is often not possible to distinguish between official and unofficial issues of different periods, and it is usually impossible to identify the mints that produced them. In this respect, wuzhu coins by themselves often contribute very little to the dating of a site. Indeed, the context, other finds and features of a site frequently offer more accurate information about its date than the coins, and in some cases may be helpful in dating the coins. Rarer and later coin-types of more precise periods and locations of issue may offer more exact information, but, as Chinese coins often remained in circulation long after their official period of issue, they must always be interpreted in the context in which they were found.

The second major problem is the quantity of coins found at sites. Hoards of coins found buried underground or in tombs in China often contain vast quantities of coins, for example, the hoard of 335 kg of coins deposited in Xuchang in the early third century (Huang Liuchun 1992). To examine such large hoards in detail requires significant resources, including expertise and funds, and these are seldom available. As a result, it is quite common for the weight of a hoard in its uncleaned state to be recorded, an estimate of the total number of coins made, and a small sample of coins examined. Such data cannot compare with the details obtained from the fuller examinations of Greek and Roman hoards. Nor are such data consistent enough for detailed studies concerning coin output, rate of circulation or rate of loss.

A third aspect concerns the creation of coins specifically for use in the after life. Coins have been placed in Chinese tombs since the Warring States period (475–221 BC). Imitation coins, made from other materials especially for this purpose, were often part of the burial assemblage. Clay imitations of gold plaques and gold cakes, along with clay imitation coins, have been found in Western Han tombs, for example at Hengyang (Hunan) (Zhou Shirong 1985) and in a tomb at Qingpu (Shanghai), and in Tomb 1 at Mawangdui (Hunan). The Mawangdui tomb also contained bamboo tablets which list the burial offerings, including *jin qian* 金錢 [gold coins or gold and coins] (Hou Ching-lang 1975). Jiang Ruoshi (1994) has established that small, light metal imitation coins were specially produced for burials in the Shaanxi and Luoyang areas.[1] It is sometimes difficult to distinguish between such burial coins and inferior unofficial issues. There was also an established custom of placing small objects of value in the mouth of the dead. Li Chaoquan's (1995) survey revealed that the following objects were used in this way: small stone and clay beads during the late neolithic; widespread use of jade and cowries during the Shang and Zhou; and coins from the Han dynasty onwards, and especially during the Sui and Tang dynasties. For example, ten of the 29 Sui tombs excavated at Anyang revealed bodies with one or two coins in the mouth (CASSIA–Anyang 1981). This custom is also known from excavations in Eastern Central Asia, particularly at sites associated with the Gaochang kingdom (see Chapters 7 and 9). Whilst Odani (1990) claims that Greek and Central Asian burials with a coin found in the mouth predate similar finds in China, it is possible that the custom developed independently in Europe and Asia.

A fourth aspect concerns the specific cultural associations with money. The widespread use of money in everyday Han dynasty life, and the vast profits made by certain individuals, led to a *de facto* money cult, the expression of which culminated in Lu Bao's essay *Qianshenlun* [The Money God] in the fourth century. The essay describes the power and influence of money, with the Money God as the personification of this idea (Hu Jichuang 1988: 322–5):[2]

> Money is a spiritual thing. It has no rank yet is revered; it has no status yet is welcomed. Where there is money, danger will turn to peace and death will give life. Where money slips away, honour will turn to baseness and life will give death. They say 'Money holds power over the spirits' – if that is true, just think of its power over men!

Coins were symbols of portable power: if the round coin represented the domed heavens and its square hole the earth, then heaven and earth were joined in the coin. From the Han dynasty onwards, amulets were made in the form of coins: some kept the wuzhu inscription and added the image of a dragon.[3] The Chinese coin-form tallied with certain philosophical ideas, such as the concept of yin and yang (front and back of the coin), and the *wuxing* [Five Directions] (north, south, east, west and centre). The *wuxing* inspired a passion for grouping things in fives, and the wuzhu inscription (wuzhu means 'five grains') can be interpreted in that light on the amulets. Philosophical ideas of the cosmos are also found on amulets of the Han and Wei dynasties, with representations of the plough constellation, and the 'Spirits of the Four Directions' (green dragon = east, white tiger = west, red bird = south, Xuanwu = north)[4] (Guo Ruoyu 1998: 3). Other coin-shaped amulets incorporated auspicious or apotropaic designs, such as the fish, symbol of abundance.

It would be unrealistic, given the young age of numismatics in China, the current level of expertise and resources, and the particular nature and problems of dealing with Chinese coin finds, to expect in a study of Chinese coins the kind of results which might emerge following a study of Greek or Roman coins. For now, the most sensible way to approach Chinese coins from an archaeological context is to follow whichever sound routes yield reliable results. For example, whilst it is impossible to do a conventional die-study on a coinage that had no dies, Thierry (1997a) has shown how careful examination of a particular series of cast coins can reveal links in the moulds, which reveal the development of that series. There is still plenty of basic groundwork to do, especially in collating all the available numismatic data, historical references and contemporary documentary evidence, and drawing sensible conclusions from these materials, even if those conclusions are sometimes sparse and not entirely satisfactory. This is also true for studying the coins of Eastern Central Asia. As the majority of coins in this study are Chinese or local issues influenced by the Chinese tradition, it is important to be aware of the history of money in China.

### Chinese coins

It is generally agreed that Chinese coinage developed independently of the Western tradition: until the late nineteenth century all Chinese coins were cast in moulds; they were usually made in a copper alloy; gold and silver coins were 'special-purpose money' often for use within the court; they have a square hole in the centre; and they have an inscription but not a pictorial design (Peng Xinwei 1965; Su Qing 1984; Thierry 1992, 1998).

Round coins first appeared in central China in the fourth century BC, during the Warring States period, and gradually spread to all the major states except Chu. The form is thought to be modelled on the round jade *bi* disks, which had round holes in the centre and were symbols of heavenly power. The states of Wei, Han and Zhao issued coins with a round hole in the centre, and the states of Yan, Qi and Qin issued coins with a square hole. Immediately prior to the unification of the Qin empire in 221 BC, round coins were present in most of the states, which no doubt facilitated the Qin unification of the currency with its own 'banliang' coin.

Discoveries of banliang coins at Yongzheng (Shaanxi), Zhangpu (Shaanxi), Yaoxian (Sichuan) and Qingchuan (Sichuan) have proved that banliang coins were already being produced about a century before the Qin unification. Thierry (1998: 27; 1999) summarizes the periodization of the early banliang: those issued during the reigns of Dukes Xian (384–362 BC) and Xiao (361–358 BC) were thick, heavy coins, with irregular characters in high relief, and a diameter of more than 30 mm; those from the reign of King Huiwen (331–325 BC) onwards were thinner and lighter, with a more regular calligraphy. However, Qin legal documentation of the mid third century stipulated the following:[5] all coins were to be used at par, and there was to be no selection of coins during transactions; state revenues were to be collected in vessels, with 1,000 coins per vessel, and each full vessel was to be sealed; coins were to be used according to the state exchange rate against gold and textiles; price tags were to be attached to all items for sale; any coins collected by non-state traders were to be placed immediately in the collecting vessels, with the market supervisor's assistance; and penalties were to be imposed upon officials who did not comply with the rules. Several sealed vessels containing 1,000 coins have been found, including one at Liutancun (Gansu) (Thierry 1999: 170–1). The inscription *banliang* translates as 'half-ounce', but, as the contemporary documents and sealed vessels prove, these coins circulated not according to weight but according to the single unit, collected officially in larger units of 1,000. The first universal Chinese coin was therefore, by intention, fiduciary. The existence of sealed pots containing 1,000 coins suggests that there was some success in the implementation of this fiduciary coinage, but it was unlikely to be enforceable in all contexts. Any disparities in the quality or quantity of coins available in circulation were probably managed by adjusting the official rate by means of discounts and premiums.

Following the Qin unification of the Warring States in 221 BC, the new empire's coinage was unified in the form of the banliang. The Qin monetary system was bi-metallic, using gold and bronze coins, and based on the weight measures *liang* 兩 [ounce] and *zhu* 銖 [grain], where 1 *liang* = 24 *zhu*. Gold was measured by the *yi* 溢 where 1 *yi* = 20 *liang*. Each banliang coin therefore had a nominal weight of 12 *zhu*.

After the fall of the Qin dynasty in 206 BC, the first Han emperor allowed the people to cast coins appropriate for their needs. The unofficial coins were smaller than the officially issued Qin coins, and, after a series of reforms, the Han government issued banliang weighing *c.*3 g and measuring *c.*25 mm. Banliang coins of the early Han period are the earliest coins found in Eastern Central Asia (see Chapter 4). After further trials, a new coin, the wuzhu, was created in 118 BC. Again, the inscription was a weight term: *wuhzu* means 'five grains'. The wuzhu coinage was widely accepted, and the majority of coins found in Eastern Central Asia are wuzhu coins, or coins modelled on the wuzhu.

The inscription 'wuzhu' persisted on coins for over seven hundred years, from the creation of the wuzhu coinage in 118 BC to its abolition in AD 621. However, there were attempts to revolutionize the coinage during Wang Mang's Xin dynasty (AD 9–23), and during the Northern Zhou dynasty (AD 557–81). The impetus to change the coinage came from the apparent contradiction of having a fiduciary coinage where the coin inscription indicated a precise weight. Wang Mang's reforms were inspired by classical texts, especially the *Zhouli*.[6] He sought to align coin-names and money-objects according to the *Zhouli*, and issued money with token values in the form of knives (in denominations of 5,000 and 500), spades (in denominations of 1,000, 500, 300, 200 and 100), round coins (in denominations of 50, 40, 30, 20, 10 and 1), turtle shells and cowries. The reforms failed for several reasons: the system itself was too complicated, the political situation was not stable enough to support it; and the correlation between the values and the objects was complicated by the rising cost of copper. The philosophy behind Wang Mang's coinage inspired the reforms of the Northern Zhou rulers (557–81), who sought to replace the wuzhu with three round coins, the inscriptions of which again harked back to ancient times: *buquan* [spade money], *wuxing dabu* [large spade of the Five Directions], *Yongtong wanguo* [circulating for ever in ten thousand kingdoms]. In spite of these reforms, the wuzhu remained the most important coin-type between the Han and the Tang dynasties.

The Tang reform of 621 abolished the wuzhu, and replaced it with the Kaiyuan tongbao coin. *Kaiyuan* meant 'new beginning', and the new inscription marked the first use in coin inscriptions of *tongbao* 通寶 [circulating treasure] meaning 'coin'. From this time on, until the early twentieth century, all Chinese coins would have a four-character inscription ending in *bao*. The Kaiyuan tongbao, like the wuzhu, was a copper alloy coin with an abstract value of one. The only way to cope with rises in the price of copper was to issue higher denomination token money. When the the higher denomination token money was in coin form, any proportional disparity in weight between the token issue and the base unit provided a profitable opportunity for coin-forgers and could lead to financial crisis (Thierry 1992: 14–15).

During the period between the Han and the Tang dynasty, when central China was fragmented into many states, there were long periods without regular coin production. None the less, enormous hoards of coins are found from this period, for example the 335 kg of coins deposited in Xuchang in the early third century (Huang Liuchun 1992). Existing coins continued to be used, and new coin-types were issued, some with wider circulation than others. Other forms of money were also adopted, in particular grain and textiles, which had had a monetary function since ancient times.

Although a convenient, portable and durable form of money, coins were not seen as desirable money-objects by all. Early debates on money focused on the inherent value of money, and its lack of any non-monetary function. The Agrarians favoured a return to barter, and the Confucians (late fourth to early third century BC) supported them, arguing for division of labour and an economy of exchange. In the *Guanzi* (attributed to Guang Gong, of the seventh century BC, but probably compiled in the Han dynasty) it was agreed that coins had only one function, to serve as money, but that this function had great political potential. The text touches on fiscal control, valuation of money, the quantity theory of money (if goods are many, they will be cheap), price control, control of money supply, speed of circulation and volume of exchange (Peng Xinwei 1965: 98–102; Hu Jichuang 1988). The *Guanzi* also included legendary accounts of the origins of coinage:[7]

> When Tang suffered seven years of drought and Yu suffered five years of floods, there were people who lacked even gruel to eat and those who were forced to sell their children. To rescue these people, Tang coined money from the metal of Mount Zhuang, and Yu did likewise from the metal of Mount Li.

The view of money as a politically created social device was still being promoted in the nineteenth century. Chinese governments issued Chinese coins for the daily needs of the ordinary people; the merchants, it was thought, could look after themselves.[8]

After the unification of the Warring States, Qin and Han discussions on money naturally concentrated on the privilege of coining; coinage had been a local issue during the Warring States period, and the Qin and Han dynasties had centralized governments. The Legalists argued in favour of a government monopoly of coinage; the Confucians argued against it, most notably in the famous court debate known as the *Yantielun* [Discourses on Salt and Iron] of AD 81.[9] There were also proposals, for example by Gong Yu (123–44 BC), for the abolition of coinage in favour of grain and textiles, so as to alleviate hardship for the people, but these were rejected. During the Eastern Han, the steep rise in the price of grain between AD 76 and 89 and insufficient government revenues available to cover expenses stimulated discussions on the relationship between money and prices. These were heightened as the situation worsened in the late Eastern Han and regularization of the coinage became urgent.

During the Jin (265–420), and Northern and Southern Dynasties (420–589), when coin production was irregular and seldom sufficient in quantity or quality, discussion again turned to the value of coins: whether the value of a coin lay in its metal content (the bullionist view), whether a coin's value was nominal rather than physical (the nominalist view), and whether 'valueless' coins should be abolished and replaced with 'useful' grain and textiles (the objectivist view). A key factor driving the objectivists was the difficulty in transporting goods to remote areas or disaster zones, even when it was financially possible to do so. The main counter-argument against objectivists was that coinage enriched the state.

Shortly after reunification, the Tang dynasty abolished the use of old coins, issuing the new, larger Kaiyuan tongbao, in the money reform of 621. Coin supply in the new empire was insufficient and the Tang dynasty money system was, by necessity, based on a dual standard of coins and textiles. Tang discussions on money consequently focused on the advantages and disadvantages of coins, grain and textiles as money; the advantages and disadvantages of private coinage; how to control the quantity of money; and the effect of the quantity of money on prices.

The Tang dynasty money reform of 621 marked a watershed in the nomenclature of coins. Prior to this, the inscriptions on most coins referred to weights (for example, *banliang*, *wuzhu*), although there was often a contradiction between the nominal and physical weight. The 621 reform abandoned the use of the *zhu* as a weight, and adopted a decimal system, with the *qian* 錢 as the key unit of weight in the new system of measures: the new Kaiyuan tongbao coin weighed one *qian*, and 10 *qian* weighed 1 *liang*.

During the Han dynasty the term *qian* was the unit for a single bronze coin, as attested in the Han dynasty wood slips from Eastern Central Asia. The term *quan* 泉 [source] is also used in the same way in these documents, albeit less frequently (see Chapter 7). The term *wen* 文 [writing] appears as a term for 'coin' in the Han dynasty text *Jiuzhang suanshu* of the third century (Peng Xinwei 1965: 227), but is not seen in the wood slips from Eastern Central Asia.[10]

Individual Chinese coins could be threaded on to a string, known in Chinese as *guan* 貫. The earliest reference to strings is in the *Hanshu* (Shihuozhi, juan 24, 1135): 'the cash of the capital districts piled up by the hundreds and ten thousands, and the strings rotted so that the coins could not be counted'. In time the *guan* came to be a monetary unit in its own right; the earliest reference to this is found in the *Weishu* (Xu Jian zhuan, juan 91, 1967): 'cash to the amount of 10,000 strings was to be conferred'. One string of coins had a notional value of 1,000 coins. In practice, the value of the string varied according to the market value of the coins, and adjustments were made, by means of a system of premiums and discounts, to manage any disparity with the notional 1,000 coins.

It was during the Tang dynasty that the compound *huobi* 貨幣 [money] also became established (Peng Xinwei 1965: 374). Prior to this, the characters *huo* and *bi* were used independently, and somewhat fluidly, to refer to goods or money.

The term *jin* 金 was used during Han times to refer to gold, as metal, as well as to a unit of 10,000 cash, which was the legally fixed cash price of 1 *jin* (Han dynasty *jin* = 240 g) of gold. During the Tang dynasty, 1 *jin* could refer to a single coin, a string of cash or an ounce of gold, depending on the context (Peng Xinwei 1965: 323).

### Other forms of money

The general acceptance that coins are small, round, or occasionally square, pieces of metal makes it rather awkward to place the bronze knife and spade money of early China, and it is often more appropriate to think in terms of Chinese money than Chinese coinage. Divinatory inscriptions on bones and turtle-shells, inscriptions on bronze ritual vessels and in the ancient literature[11] indicate that certain natural and man-made objects acquired a particular value which made them the preferred objects for exchange and payment. They were turtle-shells, cowries, pearls, leather and skins, animal horns, grain, textiles and tools. Of these, cowries, tools, grain and textiles continued to serve as money into the historical period (Thierry 1998; Peng Xinwei 1965). The cowrie is the first object for which there is a clear monetary use in China,[12] yet it is difficult to determine whether excavated cowries had a monetary or decorative or other function. The few cowries that have been unearthed in Eastern Central Asia appear to have had a decorative function and are therefore not considered as money-objects (Jiang Qixiang 1990). Similarly, while it has recently been proposed (Dai Zhiqiang and Zhou Weirong 1995) that lumps of bronze of controlled weight were part of the developmental stage for the new metal money which appeared in the Eastern Zhou period (770–221 BC) in the forms of farming hoes and hunting knives, no examples have been found in Eastern Central Asia, and these are not discussed in Chapter 4 (Daxi 1; Thierry 1997b, 1998; Dai Zhiqiang and Zhou Weirong 1997).

Although the early round Chinese coins had a weight inscription, the bamboo slips from Yunmeng prove that Chinese coins did not have an intrinsic value, but instead functioned as a medium of payment, agreed upon by the state and the people (Hulsewé 1985). Coins were not always the sole form of money, and, as long as there was general agreement, other forms of money could be used. If the coins are also seen as a money of account, then fixed quantities of coins might have equivalents in other money-objects, and payments might be in coin or another money-object.

#### *Gold and silver*

Gold and silver served as money by weight. The earliest physical evidence for the use of precious metal in China is in the form of gold plaques of the Chu state, *c*. third century BC, which were stamped and cut into small squares, usually weighing about 15 g. Clay and lead imitations of gold plaques have also been found in tombs of this period (Cribb 1979). The Qin monetary system was bi-metallic, using bronze coins and gold. Gold was measured by the *yi* (1 *yi* = 20 *liang*; 1 *liang* = 24 *zhu*), a weight term for gold inherited from the Warring States period. It was used in large payments and gifts at imperial level and among the nobility, expressed in hundreds or thousands of *yi* of gold

(Peng Xinwei 1965: 72 n21). Silver ingots in the form of traditional Chinese spade money have been unearthed in Fugou county (Henan), suggesting that silver may have functioned as a store of money (Hao Benxing 1980; 1985).[13] Silver was not coined,[14] and during the Qin dynasty was used mainly for utensils and decorative ornaments.

The Han monetary system was also bi-metallic, using gold and bronze coins, but gold was measured by the *jin* 斤, where 1 *jin* = 16 *liang*, a smaller measurement than the Qin *yi*. Various forms of Western Han gold have been found: hollow hoof-form (Cribb 1979; Huang Shengzhang 1985), gold plaques and gold cakes (Zhou Shirong 1985). Gold was widely used in imperial gifts and among the nobility during the Qin and Han, in fines as remission of punishment, to purchase rank and as a store of value in the treasury. Wang Mang bought up gold and prohibited possession of gold among the lower ranks. The situation changed during the Eastern Han, when very few gifts were made in gold.[15] During the Eastern Han, gold and silver were used together in royal gifts and in hoards of treasure. Lead imitations of Han dynasty gold ingots have also been found (Cribb 1978; Dai Zhiqiang and Zhou Weirong 1997: 795; Shaanxi-Coins 2003).[16]

Gold and especially silver became more widely used from the Jin dynasty to the Sui dynasty for the following reasons: coinage was often irregular, gold and silver had passed from the privileged nobility into wider private ownership, and there was greater foreign influence, particularly in the northwest and southeast of China. Chinese historical texts indicate that foreign gold and silver coins were used in the northwestern parts of China during the mid sixth century (*Suishu*, Shihuozhi, juan 24, 691),[17] and specimens of Byzantine gold coins (Thierry and Morrisson 1994) and Sasanian silver coins (Thierry 1993) have been found. The *liang* became the unit for gold during the Western Jin (265–316) and for silver during the Northern and Southern Dynasties. Gold and silver probably continued to be used by weight during this time. No gold and silver ingots of this period have been unearthed; however gold and silver jewellery is frequently found in tombs, especially of the Western Jin, and large quantities of gold were in demand for illuminating manuscripts and for statues in Buddhist temples during the fifth century (Peng Xinwei 1965: 231–40).

During the Tang dynasty gold and silver were secondary to coins and textiles, and usually had to be converted before use. They were used for paying taxes, bribes, imperial gifts, military expenses, rewards and in ceremonies. Increased communications with the peoples of Central Asia stimulated the use of silver in payments, and by the late Tang silver was more commonly used than gold. The Tang unit for gold and silver was the *jin* 斤, usually cast in rectangular-slab or round-cake ingot forms. Gold and silver cash were occasionally cast, but as previously these were mainly used as gifts, rewards and playthings within the court (Peng Xinwei 1965: 323–32).

### *Textiles*

Textiles have played an important role as money in China, but these are perishable forms of money and few specimens have survived. The use of textiles as money therefore is known mostly from the textual and contemporary documentary evidence.

Textiles were used in tax payments from the Warring States period (475–221 BC). The documents from Yunmeng show that by the mid third century, the *bu* 布 was a standard form of textile money, measuring 8 *chi* by 2 *chi* 5 *cun* (188 cm by 58.5 cm), and equivalent to 11 banliang coins. The frequency of prices, fines and sums of money expressed in multiples of 11 (110, 220, 660, 1,100, 2,200) suggests that textile money may have preceded certain forms of metal money, and that reckoning was originally expressed in *bu* and computed at the legal rate into coins (Thierry 1999a: 170). There is, however, some confusion in interpreting the early texts, as the same character *bu* was used both for textiles and for spade money.

Although from 221 BC the banliang replaced all other forms of coined money, gifts continued to be made in fine silk throughout the Western Han (206 BC – AD 24). During the period between the Han and the Tang dynasties, when the empire was fragmented, textiles played a major role as money. During the later years of Wang Mang's rule, silk, grain and gold officially circulated as money. During the Eastern Han (AD 25–220) lengths of silk came to be used in payments again, and textiles replaced gold as the main form of gift. Textiles were also used for rewards, making loans and travel expenses, when they could be sold to raise cash. Silk and grain were the main money-objects during the Jin dynasty and Northern and Southern Dynasties. During the 220s grain and silk served as money for six years, and in some places for as long as thirty or forty years (*Songshu*, Kong Linzhi zhuan, juan 56, 1559–60; *Tongdian*, Shihuo, juan 8, 180). During the Western Jin (265–317) official salaries were paid entirely in grain and silk. During the Northern Wei (386–534) silk served as money for over a decade during the 480s and 490s, and was used to pay land tax, bribes, relief of the distressed, salaries, loans, in purchases and rental of carts. During the Northern Qi (550–77) official salaries were reckoned in terms of silk but paid one-third in silk, one-third in grain, one-third in coin: officials of the first grade received 800 bolts of silk per annum; officials of the ninth grade received 28 bolts per annum (*Suishi*, Baiguan zhi B, juan 27, 763–4). Fines, previously payable in gold, were now payable in silk, and only if no silk was available could they be paid in coin (*Suishi*, Xingfa zhi, juan 25, 705–6). During the Northern Zhou (557–81), punishments were expressed in terms of textiles: for example, robbery (1 bolt or more), theft from one's master (40 bolts or more), petty theft (30 bolts or more) (*Zhoushu*, Wudi ji B, juan 6). Fines as remission of punishment were calculated at 12 bolts for every year of the sentence (*Suishi*, Xingfa zhi, juan 25, 763–4).

In terms of standard dimensions, in the mid third century BC 1 *bu* measured 8 *chi* by 2 *chi* 5 *cun* (188 by 58.5 cm), according to the Yunmeng bamboo slips. During the Han dynasty the standard size was 2 *chi* 2 *cun* by 4 *zhang*. Northern Wei textiles maintained this standard, as specified in the regulations of AD 473 (*Weishu*, Shihuo zhi, juan 110, 2849–70). In the Tang dynasty, the monetary system was based on a dual coin and textile standard, primarily because there were insufficient coins available. Regulations stipulated that payment for certain things should be made in textiles rather than coin: in 732 market exchanges were permitted in textiles and coins; in 735 houses, servants and horses could be exchanged for textiles and not for coins, and all other goods with a price of 1,000 cash or more could be paid for in coins or textiles; in 796 joint use of textiles and coins in the markets was specified. Textiles were also used in loans, taxes, salaries, wages, expenses, rewards, rents and bribes. The names of Tang measurements are known: the *chi* 尺 [foot]; *pi* 匹 [bolt]; *duan* 端 [length for plain cloth]; and *duan* 段 [piece], but not their actual sizes. The most commonly used unit was the *pi* bolt. When the *duan* pieces were specified, the quantities were always large (Peng Xinwei 1965: 318–22). There were obvious problems with silk as money, an often quoted example being that silk money was woven so finely that it was useless (*Jinshu*, Shihuo zhi, juan 26, 779–98).

### *Grain*

Grain was also an important form of money, but it is a perishable form, and the circumstances are less clear. The Han dynasty practice whereby the ranks of officials were expressed in measures of grain may hark back to earlier practices of using grain as money (Bielenstein 1980). During the Jin and Northern and Southern Dynasties salaries were paid partly in grain (Peng Xinwei 1965).

## Money in Eastern Central Asia

Previous studies of money in Eastern Central Asia have concentrated solely on the coin evidence (Zeymal 1992; Thierry 2000; Dong and Jiang 1991) or on specific aspects of the contemporary documentary evidence (Loewe 1967, Attwood 1991) from the region. Such mutually exclusive approaches have led to serious errors, such as Attwood's declaration that no coinage was known in the Cadota kingdom, when coins have been found at the Niya site; and Thierry's (1993) proposal that Sasanian silver coins were used as a means of storing wealth, but not as currency in Eastern Central Asia, when the Chinese documents from Turfan clearly prove that they were a major form of money there.

It is therefore essential to combine the coin evidence with the contemporary documentary evidence, within a framework of understanding of monetary practice. The contemporary documents reveal the forms of money in the region and how they were used. Furthermore, they allow us in a unique way to see how and when changes in money came about. For example, whilst some studies of the Byzantine solidi and imitations found in China have concluded that these pieces were 'objects of cult and commemorative use', perhaps with parallels to the replica shekels made for Bukharian Jews in the 1920s (Zeymal 1992; Thierry and Morrisson 1994), the dated burial inventories excavated in tombs in Turfan allow us to track changes in the supply of gold to the region, even though the inventories themselves were of imagined rather than actual goods (see Chapter 9).

The documentary evidence excavated at sites in Eastern Central Asia is extensive: in the Stein collection alone there are over 28,000 manuscripts in a variety of physical formats, and in various languages and scripts, the majority in Chinese, with a smaller number in Kharoshthi, Khotanese, Sogdian, Tibetan, Tangut, Uighur and Eastern Turkic (Whitfield 1997; Wood 1997).[18] A high proportion (about 80 per cent) of the Chinese documents are Buddhist works, reflecting the dominance of Buddhism in the region (Whitfield 1997: 230), yet the many secular documents, reflecting contemporary social and economic life, are unparalleled elsewhere in China. The extent of the documentary evidence is highlighted when the twenty-thousand-plus Han slips from Juyan are compared with the four-thousand-plus clay tablets from Persepolis (509–458 BC) and the one-thousand-plus writing tablets from Vindolanda (AD 92–120).[19]

The documentary evidence is considered more fully in Part 3 below: the Chinese wood slips found at the Juyan sites, Gansu (119 BC–AD 32), at the Shule River sites, Gansu (103 BC – AD 137), at Loulan, Xinjiang (AD 250s–330s), and at Niya, Xinjiang (AD 220s–330s) (Chapter 7); the Kharoshthi documents found at Niya and Loulan (third to fourth centuries) (Chapter 8); the Chinese paper documents found at Turfan (AD 273–768), Kucha (AD 780s) and Khotan (AD 780s to early ninth century) (Chapter 9); the Tocharian documents from Kucha and sites north of the Taklamakan Desert (seventh century) (Chapter 10); the Khotanese and bilingual Chinese–Khotanese documents from Khotan (seventh to eighth centuries) (Chapter 11); and the Tibetan documents from Mazar Tagh, Khotan, Domoko and Miran (late eighth to early ninth century) (Chapter 12). These documents, some official, some unofficial, contain first-hand evidence for money in the region. They shed light on contemporary financial and economic activity, providing specific evidence of prices, purchases, taxes, fines and salaries, and reveal that coins were not the only form of money.

The aim of this study is to examine with an open mind both the numismatic and the contemporary documentary evidence from Eastern Central Asia, and to create a new framework for money in the region to *c*.AD 800. The numismatic evidence is presented in Part 2, and begins with an introduction to one of the key sources of reference, the collection of coins acquired by Sir Aurel Stein in Eastern Central Asia. The contemporary documentary evidence is presented in Part 3.

## Notes

1. Jiang includes small Qin imitation banliang coins found in a tomb at Fengxiang gaozhuang; in the imperial tomb of Jingdi at Yangling; small Han wuzhu coins in the imperial tomb of Xuandi at Duling; small daquan wushi coins in the Han tombs at Shaogou (Luoyang) and the western suburbs of Luoyang; and small huoquan coins in a Han tomb in the western suburbs of Luoyang.
2. Mammon would be the closest Western equivalent.
3. The dragon is of immense importance in Chinese archaeology, as well as in Chinese cultural history: the Chinese popular self-reference as 'descendants of the dragon' may have its origins in the upper reaches of the Sanggan River, northern Hebei and Shanxi, six to seven thousand years ago. See Su Bingqi's 'Hua people – descendants of the dragon – Chinese: an archaeological seeking after roots' in Wang Tao (1997).
4. The god Xuanwu is represented by a combination of turtle and snake.
5. The documentation, written on bamboo slips, was discovered during excavations of a Qin tomb at Yunmeng (Hubei) in 1975. One section, the *Jin bu lu*, is devoted to the economy and money; see Hulsewé (1978, 1985).
6. The *Zhouli*, also known as *Zhouguan*, is a detailed description of the governmental and administrative structure and organization of the state of Zhou. The date of the *Zhouli* is not known, but the first reference to it is found in the *Shiji* (by Sima Qian, *c*.145–86 BC). For details see Loewe (1993: 24–32).
7. The *Guanzi* is a collection of 76 essays on political, economic and philosophical matters, written between the fifth and the first centuries BC, and brought together in the first century BC by Liu Xiang (79–8 BC). The collected articles are named after the statesman Guan Zhong (d. 645 BC). For details see Loewe (1993: 244–51). The translation, from the *Guanzi* (juan 75, Shanquan shu), is by Rickett (1998: 397).

8. Cribb (1987: 4) illustrates this point with the Imperial edict of 1854, which said: 'the currency system depends entirely on the circulation of standard cash and other forms of money without obstruction, so that [there] will be sufficient for the peoples' livelihoods in difficult times', quoting from King (1965: 151).
9. The *Yantielun* was a debate on the Han government's monopolies of the salt and iron industries, but the discussion touched on wider, often controversial, political and economic issues of the time. See Loewe (1993: 477–82) and Gale (1931).
10. The *Jiuzhang suanshu* is a collection of 246 problems with numerical solutions and the mathematical methods involved. It is the earliest surviving comprehensive arithmetical textbook, from the first or possibly late second century BC. For details see (Loewe 1993: 16–23).
11. Peng Xinwei (1965: 1–31) quotes from early texts such as the *Zhouli*, *Guanzi*, *Zhushu jinian*, *Shijing*, *Zuozhuan*, *Zhanguo ce*. For an introduction to these texts see Loewe (1993).
12. Oracle-bone inscriptions and inscriptions on bronze vessels of the Shang (sixteenth to eleventh centuries BC) and Zhou (eleventh century to 221 BC) dynasties mention 'gifts of cowries', 'putting cowries in the treasury', 'seizure of cowries', 'use of cowries' and 'double-strings of cowries'. Cowries have been found at neolithic sites, and at Shang and Zhou dynasty settlements, with complete cowries most numerous in the tombs of the mid to late Shang; and cowries with their backs removed most frequent in tombs of the Western Zhou and Eastern Zhou. There is a noticeable increase in the number of cowries and imitations found in tombs of the mid Spring and Autumn Period (770–476 BC). Imitation bronze cowries first appeared in the Shang dynasty, but the largest numbers are recorded for the Eastern Zhou (770–221 BC). Approximately 80 per cent of the total number of bronze cowries were found in Shanxi province, in the territory of the ancient state of Jin. The bronze workshop at the Houma site, which yielded 45 obverse and reverse moulds for bronze cowries, is dated to the late seventh or early sixth century BC (Zhang Tian'en 1991; Thierry 1998: 17–18; SXA 1996).
13. The Fugou deposit comprised two bronze vessels corroded together: a *ding* vessel containing 18 silver spade ingots on top of a *hu* vessel containing 392 gold plaques of the Chu state and *matijin* horse-hoof gold of the Western Han. Prior to this discovery, a Western Han well had been found at the same location. These finds suggest that the Fugou deposit was made in the Western Han period but contained items of an earlier date.
14. Indeed, China's first successful precious metal coinage was issued in 1890, in the form of struck silver dollars; see Cribb (1979).
15. Peng Xinwei (1965: 144) reckoned that Eastern Han gifts of gold amounted to only 2 per cent of the total gifts of gold during the Western Han.
16. The lead imitation ingots are round in shape. One side has an inscription in garbled, mirrored Greek script and two square stamps; the other side has a dragon design. Most Chinese numismatists believe these ingots to be one of the *bai jin san pin* [three objects in white metal] mentioned in the *Hanshu*: Shihuozhi. These have been identified as an oval piece with a tortoise scale design, a square piece with a horse design, and the round piece with the dragon.
17. Li Daoyuan's (d. 527) *Shuijing zhu*, a geographical text, also noted that the region of Jibin (= Kashmir) was rich in gold and silver, animals and precious objects. See Wang Guowei 1984.
18. The Stein manuscripts are housed in the British Library; other comparable collections of documents from Eastern Central Asia are in the Bibliothèque Nationale, Paris; the State Hermitage Museum, St Petersburg; and Beijing Library.
19. The Persepolis tablets concern Persepolis at the heart of the Achaemenid empire, and the adjacent Elymais to the west. The 114 Persepolis Treasury Tablets (492–458 BC) record payment to workers in silver from the treasury. A further four-thousand-plus tablets are known as the Persepolis Fortification Tablets (509–494 BC), and these are 'brief administrative notes concerning the supply, transfer and distribution of natural produce in the south-western Iranian heartlands, provisions that were issued as daily, monthly or sometimes extra rations to individuals or groups of workers, and also for the upkeep of animals. Each of the individuals or groups is "paid" or supplied in kind, and the "accounting" is done so subtly that the system of receipts and expenses can only be described as highly sophisticated' (Wiesehöfer 1998: 66–7). The Vindolanda tablets consist mostly of correspondence relating to everyday life at the Vindolanda fort, England, c.AD 90–130 (Bowman 1998).

Part 2

# The numismatic evidence

# 3 The Stein collection of coins from Eastern Central Asia

The key reference for this study is the collection of coins acquired in Eastern Central Asia by Sir Aurel Stein in the early twentieth century, and now housed in the Department of Coins and Medals at the British Museum. It is one of the most important collections of coins from Eastern Central Asia, owing to the range of specimens it contains and to the care taken by Sir Aurel Stein to provide accurate details of the locations and contexts in which the coins were found. This chapter introduces Sir Aurel Stein, his approach to archaeology and numismatics, and the current situation of the Stein collection of coins from Eastern Central Asia.

**Sir Aurel Stein (1862–1943)**

Sir Aurel Stein is renowned as 'the most prodigious combination of scholar, explorer, archaeologist and geographer of his generation' (Lattimore 1973). His pioneering archaeological work in Eastern Central Asia, India, Iran, Iraq and Jordan, combined with his determination to share the results of that work by publishing both popular narratives and detailed academic reports, earned him international respect, honours and awards. Today, Stein's name is most closely linked with the paintings and manuscripts of the eighth to tenth centuries which he purchased at the Caves of the Thousand Buddhas, near Dunhuang, China. But his contribution to our understanding of the history and archaeology of Eastern Central Asia was far greater than this. Following his three arduous and successful expeditions in the region in 1900–1, 1906–8 and 1913–16, he published three comprehensive scholarly publications, *Ancient Khotan* (1907), *Serindia* (1921), and *Innermost Asia* (1928). His synthesis of archaeology, geography, history, ethnography and current affairs in these publications superseded most previous Western studies of the region. To this day, they remain the 'bibles' for studying early Eastern Central Asia. The finds from these expeditions are now in various collections in the UK, Hungary and India (Wang 1999; Falconer et al. 2002).

Although Stein has largely been ignored in the history of Western archaeology, in his own time he enjoyed the highest reputation for his archaeological achievements, and received, among other distinctions, the University of Pennsylvania's Lucy Wharton Medal 1912 (previously awarded to Arthur Evans and Flinders Petrie); the Petrie Medal 1928; and the Society of Antiquaries gold medal for distinguished services to archaeology 1935 (the first recipient was Sir Arthur Evans in 1934) (Mirsky 1977; Walker 1995; Wang 2002). Leonard Woolley devoted two chapters to Stein in his popular book *History unearthed: a survey of eighteen archaeological sites throughout the world* (1958), 'designed to deal with the eighteen most important contributions to our knowledge of ancient history, and to emphasize the extent to which such contributions were due to the scientific methods of modern field-work'. Woolley wrote:

> This is the story not of one excavation but of scores of excavations conducted in the course of the most daring and adventurous raid upon the ancient world that any archaeologist has attempted . . . Stein carried out an astonishing archaeological and geographical survey of the country.

In China, a more balanced approach is beginning to emerge. In his preface to the Chinese translation of Stein's most influential publication, *Serindia*, Meng Fanren (1998) praised Stein's talent for combining geography and archaeology, his stamina in covering such wide ground, and his determination to publish his work.

**Stein's approach to archaeology and numismatics**

Stein appears to have been self-taught in archaeology and numismatics, yet his approach to both was highly professional. In the introduction to *Ancient Khotan* he wrote:

> In order to secure materials that would help us to recover this interesting chapter of lost history [of Eastern Central Asia], and to interpret it rightly, it was not enough to conduct excavations and to arrange for the deposition of what official language styles 'the archaeological proceeds' in Museums. It was at least equally important that an exact and detailed record should be kept of all observations made on the ground, and that the evidence thus secured should be published with all possible care and fullness. It is needless to emphasize for fellow-scholars the importance of this condition, which the canons of scientific archaeology impose upon any qualified worker. Yet for the benefit of others I cannot refrain from quoting the warning which an archaeological explorer of unequalled experience, Professor Flinders Petrie, has so eloquently recorded in his admirable handbook on Methods and Aims in Archaeology. 'To leave a site merely plundered, without any attempt to work out its history, to see the meaning of the remains found, or to publish what may serve future students of the place or the subject, is to throw away the opportunities which have been snatched from those who might have used them properly'.

At first glance, it may appear that Stein followed Petrie's *Methods and aims in archaeology* (1904), yet Stein had already completed his first expedition in 1901, three years before Petrie's book was published. Stein understood that the location and context of finds were essential for accurate interpretation, and was meticulous in recording such details, distinguishing which objects were found at sites, those allegedly found at sites, and purchases and gifts. In the case of the Yotkan site, he wrote (1907):

> It is scarcely necessary to point out that, even in the case of antiques bought at Yotkan or avowedly brought to me from that site, the evidence as to their origin cannot have the same value as that of finds yielded by systematic exploration under my own eyes.
>
> In respect of no other class of antiques would such full authentication be so important as in that of coin finds, for in the present state of our knowledge we must depend entirely on them for exact chronological evidence as regards the period during

> which the site of Yotkan was occupied by the Khotan capital and its débris-layers deposited. Unable to secure evidence by actual excavation, I took care to make my purchases of old coins from the site as far as possible at Yotkan itself. The quantities of coins annually washed out of the ancient strata seem to be considerable, and I had no difficulty in obtaining on my several visits to Yotkan an aggregate of close on 200 specimens. All are of copper; I did not succeed in tracing any gold or silver coins, nor even information about such.

Stein's interest in coins predated his first expedition to Eastern Central Asia. In 1886 he studied the coin collections in the British Museum and the Ashmolean Museum, Oxford, and wrote his first academic paper, 'Zoroastrian deities on Indo-Scythian coins', which was published in the *Oriental and Babylonian Record* in 1887 (Mirsky 1977). His first major publication was *Kalhana's Rajatarangini, a chronicle of the kings of Kashmir*, 1900, which comprised 1,132 pages of translation of Kalhana's history of Kashmir, introductions, extensive notes, a memoir on the ancient geography of Kashmir and a comprehensive index. In the book Stein commented on Sir Alexander Cunningham's use of coin evidence (Stein 1900; Cunningham 1846): 'In the Numismatic Chronicle for 1846 he communicated the results of his search for ancient Kashmirian coins, and proved by their analysis the great value of numismatic evidence for the critical control of Kalhana's records'. On the basis of the evidence in the *Rajatarangini*, Stein himself made a thorough investigation of the monetary system and currency of Kashmir during the period of Hindu rule. By tying in earlier and later practices, and considering the practicalities of agricultural life, Stein was able to conclude that the monetary system was not exclusively coin-based (Stein 1899):

> A monetary system based on the cowrie unit, and represented in its main bulk by a copper coinage, becomes far more intelligible if we realise that it was supplemented in all important transactions of public business and private life by the ample stores of another circulating medium, the Khari of rice.

This was a remarkable conclusion to draw in the 1890s, some fifty years before the eruption of the formalist-substantivist debate, the growth of economic anthropology and subsequent searches for a definition of money (see Chapter 2). Stein's talent lay in effective gathering of intelligence from as many sources, ancient and modern, as possible, and analysing that material with an open mind.

As a young orientalist, Stein was familiar with how the Europeans had collected coins in Afghanistan in the 1830s, and how a close examination of those coins had revealed the extent of Greek culture in the region. He knew of James Prinsep's careful study of the bilingual Indo-Greek coins which led him to the decipherment of the Kharoshthi script, and to details of the names of otherwise unknown Greek rulers, as well as non-Greek names written in the Greek script (Errington and Cribb 1992).

Stein also knew that there were similar treasures waiting to be discovered and deciphered in Eastern Central Asia. Indeed, it was at Stein's suggestion that Rudolph Hoernle wrote to the Department of Agriculture and Revenue in support of Stein's application for his first expedition to Eastern Central Asia (Mirsky 1977):

> I have now gone through nearly the whole of our collection of Central Asian antiquities . . . There are numerous points of detail on which no information can be got from the native treasure seekers . . . Some coins which I have deciphered seem to show that in the first centuries BC and AD there was a Scythian or Turki (Elighur) Kingdom which included both Khotan and Kashmir on the two sides of the Karakorum Range. Towards the end of the first century AD it was broken up into two parts: the Northern portion (Khotan) being annexed by the Chinese, the Southern (Kashmir) by the famous Indo-Scythian King, Kanishka. I have bilingual (Chinese and Indian) coins, issued by the Chinese administration of Khotan after 73 AD. Much to corroborate this and to fill in details may be discovered by European exploration.[1]

It was fortuitous then that on his first expedition Stein himself found some of these bilingual coins, which had inscriptions in the Kharoshthi and Chinese scripts, and was able to observe that 'whatever specimens of the Sino-Kharoshthi currency I could secure or see were with some doubtful exceptions confined to the Yotkan site' (Stein 1907: 204–5). The exceptions were a group of over twenty such coins which he purchased at Khotan, as having been found at other sites, near Hanguya and Ak-sipil. In his reports of this and subsequent expeditions to Eastern Central Asia, Stein wrote:

> I had endeavoured, as far as my means of reference would permit, to determine on the spot all coins found by me.
>
> (Stein 1907: xiii)

> It is scarcely necessary to point out to archaeologists how valuable for the chronological determination of the sites the indications [of coins] . . . have been.
>
> (Stein 1921: xx)

It is important to recognize that by following archaeological practices, as set out by Petrie for example (Stein 1907: ix), and by collecting coins in the fashion of explorers and scholars in India and Afghanistan, Stein was breaking new ground in Chinese numismatics. By collecting large quantities of coins, and noting precisely the details of acquisition (for example, as purchase, gift, surface find, excavation find), provenance and context, Stein was the first person to collect Chinese coins with an archaeological approach.

His approach means that there can be no mistaking coins from a genuine archaeological context, and those of spurious provenance. For example, in Karghalik Stein acquired two Roman bronze coins, two Parthian coins and an Indian Hermaius imitation. Whilst the provenance of these coins is uncertain, Stein provides a warning about dodgy coin dealers in the town (1912: I, 140–1): 'There was one who had drifted to Karghalik from Bokhara some twenty years before . . . He had brought a good number of old Bactrian, Arsacidian [Parthian], and other Greek coins with him from Bokhara, – or had since been supplied with them by friends left behind there'. When Stein wrote that he had 'endeavoured, as far as my means of reference would permit, to determine on the spot all coins found by me', he was revealing some of the difficulties in such a task. Stein did not read Chinese, and, although he would come to recognize inscriptions that turned up frequently, for the most part he had to rely on his Chinese assistants. At the time of his first expedition very little published material on Chinese coins was available in non-Chinese sources. In the introduction to the *British Museum catalogue of Chinese coins from the VIIth century*

*BC to AD 621*, published in 1892, and now regarded as full of errors and forgeries, Lacouperie (1892) wrote:

> In European literature on numismatics, on the period of Chinese coins included in the present work there are only a few papers, which cannot be referred to because they are either misleading or based upon untrustworthy sources. The only extensive work on the matter is the great Catalogue compiled in 1842 by the Baron S. de Chaudoir and M. Léontiefski at St. Petersburg.[2]

James Lockhart's *Currency of the Farther East*, which was used to identify Chinese coins from Stein's third expedition, was not published until 1907. The first comprehensive history of money in China, Peng Xinwei's groundbreaking *Zhongguo huobi shi* appeared in 1954, and its English translation by E. H. Kaplan, *A monetary history of China*, appeared in 1994.

In Stein's proposal for his fourth expedition, made to the Indian Archaeological Survey in 1925, he attempted to address some of the concerns of the Chinese intellectual world of that time. He wrote:

> The need of scientifically conducted exploration of such and other remains hitherto safely hidden in the ground is all the more urgent because in spite of traditional Chinese interest in all relics of the past the systematic recovery and study of these by means of methodical excavation and other archaeological field work has so far remained practically unknown in China. There is, however, every reason to believe that Chinese scholars of the necessary literary attainments could under competent European guidance be readily trained to apply modern Western methods of archaeological research. The employment of one or two carefully selected young literati in connection with the proposed explorations is a measure which practical considerations based upon my previous experience would in any case make highly desirable. But it might in addition serve a very useful purpose by training suitable men for employment on archaeological survey work under Chinese authority, whenever conditions may permit of this being organised.[3]

His estimate for expenses for the proposed two-and-a-half-year expedition included £2,000 for two Chinese assistants, five times the £400 proposed for two Indian noncommissioned officers. Stein was forced to abort his fourth expedition and never wrote it up (Wang Jiqing 1993, 1994; Brysac 1997, 2004).

**Identification of the coins in the Stein collection**

Stein was aware of his own limitations in identifying much of the material he collected, and was keen to enlist the help of experts. Only in this way could specialist knowledge from various fields be integrated to give a broader picture. For example, in the case of the coins from his first expedition, he wrote (1907: 203–4):

> I regret that neither during my journey nor subsequently after my collections had been deposited at the British Museum did I obtain sufficient leisure for an accurate numismatic analysis of these purchases; nor could I claim full competence for it, seeing that the vast majority of the coins secured from Yotkan belong to purely Chinese issues. A considerable number are too much worn or corroded for exact determination. Of the rest, however, 150 have been classified with the kind help of Dr. Bushell and Prof. Rapson; and the result of this preliminary analysis is sufficiently definite to be discussed here in its chronological bearing. Numismatic details in support of it will, I hope, be made accessible hereafter.

The Stein collection comprises all the coins acquired by Stein on his three expeditions to Eastern Central Asia. The finds from Stein's first and second expeditions were sent directly to London for examination and recording, and the coins arrived at the British Museum in 1901 and 1909, respectively (Mirsky 1977: 84). Government orders stated that most of the finds from the third expedition (but not including the literary material, which was destined for the India Office Library, London) were to remain in New Delhi. The coins from this expedition were therefore examined and recorded in Kashmir, and sent to the British Library with the literary material in 1924 (Stein 1928: xv). When the British Library separated from the British Museum in the 1970s they were transferred to the Museum's Department of Coins and Medals, thus bringing the entire collection together for the first time. A list of the coins from each expedition had been published, in the form of an appendix, to *Ancient Khotan* (1907), *Serindia* (1921) and *Innermost Asia* (1928), respectively.

The appendices appeared with the title 'Descriptive Lists of Coins'. They were compiled by the best oriental numismatists of the day: S. W. Bushell, E. J. Rapson, J. Allan, and, later, Stein's experienced assistant, F. M. G. Lorimer.

Stephen Wootton Bushell (1844–1909), physician to Her Majesty's Legation at Peking, is better known these days for his publications relating to Chinese ceramics than for his interest in coins. However, he was an active numismatist: his articles on Chinese coins were published in such periodicals as *The China Review* and the *Journal of the China Branch of the Royal Asiatic Society* and he was a council member of the Royal Numismatic Society from 1902 to 1904.[4] James Lockhart, in the preface to his *Currency of the Farther East* (1907), acknowledged Bushell's help in 'deciphering some of the inscriptions on the ancient coins of China'. Lockhart's catalogue was used in the preparation of at least one of the Lists of Coins; there are references to catalogue entries written in pencil in the lower left corner of the envelopes which contained the coins listed in *Innermost Asia*.[5]

Edward James Rapson (1861–1937) is well known for his ground-breaking work on ancient India. He worked at the Indian Institute in Oxford before joining the British Museum as an Assistant in the Department of Coins and Medals in 1887, where he remained until he became Professor of Sanskrit at Cambridge in 1906. When Stein returned from his first expedition, Rapson was the Kharoshthi specialist in Britain and undertook the examination and decipherment of the Kharoshthi documents Stein had found at Niya. By the time Rapson had examined the Kharoshthi documents of all three expeditions, he had increased the number of recognized Kharoshthi characters from about forty to over two hundred and eighty characters or combinations.[6]

John Allan (1884–1955) was an acknowledged world authority on oriental numismatics, and Honorary Secretary of the Royal Numismatic Society for forty years (1908–48). He joined the Department of Coins and Medals in 1907, became Keeper in 1931 and after his retirement took up the post of Lecturer in Sanskrit at Edinburgh University, which he held until he died. He was responsible for the Lists of Coins from the second and third expeditions.[7]

Florence Mary Glen Lorimer (1883–1967) was Stein's assistant, his 'Recording Angel', for thirteen years. She was employed in October 1909 to work with Fred Andrews (1866–1957), Stein's chief assistant, for an initial period of two years. She continued to work on the Stein collections until 1923, spending nine years in the British Museum and four years in Kashmir. She and Andrews wrote many of the identification slips which were later published in Stein's reports (Wang 1998).

For the most part, the identification of the coins in the three Lists is accurate, but extremely concise, and occasionally vague, and the Lists do not include such basic details as weights and measurements. A revised catalogue of the Stein collection is included in this book, listing fuller details of the coins and the contexts in which they were found.

In the 1980s Joe Cribb and Lalou Metzler rearranged the entire collection of coins to follow the order in which they are found in the Lists and noted any discrepancies. Prior to the rearrangement, the only coins to have had identification tickets with them were those which had been selected over fifty years previously to be photographed for publication in Stein's reports.[8] Each coin now has its own identification ticket, and has been ascribed a unique number which identifies it to a coin, or group of coins, in the original Lists. In spring 1993, during an intensive three-month conservation project, Celestine Enderley of the Conservation Department, British Museum, cleaned and conserved, where appropriate, all the coins in the Stein collection. Any active corrosion was stabilized and some coins were given a clear protective lacquer coating. As a result of the cleaning and conservation some of the coins now have a darker appearance, in contrast to the green-grey patina usually associated with these coins. Occasionally, two or more coins which had previously been stuck together came apart during the cleaning, thereby altering slightly the number of coins given in the original Lists. Some coins proved to have been misidentified in the Lists, the inscriptions made clear only after cleaning. A number of coins had clay packed around them, totally obscuring the inscription, and as it is possible that this was done intentionally, these coins were not cleaned. Their function remains unknown.

## The Stein collection of coins and the Silk Road

The Stein collection comprises over four thousand coins. These can be arranged in three immediately recognizable groups: (1) coins of the Chinese tradition: cast in a copper alloy, round with a square hole in the middle, with a two-character or four-character Chinese inscription, and no pictorial design; (2) coins of the Western tradition: struck in gold, silver or bronze. The pre-Islamic coins usually have a pictorial design, often figurative, and an inscription placed around the design. The Islamic coins have an inscription on either side. (3) Coins of local manufacture, modelled on the Chinese and/or Western tradition.

Almost three-quarters of the collection comprises coins of the Chinese tradition, spanning a period of about two thousand years from the Han (206 BC – AD 220) to the Qing dynasty (1644–1911). About a quarter of the collection comprises coins of the Western tradition, mainly Islamic coins. In addition, there are a small number of Roman, Parthian, Kushan and Sasanian coins, and a few imitations of Byzantine gold coins. Coins of local manufacture, modelled on the Chinese and/or Western tradition, constitute the smallest of the three main groups. It includes bilingual Sino-Kharoshthi coins, lead coins of Khotan, unidentified bronze Chinese-style coins with a non-Chinese inscription, Chinese-style coins of Qiuci, Chinese-style coins with Chinese inscriptions unique to Eastern Central Asia, and a Chinese-style coin issued by the Türgesh with a Sogdian inscription. This study concentrates on those coins which date to the period before AD 800: a total of 2,370 coins, representing almost sixty per cent of the collection.

Stein's scrupulous attention to provenance, his recording of finds on site, noting precise details of acquisition and inviting the help of specialists to identify finds makes his collection of coins from Eastern Central Asia a unique resource. Other European and Japanese archaeological explorers in Eastern Central Asia also collected coins, but these collections were not published until much later: the Oldenburg collection at the Hermitage Museum, St Petersburg (Ivotchkina 1975); the Pelliot collection, rediscovered in the 1990s in a cake tin in a store-room in the Musée Guimet, Paris (Thierry 1997a); and the Mannerheim collection at the National Museum of Finland (Talvio 1999). The Lists of Coins in Stein's reports, published in 1907, 1921 and 1928, have therefore served as the most important references for the study of Eastern Central Asian numismatics.

In terms of content, detailed provenance and accessibility, the Stein collection of coins from Eastern Central Asia is of great importance, yet it is essential to examine this collection in a much broader context. The presence of coins of the Chinese tradition, Western tradition, and local manufacture reinforces the importance of this region as a meeting-ground of very different cultures. Furthermore, the documentary evidence reveals that coins were not the only form of money in Eastern Central Asia, and that they were not always used in the same way by different peoples (see Part 3).

The archaeological surveys and excavations that have been carried out by Chinese specialists in Xinjiang since the 1920s have produced a phenomenal amount of new material. For example the hoard of wuzhu coins, weighing 45 kg, found at the Mailike'awati site, 25 km south of Khotan, raises significantly the profile of wuzhu coins in the Khotan region (Li Yuchun 1981). The Stein collection contains approximately 1,230 wuzhu coins, and to ignore this hoard is to distort the larger picture. The Stein collection forms only a small part of the much larger body of coin evidence from Eastern Central Asia, and as might be expected, Stein's collections are more representative in the regions where he spent most time. It is clear, for example, that the Stein collection contains many Sino-Kharoshthi coins, associated with Khotan, but very few Sino-Kuchan coins, associated with Kucha, where Stein spent only a few days. The following chapters in Part 2 present the coin evidence in the Stein collection in the light of more recent finds.

## Notes

1. Quoting from the National Archives of India, Department of Revenue and Agriculture (Archaeology and Epigraphy), January 1899, nos 1–2.
2. Terrien de Lacouperie (1845–94) was Professor of Chinese at University College, London. He was employed occasionally by the British Museum to work on East Asian coins, where there was no specialist in this field until Joe Cribb joined the Department of Coins and Medals, British Museum, in the 1970s.
3. Stein to Archaeological Survey of India, 16 March 1925, Archives of the Royal Geographical Society.
4. *Numismatic Chronicle* 60–4 (1900–4). For a detailed list of Bushell's publications on Chinese coins see Coole (1967: 297–8).

5. The envelopes and cloth bags were rediscovered under a pile of manuscripts from Dunhuang in the early 1970s by Peter Lawson of the British Library, and were then transferred to the Department of Coins and Medals at the British Museum. No envelopes or cloth bags remain from the first two expeditions, although there are handwritten slips detailing the coins listed in *Ancient Khotan*. These are also in the Department of Coins and Medals.
6. Obituary of Rapson in *The Eagle* 50, January 1938: 220, 224–30; also *The Proceedings of the British Academy* XXIII. The Kharoshthi documents were published in Rapson, Boyer and Senart 1920–9.
7. Obituary and bibliography of Allan in *Numismatic Chronicle*, 16th series, 16, 1955: 351–2.
8. Personal communication from Joe Cribb, Department of Coins and Medals, British Museum.

# 4 Coins of the Chinese tradition

This chapter considers the coin-types found in Eastern Central Asia that are known to have been issued in central China. It is not known what proportion of these was imported from central China, and what proportion may have been produced locally. However, some of the Chinese coins found in Eastern Central Asia are made in a very particular reddish bronze, compared with coins produced in central China, and this may be a characteristic of coins produced locally (Ivotchkina 1975; Thierry 1997a). All the Chinese types were cast, and some remains of moulds or coin-casting equipment have been found in the region (see Chapter 6).

### Cowries

Cowries served both monetary and decorative purposes in central China, and it is difficult to confirm the function of cowries found at sites (Thierry 1998). Stein found a total of seven cowries in Eastern Central Asia: at Niya (one), Endere (one), Loulan (one) and Kelpin (four). They were pierced or adapted for threading, and found in dwelling places. Stein regarded them as decorative pieces, and was right to exclude them from his Lists of Coins.

Chinese archaeologists have reported cowries in tombs dated as early as *c*.1000 BC in the lower reaches of the Kongque River, Hami and Shanshan. Other finds include ten cowries unearthed in the Han dynasty burial site in Jinxinliang, Mulei (Jiang Qixiang 1990(1): 6), and cowries arranged by the head and arms, and occasionally in the mouth, of the dead at the Alagou burial ground, near Turfan (Zhang Zhongshan 1999: 11). Cowries are not indigenous to Eastern Central Asia and were transported over long distances, just as Khotanese jades were transported over long distances to be placed in tombs in central China. In this way, cowries and jades are often seen as the earliest evidence of exchange between China and Central Asia.[1] 'Several dozen' imitation cowries carved in bone have been unearthed in the tombs of the Cheshi nobles at Jiaohe (Jie Yaohua 1999: 44), yet, as in central China, these may have served as pre-Han burial items rather than as money.

### Banliang coins (Plate 1, 1)

The earliest Chinese coins found in Eastern Central Asia are the banliang coins, a type first issued in the Qin state from the early fourth century BC, and still in production during the early Han dynasty until finally declared obsolete in 118 BC (Thierry 1999: 247–60).[2]

There are two banliang in the Stein collection: one [S.XI.A.c.36] found at Loulan and the other [S.XIV.b.1] at the eroded site northeast of the ruined town of Nanhu.[3] Both are early Han issues.

Pelliot acquired an early Han banliang (20 mm, 0.73 g) in Kucha (Thierry 2000: 129). Another banliang from Subashi Längär in the Turfan Oasis, acquired on the fourth German Turfan Expedition, is housed in the collection of the Museum für Indische Kunst, Berlin. Although the coin is quite large (30.5 mm, 4.71 g), and is probably a Qin banliang, full details of acquisition are not known, other than that it came with three wuzhu coins.[4] Chinese archaeologists have reported finds of early Han banliang at Qitai (five coins), Loulan (one) and Mulei (Dong Qingxuan and Jiang Qixiang 1990: 4–5; Jiang Qixiang 1990(1): 8; XJ–Loulan 1988: 20–1).

At least twelve banliang coins have been reported in total. With the exception of Pelliot's banliang, those with reliable provenances have been identified as issues of the early Western Han (220 BC – AD 24). The banliang in the Stein collection were found in association with later coins. As this is frequently seen in coin hoards in central China, it is likely that the banliang found in Eastern Central Asia were used contemporaneously with the later coins, and arrived with them in Eastern Central Asia after 118 BC.

### Wuzhu, clipped-rim wuzhu and derivatives (Plate 1, 2–14)

Wuzhu coins form the majority of coins found in Eastern Central Asia. They were first issued in 118 BC, and were eventually declared obsolete in AD 621. For over seven hundred years the wuzhu was the major Chinese coin in production and circulation. Precise identification of wuzhu coins remains fraught with difficulty and contention. Early identification was based upon concise descriptions in the Chinese histories; major breakthroughs have come with archaeological work in central China, where studies of wuzhu from dated tombs have begun to transform the identification process, establishing an outline chronology of wuzhu based primarily on calligraphy, the size of the coin and its hole, the reverse type, and to an extent the metal content (Thierry 1989). However, these criteria are not followed consistently, and identification of wuzhu coins remains extremely difficult: for example, bronze moulds for making coins were reused long after the first issue just as earlier coins were used as models for later issues. It is further compounded by the very long period of circulation of these coins, and the widespread clipping and private casting of wuzhu from the late Western Han onwards. Many of the wuzhu coins from Eastern Central Asia were found at surface level at sites, sometimes brought to the surface by seasonal water channels or by strong desert winds. Consequently, most are in poor condition, brittle, fragmentary, damaged, corroded or worn, and sometimes corroded together in lumps.

Stein acquired over 1,230 wuzhu coins[5] from the following sites: Yotkan, Dandan-Uiliq, Rawak, Niya, Endere, Karadong, Hanguya, Tam Öghil, Ak-sipil, Jumbe-kum, Karadobe, Mazar Tagh, Khotan, Halal-bagh, east of Yurung-kash, north of Jiya and Suya, south of Sampula, Kine-tokmak, Tatis of Ak-terek, Kök-Kumarish, Ak-terek, Khadalik, Balawaste, Mazar-toghrak, Loulan, Merdek-tim, Nanhu, Dunhuang, Yarkhoto, Farhad beg

Yailaki, Ulugh-mazar, Domoko, Chalma-kazan, Kara sai, Tarishlak, Chong Tim, Kelpin, Kudug, the Lop Desert, the Han *limes*, Kharakhoto and east of Kharakhoto, Astana, Yingpan, Korla and Kucha. Most of these sites yielded between one and thirty coins, with the sites yielding the most numerous wuzhu being the Lop Desert sites (323 coins), Loulan (214), the Rawak Vihara site and vicinity (220-plus), Yotkan (130-plus coins), and various sites around Khotan (118). Stein also reported a hoard found in 1900 about a mile from the Rawak stupa, which was unfortunately dispersed before his arrival. Eighty-seven of the wuzhu purchased at Rawak were from this hoard (Stein 1907: 482–3).

While the Stein collection indicates a greater concentration of wuzhu at sites on the southern Silk Route, this is to some extent explained by the disproportionate amount of time he spent on the route. The early Western expeditions which concentrated on the northern route reflect a similar bias towards the north. For example, Pelliot found two large hoards in the Kucha region: a hoard of two thousand wuzhu at Subashi and a hoard of 1,300 wuzhu found in a pot at Tajik (Thierry 2000).[6] Grünwedel and von le Coq acquired only 26 wuzhu during the German Turfan Expeditions between 1902 and 1914, and these coins came exclusively from the Turfan, Kucha and Aksu regions: one from Khocho (= Gaochang/Kara-khoja); three from Subashi Längär (Turfan Oasis) and eight from the Temple of Inscriptions, Subashi Längär; one from Ugh Turfan, Aksu; eleven from the guard house below Togruk Däm near Kucha; and two with unknown provenance.

Chinese archaeologists report having found wuzhu at sites throughout Eastern Central Asia, with the greatest frequency of surface finds of wuzhu being at Loulan, and the single largest hoard of wuzhu being the 45 kg mass of corroded coins at the Mailike'awati site near Khotan. At 2–3 g per coin, this would give 15,000–22,500 coins. The total number of wuzhu coins from Eastern Central Asia is not known, but already reaches into the tens of thousands.

Five large hoards have been reported in Eastern Central Asia: from Mailike'awati, Yingya'erxiang, Tajik, Subashi and Rawak. The Mailike'awati hoard, weighing 45 kg, was found in a clay vessel, 1.2 m below surface level in the northern part of the Mailike'awati site, 25 km south of Khotan. Wuzhu were also picked up at surface level. Li Yuchun (1981: 33–7) described the coins as 'Western Han wuzhu coins corroded into lumps', deposited no later than the late Western Han. However, carbon 14 tests made on charcoal from the site yielded 1525 ± 75 BP and 1460 ± 80 BP (with 1950 as base line), indicating a much later date of deposit, c.AD 350–510 (Wenwu baohu 1982: 89). The C14 date and Buddhist finds from the site indicate a date of deposition later than the Western Han. The coins have not been fully identified and, until a breakdown of the hoard is available, the likelihood that these are Eastern Han, or even later, wuzhu should not be ruled out.

The Yingya'erxiang hoard was found in spring 1999 by farmers digging water channels in Yingya'erxiang, Moyu county, in the Khotan region. Li Peng (2001) described the hoard as comprising a total of 27 kg of corroded coins, deposited during the Northern and Southern Dynasties. At 2–3 g per coin, 27 kg would represent 9,000–13,500 coins. Of the 27 kg, there were 11 kg of intact 'mostly wuzhu' coins. Li identified a sample selection of the coins as comprising early Han banliang; Western Han wuzhu; Wang Mang issues (daquan wushi, huoquan, buquan); Eastern Han wuzhu (about seventy per cent of the sample) some of which had marks (numerals, single characters, dots, lines) on them; unofficial issues and copies; many small thin coins without rims or inscriptions; Cao-Wei wuzhu; Shu wuzhu; and fenghuo coins (issued from 319). He concluded that many of the very poor quality wuzhu coins had probably been made in Eastern Central Asia. The hoard was sold to a local antique store and then on to a dealer in Beijing.

Thierry (2000) described Pelliot's Tajik hoard as comprising three distinct groups of wuzhu coins: (1) 424 Han dynasty wuzhu (38.37 per cent), mostly very worn, some with little or no trace of inscription, crudely made, with gaps due to poor metal, crudely executed inscriptions and occasionally marks added after casting; (2) 335 (30.32 per cent) clipped wuzhu with a diameter measuring 20–23 mm. Of these, 331 were Eastern Han wuzhu with clipped outer rims, and another four had clipped inner rims. Of the 127 legible coins of this group, 11 were Western Han. Group (3) comprised 346 coins (31.31 per cent) without inscription or rims, and with diameter 19–22 mm. They were all made from the reddish copper typical of later coins made in Eastern Central Asia. On account of the absence of Tang coins, the long period of use of worn coins, and the coins without inscriptions, Thierry dated the deposition of this hoard to the sixth or seventh century. Details of the Subashi hoard are not known.

Stein (1907: 482–3) heard of a hoard of Chinese coins found in a pot beneath the mud floor of a dwelling at Rawak. This hoard was large enough to have had a market value, and had been dispersed swiftly.[7] Stein was able to examine 'many dozens' of them, and purchased 87, which he identified as wuzhu coins in good condition, which had not been in circulation long. There are indeed 87 full-size Eastern Han wuzhu in good condition in the Stein collection. However, from the same group there are also some worn coins, some with clipped rims, one Wang Mang issue and possibly some later wuzhu coins, indicating that the hoard was deposited after the Han period.[8]

None of the five hoards was deposited earlier than the late Eastern Han, and none contains any Tang dynasty coins, first issued in 621. The hoards, deposited between the late second and early seventh centuries AD at different locations in Eastern Central Asia, confirm the wide distribution of wuzhu coins throughout Chinese Central Asia during this period, and probably earlier.

The Stein collection allows a closer examination of the smaller finds of wuzhu coins in context. Five areas yielded over one hundred wuzhu coins: the Lop Desert sites (323), Loulan (214), the Rawak Vihara site and vicinity (220-plus coins), Yotkan (130-plus), and various sites around Khotan (118). These finds and their contexts are considered below.

#### *Wuzhu from the Lop Desert sites and Loulan*

Stein acquired over 530 wuzhu at the Lop Desert sites and at the Loulan station L.A.:[9] most were surface finds. The single largest find comprised 211 large wuzhu in perfect condition, found northeast of Mesa L.J., on the ancient route between the station L.A. and the castrum L.E. (Stein 1928: 287–92). The coins had fallen from a caravan, and were scattered, as though falling from a swaying cart or camel, over a strip of ground 3–4 ft (*c.*1 m) wide for a distance of about 30 yds (*c.*27 m). About 50 yds (*c.*45 m) from the southeastern end of the line of coins lay a heap of Han dynasty bronze arrowheads, again in good condition and similar to Chinese arrowheads found at the Dunhuang fortifications. The juxtaposition of coins and arrowheads strongly suggested that they had fallen from a convoy coming from the Chinese side, carrying stores for troops. The combination of coins and arms on the old routes was also seen near Stein's Camp.ci, where he found five wuzhu coins and several items in copper and iron, including an iron skewer matching five found in 1907 at watch-stations of the Han *limes* west and north of Dunhuang (Stein 1928: 296–304; 1921, pl. LIV). The presence of Han dynasty coins and arrowheads confirms a definite link between the supply of coinage and military equipment.[10]

Although Stein reported 211 wuzhu found on the route, only 50 of these are represented in the Stein collection. These are Western Han types from the reigns of emperors Shaodi (86–73 BC) to Aidi (6–1 BC). They are in very good condition, and, if transported immediately after production, would indicate the early arrival of Chinese coins in the region. This would contradict the generally accepted view, followed explicitly by Zeymal (1992) and implicitly by Chinese numismatists (Jiang Qixiang 1990(1): 9), that wuzhu coins did not arrive in Eastern Central Asia before the Eastern Han (AD 25–220). The *Hanshu* (Xiyu zhuan, juan 96A; Hulsewé 1979: 91–2) records that in the 70s–60s BC the king of Loulan requested the Han government to set up an agricultural colony in his state, and that the Han government complied, sending out one major, 40 officers and other personnel. The agricultural colony was on the main route from Dunhuang to Loulan and further west until the easier route via Hami was opened in AD 73. These coins may have been intended for the new agricultural colony at Loulan, or for troops further west.

Given the importance both of Dunhuang as the westernmost Chinese station and of the *limes* fortifications guarding the routes, the quantity of wuzhu coins found at the defence stations is surprisingly small, with single coins found occasionally, but not regularly, at such sites. Presumably, there was little need for cash on watch-duty, and a greater need at the military bases, or farming garrisons (*tuntian*).

The 50 coins scattered on the road are uniquely homogenous among the coins from the Lop Desert in the Stein collection. By far the majority of finds from these sites are later issues and most are very worn. There is great variety among the Lop Desert coins: Western Han coins, worn or fragmentary later wuzhu types, found together with Wang Mang issues. Coins of different sizes were found together, as though they had once been used together. Some are full-size wuzhu, some are clipped wuzhu, and some are small coins often without inscription, commonly known as 'goose-eye' or 'chicken-eye' coins.

The terms 'goose-eye coins' (*eyan qian*) and 'chicken-eye coins' (*jiyan qian*) describe the small size of these coins (diameter ranges 10–17 mm, usually *c.*12 mm; central hole *c.*6 mm; weight 0.2–1.00 g, usually *c.*0.5 g). Where there is an inscription it is usually a crude rendering of 'wuzhu', with only half the characters visible. They appear to be modelled on clipped wuzhu coins, and lack an outer rim, although there is sometimes a rim around the square hole on one or both sides. They are crudely made, and not finished: casting sprues are often visible, and some have an exaggerated raised obverse, rendering them more robust. Whilst early historical references to 'goose-eye coins' are found in the *Suishu* (Shihuo zhi, juan 24, 690) refering to the problems caused by unofficial debased coins, the earliest archaeological context for 'goose-eye coins' is from a group of tombs at Jiayuguan, Gansu, dated AD 257–316 (Wu Rongzeng 1998).

Hoards in central China suggest that 'goose-eye coins', or reduced-size 'wuzhu', probably appeared in the Three Kingdoms period (220–65)[11] and continued to be made during the Northern and Southern Dynasties (420–589).[12] They are found in large numbers, particularly in Hebei, Henan, Shaanxi and Shandong, and clay moulds for 'goose-eye coins' have been found at Handan (Hebei province) (Wu Rongzeng 1998: 207). Wu Rongzeng suggests that the 'goose-eye coins' from the Qiuci region, Kucha, were cast there in the Northern and Southern Dynasties or later, but gives no explanation for this later dating (see Chapter 6).

Huang Wenbi (1948: 133) also reported finding six hundred 'wuzhu coins of different sizes by the old roadside' near the Kongque River in the Lop region. These numbers confirm that large quantities of coins were being transported in the region, but the great variety of wuzhu coins and derivatives found at surface level in the Lop Desert allows only broad conclusions to be drawn.

#### ***Wuzhu from Rawak and the Rawak Vihara***

The hoard of coins reported from Rawak has been discussed above. Stein also found there two separate clusters of coins which had corroded in such a way as to prove that Chinese coins were used in strings in Eastern Central Asia (Plate 1, 6). One of the clusters was intentionally separated during cleaning in 1993, and revealed an assortment of good coins alongside worn and clipped wuzhu coins (Plate 1, 7–14). There is no obvious indication from the coins themselves as to how the various wuzhu coins functioned together; whether one coin counted as one unit of currency regardless of size and appearance, or whether there was a system allowing for discrepancy by means of premium and discount rates.

At the Rawak Vihara, Stein found wuzhu coins which had been used as votive offerings, particularly at the base of pedestals of statues or inserted between the plaster mouldings and wooden boarding of the stupa base. Three wuzhu were found on the floor at the base of the seated Buddha [R.ix]; two were found below a relief [R.ix]; one was found behind another relief [R.xxviii]; one at the foot of the large statue [R.lxiv]; one in the side-wall of the gate and over sixty wuzhu in the mouldings at the foot of the stupa base (Stein 1907: 493–578). There was a predominance of coins on the west side of the stupa base, but the significance of this is not known; 22 coins and some fragments on the west, 12 on the north, 14 and some corroded together on the east, and 12 coins and numerous fragments on the south side (Stein 1907: 501). As Stein rightly noted, coins used as votive offerings were likely to be current issues, and the date of these coins marks the latest chronological limit for the abandonment of the site, though again to some time between the third and seventh century.

In his analysis of the numismatic data from the Rawak Vihara and its vicinity, Stein (1907: 205, 501) repeated an erroneous statement he had made during his analysis of the Chinese coins from Yotkan, namely that '. . . of Chinese round coins, those bearing no legend belong to the earliest type'. There is no evidence to support this claim; conversely the evidence supplied by 'goose-eye coins' suggests that round coins without inscription are more likely to be later issues. Such coins appear in the Stein collection with full-size wuzhu coins, and it is feasible that they may have been produced locally in Eastern Central Asia. Simple 'blanks' in the form of Chinese coins (without inscriptions or rims) have been found at other sites, including gold-plated examples, sewn on to headwear found at the Yingpan burials [IA.XII.f.1–3] (Stein 1928: 760) (Plate 4, 58),[13] also the embossed gold-foil disk, on an iron base [Lop Desert L.C.022] (Stein 1928: 248, pl. XXIV), and the bronze disk in the form of a Chinese coin, but thinner and concavo-convex [Lop Desert L.A.012] (Stein 1928: 220, pl. XXIV).[14] Although these specimens from Yingpan and the Lop Desert were made for decorative and/or burial puposes, they demonstrate that the simple production of coin 'blanks' could easily have been a local phenomenon. The Yingpan burials have been attributed to the Han-Jin period, so may date as late as the early fifth century.[15]

### *Wuzhu from Yotkan and other sites in the Khotan region*

Stein acquired over 130 wuzhu coins as coming from the Yotkan site. Of these, 48 were allegedly from the chance discovery of a hoard of copper coins [S.IV.A.e.1–48]. All the coins listed 'as from Yotkan' were presented to Stein or sold to him as coming from the site, where an annual washing for gold took place every summer (Stein 1912: 177, 437). Stein did not find any at the site himself.

Coins brought to Stein 'as from Khotan' included various types of wuzhu, Wang Mang, Sino-Kharoshthi, Tang, Song and Islamic coins. These were washed out of the 'culture-strata' at Yotkan, or found as 'the fragmentary débris characteristic of those completely eroded sites known as "tatis"', for example from Ak-sipil and the Hanguya tatis. It is therefore difficult to draw any detailed conclusions from the wuzhu coins from Yotkan and the Khotan region.

### Wuzhu: a discussion

Wuzhu coins are numerous, and their long period of validity and circulation renders identification and interpretation difficult. Dates of deposition of hoards and smaller groups of wuzhu coins can seldom be determined on the basis of the coins alone.

With the exception of the 211 Western Han coins which had fallen from a convoy along the route through the Lop Desert, most coins which may be identified as Western Han wuzhu were found in association with later coins, suggesting their later arrival in Eastern Central Asia. The recent discovery of early Western Han wuzhu (118–113 BC) and other Western Han objects in disturbed Cheshi tombs at Jiaohe cannot confirm an earlier date than late Western Han for the arrival of wuzhu in Eastern Central Asia, as some passage of time would be required for the Cheshi people to acquire Chinese goods (Liu Xuetang 1999: 451). Therefore, whilst it is possible that the earliest wuzhu coins may have arrived in Eastern Central Asia in the late Western Han, it is more probable that the early coins arrived together with later coins.

The majority of wuzhu coins found in Eastern Central Asia are Eastern Han standard issues, clipped wuzhu coins and copies. However, these coins remained in use until the early seventh century. In this way, the presence of wuzhu coins does not provide sufficient information for the precise dating of a site. The discovery of coin moulds at Bachu and other sites in the Kucha region (see Chapter 6) proves that 'wuzhu'-style coins were being produced locally, but unfortunately throws little light on the precise date of these coins.

Wuzhu coins are found widely distributed south of the Tianshan Mountains, with large numbers reported as surface finds from urban or settlement sites, or at sites associated with military garrisons and defence structures, such as beacon towers. Examination of the wuzhu coins and imitations in the Stein collection reveals that the ratio of full-size to crude or clipped coins (where only half the inscription is visible) at sites ranges from 50:50 to 70:30, and that a higher proportion of good coins is generally found where there were official Chinese settlements: for example, there is a high proportion of full-size coins at the Loulan sites. Although this evidence from the Stein collection can be regarded only as a sample of the much larger body of evidence, these proportions none the less compare well with the large deposits of wuzhu coins found in Gansu province, where tomb deposits of the Later Han period (AD 25–220) usually show a 50:50 ratio of good to crude or clipped coins (GSQBXH 1989: 7).[16]

The evidence from Gansu provides a useful and important comparison. There is clear evidence, despite Emperor Wudi's state monopoly on coin production from 113 BC, of local coin production in Gansu during the Han dynasty. Hundreds of thousands of wuzhu have been found at Wuwei, Huixian and Wenxian, and bronze coin moulds have been unearthed at Lintao and Nanguan, Huixian (GSQBXH 1989: 11). Han dynasty documentary evidence found at sites in Gansu shows clearly that coins were also transported over long distances, via the Hexi corridor, to the frontier sites (see Chapter 7). The documents indicate that the costs for border defence and its financial administration were mainly paid for from tax collection in central China (Chen Wunian 1998: 56), and reveal that coin supply was not always sufficient. Those slips that do refer to coin production in Gansu are concentrated around the period AD 25 when Dou Rong and his troops had occupied Gansu, when supply of coinage did not meet demand, and when Dou Rong had tried to institute a system of salary payments in grain rather than coin. At this time, illicit casting of 'small thin coins', i.e. sub-standard underweight coins, was widespread. To counter this, Dou Rong issued regulations permitting only county-level officials to cast wuzhu coins on condition they were up to the legal standard (see Juyan slips [EPF22: 38A-B, 39–41] in GS-ARC et al. 1990: 478–9) (see Chapter 7).

It is important that the proposal to restore the wuzhu in the early Eastern Han came from Gansu, namely from Ma Yuan (14 BC – AD 49), Governor of Longxi. It indicates the necessity of coinage in the northwest. Although the proposal was initially refused on the grounds that such a vast project was deemed impossible, Ma Yuan was eventually able to persuade the emperor to start coin production. Ma had previously led victorious battles against non-Chinese people in the south and against the Qiang peoples in eastern Gansu. These threats had been so serious that, when the large-scale Liangzhou rebellion later broke out in eastern Gansu (AD 110), the Chinese government even considered abandoning the northwestern frontier to the Qiang. In the end, the cost of defending Liangzhou through the period AD 107–18 alone cost the Chinese government over 24,000 million coins (Yü Ying-shih 1986: 432).

### Coins issued during the Wang Mang period (AD 9–23) (Plate 1, 15–18)

Four of Wang Mang's coin-types are found in Eastern Central Asia: the daquan wushi, the xiaoquan zhiyi, the huoquan and the buquan. These issues are similar in form to wuzhu coins. There is no evidence for any of Wang Mang's spade money in Eastern Central Asia; the unique example [IA.III.A.b.1] in the Stein collection was presented to Stein as a gift (Stein 1928: 67).

The daquan wushi [large coin worth 50] was issued AD 7–20 with the initial value of 1 daquan wushi to 50 coins (*Hanshu*, Shihuo zhi, juan 24, 1117–88). There are five specimens in the Stein collection: four were found on the Dunhuang *limes*, and one was found at the Loulan station L.A. All are small, and four are extremely small, thin and fragmentary. Clearly, they are all private castings, and, most probably, locally made.[17] A further four specimens have been reported from Qitai, another two from Loulan and an unknown number from Kucha, Hami, at sites in the Khotan region, and from Wuwei (Gansu) and Dunhuang (Gansu), but full details are not known (Zhang Zhongshan 1999: 194).

The xiaoquan zhiyi [small coin worth 1] was issued AD 9–13 to circulate alongside the daquan wushi, at the rate of 50:1 (*Hanshu*, Wang Mang zhuan, juan 99, 4039–196). There is one specimen in the Stein collection [IA.VII.c.1]. It was found at the Loulan station L.A. It closely resembles the xiaoquan zhiyi type unearthed in Luoyang (Henan province), which has a heavy rim around the hole on the reverse, diameter 14.6 mm, outer rim 1.6 mm thick, and weight 1.3 g (ZGQBDCD: Qin Han bian: 450). Another two xiaoquan zhiyi have subsequently been reported at Loulan (Zhang Zhongshan 1999: 411). Clay moulds for xiaoquan zhiyi have been found in eastern Gansu at Qingyang, Huaixian and Tongwei (Zhang Zhongshan 1999: 194); but the evidence suggests that very few of these coins found their way to Eastern Central Asia.

The huoquan was issued from AD 14. The similarity in form and size between huoquan and many wuzhu coins is striking. Indeed, in the batch of coins purchased by Stein as coming from Ak-sipil, Rawak and Jumbe-kum, all in the Khotan region, one damaged huoquan was previously misidentified as a wuzhu. This coin has a diameter of 22 mm, as do some of the clipped rim wuzhu coins, hence the misattribution. When strung together, it would have been impossible to distinguish between the smaller wuzhu and the huoquan. Huoquan are the most common of the Wang Mang types found in Eastern Central Asia. There are 28 specimens in the Stein collection. He found 22 huoquan at the sites of Niya (three), Loulan (nine) Loulan station L.A. (four), L.G. (one), the *limes* (one), Nanhu (three) and Ming-oi (one), and also purchased one huoquan at the Yotkan site, and purchased another five huoquan alleged to have come from sites in the Khotan region or at Chong Tim. There is also in the Stein collection a fragment of a buquan coin [S.XI.A.g.10].

The association of Wang Mang issues with wuzhu coins in Eastern Central Asia is striking, and parallels coin finds in central China, where Wang Mang issues are found in deposits made after the restoration of the Han dynasty in AD 25. The wuzhu was restored in AD 40, and Eastern Han deposits, such as the Leitai hoard (Gansu), show that the new wuzhu coins circulated with earlier wuzhu, huoquan and daquan wushi coins (Gan-bo-wen 1972). It is likely that the Wang Mang issues arrived in Eastern Central Asia with Eastern Han coins for the following reasons: Wang Mang coins are not found in great number in the region; they are usually found with wuzhu coins, at sites associated with official Chinese presence; there is no evidence of local coin production in the region at this time; and the documentary evidence dated *c.*AD 25 from Gansu indicates there was insufficient coin supply further to the east during the early years of the first millenium.

The total number of Wang Mang coins is rather lower than might be expected. In the winter of AD 10–11, Wang Mang is known to have increased the number of soldiers at the existing military bases in Dunhuang and Juyan, and to have mobilized troops at twelve points on the northern border in a display of power to the Xiongnu. Chinese wood slips found at Maquanwan, Gansu, reveal details of Wang Mang's attacks on Eastern Central Asia in AD 16–17 (Hu Pingsheng 2000: 16–17). The excavations of the Xuanquan zhi, a station near Dunhuang, further show that Wang Mang maintained strong links with Eastern Central Asia (see Chapter 7). The coin evidence from further east in Gansu would appear to support this: coin moulds have been found at Pingliang, Qingyang, Huaixian, Tongwei, Yuzhong, Lanzhou and Jiuquan, and large quantities of Wang Mang coins have been unearthed, for example, in the Huixian hoard of several thousand coins found in 1980 (GSQBXH 1989: 6; Zhang Zhongshan 1999: 194).

### Coins of the Wei (220–65), Jin (265–420) and Northern and Southern Dynasties (420–589) (Plate 2, 19–21)

This period corresponds to the time between the collapse of the Han dynasty (AD 220) and the subsequent fragmentation of the Han empire into smaller states and the Sui reunification in 581. There was no unity of coinage in central China during this period: some states issued coins, others did not, and many old wuzhu coins remained in circulation. For example, a type recently identified as Cao-Wei wuzhu (with the outer rim encroaching on the inscription) usually represents less than 2 per cent of the coins in hoards found in central China, indicating that these coins were issued in addition to, rather than as replacements for, existing wuzhu coins. Coin hoards deposited during the Wei-Jin period at Yecheng (the busiest market centre in north China after the destruction of the cities of Chang'an and Luoyang) comprise mostly Eastern Han wuzhu coins; those deposited at Yecheng during the Northern Dynasties comprise mostly Northern Dynasties coins, such as the Yong'an wuzhu and Changping wuzhu. Very large coin hoards of the period of fragmentation consist primarily of Eastern Han coins: for example, the Xuchang Panxiang Penlicun hoard of 335 kg, and the Luoyang Xindianxiang hoard of 45 kg (Cao-Wei keti zu 1997). Consequently, it is important to remember that Han dynasty wuzhu coins found in Eastern

Central Asia may, in fact, have a much later date of deposition than the Eastern Han coins themselves may suggest. The context and associated finds often allow for more accurate dating of a site than the coins themselves.

There are very few finds in Eastern Central Asia of coins issued by the various states prior to the Sui and Tang unification. Only three coins have definite attributions: these are the three Changping wuzhu coins issued by the Northern Qi dynasty in 553: two from the Turfan region, and one of uncertain provenance (Jiang Qixiang 1990(1): 9; Dong Qingxuan and Jiang Qixiang 1991: 8). One of the specimens from Turfan [IA.XII.a.4] was recovered by Stein among the earth and decayed matting from the disturbed Astana tomb [Ast.i.3]. This tomb had contained two bodies, the larger of which had an imitation Byzantine coin [IA.XII.a.1] in his mouth (Stein 1928: 647). It would appear then that, during this period of over 350 years, only a very small number of coins from fragmented China may have reached as far as Eastern Central Asia. It is striking that the finest examples of these, the Changping wuzhu coins, were found in tombs associated with people either Chinese in origin or accustomed to Chinese culture. Thierry and Morrisson (1994) noted a similar association of Byzantine coins and imitations in 'Chinese' tombs (see Chapter 5).

The paucity of coins from central China can be explained in part by the fragmentation of the Chinese empire and the effects of the collapse of the centralized administration on Eastern Central Asia; and in part by the substantial role of silk and grain as important forms of money in central China during this period. Grain was widely used for official salary payments and in military administrative matters; silk was used for larger transactions and coin for much smaller transactions. The histories state that 'the Hexi region [the main route from central China to Eastern Central Asia] had not used coins since the 230s' (*Jin Shi*: 86, Biography of Zhang Gui (255–314); Peng Xinwei 1965; Kaplan 1994: 187). When Zhang Zhonghua (ruled 349–55, descendant of Zhang Gui) issued Liangzao xinquan coins, there was insufficient copper in Liangzhou to cast an adequate quantity of coins, and it was too costly to transport raw copper from rich mines such as those in the Tianshan Mountains north of Qiuci (Chen Wunian 1998: 257–8). Consequently, the large hoards found in Wuwei (Gansu), deposited in the first half of the fourth century, consist mainly of old wuzhu coins: for example, the Hongsicun hoard of 45 kg, found in 1989, and the Hongxingcun hoard of 30 kg, found in 1990 (Zhong Changfa 1996). The latter hoard, ranging from Qin-Han banliang coins to fenghuo coins (issued AD 319), totalled over fourteen thousand coins of which over 50 per cent were Han standard or clipped wuzhu (2,800-plus and 4,600-plus coins, respectively) and almost 25 per cent were Wei-Jin wuzhu (5,600-plus coins).

However, the impact of Chinese coins in Eastern Central Asia during the Han period was already strong enough to stimulate local production of Chinese-style coins in Eastern Central Asia during this period of over three centuries (see Chapter 6).

### Coins of the Tang period (618–907) (Plate 2, 22–7)

Tang dynasty coins of the types Kaiyuan tongbao (first issued AD 621) and Qianyuan zhongbao (first issued 758) have been found throughout Eastern Central Asia. However, most publications on Tang dynasty coins in Eastern Central Asia have focused not on these types from central China but on the Dali yuanbao (issued during the Dali reign 766–79) and the Jianzhong tongbao (Jianzhong reign 780–3) types, and cruder coins with the single character inscription *yuan* or *zhong*, which were produced locally in Eastern Central Asia, and not in central China. These local issues are discussed further in Chapter 6.

There are 311 Kaiyuan tongbao in the Stein collection. Here and in subsequent lists, alleged finds are in square brackets. Most were found at sites, often at surface level: from Aduna-kora (four), Ak-tiken ([one]), Arkalik ([three]), Astana (one), Chalma-kazan ([two]), Chong Tim (four + [seven]), Dandan-Uiliq (six), Dawan kum tatis (one), Domoko (one), tatis north-west of Domoko (two), Dunhuang *limes* (78), east of Chong Hassar (one), Hanguya tatis ([one]), Kharakhoto (three), east of Kharakhoto (one), Kara-khoja [= Gaochang] (23), Khadalik (four), Khotan (six), Kine-tokmak ([one]), Kucha ([one]), Lachin-ata ([one]), Mazar Tagh (one), Ming-oi (seven), Miran (six), Nanhu (nine), Rawak (one), So-yang-cheng (12), tatis north of Tumshuk (two), tatis east of the Yurung-kash ([two]), Toghrak-akin (one), Toyuk ([ten]), Vash-shahri ([three]), west of Kudughun ([five]), Yarkand ([one]), Yotkan ([six]), Yar-khoto [= Jiaohe] (95) and unknown origin ([two]).

The largest finds, from Yar-khoto and the Dunhuang *limes*, are the most significant. The Dunhuang *limes* site [T.xiv.f] was a Buddhist shrine on the hillock north of the fort [T.xiv.v]. The 78 Kaiyuan were found together with two wuzhu coins and two hairpins, in a small wooden bowl beneath the reed flooring. The absence of Qianyuan coins provides a *terminus ante quem* of 758. Chinese documents found at the shrine confirm that the hoard was deposited after 650, most probably in the eighth century. The hoard must have been deposited between the mid seventh and mid eighth century.

The 95 coins from Yar-khoto were part of a group of 100 coins, which also contained four Qianyuan and one wuzhu without inscription, deposited in the upper-storey wall of a small dwelling. The presence of the Qianyuan indicates a date of deposition after 758.

These two finds therefore allow a comparison of Kaiyuan deposited before and after the middle of the eighth century. The Kaiyuan in the earlier hoard are well made, in a grey-greenish bronze, suggesting production in central China, and their good condition indicates they had not been in circulation long. The Kaiyuan in the Yar-khoto hoard are less uniformly well-made and are more worn. Kaiyuan in the earlier hoard have diameters ranging from 23 to 25.5 mm, with a majority (over 92 per cent) at 24–25 mm. The coins in the later hoard are less consistent in size, with diameters ranging from 22 to 26 mm: 62 per cent have a diameter of 24–25 mm, 24 per cent have a diameter of 25.5 mm. The average weights are 3.88 g and 3.47 g respectively, a difference of 0.4 g per coin.[18]

Four other sites yielded over ten Kaiyuan: Kara-khoja, So-yang-cheng, Arkalik and Vash-shahri. In each case the Kaiyuan were found, or purchased, with other coin-types of different periods. The Kaiyuan from the tatis near Chong Tim were found together with wuzhu coins; those acquired at Kelpin, allegedly from Chong Tim, came with Dali yuanbao and a huoquan. The Kaiyuan from So-yang-cheng were found at surface level with wuzhu and Song and Jin dynasty coins of the twelfth century. The Kaiyuan coins from Kara-khoja also suggest a twelfth-century date of deposit; they were found in a bronze cooking pot with Song dynasty coins, as part of a hoard of various metal objects in a large, octagonal stupa. The Kaiyuan from Toyuk were purchased together with six Song and 14 Qing dynasty coins. These finds confirm the reoccupation of earlier sites during the Tang dynasty and subsequent periods, and suggest that wuzhu coins may have continued to circulate in Eastern Central Asia during the Tang dynasty. They offer little information relevant to the Tang dynasty.

The seven coins from Ming-oi were, like the Dunhuang *limes* hoard, votive deposits. They were found in a shrine, at the bases of images in the shrine, in the temple corridor, an antechapel and a temple room.

In terms of their physical attributes, there are 209 Kaiyuan coins and fragments of which the diameter can be measured. The diameters range from 22 to 26 mm, with 176 coins (over 84 per cent) measuring 24.5–25 mm. Misalignment of the reverse mould is visible on 68 coins (33 per cent). When the coins are arranged by diameter size, at 0.5 mm differences, the rate of misalignment is a consistent 25 per cent of coins in each of the following groups of the same diameter size (22.5, 23, 24, 24.5, 25 mm). The weight ranges from 1.57 to 5.29 g.[19]

Some of the Kaiyuan have intentional marks on the reverse: 31 coins (15 per cent) have a crescent on the reverse. On 27 coins the crescent is found above the hole, and on four coins it is below the hole (Plate 2, 23). The coins are well made and of standard size: 30 have a diameter of 25–25.5 mm, and one has a diameter of 24 mm. Fifteen (48 per cent) of these coins came from the Yar-khoto hoard; other specimens were found at sites east of Kharakhoto (one), Ming-oi (two), Chong Tim (one), Kara-khoja (one) and Dandan-Uiliq (one). The rest were purchased or given, allegedly from sites around Khotan.

Three coins have a 'nail-mark' on the reverse; these were found east of Chong Hassar, at Yar-khoto and on the tatis north of Tumshuk. One coin [IA.IV.a.8] has the character *ping* on the reverse, indicating the Pingzhou mint (Hebei). It is a Huichang Kaiyuan, issued after 845 (Plate 2, 24).[20] However, its provenance is unreliable: it was obtained by Badruddin Khan allegedly from or near Domoko, with a group of coins containing many Song dynasty types of the twelfth century.

Qianyuan zhongbao were issued from 758, with a nominal value of 10, but new issues of Qianyuan in the late 760s had a revised value of 1, making Qianyuan equal in value to Kaiyuan (Chen Yuan and Sun Zhonghui 1991: 3). The Qianyuan found in Eastern Central Asia are all specimens with a single rim on the reverse, issued from the late 760s onwards.

There are 417 Qianyuan zhongbao in the Stein collection: from Ak-sipil ([five]), Ak-terek and Ak-terek tatis (23), Ak-tiken ([four]), Arkalik ([one]), Chalma-kazan ([11]), Dandan-Uiliq (six), Domoko and Uzun tati ([eight]), Hanguya and Hanguya tatis ([nine]), Jigda-kuduk ([one]), Kalalik ([eight]), Kara-yantak ([one]), Khadalik (79), Khotan and Khotan tatis ([28]), Kine-tokmak (two), Kumbagh ([ten]), Kucha ([three]), sites north of Jiya and Suya ([four]), west of Kudughun ([one]), Mazar Tagh (eight + [one]), So-yang-cheng (two), Togujai, Moji ([18]), Toyuk ([12]), Ushak-tal near Karashahr (one), West Lach ([one]), Yotkan ([158]), Yar-khoto (six) and unknown origin ([six]). The distribution reveals that an overwhelming majority of Qianyuan zhongbao came from sites on the southern route, particularly around Khotan. The largest group found at site came from votive deposits in a Buddhist shrine at Khadallik, where 87 coins were found, some still strung together, and comprised wuzhu, Kaiyuan tongbao, Qianyuan zhongbao and local issues dating to the Tang dynasty.

In terms of the physical attributes, the Qianyuan in the Stein collection have diameters ranging from 20 to 30 mm, with concentrations at 28–30 mm (87 coins, 20 per cent) and 21–22 mm (268 coins, 64 per cent), suggesting that there were two major sizes of Qianyuan in circulation. A much smaller concentration at 25.5–26.5 mm is represented by 13 coins (3 per cent). Thierry (1997a) has also noted three sizes of Qianyuan, albeit with slightly different ranges of diameters: over 28 mm, 24–26 mm, and 20.5–22 mm. It would appear that successive issues of Qianyuan progressively decreased in size and quality.

Misalignment of the reverse mould is visible on 89 Qianyuan (21 per cent), and similar misalignment is found together with misaligned piercing of the square hole on 46 coins (11 per cent). On one coin the square hole remains unpierced. Of the 87 Qianyuan with diameter 28–30 mm, 18 (over 20 per cent) have a misaligned reverse, and 7 (8 per cent) have both misaligned reverse and misaligned piercing of the square hole. The rate of misaligned reverse on the two main sizes is therefore fairly consistent. However, the rate soars in the group of Qianyuan with diameters 25.5–26.5 mm, where seven coins (54 per cent) have a misaligned reverse, and one coin (8 per cent) has both misaligned reverse and piercing of the square hole. Furthermore, two coins (both with diam. 21.5 mm) have casting sprues, and two coins (diam. 22 mm, 26 mm) were cast with a cracked reverse mould. If crudeness is indicative of local production, then the evidence in the Stein collection suggests that three sizes of Qianyuan zhongbao were produced in Eastern Central Asia.

## Tang coins: a discussion

The Stein collection holds over seven hundred Kaiyuan tongbao and Qianyuan zhongbao. The Pelliot collection holds fifty Kaiyuan and Qianyuan (Thierry 1997a). Chinese archaeologists have reported finds of both types throughout Eastern Central Asia, including two large finds of Tang coins near Loulan and at Lanchengzi.

Near Loulan, a group of over nine hundred Kaiyuan in very good condition was found scattered in a line along the route, suggesting a steady loss of coins spilling from moving transport (Mu Shunying 1987). Surface finds of Kaiyuan are usually reported as being found in association with other coin-types, as seen in the Stein collection. That the Loulan find consisted exclusively of Kaiyuan coins in good condition, and that over nine hundred coins were recovered, corresponding to almost one string of 1,000 coins, strongly suggests that these were coins lost from a consignment from central China.

The Lanchengzi hoard comprised 5–6 kg of coins. It was found in May 1981 at Lanchengzi, a city site strategically located between Gaochang and Yanqi, with a direct route south to Loulan. Allowing 3–4 g per coin would give an approximate total of 1,250–2,000 coins from this hoard. A sample of only eight coins was removed from this hoard: five Kaiyuan tongbao, two Jianzhong tongbao and one Dali yuanbao. As these were all issued during the Tang period, and as the city was destroyed by fire in the late Tang, it is unlikely that there were any later coins in the hoard (Jiang Qixiang 1990(1): 10–11).

The total number of Kaiyuan and Qianyuan found in Eastern Central Asia is not known, but must already exceed three thousand specimens. Those in the Stein collection indicate a distribution predominantly on the southern route. This is in striking contrast to the conclusion reached by Thierry (1997a), and to some extent it can be explained by the disproportionate lengths of time spent by Stein on the southern route and Pelliot on the northern route. However, Chinese numismatists also report a predominance of these types on the northern route, a large part of which must be explained by the Loulan and Lanchengzi hoards (ZGQBXH-SR 1995).

Of the total 728 Kaiyuan and Qianyuan coins in the Stein collection, 311 (43 per cent) are Kaiyuan tongbao and 417 (57 per cent) are Qianyuan zhongbao. The ratio of Kaiyuan to Qianyuan is quite remarkable, as the Kaiyuan is usually considered to be the more common type, both in Eastern Central Asia and in central China. Of the 50 specimens of Kaiyuan and Qianyuan in the Pelliot collection, 37 (74 per cent) are Kaiyuan and 13 (26 per cent) are Qianyuan. Of the 41 Kaiyuan and Qianyuan in the Oldenburg collection, 29 (71 per cent) are Kaiyuan and 12 (29 per cent) are Qianyuan. Chinese archaeologists and numismatists also regard the Kaiyuan as the more common type in Eastern Central Asia, yet the Stein collection suggests the opposite.

These two observations in the Stein collection demand further attention. Recent studies have proved the existence of a Chinese mint in the Anxi prefecture (modern-day Kucha) in the seventh century, which produced both Kaiyuan and Qianyuan coins, as well as other types (see Chapter 6). As Thierry (1997a) noted, there are similarities between the Kaiyuan and the middle-sized Qianyuan. However, the latter represent only 3 per cent of all Qianyuan in the Stein collection; they do not detract from the dominance of the small-size Qianyuan on the southern route. The similarities between the small Qianyuan and the locally produced Jianzhong and Dali coins further suggest that this small size of coin (20.5–22 mm) was the usual size of Chinese coins in the region, certainly in the last quarter of the eighth century. Fuller details of the more recent finds of Kaiyuan and Qianyuan in Eastern Central Asia would demonstrate whether the respective proportions of these types in the Stein collection are typical or not. The two large Tang coin deposits in the Stein collection were both found at sites associated with the northern route, and in both the Kaiyuan was the dominant type. The Tang types in the Stein collection, therefore, support the general view that the Kaiyuan were the major coin-type at sites on the northern route, but uniquely suggest that the Qianyuan may have been the major type at sites further south.

Zeymal (1992) and Thierry (1997a) regarded the Tang dynasty coins as falling into two groups: the earlier Kaiyuan tongbao, and the Qianyuan, Dali and Jianzhong types, all issued in the late eighth century, concluding that these later types prevailed over the Kaiyuan. The common view is that the later coins were produced locally in Eastern Central Asia. Ivotchkina (1975) observed that many of the late eighth-century Tang coins in the Oldenburg collection were unusually red in colour, and proposed that they were local issues.[21] This is certainly true in the Stein collection for some Kaiyuan coins and for many of the later Tang coins. Thierry (1997a) noted a similar redness in the Kaiyuan coins in the Kerish and Duldur-Aqur hoards, and proposed that the coins were produced locally, near the rich copper mines of the Kucha region. The difference in appearance among the Tang dynasty coins in the region indicates that some, especially the earlier Kaiyuan coins, were imported from mainland China and that some may have been made locally.

Historical references indicate that in central China the cost of producing Tang coins was extremely high, costing at least 750 coins in metal alone to manufacture one thousand coins, and that by 780 the cost of producing coins and transporting them to the capital ranged from 900 cash per thousand to 2,000 cash per thousand, i.e. double their face value (Twitchett 1970: 29–30).[22] It would therefore have been exceptionally costly to transport Tang coins to Eastern Central Asia, and therefore logical, economically and politically, to engage in coin production in Eastern Central Asia. Kucha was well known for its copper mines, was already producing its own coinage (see Chapter 6), and would have been an obvious location for a mint.[23] Metal analysis on a very small sample of Tang coins from Eastern Central Asia has indicated a much higher lead content than in contemporary coins from central China (Rhodes 1997), a feature that was also mentioned in the histories relating to Kucha. Jiang Qixiang (1990(1): 10–11) and Thierry (1997a: 161 n48) have suggested that the crescent mark on the reverse of many Tang coins found throughout Eastern Central Asia may be an indicator of local production, 'a local characteristic of the Anxi protectorate'. However, this and similar marks are found on many coins unearthed in central China and are not uniquely characteristic of Anxi.

As the Stein collection demonstrates, Tang coins with the same inscription but of different sizes and quality are found together. When coins of different quality are in circulation, there is a tendency either for the good coins to disappear from circulation (as per Gresham's Law, that bad coins drive out good) or for the better-quality coins to command a premium over inferior specimens. However, good coins appear to have remained in circulation alongside poorer specimens in the late eighth century in Eastern Central Asia. The coins themselves do not indicate their individual value or value relative to coins of better or poorer quality. Good coins appear to have remained in circulation in Eastern Central Asia, and the contemporary documents from Turfan merely indicate the number, and not quality, of cash coins. This suggests either that the coins circulated at par or that they circulated with premiums for the better coins and discounts for the inferior coins.

The Qianyuan zhongbao coins fall into three groups according to size: large 27–28 mm; medium 24–26 mm, and small 20–22 mm in diameter. The large Qianyuan zhongbao are well made. The small Qianyuan zhongbao are very similar to the small Dali yuanbao and Jianzhong tongbao. It would appear that successive issues of Qianyuan zhongbao decreased in size and deteriorated in quality.

Qianyuan zhongbao were issued in central China during the Qianyuan reign (758–60), which was contemporary with the disastrous An Lushan rebellion (758–63). The earliest Qianyuan coins issued in 758 had a value of 10 (i.e. 10 Kaiyuan tongbao), and served as tokens during this period of shortage of coins.[24] However, new Qianyuan zhongbao coins were cast in the late

760s, with a revised value of 1, i.e. equal in value to the Kaiyuan coin (Chen Yuan and Sun Zhonghui, Daxi 3, 1991: 13). Thierry (1997a) states that all the Qianyuan coins found in Xinjiang are 'worth-10' specimens. However, the comparable size of small Kaiyuan, small Qianyuan, Dali and Jianzhong coins, and the *terminus ante quem* provided by the Dali (766–79) and Jianzhong (780–3) coins, suggests that all four types of this size have an individual value of 1, and that the character *zhong* in the inscription merely repeats the *zhong* of the original Qianyuan zhongbao type, without representing its larger token value.[25] There can be no doubt that there was a debasement of the coinage as conditions deteriorated in the Anxi protectorate in the 760s and 770s, during its prolonged isolation from the central Tang court.

## Notes

1. For example, 756 items of Khotanese jade were found in the tomb of Fu Hao, at Yinxu, Anyang, in 1968; see CASSIA 1980: 228.
2. The earliest known mould for banliang coins is the bronze mould from Dongshecun in Fengxiang (Shaanxi province), on the southern bank of Yongshui River, corresponding with Yong, the capital of the Qin state for almost three hundred years between 677 and 383 BC (Jiang Ruoshi 1989: 3).
3. Stein's banliang from Loulan was misidentified as a wuzhu coin until cleaned in 1993. In a similar way, Stein's 'banliang' from Khadalik turned out to be a worn wuzhu coin.
4. I am grateful to Joe Cribb for sharing his notes and photographs of these coins resulting from his correspondence with Professor Härtel of the Museum für Indische Kunst, Berlin, 1983–84.
5. This figure includes both whole coins and fragments where it was possible to measure the diameter of the coin.
6. The Tajik hoard is now in the Musée Guimet, Paris.
7. The market value of the hoard was estimated at 300 Khotan tangas, which Stein noted as being equivalent to over 100 rupees.
8. There is also a small Islamic coin in with these coins. However, since some of the Rawak coins appear to be missing, it is possible that this coin has been misplaced.
9. L.A. refers to the main group of ruins at Loulan. It was a small fortified station, garrisoned by Chinese troops with the intention of guarding the route from Dunhuang.
10. The link between coinage and military pay has been observed in the Roman world; for an excellent introduction see van Heesch (forthcoming). Military expenditure was regarded as the main item of imperial expenditure; see Duncan (1993: 6).
11. See Huang Lichun (1992) on the hoard of 40 kg of coins found in the wall of the Han–Wei city of Xudu, which contained over one thousand standard coins (Eastern Han wuzhu and Three Kingdoms coins), 28 copies of huoquan, twenty thousand copies of clipped coins, and about eleven thousand goose-eye coins. No associated finds suggested a date later than the Three Kingdoms period.
12. A hoard found at Anyang, deposited in the Northern and Southern Dynasties, contained many clipped and goose-eye coins, as well as 500-plus Han wuzhu, 600-plus Eastern Han clipped wuzhu, 70-plus Three Kingdoms coins, and 1,100-plus Wei–Jin–Northern and Southern Dynasties coins. There were no Sui or Tang coins in the hoard. See Xie Shiping 1986.
13. Stein (1928: 760) lists three groups of three gilt-coins sewn on to headbands. It is not clear whether this group corresponds to Ying.III.2.03–5; Ying.III.2.06–8 or Ying.III.3.03–5.
14. These are similar to the thin silver and bronze decorative pendants found in tombs at Astana, which comprise circular, lunette- and pear-shaped plates with small holes drilled at top and bottom, for attaching by thread. See Stein 1928: pl. LXXXIX, showing Ast.i.3.012 (p. 681) and Ast.ix.2.04 (p. 706).
15. The Yingpan site lies 150 km southeast of Wuli county seat, on the southern edge of a plateau of the Kuruk-tagh Mountains. It covers 6,000 sq m, and includes a wall, beacons, stupa and cemetery. From the Western Han to the Jin period, it was an important station on the route from Loulan to the Tianshan Mountains. Investigations at the site since 1989 have yielded over two hundred sites, 120 of which have been excavated, yielding items made of wood, bronze, clay, iron, glass and silk and woollen textiles. See XJ–WWSY 1999: 190–9.
16. For example, the Han tomb at Leitai, Wuwei (Gansu), yielded 21,125 wuzhu coins, of which 11,594 were clipped wuzhu. Of a group of over ten thousand wuzhu coins found in Wenxian (Gansu), about fifty per cent were clipped coins. See GSQBXH (1989: 7).
17. Xie Shiping (ZGQBDCD: 411) has identified three periods of daquan wushi coins, according to size, with a gradual decrease in diameter and weight, and an increase in the size of the hole over time: early types (diam. 27–29.5 mm, hole 7–8.5 mm, wt 7–13 g); middle period types (diam. 26.5–28.5 mm, hole 8.5 mm, wt 5–7 g); and later types (often clipped or private castings, wt usually 2–4.5 g, though occasionally as low as 1 g). Unfortunately, this is merely a concise entry in a coin encyclopaedia; details of his source materials, and thus any regional patterns, are not included.
18. All corroded and damaged coins, as well as fragments, which would distort the average, have been excluded from this calculation.
19. All corroded and damaged coins, as well as fragments, which would distort the average, have been excluded from this calculation.
20. The term 'Huichang Kaiyuan' is used for the Kaiyuan tongbao issued after 845, which had a single-character inscription on the reverse indicating the mint of issue.
21. Tang dynasty coins cast in central China are characterized by a darker colour of bronze (*qingtong*, 'dark copper') or yellowish-pink colour (*huangtong*, 'yellow copper'). The reddish bronze (*hongtong*, 'red copper') used in the production of local coins in Eastern Central Asia can be seen in Chinese coins as late as the Qing dynasty (1644–1911), which are known popularly as *hongqian* ['red coins'].
22. The historical texts are the *Zizhi tongdian*, *Cifu yuangui* and *Xin Tangshu*.
23. Skaff (1998: 103 n113) presumed that there was also a mint at Khotan, but offered no evidence to support this.
24. A larger double-rim Qianyuan zhongbao was issued in 759, with a token value of 50, but no examples have been found in Xinjiang.
25. The expression *zhongbao* in Chinese coin inscriptions normally indicates that the coin has a value of more than 1.

# 5 Coins of the Western tradition

Coins of the Western tradition before AD 800 found in Eastern Central Asia include bronze Roman, Parthian and Kushan coins; gold Byzantine coins, imitations and derivatives; and silver Sasanian drachms, Arab-Sasanian dirhems and imitations.

**Parthian coins (Plate 3, 28–9)**

There are two Parthian coins in the Stein collection. One was issued by Phraates III, *c.*70–57 BC, Ecbatana or Rhagae mint [S.II.1], the other by Mithridates II, *c.*123–88 BC, Rhagae mint [S.II.2].[1] Stein purchased both of them at Karghalik, where the only seller he described was a dodgy coin-dealer.[2] The provenance of these coins is unreliable, and, as they may have arrived in Eastern Central Asia as late as the early twentieth century, they cannot be considered here. No other specimens are known from Eastern Central Asia.

**Bactrian and Indian coins (Plate 3, 30–1)**

At Karghalik, Stein also purchased a Scythian imitation of a bilingual tetradrachm of the Indo-Greek king Hermaius [S.II.3] (Stein 1921; Cribb 1984: 151). The provenance of this coin is not known, and the comments about the Parthian coins from Karghalik are applicable here. No other specimens are known from Eastern Central Asia.

At Yotkan, Stein purchased a bull and lion copper coin of the Indo-Scythian king Azes II (Cribb 1984: 151 [AK.II.a.50]), alleged to have come from the Yotkan site.

**Kushan coins**

The first Kushan king Kujula Kadphises (*c.*AD 30–80) issued coins in bronze, imitating Greek, Scythian, Scythian satrapal and Parthian coins. His son, Wima Takhto (*c.*80–110) introduced a new bronze coinage, also derived from Indo-Greek and Indo-Scythian issues. A distinctive Kushan coinage appeared during the reign of the next king Wima Kadphises (*c.*110–27). Wima introduced gold coins, with the king on the obverse, and a deity on the reverse, the Kushan god Wesho (= the Zoroastrian deity Vaiiush Uparo Kairiio) associated with the Indian Shiva and the Greek Heracles. Wima's coins were bilingual, in the Greek and Kharoshthi scripts, with the inscriptions on both sides identifying him as king. The coins of the fourth king, Kanishka I (*c.*127–50), were in Bactrian, written in the Greek script: the obverse inscription named him as king, and the reverse inscription named the deity on the reverse (Errington and Cribb 1992: 66–9).[3]

***Kushan gold coins***

The only gold Kushan coins known from Eastern Central Asia are the 14 quarter-dinars of Kanishka I, featuring in a pair of armlet fragments purchased by Petrovsky in 1896, alleged to have come from Yotkan, but apparently made in the eighteenth or nineteenth century. Zeymal (1992: 163–4) noted the appearance in the armlets of several coins from the same dies, a rare phenomenon among coins in circulation, and suggested that they may have been brought to Khotan soon after issue and buried as a hoard without entering circulation. It is unfortunate that the provenance of these coins is not more secure, as they might prove conclusively that gold Kushan coins did play a role in the local economy in the Khotan region, as the documents suggest (see Chapter 8). The only other evidence of gold coins at Yotkan comes from Stein's report (1907: 193) that, after gold first started appearing in the Yotkan flood-waters in the 1860s, the Khotanese Governor, Niaz Hakim Beg, sent large parties of men to wash and dig for gold there. The purchase of all gold produced in Khotan and Keriya was a monopoly of the Chinese administration, which paid diggers 110 tangas per *ser* of gold, significantly (about twenty per cent) below the market value of 138 tangas. Consequently, any finds of value, including gold coins, would have disappeared on to the black market or into the hands of a foreign buyer. Stein wrote: 'no coins or solid ornaments of gold and silver were admitted to be found now, though the discovery of such precious articles was readily acknowledged for the early years of the working'.

***Kushan bronze coins (Plate 3, 32–5)***

For Kushan bronze coins, the evidence supplied by the Stein collection is more reliable, though not watertight; all were purchased at the Yotkan site, or acquired in Khotan, as coming from Yotkan. None was found by Stein himself.

In his study of the Kushan bronze coins from Khotan, Cribb (1984) identified one Kashmir-issue bull and camel coin of Wima Takhto;[4] 24 Kashmir issues of Kanishka I, 17 drachms and seven hemidrachms struck to the reduced Attic weight standard of *c.*4 g and *c.*2 g, respectively; and three bilingual issues of Wima Kadphises, tetradrachms of the same standard, weighing *c.*16 g.

The total number of Kushan coins found in Eastern Central Asia is not known. Zeymal (1992: 162) estimated about fifty specimens, Thierry (2000: 123) about sixty, but neither gives full sources. Thierry includes two drachms of Kanishka I, acquired with Sino-Kharoshthi coins, now in the Musée Guimet. One tetradrachm of Wima Kadphises was found at Loulan (XJ-Loulan 1988; XJ-Archaeology 1985: no. 188; Dong Qingxuan and Jiang Qixiang 1991: no. 655), and a bull and camel coin of Wima Takhto was found at a site near Endere (Li Yinping 1999).[5]

The Wima Kadphises tetradrachm is the easternmost Kushan coin. It was found in the southwestern section of the Loulan site, near the three-roomed building [L.A.II], which served as the Chinese administrative headquarters of the Loulan station. Immediately to its southwest is a refuse heap [L.A.IV], which Stein (1921: 378) described as the easternmost portion of the enormous refuse heap [L.A.VI.ii], and which yielded numerous Chinese and Kharoshthi documents, dated AD 250s–330s. This is the only non-Chinese coin from Loulan, and would appear to be a rare but random find.

The majority of the Kushan coins are issues of Kanishka I. The absence of any coins of the later Kushan rulers Huvishka and Vasudeva suggests a sudden break in relations between Khotan and the Kushan kingdom in the early years of Kanishka's reign (Zeymal 1992: 157).[6]

Cribb's conclusion still holds: that the presence of the Kushan coins in ancient Khotan, and their influence as seen on the locally issued Sino-Kharoshthi coins (see Chapter 6), indicates that the rulers of ancient Khotan were in close economic contact with the early Kushan kings, and that there may have been a brief Kushan occupation of Khotan.

### Roman coins (Plate 3, 36–7)

There are two Roman bronze coins in the Stein collection. One was issued by Constantine II, AD 330–35, Antioch mint [S.II.4], the other by Constantius II, AD 340, Alexandria mint [S.II.5].[7] Stein purchased both of them from the dodgy coin-dealer at Karghalik (Stein 1912). No other specimens are known from Eastern Central Asia. There are no substantiated reports of finds of Roman bronze coins in central China; the well-known hoard of Roman bronze coins reported by Bushell (1886) was demonstrated by Thierry (2000) to be a much later deposit, probably made in the twentieth century.

### Byzantine gold coins, imitations and derivatives[8] (Plate 3, 38–9)

The Byzantine monetary system was based on the Roman pound (327.45 g). The standard gold coin was the solidus, equal to one seventy-second of a pound, created by the Roman emperor Constantine the Great (274–337). The gold was of a high degree of purity, and the fineness was well maintained. In terms of design, the obverse featured the imperial bust, and the reverse type was a cross potent on steps. Justinian II (685–95) introduced the bust of Christ as the obverse type, and the emperor, holding a cross, was removed to the reverse. The inscriptions on coins of the sixth and seventh centuries are usually in Latin, and are identificatory or religious. There are very strong references to Christianity on the coins (Grierson 1982: 1–42). The Arab-Byzantine coinage of the seventh century marks a transitional phase, during which the Christian elements of the designs and inscriptions were replaced. It ended in the 690s as a result of the monetary reform of 'Abd al-Malik, when it was decided to create a consciously Arab coinage. The introduction of Christ as the obverse type *c.*692 was unacceptable to Muslims (Grierson 1982: 144–9).

There are three imitations of gold Byzantine solidi in the Stein collection. All were derived from types of Justinian I (527–65), and all were retrieved from the mouths of occupants of seventh-century tombs at the Astana cemetery near Turfan [tombs Ast.i.3, Ast.i.5, Ast.i.6].

Thierry and Morrisson (1994) list a total of 11 Byzantine coins and derivatives found at Khotan, Astana and Yarkhoto: of types issued by Justinian I (527–65), Maurice (582–602) and Constans V (741–45). The majority are not coins but uniface imitation decorative pieces, often pierced or adapted as jewellery. Most were found in tombs, suggesting that they had a particular function in burials, and were regarded as prestigious items among the wealthy and noble people who took them to their graves.

This also appears to have been the case in central China, where about thirty Byzantine and Arab-Byzantine gold coins have been found: Xi'an, Shaanxi (11 coins), Xianyang, Shaanxi (two), Tianshui, Gansu (two), Guyuan, Ningxia (one), Luoyang, Henan (one), Cixian, Hebei (two), Zanhuang, Hebei (three), and Tumote Banner, Inner Mongolia (one). These coins and derivatives are types of Theodosius I or II (379–95, or 408–50) (one), Theodosius II (one), Leo I (457–74) (one), Anastasius I (491–518) (five), Justin I (518–27) (four), Justin II (565–78) (four), Phocas (602–10) (two), Heraclius (610–41) (two) and Arab-Byzantine coins (dated 702–47) (three) (Xu Pingfang 1996). The vast majority were found in tombs of wealthy aristocrats or high-ranking officials of the Tang dynasty, often with other gold and silver non-Chinese objects, such as Sasanian coins, cups, bowls and jewellery. The coins that did not come from tombs all came from modern-day Xi'an, formerly the site of the Tang capital, Chang'an.

Raspopova (1999) describes a similar pattern of finds of Byzantine coins and derivatives in Western Central Asia, for example at the fifth- to eighth-century Pendjikent site, Tajikistan, where imitation coins and bracteates, modelled on coins datable to no later than 629, served as funerary gifts in modest burials, and bracteates were found also in temples and private houses. At Pendjikent and other sites in Sogdiana, there could be a difference of almost two centuries between the burial date of an imitation and the date of the original coin on which it was modelled. She noted that while late Roman and Byzantine solidi influenced the coinage in Sogdiana, genuine Byzantine solidi are noticeably absent from the assemblages which include imitative coins and one-sided bracteates.

### Sasanian silver coins (Plate 3, 40–2)

The silver drachm, of reduced Attic weight, was the main denomination of Sasanian currency. The weight, almost exactly 4 g, and the fineness of the silver, were well maintained over the four centuries of the Sasanian dynasty. In terms of design, the obverse carried a portrait of the ruler, and an inscription, in Sasanian Pahlavi (Middle Persian), giving the king's name and titles, and sometimes ideograms, such as the *apud*, a symbol meaning 'may his glory increase'. Each king had his individual crown, symbolizing the *xwarrah*, or divine aura, of the ruler. The reverse bore the fire-altar with flames, with the later addition of two fire attendants, and a bust within the flames. Inscriptions on the reverse indicate the mint and date. There are very strong references to Zoroastrianism, the Sasanian national faith. The distinctive rings of dots of Sasanian coins are found on both obverse and reverse (Göbl 1983). Like the Arab-Byzantine coinage, the Arab-Sasanian coinage can be seen as a transitional coinage, ending in the 690s.

Stein collected five Sasanian drachms. One was acquired in Sistan, Iran, and is therefore beyond consideration here [IA.XVII.a.i]. One belonged to a group described as 'miscellaneous objects purchased Kara-khoja' [IA.X.d.1] (Stein 1928: 596), and its original Stein number [Kao.014] indicates that he believed it had come from Gaochang. It is a coin of Ohrmazd IV (Plate 3, 40). Only three have secure provenances: they were found in tombs at Astana: two had been placed over the eyes of a female in tomb Ast.i.3 [IA.XII.a.2–3], and one in the mouth of a female in tomb Ast.v.2 [IA.XII.e.1]. The first [IA.XII.a.2] is a coin of Ohrmazd IV (Plate 3, 41); the second [IA.XII.a.3] is a fantasy piece (Plate 3, 42). The third [IA.XII.e.1], described as in fragments, is missing.

Stein (1928: 645) described the Ast.i tombs as a separate group of tombs, without an enclosure of embanked gravel, marking the extreme northeastern extremity of the Astana cemetery. Tomb Ast.i.3 contained a pair of bodies, probably husband and wife. Both were buried with face-covers of figured silk, with a Sasanian design, and beneath the cover a pair of silver 'spectacles'. The coins were found covering the eye-sockets and below the spectacles of the female. The tomb had been disturbed. Mixed up in the general debris, Stein (1928: 647) found three small disks of silver, with square holes in the centre, imitating Chinese coins; seven thin plates of silver, crescent- or pear-shaped, manifestly part of some ornament; a thin strip of plain gold, seven glass beads and a Changping wuzhu coin (first issued AD 533) (Plate 2, 21) (see Chapter 4). On the basis of the Sasanian coin-types which were issued in the late sixth century, and allowing several years for the types (or imitations) to turn up in Astana, and the stone epitaphs dating to the seventh century found at other tombs in the Ast.i group, Stein dated this tomb to the seventh century.

The Ast.v group of tombs, with an enclosure, lay at the centre of the cemetery (Stein 1928: 659). The more important [Ast.v.1] of the two tombs described by Stein had an obituary eulogy inscribed on a large slab, for Lady Jia, native of Gaochang, in Xizhou, and daughter of an official at the rank of *zhonglang*,[9] who had died in 667 aged 75, and was buried beside her husband, Fan Yonglong (his body is now missing). She was therefore a person of status, and would have been about 38 at the time of the Chinese takeover in 640. Tomb Ast.v.2 was less grand, and also yielded a pair of bodies. The female body had a face cover made of polychrome figured silk, Sasanian in design and weave (Stein 1928: 659). In her mouth was found 'a silver coin too much decayed for exact identification, but from its size and design recognizable with certainty as a Sasanian piece. In conjunction with the inscriptional record from the adjoining tomb, Ast.v.1, this coin contributes to prove that this group of tombs is approximately contemporaneous with the group Ast.i' (Stein 1928: 659). Unfortunately, these fragments are now missing.

Stein's finds represent a very small proportion of the approximately 1,100 Sasanian and Arab-Sasanian coins found in Eastern Central Asia. The majority (947 coins) were found together with 13 crudely made gold bars, in a rock crevice near Wuqia (= Ulughqat) in the 1950s. They were found in an uninhabited area near a path on a route passing from the Ferghana valley through the Pamirs to Kashgar. The coins were described as Sasanian and Arab-Sasanian coins, many with countermarks (Li Yuchun 1959; Skaff 1998). The gold, at least, must be regarded as specie or bullion, and this may also be the case for the silver. Until the coins are examined more fully, this important find can offer only limited information.

The vast majority of the remaining Sasanian coins were found in the Turfan region: about 130 coins found at the Gaochang (= Kara-khoja) city site, and about thirty coins found in tombs at the Astana cemetery. This is a surprisingly small number of coins, when compared with the evidence for silver coins in the contemporary documents excavated at the sites (see Chapter 9).

The coins found at Gaochang came from three hoards and two single finds. The exact provenances of the hoards are not known. Two hoards, of ten and 20 coins respectively, had similar compositions, containing silver drachms of Shapur II (r. 309–79), Ardashir II (r. 379–83) and Shapur III (r. 383–88), in good condition, and showing little wear. The composition of these hoards is similar to a larger hoard found at Tépé Maranjan, near Kabul, Afghanistan (Xia Nai 1961).[10] The third hoard was dispersed before it could be studied or published, but, according to a private collector, was composed of 100 coins of the same three Sasanian rulers. The two single surface finds at Gaochang were both coins of Ardashir II. The city finds are all types issued during the fourth century.

By contrast, 17 (57 per cent) of the coins found in tombs at the Astana cemetery were issues of Khusrow II (590–628). The earliest Sasanian coin found in a tomb at Astana is an issue of Piruz (459–84), the latest silver coin is an Arab-Sasanian dirhem minted 651–*c*.700. There is a concentration of issues of the late sixth and perhaps early seventh century, which, allowing time for these types to travel eastwards to Turfan, would suggest they were used in Turfan in the seventh and even early eighth century. Indeed, the tombs yielding such coins, when dated, are of the seventh and early eighth century. More precise dates of deposition in the tombs are difficult to establish owing to multiple occupancy and disturbance. Many coins survived only because they were concealed in the mouth of a tomb occupant, and were not noticed by tomb-raiders.

Placing coins in the mouth and on the eyes was a burial custom at Gaochang, particularly, though not exclusively, for females. The Gaochang burial custom of placing coins on the eyes, then covering them with silver spectacles and a figured silk burial mask, may originally have been a Parthian custom that spread to Central Asia (Benko 1993).

About ten Sasanian coins have been found at other sites in Eastern Central Asia. A coin of Khusrow I minted 559 and an Arab-Sasanian dirhem were found at the Subashi city site, Kucha, identified as Yiluolu city of the Qiuci kingdom, and an important centre on the route east to west (Huang Wenbi 1958: 110). A coin of Piruz was acquired by Oldenburg at Karashahr (= Yanqi) (Ivotchkina 1975). Two clumps of coins, comprising in total six or seven coins of Piruz, fused together, were acquired in Khotan by Hoernle (1899), but their exact provenance is not known.

The total number of Sasanian silver coins found in Eastern Central Asia is small. Viewed independently of the documentary evidence, it is easy to assume that these, just like the imitation Byzantine coins, played a limited role in the Gaochang economy. However, the documents reveal a far wider use of silver coins in Gaochang, especially in the seventh century (see Chapter 9).

The dates of issue of the Sasanian silver coins found in Eastern Central Asia do not match those found in central China. In contrast to the fourth-century city finds and late sixth- and early seventh-century tomb finds in Eastern Central Asia, some 80 per cent of those found within China are fifth-century issues of Piruz (459–84). Within China, issues of Piruz have been found in hoards, in tombs and stupa deposits, with dates ranging from the late fourth century to the mid eighth century

(Peng Jinzhang and Sha Wutian 1998: 23). The finds of fifth- and sixth-century Sasanian coins appear to correspond not with the northern route through Qiuci and Gaochang but with another known route from Tukharistan (= Bactria) to Wakhan, across the Pamirs to Tashkurgan to Yarkand to Khotan to Shanshan, then eastwards via Dunhuang – or through the Qaidam Basin to the Koko Nor Lake – then via Lanzhou into China (Skaff 1998: 84). There is also evidence that Sasanian silver coins arrived in China by maritime routes in the late fifth century (Xia Nai 1957: 157).

### Discussion

The evidence supplied by the Western coins cannot be used in isolation, and must be considered alongside the contemporary documentary evidence (see Chapter 9) for a truer picture. Specimens of Parthian, Bactrian, Indian and Roman coins are extremely rare, and of very uncertain provenance. No Kushan gold coins of reliable provenance have been found, although the documentary evidence suggests that such coins were known on the southern route. The presence of the Kushan bronze coins, and their influence on the local Sino-Kharoshthi coins issued by the kings of Khotan, reflects the strong cultural and economic connections between Khotan and the Kushan empire.

The number of Byzantine gold coins and derivatives found in Eastern Central Asia is low, and contrasts with the documentary (see Chapter 9) and historical evidence. The contemporary burial lists from tombs at Gaochang included gold: from *c.*AD 418 gold was expressed by weight, and from *c.*551 in coin (from 100 to 10,000 coins). When the quantity of gold is expressed in coin, it is always accompanied by a quantity of silver coins. From 567 there is only one burial list which mentions gold, and in this case the quantity is expressed by weight. Tax documents from Gaochang also record transactions of gold by weight. En route to India in 629, Xuan Zang described the coinage of Aqini (= Yanqi) and Guzhi (= Qiuci) as 'gold coins, silver coins and small bronze coins'. These references demonstrate that gold coins were known and used in Eastern Central Asia between the fifth and seventh centuries, though primarily by weight. The discovery of 13 gold bars, together with 947 silver coins, in Wuqia further supports the use of gold by weight. The *Suishu* (Shihuo zhi, juan 24, 691) records that in the Northern Zhou dynasty (557–81) gold and silver coins of the Western Regions were being used in the Hexi region without prohibition from officials. This reference indicates clearly that the gold and silver was in coin form, but does not indicate whether these pieces were used as money or in other ways. During this period, gold was used in central China as money, but its normal form was as ingots or cakes, i.e. by weight. The Byzantine gold coins and imitations should therefore be regarded as specie, or perhaps as ornamental pieces for burial. The gold Byzantine coins and derivatives that have survived indicate a mostly decorative function, especially for burials. But the Wuqia find, combined with the documentary and historical evidence, indicates the use of gold bullion, rather than gold specie, as money.

The Sasanian silver coins seen in isolation would reveal their particular role in Turfan burial customs, yet the contemporary documentary evidence proves without doubt that these coins were a major form of money on the northern route in the seventh century (see Chapter 9). The emergence of the use of Sasanian silver coins as a major currency in the Turfan area reflects its important position in international trade, as Skaff (1998) has argued. Its disappearance is, however, more difficult to reckon and explain.

### Notes

1. I am grateful to Vesta Curtis for confirming the identification of these coins.
2. 'There was one who had drifted to Karghalik from Bokhara some twenty years before . . . He had brought a good number of old Bactrian, Arsacidian, and other Greek coins with him from Bokhara, – or had since been supplied with them by friends left behind there' (Stein 1912: I, 140–1).
3. There have been major breakthroughs in Kushan chronology in the last few years: Harry Falk (2001) found evidence in a Sanskrit astrological text which determined the date of the first year of Kanishka I as AD 127. Another text, the Rabatak inscription (written in Bactrian with Greek script), records the foundation of a sanctuary dedicated to the gods of the Kushan kings in the first year of Kanishka's reign, and names Wima Kadphises, Wima Takhto, Kujula Kadphises as Kanishka's father, grandfather and great grandfather, respectively. I am grateful to Joe Cribb for showing me his forthcoming article 'The Kushans, Central Asian nomadic rulers of ancient India and Bactria, 1st to 4th centuries AD'.
4. This coin was originally attributed to Kujula Kadphises (Cribb 1984), but, in the light of recent advances in Kushan chronology, has subsequently been reattributed to Wima Takhto; see note 3.
5. Li Yinping (1999) misidentified the bull and camel coin as a horse and camel coin (2.4 g, 15 mm), and noted that the (unnamed) site where it was found had once yielded a 'small corroded Sino-Kharoshthi coin'.
6. MacDowell (1968: 146) suggested that coins of the Kushan king Huvishka were found at Khotan, but these have subsequently been identified as Hun issues of Mihiragula, from Kashmir.
7. I am grateful to Roger Bland for confirming the identification of these coins.
8. The terms 'Byzantine' and 'Eastern Roman' are both used by Chinese scholars when describing the gold solidi and derivatives. Western numismatists use 'Eastern Roman' when contrasting with 'Western Roman', but it is the norm to use 'Byzantine' when referring to the period after AD 500.
9. Hucker (1985) translates *zhonglang* as Palace Attendant on the household staff of the Heir Apparent or a Prince.
10. The Tépé Maranjan hoard contained 326 coins of Shapur II, 28 of Ardashir II and 14 of Shapur III; see Curiel (1953: 101–32).

# 6 Coins of local manufacture

This chapter discusses the coins that were produced locally in Eastern Central Asia. They were modelled on coins from two distinct regions: India and the Kushan empire (originally inspired by the Greek and Hellenistic coinages), and China. The different coin-types are discussed below chronologically.

**The Sino-Kharoshthi coins of Khotan (Plate 4, 43–5)**

The Sino-Kharoshthi coins of Khotan, also known as 'Khotanese horse coins', refer to a series of coins issued by the kings of Khotan. The majority of specimens are in the Stein collection and have been published in Cribb's acclaimed study (Cribb 1984–85), in which he identified thirteen groups of Sino-Kharoshthi coins, issued by six kings of Khotan (Gurgadama, Gurga, Gurgamoya, Inaba, [ . . . ]doga and Panadosana). He suggested that the coins were probably issued during short periods at times when the kings of Khotan were able to assert their independence from Chinese, Kushan and Yarkandese rule. He proposed that the period of issue covered over a hundred years between *c.*AD 1 and 132. Whilst this date should be adjusted to *c.*AD 30–150, in the light of recent discoveries (see Chapter 5), the adjustment does not significantly alter Cribb's conclusions. It affects more adversely those who contested Cribb's date of *c.*AD 1–132 (Lin Meicun 1991; Zeymal 1992), all of whom argued against the issue of this coinage before the Chinese withdrawal from Khotan in AD 175, as recorded in the *Hou Hanshu* (Xiyu zhuan, juan 88, 2909–38). This later date cannot be substantiated.

There are 179 Sino-Kharoshthi coins in the Stein collection. None was found by Stein himself; they were purchased or presented as coming from Chalma-kazan (eight), Yarkand (one), Yotkan (78), Domoko (one), Khotan (42), 'Mazar Tagh' (one), Ak-sipil (one), Kine-tokmak (two), tatis east of Yurung-kash (six), Kucha (six), Yulduz-bagh (three) and West Lach (one). The alleged provenances therefore indicate a concentration of this coinage in the Khotan area, especially at Yotkan (over 43 per cent).

The Sino-Kharoshthi coins collected by Hoernle (152), Petrovsky (11) and Oldenburg (two) were included in Cribb's study. To Cribb's study should be added those acquired by Otani (11 coins) (Wang Lin 1987),[1] Mannerheim (76 in poor condition) (Talvio 1999),[2] Huang Wenbi (one) (Liu Wensuo 1991), and over ten coins reported in recent Chinese publications.[3] Dong Qingxuan and Jiang Qixiang (1991) published seven coins without provenance; Long Fu (1996) mentions seven coins which were found in modern-day Luopu county, in the Khotan region.[4] These raise the total of reported Sino-Kharoshthi coins close to 450 specimens. But the new data do not alter the validity of Cribb's analysis.

The Sino-Kharoshthi coins are round and struck in bronze. The basic design of this series features on the obverse a horse or camel, facing right, surrounded by a Prakrit inscription, written in the Kharoshthi script, naming the king of Khotan who issued it. On the reverse is a Chinese inscription which identifies each piece as a coin of a certain weight: 'copper coin, weight 24 grains' (*tongqian zhong nian si zhu* 銅錢重廿四銖),[5] and '6-grain coin' (*liu zhu qian* 六銖錢). Cribb (1984: 150–1) demonstrated that in the first century AD the Bactrian reduced-Attic tetradrachm and the Han Chinese ounce (*liang* = 24 *zhu*) were virtually identical in weight (15.5 g), and that the early issuers of the Sino-Kharoshthi coinage used the reduced Attic tetradrachm (15.5 g) and drachm (3.9 g) of Bactria as the models for their two sizes of coins. A smaller hemidrachm coin was also issued during the reign of King Panadosana. Kushan coins were the closest models for the Sino-Kharoshthi coinage; the intention was that the coins of Khotan should closely resemble the monetary practice of the early Kushan rulers of Bactria and the neighbouring areas of northwest India.

The bilingual elements and the comparative weights indicate that the coins were designed for use by people familiar with Kushan coins and/or Chinese coins. Both coinages must have been known in the Khotan region. The use of the term *qian* [coin] in the inscription indicates familiarity with Chinese money, and therefore offers further evidence for the arrival of wuzhu coins in the Khotan region during the Western Han. By *c.*AD 1 the Western Han wuzhu system was in disarray, with clipped and underweight coins widespread. The Eastern Han did not restore the wuzhu until AD 40, and by then the Sino-Kharoshthi coinage was already established. The Sino-Kharoshthi coins marry two completely different systems into one. This marriage would support Khotan's important role in Central Asia, and reflects Khotan's links both with northwest India, especially Gandhara, and with China. In Kushan coinage, the weight of the coin was important but was not included in the inscription as part of the design. The design featured pictorial elements, and the inscription named the issuer. In Chinese coin design the inscription was precisely a measure of weight (*wuzhu*, '5-grain'). However, the documentary evidence shows that in practice Chinese coins were reckoned not by weight, but in countable units (Chinese: *qian* or *quan*), in other words, as fiduciary money with a token value of 1 (see Chapter 2). In this way, one *qian/quan* represented one *wuzhu* coin.[5] The Chinese inscriptions on the Sino-Kharoshthi coins function in a very different way from the inscription on the Chinese wuzhu coins. They state 'this is a copper coin and it weighs 24 grains'[6] and 'this is a 6-grain coin'.[7] They identify them as coins, despite the absence of a square hole at the centre, typically found on Chinese coins. They explain how the Sino-Kharoshthi and Kushan coinages functioned, by relating the units of drachm and tetradrachm to the Chinese quarter-ounce and ounce (*liang*), respectively. As there was no Chinese term for

**Table 1**
**Equivalent values of the Sino-Kharoshthi coins and Chinese coins**

| Drachm (6-grain coins) | Tetradrachm (24-grain coins) | *Qian*/*quan* (wuzhu [5-grain] coins) | Total of *zhu*-grains |
|---|---|---|---|
| 10 | – | 12 | 60 |
| 20 | 5 | 24 | 120 |
| 30 | – | 36 | 180 |
| 40 | 10 | 48 | 240 |
| 50 | – | 60 | 300 |
| 60 | 15 | 72 | 360 |
| 70 | – | 84 | 420 |
| 80 | 20 | 96 | 480 |
| 90 | – | 108 | 540 |
| 100 | 25 | 120 | 600 |

the quarter-ounce, the solution was to use '6-grain' and, by extension, '24-grain'. The later coins issued by Panadosana are markedly different from the earlier types: he adapted the design of the 24-grain coin for use on the smaller, 6-grain size, and introduced another smaller coin, corresponding to a hemidrachm, or 3-grain coin. The intention behind the Chinese inscription on his coins also appears to be different: on both sizes, Cribb read the Chinese inscription as *yuzhi da* . . ., an incomplete inscription naming Khotan. This contrasts with the earlier Sino-Kharoshthi coins, where the inscription makes no reference to location.

The concentrated distribution of Sino-Kharoshthi coins in the Khotan region suggests the local need to exchange different currencies in Khotan, and to be able to reckon in both Kushan and Chinese currencies. Xia Nai (1962) proposed the following exchange formulae, based on the weight inscriptions on the Sino-Kharoshthi and wuzhu coins: [6 × wuzhu] = [1 × 24-grain] + [1 × 6-grain]; and [6 × wuzhu] = [5 × 6-grain]. In other words, to convert from drachms to wuzhu coins, multiply by 120 per cent; and to convert from wuzhu to drachm, multiply by 80 per cent, as in Table 1.

These formulae would require that all coins circulated at their respective face values throughout the series, and that all wuzhu circulated at par, regardless of quality. This would work only if there was an additional system for adjustment. A perfect example of this time, demonstrating adjustment on a fixed exchange equation, is seen in the fragment of silk [T.XV.i.a.3], found near Dunhuang, that can be dated to the early second century AD. It carries an inscription, giving the width, length (4 *zhang*), weight (25 *liang*) and value in coin (618 *qian*) of the roll of fine plain silk to which it once belonged. From this, it can be deduced that the value of the silk was 150 cash per *zhang* (4 × 150 = 600) or 24 cash per *liang* (25 × 24 = 600), and to the total was added a premium of 3 per cent (600 × 103 per cent = 618). As the sum of 600 cash corresponds exactly with the fixed monthly salary of a Chinese captain (*hou*) (see Chapter 7), it would appear that these values were fixed, but subject to adjustment appropriate to the circumstances. If the same was true for exchange between Chinese, Kushan and Sino-Kharoshthi coins, then, according to the fixed-rate formulae above, the captain's salary of 600 cash would exchange for 480 drachms, plus or minus any adjustment.

**Lead coins found in Khotan (Plate 4, 46–7)**

Stein acquired two lead coins from Khotan, which Cribb (1984: 135–6) described as an Indian type and a Chinese type, associated with the later coins in the Sino-Kharoshthi series.

The Indian-type lead coin [AK.XI.b.22–37] (Plate 4, 46) is a round coin, presenting on one side a horse, facing left, with foreleg raised, and above the horse appears the same symbol found on the Chinese-type lead coins. This symbol appears also at the centre of the other side, surrounded by a Kharoshthi inscription reading 'dosana' for Panadosana, thereby linking this piece with the Sino-Kharoshthi coinage.

Only one similar piece is known. It turned up in the coins-and-jade trade in Khotan in 1995, allegedly from near the Ak-sipil site (Li Yinping 1996). Larger and heavier (26 mm, 15.10 g) than the Stein example (23 mm, 12.88 g), it has a circle of dots around the rims on each side. There is no inscription naming the ruler, and a strained, enlarged version of the symbol fills the flan. On the other side, there is no symbol above the horse, which is more clearly defined than on the specimen in the Stein collection.

The Chinese-type coin [AK.XI.b.31] (Plate 4, 47) follows the arrangement of the wuzhu inscription, arranged around an elongated, rectangular central hole. The Chinese character *yu* 于 to the right of the hole stands for Yuzhi, the Chinese name for Khotan. The character to the left of the hole is more problematic: Bushell initially read it as *xian* 先 [first], then as *fang* 方 [territory, quarter] and finally settled on *tun* 屯 [settlement] (Stein 1907: 205, 575). Conrady (1920: 166–7) read it as *jin* 金, regarding the whole inscription as an abbreviation of *Yutian qian* 于闐錢 [coin of Yotkan]. Cribb (1984) read it as *fang* 方, an abbreviated form of Fangqian, the Chinese name for King Panadosana. Lin Meicun (1989) contested these readings, suggesting it read *yuan* 元 [first]. All of these are awkward readings. A more satisfactory solution would be to consider it instead as a tamgha, i.e. a tribal or personal symbol. A very similar symbol, but without the dot, appears at the centre of the Sino-Kharoshthi coins in Cribb's groups 9, 10, 12 and 13; indeed, Cribb noted its similarity with the Kharoshthi letter *cha*, which was used as a control mark on coins of the Kushan kings Kujula and Kanishka. The symbol links this coin to the Indian-type coin, and thereby to Panadosana, and the Sino-Kharoshthi series. It is symbolic of Khotan, or the people of Khotan. If the symbols, with and without the dot, are regarded as variations of the same, then the design of the Chinese-type lead coin can be reinterpreted. The issuers followed the form of the Chinese wuzhu, but adapted it by elongating the hole at the centre, and replaced the wuzhu inscription with a bilingual or bicultural inscription, wherein the Chinese character represented the Chinese name for Yotkan, and the other symbol represented the tribal tamgha of the Yotkan people. These coins can therefore be seen as local bilingual or bicultural coins of Khotan, modelled on the Chinese rather than the Kushan coinage.

The specimen in the Stein collection [AK.II.a.4] (5.45 g, diam. 24 mm, hole 10 × 5 mm) has a definite rim around the hole on both obverse and reverse. Three similar specimens from Khotan are known: one in the Hoernle collection (Cribb 1984, 1985); one in the Hedin collection (Conrady 1920); and one found in Luopu county, Khotan, now in the China Numismatic Museum, Beijing (Li Yinping 1995; 2002). Chinese archaeologists have found more specimens, particularly in Luopu county, Khotan. However, a large quantity of forgeries of these coins, produced in a village in Khotan, appeared on the market in Urumqi in 1996 (Qian Boquan 1998). As a result of this, there has been a reluctance to publish lead coins unless the authenticity is absolutely sure, and only one coin has been published with a photograph. This coin (2.2 g, diam. 21 mm, hole 11 × 8 mm) was found in Luopu county, is smaller than the Stein specimen, and has no rims (Li Yinping 2002). An even smaller specimen (1.3 g, diam. 16 mm, hole 8 × 5 mm), with an outer rim, has been published with a line drawing (Qian Boquan 1998).[8]

A new Chinese-type lead coin came to light in Luopu county in the 1990s (Li Yinping 1995; Qian Boquan 1998). It is similar in appearance to the other lead Chinese-types (6.9 g, diam. 23 mm, hole 13 × 5 mm), and appears to be genuine, but has a different inscription. The character on the right of the hole is *yu* 于 representing Yutian, as before. The symbol on the left of the hole [symbol] has not been identified. If the symbol [symbol] on the other lead type is a tamgha representing the people of Yotkan, then it would follow that this symbol [symbol] may function in the same way.

### Unidentified bronze Chinese-type coin with non-Chinese inscription (Plate 4, 48)

In the Stein collection there is one bronze Chinese-type coin [S.XXX.d.5], with a four-character inscription arranged around the hole as on a Chinese coin. But the inscription, which has not been deciphered, is clearly not Chinese. The coin (1.41 g, 16 mm) has rims around the edge and the hole on the obverse; the reverse is plain and uneven. It was brought from the Mazar tagh site.

A similar, but smaller, specimen (0.6 g, 14 mm) was found by Chinese archaeologists in the desert south of the Ak-sipil site in 1997 (Li Yinping 1997, 1998). It has the same inscription, rims and reverse as the Stein specimen. The reading of the inscription remains problematic. Li (1997) erroneously read the inscription as Kharoshthi script *3 hra ch'a sra* which he translated as '3 hra qian' or '3 hra coin', taking *hra* to be a local measure term, equal to 1 *zhu*, thereby making this piece a 3-grain coin, equal to the hemidrachm, in the Sino-Kharoshthi series. In terms of the size and arrangement of the four-character inscription, the closest model is indeed the Chinese xiaoquan zhiyi [small coin worth-1] issued in AD 9, but these coins are extremely rare in Eastern Central Asia (see Chapter 4). However, the script is not Kharoshthi, and might be closer to Brahmi, which was also used in Eastern Central Asia. Furthermore, two of the four 'characters' could be read as Pahlavi: [symbol] could be derived from the Pahlavi word 'pd, *abd*, meaning 'excellent' found on Sasanian coins (see below), and [symbol] could read 'k'.[9] The character on the left [symbol] could read as a miswritten Chinese 五 meaning '5'. However, these suggestions are all tentative and the reading remains uncertain, as does its attribution.

### Local Chinese-type issues

The Chinese inscriptions on the coins from Khotan provide the earliest evidence in Eastern Central Asia for locally produced coins influenced by the Chinese coinage. Stein (1907: 501) presumed that Chinese coins were made in Eastern Central Asia, but found no direct evidence for their manufacture.[10] However, new evidence for local production of Chinese-style coins, in the form of coin moulds and equipment, has come to light at sites on the northern route, and local manufacture is now indisputable. Much of the evidence has come from sites around Kucha, which corresponds to the territory of the earlier kingdom of Qiuci. It is for this reason that the locally produced 'wuzhu' coins are known as Qiuci coins.

### Qiuci coins

The discovery of over ten thousand locally made coins, modelled on the wuzhu, and of numerous coin moulds, at urban and monastery sites in the Kucha region has shown that there were mints in the ancient kingdom of Qiuci producing Chinese-style coins before the Tang dynasty. Ancient copper mines have also been located in the region (Mei Jianjun 2000).

The Qiuci coins fall into three main groups: (1) Qiuci small coins, usually without inscription; (2) Qiuci wuzhu coins, with a modified *wuzhu* inscription; and (3) Qiuci-script wuzhu coins, which always have a non-Chinese inscription, and usually also have a Chinese inscription. Moulds have been found for the first two groups, but not for the third. The terms used to describe these coins are not fixed, and it is difficult to distinguish between them in reports. The most significant finds of types (1) and (2) are at Toksun-sarai, Bachu county (coins, moulds for different sizes of coins and coin-making equipment) (Plate 5, 1–2); Chong Tim (coins and moulds); Xiaohanna site, Kucha (100 coins, moulds and equipment); in a cave at Wenbashi, Baicheng (over four hundred moulds); Luntai city site (over two hundred coins); at Bacheng, Kucha (10,064 coins in a clay pot) (Jiang Qixiang 1999).

#### *Qiuci small coins (Plate 5, 3–4; Plate 6, 5–7)*

The Qiuci small coins are cruder versions of the wuzhu form: they are smaller (10–15 mm in diameter), often thinner versions, usually without inscription or outer rim, but sometimes with a rim around the central square hole. Qiuci small coins and moulds have been found in Kucha (Kumtura, Yuqitu'er, Yisitana and Senmusaimu sites), Xinhe (Tuokelake'aiku and Suokakule sites), Wensu (Kayigu site), Keping (Kesunle, Majiankele and Qiongtimu [= Chong Tim] sites), and in Baicheng (Kesun'er and Wenbashi sites).[11] The remaining fragments of the moulds are thin, approximately 2 mm deep, made of grey or reddish-grey clay, and have impressions on one side only. They would have produced coins with a plain, flat reverse. At Daheitaikeqin (= Tangwangcheng), Kucha, Dawangkumu and Qiongtimu, the mould fragments were found stacked together in six to eight layers. The moulds at Dawangkumu showed traces of the clay casing which had held the layers together, and the pouring runners were still attached to the moulds from Wenbashi (Zhang Ping 1989, 1991).

The moulds for Qiuci small coins demonstrate that the master coins used to make the impressions in the mould were not of a consistent size, which would explain the wide variety in size and shape of these rather crude coins. The full-size moulds would have measured approximately 200 by 120 mm, each accommodating about one hundred coins, which suggests that each stack could yield up to one thousand coins (Zhang Ping 1991). This method of stacked layers of moulds was used in central China during the Han dynasty (HN-Museum 1978). The lack of gullies and of impressions for the reverse of the coin indicate a fairly primitive level of coin casting. It is for this reason that they are assumed to be the earliest Chinese-style coins made in Qiuci.

Outside Eastern Central Asia, the earliest datable context for such coins is found in the tombs dating 257–316 at Jiayuguan, Gansu (Wu Rongzeng 1995). Similar coins were produced also in central China. There are many similar specimens of 'small coins' in the Stein collection, but it is impossible to identify which were local issues, and which were imported from central China. As the identification of this type remains problematic, they provide very limited evidence for studying the local money tradition of the region.

### Qiuci wuzhu coins

The Qiuci wuzhu coins have a modified inscription, where *zhu* 銖 is written *zhu* 朱 without the medal radical *jin* 金. This is a characteristic sometimes found on Chinese coins of the Jin period (265–420). The Qiuci wuzhu coins range in size from 14–20 mm, often with an enlarged square hole (6.5–9 mm) (Jiang Qixiang 1990(1); Dong Qingxuan and Jiang Qixiang 1991: 16; Zhang Ping 1991: 136, 145; Thierry 2000). Zhang Ping (1991) observed that the larger coins were made with shallow outer rims, and suggests that the smaller coins imitated, in reduced size, the clipped coins of the Eastern Han.

Qiuci wuzhu coins are less common than the Qiuci small coins. They have been found at the following sites: Subashi, Tangwangcheng and Dunmailiqite, all in Kucha, and at Toksun-sarai, in Bachu county (Zhang Ping 1991: 136). The most significant finds were made at Toksun-sarai in 1959, when Qiuci wuzhu coins, moulds, crucibles and wuzhu coins were found together at this site in the former territory of Weitou, in the southeast of the Qiuci kingdom.

The moulds for Qiuci wuzhu coins indicate that different sizes of coin were being made. The crudeness of the moulds suggests that the variation in size was not deliberate, and was therefore not essential for the circulation of this coinage. This indicates either that the coins circulated at par or that there was a system of adjustment.

As these coins present the same problems as the 'small coins', specimens of this type in the Stein collection are included in the general discussion on wuzhu coins (see Chapter 4). I have discussed them here because there was clearly local manufacture of these coins, and they therefore differ in some aspects from the mainstream coinage of central China.

### Qiuci-script coins (Plate 4, 49–50)

Qiuci-script coins are finely made, and indicate a more sophisticated casting technology than the Qiuci small coins, and Qiuci wuzhu coins. They have inscriptions, and inner and outer rims on both obverse and reverse. The inscriptions are in two scripts: Chinese on one side and what appears to be a local script on the other. The Chinese inscription reads *wuzhu*, as on wuzhu coins. The reading of the non-Chinese inscription is problematic. Numismatists in Xinjiang privately consider that the local script might be a phonetic rendering of the name Qiuci; however, this theory has not been substantiated.[12] Ji Xianlin (Kucha WGS 1987: 34), proposed that the more complex figure represented '50' in the Tocharian A or B language, written in Brahmi script, and that the circle represented a weight unit equal to one-tenth of a *zhu*, thereby rendering the Chinese and local inscriptions equal in value. There is, however, no evidence for this. Thierry (2000: 132) rejected this reading on the basis that these symbols are not known in documents from Kucha, and that the association of the complex symbol with the Brahmi letter is forced, and untenable.

If we consider the possibility that the inscription is not Brahmi but Pahlavi, then the inscription on the Qiuci coins can be seen as derived from the Pahlavi word 'pd, *abd*, meaning 'excellent'. It is often found in addition to the expression *Xvarrah abzud* meaning '[May his] glory [be] increased' and became a standard feature of Sasanian coin design from the rule of Khusrow I (531–79).[13] Its first regular position was behind the king's head; and from the rule of Khusrow II (590–628) it appeared in the outer margin of the coins. Silver coins, in the form of Sasanian dirhems and imitations, were an important currency on the northern route in the early seventh century (see Chapter 5), with issues of Khusrow II accounting for 50 per cent of all Sasanian coins found there. Contemporary documents (see Chapter 9) demonstrate that circulation of Sasanian coins in Turfan began in the 580s, and peaked in the period from the 620s to the 650s. Silver coins also circulated in Qiuci at this time: en route to India, in AD 629, Xuan Zang observed that 'gold coins, silver coins and small copper coins' were used in the kingdoms of Aqini (= Yanqi/Karashahr) and Qiuci (= Kucha). The importance of Sasanian coins in the region would explain the adoption of *abd* on Qiuci coins. This new interpretation would suggest an issue date of the early seventh century for the Qiuci script coins. The description 'small copper coins' indicates coins that were small, when compared with Chinese wuzhu and Tang coins, with which Xuan Zang would have been more familiar in central China. The description 'small copper coins' would apply to any of the Qiuci coins.

The arrangement of the Chinese and Qiuci script on the coins falls into main five types, which Thierry (2000) named A–E. The identification of *abd* allows us to expand these to include sub-groups according to the alignment of *abd* with the Chinese script (see Table 2). The Qiuci script is always found on the side with sharp inner and outer rims. By contrast, on the two examples of type D coins in the Stein collection, the Chinese inscription is barely visible. This suggests that the Qiuci script side was the more important side.

**Table 2**
**Qiuci-script coins [I = inner, O = outer]**

| Type | Side A scripts | Side A rims | Side B scripts | Side B rims | Alignment | Possible Chinese prototype |
|---|---|---|---|---|---|---|
| A | Chinese and Qiuci | I & O | – | no rims | 180° | clipped wuzhu (3rd to early 4th c.) |
| Ba | Chinese | O | Qiuci | I & O | 180° | – |
| Bb | Chinese | O | Qiuci | I & O | 0° | – |
| C | Chinese | O | Qiuci | I & O | 180° | Cao-Wei wuzhu (220–65)[14] |
| Da | Chinese | I & O | Qiuci (mirrored) | I & O | 180° | Shu-Han wuzhu (221–63) |
| Db | Chinese | I & O | Qiuci (mirrored) | I & O | 0° | – |
| E | Qiuci | I & O | – | no rims | – | – |

Thierry notes the similarity of type C Quici-script coins to wuzhu issued during Western Wei rule (535–56); however, they are closer to the wuzhu coins under Cao-Wei rule (220–65). Both have large square holes, with no inner rim on the obverse, and the Chinese characters touch the sides of the square hole. On Cao-Wei wuzhu, the triangular head on the *zhu* 銖 is small and equilateral and the inner and outer rims on the reverse are clear and sharp (Cao-Wei 1998). On Western Wei coins, the triangular head of the *zhu* 銖 is elongated, and the reverse rims are less clearly defined. The Qiuci-script coins therefore appear to have been modelled on Chinese coins of the third and early fourth centuries.

Stein acquired four Qiuci script coins: three were purchased from Korla [IA.XV.a.16–18] (Thierry type E), and one came from Yulduz-bagh [IA.XV.c.18] (Thierry type A). Those from Korla have no Chinese inscription (Thierry type E). This represents a very small sample of the known Qiuci-script coins. While the total number is not known, the largest find of Qiuci-script coins comprised over ten thousand coins deposited in a clay waterpipe, together with Han wuzhu coins, clipped rim wuzhu and Qiuci small coins, at the Dunmailimaiqite site, Kucha, and smaller quantities of Qiuci script coins have been found at the Subashi and Kumtura sites, Kucha, and at the Kuona site, Luntai (Xue 1987). Occasional finds of Qiuci-script coins have been made beside the road from Keping (= Kelpin) to Bachu (Liu Jinwen 1985).

***Qiuci coins: a discussion***

Well over ten thousand Qiuci coins have been found in Eastern Central Asia, mostly concentrated at sites on the northern route, especially in Kucha and Bachu counties. This indicates significant coin production in the ancient kingdom of Qiuci, and reveals that the majority of the coins remained within the territory of the kingdom. This is particularly true for the Qiuci-script coins. The *abd* indicates that the Qiuci-script coins were made after the mid sixth century. The new style of coinage, with greater attention to manufacture, serves to distinguish them from the Qiuci small coins and Qiuci wuzhu coins. The similarly crude manufacture of the Qiuci small coins and Qiuci wuzhu coins suggests either that they were contemporary or that during various stages of early local coin production there was no need or desire to improve the quality. Jiang Qixiang (1999: 427) observed that Qiuci small coins have been found within the former territory of Qiuci and as far as Yutian, Khotan, and suggested that they probably had a wider circulation than Qiuci wuzhu coins. Fuller details of these coins are required before more concrete conclusions may be drawn.

The three main types of Qiuci coins are often found at sites with Sui or Tang dynasty remains. They have been found with Kaiyuan tongbao and Dali yuanbao, the latter of which were issued in the eighth century (Zhang Ping 1991; Huang Wenbi 1983), indicating that these coins remained in circulation in the eighth century.

**Gaochang jili (Plate 4, 51)**

Stein acquired one Gaochang jili coin [IA.X.d.4] in Kara-khoja (= Gaochang), among miscellaneous objects purchased from local cultivators or from petty dealers who had found them while digging for earth, manure or treasure at the Gaochang and Astana sites. Today, over forty specimens are known (Zhang Zhongshan 1999: 40). With one exception,[15] all were found within the Turfan region, mostly from the Gaochang site or Astana cemetery. Gaochang was the name adopted by the Jushi kingdom in 460, and used until the Chinese takeover in 640. The Chinese inscription *Gaochang jili* translates literally as 'Gaochang: auspicious, advantage'.

All specimens are heavy and rather chunky, with weights ranging from 6.2 to 13.76 g, though most weigh *c.*9–10 g, and have a diameter of 26–27 mm. All appear to be individually cast, and no piece is identical to another. As Thierry has shown (2000: 135–6), the reduced size of the square hole, the rims on both sides, the thicker heavier rims, the use of clerk script in the calligraphy and the replacement of the *wuzhu* inscription with a more esoteric inscription all indicate that these pieces were probably made in the late sixth or seventh century. In terms of the good wishes expressed in the inscription, they follow the example of the Chinese coin with the inscription *Yongtong wanguo* [may this piece circulate forever through ten thousand countries], issued 579–80 by the Northern Zhou. The same principle was adopted for the Kaiyuan tongbao coin issued in 621, which is described in its inscription as a 'circulating treasure of the beginning of the new era'.

The date of the Gaochang jili was determined when one specimen (26 mm, 12.5 g) was found under the body in Tomb 519 at Astana. The occupant was Qu Wenzi, a lady of the Qu royal family, and the wife of Zhang Longye. The tomb was intact and its tombstone was dated 642. It yielded official documents, written in Chinese, from the Gaochang kingdom immediately prior to the Chinese takeover in 640. The documents were all dated to the reign of Qu Wentai (620–40)

(Jiang Qixiang 1990(3): 9; XJ-Museum et al. 1975: 17). It is likely that the Gaochang jili pieces were issued during his reign.

On the basis of the inscription and the rarity of this type, it is likely that the Gaochang jili was made not to function as a coin but as a coin-shaped piece with a non-monetary function, perhaps an amulet wishing for good luck or a piece made specifically for burial (Jiang Qixiang 1990(3)). Thierry (2000: 136) proposed that it might have served a political, celebratory or commemorative purpose, though did not identify a specific occasion. Yet events in the 620s provide ample reason for celebration. Following the coup d'état in Gaochang in 614, Qu Boya and his son, Qu Wentai, sought refuge with the Western Turks. In 620 they succeeded in restoring the Qu dynasty, with Qu Boya as king, and Qu Wentai in charge of administration, and began to use the new reign name Chongguang [Double Glory] (Wang Su 1998: 452). The Gaochang jili piece was most probably issued to commemorate the restoration of 620.

The parallels that appear to exist between the Qiuci-script coins and the Gaochang jili demonstrate the desire by the larger kingdoms on the northern route to issue new types of coins in the early seventh century. The impetus must have followed the series of major political changes both east and west in the early seventh century. The reunification of the Chinese empire under the Sui ended almost 300 years of fragmented rule; in 618 the Tang dynasty was established, and in 621 the new Kaiyuan tongbao coinage was announced, replacing the wuzhu coinage of seven centuries. The series of political changes further west were also far-reaching: the emergence of the Turks *c.*560, the Byzantine-Sasanian wars, the unprecedented splendour of the Sasanian ruler Khusrow II (591–628), followed, in the 620s, by the defeat of Persians everywhere at the hands of the Byzantine armies of Heraclius; and the rise of the Arabs.

The Qiuci-script coins may help also in the interpretation of the Gaochang jili inscription. The characters *ji* and *li* express a wish for auspiciousness and advantage. If the Pahlavi reading of 'pd, *abd*, meaning 'excellent' on the Qiuci script coins is correct, then these coins further reflect the strength of Sasanian culture and Zoroastrian religion on the northern route, as observed in other aspects of life at Qiuci and Gaochang.

### Dali yuanbao (Plate 4, 52–3)

In the Stein collection there are 92 Dali yuanbao, from the Ak-terek tatis ([four]), Arkalik ([one]), Chalma-kazan ([four]), Chong Tim ([six]), north of Jiya and Suya ([one]), Khadallik (14), Khotan ([six]), Mazar Tagh (one), 'Mazar Tagh' ([two]), Ming-oi (six), Toghrak-akin (four), Togujai, Moji ([three]), Yotkan ([35]), the tatis east of Yurung-kash ([two]), and unknown provenance ([three]). The vast majority came from sites on the southern route, with over 38 per cent alleged to have come from the Yotkan site, and over 15 per cent from Khadallik. This contrasts markedly with the majority of finds, which are concentrated on the northern route, and can be explained by the disproportionate length of time Stein spent on the southern route.

The specimens in the Stein collection range in size from 19–24.5 mm, with concentrations at 21.5 to 22 mm (51 per cent) and 24 mm (20 per cent). This accords with Thierry's (1997) conclusion that there were two sizes of Dali yuanbao coins (large *c.*23.5 mm; small 21.5 to 22 mm).

### Jianzhong tongbao (Plate 4, 54)

In the Stein collection there are 36 Jianzhong tongbao: from Chalma-kazan ([one]), Khadalik (one), Khara-khoja (two), Kucha (one), Ming-oi (12), Toghrak-akin (16), Yar-khoto (one), Yotkan ([two]). The majority of these coins were found on the northern route.

The specimens in the Stein collection range in size from 20.5–25 mm, with a concentration at 21–21.5 mm (55 per cent). This accords with Thierry's smaller size (20–21.5 mm) but not his larger size (22.5 mm), which is represented in the Stein collection by only three coins (8 per cent).

### Coins with the single character *yuan* 元 or *zhong* 中 (Plate 4, 55–6)

These are small bronze Chinese-type coins, often found together with Dali yuanbao and Jianzhong tongbao, which have a single character inscription *yuan* or *zhong*, positioned above the hole. This placement corresponds with the position of the first character in Chinese coin inscriptions. These types are not found in central China, and are consequently believed to be local derivatives of the Dali yuanbao and Jianzhong tongbao, borrowing the characters *yuan* and *zhong*, respectively.

In the Stein collection there are five *yuan* coins: found at Ming-oi [S.XXII.b.3] and Toghrak-akin [IA.XVI.c.21, 23, 24, 26]. They range in size from 20–20.5 mm and weigh 1.72–2.01 g. There are three *zhong* coins: one from from Ming-oi [S.XXII.b.1] and two from Toghrak-akin [IA.XVI.c.17, 25]. They range in size from 20.5 to 21 mm. The Pelliot collection has eight *yuan* coins, all *c.*20 mm, all from Kucha, and no *zhong* coins. These coins are crudely made, have no rims and often have an irregular edge. The characters *yuan* and *zhong* are the simplest characters in the two inscriptions, and would have been the easiest to reproduce clearly.

### Dali yuanbao, Jianzhong tongbao, yuan and zhong coins: a discussion

The inscriptions on the Dali yuanbao and Jianzhong tongbao indicate that they were issued in the Dali (766–79) and Jianzhong (780–3) reigns of the Tang dynasty. Numismatists treat them as local issues of Eastern Central Asia because these types are not mentioned in the Chinese histories. They were not produced in central China and are very rarely found there.[16]

Three independent studies (Wang Yongsheng 1995; Thierry 1997a; Rhodes 1997) have proved that these coins were produced at a Chinese mint in the Anxi protectorate, with its seat at Qiuci (modern-day Kucha) during a period of almost twenty years when the Tibetans dominated Hexi (modern-day Gansu), severed communications between central China and Eastern Central Asia, and isolated the Anxi protectorate. The military commanders of both the Anxi and Beiting protectorates had been called back to defend the Chinese capital, Chang'an, during the An Lushan rebellion (758–63), and in 766 the Tang court ordered Guo Xin, Capital Liaison Officer (*liuhou*) of the Four Garrisons, to assume supreme authority, both military and civilian, in the Anxi protectorate. Although isolated from central China, the Anxi protectorate under Guo Xin remained politically loyal to the Tang court. With coin supply from the mainland interrupted, the decision was taken locally and independently to produce coins, needed by the isolated Chinese administration. The use of the current Chinese reign-names (*nianhao*) in the coin inscriptions was a political statement, boldly declaring that the Anxi protectorate was still a territory of the Chinese empire, and that it remained loyal to China.

Thierry (1997a) successfully identified mould-links within the groups, and showed how Dali yuanbao and Jianzhong tongbao were cast from moulds made with impressions from altered Tang dynasty coins. The common characters on the coins are presented below in italics:

- Kai*yuan* tong*bao* were used to make moulds for large Dali *yuanbao*.
- Small Qian*yuan* zhong*bao* were used to make moulds for small Dali *yuanbao*.
- Kaiyuan tong*bao* were used to make moulds for large Jianzhong tong*bao*.
- Small Qianyuan zhong*bao* were used to make moulds for small Jianzhong tong*bao*.

He also showed how links in the calligraphy and repetition of flaws among the Dali and Jianzhong coins indicated that these coins were made from moulds with impressions of the same 'master-coins', further evidence that these coins were made within a limited geographical area.

The mould-links between the Kaiyuan, Qianyuan and Dali yuanbao would also explain why the Dali and Jianzhong inscriptions read clockwise rather than top-bottom-right-left, as on the Kaiyuan tongbao.[17]

Metallurgical analysis of a small sample of Dali yuanbao revealed a lead content of 38–60 per cent, much higher than that of contemporary coins from central China (usually below 20 per cent). An even higher lead content (43–74 per cent) was found in some of the Qianyuan coins, indicating that the Anxi mint probably also produced Qianyuan zhongbao coins (Rhodes 1997).[18]

The four types, Dali yuanbao, Jianzhong tongbao, *yuan* and *zhong* coins, were all produced locally in the Anxi protectorate. They are a distinct group of local issues, and are often found together with Kaiyuan and Qianyuan coins. A total of over a thousand specimens of the four types have been found (Wang Yongsheng 1995; Thierry 1997a), about eight hundred of these (80 per cent) at sites on the northern route, particularly at sites in the Kucha region. The Anxi proctectorate included the Four Garrisons of Kucha, Karashahr, Kashgar and Khotan, and almost all known specimens are from within this territory. The circulation of these coins was clearly limited to the Anxi protectorate.

## Türgesh coins (Plate 4, 57)

Türgesh coins are part of a distinctive group known as Sino-Sogdian coins, because they were clearly modelled on the Chinese Kaiyuan tongbao coin but were issued by Sogdians or Turkic princes in Sogdian towns, and usually have a Sogdian inscription and a tamgha, or tribal symbol, on the reverse. The Türgesh coins are the easternmost types of the Sino-Sogdian coins. They were issued by the Türgesh tribe, a branch of the Western Turks, and were made by Sogdians in Suiyab and Talas, inspired by the Sino-Sogdian coins issued in Samarkand (Thierry 1999).

There are two Türgesh coins in the Stein collection: one was purchased at Yotkan, allegedly from that site [AK.II.a.59], the other allegedly came from one of the sites south of Kelpin [S.XXXI.d.25]. Both are Türgesh type II, according to Thierry's classification. Type II coins typically have a diameter of 24–25 mm, weigh *c*.5 g, and have a high copper content of at least 80 per cent, but usually *c*.90 per cent, and are very well made. The inscription comprises four words 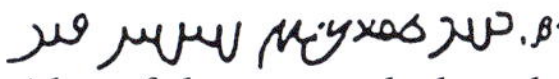. βγy twrgys γaγan pny arranged at the four sides of the square hole, which translate as 'coin of the celestial qaghan of the Türgesh'. The reverse features a tamgha, or tribal symbol 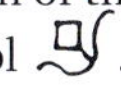.

Type II coins are the most common Türgesh coins, represented in Thierry's list by over fifty specimens. In terms of distribution, most have been found in the Ak-Peshim and Krasnoretchensk region in Kyrgyzstan, which corresponds to the political centre of the Türgesh khanate. But specimens have been found also far beyond the Türgesh khanate itself: in Talas (Kazakhstan), Pendjikent (Tajikistan), at the Bit-Tepe site and in the Sur-Darya valley (Uzbekistan). In Eastern Central Asia, specimens have been found in Khotan, Kashgar, Kelpin, Kucha, Mulei and Turfan. In central China, specimens have been found at Qingyang, Lixian, Yongchang, and between Anxi and Dunhuang (Gansu province) and at Qishan (Shanxi province).

The quality of type II coins and the extent of their distribution suggests that they were issued at the height of power of the Türgesh tribe, namely during the reign of Sulu (716–37). In this way, the tamgha on the reverse of the coins would represent Sulu (as a personal symbol) or his clan (as a clan symbol). It is likely that the type II coins were made at the political centre of the Türgesh khanate, at Suiyab (= Suye, Suiye). In 657 the Chinese administration had named Suiyab as one of its Four Garrisons of Eastern Central Asia, but had to struggle to hold on to it. Eventually, in 719 Sulu forced the Chinese to leave Suiyab, and made his royal palace here. It is likely that Chinese coins were in circulation there. The Sino-Sogdian coins of Samarkand had already set a precedence for bilingual coins with a Chinese form and a Sogdian inscription (Smirnova 1981). The Türgesh type II coins issued by Sulu therefore represent the currency of a new political power at Suiyab.

### Notes

1. These can be classified from Wang Lin (1987), centre plates, as the following types: (no. 1) Cribb 1, (nos 2, 5, 6) Cribb 2, (no. 3) Cribb 4, overstrike on Hermaius imitation, (no. 4) Cribb 2 or 4, (nos 7–8) Cribb 5, (no. 9) Cribb 5–6, (no. 10) Cribb 1–6, (no. 11) Cribb 7–8.
2. Talvio (1999: 118) published three of these coins, which can be classified as (nos 1–2) Cribb 5, (no. 3) Cribb 10.
3. The Hoernle collection is now in the Department of Coins and Medals, British Museum. The Petrovsky and Oldenburg collections are in the State Hermitage Museum, St Petersburg. The Otani specimens are in the Lushun Museum, Dalian, China. The Mannerheim coins are in the National Museum of Finland, Helsinki; see Talvio (1999). Huang Wenbi's coins are in the National Museum of Chinese History, Beijing.
4. Four of these are in the Cultural Relics Office, Khotan.
5. This is even more explicit in Chinese coin inscriptions issued in the Shu-Han state (AD 221–63) which had the inscription *zhibai wuzhu*, literally 'worth 100 wuzhu', i.e. worth 100 wuzhu coins, and not worth 500 *zhu*.
6. A silvery finish has been noted on three Sino-Kharoshthi drachm/6-grain coins: one in the Hermitage collection, one in the British Museum collection, and one recent find, of uncertain provenance and authenticity, published by Qian Boquan (1999). The silvery appearance has been discussed by Cribb (1984: 143 n57).

7. They appear to combine features of both the wuzhu and Wang Mang coinages: by indicating the weight, as on wuzhu, and by identifying them as coins, by using the character *qian* in the inscription. Although the interchangeable character *quan* is seen on the Wang Mang coinage (*daquan wushi*,'large coin [worth] 50'; *xiaoquan zhi yi*, 'small coin worth 1'; and *huoquan*, 'trade coin'), the character *qian* is not seen on Chinese coins before the *Taiping baiqian* coinage of AD 256. The use of *qian* on the Sino-Kharoshthi coins represents the earliest appearance of this character on coins.
8. This coin, allegedly found before 1996 but of unknown provenance, is now in a private collection.
9. I am grateful to Joe Cribb for his comments on the inscription, and to Vesta Curtis for her help with the Pahlavi.
10. Stein (1907: 501) wrote: 'It is thus difficult to determine the date when the current use of wu-chu coins, whether imported from China or locally coined, is likely to have ceased in Khotan'.
11. These were discovered during archaeological surveys in the Aksu region; see Zhang Ping (1991). Full details have not been published.
12. Personal communication with Jiang Qixiang and others in Xinjiang in 1994.
13. I am grateful to Vesta Curtis for confirming that the symbol could be Pahlavi, and for working out this solution with me.
14. This has been adjusted from Thierry's identification.
15. This was found among the lavish burial goods, some dated to the eighth century, in the tomb of the Prince of Bin, near Hejiacun, Shaanxi; see Shaanxi Museum (1972).
16. The exceptions are one Dali coin and seven hundred Qianyuan coins found in a hoard of 1,000 kg of coins with a *terminus post quem* of 1189, in Huolu, Hebei province, and one Dali coin found in Lai'an county, Anhui province (Thierry 1997a: 151).
17. Chinese coin inscriptions are usually arranged top-bottom-right-left of the hole. The earliest appearance of a clockwise inscription, top-right-bottom-left of the hole, is on the *daquan* coins issued by the Wu state from AD 238.
18. The analysis was done as part of a larger project looking at the metal content of Chinese cash coins from the third century BC to the twentieth century; see Wang et al. (2004).

Part 3

# The documentary evidence

# 7 Chinese documents: wood slips, first century BC to fourth century AD

## Wood slips

The earliest Chinese documents found in Eastern Central Asia are tall, narrow strips of wood, with a vertical handwritten inscription in ink, known as wood slips (*mujian*). It was standard practice in Qin and Han dynasty China to tie bamboo- or wood slips together to form longer documents and records. When found at sites, the bindings have often disintegrated and the documents have to be reconstructed slip by slip.[1] The total number of wood slips found in China escalates with each new discovery (Wang Tao 2000). The total found throughout China was estimated in 1990 at fifty thousand, of which over thirty thousand (approximately 60 per cent) were found in Xinjiang and Gansu. Most of these were from the Han dynasty fortifications at Juyan (Gansu) and sites nearby. Other large collections have been found at the Han dynasty fortifications along the Shule River near Dunhuang (Gansu) and at the Loulan and Niya sites (Xinjiang).[2]

He Shuangquan (1989: 150) arranges the slips dated to the Han dynasty found throughout China in five periods: (I) early Western Han (206–141 BC, no examples from Juyan and Dunhuang); (II) mid Western Han (140–33 BC, examples from Juyan); (III) late Western Han (32 BC – AD 8, examples from Juyan, Wuwei, Dunhuang and Niya); (IV) Wang Mang era (AD 9–24, examples from Juyan, Wuwei and Dunhuang); (V) Emperor Guangwudi, Eastern Han (AD 25–32, examples from Juyan and Dunhuang). The majority of dated slips found throughout China are from periods II–IV (140 BC – AD 24), late Western Han and Wang Mang periods. This corresponds well with the dated slips from Juyan, where the earliest slips are dated 119 BC (Xu Pingfang 1978: 27) and the latest slips continue further into the Eastern Han and are dated AD 32.

However, although some wood slips from Eastern Central Asia can be dated as early as period III, the majority of wood slips from Loulan and Niya are from a later period, and are dated AD 252–330s, indicating that the practice of using wood slips continued much later in Eastern Central Asia than in the rest of China.

The content matter of the wood slips is varied, and includes classical texts, laws and regulations, administrative matters of the military garrisons, private correspondence and burial lists (Li Junming and He Shuangquan 1990: 2). Among the administrative affairs are registers, ledgers, official correspondence and laws. The slips from Juyan indicate that, although there was a large military population at the borders, the administration of these regions followed the same hierarchy as central China: from central government (*zhongyang*) to prefecture (*jun*) to county (*xian*) to township (*xiang*) to village (*li*) (He Shuangquan 1989; Hucker 1985: 13–14). Civil administration was managed at village level, with the head of the village (*lizheng*, *lishi*) responsible for the organization of farming, punishments, fines, security, tax collection and transfer of receipts and payments up to the township government. Similar in size and rank to the village was the market (*shi*), also mentioned in the documents. Both village and market were usually walled enclosures, as excavations in Gansu have confirmed, with government offices stationed in the markets rather than the villages (He Shuangquan 1989: 171–86). Many of the documents record the movement of personnel, goods and money between the different levels of administration.

This chapter considers the evidence for money in the wood slips, looking first at the earlier slips from Juyan and Dunhuang, then at the later slips from Loulan and Niya. The sheer quantity of the slips excavated at Juyan and the light they shed on the minutiae of everyday economic and financial life at this border with its well-established system of accounting and record-keeping is phenomenal. It provides unique first-hand information from which to assess the much smaller quantity of similar data from Dunhuang, Loulan and Niya.

## The wood slips from Juyan

### *The sites*

Juyan is known today as Ejina Banner (Ejin Qi), in Inner Mongolia, and lies 90 km northeast of Jinta county, Gansu. The name Juyan originates in the Juyan tribe of the Xiongnu, who surrendered when the Han army defeated the Xiongnu in 102 BC. The Han court then installed a county-level administration at Juyan. Juyan was one of the nine counties in Zhangye prefecture and comprised two townships and 82 villages. It was temporarily renamed Jucheng during the Wang Mang period (AD 9–24), and was gradually abandoned from AD 31 (He Shuangquan 1989: 161–7).

The Juyan sites were built alongside the Ruoshui River and near the Juyan Lake (see Maps 6–7). The river originates in the Qilianshan Mountains, and flows north through the prefecture-seat of Zhangye, where it splits east–west. From here, the river flows in a northwesterly direction through the desert to the Juyan Lake. The Han court fought the Xiongnu for this strategic location and set up farming garrisons on the fertile land (GS-Archaeology et al. 1990).

### *The wood slips*

The total number of wood slips from Juyan is estimated at approximately 31,000 (He Shuangquan 1989: 147). The most significant finds from the Juyan sites have been the ten-thousand-plus slips found by the Sino-Swedish Expedition in the 1930s; the 19,400-plus slips excavated at Jianshui jinguan, Jiaqu houguan and Jiaqusai disisui san chu between 1972 and 1974; the 173 slips found north of Bukentuoni in 1976; and 22 slips found again at Jiaqu houguan in 1982 (GS-Archaeology et al. 1990). The concentrations of wood slips, for example at Jiaqu houguan, correspond with the locations of administrative or military buildings.

For convenience, the following abbreviations are used throughout this chapter: HJ = *Hejiao* (Xie Guihua et al. 1987); XJ = *Xinjian* (GS-Archaeology et al. 1990).

### *Evidence for money*

The evidence for money in the Juyan slips is overwhelming; there can be no doubt that everyday life at Juyan involved money and that coins were the major form of money, as was the case throughout most of the monetized Han empire. Textiles and grain were also used in payments, but to a lesser extent. Fines were expressed in gold. These payments and charges may have been expressed in terms of measures of textiles, grain and gold, yet their equivalent value is also given in coin (*qian* or *quan*). One document [HJ p. 162, 95:8] is an order that values and prices at Juyan should be reckoned in coin (*quan*), and the same is suggested in the titles of the account books (*qian caiwu zhiqian churu bu* 錢財物直錢出入簿, 'double-entry ledger for coins and goods, expressed in coin') [XJ p. 178, EPT51:88].

The two characters *qian* and *quan* both mean 'coin'. At first glance, it is easy to presume that *qian* refers to the wuzhu coins of the Han dynasty and *quan* to the various coins of the Wang Mang period (AD 7–24). Not only did Wang Mang attempt to abolish the wuzhu coin in AD 9, but the term *quan* appears in all the inscriptions but one of the coins he issued.[3] However, closer examination reveals that *quan* and *qian* are found in the same documents and that both terms were used in documents that predate the Wang Mang period. The distinction is therefore difficult to explain, and it would seem that *quan* and *qian* were interchangeable at Juyan.

Given that the location of the Juyan site was within Chinese territory, under Chinese civil or military administration, that the coins found at these sites are either Han or Wang Mang types and that very large quantities of coins were recorded in the slips (often over one thousand coins), it is clear that *qian* and *quan* refer to Chinese coin-types of the Han dynasty and Wang Mang period. The most likely types are the Han wuzhu, and the Wang Mang issues: huoquan, daquan wushi and xiaoquan zhiyi. This concurs with the actual coin evidence from the Juyan sites. The wuzhu and the huoquan are similar in form, design, weight and measurements, and may have circulated together. Consequently, whilst the slip about reckoning in coin quoted above [HJ p. 162, 95:8] can be interpreted as distinguishing *quan* from *qian*, it is probably better interpreted as distinguishing coins from other forms of money.

Although the bookkeeping evident in the wood slips suggests well-established routine practices with *qian* or *quan* indicating a consistent coinage, a small number of slips indicate that the situation was in reality more complicated. Different names for coins indicate a probable disparity in their value: for example in the slips [EPF 22:1–36] produced at the end of Wang Mang's rule and during the early Eastern Han, *xingqian* 行錢 [circulating coins] are contrasted with *Lude qian* 觻得錢 [coins of Lude county]. Although it is impossible now to determine the criteria for *xingqian* and *Lude qian*, the distinction suggests a physical difference, and furthermore that values of particular coins may have varied according to location, with some at a premium and others at a discount. Lude was a centre where desirable Chinese goods were available; perhaps coins of Lude

**Table 3**
**Amounts exceeding 100,000 coins**

| Amounts over 100,000 coins | Reference |
|---|---|
| 9,600,000 *qian* | [XJ p. 361, EPT59:37] |
| 6,008,000 | [HJ p. 322, 208:5] |
| 5,650,100+ | [XJ p. 251, EPT52:330] |
| 2,000,000+ (sale of irrigated land) | [XJ p. 154, EPT50:33A] |
| 2,000,000 *quan* | [XJ p. 53, EPT9:1] |
| 1,473,000 *qian* | [HJ p. 242, 146:73] |
| 1,300,00 *qian* | [XJ p. 360, EPT59:26] |
| 400,000 | [HJ p. 51, 33:8] |
| 298,100+ (value of textiles) (84 BC) | [HJ p. 82, 47:3] |
| 154,200+ *qian* | [XJ p. 371, EPT59:181] |
| 100,000+ (payment to hired local soldier) | [XJ p. 492, EPF22:224] |

were also desirable? Other distinctions of coins include the terms *daquan* 大泉 [large coins] [HJ p. 401, 240:26; HJ p. 390, 237:24], *xiaoquan* 小泉 and *xiaoqian* 小錢 [small coins] [HJ p. 130, 74:8; XJ p. 370, EPT59:163], and *siquan* 私泉 [unofficial coins] [HJ p. 555, 412:2]. The dates of these slips are probably contemporary with the wood slips dated to the end of Wang Mang's rule and the early Eastern Han, which indicate problems at this time with substandard coins and very large quantities of low value coins – often in thousands, or tens of thousands. The descriptions *daquan* and *xiaoquan* are again suggestive of the daquan wushi (AD 7–14) and xiaoquan zhiyi (AD 9–14) coins issued by Wang Mang, but do not confirm that the slips are refering to these coin-types. Indeed, the small coins are called *xiaoqian* in one example and *xiaoquan* in another, which strongly suggests that the meaning 'small coins' rather than 'xiaoquan zhiyi coins' was intended. The meaning of *chunqian* is not known, but perhaps simply indicates new coins issued at the beginning of the financial year.

### *Quantity and supply of coins*

The documents record vast quantities of coins, and there are twelve examples where the amounts total over one hundred thousand coins (see Table 3).

The salaries of personnel stationed at the Juyan sites demanded substantial quantities of coins. Two terms are used for salaries: *feng* 奉 and *lu* 祿, and only occasionally are they found together in the same document. For example, one slip, dated 54 BC, is explicitly headed 'Register of *feng-lu*, 8th month of the 4th year of the Wufeng reign' [XJ p. 21, EPT5:47]. The term *feng* appears always with quantities of coin (*qian*), and is expressed as *fengyongqian* 奉用錢, *fengqian* 奉錢 or *yongqian* 用錢. The term *lu* appears with quantities of coins, textiles, grain and even salt, and is expressed as *lubo* 祿帛 or *luyongbo* 祿用帛 [salary-silk], *lubu* 祿布 [salary-cloth], *lusu* 祿粟 [salary-grain] and *luyongyan* 祿用鹽 [salary-salt]. It would appear that salary entitlement was noted in coin and expressed in terms of *feng*, and that the actual payment was either in coin (*feng* or *lu*) or in kind (*lu*).

The references to salary entitlements and payments are very numerous, yet most examples are fragmentary and give an amount in coin without an official title or date. Most references to salary payments are expressed in coin (*qian*), and a list of

**Table 4**
**Official or military salaries at Juyan**

| Rank | Salary (*qian*) | Date | Reference |
|---|---|---|---|
| *Zhangye-Juyan duwei* | 12,000 | (n.d.) | [XJ p. 393, EPT59:539] |
| *Houzhang* | 1,200 | (n.d.) | [XJ p. 189, EPT51:207] |
| *Houzhang* | 1,200 | (n.d.) | [XJ p. 192, EPT51:234] |
| *Houzhang* | 1,200 | (n.d.) | [XJ p. 205, EPT51:409] |
| *Hou* | 6,000 | (54 BC) | [XJ p. 21, EPT5:47] |
| *Shili* | 1,200 | (54 BC) | [XJ p. 21, EPT5:47] |
| *Lingshi* | 900 | (54 BC) | [XJ p. 21, EPT5:47] |
| *Weishi* | 600 | (54 BC) | [XJ p. 21, EPT5:47] |
| *Wei* | 2,000 | (54 BC) | [XJ p. 21, EPT5:47] |
| *Li* (multiple?) | 4,800 | (n.d.) | [XJ p. 189, EPT51:207] |
| *Li* (multiple?) | 5,400 | (53 BC) | [HJ p. 509, 311:34] |
| *Houshi* | 600 | (n.d.) | [XJ p. 189, EPT51:207] |
| *Houshi* | 900 | (n.d.) | [XJ p. 192, EPT51:234] |
| *Houshi* | 900 | (n.d.) | [XJ p. 36, EPT6:1] |
| *Buqin duizhang* | 600 | (n.d.) | [XJ p. 192, EPT51:234] |
| *Dangqu duizhang* | 1,200 | (n.d.) | [XJ p. 192, EPT51:234] |
| *Duizhang* | 600 | (n.d.) | [XJ p. 205, EPT51:409] |
| – | 1,800 | (59 BC) | [HJ p. 262, 159:22] |
| – | 720 | (81 BC) | [HJ p. 347, 216:7] |
| – | 600 | (59 BC) | [HJ p. 73, 42:12] |
| – | 600 | (63 BC) | [HJ p. 561, 433:33&48] |
| – | 600 | (71 BC) | [HJ p. 597, 498:8] |
| – | 600 | (80 BC) | [HJ p. 597, 498:8] |
| – | 480 | (81 BC) | [HJ p. 624, 513:38] |
| – | 480 | (81 BC) | [HJ p. 624, 513:40] |
| – | 480 | (81 BC) | [HJ p. 157, 90:60] |
| – | 400 | (81 BC) | [HJ p. 499, 303:45] |
| | 360 | (81 BC) | [HJ p. 499, 303:49] |

those including official title and/or date is given in Table 4. Salary payments in textiles, grain and salt are discussed later in this chapter.

The recorded quantities of coins are clearly enormous, and the source of coins at Juyan needs to be determined. Two important slips from Juyan [XJ p. 478, EPF22:38A–39], found in Building 22 at the site known as Pochengzi, provide crucial evidence that officials at the borders were permitted to cast coins *c.*AD 30. The first [XJ p. 478, EPF22:38A] is dated AD 30 and states that there is unofficial casting of small, thin coins that are inferior to the regulatory standard, thieves are opening up graves and brazenly selling the contents and that, as no one is taking responsibility, the people are suffering badly. The second [XJ p. 478, EPF22:39] is a regulation, stating that henceforth only officials at county level may cast coins, and that these must meet the regulatory standard. Clearly, coins were being cast at Juyan immediately after the assassination of Wang Mang (AD 25) and the restoration of the Han dynasty (GS-Archaeology et al. 1990: 478). There are two further references to local coin production. Neither is dated, though one [HJ p. 26, 16:11] includes the Eastern Han official title of the Commandery Governor (*taishou*) so must date later than AD 25. It records the decision of the Commandery Governor, the generals (*jiangjun*) and envoys (*shizhe*) that substandard coins should not be used, and that they should be replaced with wuzhu coins. The second [HJ p. 33, 20:12A] would also appear to be from the same period; it is an announcement from the Defender (*duwei*) about local coin production. These four slips describe coin production in difficult circumstances after the restoration of the Han dynasty (AD 25), and just a few years before the gradual abandonment of Juyan began. There is no other evidence for local coin production at Juyan.

**Table 5**
**Accumulated pay in the form of salary arrears**

| Length of arrears | Salary payments (per month) | Reference |
|---|---|---|
| 277 months + 3 days (= > 23 years) | 600 | [HJ p. 156, 89:14] |
| 108 months (= 9 years) | 700 | [XJ p. 227, EPT52:6] |
| 12 months + 19 days | 600 | [XJ p. 193, EPT51:238] |
| 12 months | 1,200 | [HJ p. 149, 84:30] |
| 8 months | 1,200 | [HJ p. 616, 509:19] |
| 3 months | 3,000 | [HJ p. 210, 127:28] |
| 3 months | 1,200 | [HJ p. 55, 35:5] |
| 3 months | 900 | [HJ p. 6, 4:20] |
| 3 months | 600 | [XJ p. 241, EPT52:181] |
| 3 months | 600 | [HJ p. 39, 26:19 & 30] |
| 3 months | 600 | [HJ p. 146, 82:33] |
| 3 months | 900 | [HJ p. 175, 104:35; 326:12] |
| 3 months | 600 | [HJ p. 445, 266:1] |
| 3 months | 600 | [HJ p. 597, 498:8] |
| 3 months | 600 | [HJ p. 611, 507:4] |
| 3 months | 600 | [HJ p. 627, 515:12] |
| 3 months | 200 | [XJ p. 199, EPT51:309] |
| 3 months | – | [HJ p. 117, 68:13] |
| 2 months | 700 | [HJ p. 162, 95:10] |
| 2 months | 480 | [HJ p. 631, 516:30] |
| salary arrears (details unclear) | – | [HJ, p. 636, 520:6] |

The wood slips confirm that coins used in salary payments had been collected as tax. Many slips mention both *fengyongqian* 奉用錢 [salary-coins] and *fuqian* 賦錢 or *fuquan* 賦泉 [tax-coins]. Special registers known as *fuqian churu bu* 賦錢出入簿 were used to keep track of the 'tax-coins' paid in and taken out [HJ p. 55, 35:8A], and there were 'salary-and-tax name lists' (*fengfu mingji* 奉賦名籍) [HJ p. 128, 73:16]. The intention was that collection and redistribution of coins in this way should be kept in balance.

However, local supply of coinage was not always sufficient. Although salaries were reckoned by the month, they were not paid strictly by the month. Some documents show salary payments partially reduced on account of a previous advancement, as Loewe (1967: I, 97) has shown. Others show accumulated pay in the form of salary arrears ranging from two months to over twenty-three years,[4] with a high frequency of three months' cumulative pay (see Table 5). The slips recording arrears of salary payment are uniquely important because they

**Table 6**
**Salary payments in textiles or grain**

| Salary payment | Quantity | Reference |
|---|---|---|
| Part in *feng-qian*. part in textiles | – | [XJ p. 36, EPT6:6] |
| *Luyongbo* | 18 *pi* 2 *chi* short by ½ *cun* (worth 14,443 coins) | [HJ p. 324, 210:27] |
| *Luyongbo* | 18 *pi* 1 [*cun*] | [HJ p. 576, 480:11] |
| *Luyongbo* | 1 *pi* 4 *cun* | [HJ p. 445, 266:15] |
| *Lubo* | 1 *pi* | [XJ p. 104, EPT43:41] |
| *Lubo* | 1 *pi* | [HJ p. 67, 39:30] |
| *Lubo* | 1 *pi* | [HJ p. 550, 394:1] |
| *Lubo* | 3 *zhang* 3 *chi* | [XJ p. 36, EPT6:5] |
| *Lubo* | 3 *zhang* 3 *chi* | [XJ p. 36, EPT6:6] |
| *Lubo* | 3 *zhang* 3 *chi* | [XJ p. 40, EPT6:76] |
| *Lubo* | 3 *zhang* 3 *chi* | [XJ p. 98, EPT40:199] |
| *Lubo* | 3 *zhang* 3 *chi* | [XJ p. 425, EPT65:79] |
| *Lubo* | 3 *zhang* 3 *chi* | [HJ p. 162, 95:7] |
| *Lubo* | 3 *zhang* 3 *chi* | [XJ p. 104, EPT43:46] |
| *Lubo* | 3 *zhang* . . . | [XJ p. 36, EPT6:2] |
| *Lubo* | – | [XJ p. 381, EPT59:336] |
| *Lubo* | – | [HJ p. 445, 266:9] |
| *(Lu)bo* | 2 *zhang* 6 *chi* | [XJ p. 78, EPT27:10] |
| – | 2 *zhang* 2 *chi* | [XJ p. 49, EPT7:51] |
| *Lubu* | 2 *pi* . . . | [XJ p. 378, EPT59:297] |
| *Lubu* | 3 *zhang* 6 *chi* | [XJ p. 78, EPT27:10] |
| *Lusu* | – | [XJ p. 27, EPT5:161] |
| *Lusu* | 10 | [XJ p. 58, EPT10:47] |
| *Lusu* (measured in *hu* and *dou*) | – | [XJ p. 47, EPT7:27] |
| *Lusu* (expressed in *shi*-bushel) | – | [XJ p. 482, EPT22:72–76] |
| [Salary for '2,000 bushel official'] | – | [XJ p. 55, EPT10:2A] |
| *Luyan* | – | [HJ p. 252, 154:10] |

identify the sources of these coins as the treasuries in the capital city and prefectures. Two documents refer to 'Henei tax-coins' [HJ p. 597, 498:8; and HJ, p. 636, 520:6]. The former is dated 80 BC. As Sawara (1995: 561–3) has rightly shown, they prove that the government was prepared to send out coins over long distances at exceptional times when local supply was insufficient. The origins of such coins and textiles were recorded at every stage of their passage, and the special attention paid to these temporary supplements indicates that their supply was exceptional rather than regular. They may also be connected with the fan-shaped wooden pieces found at Juyan, which Loewe (1967: I, 72) believed to be labels for containers of coins. These findings confirm that some Chinese coins were being transported at least as far to the northwest as Juyan during the first century AD, albeit in exceptional circumstances.

### *Bookkeeping*

As the salary records confirm, a well-established system of bookkeeping is manifest in the Juyan wood slips, and there are regular, standard patterns for recording transactions involving coins. The phrase *neng shu hui ji* 能數會計 [good at numbers and keeping accounts] appears frequently as the criteria for recruiting bookkeepers [e.g. HJ p. 658, 562:2].

Many of the Juyan documents record the transfer or movement of money, and again the accounting formulae are well-established and straightforward. Lists of goods, payers and payees were compiled in registers, known as *ji* 籍 and *bu* 簿, where *ji* usually served to record official and personal names, and *bu* served as an account book of incomings and outgoings. For example, *ji* record those troops who have been paid, and *bu* record the movement of coins (*qian* or *quan*) and other goods (*caiwu* 財物). The movement of money was carefully recorded at every stage of its passage.[5] There may have been a system of marking slips recording transfer of money. The tips of some slips were painted red: for example a slip recording a consignment of coins (*diaoqian* 調錢) [XJ p. 107, EPT43:98], and registers of tax-coins (*fuqianbu* 賦錢簿) and goods (*caiwubu* 財物簿) [XJ p. 480, 22:54A and 55B].[6]

There are too many wood slips from Juyan to list all the economic and financial activities recorded on them. A selection of the most frequent occurrences is given below: salary payment, taxation, fines, 'horse money', prices of goods, service and compensation, markets and private enterprise, and loans. The frequency of these activities reveals consistent patterns which allow a deeper understanding of how money was used.

### *Salary payment*

The slips show that salaries were paid in coin, textiles, grain or salt. By far the majority were paid in coin, with smaller numbers in textiles, and even fewer in grain. Only one slip records a salary paid in salt [HJ p. 252, 154:10]. Salaries paid solely in coin have been discussed earlier. Some salaries appear to have been paid part in coin (*fengqian*) and part in textiles (*lubo*), [e.g. XJ p. 36, EPT6:6] (see Table 6). Salaries paid in textiles are differentiated as *lu(yong)bo* [salary-silk] and *lubu* [salary-cotton]. They are measured by length: *pi* 匹 > *zhang* 丈 > *chi* 尺 > *cun* 寸, with the most frequent quantity of *lubo* being 3 *zhang* 3 *chi*. The largest quantity of *luyongbo* is 18 *pi* 2 *chi* short by $\frac{1}{2}$ *cun* (in total worth 14,443 coins).

Only three slips mention salaries paid in grain (*lusu* 祿粟): they confirm that some salaries were occasionally reckoned or paid in grain, measured in *hu* 斛 and *dou* 斗. One slip [XJ p. 482, EPT22:72–76] expresses salary payment for Juyan officials as *lusu* 祿粟 [salary-grain], with quantities measured in *shi* 石 [bushels]: Juyan *duwei* 60 *shi*, Juyan *duweicheng* 30 *shi*, Juyan *ling* 30 *shi*, Juyan *cheng* 15 *shi*, Juyan *zuoyouwei* 15 *shi*. Another mentions a 2,000-*shi* official [XJ p. 55, EPT10:2A]. This relates to the abstract ranking system of the Han dynasty, which Bielenstein (1980: 4, 125–31) explains as an 'arbitrary scale which must have originally expressed the salary in kind due to the officeholder, but later ceased to do so and became simply a tool for the ranking of office and their incumbents, and for the determination of privilege and protocol. Salaries were fixed in relation to the scale, in the sense that these increased (although not proportionately) with each higher step.' Unfortunately, there is not sufficient consistent data regarding these titles, amounts and dates to expand on this single document from Juyan.

One document [XJ, EPT59] from Juyan uniquely contains a list of payments to officials for the month corresponding to late October to early November AD 11, where the money-object is expressed as *da-huang-bu* 大黃布 [large yellow cloth]. Where clearly legible, all the payments are for 13 *da-huang-bu* or for multiples of 13 *da-huang-bu*. This suggests that payment was a standard 13 *da huang bu* per person, regardless of rank. It is interesting that the largest quantity of *luyongbo* recorded was worth 14,443 coins, an amount which is again divisible by 13 (1,111 × 13 = 14,443) (see Table 7).

As this document [XJ, EPT59] is dated AD 11 (Wang Mang year 4, xinwei), and, as Wang Mang's largest spade money, issued AD 10, had the inscription *da-bu-huang-qian* [large spade yellow (worth) thousand], there is a temptation to read these payments as 13 pieces of spade money per person,[7] but the contexts do not allow this. First, the spade money is the largest in a series of ten, on all of which the arrangement of the inscription is identical, with *bu* as the second character,[8] so the inversion of *bu* and *huang* in *da-huang-bu* would appear forced and would need to be explained. Second, the term *huang-bu* [yellow cloth] is also found as a textile used to make shirts and trousers [e.g. XJ p. 234, EPT52:93; XJ p. 238, EPT52:139]. Third, at face value 13 spades would be equivalent to 13,000 coins, or a staggering 21.67 times the more normal salary of 600 *qian* per month for an official of the rank of *hou* [captain]. Fourth, although the *da-bu-huang-qian* is the most common of the ten spades of Wang Mang's AD 10 reform, the largest finds of this type throughout China total just 156 from Gaomi (Shandong), and over one hundred from Jingjiashan Tomb M2, Nanchang (Jiangxi), both in eastern China (Zhu Huo 1992: 191). In this light, even the preliminary total of 2,093 spades from the Juyan

**Table 7**
**Payments of *da-huang-bu***

| Rank | Payment of *da-huang-bu* | Reference (XJ, pp. 358–416, EPT 59) |
|---|---|---|
| *Houshi* | 13 | [XJ EPT59:191] |
| *Houshi* | 13 | [XJ EPT59:192] |
| *Houshi* | 13 | [XJ EPT59:197] |
| *Houshi* | 13 | [XJ EPT59:210] |
| *Shishi* | 13 | [XJ EPT59:193] |
| *Weishi* | 13 | [XJ EPT59:194] |
| *Weishi* | 13 | [XJ EPT59:195] |
| *Shili* | 13 | [XJ EPT59:196] |
| *Shili* (x 11) | 143 (= 13 x 11) | [XJ EPT59:220–1] |
| [*Dui?*] *zhang* | 13 | [XJ EPT59:198] |
| – | 13 | [XJ EPT59:199] |
| (Details unclear) | – | [XJ EPT59:200] |
| *Duizhang* | – | [XJ EPT59:201] |
| *Duizhang* | – | [XJ EPT59:211] |
| *Duizhang* | 13 | [XJ EPT59:202] |
| *Duizhang* | 13 | [XJ EPT59:203] |
| *Duizhang* | 13 | [XJ EPT59:204] |
| *Duizhang* | 13 | [XJ EPT59:205] |
| *Duizhang* | 13 | [XJ EPT59:206] |
| *Duizhang* | 13 | [XJ EPT59:207] |
| *Duizhang* | 13 | [XJ EPT59:208] |
| *Duizhang* | 13 | [XJ EPT59:209] |
| *Duizhang* | 13 | [XJ EPT59:212] |
| *Duizhang* | 13 | [XJ EPT59:213] |
| *Duizhang* | 13 | [XJ EPT59:214] |
| *Duizhang* | 13 | [XJ EPT59:215] |
| *Duizhang* | 13 | [XJ EPT59:216] |
| *Duizhang* | 13 | [XJ EPT59:217] |
| – | 13 | [XJ EPT59:218, 219, 227] |
| *Houzhang* | 13 | [XJ EPT59:222] |
| *Li* (× 9) | – | [XJ EPT59:223–5] |
| *Li* (× 9) | 117 (= 13 × 9) | [XJ EPT59:228] |
| *Li* (× 107) | 13[91] (= 13 × 107) | [XJ EPT59:226A] |

documents would appear excessive. The payments in *da-huang-bu* therefore must refer to a specific item, perhaps simply a length of yellow cloth, given in payment, and with a monetary value closer to a more usual salary of 600 *qian*.[9] The absence of proportionate differentiation of payment of *da-huang-bu* among the different ranks suggests that the *da-huang-bu* may have been a government bestowal to all officials, perhaps to mark an important imperial occasion or as a kindly impulse.[10]

### *Taxation*

As mentioned above, taxation is almost always expressed in coin: 'tax-coin' (*fuqian*), and associated with salary payments (*feng*). It is not clear if, and how, 'tax-coins' were collected locally. The majority of cases refer to 'tax-coins' transported to Juyan from central China. One example notes the movement of over 14,300 'tax-coins' [HJ p. 230, 139:28]. It is interesting

**Table 8**
**Fines**

| Fines (in gold) | Reference |
|---|---|
| Half-*liang*, 1 *liang*, 2 *liang* | [XJ p. 554, EPS4:T2:8B] |
| 2 *liang*, worth 1,000+ [coins] | [HJ p. 366, 227:13] |
| 4 *liang*, worth 2,500 [coins] | [XJ p. 337, EPT57:1] |
| 4 *liang* | [XJ p. 22, EPT5:60] |
| 4 *liang* | [HJ p. 42, 27:24] |
| Worth 2,500 [coins] | [HJ p. 379, 231:115A] |
| Worth 5,000 [coins] | [HJ p. 379, 231:115B] |

that the number 14,300 is a multiple of both 11 and 13 (11 × 1,300 = 14,3000; 13 × 1,100 = 14,300). The same is true for the largest quantity expressed in *luyongbo*, worth 14,443 coins (11 × 1,313 = 14,443; 13 × 1,111 = 14,443) [HJ, p. 324, 21:27] (see Table 6).

### *Fines*

Fines are indicated by the term *fa* 罰. When the payment is specified the term is always expanded to *fajin* 罰金 [fine in gold]. In five examples payment is explicitly stated in gold, measured by weight in units of *liang* 兩, and in two of those examples the equivalent in coin is given. Only two examples express the fine in terms of coin (see Table 8). According to these examples, 1 *liang* of gold was equivalent to 625 coins, just slightly higher than one month's salary (of 600 coins) for an official of *hou* [captain] rank. The most frequent fine of four *liang* of gold (or 2,500 coins) was therefore equivalent to over four months' salary for a *hou*. The fact that the fines are expressed first in gold and then in coin suggests that fines may once (perhaps traditionally) have been payable in gold, and that with the greater availability of coins they later came to be paid in coin. The actual calculations can be seen as [625 = 600 + 25] or [625 = 600 + ($^1/_{24}$ × 600)]. This tallies well with the equivalent values of silk and coin where 1 *liang* of silk had a value of 24 coins (25 *liang* of silk = 25 × 24 coins = 600 coins) seen on a silk fragment from Dunhuang (see below).

### *'Horse money'*

'Horse money' (*maquan* 馬泉 or *maqian* 馬錢) was paid into the treasury following the death of a horse while on the road. There were strict procedures whereby all horses taken out on the road had to be checked back into the stables; if a horse died while out of the stables, its body (flesh, bones and skin) was sold and the money received was handed in to the authorities (see Table 9).

**Table 9**
**Horse money**

| Horse money | Quantity | Reference |
|---|---|---|
| *Maquan* | 350 *mei* | [XJ p. 68, EPT17:36A] |
| *Maquan* | 5,900+ *mei* | [XJ p. 86, EPT40:11A] |
| *Maquan* | 4,000 *mei* | [XJ p. 88, EPT40:37A] |
| *Maqian* | 5,000 | [XJ p. 295, EPT53:232] |
| *Maqian* | 9,500 | [HJ p. 55, 35:4] |
| *Maqian* | – | [HJ p. 125, 72:4] |
| *Maqian* | 5,500 | [HJ p. 238, 143:19] |
| *Maqian* | – | [HJ p. 239, 145:1] |

### *Prices of goods*

A lengthy table showing prices and values of goods is attached to the end of this chapter (see Table 17). The data in the table should be used with caution as the slips are mostly without date, and the transactions cover a period of approximately one hundred years (119 BC to AD 32), during which time prices are likely to have fluctuated. Furthermore, the table does not distinguish between official supplies and private enterprise. However, the data are important in that they allow a broad view of values and prices during the period. It is even more significant that some general patterns have emerged and these provide unique contemporary evidence for economic life at Juyan. The most expensive items in the table are land, livestock, carts, slaves, textiles and clothing. The slips indicate that most items were valued in coin, usually expressed as *qian*. Grain, livestock, fodder and land were always valued in coin. Textiles, clothing, shoes, meat,[11] fish and wine were valued in coin and occasionally in grain.

### *Service and compensation*

In addition to the official salaries discussed above, there was also official employment of local people, for example to fight in battle, and private employment of individuals from elsewhere in China, for example, as fishermen and agents (see below). One document states that when a hundred Xiongnu people fought against the Qiang they were each paid 100,000 coins [XJ p. 492, EPF22:224]. Another records that thirty thousand coins were provided for the burial of a person killed in battle against the Qiang [HJ p. 448, 267:19].

Two slips give the price of slaves as 20,000 coins for a young girl slave (*xiaobi*) [HJ p. 61, 37:35], and 3,000 coins for two children (*xiaonu*) [HJ p. 61, 37:35]. Another slip gives the value of infants at 104 and 130 coins [HJ p. 201, 123:22].

### *Markets and private enterprise*

The slips distinguish between official (*guan* 官) and private (*si* 私) business, which was often expressed as 'private enterprise for the family' (*wei jia sishi* 為家私事). They record activity at the markets of Juyan, Jianshui and Lude. There are numerous examples of private enterprise (*sishi* 私事) in the Juyan slips (see Table 10). One slip records someone buying silk for another person [XJ p. 236, EPT52:112]. Another slip refers to a textile merchant [HJ p. 259, 157:24A] and another to an official and his enterprise [XJ, p. 475–8, EPT22]. One slip records the purchase of silk by the chief of some non-Chinese people (*huzhang*) [HJ p. 348, 217:15–19]. There are also two examples of people 'travelling on a private seal' (*yi siyin xing* 以私印行) [HJ p. 491, 299:6 and HJ p. 501, 306:4A and 5:9A]. These may be seen as travel documents similar to the official passes, or passports, found at Xuanquan (see below). They probably indicated that the traveller was not on official business and was therefore personally liable for his own affairs.

One series of slips [XJ, p. 475–8, EPF22:1–36] provides a clear illustration of private enterprise in the form of a court case between an official Li Jun and a commoner En, during the

**Table 10**
**Private enterprise**

| Private enterprise | Reference |
|---|---|
| Private enterprise for the family | [HJ p. 45, 29:6] |
| Private enterprise for the family | [HJ p. 351, 218:27] |
| Private enterprise for the family | [HJ p. 454, 270:20] |
| Private enterprise for the family | [HJ p. 552, 403:12] |
| Private enterprise for the family, at Juyan | [HJ p. 406, 243:20] |
| Private enterprise at Juyan | [HJ p. 407, 243:34] |
| Private clothing (*siyi*) | [HJ p. 461, 23:27B] |
| Buying silk for another person | [XJ p. 236, EPT52:112] |
| Textile merchant | [HJ p. 259, 157:24A] |
| Chief of non-Chinese people (*huzhang*) buying silk | [HJ p. 348, 217:15–19] |
| Travelling on a private seal | [HJ p. 491, 299:6] |
| Travelling on a private seal | [HJ p. 501, 306:4A & 5:9A] |
| Private enterprise: court case between the official Li Jun and En | [XJ p. 475–8, EPF22:1–36] |

Wang Mang period (GS-Juyan 1978a–b). It records how Li Jun commissioned En to sell five thousand fish[12] on his behalf for an agreed total of 400,000 coins (*xingqian*), involving a round trip of some twenty days from Juyan to Lude. Li Jun advanced En 27 *shi* of grain and loaned him an ox. En sold the fish, but failed to raise the 400,000 coins. In an attempt to meet the agreed total, he sold the ox and engaged in trade of goods, but still fell short of the agreed amount. En's son had been working as a fisherman for Li Jun for over three months, and his wages (reckoned at 55,400 coins) were put towards raising the 400,000 coins. When finally the 400,000 coins had been raised, and En's means were exhausted, Li Jun then took him to court for failing to return the loaned ox. The court ruled that Li Jun's demand was inappropriate and had him demoted.

The neutrality with which these facts are discussed suggests that, other than Li Jun's unreasonable demand for the ox, all the other actions were not in themselves unusual. The official was able to engage in private money-making activities, employing both En and his son to do different jobs and with different methods of payment. The son's pay was reckoned at the *per diem* market rate; the father's pay was to come from the sale of the fish. En, a sixty-year-old from Yingchuan prefecture (modern-day Yexian, Henan province), was able to travel freely between settlements with a loaned ox, and a presumably conspicuous load of five thousand fish. He was able to sell the ox, which he did not own, and to use the funds to purchase goods of Chinese origin. This document shows that officials and commoners alike were free to engage in trade.

***Credit and debt***

The Juyan slips make frequent mention of credit and debt in the form of accumulated payment of salary in arrears (see above), lending at profit, and buying and selling on credit.

There is substantial evidence for buying and selling on credit (*shi* 貰 or *shimai* 貰買，貰賣), with payment deferred or by instalment. Proof of payment was confirmed by means of written contracts (*quanyue* 券約) or by record in the

**Table 11**
**Buying and selling on credit (*shi* or *shimai*)**

| Type of transaction | Reference |
|---|---|
| *Shi* | [XJ p. 527, EPF22:779] |
| *Shi* | [HJ p. 22, 14:14] |
| *Shi* | [HJ p. 317, 203:26] |
| *Shi* | [HJ p. 318, 203:48] |
| *Shimai* | [XJ p. 334, EPT56:402] |
| *Shimai* | [XJ p. 546, EPC:3] |
| *Shimai* | [XJ p. 327, EPT56:293] |
| *Shimai yiwu* | [XJ p. 189, 51:210A] |
| *Shimai yiwu* | [XJ p. 301, EPT54:2] |
| *Shimai yiwu* | [HJ p. 98, 56:16] |
| *Shimai yiwu* | [HJ p. 174, 104:21] |
| *Shimai yicaiwu* | [XJ p. 231, 51:55] |
| *Shimai yicaiwu* | [XJ p. 293, 51:186] |
| *Shimai yicaiwu* | [XJ p. 352, EPT58:45A] |
| *Shimai yicaiwu* | [HJ p. 17, 10:34A] |
| *Shimai yicaiwu* | [HJ p. 79, 45:24] |
| *Shimai yicaiwu* | [HJ p. 331, 213:15] |
| *Shiyi chu* | [XJ p. 555, EPS4:T2:22] |

account-books (*bu* 簿 or *ji* 籍). This form of credit seems to have been co-ordinated by the stores (*zang* 藏) of the military stations, and to have been used by the military personnel. There were restrictions: the term *shimai* also appears in the negative, suggesting that credit was sometimes refused [XJ p. 329, 316; HJ p. 92, 52:58; HJ p. 663, 564:26]. Several slips refer to amnesties for debtors, and two slips announce a prohibition on *shimai* [XJ p. 251, EPT51:334 and HJ p. 4, 4:1].

In *shimai* transactions the goods are specified as 'garments wealth goods' (*yicaiwu* 衣財物) or 'garments-goods' (*yiwu* 衣物) (see Table 11). Indeed, out of 24 examples of *shimai* transactions, 22 refer to textiles or garments; the other two refer to the following accoutrements: sword, staff and whip. These confirm that textiles or garments were the main category of goods bought and sold on credit. A *shimai* transaction might involve a single item or several items. For example, one slip lists the seller's items as one black lined robe, one long robe of *jian* silk, one pair of black trousers and another black garment [HJ p. 321, 206:28] (see Table 12).

Written contracts [e.g. HJ p. 254, 155:13A] determined the payment terms, usually to be paid in full in coin within a few months. Examples include a pair of trousers worth 550 to be fully paid for in coin by spring [XJ p. 342, 57:72]; another pair of trousers worth 270, of which 200 has already been paid and another 70 is owed [XJ p. 181, 51:12]. In 37 BC an official from Jiaqu purchased from a soldier a garment valued at 750, and the contract specifies that the full amount should be paid in coin by spring [HJ p. 38, 26:1]. Another contract records the purchase by a soldier of black cloth worth 353 in the seventh month, and specifies that the full amount should be paid in coin by the twelfth month [HJ p.436, 262:29]. Payment by spring or the twelfth month in effect meant payment by the end of the financial year; in line with the duty of the imperial Chancellor to present the financial documents in the capital on the first day

**Table 12**
**The goods exchanged in *shi* or *shimai* transactions**

| Object of *shimai* | Value in coin | Reference |
|---|---|---|
| 1 official's *pao* robe | worth . . . | [XJ p. 415, EPT59:923] |
| 1 *pao* robe | – | [XJ p. 115, EPT43:255A] |
| 1 black *duan*-silk lined *pao* robe | 2,500 | [HJ p. 122, 69:1] |
| 1 black lined *pao* robe | 1,800 | [HJ p. 321, 206:28] |
| 1 *jian*-silk long *pao* robe | 2,000 | [HJ p. 321, 206:28] |
| 1 white *chou*-silk *ru* jacket | 500 | [XJ p. 198, 51:302] |
| 1 pair of black trousers | 900 | [XJ p. 553, EPS4:T1:21] |
| 1 pair of black trousers | 1,100 | [HJ p. 321, 206:28] |
| Black trousers | 270 | [XJ p. 181, 51:125] |
| 1 pair of trousers | 550 | [XJ p. 342, 57:72] |
| 1 *pi* of *chunlü* (?) | 1,000 | [HJ p. 183, 112:27] |
| Black . . . | 750 | [HJ p. 321, 206:28] |
| Black *fu* (?) | – | [XJ p. 295, EPT53:221] |
| *Bu fu* (?) | – | [XJ p. 215, 51:540] |
| Black *bu*-cloth | – | [XJ p. 546, EPC:3] |
| 1 *jin* of *xi* (?) | 350 | [HJ p. 319, 206:3] |
| 4 *dou* of *mai* (?) | 38 | [HJ p. 319, 206:3] |
| 1 official *xi* (?) | – | [HJ p. 154, 88:13] |
| 3 *pi* of *lian*-silk | – | [HJ p. 254, 155:13A] |
| 2 *mei* of *ji* and *xu* | 300 | [XJ p. 195, 51:249] |
| 3 *pi* of *qi* (?) | 1,000+ | [XJ p. 307, EPT56:10] |
| Clothes | 1,000s | [XJ p. 315, EPT56:113] |
| Sword | 700 | [HJ p. 455, 271:1] |
| Staff and whip | – | [XJ p. 519, EPF22:645] |

of the New Year, which from 103 BC was the first day of the first month (Bielenstein 1980: 8).

## The wood slips from Dunhuang and Jiuquan

### *The sites*

Dunhuang and Jiuquan lie in the northwest of Gansu province. Han dynasty Dunhuang prefecture corresponds today to the eastern borders of Xinjiang, and Dunhuang and Anxi counties in Gansu. The Jiuquan prefecture of the Han dynasty corresponds today to the area including Yumenzhen, Chijinbao, Jiuquan and Jinta in Gansu. Dunhuang was the last important Chinese centre on the route from China to Central Asia (see Maps 6–7).

In the Han dynasty Dunhuang prefecture comprised four *duwei* (adminstrative regions): Yumen, Yangguan, Zhongbu and Yihe. Jiuquan prefecture comprised three *duwei*: Xibu duwei (in the west), Beibu duwei (in the north), and Zhongbu duwei (in the centre) (Lin Meicun and Li Junming 1984). The Dunhuang and Jiuquan wood slips were recovered from the line of beacon towers and fortifications built during the Han dynasty along the Shule River, from east of the Yushuquan Basin to west of Dunhuang, during the Han dynasty to guard the route to the west and protect the settlements of Dunhuang and Jiuquan. The salt marshes a little further to the west were extremely difficult territory to cross and served as a natural defence.

**Table 13**
**Wood slips from watch-station T.VI.b that mention coins**

| Mention of coins | Reference |
|---|---|
| 1 long official *pao* robe, price 1,000 (60 BC) | [Shule 63] |
| 1 long official *pao* robe, price 287 | [Shule 76] |
| 1 *xi* suit, price 450 | [Shule 76] |
| Paid out 150 *qian* | [Shule 79] |
| Gift of 10 *jin* of gold | [Shule 127] |
| (1)23 *jin* price 270+ | [Shule 163] |
| 1 long official *bu*-cloth *pao* robe, price 1,300 (60 BC) | [Shule 170] |
| 500+ *qian* | [Shule 215] |
| 4 months' salary (= 2,400 *qian*) in arrears | [Shule 219] |
| Non-Chinese soldier owes 240 *qian* | [Shule 261] |

### *The wood slips*

Stein found over nine hundred wood slips at the Shule River sites near Dunhuang and Jiuquan in 1907 and 1915. These have been studied by Chavannes (1913), Maspéro (1953) and Loewe (1967) in Europe, and by many scholars in China, including Zhang Feng (1931) and Lin Meicun and Li Junming (1984).[13] Over two thousand more wood slips have been found since Stein's time. The Scientific Expedition to the North West (*Xibei Kexue Kaochadui*) found 49 wood slips in 1944. The Jiayuguan City Cultural Relics and Heritage Office (*Jiayuguan shi wenwu baoguan suo*) found 91 wood slips near Yumen in 1977. The Gansu Provincial Cultural Relics Team (*Gansu sheng wenwu gongzuodui*) and the Dunhuang Cultural Office (*Dunhuang wenhuaguan*) found 1,027 wood slips at Maquanwan in 1979. In the 1980s the Dunhuang Museum also collected over two hundred wood slips. In addition, between 1990 and 1992 the Xuanquan zhi site was excavated, yielding over 23,000 wood slips; these are discussed separately below.[14] For convenience, the following abbreviation is used below for woodslips from the Shule River sites: Shule (= Lin Meicun and Li Junming 1984).[15]

The majority of these slips are from the Han dynasty, with the dated slips covering the period 103 BC to AD 137 [Shule 672 and 443, respectively]. One undated slip [Shule 435] may predate 103 BC; it tells of 'the defender (*duwei*) of Jiuquan and Yumen protecting the people' and refers to the reign of Wudi, before Dunhuang had become a prefecture. The majority of the dated slips from these sites are from 60–57 BC, and are therefore contemporary with the slips from Juyan. A very small number of slips may postdate the Han dynasty [e.g. Shule 933] on the grounds of their later calligraphic style (Lin Meicun and Li Junming 1984).

Although the total quantity of slips from Dunhuang and Jiuquan is much smaller than the vast quantity found at the Juyan sites, the evidence for money in these documents is remarkably similar. Registers and log books were used to keep track of incomings and outgoings. Two slips refer to monthly salaries paid in coin, at 600 coins [Shule 509] and 1,200 coins [Shule 219], the latter paid in arrears. One slip confirms the practice of paying 'horse money' in Dunhuang, here to the value of 3,000 *qian* [Shule 480]. Accounting practices are similar, and, as at Juyan, evidence for prices or values is most frequent for textiles and garments (see examples below). One slip [Shule

**Table 14**
**Payments in the wood slips from Dunhuang and Jiuquan**

| Payments | Reference |
|---|---|
| 50, buy axe pay out 100, buy silk pay out . . ., 48 *qian*, . . ., price 650, 10 *chi* cloth price 60 | [Shule 692] |
| Purchase. .23 *jin* in weight, price 270 | [Shule 163] |
| . . .8 . . .*qian*, . . .12 *qian*, gentleman's room 17 . . . | [Shule 530] |
| List of agricultural produce, total 2,000, entered 220 and another 1,000+ | [Shule 581] |
| Owing 1,810 *qian* (AD 1) | [Shule 322] |
| Exchange rate of 13 *qian* 5 *fen* | [Shule 354] |
| Purchase of a horse | [Shule 371] |
| Purchase of horses | [Shule 514] |
| The office took the amount calculated earlier; the balance was restored | [Shule 90] |
| Paid out 1,100 *qian* | [Shule 706] |
| Paid out 96 *qian* | [Shule 706] |
| . . . worth 120 [coins] | [Shule 706] |
| A kind of hemp @ 10 [coins] per *jin* | [Shule 301] |
| Grain prices: 5 *sheng* of *liang mi* @ 100 (1 @ 20) | [Shule 581] |
| 6 cups @ 120 (1 cup @ 20) | [Shule 581] |
| 1 *shi* of . . . @ 100+ | [Shule 581] |
| . . . @ 50 | [Shule 581] |
| 90 *qian* owed, 40 *qian* owed | [Shule 842] |
| Worth 400, already received 300 *qian* | [Maspéro 1953: 42, no. 117] |

170] is a contract dated 60 BC, in which a man from Guanghan (in modern-day Sichuan province) is selling a Chinese-style cloth robe to a non-Chinese head of troops for 1,300 *qian*, to be paid for in full by the first month. This document is similar to the Juyan *shimai* contracts, and furthermore confirms that non-Chinese local people were hired at Dunhuang, and that they could buy garments on credit from Chinese people who had come from southwest China.

Ten slips from a single watch station [T.VI.b] mention coins (see Table 13). These are not unique; there are several wood slips from Dunhuang and Jiuquan which refer to payments of coins (see Table 14). The slips support the evidence from Juyan and confirm that economic life was probably similar in the two regions.

One document [Stein T.xv.a.i.3, doc.539 (= Shule 439)] from the refuse heap below the watch-tower [T.xv] is particularly significant. It is one of two strips of undyed silk, found together and originally from the same larger piece of silk. One bears the impression of a Chinese seal and retains the selvedge at each end, indicating the original width of the roll was 50 cm. It has a Chinese inscription stating that it is a roll of silk from Kangfu in the kingdom of Rencheng: width 2 *chi* 2 *cun*, length 4 *zhang*, weight 25 *liang*, value 618 (Stein 1921: 373–4, 700–1). The kingdom of Rencheng corresponds to modern-day Jining, Shandong province; it was established in AD 84, and was abolished in the Jin dynasty (265–420).[16] This slip confirms precisely the exchange value of silk and coin in the late first century or early second century AD. It is also important that the width of the silk fragment with the selvedge matches that of the roll of silk found by Stein at Loulan [LA.I.002], confirming that 50 cm was probably a standard measurement for silk (Stein 1921: 373–4, 701). The total value in coin of this roll of silk was 618 coins, or 600 × 103 per cent. It was equivalent to the monthly salary of a captain (*hou*), with a premium of 3 per cent. This calculation confirms that 1 *liang* of silk had a value of 24 coins (25 × 24 = 600), and that 1 *zhang* of silk had a value of 150 coins (4 × 150 = 600). If these calculations are considered as the standard exchange rate then the addition of a premium of 3 per cent can be seen as an adjustment to the standard rate.

#### *The wood slips from Xuanquan, Dunhuang prefecture*

Excavations between 1990 and 1992 at the Xuanquan site have yielded a further 35,000 wood slips, including 23,000 with inscriptions (GS-Archaeology 2000a–c). The wood slips have been published only in part so far (Hu Pingsheng and Zhang Defang 2001), but first reports indicate that approximately 10 per cent are dated, indicating a continuous period of occupation at the site in three distinct periods: (early) 111–92 BC; (height) 86–29 BC; (decline) to AD 107. It was then abandoned for a while, before the site was reoccupied as a postal or relay station, with some new construction on the original site, during the Wei-Jin period.

The Xuanquan site lies midway between Anxi and Dunhuang (64 km east of Dunhuang and 60 km west of Anxi) with the Great Wall and the Shule River to the north. The distance between Anxi and Dunhuang was too great to travel in one day, making Xuanquan the overnight resting place for traffic heading east or west. Official passes were required by all travellers, and many of the documents found here are legal and government documents, travellers' identification documents and private correspondence. Those documents that have been published show similarities with the wood slips from Juyan and Dunhuang. The following examples are from Hu Pingsheng and Zhang Defang (2001). One document dated 50 BC states that lost or damaged goods and coins are to be recorded, along with the name of the person responsible, and that he is to be personally liable for the loss [B.II.0115.4:87]. Another refers to transport costs, which included the maintenance of horses and carts, and to the office responsible for coins and goods in the stores (*shaonei*) [I.0210.1:96]. There are numerous lists. One notes the price of a chicken at 80 coins [I.0112.3:125]; this compares with the price of a fish (also 80 coins) at Juyan [XJ,p. 475–8, EPF22:1–36]. Another, dated 62 BC, notes that 28 chickens were received, 15 were purchased and the price was 2,215 coins [I.0112.3:129]; this would put the price per chicken at approximately 145–150 coins. There are also documents which refer to horses and 'horse money'. Three are dated to 32 BC: one is a list of horses, including privately owned horses [V.1610.2:11–20]; the second, dated 32 BC, states that a nine-year-old horse died of sickness, and its bones and flesh were sold for 210 coins [I.0111.2:2]; and the third states that the flesh and bones of five dead horses were sold for 2,740 coins (= 548 coins per horse) [I.0116.2:69]. Wuzhu and Wang Mang coins have been found at the site, but no details have been published yet.

## Excavated documents from Loulan and Niya

### *The sites*

The Loulan and Niya sites are two of the most important archaeological sites in Xinjiang. Loulan (Kharoshthi: Kroraina) occupied a strategic location: lying west of Dunhuang, it offered direct access to routes north and south of the Tarim Basin and beyond. The Loulan state paid allegiance to both the Xiongnu and the Han empire, until Chinese troops took the state in 77 BC, after which it was known as Shanshan. The principal ruins at Loulan are the remains of the small fortified station [L.A.], garrisoned by Chinese troops with the intention of guarding the route from Dunhuang to the main line of oases north of the Tarim River. It was first opened *c.* 110 BC and was in use throughout the Han dynasty. The route from Dunhuang to Loulan meant crossing very difficult terrain, and the route declined in importance when the Chinese took control of Hami and gained access to Eastern Central Asia by a much easier route.[17]

The Niya site lies in the desert *c.* 140 km to the north of modern-day Minfeng. The area around Niya has been identified with the kingdom of Jingjue. The Niya site itself measures approximately 22.5 km (north–south) by 6.5 km (east–west). There is a stupa at the centre of the site, a cemetery in the northern part of the site; most other remains are of dwellings.[19] It has been identified with the city of Cadota, capital of the Shanshan kingdom, mentioned in the Kharosthi documents found at the site. The site flourished during the Eastern Han and Jin dynasties, and was deserted in the early fourth century after the collapse of the Shanshan kingdom (Atwood 1991). Although some Chinese archaeologists (for example, Liu Wensuo 1992b) maintain that no Western Han remains have been found at the site, the documents from Stein's fourth expedition, examined only recently, do include Western Han wood slips from the Niya site and therefore confirm that the Niya site was occupied in the Western Han period (Lin Meicun 1998; Wang Jiqing 1998).

### *The wood slips*

Over seven hundred Chinese documents have been found at Loulan and Niya from the expeditions of Hedin in 1901, Stein in 1906, 1914 and 1930–1,[20] and Otani in 1909. The vast majority of these are from the Loulan L.A. site. In 1980 the Xinjiang Loulan Archaeological Team found a further 64 Chinese documents (63 wood slips and one paper document) together with a single Kharoshthi document in an official dwelling at Loulan (Hou Can 1988). Lin Meicun and Li Junming (1984: 98–102) include another 71 slips from the Lop region. Only a small number of Chinese documents have been found at Niya: most are in the Stein collection, which contains 58 specimens (Lin Meicun 1985: 2). Most recently, the Sino-Japanese teams excavating at Niya have found a small number of wood slips (Zhong-Ri 1996, 1999). For convenience, the references below have been abbreviated to Loulan or Niya, according to provenance; both are from the running numbers in Lin Meicun's (1985) collection of documents from the two sites.

The dates of the Loulan and Niya documents are later than those from Juyan and Dunhuang. Although the earliest dated document from Loulan is of AD 252 [Loulan 61], it is post-dated but close enough to the next dated document of 265 [Loulan 240] to confirm that the earliest documents from Loulan date to the 250s–260s (Hu Pingsheng 2000: 154). The latest dated document from Loulan is of 331 [Loulan 13].[21] Following a study of the dates, ranks and personal names in the documents from Loulan and Niya, Hu Pingsheng (2000: 218) arranged the documents in three periods of Chinese rule: (1) Cao-Wei period (220–80); (2) Early Jin period, early years of the Taishi reign (265–74); (3) Former Liang period (310–30). He noted that periods 1 and 2 are consecutive, but identified a gap of almost forty years (272–310) between periods 2 and 3. He suggested that during this gap the Chinese court could not support the post of the Head of the Western Regions (*Xiyu changshi*) at Loulan and so abolished it.

The contents of the documents mainly concern the administration of the military garrisons there, with a smaller number of items of official and personal corrrespondence (Lin Meicun (1985: 3–5). They indicate that the administration of Loulan especially during the Taishi reign was of a military rather than civilian nature, and that the system of military personnel was very similar to that described in the Chinese histories (*Jinshu*, Zhiguan zhi). The documents suggest that the Head of the Western Regions at Loulan was stationed there to manage the troops at the state farming garrison and to communicate with other states in Eastern Central Asia, and that there were no civilians from central China in Loulan to look after. The only civilians in this area were the local non-Chinese (*hu*) people, who had their own king (*huwang* or *hunaxian*) (Hu Pingsheng 2000: 124–6, 188–90).

Many documents indicate a deterioration in the conditions for the troops stationed at Loulan: daily grain rations gradually fell from 1 *dou* 2 *sheng* to 5 *sheng*, and from 269 textiles were distributed instead of grain rations (Hu Pingsheng 2000: 188–93). Such difficulties in maintaining the garrisons would explain the Chinese withdrawal from the late third century.

***Evidence for money in the wood slips from Loulan***

Some 670 Chinese documents were found by Hedin, Stein and Otani at or near Loulan,[22] and a further 70 have been found by Chinese archaeologists in the Lop Nor region (Lin Meicun and Li Junming 1984: 98–102).

The documents from Loulan were written on wood, paper and silk, and the dated documents cover the years 252–331. The earliest is a paper fragment dated 252 [Loulan 61]; the latest is a wood-slip dated 331 [Loulan 13].[23] Most of the wood slips are from the period 263–70; the paper fragments are from the same period and later to 331 (Maspéro 1953: 52). They are therefore three hundred years later than the latest slips from Juyan, and one to two hundred years later than the latest slips from Dunhuang and Jiuquan.

The slips are mostly official documents relating to the Chinese administration established in Loulan *c.*AD 263, under the Head of the Western Regions. The subject matter of the inscriptions relates mainly to the administration of the military garrisons, and there is a smaller amount of official and personal corrrespondence (Lin Meicun 1985: 3–5). Some documents indicate practices similar to those seen at Juyan and Dunhuang. For example, the twelve horse-hides paid in to the stores [Loulan 581] may be associated with the custom of 'horse money' seen at Juyan and Dunhuang, accounting for each horse that went out on the road. Maspéro (1953: 53) noted that the Chinese documents from Loulan do not concern the indigenous kingdom of Shanshan, only the civil and military Chinese administration, installed beside and outside the indigenous administration. This contrasts with the wood slips from Dunhuang and Jiuquan, which tell of frequent interaction among the Chinese and local population.

However, Loulan was not an isolated settlement. Several documents record the use of objects, especially iron tools, made by non-Chinese people: a large saw [Loulan 418], 28 small saws [Loulan 371], 16 small saws [Loulan 561] and 395 spades [Loulan 348]. However, it is not clear whether these were acquired in the vicinity of Loulan or brought in over longer distances. There was some transfer of furs (e.g. sable) [Loulan 340] and skins (e.g. calf-hide) [Maspéro 1953: 69, no. 204], though again the contexts are unclear.

The slips from Loulan also indicate that non-Chinese people were able to acquire Chinese goods: for example, the non-Chinese person who had various different kinds of silk: 10 *pi* 2 *zhang* of fine white silk (*baijuan*), 1 *pi* of fine yellow silk (*huangjuan*), 1 *pi* of fine white silk (*lian*) and 2 *pi* of cloth (*bu*) [Loulan 373].

Important foreign visitors to Loulan were the responsibility of at least one official, the Head of Hospitality (*kecao*), mentioned in two wood slips. The first records a payment of two calf-hides to the Head of Hospitality [Maspéro 1953: 69, no. 204]. The second records an announcement by the Head of Water (*shuicao*) that the cost of the vegetables eaten by the heads of the previous administration came to 1 *pi* of silk, which must be paid to the Head of Hospitality [Maspéro 1953: 73, no. 228].

The latter document is extremely interesting as it indicates that payment at official level within Loulan was made in textiles. This is surprising as numerous visitors to the Loulan site, including Stein, have reported seeing lots of coins on the ground (see Chapter 4). From the coin evidence alone it would be easy to assume that coins were the only form of money at Loulan. However, the documents found at Loulan indicate that this was probably not the case. Only three documents mention coins: one, dated 240, records that 200 coins were paid for 10,000 *shi* of grain [Loulan 13].[24] The other gives a price reckoned in 'Dunhuang coins', but unfortunately the context of this price is not clear [Loulan 556]. The specification of 'Dunhuang coins' probably indicates that better-quality Chinese coins were valued at a premium. The third document [Loulan 594] throws light on the equivalent values of coins and grain. It appears to be a list of items, listing rice and grain on one side, and other goods on the other side. The document is incomplete, and its purpose, date and origin are not known. However, it indicates that the value of rice ranged between 100 to 135 [coins] per *dou*, and that the total value of the goods on both sides of this incomplete list would exceed 10,200 [coins]. It is the only document indicating a large quantity of coins at Loulan.

**Table 15**
**Transactions reckoned in textiles at Loulan**

| Transaction | Reference |
|---|---|
| 1 *pi* of silk (as payment for vegetables eaten) to be paid to the *kecao* | [Maspéro 228] |
| 2 items of long textiles and 14 of short textiles sent to the store | [Loulan 515] |
| Goods, grain and *hu* cow(s), price several *pi* of silk | [Loulan 57] |
| Contract about borrowing goods, 18 *pi* of loan-textiles? | [Loulan 433] |
| Entered 319 *pi*, now for buying 4,326 *pi* for the master | [Loulan 235] |
| Remaining: 7 + 1 *pi* . . ., and 13 *pi* . . . | [Loulan 292] |
| Clothing: price 3 *pi* of coloured silk | [Loulan 553] |

Whilst only three documents record transactions reckoned in coin, seven documents record transactions reckoned in textiles (see Table 15). These documents confirm that *pi* was the standard unit for silk from the mid third to the mid fourth century in Loulan and that payments could be made in silk for food, grain, goods, clothing and livestock, and that textiles were also used in loans. Three further examples provide evidence of buying and selling silk: a list of sales (4 + 5 *pi*) and purchases (10 + 6 + 15 + 10 + 6 *pi*) of silk [Loulan 598; Maspéro 239]; a petition relating to a sale of silk for which the buyer has not yet paid [Loulan 40]; and a set of instructions to a silk buyer, listing in order of preference the types of silk he should buy [Loulan 55]. There can be no doubt that textiles were bought and sold by people at, or passing through, Loulan, and that textiles served as an important form of money at Loulan.

The documents recording transactions reckoned in grain are even more surprising, and suggest that grain may also have been more important than coins when making payments and loans at Loulan. One document [Loulan 411] is two-sided: one side lists a number of goods and their values in grain, and the other lists personal names and amounts of grain. The goods include 2 *dou*-worth of *bu*-cloth and 2 *dou*-worth of shoes. The reverse lists the following allocations of grain: 16 *dou*, 4 *dou*, 2 *dou*, 14 *dou*, 20 *dou*, 1 *dou*, 2 *dou*, 2 *dou*, 2 *dou* and 4 *dou*. Although the document is incomplete and the relationship between the lists on the front and back is not clear, it proves that

**Table 16**
**Physical descriptions of the bearers of documents at Niya**

| Description of the bearer | Reference |
|---|---|
| Hu Zhizhu, of the Yuezhi kingdom, middle-aged, 49 years, black | [Niya 673] |
| Male, young, 25 years, two ox-carts, 2 oxen | [Niya 675] |
| Middle-aged, black, big eyes, moustache and beard | [Niya 693] |
| 56 years, one slave, moustache and beard, white, cloth breeches, hemp shoes | [Niya 701] |
| 14 years, small, cloth breeches | [Niya 707] |
| 56 years, one slave, middle-aged, moustache and beard, white, cloth . . . | [Niya 715] |

purchases were sometimes paid for in grain. One document records a loan of grain to be repaid with interest [Loulan 465].

There were, of course, strong links with Dunhuang, the nearest Chinese settlement, and two documents appear to indicate trade with Dunhuang. One is dated 269 and records a payment of 10 *pi* of Dunhuang fine coloured silk (*lingcai*) [Loulan 191]. The other records selling goods to Dunhuang [Loulan 137].

In spite of the large quantities of Chinese-type coins reported at the Loulan sites, only these three documents suggest that coins may have played a significant role in financial transactions at Loulan. The documentary evidence alone suggests that coins, grain and textiles were used as money in this region from the mid third to the mid fourth century, and that grain and textiles were more frequently used as money than coins, at least in the recorded transactions.

***Evidence for money in the wood slips from Niya***

Stein found 58 Chinese documents at Niya on his four expeditions, and few have been found since. The majority of the documents record the movement of people. Several note locations in the Hexi corridor, and one appears to be a list of centres on the way from central China out to the west: Wuwei, Xiping, Xijun, Zhangye, Jiuquan, Dun[huang] [Niya 697]. Another lists kingdoms of the Western Regions: Shanshan, Yanqi, Qiuci and Shule [Niya 684] and two more mention the kings of Yutian [Niya 678] and Shanshan [Niya 709]. At least six documents are passes and describe the physical appearance of the bearer (see Table 16).

Other documents tell of the loads carried: ginger (*jiang*), 'southern elm' (*nanlang*) and, more significantly, 'money-goods' (*huowu*), though no description of those goods is given [Niya 680]. Two documents [Niya 687, 713] report private or unofficial business (*sixing*), probably a shortened version of the *yi si yin xing* [travelling on a private seal] found in the Juyan slips mentioned above.

Eight double-sided documents record how named persons paid their respects and made requests (to the court or religious centre?), with a gift, usually a reddish kind of gemstone (*langgan*) [Niya 718–24, 726].

Stein found 70 Chinese documents at the Niya site during his third expedition. Only one of these is dated, to AD 269 [Niya 706], and only one document [Niya 701] mentions coins, but it is incomplete and the meaning is unclear. The Chinese documents from the Niya site do not suggest widespread use of any particular form of money and record remarkably little about the economic life at Niya. This is in marked contrast to the seven-hundred-plus Kharoshthi documents found there, which offer very vivid evidence of the economic life of the indigenous people of Niya (see Chapter 8).

**Notes**

1. For a description of the various formats of Han slips see Li Junming and He Shuangquan (1990: 3) and Loewe 1967.
2. Li Junming and He Shuangquan (1990) estimate a total of fifty thousand slips found since the late nineteenth century. GS-Archaeology et al. (1990: 1) lists finds of slips from Juyan: over ten thousand found by the former Xibei kexue kaochatuan in the 1930s; over 19,400 excavated at Jianshui jinguan, Jiaqu houguan and Jiaqusai disisui san chu between 1972 and 1974; 173 slips found north of Bukentuoni in the Ejina Banner area in 1976; and 22 slips found again at Jiaqu houguan in 1982. Other finds of slips elsewhere in Gansu province and in Xinjiang raise the total found in Eastern Central Asia to well over thirty thousand. According to Whitfield (1997: 229), 'the 1,300 Chinese wood slips catalogued by Chavannes and Maspéro represent fewer than half of the total', with the British Library housing a further '2,000 completely uncatalogued fragments', and 'five drawers of slip fragments with site marks only'.
3. The coins were the daquan wushi [large coin 50] (AD 7), xiaoquan zhiyi [small coin worth 1] (AD 9), xuanquan yishi [dark coin 10] (AD 10), youquan ershi [young coin 20] (AD 10), zhongquan sanshi [middle coin 3] (AD 10), zhuangquan sishi [strong coin 40] (AD 10), and huoquan [money coin] (AD 14). In his first currency reform (AD 7) Wang Mang retained the wuzhu, supplementing it with the daquan wushi and two knife coins. His second reform (AD 9) abolished his earlier knife coins and wuzhu, rendering the daquan wushi and xiaoquan zhiyi the official coin types. The xuanquan, youquan, zhongquan and zhuangquan coins were issued during his third reform (AD 10). His fourth reform (AD 14) abolished the daquan and xiaoquan types, replacing them with the huoquan [money coin] and huobu [money spade].
4. Arrears of salary payments are not unique to Juyan; in Britain, in 1438 during the reign of Henry VI, the Crown's judicial officials claimed not to have been paid for eleven years; see Griffiths (1981: 310). I am grateful to Barrie Cook for this reference.
5. Movement of coins may have paralleled the movement of grain. Grain storage was organized at Chengcang, which operated at county (*xian*) level. Grain was supplied from Chengcang to local granaries, where it was distributed down to individuals in specified rations. Grain was released only upon sight of the correct documentation, and records were kept at each stage. Travelling personnel were also issued with documentation which they could present in different towns and thereby receive rations (Li Junming 1998: 32).
6. The association of red with financial documents appears to be persistent; one of the documents excavated at Turfan [66TAM59: 416], regarding a loan of grain, had two characters written in red ink (see Chapter 9). Many of the bamboo tallies used as money in southeast China in the early twentieth century also had painted red tops.
7. The following Wang Mang types have been found in Gansu province: daquan wushi, yidao ping wuqian, qidao wubai, da-bu-huang-qian spades, xiaoquan zhiyi, huoquan and huobu, but quantities are not indicated. See GSQBXH (1989).
8. The series is xiao-bu-yi-bai (worth 100), xuan-bu-er-bai (worth 200), you-bu-san-bai (worth 300), xu-bu-si-bai (worth 400), cha-bu-wu-bai (worth 500), zhong-bu-liu-bai (worth 600), zhuang-bu-qi-bai (worth 700), di-bu-ba-bai (worth 800), ci-bu-jiu-bai (worth 900), da-bu-huang-qian (worth 1,000).
9. The meaning of *da-huang* is not known. *Da-huang* is the Chinese term for rhubarb, which is most commonly known for its medicinal properties, but may be used also as a dye. In this way the cloth and clothes could be a distinctive yellow/red colour, perhaps for a special purpose. Stein (1921: 758) also mentions a *da-huang* variety of crossbow appearing in the documents from the *limes*, but again the meaning of *da-huang* is not clear.
10. For examples of bestowals during the Han dynasty see Bielenstein (1980: 195–7).

11. Hu Pingsheng (2000: 138–52) notes in the Juyan slips a strong adherence to the Qin dynasty instructions on official horse- and cattle-rearing. For example, when an animal was killed, the meat and fat were to be sold, and the money to be paid in to the relevant office along with the animal's tendons, saddle or horns. This is seen in mid to late Western Han documents [Ju 286:19A and 19B] where the weights of meat and fat are listed and the price noted.
12. Another slip [XJ p. 124, EPT44:5] also refers to a large quantity (2,270) of fish.
13. He Shuangquan (1989: 147) proposes a total of two thousand slips from different sites in Dunhuang, but gives no breakdown of figures or sources. Lin Meicun and Li Junming (1984) provide a summary and bibliography of studies on the Shule documents (many fragmentary), summary and plans of the sites where they were found.
14. http://www.ndcnc.gov.cn/dunhuang/dunhuanghanjian.htm, accessed 12 February 2004.
15. For a bibliography of work on Han slips see Shu Xue (1978); and Lin Meicun and Li Junming (1984).
16. See Chavannes (1913: 118 n539), on the data presented in the *Hou Hanshu* (juan 31).
17. Stein (1921, ch. 9) discusses in detail the historical references to Loulan in the *Hanshu* and *Shuijing zhu* (ed. by Li Daoyuan).
18. Stein and the Chinese scholars Wang Guowei and Luo Zhenyu identified the Niya site with Jingjue. The small kingdom of Jingjue is reported in the *Hanshu* (Xiyuzhuan) and *Hou Hanshu* (Xiyuzhuan) to have existed during both Western and Eastern Han times. During the early 1990s oil exploration engineers and hydrologists working in the desert to the north of the Niya site reported the discovery of a large site, 'the new Niya site', in the desert. Small finds from 'the new Niya site' are housed in the Xinjiang Museum (Liu Wensuo 1992b: 82).
19. For full details see Stein (1907, 1921, 1928) and Zhong-Ri (1996, 1999).
20. Stein also found wood slips at Niya on his fourth expedition, 1930–1. These are known only from photographs, see Wang Jiqing 1998; their current location is not known.
21. Loulan numbers refer to the running list of transcriptions in Lin Meicun (1985). [Loulan 61] = Conrady 16,1, [Loulan 240] = Conrady 51, [Loulan 13] = Chavannes 886.
22. The 670-plus include 277 from Hedin's second expedition, 349 from Stein's third expedition, and 44 from Otani's second expedition. Hedin entrusted the Chinese wood slips from Loulan to Karl Himly for research, and when Himly died they were passed on to Conrady, who published them in *Documents and small finds discovered by Hedin in Loulan* (1920); see also Tomiya (2001). Maspéro studied the slips found by Stein at Loulan and Niya and published them in 1953.
23. The date is given as Jianxing year 18. Jianxing was a reign period of the Western Jin, which ceased in its fourth year, when the Western Jin collapsed. The Former Liang dynasty continued to use this reign period until 349, and Jianxing year 18 corresponds to the seventh year of Zhang Jun's rule.
24. The date is given in Chinese as Jianxing year 18, which would correspond with AD 240. The Jianxing reign period lasted only 15 years, although it continued to be used in Loulan.

**Table 17**
**Prices of goods at Juyan**
**(XJ = Xinjian [GS–ARC et al. 1990]; HJ = Hejiao [Xie Guihua et al. 1987])**

| Type of goods | Unit of account | Cost or price | Actual transaction | Reference |
|---|---|---|---|---|
| **Grain** | | | | |
| Water-chestnuts (*biqi*) | Coin | 1 *dou* @ 35 | 1 *dou* @ 35 | [HJ p. 437, 262:34] |
| Seed (*rongjie*) | Coin | 1 *dou* @ 30 | ½ *dou* @ 15 | [HJ p. 437, 262:34] |
| Grain (*liang*) | Coin (*qian*) | 1 *shi* @ 110 | 2 *shi* @ 220 *qian* | [HJ p. 334, 214:4] |
| Millet (*shu*) | Coin (*qian*) | 1 *shi* @ 105 | 2 *shi* @ 210 *qian* | [HJ p. 334, 214:4] |
| Barley (*damai*) | Coin (*qian*) | 1 *shi* @ 110 | 1 *shi* @ 110 *qian* | [HJ p. 334, 214:4] |
| Grain (*qu*) | Coin (*qian*) | 1 *dou* @ 23 | 5 *dou* @ 115 *qian* | [HJ p. 334, 214:4] |
| Grain | Coin (*qian*) | 1 *shi* @ 75 | 2 *shi* 2 *dou* @ 170 *qian* | [XJ p. 26, EPT4:134] |
| Grain | Coin (*qian*) | 1 *shi* @ 75 | 2 *shi* 4 *dou* @ 190 *qian* | [XJ p. 26, EPT4:134] |
| Grain | Coin | 1 *dou* @ 11 | 5 *dou* @ 55 | [XJ p. 176, EPT51:71] |
| Grain | Coin | 1 *dou* @ 10.6 | 30 *dou* @ 318 | [XJ p. 177, EPT51:82A] |
| Grain | Coin (*qian*) | 1 *dou* @ 24 | 7 *dou* @ 168 *qian* | [XJ p. 191, EPT51:223] |
| Grain | Coin | – | 24 | [XJ p. 193, EPT51:235A] |
| Grain | Coin | 1 *shi* @ 35 | 66 *shi* @ 2,310 | [HJ p. 495, 303:3] |
| Grain | Coin (*qian*) | – | 30 *qian* | [HJ p. 58, 36:7] |
| Grain | Coin | 1 *shi* @ 185 | 2 *shi* @ 390 | [HJ p. 38, 26:9A] |
| Grain (*mai*) | Coin | 1 *shi* @ 120 | 3 *shi* @ 360 | [HJ p. 38, 26:9A] |
| Grain (*mai*) | Coin | 1 *dou* @ 38.4 | 5 *dou* @ 192 | [HJ p. 521, 332:11] |
| Grain (*gu*) | Coin | – | 60 *shi* 6 *dou* 6 *sheng* @ 2,123 | [HJ p. 31, 19:26] |
| Threshed grain? (*shichong*) | Coin (*qian*) | 1 *shi* @ 66.7 | 600 *shi* @ 40,000 *qian* | [XJ p. 309, EPT53:36] |
| Threshed grain? (*shichong*) | Coin (*qian*) | 1 *shi* @ 66.7 | 900 *shi* @ 60,000 *qian* | [XJ p. 309, EPT53:37] |
| **Textiles or clothing** | | | | |
| (–)-*chi* | Coin | – | 5 *chi* (or more) @ 450 | [XJ p. 378, EPT59:284] |
| (?)-*pi* | Coin | 1 *pi* @ 1,200 | 6 *pi* 1 *zhang* | [HJ p. 364, 225:45] |
| (?)-*pi* | Coin | 1 *pi* @ 1,200 | 1 *pi* @ 1,200 | [XJ p. 214, EPT51:531] |
| (?)-*pi* | Grain | 1 *pi* @ 1 *dou* | 1,068 *pi* (–) | [XJ p. 220, EPT51:647] |
| (?)-*pi* | Coin | 1 *pi* @ 300 | 2 *pi* @ 600 | [XJ p. 261, EPT52:493B] |
| (?)-*pi* (84 BC) | Coin | 1 *pi* @ 1,200+ | 247 *pi* 8 *chi* @ 298,100(+) | [HJ p. 82, 47:3] |

(*cont.*)

**Table 17**
**(*cont.*)**

| Type of goods | Unit of account | Cost or price | Actual transaction | Reference |
|---|---|---|---|---|
| (–) | Coin (*qian*) | – | 2 *zhang* 2 *chi* @ 1,600 *qian* | [HJ p. 231, 140:1B] |
| (–) | Coin | – | 3 *zhang* 3 *chi* @ 350 | [HJ p. 269, 168:10] |
| Light-coloured textile (*piao*) | Coin | 1 *pi* @ 800 | 1 *pi* @ 800 | [HJ p. 479, 284:36] |
| Textile (*daisu*) | Coin | 1 *pi* @ 23 | 1 *zhang* 6 *chi* @ 368 | [HJ p. 479, 284:36] |
| White silk (*bailian*) | Coin | 1 *pi* @ 700 | 2 *pi* @ 1,400 | [HJ p. 479, 284:36] |
| Silk (*lian*) | Coin | 1 *pi* @ 1,000 | 1 *pi* @ 1,000 | [HJ p. 479, 284:36] |
| Silk (*bo*) | Coin | 1 *pi* @ 410 | 1 *pi* @ 410 | [HJ p. 67, 39:30] |
| Silk (*bo*) | Coin | 1 *pi* @ 477 | 1 *pi* @ 477 | [XJ p. 381, EPT59:345] |
| Silk (*bo*) | Coin | 1 *pi* @ 450 | 2 *pi* @ 900 | [HJ p. 155, 89:12] |
| Silk (*bo*) | Coin (*qian*) | – | 1,090 *pi* 2 *chi* 5 *cun dabancun* @ 354,200 *qian* | [HJ p. 615, 509:15] |
| Henei silk (Henei 20-*liang bo*) | Coin | – | 8 *pi* 1 *zhang* 3 *chi* 4 *cun* @ 2,978 | [HJ p. 496, 303:5] |
| Henei silk (Henei 20-*liang bo*) | Coin | – | 36 *pi* 2 *zhang* 2 *chi* 2 *cun dabancun* @ 13,068 | [HJ p. 615, 509:8] |
| Silk (*di* 26 *liang bo*) | Coin | – | 5 *pi* 2 *chi* @ 1,000+ | [HJ p. 639, 522:2] |
| Cloth (*bu*) | Coin | 1 *pi* @ 400 | 1 *pi* @ 400 | [HJ p. 503, 308:7] |
| Cloth (*bu*) | Coin (*qian*) | 1 *pi* @ 400(+) | 1 *pi* @ 400(+) *qian* | [XJ p. 51, EPT8:25] |
| Cloth (*bu*) | Coin (*qian*) | 1 *pi* @ 500 | 1 *pi* @ 500 *qian* | [XJ p. 283, EPT53:52] |
| Cloth (*bu*) | Coin | 1 *pi* @ 750 | 1 *pi* @ 750 | [XJ p. 363, EPT59:64] |
| Cloth (*bu*) | Coin | 1 *pi* @ 750 | 2 *pi* @ 1,500 | [XJ p. 364, EPT59:70] |
| Cloth (*bu*) | Coin | 1 *pi* @ 400 | 1 *pi* @ 400 | [XJ p. 400, EPT59:660] |
| Black cloth (*zaobu*) | (Coin) | – | 2 *pi* | [XJ p. 230, 139:32] |
| 'Quail-thread' (*chunlü*) | Coin | 1 *pi* @ 1,000 | 1 *pi* @ 1,000 | [HJ p. 183, 112:27] |
| 'Longevity . . .' (*guangdi wannian*) | – | – | – | [HJ p. 183, 112:27] |
| *Qibu?* | Coin | 1 *pi* @ 333.3 | 3 *pi* @ 1,000 | [XJ p. 307, EPT56:10] |
| Guanghan cloth (*Guanghan babu*) | Coin | 1 *pi* @ 220+ | 19 *pi* 8 *cun dabancun* @ 4,320 | [HJ p. 160, 90:56, 303:30] |
| *Babu* | Coin | 1 *pi* @ 290 | 1 *pi* @ 290 | [HJ p. 485, 287:13] |
| *Babu* | Coin | 1 *pi* @ 28.75 | 8 *pi* @ 230 | [HJ p. 508, 311:20] |
| *Jiubu* | Coin | 1 *pi* @ 110.3 | 3 *pi* @ 331 | [HJ p. 472, 282:5] |
| *Zhongwen bu* | Coin | 1 *pi* @ 300 | 2 *pi* @ 600 | [XJ p. 311, EPT53:72A] |
| *Zhongwen bu* | Coin | 1 *pi* @ 300 | 2 *pi* @ 600 | [XJ p. 311, EPT53:72A] |
| *Zhongwen bu* | Coin | 1 *pi* @ 300 | 2 *pi* @ 600 | [XJ p. 311, EPT53:72A] |
| *Zhongwen bu* | Coin | 1 *pi* @ 300 | 2 *pi* @ 600 | [XJ p. 311, EPT53:72A] |
| *Zhongwen bu* | Coin | 1 *pi* @ 300 | 2 *pi* @ 600 | [XJ p. 311, EPT53:72A] |
| *Zhongwen bu* | Coin | 1 *pi* @ 300 | 2 *pi* @ 600 | [XJ p. 311, EPT53:72A] |
| *Zhongwen bu* | Coin | 1 *pi* @ 300 | 1 *pi* @ 300 | [XJ p. 311, EPT53:72A] |
| *Zhongwen bu* | Coin | 1 *pi* @ 300 | 1 *pi* @ 300 | [XJ p. 311, EPT53:72A] |
| *Bu* | Coin | – | 3 *pi* @ 1,000+ | [XJ p. 306, EPT56:10] |
| Textiles: (*ji/xi*) | Coin (*qian*) | 1 *ji/xi* @ 400 | 1 *ji/xi* @ 400 *qian* | [XJ p. 156, EPT50:56B] |
| Textiles: (*ji/xi*) | Coin | 1 *jin* @ 350 | 1 *jin* @ 350 | [HJ p. 319, 206:3] |
| Wadding (*xu*) | Coin | 1 *jin* of each @ 200 | 2 *jin* @ 400 | [HJ p. 155, 89:3] |
| Wadding (*xu*) (84 BC) | Coin | – | 2 *jin* 8 *liang* @ 400 | [HJ p. 503, 308:7] |
| Textiles | Coin | 1 *liang* @ 270 | 1 *liang* @ 270 | [XJ p. 181, EPT51:125] |
| Textiles | Coin | – | – | [XJ p. 250, EPT52: 323] |
| Black textiles (*zao*) | Coin | 1 *chi* @ 19.25 | 4 *chi* @ 77 | [HJ p. 148, 84:5] |
| Black textiles (*zao*) | Coin | – | 1 *zhang* 6 *chi* @ 1,900+ *qian* | [HJ p. 255, 156:34] |
| Black textiles (*zao*) | Coin | 1 *zhang* @ 2,000 | 2 *zhang* 5 *chi* @ 5,000 | [HJ p. 479, 284:36] |
| Black silk (*zaolian*) | Coin | 1 *pi* @ 1,200 | 1 *pi* @ 1,200 | HJ p. 55, 35:6] |

**Table 17**
**(*cont.*)**

| Type of goods | Unit of account | Cost or price | Actual transaction | Reference |
|---|---|---|---|---|
| Silk (*jian*) | Coin | 1 *pi* @ 600 | 1 *pi* @ 600 | [XJ p. 539, EPW34] |
| Silk (*jian*) | Coin | 1 (?) @ 800 *qian* | 1 (?) @ 800 *qian* | [HJ p. 266, 163:3] |
| Silk (*jian*) | Coin | – | – | [HJ p. 359, 221:19] |
| Raw silk (*xiaoji/xi*) | Coin | 1 *jin* @ 222 | 2 *jin* @ 444 | [HJ p. 436, 262:28A] |
| Textiles | Grain | – | – | [HJ p. 296, 185:15, 217:10] |
| Red cloth? (*jiang*) | Grain | – | – | [XJ p. 441, EPT65:330A] |
| Red silk cord (*tiji*) | Coin | 1 cord @ 25 | 1 cord @ 25 | [XJ p. 359, EPT59:7] |
| Unspun floss (*luoxu*) | Coin | 1 *jin* @ 70 | 2 *jin* @ 140 | [XJ p. 360, EPT59:21] |
| Wadding/floss (*xu*) | Coin | 1 *mei* @135 | 1 *mei* @ 135 | [XJ p. 361, EPT59:38] |
| Wadding/floss (*xu*) | Coin (*qian*) | 1 *jin* @ 10.4 | 232 *jin* @ 2,420 *qian* | [XJ p. 195, EPT51:257] |
| Wadding/floss (*xu*) | Coin | 1 *mei* @ 150 | 2 *mei* @ 300 | [XJ p. 195, EPT51:249] |
| Wadding/floss (*xu*) | Coin | 1 *tuo*-bag @ 50 | 3 *tuo*-bags at 150 | [XJ p. 206, EPT51:414] |
| Long black robe (*zaopao*) | Coin | 1 robe @ 1,900 | 1 robe @ 1,900 | [XJ p. 199, EPT51:314] |
| Long black lined robe (*zaolianfupao*) | Coin | 1 *ling* @ 2,500 | 1 *ling* @ 2,500 | [HJ p. 122, 69:1] |
| White lined long official robe (*baifupao*) | Coin | 1 *ling* @ 1,800 | 1 *ling* @ 1,800 | [HJ p. 321, 206:28] |
| Long official robe (*guanpao*) | Coin (*qian*) | 1 robe @ 1,200(+) | 1 robe @ 1,200(+) *qian* | [XJ p. 65, EPT16:11] |
| Long official robe (*guanpao*) | Coin | 1 *ling* @ 1,500 | 1 *ling* @ 1,500 | [HJ p. 256, 157:5A] |
| Long official robe (*guanpao*) | Coin | 1 *ling* @ 1,450 | 1 *ling* @ 1,450 | [HJ p. 671, jiafu 22] |
| Long official robe (*guanpao*) | Coin (*qian*) | 1 robe @ 500 | 1 robe @ 500 *qian* | [HJ p. 426, 257:17] |
| Long official robe of cotton (*guanbupao*) | Coin | 1 robe @ 450 | 1 robe @ 450 | [XJ p. 384, EPT59:374] |
| Long official robe of silk (*jianchangpao*) | Coin | 1 *ling* @ 2,000 | 1 *ling* @ 2,000 | [HJ p. 321, 206:28] |
| Long robe (*pao*) | Coin | 1 robe @ 1,000 | 1 robe @ 1,000 | [XJ p. 361, EPT59:31] |
| Long lined robe (*fupao*) | Coin | 1 *ling* @ 400 | 1 *ling* @ 400 | [HJ p. 84, 49:10] |
| Short coat of fine silk (*baichouru*) | Coin (*qian*) | 1 coat @ 500 | 1 coat @ 500 *qian* | [XJ p. 198, EPT51:302] |
| Short coat of fine silk (*lianru*) | Coin (*qian*) | 1 coat @ 830 | 1 coat @ 830 | [XJ p. 399, EPT59:645] |
| Short coat of woven silk (*zengru*) | Silk (*bo*) | 1 coat @ 1 *pi* | 1 coat @ 1 *pi* | [XJ p. 424, EPT65:65] |
| Lined short coat (*furu*) | Coin (*qian*) | – | – | [HJ p. 426, 257:17] |
| Short coat (*ru*) | Grain | 1 coat @ 3 *jin* | 1 coat @ 3 *jin* | [XJ p. 442, EPT65:330A] |
| Short coat (*ru*) | Coin | 1 coat @ 2,600 | 1 coat @ 2,600 | [HJ p. 188, 116:40] |
| Black cloth shirt (*zaoyi*) | Coin | 1 shirt @ 390 | 1 *shirt* @ 390 | [XJ p. 233, EPT52:91B) |
| Unlined shirt (*danyi*) | Coin (*qian*) | 1 shirt @ 248 | 1 *shirt* @ 248 *qian* | [XJ p. 386, EPT59:413] |
| Unlined shirt (*danyi*) | Coin | 1 shirt @ 100 | 1 *shirt* @ 100 | [XJ p. 444, EPT65:380] |
| Black unlined cloth shirt (*zaobu-zhang-danyi*) | Coin | 1 *ling* @ 353 | 1 *ling* @ 353 | [HJ p. 436, 262:29] |
| Suit in black (*zaoxi*) | Coin | 1 suit @ 2,000 | 1 suit @ 2,000 | [XJ p. 233, EPT52.91B) |
| Suit (*xi*) | Coin | 1 suit @ 900 | 1 suit @ 900 | [XJ p. 337, EPT57:3A] |
| Suit (*xi*) | Coin | 1 suit @ 1,250 | 1 suit @ 1,250 | [XJ p. 394, EPT59:555] |
| Long robe (*pao*) | Coin | 1 robe @ 1,300 | 1 robe @ 1,300 | [XJ p. 233, EPT52:91B) |
| Long cloth robe (*bupao*) | Coin | 1 robe @ 450 | 1 robe @ 450 | [XJ p. 318, EPT53:152] |
| Cloth trousers (*buku*) | Coin | 1 pair @ 400 | 1 pair @ 400 | [XJ p. 337, EPT57:3A] |
| Cloth lined trousers (*bufuku*) | Coin (*qian*) | – | – | [HJ p. 426, 257:17] |
| Black lined trousers? (*zaofuku*) | Coin | 1 pair @ 700 | 1 pair @ 700 | [XJ p. 341, EPT57:57] |
| Black trousers (*zaoku*) | Coin | 1 pair @ 900 | 1 pair @ 900 | [XJ p. 533, EPS4.T1:21] |
| Black trousers (*zaoku*) | Coin | 1 pair @ 1,100 | 1 pair @ 1,100 | [HJ p. 321, 206:28] |
| Trousers (*ku*) | Coin | 1 pair @ 550 | 1 pair @ 550 | [XJ p. 342, EPT53:72] |
| Trousers (*ku*) | Grain | 1 pair @ 15 *shi* | 1 pair @ 15 *shi* | [XJ p. 435, EPT65:229] |
| Trousers (*ku*) | Coin | 1 pair @ 700 | 1 pair @ 700 | [HJ p. 145, 82:11] |
| Trousers (*ku*) | Coin (*qian*) | 1 pair @ 500 | 1 pair @ 500 *qian* | [HJ p. 426, 257:17] |
| Trousers-*guo* (*kuguo*) | Coin | – | 100 | [HJ p. 527, 335:52] |
| Leather trousers? (*weiku*) | Coin | 1 pair @ 600 | 1 pair @ 600 | [XJ p. 233, EPT52:91B) |

(*cont.*)

**Table 17**
**(*cont.*)**

| Type of goods | Unit of account | Cost or price | Actual transaction | Reference |
|---|---|---|---|---|
| Leather trousers? (*piku*) | Coin | 1 pair @ 300 | 1 pair @ 300 | [XJ p. 233, EPT52:91B) |
| Leather (–) (*pi*–) | Coin | 1 unit @ 600 | 1 unit @ 600 | [XJ p. 233, EPT52:91B) |
| Bag (*tuo*) | Coin | 1 bag @ 200 | 1 bag @ 200 | [XJ p. 233, EPT52:91B) |
| Sheet leather? (*zhangwei*) | Coin | 1 unit @ 300 | 1 unit @ 300 | [XJ p. 233, EPT52:91B) |
| Black garment (*zao* . . .) | Coin | – | 750 | [HJ p. 321, 206:28] |
| Garment | Coin | 1 unit @ 1,470 | 1 unit @ 1,470 | [XJ p. 242, EPT52:188] |
| Garment | Coin | 1 unit @ 600 | 1 unit @ 600 | [XJ p. 242, EPT52:188] |
| Garment | Coin | 1 unit @ 290 | 1 unit @ 290 | [XJ p. 242, EPT52:188] |
| Garment | Coin | 1 *ling* @ 600 | 1 *ling* @ 600 | [XJ p. 445, EPT65:387] |
| Garment | Coin (*qian*) | 1 unit @ 500 | 1 unit @ 500 *qian* | [HJ p. 426, 257:17] |
| Garment (37 BC) | Coin | 1 @ 750 | 1 @ 750 | [HJ p. 38, 26:1] |
| Garments | Coin | – | 90,100+ | [XJ p. 254, EPT52:387] |
| Garments | Coin (*qian*) | – | 1,100+ *qian* | [XJ p. 318, EPT53:152] |
| **Meat** | | | | |
| Beef | Coin | – | 100 | [XJ p. 193, EPT51:235A] |
| Beef | – | – | 100 *jin* | [HJ p. 452, 269:3] |
| Stomach | Coin | 1 *jin* @ 3 | 8 *jin* @ 24 | [XJ p. 193, EPT51:235A] |
| Rack of ribs | Coin | – | 70 | [XJ p. 193, EPT51:235A] |
| Sacrificial meat | Coin | – | 68 | [XJ p. 193, EPT51:235A] |
| Sacrificial meat | Coin | – | 30 | [XJ p. 193, EPT51:235A] |
| Cow's head | Coin | 1 cow's head @ 80 | 1 cow's head @ 80 | [XJ p. 193, EPT51:235A] |
| Head | Coin | 1 head @ 60 | 1 head @ 60 | [HJ p. 483, 286:19B] |
| Lung | Coin | – | 60 | [HJ p. 483, 286:19B] |
| (?) (*kuan*) | Coin | – | 30 | [HJ p. 483, 286:19B] |
| Liver | Coin | – | 50 | [HJ p. 483, 286:19B] |
| Hoof | Coin | – | 20 | [HJ p. 483, 286:19B] |
| Neck | Coin | – | – | [HJ p. 483, 286:19B] |
| Heart | Coin | – | 30 *jin* | [HJ p. 483, 286:19B] |
| (?) (*huangjiang*) | Coin | – | 10 | [HJ p. 483, 286:19B] |
| Udder | Coin | – | 20 | [HJ p. 483, 286:19B] |
| Tongue | Coin | – | 20 | [HJ p. 483, 286:19B] |
| (?) (*jie*) | Coin | – | 10 | [HJ p. 483, 286:19B] |
| Intestines (*changyi*) | Coin | – | 40 | [HJ p. 483, 286:19B] |
| Meat | Coin | 1 *jin* @ 4 | 541 *jin* @ 2,164 | [HJ p. 483, 286:19A) |
| Meat | Coin (*qian*) | 1 *jin* @ 30 | 10 *jin* @ 300 *qian* | [XJ p. 273, 198:11A] |
| Meat | Coin | 1 *jin* @ 7 | 100 *jin* @ 700 | [XJ p. 675, yifu 29A] |
| Meat | Grain | 5 *jin* @ 1 hu | 120 *jin* @ 24 hu | [XJ p. 90, EPT40:76A&B] |
| Meat | Grain | 5 *jin* @ 1 hu | 10 *jin* @ 2 hu | [XJ p. 102, EPT43:33A&B] |
| Meat | Grain | 1 *jin* @ 0.7 | 50 *jin* @ 7 *shi* 5 *dou* | [XJ p. 506, EPT65:456] |
| Meat | Coin | 1 *jin* @ 3.3 | 30 *jin* @ 100 | [XJ p. 193, EPT51:235A] |
| Meat | Coin | 1 unit @ 1.04 | 136 units @ 142 | [XJ p. 234, EPT52:99] |
| Meat | Coin (*qian*) | – | 66 *qian* | [XJ p. 383, EPT59:364B] |
| Meat | Coin (*qian*) | – | 70 *qian* | [HJ p. 261, 159:4] |
| Meat | Coin (*qian*) | 1 *jin* @ 6.6 | 15 *jin* @ 100 *qian* | [XJ p. 555, EPS4.T2:15] |
| Meat | Coin (*qian*) | 1 *jin* @ 6.6 | 15 *jin* @ 100 *qian* | [XJ p. 555, EPS4.T2:15] |
| Meat | Coin (*qian*) | 1 *jin* @ 6.6 | 15 *jin* @ 100 *qian* | [XJ p. 555, EPS4.T2:15] |
| Meat | Coin (*qian*) | 1 *jin* @ 6.6 | 15 *jin* @ 100 *qian* | [XJ p. 555, EPS4.T2:15] |
| Meat | Coin (*qian*) | 1 *jin* @ 6.6 | 15 *jin* @ 100 *qian* | [XJ p. 555, EPS4.T2:15] |
| Meat | Coin (*qian*) | 1 *jin* @ 6.6 | 15 *jin* @ 100 *qian* | [XJ p. 555, EPS4.T2:15] |
| Meat: stomach (*weishen*) | Coin | 1 *jin* @ 4 | 12 *jin* @ 48 | [XJ p. 193, EPT51:235A] |

**Table 17**
**(*cont.*)**

| Type of goods | Unit of account | Cost or price | Actual transaction | Reference |
|---|---|---|---|---|
| Meat: kidney | Coin | 1 kidney @ 42 | 1 kidney @ 42 | [XJ p. 193, EPT51:235A] |
| Intestines | Coin | – | 27 | [XJ p. 193, EPT51:235A] |
| Animal fat/lard | Coin | 1 *jin* @ 6 | 63 *jin* @ 378 | [HJ p. 483, 286:19A] |
| Animal fat/lard | Coin (*qian*) | 1 *jin* @ 17 | 10 *jin* @ 170 *qian* | [XJ p. 222, 133:10] |
| Animal fat/lard | Coin (*qian*) | 1 *jin* @ 30 | 6 *jin* @ 180 *qian* | [XJ p. 96, EPT40:163] |
| **Livestock** | | | | |
| Ox | Coin | 1 ox @ 3,500 | 1 ox @ 3,500 | [XJ p. 285, EPT53:73] |
| Working ox (*yongniu*) | Coin | 1 ox @ 2,500 | 2 oxen @ 5,000 | [HJ p. 34.5, 24:1B] |
| Working ox (*funiu*) | Coin | 1 ox @ 3,000 | 2 oxen @ 6,000 | [HJ p. 61, 37:35] |
| Sheep | Coin (*qian*) | 1 sheep @ 250 | 1 sheep @ 250 *qian* | [XJ p. 191, EPT51:223] |
| Sheep | Coin (*quan*) | 1 sheep @ 900 | 1 sheep @ 900 *quan* | [HJ p. 556, 413:6A] |
| Sheep | Coin (*quan*) | 1 sheep @ 975 | 1 sheep @ 975 *quan* | [HJ p. 556, 413:6A] |
| Sheep | Coin (*quan*) | 1 sheep @ 1,000 | 1 sheep @ 1,000 *quan* | [HJ p. 556, 413:6A] |
| Sheep | Coin (*quan*) | 1 sheep @ 1,000 | 1 sheep @ 1,000 *quan* | [HJ p. 556, 413:6A] |
| Dog | Coin | 1 dog @ 500 | 1 dog @ 500 | [HJ p. 267, 163:6] |
| Chicken | Coin (*qian*) | 1 chicken @ 36 | 5 chicken @ 180 *qian* | [XJ p. 191, EPT51:223] |
| Camel | Coin (*qian*) | 1 camel @ 18 | 4 camels @ 72 *qian* | [XJ p. 191, EPT51:223] |
| Working horses (*yongma*) | Coin | 1 horse @ 4,000 | 5 horses @20,000 | [HJ p. 61, 37:35] |
| 10-year-old horse | Coin (*qian*) | 1 horse @ 4,000 | 1 horse @ 4,000 | [HJ p. 256, 157:1] |
| Horse | Coin | – | – | [HJ p. 33, 20:8] |
| **Land and property** | | | | |
| Irrigated land | Coin | – | 2,000,000 | [XJ p. 154, EPT50:33A] |
| Residence (*zhai*) | Coin | 1 *qu* @ 3,000 | 1 *qu* @ 3,000 | [HJ p. 34.5, 24:1B] |
| Residence (*zhai*) | Coin | 1 *qu* @ 10,000 | 1 *qu* @ 10,000 | [HJ p. 61, 37:35] |
| Cultivated land (*tian*) | Coin | 1 @ 10,000 | 5 @ 50,000 | [HJ p. 61, 37:35] |
| Cultivated land (*tian*) | Coin | 1 *mu* @ 100 | 50 *mu* @ 5,000 | [HJ p. 34.5, 24:1B] |
| **Fodder** | | | | |
| Fodder | Coin (*qian*) | 1 *su* bundle @ 8.5 | 10 *su* bundles @ 85 *qian* | [XJ p. 161, EPT50:140B] |
| Fodder | Coin (*qian*) | 1 *su* bundle @ 9 | 3 *su* bundles @ 27 *qian* | [XJ p. 161, EPT50:140B] |
| Alfalfa | Coin (*qian*) | – | 59 *qian* | [HJ p. 510, 312:10A] |
| Alfalfa | Coin | 1 *su* bundle @ 0.3 | 3,000 *su* bundles @ 900 | [XJ p. 178, EPT51:88] |
| Alfalfa | Coin | 1 *su* bundle @ 0.3 | 2,000 *su* bundles @ 600 | [XJ p. 178, EPT51:88] |
| Alfalfa | Coin | 1 *su* bundle @ 1.2 | 150 *su* bundles @ 180 | [XJ p. 239, EPT52:149A] |
| Alfalfa | Coin | 1 *su* bundle @ 0.12 | 4,500 *su* bundles @ 540 | [XJ p. 239, EPT52:149A] |
| **Other** | | | | |
| Stone for grain sacrifice (*fanshi*) | Coin (*qian*) | – | 750 | [HJ p. 334, 214:4] |
| 6-*chi* reed-mat (*xi*) | Coin | 1 *chi* @ 22.5 | 6 *chi* @ 135 | [XJ p. 161, EPT50:144] |
| Ghee | Coin (*qian*) | 1 *jin* @ 22.3 | 3 *jin* @ 67 *qian* | [HJ p. 448, 267:12] |
| Mat edging | Coin | 1 @ 150 | 2 @ 300 | [HJ p. 447, 267:7] |
| Animal glue | Coin (*qian*) | 1 *jin* @ 53.4 | 23 *jin* @ 1,330 *qian* | [HJ p. 372, 229:8] |
| (?) | Coin (*quan*) | 1 (?) @ 4.35 | 92 (?) @ 400 *quan* | [XJ p. 167, EPT50:222] |

(*cont.*)

**Table 17**
**(*cont.*)**

| Type of goods | Unit of account | Cost or price | Actual transaction | Reference |
|---|---|---|---|---|
| Wine | Coin (*qian*) | – | 130 *qian* | [XJ p. 191, EPT51:223] |
| Wine | Grain | 1 *dou* wine @ 2 *dou* grain | 2 *shi* 3 *dou* @ 4 *shi* 6 *dou* | [XJ p. 506, EPF22:457A] |
| Onions | Coin (*qian*) | 1 *su* bundle @ 4 *qian* | 40 *su* bundles @ 160 *qian* | [HJ p. 49, 32:16] |
| Beans | Coin (*qian*) | – | 3 *shi* @ 121 *qian* | [HJ p. 510, 312:10A] |
| Bean product (*douchi*) | Coin (*qian*) | 1 *dou* @ 25 | 1 *dou* @ 25 *qian* | [HJ p. 334, 214:4] |
| Castor-oil plant | Coin | 1 @ 20 | 1 @ 20 | [HJ p. 514, 317:24] |
| Cow-hide | Coin (*qian*) | 1 hide @ 300 | 1 hide @ 300 *qian* | [XJ p. 199, EPT51:321] |
| Sheep-skin (*yangwei*) | – | 7 *mei* | – | [XJ p. 441, EPT65:322] |
| Bow(s) | Coin | – | 550 | [XJ p. 429, EPT65:126] |
| Bow-string | Coin | 1 @ 2 | 14 @ 28 | [HJ p. 514, 317:24] |
| Sword | Coin | 1 @ 650 | 1 @ 650 | [HJ p. 427, 258:7] |
| Sword | Coin | 1 @ 700 | 1 @ 700 | [HJ p. 455, 271:1] |
| Furs (*xiqiu*) | Coin | 1 @ 380 | 1 @ 380 | [HJ p. 427, 258:7] |
| Skins | Coin | 1 *dou* @ 150 | 1 *dou* @ 150 | [HJ p. 436, 262:28B] |
| Room (*fang*) | Coin | – | 970 | [XJ p. 242, EPT52:193A] |
| Wood | Coin (*qian*) | 1 *chi* @ 23.5 | 8 *chi* 5 *cun* @ 200 *qian* | [XJ p. 247, EPT52:277] |
| Wood | – | – | – | [XJ p. 428, EPT65:120] |
| Casket/coffin? (*du*) | Coin (*qian*) | – | 2,200 *qian* | [XJ p. 385, EPT59:392] |
| Pony-carts (*zhaoche*) | Coin | 1 cart @ 5,000 | 2 carts @ 10,000 | [HJ p. 61, 37:35] |
| Ox-carts (*niuche*) | Coin | 1 cart @ 2,000 | 2 carts @ 4,000 | [HJ p. 61, 37:35] |
| Vegetables (*jiao*) | Coin (*qian*) | 1 bundle @ 1.5 | 20 bundles @ 30 *qian* | [HJ p. 233, 140:18B] |
| Vegetables (*cai*) | Coin (*qian*) | – | 216 *qian* | [HJ p. 261, 159:4] |
| Vegetables (*cai*) | Coin (*qian*) | – | 216 *qian* | [HJ p. 261, 159:4] |
| Ginger | Coin | 1 *sheng* @ 20 | 2 *sheng* @ 40 | [HJ p. 604, 505:16] |
| (?) (*qu*) | Coin | 1 *dou* @ 9.5 | 4 *dou* @ 38 | [HJ p. 319, 206:3] |
| – | Barley (*damai*) | – | 45 measures of barley | [XJ p. 415, EPT59:914A] |
| – | Coin (*qian*) | 1 *mei* @ 152 | 8 *mei* @ 1,216 | [XJ p. 428, EPT65:114] |
| – | Grain | – | 33 *shi* | [XJ p. 441, EPT65:330A] |
| Shoes | Grain | – | 1 pair | [XJ p. 441, EPT65:330A] |
| Fish | Grain | – | 30 fish @ 3 *dou* (+?) | [XJ p. 421, EPT65:33] |
| Fish | Coin | – | 30 *mei* @ 100+ | [HJ p. 462, 274:26A–26B] |
| Fish | Coin | – | 30 *mei* | [HJ p. 462, 274:26A–26B] |
| Reed (*wei*) | Coin (*qian*) | 1 *mei* @ 23 | 1 *mei* @ 23 *qian* | [HJ p. 148, 84:5] |
| Female slave (*xiaobi*) | Coin | 1 slave @ 20,000 | 1 slave @ 20,000 | [HJ p. 61, 37:35] |
| Young slaves (*xiaonu*) | Coin | 1 slave @ 1,500 | 2 @ 3,000 | [HJ p. 61, 37:35] |
| Infant (*ying*) | (–) | 1 @ 130 | 1 @ 130 | [HJ p. 201, 123:22] |
| Infant (*ying*) | (–) *mei* | 1 @ 104 *mei* | 1 @ 104 *mei* | [HJ p. 201, 123:22] |
| Knife (*cimadao*) | Coin | 1 @ 7,500 | 1 @ 7,500 | [HJ p. 436, 262:28B] |
| Iron goods | – | – | – | [XJ p. 228, EPT52:15] |
| 2-*cun* iron knife | Coin | 1 knife @ 30 | 1 knife @ 30 | [XJ p. 359, EPT59:7] |
| Iron cup? (*tiedou*) | Coin | 1 cup @ 90 | 1 cup @ 90 | [XJ p. 359, EPT59:7] |

# 8 Kharoshthi documents, third and fourth centuries

## The Kharoshthi script

The Kharoshthi script was developed out of Aramaic, the official script of the Achaemenid administration, during the late Achaemenid period, for transcribing the local language of the eastern reaches of the Achaemenian empire (western regions of modern-day India). The Kharoshthi script is closely linked to the Middle Indo-Aryan (or 'Prakrit') dialect Gandhari, a name invented by Bailey (1946) to encompass its development and use in Gandhara and Gandhara-influenced regions, and because Gandhari is a distinctly separate language from the other members of the Middle Indo-Aryan family. Salomon (1996) describes Kharoshthi as 'a regional script', contrasting it with Brahmi, which was widely used in South Asia, except in the northwest, where Kharoshthi prevailed. It was an official script of the Kushan empire. From the second century BC to the third century AD Kharoshthi was the main medium of writing in the northern Punjab, Gandhara and the Kabul region (modern-day northern Pakistan and eastern Afghanistan). In the third century it fell out of use in these regions, and was replaced by derivatives of Brahmi. However, use of Kharoshthi had also spread further north to Uzbekistan and further east to Eastern Central Asia. The Kharoshthi documents of the third to fourth century AD found at sites in the south of the Tarim Basin are the last significant body of documents written in the Kharoshthi script before it died out. They are (with one exception from Endere, Burrow 1940: §661)[1] written in a local variety of Gandhari Prakrit, sometimes described as Niya or Kroraina Prakrit (Burrow 1937: v; Salomon 1998a: 159). A much smaller quantity of documents in the Kharoshthi script is known from sites north of the Tarim Basin, and these are believed to be of a later date. They remain unpublished and are not considered here (Salomon 1998a: 45; Lin Meicun 1988: 18). Details of the current locations of all Kharoshthi documents excavated in Eastern Central Asia have been published by Lin Meicun (1992).

The numerical notation of Kharoshthi was determined by Dowson (1863), who corrected Cunningham's assumption that the numbers followed a decimal or place-value system (Salomon 1998a: 218). There are symbols only for 1, 4, 10, 20, 100 and 1,000, and all other numbers are indicated additively, so that 15 is written 10 4 1, and multiplicatively for hundreds and thousands, so that 8,000 is written 4-4-1,000. It is noteworthy that the sign for 1,000 is known only from the Eastern Central Asian Kharoshthi documents (Salomon 1998a: 64).

## The Kharoshthi documents: discovery, date and contents

Opinions as to why Kharoshthi script has been found in Eastern Central Asia are changing as Chinese scholars question earlier Western approaches. Brough's (1965) suggestion that the Kharoshthi script shows Shanshan to be the eastern extent of the Kushan empire is fiercely challenged by Ma Yong (1990) and Lin Meicun (1988: 12; 1996: 188–9), who argue that the Shanshan kingdom never came under the Kushans, and that Kharoshthi was used in Shanshan by Kushan or Yuezhi immigrants who moved eastwards after the Han court withdrew its frontier troops from the Tarim Basin c.AD 175. Their argument is based upon later texts which note that the father of a Yuezhi man, Zhi Qian, went to Luoyang during the later reign of Huandi (147–67) or early reign of Lingdi (168–89) (*Gao seng zhuan*, juan 1, Kang sen zhuan, 14–21).

Salomon (1998a: 45-6) maintains that the spread of the Kharoshthi script is closely linked with the spread of Buddhism, under the patronage of the Kushan rulers, and notes that the Kharoshthi inscriptions with a dedicatory or memorial content which have been found in China 'are often hardly distinguishable in form from similar inscriptions from India, and presumably reflect the presence of Gandhari-speaking Indian monks in the Buddhist monasteries of these places'.

Most of the Kharoshthi documents from Eastern Central Asia are written in ink on wooden or leather tablets. The exceptions are the Kharoshthi inscriptions on textiles from Loulan, Miran and Dunhuang. Those from Loulan include a small silk bag from Loulan L.A. [L.A.vii.059] (Stein 1928: 223, pl. XVII; Rapson et al. 1997: §756); a strip of fine silk from Loulan L.A. [L.A.vi.ii.0236] (Stein 1921: 436; Boyer et al. 1920–29: §697); and a piece of silk bearing a good-luck inscription in Chinese from Loulan L.B. (Hou Can 1988; Lin Meicun 1988). Those from Miran include a silk banner [M.III.0015] (Stein 1921: 495; pl. xxxix) and a piece of silk found at the remains of a Buddhist temple (Huang Wenbi 1983). Some Kharoshthi writing has been found among the wall-paintings at Miran (Stein 1921: 529–32; Boyer 1911). One fragment of fine silk found at Dunhuang also has a Kharoshthi inscription [T.xii.a.ii.20; KI 708] (Stein 1921: 777, pl. xxxix).

The vast majority (almost one thousand specimens) of Kharoshthi documents from Eastern Central Asia were found by Stein during his first three expeditions, and are now housed in the British Library and the National Museum of India, New Delhi. Boyer et al. (1920–29) published 764 of these Kharoshthi documents, including six documents acquired by Huntington at Niya. Of these documents, 709 are from Niya, 48 from the Lop desert sites, six from Endere and one from a Dunhuang beacon site. Stein found a further 18 documents at Niya in 1930; these were confiscated in China, but studied from photographs (Burrow 1939).

Stein's contemporaries found surprisingly few Kharoshthi documents: in March 1901 Hedin found one Kharoshthi document, and Kharoshthi on the reverse of a Chinese document found in the Lop Nor area, now in the Swedish Ethnographical Museum (Conrady 1920). Huntington found six Kharoshthi documents at Niya in 1905, now in the Huntington

Library, Los Angeles (Huntington 1907: 203–4, plate facing p. 204; Boyer et al. 1920–29: K.758–763).

Lin Meicun's survey (1988: 19–22) adds about another hundred Kharoshthi documents found by Chinese individuals or teams, now housed in the Xinjiang Museum, the Khotan Cultural Relics Office, the Xinjiang Academy of Social Sciences: Institute of Archaeology, the Gansu Provincial Museum and the National Museum of Chinese History. These include one inscription on stone (broken in three parts), purchased in Luoyang (Brough 1961); 66 Kharoshthi documents found at Niya by the Xinjiang Museum Archaeological Team in October 1959 (XJ-Museum 1961); 40-plus documents found on the southern edge of the Tarim Basin, of which only two fragments were collected, now in the Gansu Provincial Museum (Ma Yong 1980); a wooden tablet from the Loulan L.A. site, and the silk bearing a good-luck inscription in Chinese found with a Kharoshthi inscription from the Loulan L.B. site (Hou Can 1988; Lin Meicun 1988); one Kharoshthi wooden tablet found in the corner of a house at the Niya site in 1981 (Salomon 1986); numerous wooden tablets found at the Niya site in 1981; and one document from Toksun-sarai (Lin Meicun 1988: 70 n2). The Sino-Japanese excavations at Niya between 1988 and 1997 also recovered nine documents (Zhong-Ri 1996, 1999).[2]

With the exception of one document [Burrow 1940: §661], the Kharoshthi documents from Niya and Loulan are written in Niya (or Kroraini) Prakrit. Burrow (1937: v) notes that the language is uniform throughout the rest of the Kharoshthi documents he translated (Burrow 1940), and, on the basis of Rapson's Table of Kings and Regnal Years (1929: 326–8) suggests that the documents cover a period of at least 88 years. Rapson's succession of kings is as follows (with the latest regnal year in parenthesis): Pepiya (8), Tajaka (3), Amgoka (46 or 36), Mahiri (28) and Vashmana (11).

Two documents from the Niya site suggest more specific dates: (1) a Chinese wood slip dated AD 269 [N.xv.326] which was found with Kharoshthi wooden tablets (Stein 1907: 205, 537, pl. cxii) and (2) a Kharoshthi divorce document naming King Sulica of Shanshan, whom Lin Meicun (1989a) believes to be the sixth king, ruling *c.*336–59. Lin Meicun (1996: 194–6) identifies a total of seven Shanshan kings, and claims that Kharoshthi script was used in the Shanshan kingdom from the Eastern Han (25–220) and was abandoned only at the beginning of the fifth century when Shanshan was attacked and the inhabitants were forced to flee. However, the concrete evidence from the two dated documents from Niya gives a secure dating to the third and fourth centuries only.

The standard translations of the Kharoshthi documents are Burrow's (1940) English translation and Lin Meicun's (1985) Chinese translation. Early investigations of the documents focused on linguistics, especially the mix of ancient Indian and Iranian elements (Burrow 1939; Thomas 1924, 1946; Lüders 1936; Bailey 1949). The rich information contained within the documents has been considered by Brough (1965), Agrawala (1952, 1954) and Atwood (1991), though seldom in conjunction with the archaeological evidence.

The Kharoshthi documents from Niya, Loulan and Endere throw light on life in the Shanshan kingdom in the third and fourth centuries AD. They are mostly official and financial records, in the form of legal or administrative documents, such as court rulings on disputes, contracts of sale and records of loans, tax collection, hire and rent. A smaller number are letters between individuals or family members. Many of the documents reveal exchange and conversion values, and provide an insight into the monetary and economic customs of the kingdom.

**References to money in the Kharoshthi documents**

On the basis of the Kharoshthi documents alone, there are two schools of thought. Agrawala (1954: 220–3) argued that the terms *sadera* (*satera*), *drakhma* (*trakhma*), *dhane*, *masa* (*masha*) and *muli* found in the documents refer to 'various indigenous and foreign coins', dropping his earlier tentative suggestion (Agrawala 1951: 104) that the term *kampo* might also be a coin-name. Surveying the dated documents (in the order of kings Tajaka, Pepiya, Amgoka, Mahiri, Vashmana), he noted that these terms do not appear during the reign of Tajaka, that *muli* first appear during the reign of Pepiya, that *muli* are frequently mentioned during the reign of Amgoka, that *muli*, *suvarna-sadera*, *trakhma* and *masha* are all mentioned during the reign of Mahiri, and that *muli* are frequently mentioned in the reign of Vashmana. Burrow (1940) noted that *muli* means price or worth, but as he took it to be worth one-twelfth of a *sadera* or gold stater coin (Burrow 1937: 111), surely implied that it might be a coin. Thierry (2000) followed Burrow: he accepted the references to gold staters, but noted that there are no references to bronze coins. Lin Meicun (1993: 97) assumed that *muli* means a bronze coin, in the same way that the Chinese term *qian* refers to a coin.

Atwood (1991: 190–1), on the other hand, boldly stated that 'the economy of Shanshan had little room for money. No coinage as such was known in the Cadota kingdom.' He argued that *sadera* and *drakhma* were weights rather than coins, and that gold was used for purchasing goods only by travellers, namely monks and merchants. In one case, Burrow (1940) and Bailey (1949: 128) took *dhane*, *sadera* and *drakhma* to be weights (Burrow 1940: §702). Bailey, in correspondence with Agrawala (1954: 220 n5; 223), also doubted that *muli* was a coin, preferring to stay close to the original Sanskrit *mulya*, meaning price or value.

These terms are discussed below. For convenience, references to documents in Burrow (1940) are presented below in the form [§1].

***Suvarna sadera (satera)***

Four documents from different locations at the Niya site mention *suvarna sadera* (*satera*).[3] Burrow [§324, §419, §12, §431–2] translated *suvarna sadera* as 'gold stater'. In this way, a Chinese man paid two gold staters (*suvarna satera*) and 2 drachms (*trakhma*) for a man [§324], and Anamda used a gold stater (*suvarna sadera*) to purchase land [§419]. These examples and the two gold coins (*suvarna sadera*) mentioned in witnessed circumstances [§12], and the lack of a single gold coin (*suvarna sadera*) requested by the queen [§431–2], show that gold staters were rare and of high value:

> His majesty the king gives instructions to the *cuvalayina* Maltsuta as follows: The *sothamga* Sugita informs us here that his son Livarazma found in a gold *sakasya* (?) one *kampo* (?) and two *suvarna sadera*, and that many people of Cadota and the mountains are witnesses. In that matter the *tagastas* are cheating (*nikaremti*) the owners. When this sealed wedge-tablet reaches you, etc. . . . the *tagastas* are to be stopped from doing injustice to the people [§12].

In the fourth year of his majesty the great King Mairi the son of heaven, on the 13th day of the third month, at this date (?) the Supis came to Calmadana; they plundered the kingdom and carried off the inhabitants. The Supis seized a man called Samrpina, a slave of the *vasu* Yonu and sent him as a present to Cinasgasi (the Chinaman Sgasi). Cinasgasi (provided) from here, as a recompense for the man, 2 *suvarna satera* and 2 drachmas. (Consequently) that man became the rightful property (?) of Sgasi. His own master, the *vasu* Yonu, did not wish to remove the man himself, and permission was given to Sgasi to sell him to others. Considering this Cinasgasi sold this man to Katge. As the price of the man [ . . .] and one bow is right, Cinasgasi has sold well and Katge has bought well [§324].

Document concerning purchase of a vineyard: They sold a vineyard of four *apcira*, and another piece of *letga kuthala* land in the *misi* land. The whole amount is five (pieces of land). Anamda bought it and paid the price, 1 *suvarna sadera* and another 2 *muli*, and a later amount of 12 *muli*. They agreed on equal terms. It was well bought and well sold . . . [list of witnesses given] . . . The fine [for any attempt to argue the authority of the document] is five pieces of cloth, and the punishment fifty strokes [§419].

The *suki* wine of the people of Yave *avana* is to be separately measured out. Of the people of the *apsu* Saca, and of all the people of Yave *avana*, the original *suki* wine is 19 *khi* (each). It has been collected for two years. In the third year a letter came from the *vasu suvesta* Marega (to the effect that) this wine was all to be sold for clothing and bedding. Of this wine Parsu bought the price, one horse five years old, and with that horse he received five *khi* of wine and two *agisdha*. Another second horse the *ageta* Spaga took from here to there, and the *suvesta* Marega received it. With the horse was one *kojava* and one *agisdha*. A third horse I send from the *tomgha* Saja. The *suvesta* Marega received it. (It is) four years old. Along with that horse one *avale*, two *kojava*, and also one *agisdha* were sent there. The total is forty-four, (also) one white *kojava*. These objects were all packed there in the capital by the *tomgha* Saja. In addition four *kavaji* made of felt and one *raji*. On another occasion the queen came here. She asked for 1 *suvarna sadera*. There is no gold. Instead of it we gave carpet (*tavastaga*) thirteen hands long. Seraka took it. Many people here know this matter as witnesses. (Also) one *artavasa* [§431–2].

Agrawala (1954: 225–6) contrasted the explicit use of *suvarna sadera* in the Niya documents with the simpler *sadera* in Indian documents. Arguing that as staters in India were always gold[4] there was no need to add *suvarna*, he suggested that in Shanshan there might also have been gold staters and simple staters. Yet, there is no evidence to suggest that there were 'simple staters' in Shanshan, and the converse may be equally true, that the fuller term *suvarna sadera* may have been used to indicate both gold and coin, with the stress on the coin rather than the gold, as in 'gold that has been coined or weighed' rather than a 'coin made of gold'. This interpretation would explain why the queen was told there was no gold, rather than no gold coins [§431–2], and would also eliminate Agrawala's supposition that the omission of *sadera* is a scribal error.

No gold coins have been found at sites in the territory of ancient Shanshan, and the four references to *suvarna* show that gold was rare and was valued: a gold necklace [§113]; some gold that has been left with someone for forwarding [§177]; a notice that gold should be sent to the mountains, where it is sought after, and that it should be sold according to the price there [§140]; and notice of a person trying to recover a debt of gold lent before the kingdom was plundered [§494].

*Sadera* appears in only one other document [§702], from Loulan L.B. (Stein 1921: 444 [= L.B.iv.i.6]). It is a letter announcing of the birth of a baby boy, and asking for '3 *dhane* of pepper (marica), 1 *drakhma* of ginger, 2 *drakhma* of pepper (pipali), 1 *dhane* of *tvaca*(?), 1 *dhane* of small cardamoms and 4 *sadera* of sugar' to be sent. Bailey (1949: 128) and Burrow (1937: 141) interpreted this list as a medical prescription, and read *sadera*, *drakhma* and *dhane* as weight terms. This is supported by fragments of Kuchean texts which mention *trakam* (drachm) and *satera* in a medical context (Filliozat 1948, quoted in Bailey 1949). The prescription is no doubt for the mother, who is described as having 'survived the pains of childbirth in safety and good health'.

Agrawala's alternative interpretation (1954: 225–6) that *sadera*, *dhane* and *drakhma* in one document [§702] are Persian coin-names, in a letter from a son to his father asking for goods from a distant place and refering to prices in Persian currency, is contrived. His argument against their being weight terms on the grounds that 'the correspondent would hardly have requested their supply in such a negligible quantity' hangs on his presumption that the destination is distant, and that his foreign-sounding name is possibly Iranian (Burrow 1937: 90). Yet, the correspondent writes that the mother 'has survived the pains of childbirth in safety and good health. A son has been born. You must all be pleased.' The letter announces good news from an official (*cuvalayina*) to his superior (*gusura*) over an unspecified distance. The list of items is medicinal, and, given the context, is probably a restorative for the mother. As such, the 'negligible quantity' of ingredients merely confirms the good news.

To sum up, *sadera* on its own is used in the documents as a weight term and not as a coin-name. *Suvarna sadera* may refer specifically to a gold coin (gold stater), or perhaps to a stater-weight of gold.

#### *Drakhma (trakhma)*

Two documents refer to *trakhma* [§324] and *drakhma* [§702], both mentioned above. In one [§702], from Loulan, *drakhma* is clearly a weight term; in the other [§324] from Niya, *trakhma* has been interpreted as a coin-name, but could also be a weight term. If *suvarna sadera/satera* is found to be a gold coin, then it follows that *trakhma* (*drachma*) is also likely to be a coin. However, the only non-Chinese coin so far discovered at Niya or Loulan is the tetradrachm of Wima Kadphises found in the refuse heap at Loulan (see Chapter 5). The evidence is therefore too minimal to conclude at this stage that the term *drackma* refers specifically to a coin.

#### *Masa*

Three documents mention *masa* [§149, §500, §661] and in large quantities: 2,500, 2,800 and 8,000 *masa* respectively. One document [§149] from Niya is a list of property stolen from a fugitive: 2,500 *masa*, four roughly woven cloths, three woollen cloths, one silver ornament, two jackets, two *somstamni* (?), two belts and three Chinese robes. Document [§500] from Niya is a fragment about a man of Niya who received a loan of 2,800 *masa* from a monk. Document [§661] from Endere concerns the sale by a city-dweller of a camel with special marking for 8,000 *masa*, the price paid in full in *masa*.

The meaning of *masa* is still not fully understood. Burrow (1937, 1940) does not translate *masa*. Konow (1936: 237) interpreted *masha* as a 'weight of gold'. Agrawala (1954: 226) argued that *masha* was an Indian silver coin, with 16 *masha* (*masaka*) = 1 *karshapana* (*kahapana*) coin during the Kushan period in India. The large quantities of *masa* render it unlikely that they are gold coins, although Sanskrit *mashaka* means 'bean or weight of gold' (Monier-Williams 1899: 814); Sanskrit *másha* means a particular weight of gold (= 5 *krishnalas* = one-tenth of a *suvarna* = 17 grains troy) (Monier-Williams 1899: 814). This would be too high. Following these terms, the 2,500 *masa* would correspond to 250 *suvarna*, the 2,800 *masa* to 280 *suvarna* and the 8,000 *masa* to 800 *suvarna*. These figures appear excessive given the rarity of gold in the documents.

There is a plausible solution: that *masa* refers to Chinese coins. The *masaka* was the chief copper coin of ancient India (Allan 1936: clx–clxi), and the Indian term *masha* originally meaning *Phaseolus* bean, but used to denote a small coin (Cunningham 1891: 45), persisted until the early twentieth century where it is found as *mace*, meaning one-hundredth of a Chinese ounce (Cribb 1987: 105). The only coins found at the Niya site are Chinese bronze coins of low value. By the Han dynasty, Chinese coins were measured by the individual coin (*qian* or *quan*) or by the string (*guan*) of 1,000 coins, knotted in ten batches of 100.[5] In this way, the 2,500 *masa* would correspond to 2.5 strings, the 2,800 *masa* to 2.8 strings and the 8,000 *masa* to 8 strings of Chinese coins. Although the total number of coins retrieved from Niya is not known, and Stein found only 32 Chinese coins at Niya, the larger finds of Chinese coins from the southern route would support this argument: for example, the find of 45 kg of wuzhu coins found at Mailike'awati would correspond to 16,304 coins at the weight (2.76 g) of an Eastern Han wuzhu coin [S.VIII.a.2] found by Stein at Niya (see Chapter 4).

The Kharoshthi documents indicate that certain types of people had access to *masa*: one example relates to property stolen from a fugitive, i.e. someone from outside Niya [§661]; another describes a camel-seller as 'a man of the city' [§149]; and a third specifies a man of Niya borrowing from the monk Mochapriya [§500]. Mochapriya is mentioned in three other documents [§386, §494, §502], two of which confirm his engagement in loans and borrowing. One [§494] confirms his right not to repay a loan of gold after the kingdom was plundered by the Khotanese; and the other [§502] relates to his lending out water. From these documents it is clear that fugitives, monks and 'men of the city' had access to Chinese coins.

The dates of the three documents are not clear: [§149] refers to the ninth year of an unspecified reign; [§500] to the seventeenth year of Mahiri (Rapson's fourth king); and [§661] is dated to the third year of King Hinjhadeva Vijita Simha of Khotan, which Thomas (1946: 523) placed in the late third century, after the Khotanese conquest of Shanshan.

### *Muli*

The most frequent unit of account in the Kharoshthi documents is the term *muli*, which Burrow (1937: 111–12) concluded meant 'price' in general as well as a particular unit of value. The word *muli* developed out of the Sanskrit term *múlya*, meaning price, worth, value, or a sum of money given in payment (Monier-Williams 1899: 827). Burrow noted that the locative of *muli* was used alongside the name of an object serving as payment to indicate how many *muli* it was worth. However, the documents do not reveal the physical nature or the material object of *muli*.

**Table 18**
***Tavastaga* carpets**

| *Tavastaga* carpets | Reference |
|---|---|
| *Tavastaga* (13 hands long) given to queen instead of 1 gold stater | [§431–2] |
| *Tavastaga* (13 hands long) valued at 12 | [§579] |
| *Tavastaga* (12 hands long) | [§527] |
| *Tavastaga* (8 hands long) | [§578] |
| *Tavastaga* (6 hands long) given in part payment for a vineyard | [§581] |
| *Tavastaga* (4 hands long) given in part payment for royal camels | [§583] |
| *Tavastaga* (12 hands + 11 hands long) given in part payment for a woman | [§590] |
| *Tavastaga* to be purchased in the mountains | [§633] |
| 1 *tavastaga* on deposit [line in ink drawn through entry] | [§534] |
| 3 *tavastaga* to be brought from a different location | [§622] |

The temptation is to consider *muli* as a bronze coin, although the documents neither support nor refute this. It is an assumption (Khotanese *mura* = Kharoshthi *muli* = Chinese *qian*) that Lin Meicun (1993: 97) slipped into his notes on an eighth-century bilingual Chinese-Khotanese document from Khotan [H.16.2.2] (see Chapter 10). The Chinese and Khotanese texts on the document are similar, except for the omission in Khotanese of the Chinese section recording payment of 3,000 coins (Lin Meicun 1993: 93), 'reckoned in thousands' (Lin Meicun 1993: 93).

Burrow (1937: 111) deduced that 1 *muli* is equivalent to one-twelfth of a gold stater. His argument was based on two documents: [§431] in which the queen asks for 1 gold stater, but is given carpet measuring 13 hands in length; and [§579] in which the price received for a sale of land was 13 hands of carpet valued at 12. However, the documents are not related ([§431] is from N.xii.ii.I; [§579] is from N.xxiv.viii.82) and there is no indication of common date. Furthermore, Burrow took it as certain that the carpet given to the queen was an established equivalent to 1 gold stater, and that the value of a carpet was a consistent 12 *muli*. Thierry (2000) questioned the consistency of the carpet, but did not check the documents. In fact, both documents specify *tavastaga* carpets. Among the Kharoshthi documents there are ten references to *tavastaga* carpets (see Table 18). From this larger body of evidence we can deduce that *tavastaga* carpet was used in making payments or part-payments; it was usually measured by length (between 4 and 13 hands long) though sometimes in countable units (one to three units), and was available for purchase in the mountains. There is only one reference to 13 hands of *tavastaga* carpet valued at 12 *muli*, making it difficult to substantiate Burrow's deduction that 1 *muli* equals one-twelfth of a gold stater. Furthermore, at this rate, the payment of 24 *muli* and 2 drachma (= 2 gold staters and 2 drachma) for one man [§324] appears to be out of line with other prices or equivalents given in the documents: girl at 45 *muli* [§551], camel at 30–50 *muli* [§571, §551, §437, §590, §589, §590, §592], hire of camel at 13 *muli* [§505], horse at 30–40 *muli* [§580, §495], 13 hands of

**Table 19**
**Payments**

| Items purchased/Context | Form of payment | Note | Reference |
|---|---|---|---|
| 16 *muli* 15 *khi* of food | 1 jacket | After the food was distributed, 1 *muli* remained | [§343] |
| 1 *kojava* rug | Royal corn | – | [§448] |
| 3 *tavastaga* carpets | Corn | – | [§622] |
| Court case involving 12 hands of carpet and 6 *milima* of corn | Corn | 3 *milima* to be paid now, 3 *milima* in the autumn | [§527] |
| 1 cow | Corn | Measured in *milima* | [§122] |
| 1 camel | 100 *milima* of corn | Payment deemed excessive | [§468] |
| Army maintenance | 4 *milima* 10 *khi* of corn, 3 sheep | – | [§479] |

**Table 20**
**Wages paid in grain**

| Wages paid in grain | Reference |
|---|---|
| . . . In Peta-nagara there is corn for paying wages (to the extent of) *milima* . . . Further there is corn for the wages of the guard, *milima* 3, and corn for his food, 1 *milima* 10 *khi*. When this Jamavam[na] arrives there, quickly 15 *milima* of corn is to be given to Jamavamna and Thuvaya; no obstruction is to be made | [§25] |
| The asa have not received their wages. It is 1 *milima* and 10 *khi* | [§476] |
| Pay *sikhi*-corn as hire for man's work | [§532] |

**Table 21**
**Packed corn**

| Packed corn | Reference |
|---|---|
| Complaint that two people have eaten one parcel of corn belonging to another | [§68] |
| Three people each pay 3 *milima* of packed [corn] | [§131] |
| If the tax payment gets plundered on the way, you will pay it from your own farm, parcel for parcel | [§154] |
| I, the great king, have allowed half of the packed corn as a grant to the *cozbo* Samasena. The other half is to be brought. The half that has been relinquished is to be provisions for L | [§235] |

*tavastaga* carpet at 12 *muli* [§579], cow at 10 *muli* [§327], *kojava* rug at 5–10 *muli* [§327, §222], 10 *khi* of wine at 10 *muli* [§571].

However, a list of names with payments [§210] shows that 1 *muli* was equivalent to 1 *milima* (= 20 *khi*) of grain. Indeed, the term *muli* occasionally stands in for the term *milima* [§343], and the following examples indicate that grain was used in various kinds of payments: for purchasing a *kojava* rug [§448], *tavastaga* carpets [§622], a cow [§122], a camel [§468]. One court case involved 12 hands of carpet and 6 *milima* of corn [§527] (see Table 19). In another example land was bought for one Khotanese *alena* rug and 5 *milima* of corn, with the price reckoned at 15 [*muli*] [§549].

Grain was also collected in for tax purposes and redistribution. Taxes were payable in grain, or in an equivalent amount in other goods [§309], for example, wine or silk [§225]. When paid in grain they were measured in *milima* and *khi* [§291], often expressed as several hundreds of *milima* [§292]. One tax payment appears to involve women and grain, though the details are unclear [§165]. Tax payments sometimes accumulated and were paid in arrears [§140, §207]. Other documents record tax collection [§547, 348]. Tax was collected at different locations; one document states that tax collection at one place is to be split, with one-third taken to the capital and two-thirds deposited at Pisali [§291]. Another orders corn to be collected and deposited in all the offices of the city [§272]. Where transport of grain was required, a camel load was reckoned as 3 *milima* of corn [§291].

Tax payments and loans are mentioned together in [§59], which would suggest that the collection points also lent out from their stores. In some documents it is not clear whether the amounts are being paid into or out of the stores [§98, §536]. Lists of names and their payments were drawn up [§210]. One document indicates collection of grain by the elder, who is then to hand it over to a monk [§477].

Grain was loaned out at interest [§79, §140, §539], which in one case appears to have been double the original value of the loan [§142]. In another example, the loan was made in grain, but a camel was expected as the repayment [§530]. Interest could be paid in several instalments [§102]. Grain was also used to pay wages (see Table 20).

Several documents mention 'packed corn' and individual parcels of corn [§59, §68, §131, §151, §235] (see Table 21), but there is not sufficient evidence to suggest that these were of a particular standard size and pre-packed. Indeed, one document specifies the weighing out of grain in offices [§207].

To sum up, grain is the only commodity for which there is direct conversion. It was used for making payments, for wages, loans, taxation and redistribution. It was measured by weight in *milima* and *khi*, and was convertible at the rate of 1 *muli* = 1 *milima* = 20 *khi*. Measurements in *khi* are usually in multiples of 5, expressed as 5, 10 or 15 *khi*. Measurements of *milima* range from 1 to several hundred. A camel load appears to have been 3 *milima* [§291]. The largest payment for a single item was 100 *milima* for a camel, deemed excessive [§468]. Apart from this example, the prices and tax payments do not vary enormously, suggesting that these quantities were within a normal range, rather than exceptional examples.

However, there are patterns for exchange of other items, for example in sales of slaves, animals and land (see below). Other forms of financial transaction also existed. Some of these are associated with traditional customs, and the most striking of these is the 'milk payment', being the payment of one horse for an adopted child [§11, §45, §331, §415, §434, §553, §741]. This custom distinguished between slaves and free people; the milk payment did not apply to adoption of children among slaves [§39] and adopted children could not be made slaves, sold or pledged [§569]. On one occasion a camel was given as a 'milk payment' [§569].

In the following sections I will discuss some of the financial and economic activities revealed in the Kharoshthi documents.

## Financial and economic activities seen in the Kharoshthi documents

### *Sales of slaves*

Slaves occur frequently in the documents [§106, §130, §133, §143, §144, §152, §320, §322, §328, §358, §364, §491, §506, §528, §538, §550, §666, §696, §709]. Where the prices are given, we can see that camels were used as the main form of payment for slaves: male slaves [§575], women slaves [§209, §590], girl or child slaves [§625, §589, §592, §437]. Silk, carpets and rugs were also used to purchase slaves. For one woman, 41 rolls of silk were paid [§2]. Other slaves were paid for in a combination of camels, horses, carpets, rugs and grain [§575, §590, §591, §592, §575]. All transactions for girls were made in camels; for women they were mostly made in camels with occasional payments in textiles or *tavastaga* carpets, and camels were used in part-payment for men (see Table 22).

**Table 22**
**Purchases of slaves**

| Slave purchased | Payment | Reference |
|---|---|---|
| 1 woman | 41 rolls of silk | [§2] |
| 1 woman | 1 7-year-old camel | [§209] |
| 1 woman | 1 *viyala* camel (40 *muli*)<br>12 hands of *tavastaga* carpet<br>11 hands of *tavastaga* carpet<br>8 sutra *muli* | [§590] |
| 1 child | 1 8-year-old camel | [§625] |
| 1 girl | 1 1-year-old camel (worth 40 *muli*) | [§589] |
| 1 girl | 1 *amklatsa* camel (worth 30 *muli*)<br>1 Khotanese *kojava* rug | [§592] |
| 1 girl | 45 *muli* (paid 1 camel worth 42 *muli*) | [§437] |
| 1 girl | – | [§551] |
| 1 man | – | [§436] |
| 1 man | 1 3-year-old camel<br>5 *milima* of corn, 3 other goods | [§575] |
| 1 man | 1 5-year-old camel<br>1 5-year-old horse, 25 *atga* (?) | [§591] |

### *Animals*

The animals mentioned in the documents are camels, horses, cattle [§157, §676], sheep [§568, §584, §585] and goats [§633]. The most important were camels and horses, which were frequently used in purchases of land (see below). Agrawala (1952: 103) concluded that 'animals like cows and camels were media of exchange. In fact, the term *vita* (Sanskrit. *vitta* [= acquisition, wealth, property, goods, substance, money, power] is affixed to these animals, showing that they were the main form of wealth.'

Camels were used in payments to purchase slaves [§209, §590, §625, §589, §592, §437, §575, §591], to purchase land [§422, §571, §624, §655, §715] and in payment of taxes [§16, §163, §165]. Camels were purchased with corn [§335, §348, §468, §526, §530]. The usual price of a camel was 30–42 *muli* (the reckoning used to purchase slaves), with 100 *milima* of corn (= 100 *muli*) deemed excessive [§468]. In one example, 8,000 *masa* was paid for a camel with a special marking [§661]. Camels were the main form of transporting goods, and camel hire is a frequent topic in the documents [§52, §83, §359, §382, §340, §505, §516].

Four documents give the price of hiring a camel as one white *arnavaji* textile (8 hands long) [§83]; 1 *posara* (?) [§382]; 1 *muli* [§382]; and 13 *muli* [§505]. It is not possible from these figures to ascertain whether there was a standard price for hiring camels.

There was always the danger that camels might die, be lost or be carried off by an armed band [§195]. When a camel died, it was the practice for the last keeper of the camel to pay recompense to the owner [§40, §570, §578]. If a camel died while in state employment, the recompense was paid out from the administration [§435]. Recompense for the death of a camel appears to have been another camel [§570] or a carpet [§578]. In one example [§578], S gave P a camel to break in, the camel died, so P gave a woman to S, and, in return for the woman, S gave to P (according to the custom of *pratiprahuda*, see below under gifts) 8 hands of *tavastaga* carpet.

The 'milk payment' of one horse for an adopted child has been mentioned above. Horses could be hired [§213]; they were used to transport wine [§333]; and were presented as a gift to the King of Khotan [§214]. Indeed, there were royal stables [§600]. Occasionally horses were stolen [§545]. In one example [§24] Caule is recovering a debt of a horse from Sugita's slave, but Caule does not want the horse back; instead he wants the house and land given to Sugita by the king. The document [§431–2] considers the exchange of horses for wine.

Land could be owned by freemen, monks [§473] and even slaves [§574]. It could be inherited [§187, §260] or bought [§255]. The cost of land varied according to the kinds of crops it could support, and the land was measured according to its capacity for seed [§186]. The following were all used to buy land: horses [§495, §586, §648, §654, §580, §582], camels [§422, §624, §715, §571], cow in calf [§186] and *tavastaga* carpet [§579]. Sometimes a combination of goods was used when buying land: horse and wine [§574], camel and other goods [§655], Khotanese *alena* rug and corn [§549], *tavastaga* carpet, *kavaji* (?), sheep and corn [§581] and wine and other goods [§652]. In some cases, the value of the goods exchanged for land were reckoned in *muli* [§495, §580, §571, §655, §549, §579]. These indicate that a horse was worth 30–40 *muli* [§495, §580],

**Table 23**
**Payments for land**

| Nature of payment | Reference |
|---|---|
| 1 horse (worth 30 *muli*) | [§495] |
| 1 horse | [§586] |
| 1 horse | [§648] |
| 1 horse | [§654] |
| 1 4-year-old horse (worth 40 *muli*) | [§580] |
| 1 horse and 1 *milima* of wine | [§574] |
| 3 horse (?) (worth 15) | [§582] |
| 1 camel | [§422] |
| 1 camel | [§624] |
| 1 9-year-old camel | [§715] |
| 1 2-year-old camel (worth 50 *muli*) | [§571] |
| 1 4-year-old camel + *raji* 2 *amila* (?) (total worth 90 *muli*) | [§655] |
| 1 cow-in-calf | [§186] |
| 1 Khotanese *alena* rug and 5 *milima* of corn (total worth 15 *muli*) | [§549] |
| 13 hands of *tavastaga* carpet (worth 12 *muli*) | [§579] |
| 6 hands of *tavastaga* carpet, 1 *kavaji*, 2 sheep, 1 *milima* of corn | [§581] |
| 10 *khi* of wine, 3 *agisdha* (?) | [§652] |

and a camel was worth 50 *muli* [§571] (see Table 23). Land was also rented out. One document states that rent was paid in ghee [§496]. Others indicate that some lands were subject to particular taxes [§374, §677].

***Taxation***
Many documents relate to taxes [§57, §70, §158, §164, §179, §275, §307, §315, §317, §390, §450, §468, §481, §725] and tax collectors [§33, §90, §198, §272, §520, §567]. The tax terms are numerous and many are unidentified. Taxes were paid in the following: camels [§42]; ghee [§42, §162, §165, §207, §714]; wine [§168, §206, §207]; grain [§59, §207]; cows [§207]; sheep [§162, §207, §714]; jars of pomegranates [§315, §617]; madder [§315, §385]; baskets and sacks [§207]; carpets and rugs [§207, §714], felt garments [§382, §385] and textiles [§385, §714]. These were probably all local products.

Several documents refer to arrears of tax payments [§162, §207, §211] and some substitution of goods was allowed: for example one [§382] allows a felt garment to be paid instead of ghee.

***Loans***
Loans, payable with interest, were common [§100, §140, §272, §370, §588], and two documents tell of people 'harassing each other on account of old debts' [§272, §357]. Two documents refer to debts expressed in *muli*: both are for 20 *muli* [§393, §576]. The items on loan include food [§142]; grain [§539]; wine [§345, §539, §622]; *thubadanna* (?) [§378]; water [§502, §604]; and sheep [§539]. The majority of loans involved corn or food (see Table 24). There was limited liability for some loans: for example, the property of a master was not to be used to repay the debt of his slave [§24]. One document [§35] tells of a debt of silk, which cannot be investigated until the merchants arrive from China. Another document [§660] notes that a man has returned from the capital and lists various rolls of silk and other items that have changed hands. It would seem then that loans were not limited to local residents, and may have involved outsiders.

***Specific references to times of war and plunder***
In principle, property taken during a time of war was not regarded as theft. This is seen in the reference to a hoard, which was disturbed by dogs and foxes and dug out of the ground by two people who were subsequently accused of theft [§17]. There was also a law that anything given or received before plundering could not be the object of a legal dispute [§494].

***Gifts***
There are numerous references to gifts and giving, from diplomatic to official level and within the family. Often the term 'gift' appears to express the action of 'handing over': for example, handing over a girl [§114]; a woman and her children [§415]; *hasga* (?) [§542]; crop-land [§572]; land [§656]. Sometimes there is an indication of a payment expected in return. For example, a gift of one *kojava* rug worth 10 *muli* is expected in return for some land [§223]; a coat is expected in return for a silk item [§316]. Two sheep and three *hastavarsaga* were given in return for a horse [§243].

Honorific gifts and provisions were provided for envoys from state funds [§22]. Gifts to and from royalty include the gift of a horse to the king of Khotan [§214] and a royal cow as a present [§122]. One letter sent to a superior makes several references to gifts [§288]:

> At the feet of the master, dear to men and gods, honoured by men and gods, the Bodhisattva in person, the great *cozbo* Somcaka, the *cozbo* Yili and Namilgaae pay respect and send the health of his divine body, much, immeasurable and such is our statement:
>
> It is a long time since we were able to send you a letter and a present. For that reason we earnestly beg your indulgence. Nothing should be unknown to your divine knowledge. This *sramanera* Cakvala has been sent to you to convey [wishes of] good health to your divine body. Whatever communication he makes to you there, by all means his words must be listened to. Let this *sramanera* be under your care. Let them do nothing in disregard of him. We have sent a small present so that you need not worry about a present. Later we will send a letter and present in the hand of Dharmapriya, which will be worthy of you – from Yili one rope, and from Namilgaae one *lastuga*.
>
> To the feet of his dear brother the *cozbo* Budharachi of unlimited merit, who abides in (my) heart, Dharmapriya sends health, much.

The formulae for sending gifts appear to indicate at least two different types, although the motive for distinguishing between the two formulae is unclear. One set has the formula *prahuda prahidemi* (or similar). Of these nine letters, two are addressed to a high-ranking *cozbo* [§165, §399] and one from a father to his son [§109] (see Table 25).

The other set has the formula *manasikara* (or similar), which Burrow translates as 'token of remembrance'. Of these ten letters, five are addressed to a high-ranking *cozbo* [§140, §161, §338, §370, §585] (see Table 26). The small silk bag [L.A.vii.059] found at the Loulan site L.A. with a Kharoshthi inscription on both sides includes the expression *manasi*[*m*]*karo matra praharasa*, suggesting that this bag may

**Table 24**
**Loans**

| Nature of loan | Circumstances | Reference |
|---|---|---|
| Loan of corn (2 lots) to L | The amount of that corn which has been used up or given to others has been entered on a tablet. The amount of corn remaining from that is 5 *milima* 10 *khi*. That corn is to be demanded of Samghasena along with interest. Reckoning of the *vasdhigaim* corn and field-corn is to be made separately | [§140] |
| Loan of corn (10 *khi*) from *panimcana* | A reckoning of that is to be made along with the interest. As regards the previous corn, reckoning is to be made in detail for each year individually. As regards last year's corn in C's hand, K knows how much came off the threshing floor. Also a reckoning is to be made of the corn C has | [§140] |
| Loan of corn | 2 interest instalments are mentioned | [§102] |
| Loan of food (1 *milima* 10 *khi*) | As formerly, they pay there double what they receive here. By that arrangement the food is to be repaid | [§142] |
| Loan of corn (30 *milima*) | Monk A gave the thief B to L as being equivalent to the value of 110 *muli* of the corn A had received on loan and the twelve lengths of cloth (etc.) that had been stolen | [§345] |
| Loan of corn | S loaned 3 *milima* of corn to K. They agreed on a camel as the price. K never gave the camel. Now he must return the camel plus allowance for the years past, or return corn plus interest | [§530] |
| Loan of corn | – | [§79] |
| Loan of corn | Interest payable | [§539] |
| Loan of corn | A decision is to be made about the corn from the mountains; do it carefully or you will have to pay this corn out of your own | [§635] |

**Table 25**
**Gifts sent with letters (set 1)**

| Formula in letter | Gift | Reference |
|---|---|---|
| *Prahuda pra[hi]ta* | 1 arrow (for good luck) | [§231] |
| *Prahuda prahidemi* | 1 arrow (again) | [§399] |
| *Prahuda harmai* | 1 present | [§667] |
| *Prahuda prahidemi* | 1 present | [§499] |
| *Prahuda prahidemi* | 1 present | [§165] |
| *Prahoda prahidemi* | 1 present | [§188] |
| *Prahidemi prahuda* | 2 presents | [§153] |
| *Prahida prahuda* | 1 *hastavarsaga* textile | [§311] |
| *Prahadavya prahida* | 1 *aridi* (to mother)<br>1 *aridi* (to father)<br>*sidha* salt (to Sugita)<br>*aridaga* (?) (to Sarvasriae<br>(?) + *alamgila* (?) (to Samapriae)<br>1 jewel (to Sampriae)<br>1 jewel (to Suvornapriae) | [§109] |

**Table 26**
**Gifts sent with letters (set 2)**

| Formula | Gift | Reference |
|---|---|---|
| *Manasikara prahita* | 1 Chinese turban | [§353] |
| *Mamnasikara prahi* | 1 portion of ginger | [§354] |
| *Manasimkaro matra prahi(da)* | 1 *hastavarsaga* textile<br>5 (?) | [§370] |
| *Manasimgaramatra prahida* | 1 *hastavarsaga* textile | [§338] |
| *Manasikara matra prahuda* | 1 *chotaga*<br>1 *lastuga* textile | [§161] |
| *Mamnasim karo prahuda* | 1 *lespa*<br>3 *sira*<br>1 *vatu* | [§140] |
| *Prahita manasitkara matra* | 1 bow-string | [§252] |
| *Prahita mamnasikamro* | 1 *lastuga* textile | [§585] |
| *Prahuda manasikara* | 1 gift | [§177] |
| *Manasigara matra* | 1 *lastuga* textile | [§184] |

once have contained such a memento (Stein 1928: 223, pl. XVII; Rapson et al. 1997: 756).

The absence of gifts is also noted. One letter [§690] indicates that family members expected presents: 'Other relations have received small presents. We have been ignored.' Another [§573] requests no gift, 'not even a hair'. Six letters conclude with the instruction 'not to worry about a gift' [§109, §159, §246, §288, §320, §335].

***Theft of property***

Four documents report thefts of property, in two of which the thief was a slave (see Table 27).

Slaves themselves were also stolen, for example when the Supis seized a slave, and sold him to a Chinese man [§324].

***Punishment***

Punishment was generally in the form of fines and blows (see Table 28). It appears that blows were counted in fives or tens (15, 30, 50, 70, 110 blows). Fines were in the form of people, animals and food. In Cadota there appears to have been a problem with disobedient novices, who were fined in rolls of silk for various offences (see Table 29).

**Table 27**
**Thefts of property**

| Items stolen | Thief | Action taken | Reference |
|---|---|---|---|
| 4 roughly woven cloths<br>3 woollen cloths<br>1 silver ornament<br>2,500 *masa*<br>2 jackets<br>2 *somstamni* (?)<br>2 belts<br>3 Chinese robes | – | – | [§149] |
| Many items of clothing and textiles<br>4 golden *dare* (?) | Slave | – | [§318] |
| 12 lengths of silk<br>3 *urnavarande*<br>2 ropes<br>3 felt garments<br>4 sheep<br>1 *aresa*<br>(Total value: 100 *muli*) | Monk's slave | The monk was to pay back in full. He already owed the court a fine of one cow. The monk handed over the thieving slave as being equivalent to the value of 110 *muli* of corn which he had received on loan and the 12 lengths of cloth that had been stolen | [§345] |
| 7 strings of pearls (*mutilata*)<br>1 mirror<br>1 *lastuga* of multi-coloured silk<br>1 *sudi* ear ornament | – | – | [§566] |

**Table 28**
**Fines and punishments**

| Offence | Punishment (blows/strokes) or fine | Reference |
|---|---|---|
| Assault and breaking a bone | 70 blows<br>1 young man | [§187] |
| Cutting down other people's trees to sell | 1 horse | [§482] |
| Cutting branches off other people's trees | 1 cow | [§482] |
| Stealing and eating one 6-year-old cow | 1 × 6-year-old cow<br>1 × 3-year-old cow with calf<br>50 blows | [§676] |
| – | 1 sheep<br>30 blows | [§204] |
| – | I cow | [§345] |
| Non-attendance | 10 *khi* of rations<br>15 blows | [§462] |
| Questioning a court ruling | 30 lengths of cloth | [§345] |
| Disputing a divorce agreement | 1 × 4-year-old horse<br>110 blows | [Lin Meicun 1989a] |

***Contracts and penalties***

A number of the Kharoshthi documents are contracts. Typically, these were witnessed and rendered effective by the cutting of a string [§186]. The contracts describe the goods that are changing hands, clarify ownership and indicate the longstanding authority of the contract. Sometimes the document includes a penalty that must be paid for reneging on the contract: sometimes a vague 'penalty will be incurred' [§568]; sometimes 'as the law of the kingdom demands' [§661]. Some penalties are more specific (see Table 30).

**Discussion**

Examination of the Kharoshthi documents reveals that there were established monetary practices in the Shanshan kingdom, and that these were often very different from those of China, as seen in the wood slips (see Chapter 7). But it is clear that there was trade between Shanshan and China, and that this had some impact on the money practices of Shanshan.

The only references to coins in the Kharoshthi documents from Eastern Central Asia are to gold coins in the documents found at Niya. There are no specific descriptions of or

**Table 29**
**Punishment for offences by monks as listed in document [§489]**

| Offence | Fines (in rolls of silk) |
|---|---|
| Non-participation in activities of the religious community | 1 |
| Non-participation in the *posatha* ceremony | 1 |
| Inappropriate clothing (wearing 'householder's dress') | 1 |
| Physical violence: light blow | 5 |
| Physical violence: moderate blows | 10 |
| Physical violence: excessive blows | 15 |

**Table 30**
**Penalties for disputing sales**

| Transaction | Penalty for disputing a sale | Reference |
|---|---|---|
| Sale of man | 1 castrated horse and 50 blows | [§591] |
| Sale of land | 1 gelding and 70 blows | [§571] |
| Sale of land | 1 horse and 70 blows | [§580] |
| Sale of girl | 1 4-year-old gelding and 50 blows | [§437] |
| Sale of land | 5 pieces of cloth and 50 blows | [§419] |
| Sale of pot | 12 lengths of cloth | [§348] |
| Sale of woman | 1 *vito* (?) horse and 70 blows | [§209] |

references to bronze coins, although Chinese bronze coins have been found at the sites. The true meaning of *masa* needs to be established to prove whether this refers to Chinese coins. The main unit of account in the documents is the term *muli*, but the origins of this word are not known. *Muli* has an equivalent in grain, where 1 *muli* = 1 *milima* of grain, and 1 *milima* = 20 *khi*. Measurements of *khi* are always in multiples of 5, expressed as 5, 10 or 15 *khi*, but effectively serving as quarter, half and three-quarter measurements respectively. It is interesting that the fines for disobedient monks at Cadota were one, five, ten and fifteen rolls of silk.

Grain was certainly used in payment for goods, wages, tax purposes and loans. Grain payments were made at the time of exchange, or in instalments, which may have been arranged according to the agricultural year. The documents indicate that animals, carpets, textiles and wine were also used in payments. The documents served to record the transactions or to settle cases brought to the court. Some documents are thus the formal recording of barter. Certain patterns have emerged in the documents, showing a hierarchy (albeit a hazy one) of items used in payment. Corn was a major medium of exchange, and was used to purchase camels. Camels were the most common form of payment for slaves. Horses, camels, carpets, corn and wine were used to purchase land.

Taxation appears to have been in whatever animals, crops or goods were bred, harvested or manufactured locally. Tax collection allowed for substitution of goods and payment was sometimes in arrears. References to changing to a single tax collection point suggest that collections were previously made at various locations. Loans were fairly common.

Slaves were able to buy and sell land and engage in similar economic activities to their owners. A slave was responsible for his own loan, and his liability for a loan could not be computed to his owner. However, there are clear distinctions between slaves and freemen: for example an adopted free child could not be treated as a slave, and a slave child adopted by a slave did not merit a 'milk payment'.

Reports of theft often accused a slave, and the list of items stolen usually included carpets, textiles or clothes. Punishment for various offences usually involved a fine and/or physical punishment. The fines included people, horses, cows, sheep, rations and silk, and the most elaborate description of fines is for disobedient monks not attending activities, where the fines are one, five, ten or fifteen rolls of silk (i.e. in multiples of five). Punishment was also due for breaking a contract, and the penalty is specified as a horse (often a gelding), textiles and physical blows. Horses, carpets and textiles appear to have had a specific function in the payment of fines and penalties.

There was also a well-established custom of sending a gift with a letter, and, although two distinct patterns of language surrounding gift-sending are discerned, the intentions behind the two are not clear.

**Notes**

1. This document was found at Endere and shows differences in alphabet and dialect. Endere was in the kingdom of Khotan, where a different form of Prakrit was used.
2. See Zhong-Ri 1996, di yi juan, 269–338 (in Japanese) and Zhong-Ri 1999, di san juan (Chinese version): 139–53.
3. Burrow §12 = Boyer et al. (1920–29: 43) from N.i.61; see Stein (1907: 388). Burrow §324 = Boyer et al. (1920–29: 324) from N.xv.158; see Stein (1907: 406). Burrow §419 = Boyer et al. (1920–29: 419) from N.xxi.7+4; see Stein (1907: 414). Burrow §431–2 = Boyer et al. (1920–29: 431) from N.xiii.ii.I; see Stein (1921: 248).
4. See also Thomas (1924: 671–2 and 1926: 507) for the continued use of *sadera* as a coin-name or weight, e.g. into Uighur Turki 'six satir of silver' in a document purchased by the German expedition of 1902–3; 'sadera' in Armenian; and 'sadera' in the Indian text *Ganita-sara-samgraha* of Mahavira.
5. The earliest record of a string being used with coins is in the *Hanshu* (Shihuozhi), which states how, in 140 BC, coins were piling up in the capital and their strings were rotting so that the coins could not be counted. However, Peng Xinwei (1965: 214 n2) notes that the monetary unit of 1 string of 1,000 coins became current after the Han, citing the reference in the *Weishu* (juan 91, Xu Jian zhuan), that in year 22 Gaozu ordered cash to the amount of 10,000 strings to be conferred.

# 9 Chinese documents: paper documents, fourth to eighth centuries

Most of the Chinese paper documents found in Eastern Central Asia have come from sites in the Turfan region, some acquired by Western and Japanese explorer archaeologists in the early twentieth century, and many more by Chinese teams. Between 1959 and 1975 Chinese archaeologists excavated over 450 tombs at the Astana and Kara-khoja cemeteries, about 40 km east of Turfan city. These sites are associated with the Gaochang city site, which was the capital of the Gaochang kingdom. The dominant culture of the Gaochang kingdom was Chinese, and Chinese customs and practices were encouraged in particular by the third ruler of the kingdom, Qu Boya. The tomb occupants at the Astana cemetery were predominantly Chinese, or if not Chinese, they had adopted Chinese burial practices. The Chinese took Gaochang in 640 and divided the kingdom into five sub-prefectures, known collectively as Xizhou.[1]

Excavation at Astana and Kara-khoja has been mostly salvage archaeology; only one tomb was found intact; the rest had been disturbed. The documents, however, were of little interest to the grave-robbers, who ignored over ten thousand fragments of Chinese documents dating from AD 273–768. Chinese historians have pieced together the fragments to form 1,600 documents, which have been published as *Tulufan chutu wenshu* (Tang Changru 1981–92). Of these documents, almost 250 (15 per cent) are contracts (Yamamoto and Ikeda 1987: 10). Approximately 5 per cent of the Turfan contracts predate the establishment of the Gaochang kingdom in AD 502, 30 per cent are from the period of the Gaochang kingdom under the ruling Qu family (AD 502–640), and 65 per cent are from the period after the Chinese takeover of Gaochang in AD 640. These excavated documents are straightforward records of actual transactions, and provide first-hand evidence of economic life and customs in the region. Some were placed in the tombs intentionally; others have survived by chance, often recycled as paper shoes (see Plate 8). Consequently, they form the only group of randomly preserved documents from the seventh and eighth centuries in China (Hansen 1995: 1–22). In addition to the contracts, several tombs also yielded burial lists: some are true inventories of the actual objects in the tombs, others are apparently wishful inventories of imaginary objects. In this respect the burial lists are multi-functional, serving as the practical documentation of objects, but also revealing the material desires of the time.

Paper documents have also been found in other regions of Eastern Central Asia, for example in Kucha and Khotan. These are far fewer in number than the larger body of documents from Turfan. The Chinese contracts from Turfan are dated 367–741; those from Kucha are dated in the 780s; and those from Khotan are dated in the 780s and possibly into the first years of the ninth century.

This chapter examines the contracts and tomb inventories from Turfan, Kucha and Khotan, considering the evidence from these three different locations and different periods. It looks primarily at the basic function of the individual contracts[2] – in terms of purchase, loan, lease or hiring labour, and the media of payment involved – and tomb inventories, with the aim of ascertaining the forms of money that were used and the general patterns of their use.

For convenience, references to the individual documents give the document registration numbers which expand as follows: 64TAM4:39 = 1964 Turfan Astana Mu [= tomb] no.4, object no.39. The following abbreviations have been used in this chapter: Y&I (Yamamoto and Ikeda, 1987) and TCW (*Tulufan chutu wenshu*). Details of particular documents are given in the tables.

It should be stressed that the documentary evidence from Turfan is extensive, and that the contracts and loans discussed here are part of a much larger body of material, which in turn can be compared against the Tang dynasty texts relating to taxation, land distribution and other important aspects of economic life. Recent work on these documents, in particular by members of the three-year US-Chinese project 'The Silk Road Project: Re-uniting Turfan's scattered treasures' has transformed our understanding of life at Gaochang.[3] In this chapter, I have focused on the contracts and burial lists as these provide primary evidence for the different forms of money that were used in the most basic financial transaction, i.e. payment. Many of these documents are dated and allow us to track the rise and fall of different forms of money.

### The contracts from Turfan (see Tables 31–4)

The history of contracts in China and their formats and stylistic features have been discussed by others (Yamamoto and Ikeda 1987; Hansen 1995), and are not included here. But it is important for the Chinese contracts to be seen in the contexts of place, date and culture. Most were retrieved from tombs in the Astana and Kara-khoja cemeteries associated with the Gaochang kingdom, in the Turfan region. Apart from one Sogdian contract, there are no other surviving contracts in other languages from Turfan with which to compare them, and this method of recording an agreement of exchange appears to have originated in central China, perhaps continued in the Turfan region by the many Chinese who settled there. Indeed, Hansen (1995: 1–24) notes a similarity of contractual language in the documents from Turfan and central China, and linguistically sees no foreign influence on the wording of the Turfan contracts.

The contracts were drawn up independently of the state authorities; indeed the Chinese state was reluctant to intervene in private contracts, even after the promulgation in 653 of the Tang Code (*Tanglü*), a comprehensive code of laws according to Confucian principles. This is explicit in many contracts where the text concludes with the phrase 'Officials have government

**Table 31**
**Contracts of sale, Turfan**

| Date | Transaction | Price agreed | Penalty | Special considerations | References |
|---|---|---|---|---|---|
| 273 | Coffin | 20 *pi* of *lian* silk | – | – | 66TAM53:9 / Y&I: §1 |
| 367 | Camel | 1 camel | 10 *zhan* carpets | – | Hou Can 1982 / Y&I: §2 |
| 509 | Slave, 25-year-old female | 3.5 *zhang* of Qiuci *jin* brocade | 7 *zhang* of Qiuci *jin* brocade | – | 75TKM99:6(a) / Y&I: §3 |
| 541 | Land | – | – | – | 66TAM48:23 / Y&I: §4 |
| Gaochang period | Vineyard | *Die* cloth | – | – | 67TAM90:32 / Y&I: §5 |
| 627 | Farming employee, aged 20+ | 380 silver coins | Double the price | 280 silver coins paid, 100 to be paid on 2nd day of 1st month. Overdue payment incurs interest at 10% per month | 60TA338:142(a) / Y&I: §6 |
| 628 | Plot of land for house | 4 silver coins per 10 *bu* | Double the price | – | 69TAM135:2 / Y&I: §7 |
| 631 | House | 300 silver coins | Double the price | – | 64TAM10:37 / Y&I: §8 |
| 637 | Garden | 20+ silver coins | 100 silver coins | Paid in instalments, with interest | 64TAM15:292 / Y&I: §9 |
| Gaochang period | Vineyard | 50 silver coins | Double the price | – | 69TAM140:184 / Y&I: §10 |
| Gaochang period | Field | – | – | – | 60TAM316:081(a) / Y&I: §11 |
| Gaochang period (or early Tang) | Vineyard | 30 coins (*kongqian*) | – | – | 69TAM117:572 / Y&I: §12 |
| 638 | Field | 390 (silver) coins | Double the price | Corvée obligations transferred with ownership of land | Otani 3464, 3466, 2405, 3460, 3465 / Y&I: §13 |
| 638 | Field | 120 (silver) coins | Double the price | – | Otani 1469, 3461, 3458, 3459, 3463, 3461 / Y&I: §14 |
| 638 | Vineyard | (Incomplete) | – | – | Otani 3468 / Y&I: §15 |
| 638 | Vineyard | (Silver) coins | – | – | Otani 1494, 3462, 1500, 1492, 3470, 3457 / Y&I: §16 |
| Gaochang period or early Tang | (?) | 6 *pi* of *lian* silk | 20 *pi* of white *lian* silk | – | 69TAM117:571 / Y&I: §17 |
| Zhenguan period (640–9) | House | 10 silver coins | Double the price | – | 59TAM301:154–3 / Y&I: §18 |
| 644 | House | 5 silver coins | Double the price | – | 60TAM338:145 / Y&I: §19 |
| 649 | Horse | (Incomplete) | – | – | 60TAM337:118 / Y&I: §20 |
| 649 | Horse: red with black mane and tail | (Silver) coins | – | – | 60TAM337:116 / Y&I: §21 |
| 647–50 | Horse | White *lian* silk | – | – | 60TAM337:117 / Y&I: §22 |
| 650 | Slave | *Lian* silk? | – | – | 60TAM337:1110 / Y&I: §23 |
| post-640 | House | Silver coins | Double the price | – | 60TAM337:114(a) / Y&I: §24 |

**Table 31**
**(*cont.*)**

| Date | Transaction | Price agreed | Penalty | Special considerations | References |
|---|---|---|---|---|---|
| 661 | Slave | 6 *pi* of *shuilian* silk 5 silver coins | – | – | 64TAM4:44 / Y&I: §25 |
| 662 | Slave | *Lian* silk | – | – | 60TAM317:30–7 / Y&I: §26 |
| 662 | Ox | Ox | – | – | 60TAM317:30–6 / Y&I: §27 |
| 668 | Hay: 90 bundles | 40 silver coins | 60 silver coins | If borrower does not repay or absconds, value of original price to be extracted from his family's assets | 64TAM4:32 / Y&I: §28 |
| 673 | Camel: 10-year-old | 14 *pi* of silk | – | Unit Leader Du of Qianting, Xizhou, bought camel from Sogdian, with intention of registering it and thus acquiring market certificate* | 64TAM35:21 / Y&I: §29 |
| 695 | Horse | – | – | – | Y&I: §30 |
| 731 | Slave: 11-year-old female | 40 *pi* of *lian* silk | – | Slave was bought in Xizhou; document is certificate stamped with mark of the Xizhou *dudufu* | TAM509:8–12–2 / Y&I: §31 |
| 732 | Slave: 13-year-old female (non-Chinese) | 40 *pi* of *dalian* silk | – | Sale guaranteed by 5 people | Y&I: §Ad.13 |
| 733 | Horse: 6-year-old, red with black mane and tail | 18 *pi* of *dalian* silk | – | Bought at Xizhou | TAM509 / Y&I: §32 |
| 741 | Ox: 4-year-old | 8 *pi* of *dalian* silk | – | Buyer is Zhenyuan Monastery | Calligraphy Museum, Japan / Y&I: §33 |

* It is possible that this transaction was effected primarily to get a market certificate, without which the camel would not have been allowed through the border checks (draught animals had a potential role in battle).

law; commoners have private contracts' (*guan you zhengfa, ren cong siqi* 官有政法，人從私契) [e.g. 64TAM4:39]. This phrase is more elaborate than the simpler phrase 'the people have private needs' (*min you siyao* 民有私要) found in contracts prepared during the period of the Gaochang kingdom [e.g. 72TAM153]. Hansen (1995: 5–6) contrasts the Chinese ideal 'for individuals to draft a private agreement without depending on the judicial system to enforce it' with MacCormack's (1990: 235) definition of a modern Western contract as 'an agreement between two or more parties which the law makes enforceable, provided certain conditions are met'.[4] This is a fundamental distinction between early Chinese contracts and the modern Western view of contracts. In this light, the inclusion in the Chinese documents of an agreed penalty for reneging on a contractual obligation appears all the more necessary.

#### *The contents of the contracts*

Regular features of the contracts included the date, place and names of the people making the contract, names of witnesses, details of the contractual arrangement and, where appropriate, the rate of interest to be paid. Most contracts also included a penalty to be paid if either party changed his mind and wished to cancel the contract. The penalty is usually expressed as double the original price agreed, and is paid by the person cancelling to the other party.

Yamamoto and Ikeda (1987: 35–8) have classified the contents of the contracts found at Turfan, Kucha and Khotan as follows: tenancy contracts (92); loan contracts (69); purchase and sales contracts (33); employment contracts (25); lease contracts (11); piecework contracts (three); exchange contracts (two); receipts for cash (two), wills (one); miscellaneous, including contract with non-Chinese (one); and contents unclear (29). The documents from Kucha (11), Khotan (eight) and Dunhuang (four) are almost all loan contracts. The documents reveal that coins, textiles and grain were used in payment. Grain and textiles require more detailed studies in their own rights; here 'grain' is used inclusively for wheat, barley, millet and rice, husked or unhusked,[5] and the textile terms are indicated by precise Chinese terminology and concise English type, e.g. *lian* silk. The coins are described in the documents simply as gold, silver or copper coins, and can be seen in the light of the numismatic evidence presented in Part 2.

### *Pre-Gaochang kingdom (pre-AD 502)*

Four Chinese documents excavated at Turfan predate the establishment of the Gaochang kingdom (AD 502). The two earliest ones relate to purchases: the first, dated 273, concerns the purchase of a coffin, for the price of 20 *pi* of *lian* silk [66TAM53:9; Y&I: §1]. The second, dated 367, concerns an exchange of camels, expressed as a sale, in which two men swap one camel for another, at no gain. The penalty for cancelling the contract is ten *zhan* carpets [Y&I: §2] (Hou Can 1982). It is reasonable to assume that one of the men was travelling away from home, and needed to exchange a tired camel for a rested camel for the next leg of his journey (see Table 31). The third, dated 418, is a contract for the rental of three baskets of mulberries for silkworms, and the price is again reckoned in carpets [63TAM1:16; Y&I: §35] (see Table 32). The fourth, dated 423, is a contract for hiring short-term agricultural labour, and the payment is expressed in rolls (*pi*) of *dajuan* silk [TCW 1:39] (see Table 34).

In all four documents, payment is expressed exclusively in carpets or silk, indicating that these were probably the major forms of money in Turfan from the late third century to the early fifth century. The earlier Kharoshthi documents (see Chapter 8) show that carpets (Kharoshthi: *kojava*; *tavastaga*) were used in payments at sites along the southern route in the third century, which suggests that the use of carpets in payment at Turfan may have been part of a wider local tradition.[6] The Chinese wood slips from Loulan and Niya (see Chapter 7) have already shown how textiles served as a form of money in Eastern Central Asia from the mid third to the early fourth century. The Turfan contracts confirm that silk was also used in payments in Turfan at this time, and continued to be used into the early fifth century.

### *Gaochang kingdom (AD 502–640)*

Approximately one-third of the Turfan contracts are from the period of the Gaochang kingdom (502–640). Sales contracts are for vineyards (five),[7] fields (three), houses (two), slaves or farmhands (two), gardens (one) and land (one) (see Table 31). Two payments are expressed in textiles: in 509 a twenty-five-year-old female slave was sold for three and a half *zhang* of Qiuci *jin* brocade [75TKM99:6(a); Y&I: §3]; and the payment for a vineyard was made in textiles [67TAM90:32; Y&I: §5]. In another document the penalty for cancelling the contract (and probably also the agreed payment) was reckoned in *houjuan* silk [60TAM316:081(a); Y&I: §11]. Payments for all other purchases were expressed in silver coins, ranging from four to 390 silver coins, occasionally paid in instalments.

The three earliest loan contracts from this period concern loans of textiles: a piece of *jin* brocade loaned in 506, interest payable in *xingbu* cloth [75TKM88:1(b); Y&I: §36]; a piece of *jin* brocade loaned in 514, interest payable in *jin* brocade [75TKM99:6(b); Y&I: §37]; and some cotton loaned in 551, interest payable in *jin* brocade [60TAM326:014; Y&I: §38]. All subsequent loans are of grain (12), accommodation (four) and silver coins (four) (see Table 32). Loans of silver coins ranged from 2 to 12 coins. Just as interest on the textiles was payable in textiles, interest on grain loans was payable in grain; on accommodation and coin loans the interest was payable in coins. The usual penalty for cancelling a contract was double the original loan, or rent, and, if payment was not forthcoming, the equivalent value of the original loan was extracted from the assets of the borrower's family. Some loans were taken out by individuals, some by groups of up to eight people.

Thirty-five contracts concern lease of land during the Gaochang kingdom, described as fields (25), trees (four), vineyards (three), vegetable plots (two) and orchards (one) (see Table 33). The means of payment is known for 28 (80 per cent) of these; 15 were paid in grain, 12 in silver coins, and one in a kind of sauce. Payments for vegetable plots, trees, vineyards and orchards were made in silver coins. For fields they were made in either grain or silver coins, ranging from two to 25 silver coins. This suggests that superior quality land for higher-value cash crops was leased out for silver coins, and more ordinary fields were leased out for grain.

Six contracts concern seasonal labour, with payment in grain or food and silver coins (see Table 34). Three are for agricultural work: one (dated 565 or 625) reports payment in grain [TCW 1:39]; another (dated 613) in 20 silver coins, paid in advance [TCW 4:156]; and the third (dated 631) in 6 silver coins, also paid in advance [TCW 3:281]. For looking after sheep on the land, payment was in coin and grain or food; for looking after sheep in the monastery the payment was made in grain or food [TCW 3:207]. Payment for an unidentified task was made in food and silver coins, in instalments [TCW 4:39]. The payments were split evenly between grain or food (two), silver coins (two), and part grain part silver coins (two), with grain or food probably playing a larger role when food and lodging was provided, as for the shepherd working at the monastery.

### *Chinese rule (AD 640–780s)*

Seventeen documents record purchases after 640: horses (five), slaves (five), houses (three), cattle (two), camel (one), and hay (one) (see Table 31). Apart from one ox which was exchanged for another, all the payments were made in silk or silver coins. Where specified, the houses were paid for in silver coins, the horses in silk or silver coins; one slave was paid for in silk and silver coins, but the other slaves, the camel and one ox were paid for in silk, and the graveyard in *zaxin* (unidentified). There appears to have been a hierarchy whereby premium purchases were paid for in silver coins, and less important purchases in silk.

There are 34 loan contracts after 640: loan of silver coins (11), grain (seven), houses (five), unspecified coins (three), copper coins (three), *lian* and *jinlian* silk (two), ox and cart (one) and unknown items (one) (see Table 32). Interest was payable on the loans; the penalty for non-payment was the equivalent value of the original loan extracted from the assets of the borrower's family. Exactly 50 per cent of the loans were specified in coin, mostly in silver (*yinqian* 銀錢 or *wen* 文), ranging from 2 to 48 coins per loan, with five loans of 10 silver coins. At the beginning of the eighth century there was a sudden change to copper coins. Three loans are expressed in copper coins (*tongqian* 銅錢 or *qian* 錢), and the penalties are more varied. The first, dated 703, has a penalty payable in land or assets [64TAM35:15; Y&I: §89]; the second, dated 708, has a penalty of double the loan ($2 \times 320 = 640$ copper coins)

**Table 32**
**Contracts of letting and hiring, Turfan**

| Date | Goods loaned | Terms agreed | Other | References |
|---|---|---|---|---|
| 418 | 3 baskets of mulberries | Reckoned in carpets | – | 63TAM1:16 / Y&I: §35 |
| 506 | 1 *zhang* of yellow Qiuci *zhong jin* brocade, made in Gaochang | To repay 1.5 *zhang* of *jin* brocade by 30th day of 2nd month, interest at 3 *zhang* of *xingbu* cloth per month | Borrower is brother of Buddhist monk | 75TKM88:1(b) / Y&I: §36 |
| 514 | ½ *zhang* of white *jin* brocade | To repay half *zhang* of *jin* brocade by 30th day of 10th month; thereafter interest payable at 1 *zhang* of *shengbu* cloth per month | – | 75TKM99:6(b) / Y&I: §37 |
| 551 | 60 *pi* of cotton 40 *chi* of *jin* brocade | To repay by 30th day of 8th month, thereafter interest payable at ( . . . ) and 4 *chi* of *jin* brocade per month | – | 60TAM326:014 / Y&I: §38 |
| 583 | Grain | To repay by 8th month; monthly interest payable | 8 people borrowing (one of borrowers was brother of Buddhist monk); family will be responsible | Y&I: §39 |
| (593?) | 12 silver coins | To repay 24 silver coins within 9 months | If borrower fails to repay or absconds, value of original price to be extracted from his family's assets | O.4886 / Y&I: §40 |
| 597 | House | Coins | If borrower fails to repay by deadline, then he must pay double | 72TAM153:35(b) / Y&I: §41 |
| 598 | Grain | Grain | If borrower fails to repay by deadline, then he must pay double | 60TAM313:091–1 / Y&I: §42 |
| 598 | Loan | – | 7 people borrowing | 60TAM313:091–2 / Y&I: §43 |
| 602 | 2 silver coins | To repay in coins and grain | If borrower fails to repay or absconds, value of original price to be extracted from his family's assets | 64TAM34:12, 14 / Y&I: §44 |
| 602 | Grain | – | If borrower fails to repay by deadline, then he must pay double | 64TAM34:101 / Y&I: §45 |
| 602 | Grain | Interest payable in grain | If borrower fails to repay by deadline, then he must pay double | 64TAM34:102 / Y&I: §46 |
| Gaochang period | Grain | Interest payable in grain | If borrower fails to repay by deadline, then he must pay double. If borrower fails to repay or absconds, value of original price to be extracted from his family's assets | 64TAM34:11 / Y&I: §47 |
| Gaochang period | *Die* cloth (by weight); 3 *pi* of *bacongbu* cloth | To repay within 8 months; interest payable in *die* cloth | If borrower fails to repay by deadline, then he must pay double | 64TAM34:13 / Y&I: §48 |
| 606 | Grain | Interest payable in grain | 5 people borrowing. If borrowers fail to repay by deadline, then they must pay double. If borrower fails to repay or absconds, then extract value of original price from family assets | 60TAM321:011, 012 / Y&I: §49 |

(*cont.*)

**Table 32**
***(cont.)***

| Date | Goods loaned | Terms agreed | Other | References |
|---|---|---|---|---|
| 606 | Grain | Interest payable in grain | 6 people borrowing. If borrowers fail to repay by deadline, then they must pay double. If borrower fails to repay or absconds, then extract value of original price from family assets | 60TAM321:15 / Y&I: §50 |
| 606 | Silver coins | Interest payable | – | 60TAM321:014 / Y&I: §51 |
| 606 | (Silver) coins | – | If borrower fails to repay or absconds, then extract value of original price from family assets | 60TAM321 / Y&I: §52 |
| 610? | Grain | Interest payable in grain | 2 people borrowing. If fail to repay or absconds, then extract value of original price from family assets | 60TAM320:131, 122 / Y&I: §53 |
| 611 | Grain | Interest payable in grain | 8 people borrowing | 60TAM320:132,133, 134 / Y&I: §54 |
| 620 | Grain | – | – | 60TAM339:502 / Y&I: §55 |
| 624 | 1 cartload of sheep dung and 5 cartloads of kindling | To repay in grain | If borrower fails to repay by deadline, then he must pay double | 67TAM80:13 / Y&I: §56 |
| Gaochang period | Rooms | Silver coins, interest payable at one-fifteenth per month | 2 nuns borrowing | 67TAM364:92 / Y&I: §57 |
| Gaochang period | Rooms | – | – | 69TKM38:4 / Y&I: §58 |
| Gaochang period | Rooms | – | – | 72TAM153:41 / Y&I: §59 |
| Gaochang period | Grain | – | If borrower fails to repay or absconds, then extract value of original price from family assets | 60TAM092(a) / Y&I: §60 |
| Gaochang period | Grain | – | If borrower fails to repay or absconds, then extract value of original price from family assets | 64TAM25:12 / Y&I: §61 |
| Gaochang period | (Silver) coins | To pay back 7½ (silver) coins by certain date, thereafter interest payable monthly | If borrower fails to repay by deadline, then he must pay double. If fails to repay or absconds, then extract value of original price from family assets | 72TAM153:35(a) / Y&I: §62 |
| Gaochang period | (Silver) coins | – | If borrower fails to repay by deadline, then he must pay double. If fails to repay or absconds, then extract value of original price from family assets | 72TAM153:42 / Y&I: §63 |
| Gaochang period | (Silver) coins | – | If borrower fails to repay or absconds, then extract value of original price from family assets | 72TAM153:44 / Y&I: §64 |
| 640 | House | 15 silver coins, interest payable at $\frac{1}{15}$ per month | – | 64TKM1:33(a2) / Y&I: §65 |
| 648 | House | Rent payable in (silver) coins | – | 72TAM204:18 / Y&I: §66 |
| 659 | Grain | – | – | 64TAM20:34 / Y&I: §67 |

**Table 32**
**(*cont.*)**

| Date | Goods loaned | Terms agreed | Other | References |
|---|---|---|---|---|
| 660 | 10 silver coins | To repay in silver coin, interest payable at 10% per month | If borrower fails to repay or absconds, then extract value of original price from family assets | 64TAM4:38 / Y&I: §68 |
| 661 | 30 *pi* of *lian* silk | Interest payable at 4 *pi* per month, or 5 *pi* per month if payment is late | If borrower fails to repay or absconds, then extract value of original price from family assets | 64:TAM4:34 / Y&I: §69 |
| Tang | (Silver) coins | – | – | 69TAM137:1–5 / Y&I: §70 |
| 664 | Ox and cart | – | 6 people borrowing | 60TAM338:322 / Y&I: §71 |
| 665 | 10 (silver) coins | Interest payable at 10% per month | If borrower fails to repay or absconds, then extract value of original price from family assets | 67TAM363:9 / Y&I: §72 |
| 665 | 3 *pi* of *jinlian* silk | Interest-free if loan returned within 10 days, thereafter interest payable monthly | If borrower fails to repay or absconds, then extract value of original price from family assets If *lian* silk is taken to Anxi and rewards are received, then only repay 2 *pi*, if no rewards only goods, then repay 3 *pi*. | 64TAM4:36 / Y&I: §73 |
| 665 | 48 silver coins<br>24 silver coins | Interest-free if loan returned within 10 days. thereafter interest payable monthly | 2 borrowers. If borrowers fail to repay or abscond, then extract value of original price from family assets | 64TAM4:53 / Y&I: §74 |
| 664–5 | Loan | – | – | 64TAM4:51, 52 / Y&I: §75 |
| 666 | 10 silver coins | Interest at 10.5% per month | If borrower fails to repay or absconds, then extract value of original price from family assets | 64TAM4:39 / Y&I: §76 |
| 668 | 20 silver coins | Interest at 10% per month | If borrower fails to repay or absconds, then extract value of original price from family assets | 64TAM4:40 / Y&I: §77 |
| 670 | 40 silver coins | Interest at 10% per month | If borrower fails to repay or absconds, then extract value of original price from family assets | 64TAM4:41 / Y&I: §78 |
| 670 | 10 silver coins | Interest at 10% per month | If borrower fails to repay or absconds, then extract value of original price from family assets | 64TAM4:37 / Y&I: §79 |
| 673 | Silver coins | Interest payable | If borrower fails to repay or absconds, then extract value of original price from family assets | 64TAM19:45, 46 / Y&I: §80 |
| 674 | 20 silver coins | Interest at 10% per month | – | 64TAM19:36 / Y&I: §81 |
| 674 | 10 (silver) coins | – | – | 60TAM330:26–4 / Y&I: §82 |
| 677 | 8 silver coins | Interest at 1/8 per month | If borrower fails to repay or absconds, then extract value of original price from family assets | 67TAM363:7–2 / Y&I: §83 |
| Tang | Coins | – | – | 65TAM40:33 / Y&I: §84 |
| Tang | Coins | – | – | 65TAM40:30 / Y&I: §85 |

(*cont.*)

**Table 32**
**(*cont.*)**

| Date | Goods loaned | Terms agreed | Other | References |
|---|---|---|---|---|
| Tang | House | To repay in coins, in instalments | Penalty payable in coins | 65TAM40:28 / Y&I: §86 |
| Tang | House | – | – | 65TAM42:92 / Y&I: §87 |
| Tang | House | – | Penalty for reneging on contract is 24 silver coins | 65TAM40:29 / Y&I: §88 |
| 703 | 320 copper coins | Interest to be paid according to the law | Otherwise repay in land | 64TAM35:15 / Y&I: §89 |
| 708 | 320 copper coins | To repay . . . 64 coins' worth of food by the eighth month, 64 coins' worth of food by the ninth month | If borrower fails to repay by deadline, then he must pay double. If borrower fails to repay or absconds, then extract value of original price from family assets | 75TAM239:12 / Y&I: §90 |
| Tang | Grain | Interest at 10% per month | If borrower fails to repay or absconds, then extract value of original price from family assets | Ast.ii.4.081 & 079b / Y&I: §91 |
| Tang | Grain | Interest payable | – | 67TAM78:39 / Y&I: §92 |
| 720 | Grain | Interest payable | If borrower fails to repay or absconds, then extract value of original price from family assets | 72TAM184:6 / Y&I: §93 |
| Tang | Grain | For every 5 units borrowed, must repay 7 units | If borrower fails to repay or absconds, then extract value of original price from family assets | Otani 1036 / Y&I: §94 |
| Tang | Grain | – | – | M.364 / Y&I: §95 |
| 765 | Grain | – | Official document of joint mutual security groups in Jiaohe district, begging to borrow with interest from price-regulating granaries | D. A.TIII 315 / Y&I: §96 |
| Tang | Loan | Interest payable | – | Otani 8060 / Y&I: §97 |
| Kaiyuan period (713–41) | Coins | – | – | 72TAM184 / Y&I: §Add12. |

[75TAM239:12; Y&I: §90]; and the third, dated early eighth century, is incomplete [72TAM184; Y&I: §Ad.12] (see Table 32).

The functions of the loans were seldom stated, but two loans of silk, one in silk and one in silver coins, were used to make journeys [64TAM4:36; Y&I: 73 and 64TAM4:53; Y&I: §74]. The two contracts, both dated 665, stated that, if the borrower returned to Xizhou (Turfan) within ten days, then the loan was interest-free. Thereafter a monthly interest charge was payable. The ultimate penalty was the value of the original loan extracted from the borrower's family assets. The loan of silk (3 *pi*) had an extra clause: if the silk was taken to Anxi (= Kucha, the *duhufu* or administrative centre, 658–70) and rewards were received, then the borrower was to return only 2 *pi* of silk. If no rewards were received, then the full 3 *pi* was be repaid.[8] The documents were found together in the same tomb [64TAM4] of the soldier and moneylender Zuo Chongxi, buried in 673. It would seem that Zuo himself had business in Anxi, and was keen that the borrower of the silk might save him a journey to Anxi. He was prepared to offer him an interest-free loan and a discounted repayment if he succeeded in acting as courier for him and brought the rewards back with him.

A total of fifteen contracts were found rolled up in a bundle in Zuo's tomb. One is illegible; the rest concern the purchase of a fifteen-year-old slave (one), the purchase of ninety bundles of hay (one), Zuo's lending out of money or silk (eight), and Zuo's renting land from the poor (four). As the usual custom was for contracts to be recycled or destroyed at completion, it is assumed that Zuo hoped they would be completed, or prove ownership, in his next life. Zuo Chongxi and his contracts are discussed more fully by Hansen (1995: 33–9) and Chen Guocan (1983a, 1983b).

Forty-nine documents record the leasing of land: fields (43), vineyards (four), vegetable plots (one) and houses (one) (see Table 33). Where specified the repayments were made as follows: vegetable plot and house in silver coins, vineyards in silver coins until the beginning of the eighth century and then in copper coins; and fields in grain (17), in silver coins (seven), in grain and silver coins (one) and in copper coins (two).

**Table 33**
**Contracts of leasing land, Turfan**

| Date | Type of land leased | Rent agreed | Penalty for missing deadline | References |
|---|---|---|---|---|
| 584 | Field | 5 silver coins | – | 60TAM326:016 / Y&I: §98 |
| *c.* 584 | Field | 16 silver coins | If borrower misses deadline, then he must pay double | 60TAM326:017, 018 / Y&I: §99 |
| *c.* 584 | Field | Grain | If borrower misses deadline, then he must pay double | 60TAM326:013 / Y&I: §100 |
| 586 | Vegetable garden | 5 silver coins | – | 67TAM364:102 / Y&I: §101 |
| 587 | Trees | Coins | If borrower misses deadline, then he must pay double | 67TAM365:5 / Y&I: §102 |
| 588 | Field | 9 silver coins | – | 60TAM308:81 / Y&I: §103 |
| 588 | Field | Grain | – | 60TAM365:71 / Y&I: §104 |
| 588 | Date-trees | – | 2 silver coins | 67TAM364:11 / Y&I: §105 |
| *c.* 588 | Field | Grain | If borrower misses deadline, then he must pay double | 67TAM364:5 / Y&I: §106 |
| 589 | Field | Grain | – | 67TAM365:72 / Y&I: §107 |
| 589 | Field | Grain | If borrower misses deadline, then he must pay double | 67TAM365:14 / Y&I: §108 |
| 586–9 | Trees or vineyard | – | – | 67TAM365:91 / Y&I: §109 |
| 586–9 | Field? | Coin | If borrower misses deadline, then he must pay double | 67TAM365:92 / Y&I: §110 |
| 586–9 | Field | 25 silver coins | – | 67TAM364:15 / Y&I: §111 |
| 586–9 | Field | – | – | 67TAM364:7 / Y&I: §112 |
| 596 | Field | Grain | – | 72TAM153:39, 40 (a) / Y&I: §113 |
| 616 | Field | Grain | If borrower misses deadline, then he must pay double | 72TAM151:94 / Y&I: §114 |
| 616 | Field | Grain | If borrower misses deadline, then he must pay double | 72TAM151:13 / Y&I: §115 |
| 619 | Field | – | – | 73TAM116:56 / Y&I: §116 |
| 620 | Field | – | – | 73TAM116:58, 59 / Y&I: §117 |
| 623 | Vegetable garden | 2 silver coins | If borrower misses deadline, then he must pay double | TCW 3:310 / Y&I: §118 |
| 623 | Field | Grain | If borrower misses deadline, then he must pay double | 69TAM140:185 / Y&I: §119 |
| 625 | Trees | 8 silver coins | Late payments incur charge of 10% | 60TAM338:144 / Y&I: §120 |
| 629 | Field | Grain | – | 72TAM155:31 / Y&I: §121 |
| 629 | Field | 20 silver coins | – | 69TAM338:141 / Y&I: §122 |
| 632 | Field | Grain | If borrower misses deadline, then he must pay double | 69TAM117:573 / Y&I: §123 |
| Gaochang period | Orchard | Silver coins | If borrower misses deadline, then he must pay double | 72TAM153:38(a) / Y&I: §124 |
| Gaochang period | Vineyard | 7 silver coins | If borrower misses deadline, then he must pay double | 67TAM364:6 / Y&I: §125 |
| Gaochang period | Vineyard | Sauce | If borrower misses deadline, then he must pay double | 72TAM153:36, 37 / Y&I: §126 |
| Gaochang period | Field | Grain | – | 69TAM135:7 / Y&I: §127 |
| Gaochang period | Field | Grain | If borrower misses deadline, then he must pay double | 64TAM25:13 / Y&I: §128 |
| Gaochang period | Field | Grain | If borrower misses deadline, then he must pay double | 66TAM48:22 / Y&I: §129 |
| Gaochang period | Field | Grain | – | 72TAM155:32 / Y&I: §130 |
| Gaochang period | Field | (Silver) coins | – | 67TAM364:12 / Y&I: §131 |
| Gaochang period | Field | – | – | 67TAM364:91 / Y&I: §132 |

(*cont.*)

**Table 33**
**(*cont.*)**

| Date | Type of land leased | Rent agreed | Penalty for missing deadline | References |
|---|---|---|---|---|
| 640 | Field | Grain | – | 64TAM15:23 / Y&I: §133 |
| 641 | Field | Grain | – | 64TAM15:16 / Y&I: §134 |
| 642 | Field | Grain | – | 69TAM117:57/11 / Y&I: §135 |
| 642 | Field | Grain | If borrower misses deadline, then he must pay double | 69TAM117:57/10 / Y&I: §136 |
| 643 | Field | Grain | If borrower fails to repay, then take from family assets | 59TAM301:15/4/1,2 / Y&I: §137 |
| 648 | Field | Grain | – | 64TAM24:26 / Y&I: §138 |
| 649 | Field | 16 silver coins | – | 64TAM10:34 / Y&I: §139 |
| *c.*649–50 | Field | Silver coins | – | 64TAM10:35 / Y&I: §140 |
| 651 | Field | Grain | – | 64TAM24:28 / Y&I: §141 |
| 653 | Field | 6 silver coins | – | 64TAM10:36 / Y&I: §142 |
| 653 | Field | 24 silver coins | – | 64TAM10:33 / Y&I: §143 |
| *c.*649–53 | Field | – | – | 64TAM10:51 / Y&I: §144 |
| 658 | Field | Grain | – | 67TAM74:1–4 / Y&I: §145 |
| 658 | Field | – | – | 67TAM74:1–2 / Y&I: §146 |
| 658 | Field | – | – | 67TAM74:1–9 / Y&I: §147 |
| 659 | Field | Grain | – | Otani 2828 / Y&I: §148 |
| 660/654 | Field | 15 silver coins | To pay in instalments | 64TAM10:40 / Y&I: §149 |
| 655 | Field | Grain | If borrower misses deadline, then he must pay double | 69TAM137:1–2, 1–4(1) / Y&I: §150 |
| *c.*660 | Field | (Silver) coins | – | 69TAM137:1–1, 3 / Y&I: §151 |
| 661 | Vegetable garden | (Silver coins) | To pay in instalments | 64TAM4:42 / Y&I: §152 |
| 661 | Field | – | If borrower misses deadline, then he must pay double | 64TAM10:39 / Y&I: §153 |
| 662 | Field | (Silver) coins | – | 60TAM317:30–4 / Y&I: §154 |
| 662 | Field | Grain | – | 60TAM317:30–1 / Y&I: §155 |
| 661–5 | Field | Grain | – | 60TAM332:9–4 / Y&I: §156 |
| 663 | Land | (Silver) coins | Penalty of 50 coins | 60TAM337:18(a) / Y&I: §157 |
| 666 | Field | – | – | 64TAM4:43 / Y&I: §158 |
| 666 | Vineyard | 35 (silver) coins | – | 64TAM4:45 / Y&I: §159 |
| 668 | Field | – | – | 60TAM330:26–1 / Y&I: §160 |
| 670 | Field | Grain + 30 silver coins | – | 64TAM4:33 / Y&I: §161 |
| 668–74 | Field | – | – | 60TAM330:26–3 (1) (2) / Y&I: §162 |
| 668–74 | Vineyard | – | – | 60TAM330:26–2 / Y&I: §163 |
| 651–76 | Field | – | – | 64TAM19:47 / Y&I: §164 |
| mid 7th c. | Field | Grain | If borrower misses deadline, then he must pay double. If he fails to repay or absconds, then extract from family assets | 64TAM15:22 / Y&I: §165 |
| mid 7th c. | Field | – | – | 64TAM15:27 / Y&I: §166 |
| mid 7th c. | Field | – | – | 59TAM301:142–2 / Y&I: §167 |
| mid 7th c. | Vegetable garden | (Silver) coins | – | 65TAM40:35 / Y&I: §168 |
| 677? | Field | – | – | 67TAM363:7–4 / Y&I: §169 |
| 681 | Field | – | – | 69TAM117:57/12 / Y&I: §170 |
| 687 | Field | Grain | If borrower misses deadline, then he must pay double | 64TAM35:20 / Y&I: §171 |
| 7th c. | Vineyard | 20 (silver) coins | – | Otani 3101, 3103, 3104 / Y&I: §172 |

**Table 33 (*cont.*)**

| Date | Type of land leased | Rent agreed | Penalty for missing deadline | References |
|---|---|---|---|---|
| 692 | Field | Grain | If borrower misses deadline, then he must pay double | Ast.iii.4.090 / M.314 / Y&I: §173 |
| 703 | Vineyard | Copper coins | To pay in instalments of 480, 640, 800, 800 | 67TAM93:2 / Y&I: §174 |
| 736 | Field | Grain | If borrower misses deadline, then he must pay double | Otani 3107 / Y&I: §175 |
| c. 736 | Field | – | – | Otani 3107 / Y&I: §176 |
| 746 | Field | 450 coins | If borrower misses deadline, then he must pay double | Calligraphy Museum, Japan / Y&I: §177 |
| 748 | Field | – | – | 73TAM506:04–2 / Y&I: §178 |
| 8th c. | Field | Grain | – | 73TAM506:04–16 / Y&I: §179 |
| Tang | Field | – | – | 67TAM78:46 / Y&I: §180 493, 494 / 60TAM337:119 / Y&I: §180–8 |
| Tang | Field | – | – | 67TAM78:513 / Y&I: §181 |
| Tang | Field | – | – | 64TAM78:512 / Y&I: §182 |
| Tang | Field | – | – | 67TAM78:493 / Y&I: §183 |
| Tang | Field | – | – | 60TAM337:119 / Y&I: §184 |
| Tang | Field | – | – | 60TAM313:094 / Y&I: §185 |
| Tang | Field | – | – | Otani 3102 / Y&I: §186 |
| Tang | Field | – | – | Otani 3105 / Y&I: §187 |
| Tang | Field | – | – | Or. 8212–910 / Kao.091 / Y&I: §188 |
| Tang | Field | – | Penalty payable in coins | Otani 4914 / Y&I: §189 |

Payments in coins range from 6 to 35 silver coins, and from 450 to 800 copper coins. Repayments for leasing land were therefore made in coin and grain, with a change from silver to copper coins from the beginning of the eighth century. The distinction between repayments in coin and grain suggests that superior-quality land, possibly for higher-value cash crops, was leased out for coins, and more ordinary field-land for grain.

The majority (69.5 per cent) of short-term labour contracts are from the period under Chinese rule, and there is a marked difference in the contracts after 640 (see Table 34). The nature of the work changed from agricultural seasonal labour to beacon-watch (13), delivering silk (two) and taking horses to pasture (one). By then, it was standard practice to pay for short-term labour in silver coins. The highest payment for labour during this period was 20 silver coins. Keeping watch at a beacon was measured at 15 days to the watch, with payment at 4 to 10 silver coins, usually paid in advance. Yang Jiping (1997) suggests that the usual payment for one watch was 4 to 5 silver coins, and that the fee later rose because of a decrease in the value of silver coins, but this should be regarded with caution as not all the documents are dated. The change in the nature of the work is probably associated with the different system of taxation introduced by the Chinese after 640, including a labour tax, which Yang suggests replaced the Gaochang tax payments in silver coin (e.g. *dingzheng qian*). The contracts for beacon-watch were private arrangements hiring substitutes to do watch-duty. In these cases, the person actually doing the watch-duty (and not the taxpayer) was considered responsible for any mishaps during that period of duty. By transferring responsibility from the taxpayer to the hired person, the Chinese government at Gaochang acknowledged, possibly even approved, the practice of subcontracting out tax obligations. Taking horses out to pasture and delivering silk may also have been tasks that were subcontracted out.

### The contracts from Kucha, Khotan and Dunhuang (see Tables 35–7)

The Chinese contracts found at Kucha, Khotan and Dunhuang appear to support the observations drawn from the evidence from Turfan, although these are far fewer in number and of a slightly later date.

Eleven contracts have been retrieved from Kucha [Y&I: §236–246], all of which are dated to the second half of the eighth century (see Table 35). Eight of these are loan contracts, including seven for loans of coins. One is dated to the Dali period (766–79); four documents are dated 781;[9] one to 782 and one to 786. The earliest (dated 766–79) is for a loan of 500 coins; four (781) and probably the incomplete document (782) are for 1,000 coins; and one (786) is for 15,000 coins. The coins are expressed as *qian*, and although no further description of the coins is given, the large quantities, measurable in units and half-units of one thousand indicate these must be Chinese-style bronze coins. There are also two incomplete documents concerning a loan of grain, and hiring labour.

Eight contracts have been found at Khotan, dated from 782 to the end of the eighth century (see Table 36). All record loans: of grain (one), coins (six), and a donkey (one). One loan of 500 coins also records the mortgaging of an ivory comb [Y&I: §248].

**Table 34**
**Contracts of hiring labour, Turfan (adapted from Yang Jiping 1997)**

| Date | Labour required | Payment | Special considerations | References |
|---|---|---|---|---|
| 423 | Short term agricultural work | *pi* rolls of *dajuan* silk | – | TCW 1:39 |
| 565 or 625 | Short term agricultural work | Grain | 2nd month: grain for (?) people<br>3rd month: grain for 20 people<br>4th month: grain for 6 people<br>5th month: grain for 10 people<br>6th month: grain for 6 people<br>7th month: grain for 10 people | TCW 3:225–234 |
| 574 or 586 | To look after sheep on the land | (Silver) coins and food | Food paid in advance, coins paid after | 60TAM326:019 / Y&I: §190 / TCW5:155 |
| 613 | Agricultural labour | 20+ silver coins | Paid in advance | TCW 4:156 |
| 624 | To look after sheep in the monastery | Food | Paid in advance | TCW 3:207 |
| 631 | Agricultural labour | 6 (silver) coins and tools | Paid in advance | TCW 3:281 |
| 637 | (Uncertain) | 7 silver coins and food | Paid part in advance, part after | TCW 4:39 |
| 642 | Beacon watch-duty | 5 silver coins | Paid in advance | TCW 4:120 |
| 643 | Beacon watch–duty | 4 silver coins | – | TCW 4:147 |
| 655 | Beacon watch-duty at Hetou for 1 watch of 15 days | 5 (silver) coins | Paid in advance | TCW 5:57 |
| 655 | Beacon watch-duty for 15 days | 7 (silver) coins | 4 (silver) coins paid in advance | TCW 5:59 |
| 655 | Beacon watch-duty at Fuxian for 1 [watch] of 15 days | (Uncertain) | Paid part in advance, part after | TCW 5:61 |
| 655 | Beacon watch-duty for 1 watch of 15 days | 6 silver coins | Paid in advance | TCW 5:62 |
| 655 | Beacon watch-duty for 1 watch | 4 silver coins | Paid in advance | TCW 5:84 |
| 656 | Beacon watch-duty for 15 days | Silver coins | Paid in advance | TCW 5:111 |
| 658 | Beacon watch-duty for 15 days | 7 silver coins | Paid in advance | TCW 5:142 |
| 662 | To deliver silk | Silver coins | Paid part in advance, part after | TCW 6:182 |
| 662 | To deliver silk | (Uncertain) | (Uncertain) | TCW 6:183 |
| c.668 | Beacon watch-duty for 1 watch of 15 days | 8 silver coins | Paid in advance | TCW 5:164 |
| Gaozong | To pasture horses | 14 silver coins | Paid in instalments | TCW 6:590 |
| Wuzhou period | Beacon watch-duty at Jiaohe for 1 watch of 15 days | Silver coins | Paid in advance | TCW 7:270 |
| Wuzhou period | Beacon watch-duty at Shenshan for 1 watch of 15 days | 10 silver coins | Paid in advance | TCW 7:271 |
| Tang | Beacon watch-duty at Jiaohe | 10 silver coins | Paid in advance | TCW 7:272 |
| Tang | Beacon watch-duty | Coins | – | TCW 7:273 |
| Tang | Beacon watch-duty | Coins | Paid part in advance, part after | TCW 9:226 |
| Tang | Beacon watch-duty | – | Paid in advance | TCW 9:227 |
| Tang | (Beacon watch-duty) | Coins | – | TCW 9:229 |

Other coin loans are for 1,000 [Y&I: §249] and 15,000 [Y&I: §250 and Y&I: §251]; two other coin loans are incomplete. Interest was payable in grain on the grain loan, and in coin on the coin loans and donkey loan. The amounts of 15,000 coins match the largest quantity of coins loaned at Kucha. As in the Kucha documents, the coins must be Chinese-style bronze coins. The documents from Khotan should also be considered in the light of contemporary Khotanese and bilingual Chinese–Khotanese documents (see Chapter 11).

One contract from Dunhuang concerns the sale of a thirteen-year-old non-Chinese slave, paid for in textiles (Y&I: §256) (see Table 37). It resembles seven official passes excavated in front of Cave 122, and may once have been attached to such a pass, probably as proof of ownership of the slave (Hansen 1995: 50).[10]

**The tomb inventories from Turfan (see Table 38)**

A total of 43 tomb inventories have been found at the Astana and Kara-khoja cemeteries, Turfan (*TCW*; Hansen 1998b). The earliest dated documents are from 384, and the latest from the 640s. They cover the period before the Gaochang kingdom, the Gaochang kingdom and the early years after the Chinese

**Table 35**
**Documents from Kucha**

| Date | Loan/Hire | Terms agreed | Special considerations | Reference |
|---|---|---|---|---|
| 780 | Loan of grain | – | – | Huang Wenbi 1958: 94 / Y&I: §237 |
| 781 | Loan of 1,000 coins | To repay 200 coins per month for 6 months (total of 1,200 coins) | If borrower fails to pay, the guarantors are responsible | Otani 8047 / Y&I: §238 |
| 781 | Loan of (1,000) coins | – | – | Otani 8048–8054 / Y&I: §239 |
| 781 | Loan of (1,000) coins | To repay 200 coins per month for 6 months (total of 1,200 coins) | – | Otani 8056 / Y&I: §240 |
| 781? | Loan of coins | – | – | Otani 8055 / Y&I: §241 |
| Tang | Loan of textiles | – | Document relating to contract in Kuchan language | Y&I: §243 |
| Tang | Hiring labour | – | – | Y&I: §246 |
| Dali period (766–79) | 500 coins | – | – | Stein S.5872, S.5870 / Y&I: §248 |
| 782 | 1,000 coins | – | – | Stein S.5876 / Y&I: §249 |
| 786 | 15,000 coins | – | – | JASB LXX–1, ex.1 / Y&I: §250 |

**Table 36**
**Loan documents from Khotan**

| Date | Loan | Terms agreed | Special considerations | Reference |
|---|---|---|---|---|
| 782 | Grain | To repay within 9 months | Otherwise lender will take borrower's livestock to the value of the loan | Stein S.5871 / Y&I: §247 |
| Dali period (766–79) | 500 coins | To repay with interest | Borrower pledges an ivory comb | Stein S.5872, 5870 / Y&I: §248 |
| 782 | 1,000 coins | Interest payable at 10% per month | Otherwise lender will take borrower's livestock to the value of the loan | Stein S.5867 / Y&I: §249 |
| 786 | 15,000 coins | To repay 16,000 coins within 8 months | Otherwise lender will take borrower's livestock to the value of the loan | Hoernle 1899, no. 1 / Y&I: §250 |
| 787 | 15,000 coins | – | – | Stein S.5869 / Y&I: §251 |
| 790 | Coins | – | – | Stein S.5862 / Y&I: §252 |
| Zhenyuan period (785–804) | Coins | – | – | Stein S.6967, 6971 / Y&I: §253 |
| c.790 | Donkey | – | – | Stein S.6972 / Y&I: §254 |

takeover. Most of the tombs had been disturbed and only occasionally is it possible to verify the inventories against the objects found in the tombs. While it is likely that some of the items in the lists related to real objects, the enormous quantities quoted in others suggest that there was an element of fantasy involved. There may have been an expected set of items, including for example the fantastic 1,000,000,000,000 *zhang* of 'silk for climbing up to heaven' (*pantianxi* 攀天系) which is found frequently in the inventories between 543 and the 640s [e.g. 72TAM170:9; and 64TAM15:6], and was clearly a part of the desired burial assemblage.[11] However, most items on the inventories are individual garments or accessories, or quantities of money, which would be needed in the next world. Table 38 lists only the gold, silver, copper coins and textiles mentioned in the documents. It reveals a number of important developments between 384 and the 640s.

The two earliest inventories, dated 384, belonged to a man and his wife, buried in Tomb 305. Both lists include many items, ending with two copper coins and silk. The man's inventory indicates 'two copper coins for holding in the hand' and six bolts of silk. The woman's inventory indicates two copper coins without specifying their location, and two *liang* of yellow silk. It is interesting that his silk is measured by length, and hers by weight. There is no mention of gold, silver or textiles.

One inventory of the early fifth century includes the phrase 'sufficient copper coins' (*tongqian zifu* 銅錢自副), perhaps referring to small copper coins made specially for burial purposes,[12] or to imagined coins. In either case, there was an intention to present (or at least represent) copper coins in the tomb.

Two inventories from different tombs, both dated 620, each list 14 *laqian*. As *la* refers to sacrifices made after the twelfth

**Table 37**
**Documents from Dunhuang**

| Date | Activity | Terms agreed | Special considerations | Reference |
|---|---|---|---|---|
| (744–58) | sale of 13-year-old non-Chinese slave | Buyer paid in textiles | It is possible that this was a market certificate once attached to an official pass (7 official passes dated 748 were excavated in front of Cave 122) | Y&I: §256 |
| 782 | 1,000 coins | – | Novice Ma at Huguo Monastery | Stein S.5867 / Giles 1957: §7529 |
| 782 | 17 piculs of grain | – | | Stein S.5871 / Giles 1957: §7531 |
| 787 | Loan (incomplete) | – | Dated Jianzhong year 8, which corresponds to Zhenyuan year 3 | Stein S.5869 / Giles 1957: §7563 |

month, these coins may have been a kind of temple coin. The significance of 14 *laqian* is not known.

Gold first appeared in the inventories in 418. Before the Gaochang kingdom was established in 502, gold was measured by weight, first expressed by the *liang* and later by the *jin*. Silver also first appeared in the pre-Gaochang period, reckoned by weight (*jin*). Gold and silver continued to be measured by weight in the early years of the Gaochang kingdom. Gold and silver were first expressed in terms of coins in the inventory dated *c.*551. In this document, gold was presented in two forms: both by weight and in coin. Thereafter, it is usual to see gold and silver expressed in coins; only one later inventory, dated 592, refers to gold and silver both by weight (the gold in *jin*, the silver in *liang*) and in coin. The quantity of gold coins ranges from 100 to 10,000. The quantity of silver coins ranges from 100 to 1,000,000. By contrast, the contracts from Turfan listed above refer to relatively small numbers of silver coins, up to a maximum of 390 silver coins (see above). The larger quantities of gold and silver coins listed in the tomb inventories must therefore be representational rather than actual. The quantities stated in the tomb inventories can also be compared with the gifts presented to the Buddhist monk Xuan Zang by the king of Gaochang: 100 *liang* of gold, 30,000 silver coins, and 500 *pi* of *ling* silk and *luo* silk (*Datang Dacisi si san cang fa shi zhuan*; Beal 1911: 30).

Textiles appear regularly in the inventories. In the earliest inventory, dated 384, yellow silk was held in the hand (perhaps a precursor to the *pantianxi*?). Cloth and silk appeared in larger quantities from 418. The tomb of Lady Peng, dated 459, lists 99,999 *pi* of *zacaijuan* silk and 99,999 *liang* of cotton (?). It is unique in several ways: the burial list was written on silk rather than on paper, and the tomb also contained 69 mini-bolts of silk of different designs. Most of the mini-bolts measured 2–5.5 cm in width, and the largest piece measured 13.5 × 5.5 cm. (Turfan WGS 1994). Textiles remained a very important part of the burial assemblage, reckoned in units of 100, 1,000, and 10,000, and by 591–2 in units of one million and even 10 million.

The inventories dated 567–92 do not mention gold or silver at all, and the massive quantities of textiles expressed in the inventories of the early 590s appear in great contrast to this absence. Whilst the break of over twenty years may appear significant, the contracts none the less indicate that silver coins were being used in the 580s to pay for leases of land. In this respect, although the documents are contemporary, the evidence in the contracts and the tomb inventories is contradictory. The contracts should be seen as evidence of actual everyday life; and the tomb inventories as wishful thinking for the next life.[13] Gold coins do not feature in the contracts at all, yet the inventories indicate that they were highly desired and that they represented purchasing power. Silver coins feature in both contracts and burial lists. Silver appears first in the inventories in the early sixth century, reaching one million silver coins in 548, but silver does not appear in any form in the contracts until the 580s. Clearly, the knowledge of and desire for gold and silver coins preceded and remained far greater than their general availability.

### Discussion: the contracts and the tomb inventories in perspective

From the evidence of the Turfan contracts alone, the following patterns emerge. From the late third century to the early sixth century, silk and carpets were the main forms of money, for purchases, loans and hiring labour.[14] After the establishment of the Gaochang kingdom in 502, textiles continued to be the main form of money, for purchases and loans, although the types changed from silk and carpets to silk and cloth (cotton or linen).[15] In the mid sixth century, a change occurred, and silver coins and/or grain replaced textiles and carpets, as the means of paying for loans, lease of land and hiring of labour. There appears to have been a hierarchy, with silver coins preferred for transactions of superior quality. As Jiang Boqin (1994: 36) has suggested, the economy of the Gaochang kingdom appears to have followed a silver standard.

After the Chinese takeover in 640 several changes took place. Silver coins remained the superior form of money, but silk largely replaced grain as the secondary form. Labour was paid for in silver coin; purchases were paid for in silver coins and/or silk; and loans were made mostly in silver coins and silk. There is a sudden watershed *c.*700 when copper coins replaced silver coins. The coin evidence found at the sites indicates that the silver coins must have been Sasanian drachms, or imitations, and the copper coins must have been Chinese coins, or local issues in the Chinese style.

The contracts form only about 15 per cent of the documents recovered from Turfan, and the tomb inventories an even smaller percentage, yet they identify the forms of money that

**Table 38**
**Tomb inventories from the Astana and Kara-khoja cemeteries, Turfan**

| Date | Gold | Silver | Copper coins | Textiles | Held in hand | Reference |
|---|---|---|---|---|---|---|
| 384 | – | – | 2 copper coins | – | 2 *liang* of yellow hand silk | 59TAM305:8 / TCW 1992:I, 3 |
| 384 | – | – | 2 copper coins | – | 2 copper coins | 59TAM305:17 / TCW 1992:I, 3 |
| 418 | 1,000 *liang* | – | – | 100 *pi* of *zhengbo sijuan* silk | Yellow *si* silk | 63TAM1:11 / TCW 1992:I, 5 |
| Longxing period *c.*423 | – | – | – | – | – | 75TKM96:15 / TCW 1992:I,29 |
| Early 5th c. | – | – | – | 100 *pi* . . . | – | 66TAM59:2 / TCW 1992:I. 12 |
| 425 | 1,000 *liang* | – | – | – | – | 75TKM96:17 / TCW 1992:I, 28 |
| 436 | – | – | – | – | – | 66TAM62:5 / TCW 1992:I, 47 |
| 459 | – | – | – | 99,999 *pi* of *zacaijuan* silk<br>99,999 *pi* of cotton (?) | – | Turfan WGS 1994 |
| Early 5th c. | – | – | – | – | – | 75TKM91:3 / TCW 1992:I, 55 |
| Early 5th c. | 1,000 *jin* | – | *Tongqian zifu* | 1,000 *pi* of *sejin* silk | 3 *zhang* of yellow *si* silk | 63TAM2:1 / TCW 1992:I, 85 |
| Jianping year 6 | – | – | – | 100,000 *pi* of *zase* textiles | – | 75TKM99:7 / TCW 1992:I, 90 |
| (?) | 100 *jin* | 100 *jin* | – | 100 *jin* of *si* silk | – | 75TKM99:16 / TCW 1992:I, 91 |
| Gaochang period | – | – | – | 100 *pi* . . .<br>10,000 *pi* of *jin* brocade | – | 75TKM90:19 / TCW 1992:I, 116 |
| *c.*551 | . . . *jin* of gold; 2,000 gold coins | 1,000 silver coins | – | 100 *pi* of *baijuan* silk; 1,000 *jin* of *luansi* silk | – | 59TAM303:01 / TCW 1992:I, 129 |
| 538 | 1,000 *jin* | 100 *jin* | – | *Xijin* silk | – | 73TAM524:34(h) / TCW 1992:I, 130 |
| 543 | 100 gold coins | 100 silver coins | – | 40 *pi* of *baijuan* silk<br>200 *pi* of *budie* cloth | – | 72TAM170:9 / TCW 1992:I, 143 |
| 548 | 10,000 gold coins | 1,000,000 silver coins | – | 1,000 *zhang* of *dajin* brocade<br>10,000 *pi* of *dalian* silk<br>1,000 *jin* of *jin* silk<br>10,000 bundles of *juan* silk | – | 72TAM170:77 / TCW 1992:I, 144 |
| 548 | 100 gold coins | – | – | 100 *pi* of *baijuan* silk<br>100 *pi* of *leishi* textiles<br>100 *pi* of *leidie* cloth<br>100 *pi* of *xinglei* textiles | – | 60TAM313:07/2 / TCW 1992:I, 200 |
| 557 | – | – | – | 100 *pi* of *baijuan* silk | – | 73TAM524:28 / TCW 1992:I, 131 |
| 558 | 300 gold coins | 500 silver coins | – | 100 *zhang* of *dajin* silk<br>100 *pi* of *ling* silk<br>100 *pi* of *luo* silk<br>100 *pi* of *juan* silk<br>100 *pi* of *qi* silk | – | 72TAM169:32 / TCW 1992:I, 207 |

(*cont.*)

**Table 38**
**(*cont.*)**

| Date | Gold | Silver | Copper coins | Textiles | Held in hand | Reference |
|---|---|---|---|---|---|---|
| 562 | 1,000 gold coins | 1,000 silver coins | – | 100 *pi* of *zajin* silk<br>700 *pi* of *juan* silk<br>600 *jin* of *jin* silk<br>1,500 *pi* of *die* cloth | – | 72TAM170:88 / TCW 1992:I, 145 |
| 567 | – | – | – | – | – | 67TAM88:12 / TCW 1992:I, 198 |
| 576 | – | – | – | – | – | 72TAM169:42 / TCW 1992:I, 208 |
| 591 | – | – | – | 10,000,000 *duan* each of several types of textiles<br>10,000,000 *pi* each of several types of textiles | – | 73TAM517:25 / TCW 1992:I, 254 |
| 592 | – | – | – | 1,000,000 *pi* each of several types of textiles<br>1,000,000 *duan* of *caijin* silk | – | 69TKM38:1 / TCW 1992:I, 251 |
| 592 | 1,000 *jin*<br>1,000 gold coins | 100 *liang*<br>100 silver coins | – | 1,000 *zhang* of *jin* silk<br>10,000 *pi* of *juan* silk<br>100 *pi* of *bailing* silk<br>100 *pi* of *xibu* cloth<br>100 *pi* of *xidie* cloth | – | 60TAM335:10 / TCW 1992:I, 253 |
| 596 | 10,000 gold coins | 10,000 silver coins | – | 100 *zhang* of *beijin* silk<br>1,000 *duan* of *zasecaijin* silk | – | 66TAM48:2 / TCW 1992:I, 334 |
| 597 | 1,000 gold coins | 1,000 silver coins | – | 100 *zhang* of *beijin* silk<br>1,000 *zhang* of *caijin* silk | – | 73TAM517:24 / TCW 1992:I, 255 |
| Gaochang period | – | – | – | 10,000 . . .<br>10,000 . . . 100 *jin* of *jin* brocade | – | 60TAM313:07/1 / TCW 1992:I, 289 |
| 604 | 1,000 gold coins | 1,000 silver coins | – | 10,000 *pi* of *jincai* silk | – | 66TAM48:1 / TCW 1992:I, 335 |
| 605 | 1,000 gold coins | 1,000 silver coins | – | 1,000 *zhang* of *baifujin* brocade<br>1,000 *duan* of *lingjuan* silk<br>1,000 *duan* of *zasejin* silk | – | 64TAM23:16 / TCW 1992:I, 306 |
| 605 | 10,000 (gold) coins | (silver) coins | – | Yellow . . . | – | 64TAM333:08/1–08/4 / TCW 1992:I, 307 |
| 607 | 10,000 gold coins | 10,000 silver coins | – | 1,000 *duan* of *jincai* silk | – | 73TAM520:4 / TCW 1992:I, 311 |
| 613 | 10,000 gold coins | 10,000 silver coins | – | 10,000 *pi* of *jincai* silk | – | 67TAM370:1 / TCW 1992:I, 331 |
| 617 | – | – | – | 1,000 *jin* of *zasejin* silk | – | 73TAM113:1 / TCW 1992:I, 332 |
| 617 | 100 gold coins | 100 silver coins | – | 50 *zhang* of *jin* brocade<br>100 *pi* of *juan* silk<br>1,000 *duan* of *lian* silk | – | 66TAM48:3 / TCW 1992: I, 336 |

**Table 38**
**(*cont.*)**

| Date | Gold | Silver | Copper coins | Textiles | Held in hand | Reference |
|---|---|---|---|---|---|---|
| 620 | 1,000 gold coins | 1,000 silver coins | – | 1,000 *jin* each of *zaji* silk; 100 *pi* each of . . . 100 *pi* of . . . 1,000 *pi* of *xiubu* cloth 1,000 *pi* of *xingbu* cloth 1,000 *pi* of *die* cloth | – | 64TAM31:12 / TCW 1992:I, 358 |
| 620 | – | – | 14 *laqian* | 1,000 *pi* of *baijuan* silk 10,000 *zhang* of *beijin* silk | – | 72TAM205:2 / TCW 1992:I, 360 |
| 620 | 10,000 gold coins | 10,000 silver coins | 14 *laqian* | 1,000 *zhang* of *beijin* silk; 500 *pi* of *zase* silk 500 *pi* of *ling* silk | – | 73TAM116:19 / TCW 1992:I, 370 |
| 620 | – | – | – | 1,000 *duan* of *ling* silk 1,000 *duan* of *lian* silk 200 *zhang* of *beijin* silk 10,000 *pi* of *xijin* silk | – | 72TAM151:6 / TCW 1992: II, 85 |
| 633 | 10,000 gold coins | 10,000 silver coins | – | 1,000 *pi* of *linglian* silk | – | 72TAM173:1 / TCW 1992:I, 421 |
| Gaochang period | – | – | – | Several 100 *pi* of . . . 300 *pi* of *baidie* cloth | – | 60TAM310:03/1 / TCW 1992:I, 460 |
| Tang *c.*640s | 'Sufficient' | 'Sufficient' | – | 1,000 *duan* of *bailian* silk; 10,000 *duan* of *zasewu* silk | – | 64TAM15:6 / TCW 1992:II, 20 |
| Tang *c.*640s | 100,000 coins (gold and silver) | | – | – | – | 59TAM301:17 / TCW 1992:II, 81 |

were used, and reveal significant patterns in the currency at Gaochang/Xizhou over a period of about four hundred years. The remaining documents from Turfan include census and registration documents, details of taxation, land ownership and other aspects of Turfan life. The contents of these documents support the findings from the contracts and tomb inventories, and fill out the picture in more detail.[16]

The picture of economic life at Dunhuang and Turfan appearing from the contents of the excavated documents is huge. In this chapter I have considered only the contracts and tomb inventories, as these are paramount for determining the forms of money used. But there are also many documents relating to taxation and other financial and economic activities, and it would be useful to explore these more fully. To give just one example of how the findings from this chapter can be expanded by the other documents, we can compare the six tomb inventories which list gold and silver by weight, and compare them with six tax documents from Turfan. These record transactions in gold, in weight units of *liang* (4, 8.5, 9, 9.5, 10 *liang*), for which a 'weight-value tax' (*chengjiaqian*) was payable, at the rate of 1 silver coin per 4 to 5 *liang* of silver. Six documents from Turfan record sales of silver, in units of *jin* and *liang* (2, 2, 2, 2 *jin* 1 *liang*, 5 *jin* 2 *liang*, 8 *jin* 1 *liang*) and the tax was at the rate of 1 silver coin per *jin* of silver. The 'weight-value tax' was also paid on other goods, for example, 1 silver coin per 10 *jin* of silk, 1 silver coin per 40 *jin* of perfume, and 1 silver coin per 50 *jin* of sal ammoniac (Zheng Xuemeng 1986; Jiang Boqin 1994: 35).

According to the *Weishu* (Shihuozhi), public weighing scales were hung at the gate to every market in China from county level upwards during the Northern Dynasties (386–581), and the Gaochang court also adopted this practice. It is significant that the people who made these transactions and paid the tax were not Chinese but Sogdian or Turkic, or from Gaoche or Qiuci.[17] They did not appear in the Gaochang/Xizhou census registers, but were traders, who appear to have been taxed in a different way to residents. Jiang Boqin (1994: 175–9) regards them as part of a network of traders passing on substantial quantities of goods. In addition to the weighed gold and silver mentioned above, they also dealt in copper (41 *jin*); silk (10, 50, 60, 80 *jin*); perfume (33, 52, 65, 92, 172, 252, 362, 572, 800 *jin*); and also in medicine: *yuyinjin* medicinal root (87 *jin*); sal ammoniac (11, 50, 172, 201, 241, 251 *jin*); and medicine (144 *jin*).

## Notes

1. For further details see Zhang Guangda and Rong Xinjiang (1998) and Hansen (1998a).
2. It ignores the 'tomb contracts' that were made with the gods, rather than with people. For details of tomb contracts see Hansen (1995: ch. 6) and Dien (1995).
3. The project is introduced in Hansen (1998a). Publications resulting from the project include Hansen (1998b), Zhang Guangda and Rong Xinjiang (1998), Skaff (1998), Sheng (1998) and Deng (1999).

4. Yamamoto and Ikeda (1987) and Hansen (1995) both provide a brief history of contracts in China; Hansen also compares and contrasts Chinese and Western concepts and practices.
5. In his study of grain at Turfan, Trombert (2002b) detects a hierarchy of grain: in descending order, wheat, unhusked barley, husked barley, millet.
6. A later contract from Turfan, dated AD 541, concerns a sale of land, the price of which is reckoned in *die*, which may also be a kind of carpet [66TAM48:23; Y&I 1987: §4].
7. For a detailed study of wine and viticulture at Turfan see Trombert (2001, 2002a).
8. Hansen (1995: 35) incorrectly reads this as taking the silk to Xizhou.
9. These four documents are dated Dali year 16, although the Dali period lasted only 14 years.
10. The majority of contracts from Dunhuang were from the ninth and early tenth centuries, for loans of grain, seed or textiles made by monks exclusively to local people who were struggling to maintain their very existence. Whilst Dunhuang may have been a very important international centre, Trombert (1995) has shown that loans from the Dunhuang monasteries were not made to merchants covering long distances, and that the specific nature and fixed range of textiles listed in the Dunhuang loan documents prove the continuing practice in the region of using textiles as money.
11. The two wooden cylinders wrapped in silk, one found in the male right hand and one found lying between the male and female in the seventh-century tomb Ast.i.6 at the Astana cemetery, may be symbolic representations of bolts of silk. In the mouth of the female was found an imitation gold Byzantine coin [IA.XII.c.1], and near her head were two wuzhu coins in perfect condition [IA.XII.c.2–3] (Stein 1928: 649). These items may be representative of the larger quantities stated in tomb inventories. Fastened to the ceiling of this tomb, by means of a twig, was a rag of rotten silk, placed there quite intentionally.

    Hansen (1998b: 51) suggests that the references for rising to heaven seen in the burials at Astana may reflect the Buddhist concept of rising to heaven, as contrasted with the Chinese concept of descending to the next world.
12. See Chapter 3, note 20.
13. The tomb inventories are probably related to the paper offerings – representing gold, silver, coins and textiles – that were burned (and continue to be burned) for the benefit of the ancestors in the spirit world. Tang Lin's *Mingbaoji* of the seventh century is the earliest record of this custom, which was already well established by then. See Hou Ching-lang (1975: 5–8) for details.
14. Jiang Boqin (1994: 67) suggests that *zhan* carpets were one of the many kinds of goods sold by Sogdian merchants in the markets in central China.
15. For details on the history of cotton in Eastern Central Asia see Trombert (1996). He notes that by the early sixth century cotton was being cultivated and woven in Turfan (though nowhere else in Eastern Central Asia) and that the cotton weaving industry was dominated by non-Chinese communities, such as Uighurs and Sogdians. Cotton was used in official payments (e.g. tax payments) and in large-scale commercial transactions. Indeed, Chinese documents of the Tianbao reign (742–56) found in the Astana and Kara-khoja cemeteries indicate that the finest silks and cottons were comparable in price: 45 coins per *chi* of fine silk [O.3073] and 44 coins per *chi* of fine cotton [O.3057].
16. Chinese historians have been working on these documents since 1975. Their findings have been published in *Dunhuang Tulufan wenshu chutan* (Wuhan 1983), *Dunhuang Tulufan chutu jingji wenshu* (Han Guopan 1986) and specialist journals such as *Dunhuang Tulufan yanjiu*.
17. In order to keep this study manageable and focused on money, I have not looked at issues of ethnicity or cultural backgrounds of the different peoples at Turfan and elsewhere in the region. However, there is a growing literature in this area; for example, for an introduction to work on Sogdians in China and Eastern Central Asia see Trombert (2003), and on the Sogdian trade diaspora see Skaff (2003).

# 10 Tocharian documents, seventh century

The Tocharian group of Indo-European languages comprises two distinct groups known as Tocharian A and Tocharian B, both of which were written in the Brahmi script. Tocharian documents have been found at sites north of the Taklamakan desert: Tocharian A documents in the Yanqi and Turfan regions, Tocharian B documents at sites stretching from Maralbashi to Turfan. As Tocharian B documents are generally found further to the west than Tocharian A documents, and as they refer frequently to Kucha (Tocharian $\mathrm{k}_{u}$’siññe), Tocharian B has also been called Kuchean. The language, presentation and content matter of Tocharian A and Tocharian B documents is quite different. Tocharian A documents are primarily religious, specifically Buddhist, in context, and are mostly written on *pothi* leaves. By contrast, Tocharian B documents include secular concerns, presented in a more vernacular language, written in a more cursive style of Brahmi, on paper scrolls or wooden tablets. It has been suggested that at the time of documentation Tocharian A was a dead, liturgical language preserved in the monasteries in Turfan, whilst Tocharian B was a living language in Kucha.[1] The Tocharian B documents date to the early to mid seventh century. Pinault (1998) suggests a date of *c*.650 by which time Qiuci had lost its independence from China, and the administration of the region was in the hands of petty kings under the Tang empire.

Tocharian manuscripts were first discovered in the 1890s. The majority were found in Turfan by Prussian expeditions in 1903–4 and 1906–7, and in Kucha by a French expedition of 1906–9. Very small quantities were found by Stein (Stein 1928, pl. CXXIII), Rudolph Hoernle, Beresovsky (1994), Otani, Huang Wenbi (Huang Wenbi 1958), and Pelliot (Pinault 1998). Whilst the majority of Tocharian A documents have been published (Sieg and Siegling 1921), they are religious in content and not relevant to this study. The important collections of Tocharian B documents are in the Staatsbibliothek Preussischer Kulturbesitz and the Museum für Indische Kunst in Berlin; the British Library; the Asian Institute of the Russian Academy of Sciences, St Petersburg; the Library of the Ryukoku University, Kyoto; the Tokyo National Museum; the Xinjiang Museum, Urumqi; and the Bibliothèque Nationale, Paris (Pinault 1994, 1998). Some, but not all of the Tocharian B documents have been published, and the resulting knowledge is somewhat patchy.

Tocharian B documents include monastery records (on paper and wood), commercial and administrative correspondence, caravan or customs passes (on wood), tally-sticks (made of wood, with notches cut into them); and wooden labels that had originally been attached to offerings made to monasteries, inscribed with the names of the donors and descriptions of contents. As Pinault (1998) notes, the extensive copying and recital of Buddhist texts, and the decoration of Buddhist temples and monasteries that took place in sites north of the Taklamakan Desert reflects the prosperity of these Buddhist communities, and suggests that they had plentiful resources and donations. Indeed, the royal family and the local elite were interested in Buddhism: kings and princes appear as donors in wall-paintings, and the aristocracy are known to have adopted Buddhism and to have translated Sanskrit texts into Chinese. Most of the Tocharian B documents have been found in a religious context, for example in the archives at the Duldur-Aqur monastery, and at the Buddhist remains of Kucha, Ming-oi, Kizil and Subashi. They therefore throw some light on the economic life of the religious communities north of the Taklamakan in the seventh century.

Close examination of the names on the documents has revealed that the caravan passes were written by officials of the kingdom of Qiuci, and account registers and letters were probably written by monks. The labels and tally sticks were also found in religious contexts, which links them either to the monks or to employees of the monasteries.

In the Tocharian B documents, there appear to be two terms for money: *cane* and *kusane*. *Cane* is derived from the Chinese *qian* [*dz’i̲an / *dz’i̲än / ts’i̲en of *c*.600 (Karlgren 1957)] (Naert 1965). The coins found at sites north of the Taklamakan Desert are precisely coins of the Chinese tradition, in particular the distinctive Qiuci coinage (see Chapter 5). The term *cane* appears most frequently in the fragments of account registers from Duldur-Aqur, many of which show signs of fire damage. The registers cover a full year, or sometimes half-year, of transactions, and follow the formula: date (month and day), name of person making the transaction, the name of the witness or guarantor, and a signature or measure of thumb. The ‘measure of thumb’ probably corresponds with the ‘drawing of finger-joints’ found on Chinese contracts (Hansen 1995). This feature, akin to the modern-day practice of taking fingerprints, is one of many similarities that Pinault (1998) has drawn with economic management at Chinese monasteries. *Kusane* also refers to coins. Its etymology is unknown (Adams 1999: 186). It appears repeatedly in the document [T.III.MQ.179.1–5] (Sieg and Siegling 1953: 303–4, Sieg 1950) which appears to be a list. Each line of text ends with a form of *kusane* and a number, which ranges from 250 to 801,900 (500 / 500 / 500 / 306,940 / 700 / 750 / 750 / 500 / 700 / 1,400 / 550 / 310 / 150 / 250 / 405,900 / 5,000 / 6,000 / 6,000 / 801,900 / 3,067). This document has yet to be translated and its context is not clear however, the inclusion of three numbers over 100,000 (306,940 / 405,900 / 801,900) indicates enormous quantities of coins.[2] The two terms *cane* and *kusane* must refer to the Qiuci coins found in large quantities at sites north of the Tarim Basin.

Donations feature strongly in the documents. They were received in the form of natural produce (for example, grain and oil) and in coin. Donations were a major form of income to the monasteries, and were an important mechanism for economic and financial transactions. Some donations were retained by the monastery, some, especially those in kind, were sold for coin. The top level of donors were merchants and princes. Other donors included various lay-people. Some names appear frequently, suggesting that these people brought donations to the monasteries on a regular basis. Indeed, some lay-people appear to have played a significant role in the economic management of the monasteries. The *vinaya*, or framework of rules upon which a Buddhist monastic community was built, prohibited three commercial activities in particular: contact with gold and silver, trading in precious metals, and buying and selling. When viewed in this light it is clear that, while donations were an important part of religious life at the monasteries, they also provided a convenient mechanism for managing the financial affairs of the monastery, and that the names which appeared frequently were probably those of intermediaries who acted as agents between the religious and the secular world. Various schools of Buddhism flourished in the monasteries north of the Taklamakan, and some were less strict than others. For example, monks following the *vinaya* of the Mahasamghikas were allowed to engage in commerce and trade as long as it was for acts of piety. In general, however, the Buddhist clergy could not engage in financial and economic affairs without the help of groups of merchants and artisans who were loyal to the monastery.

Account registers indicate the use of provisions collected in by the monasteries: for consumption by monks, for consumption by workers or intermediaries (both were dependants of the monasteries), religious needs (including oil for lamps), gifts or loans of grain to lay-people, payment in kind for labour and other services, and conversion of donations into coin. People who worked for the monastery were paid in kind or in coin. The flour mills, in particular, appear to have played a major role in economic life, and millers too were paid in kind or in coin. Pinault (1998) compares the large flour mills at sites north of the Taklamakan with similar mills in China, which were controlled by rich lay-people and large monasteries, and which were an important source of revenue.

Revenue for the monasteries came from various sources: donations in coin, interest on investments and loans, conversion of donations of provisions into coin, and tenant farming by lay-people on garden-lands and orchards. Rich lay-people gave gardens to the monastery, but, as the monks were forbidden to engage in agricultural work, the monasteries had to rent the land out to lay-people. Again, this practice was also known in China. The Tocharian word *werwiye* refers to those lands dependent on the monastery, the yields of which were measured in terms of grain, fruit and vegetable produce, and the income of which was reckoned in coin. One document found by Huang Wenbi at Maralbashi lists: 'from the gardens, from Kwemtoko, I received the payment of 2,000 coins' (Huang 1958: HW.4.6).

A monastery could give grain in exchange for other provisions or produce, but goods and services were mostly paid for in coin. One document [PK.DA.M.507 (40–42)] from Kucha in the Pelliot collection lists many transactions involving payments in coin:

> On the 20th day of the 4th month, I purchased some *tun* for 3 [coins], Sudhana witnessed it.
> On the 15th of the 5th month, I purchased some *tun* . . ., Kercapiske witnessed it.
> On the 9th of the 6th month, I purchased some *tun* . . ., Jnanasena witnessed it.
> On the 11th, Kercapiske went to mill some grain, I gave him 25 coins to pay for it.
> On the 21st, Kercapiske went to mill some grain, I gave him 27 coins to pay for it.
> On the 6th of the 9th month, I purchased some *tun* for 2 [coins].
> At Pravarana festival, for the Buddha's lamp, I purchased 2 *sank* of oil for 12 [coins].
> On 23rd of the 8th month, I purchased some *tun* . . ., for 5 [coins], Kercapiske witnessed it.
> On the 13th of the 10th month, I purchased some *tun* for 3 [coins], Sudhane witnessed it.
> In *warsanne* (= 11th month), at full moon, I purchased some *tun* . . ., Buddha witnessed it.
> On the 21st of the 9th month, for the musicians (?), I paid 50.
> In *rapanne* (= 12th month), the 13th, I gave 3 coins to Indravarman, to pay for the milling.

The geographical location of Qiuci favoured commercial development. The caravan passes show that the Qiuci kingdom controlled the passage of goods and merchandise through this part of Eastern Central Asia. Furthermore, Buddhist monks who travelled from China to India also passed through Qiuci, for example, Xuan Zang, who in 629 observed that 'gold coins, silver coins and small copper coins' were used in the kingdoms of Aqini (= Yanqi) and Qiuci (= Kucha). The dated documents in Tocharian B are from the early seventh century, and the coins found at the sites support Xuan Zang's observation at least in terms of the small copper coins.

The role of the monastery as a financial institution is well known in central China during the Tang dynasty (Gernet 1956; Twitchett 1970). In particular, there are similarities in financial administration at monasteries in the Tokharian B documents and the Chinese documents from Dunhuang (Pinault 1998).

## Notes

1. See 'Tocharian languages', *Encyclopaedia Britannica*, http://www.search.eb.com/eb/article?eu=118119 (accessed 7 June 2002).
2. One suggestion is that *kusane* derived from the name of the Kushan dynasty; see L. Isebart (1980: 76–77, 265), but this is difficult to reconcile with the archaeological finds which suggest that only Chinese type coins were known in the region at this time. I am grateful to Ursula Sims-Williams for her help with these coin-terms and in locating the references.

# 11 Khotanese and Chinese documents, seventh and eighth centuries

Khotanese, also known as Khotan Saka or Khotanese Saka, belongs to the eastern group of Middle Iranian languages.[1] It was written in the Central Asian Brahmi script, which had developed from the Indian Brahmi script, and is known in both formal and cursive styles. The majority of the Khotanese documents have come from religious sites, such as shrines and monasteries, within the kingdom of Khotan and at Dunhuang; many are religious texts in the form of *pothi* leaves. Secular and other documents were often written on the back of Chinese scroll documents (usually unrelated to the Chinese text on the other side) (Emmerick 1979: 6–8), and a smaller number of documents were written on wood. The wooden documents are generally more temporary in nature than those written on paper, and many of these were orders from officials (Kumamoto 1996b; Skjærvø 2002: lxxii–lxxiii). The Khotanese documents from Khotan have been dated to the seventh to early ninth centuries, and those from Dunhuang to the late ninth to the late tenth century. This chapter considers only the earlier, secular, documents from Khotan.[2] These include orders, petitions, contracts, personal letters, documents of a financial or economic nature, and lists of names. There are also a few box-shaped wooden documents with sliding lids; this was one of the forms used for contracts, for example, for payment for the use of water [Or.9268A] and for the adoption of a boy [Or.9268B].

There are three major collections of early Khotanese documents: (1) those collected by Petrovsky and Malov, forming the St Petersburg Collection, at the Institute of Oriental Studies, Russian Academy of Sciences (Emmerick and Vorob'ëva-Desyatovskaja 1995); (2) those collected by Hedin, now at the Ethnographical Museum, Stockholm (Bailey 1961); and those received by Hoernle or collected by Stein, now at the British Library, London (Skjærvø 2002). For convenience, the following abbreviations have been used in this chapter [SI.P.] = St Petersburg Collection (Ser-India, Petrovsky); [SI.M.] = St Petersburg Collection (Ser-India, Malov); [SI.O] = St Petersburg Collection (Ser-India, Oldenburg); [Or.] = British Library; [IOL] = India Office Library collection, now at the British Library; and [H] = Hedin. It should be pointed out that many secular documents are not fully understood and need further clarification.

Other documents from this period discussed in this chapter include the bilingual Khotanese–Chinese documents that were collected by Nils Ambolt in Domoko[3] and the eighth-century Chinese documents collected by Stein in Khotan and at Dandan-Uiliq (see Skjærvø 2002: xlvii).

### References to money in the Khotanese documents

In the Khotanese documents two terms are used to indicate money: *dramma* [H:3] is used in the more general sense of money and *mura* is used specifically to mean coins.

#### *Dramma*

*Dramma*, probably derived from the Greek δραχμή (Bailey 1961: 70), appears in several documents [Or.11252/4; Or.12637/17; Or.12637/60; Or.9268A; IOL Khot 3/5; IOL Khot 23/14; IOL Khot 177/3; IOL Khot Wood 1; SI.P. 93.11]. In three documents it is used in the context of money being withdrawn [IOL 11252/4; Or.12637/17; Or.12637/60]. In two documents the term *drammaja* is found in the context of money-making, or profit-making, and is followed by a specific quantity of *mura* [Or.9268A; IOL Khot 3/5]. In one case, *drammai* is followed by a specified quantity of cloth (*thau*) [IOL Khot 177/3].

#### *Mura*

The term *mura* appears frequently in the Khotanese documents. Lüders (1919) proved that *mura* (*muri*, *murai*) meant small, copper Chinese-style coin, and that *mura* derived from *mudra* [seal] which is found in Niya-Prakrit, where *kilamudra* refers to sealed wooden tablets. The documents indicate that large quantities of *mura*, occasionally expressed as *savi mura* [copper coin], were used. They indicate that coins were used in payments, and that the value of other objects was also reckoned and stated in *mura*. From the frequent references to large quantities of coins in the documents there can be no doubt that Chinese, or Chinese-style, coins were widely used in the Khotan area. The coins found at sites in the same area confirm that *mura* must refer to the Tang dynasty coin-types made in central China and, perhaps more likely, the Chinese-style coins made locally in Eastern Central Asia (see Chapters 4 and 6). The Khotanese documents suggest that very large quantities of these coins were in general circulation. Tables 39 and 40 indicate amounts in excess of 1,000 *mura* and 10,000 *mura*, respectively. The single largest amount is 113,000 *mura* [SI.P. 97.4]. The vast quantities of *mura* and the reckoning in thousands is immediately suggestive of the unit of 1,000 coins. It is particularly interesting therefore to note the use of the term *ysa'ca*, meaning 'one thousand' and translated as 'thousander' by Skjærvø (2002) and Emmerick and Vorob'eva-Desyatovskaja (1995). The term *ysa'ca* is used only for numbers above 10,000: for example, 12,000 is expressed as 12 *ysa'ca* [SI.P. 94.3] (see Table 40). The unit of 1,000 *mura* and the use of the special term *ysa'ca* would accord with the Chinese unit of a string of 1,000 coins and the *srang* of *dmar* seen in the Tibetan documents (see Chapter 12).

The large sums of *mura* in the documents suggest that the individual coins were of low value. This is confirmed in a document which lists the items a man took for his wife who had been resettled in a new place: 'he took for her whatever things there were worth even a single copper *mura*' [Or.8212/162]. Occasionally a sum is expressed with the phrase 'minus one or two' [Or.11344/14; IOL Khot 44/5].

**Table 39**
**Large quantities of *mura* (exceeding 1,000 *mura*)**

| Large quantities of mura | Date | Reference |
|---|---|---|
| 1,640 *mura*<br>2,250 *mura*<br>1,640 *mura* | – | [H:1] |
| 14,000 *mura*<br>14,000 *mura* | – | [H:12][4] |
| 3,000 *mura*<br>14,000 *mura* | – | [H:16] |
| 2,500 *mura* | – | [H:26] |
| 2,045 *mura*<br>1,590 *mura* | – | [H:33] |
| 1,109 *mura* | – | [H:39] |
| 3,204 *mura* | – | [H:41] |
| 1,370 *mura* | – | [H:55] |
| 2,000 *mura* | – | [H:60] |
| 4,000+ *mura* | – | [SI.P. 93.3] |
| 5,000 *mura* | – | [SI.P. 94.1] |
| 5,000 *mura* | – | [SI.P. 94.3] |
| 2,000 *mura* | – | [SI.P. 94.9] |
| 5,000+ *mura* | – | [SI.P. 94.16] |
| 3,875 [*mura*] | – | [SI.P. 97.4] |
| 1,110 *mura* | – | [SI.P. 99.2] |
| 5,000+ *mura* | – | [SI.P. 101.9] |
| 2,000 *mura* | – | [SI.P. 101.31.5] |
| 1,000 [*mura*]<br>4,000 [*mura*]<br>2,000 [*mura*]<br>2,000 [*mura*]<br>1,000+ [*mura*] | – | [SI.P. 103.18] |
| 3,200 *mura*<br>4,200 *mura*<br>2,500 *mura* | – | [SI.P. 103.19] |
| 1,000+ *mura*<br>1,000+ *mura* | – | [SI.P. 103.25] |
| 7,070 *mura*<br>2,000 *mura* | – | [SI.P. 103.29] |
| 1,300 *mura* | – | [SI.M. 52] |
| 5,000 *mura* | – | [SI.P. 103.36] |

| Large quantities of mura | Date | Reference |
|---|---|---|
| 1,200+ [*mura*]<br>4,000 [*mura*]<br>3,000 *mura* | – | [SI.P. 94.23] |
| 1,000+ *mura* | – | [SI.P. 98.7] |
| 1,000 *mura* | – | [SI.P. 103.7] |
| 1,800+ [*mura*] | – | [SI.M. 26] |
| 2,200 *mura* | – | [SI.P. 103.49] |
| 5,000 *mura* | – | [Or.6393/1 (M.9)] |
| 10,000 *mura* | – | [Or.6394/1 (M.9)] |
| 1,370 *mura* | 778–9 | [Or.6394/2 (M.9)] |
| 5,000 *mura* | 784 | [Or.6395/1 (M.10)] |
| 5,500 *mura* | 779 | [Or.6395/2 (M.9)] |
| 1,000 *mura* | – | [Or.6397/1 (G.)] |
| 3,000 *mura* | – | [Or.6399/1.2 (G.1)] |
| 8,800 [*mura*] | – | [Or.6400/1.2 (G.1)] |
| 1,850 *mura*<br>3,750 [*mura*] | – | [Or.6400/1.5 (G.1)] |
| 1,000 [*mura*]<br>2,000 *mura* | – | [Or.6400/2.2 (G.1)] |
| 3,280 [*mura*]<br>3,300 [*mura*]<br>3,000 *mura*<br>3,300 [*mura*]<br>10,000 *mura* minus 1 or 2 | – | [Or.11252/23] repeated in [Or.11344/14] |
| 1,000 *mura* | – | [Or.11252/38] |
| 9,000 [*mura*] | – | [Or.11344/15] |
| 2,977 *mura* | – | [Or.12637/12.1] |
| 8,396 *mura* | – | [Or.12637/21.1a] |
| 9,000(+) [*mura*]<br>3,000 *mura* | – | [IOL Khot 51/6] |
| 2,000 *mura* | – | [IOL Khot 53/2] |
| 2,000 *mura*<br>1,000 *mura* | – | [IOL Khot 173/9] |
| 1,500 *mura*<br>1,200 *mura* | – | [IOL Khot Wood 29] |
| 1,000 *mura* | – | [OIOC Photo 392/57 (T.O.20)] |

There are too many references to smaller quantities of *mura* in the Khotanese documents to list them all here. One document [SI.P. 103.52] lists the accounts drawn up by a monastery and gives a useful indication of relative prices:[5]

> I bought pepper (for) 5 *mura*, cumin (for) 6 *mura*, peas (?) for 15 *mura*, rice (for) 38 *mura*, herbs (for) 26 *mura*. I gave Namauda 8 *mura* and Asalai 15 *mura*. This (was) the purchase in the year of the Acarya Punasida.
>
> This is the issue of *mura* for sesame expended in the year of Acarya Abayasida. I bought 3 (lots of sesame) for cooking (for) 169 *mura*. I gave Samgadatta 90 *mura* for licquor. Jsanara forwarded 30 *mura* (for purchases of sesame). I bought pepper and salt (for) 8 *mura*. Haskastara requested 15 *mura*.
>
> This is the issue of those *mura* that I paid for wheat. Haskastira received 100 *mura* and Saphumga (also). Samdrram received 30 *mura*. Maskidara received 15 *mura*. Sudaram received 20 *mura*. Budarma received 20 *mura*. Samgadatta received 25 *mura*. Marsala received 30 *mura*. Amsuka received 30 *mura*. Asale received 10 *mura*.
>
> Acarya Amrritasida received 50 *mura*. Punaprraba received 30 *mura*. Budarman received 6 *mura*. Amstara received 20 *mura*. I bought a filter (for) 10 *mura*. Namauda received 20 *mura*. The Svanakas received 35 *mura*. I bought herbs (for) 15 *mura*. Acarya Punasida received 50 *mura* for a cloak.
>
> I paid 10 *mura* for the oil maker (?). Asnekule received 30 *mura*. I bought salt (for) 4 *mura*. I bought 5 bags (for) 200 *mura*. Asalai received 80 *mura* (and) . . . a pen. I bought rice and bread (for) 25 *mura*. Marsala received 165 *mura* (for) a saw and built one cowpen.

The largest amounts in these accounts are the 165 *mura* for a saw, the 90 *mura* for licquor and the 169 *mura* for three lots of sesame for cooking.

**Table 40**
***Mura* reckoned in 'thousanders' (*ysa'ca*)**

| References to 'thousanders' | Reference |
|---|---|
| 20 thousanders | [H:3] |
| 14 thousanders 310 | [H:13] |
| 40 thousanders | [H:19] |
| 22 thousanders 120 | [H:57] |
| 12 thousanders | [SI.P. 94.3] |
| 113 thousanders 730 | [SI.P. 97.4] |
| [. . .] 8 thousanders 840 | [SI.P. 99.2] |
| [. . .] thousanders 980 | [SI.P. 99.7] |
| 30 thousanders | [SI.P. 103.10] |
| 14 thousanders 130+ *mura*<br>29+ thousanders | [SI.P. 98.2] |
| 20 thousanders 800 | [Or.6398/2 (G.1) |
| 44 thousanders | [Or.11252/30] |
| 24 thousanders<br>30 thousanders<br>30 thousanders<br>[. . .] thousanders 900 | [Or.012637/23] |
| 20 thousanders | [OIOC Photo 392/57 (T.O.34)] |

***Money collectors and accountants***
The term *murahamga* is found in several documents (see Table 41), and has been translated as 'money collector' and 'tax collector' (Emmerick 1996: 116). In two documents [SI.P. 103/41 and SI.P. 103/43] the correspondence is addressed to a named person 'and the (other) money collectors'. This suggests that the *murahamgha* were co-ordinated in groups, probably one per locality, and that the named person was the head of the group and was responsible for liaison between the central administration and the other *murahamgha*, as well as the people of his own locality. Another document [OIOC Photo 392/57 (T.O.34)] concerns a request from a *murahamgha* to a *spata* official for a total of 20,000 *mura*. The *spata* then issues orders, and is aware that there will be interest to pay. It is not clear in this document whether the *murahamgha* was charging interest himself or whether he was acting as an agent.

In addition to the *murahamgha* there were 'accountants' [*phani-kvani* and *khrram bana*]. The term *phani-kvani* is found in three documents [SI.P. 95.11; SI.P. 96.15; SI.P. 103.24]. The contexts, though not entirely clear, suggest that they may have been responsible for keeping accounts of grain and agricultural produce brought to the stores. The other term *khrram bana* is found in one document [Or.12637/14.2] in the context of 'sealing their names on inspection'. Emmerick (1985: 303) suggested there might be a link here with the Tibetan *khram-dpon*. The role of the accountant was clearly different from that of the *murahamgha*: the accountants may have been closely associated with the stores of the state, and the *murahamgha* with the localities they represented. Some documents indicate the number of men or 'half-men' (meaning older men or children), and the quantities of goods they were required to deliver [e.g. Or.6400/1.3 (G.1)]. From one document [Or.6396/2 (G.G.M.1)], it would seem that 'half-men' also paid half the full rate of tax: 41 full-men were to deliver 213 *mura*, and 12 half-men were to deliver 106 *mura*.

***Vouchers and receipts***
Several documents refer to vouchers, apparently issued in official circumstances, for example as a record of a deposit in the stores in Gaysata [SI.P. 103.48].[6] The usual term for voucher is *ksau* (plural *ksauva*) (Skjærvø 2002: lxxviii; Bailey 1961: 55), seen in several documents (see Table 42). Also associated with *ksauva* is the term *chau-pam*, seen in two documents [SI.P. 103.46; SI.P. 103.49]. *Chau* is derived from the Chinese *chao* meaning 'receipt' (鈔) (Bailey 1961: 72; Emmerick and Vorob'ëva-Desyatovskaja 1995: 155; Skjærvø 2002: lxxviii). It would be worth investigating if *pam* is also derived from a Chinese root, possibly from *ban* (版), meaning 'tablet' or 'ticket', for which the reconstructed pronunciation in Middle Chinese is *pan.[7]

The vouchers seem to have functioned as receipts or proof of payment or delivery of goods. However, the terms *ksauva* and *chau-pam* do not appear in documents specifying tax payments (see Table 48), suggesting that the vouchers were used for particular transactions, which were not related to taxation. One document [SI.P. 103.48] records the deposit of sheepskins for storage in Gaysata in return for a voucher. The document accusing the official of incompetence [H: 3] in particular shows the importance of vouchers for keeping financial records and balancing account books.

***Deferred payments***
Not all payments were made in full and on time. The Khotanese documents reveal that credit played an important part of everyday life: there are examples of loans, part payments, deferred payments and outstanding payments (see Table 43). It is likely that some of the delays in payment or delivery were associated with the agricultural calendar: for example, people would have more grain available after harvest-time. Orders from officials demanding payment or delivery sometimes specified that the money or goods were to be delivered within five days or strong penalties would be incurred. Penalties often involved a beating with a specificied number of strokes of the stick.

Many documents concern deferred payments, usually with interest (*ysantha*). Advances were also available, to be repaid with double the amount borrowed. They indicate that delayed payments were a regular feature of economic life in the Khotan region, that credit played an important role, and they explain the need for vouchers and more formal contracts.

Some financial arrangements involved the drawing up of a more formal contract.[8] Such arrangements included purchases of land, adoption, and purchase of adults, especially adult working capacity (see Table 44) (Skjærvø 2003). There were conditions attached to the purchase of land, more specifically that the land should be cultivated in a particular way. The periods noted in these documents are defined as 'autumns', and may refer to annual harvests. In one document [Or.6397/1 (G.1)], the price of the land was reckoned in *mura*, in another [Or.6393/2 (M.9)] the seller could repurchase the land when he had sufficient grain or textiles to do so. These documents suggest that sales of land could be paid for in *mura*, grain and textiles. In an adoption contract [Or.9268B], the desired price

**Table 41**
***Murahamgha* (money collectors)**

| Details | Money-form collected | Reference |
|---|---|---|
| Names tax collector Kasaka | – | [SI.P. 103.17] |
| Names nine tax collectors and quantities of tax handed in or owed | Sacks (1 sack per 10 men)<br>Ropes (1 rope per 10 men)<br>*Aysdam* (1–3.5 *kha*) | [IOL Khot Wood 58] |
| Money collectors | – | [SI.P. 97.1] |
| Names money collector Jsajsaka and some payments | Cloth | [SI.P. 98.8] |
| Money collector | – | [SI.P. 99.8] |
| Money collectors at the Inner Fort | *Mura* | [SI.P. 101.1] |
| Money collector | – | [SI.P. 101.21] |
| Money collector | – | [SI.P. 101.31.2] |
| Money collectors | Cloths | [SI.P. 103.12] |
| Money collectors | – | [SI.P. 103.30] |
| Names money collectors Sidaka and Arrtaa. Dispute with the money collectors, order to bring the *mura* in person within 6 days | *Mura* | [SI.P. 103.37] |
| Names Sidaka 'and the (other) money collectors' | – | [SI.P. 103.41] |
| Names Punargam and other money collectors. Concerns debts at the Inner Fort | – | [SI.P. 103.43] |
| Money collectors | – | [SI.M.11.1] |
| Names money collector Darmadatta. Requests *mura* | *Mura* | [IOL Khot Wood 21] |
| Names money collector Marsakas | – | [Or.6401/1.3 (G.1)] |
| Money collector | – | [Or.8212/1717] |
| Money collectors have asked the *spata* official for 20,000 *mura*. The *spata* issues orders and is aware that there will be interest to pay. He also insists that horses should be purchased | *Mura* | [OIOC Photo 392/57 (T.O.34)] |

**Table 42**
**Vouchers or receipts**

| Details | Voucher | Reference |
|---|---|---|
| 5,000 delivered, he demanded a voucher for it | *Ksau* | [SI.P. 93.27] |
| Voucher issued . . . he gave cloths making up the total (?): 15 | *Ksau* | [SI.P. 98.1] |
| Voucher for 15 (sheep)skins . . . winter garments to be stored in Gaysata (confirmed by Chinese text) | *Ksau* | [SI.P. 103.48] |
| Royal cloths . . . cloths . . . voucher of the minister | *Ksau* | [SI.P. 96.10] |
| . . . entered the *samtira* and . . . not yet received the vouchers for them . . . from the Sogdians he received the sum . . . | *Ksauva* | [Or.11344/16] |
| I have no writ for vouchers for woollen cloths and another amount of 1,000 | *Ksauva* | [Or.11344/18] |
| . . . sealings (?) for it half vouchers (?) for him . . . the cloth is old (?) | *Ksauvai* | [Or.12637/51] |
| As soon as the order arrives, send the thing to me, gather in the (unknown thing?) quickly, then gather the vouchers and give them to the man, whatever amount he brought here. I gave you an order regarding the vouchers previously, but you have not given them to me . . . if the vouchers and those *mura* do not arrive . . . | *Ksauva* | [OIOC Photo 392/57 (T.O.34)] |
| According to the vouchers the cloths sold were 23 and. . . . The Sogdians have sold 2½ cloths, though there are no vouchers yet (for them) | *Ksau* and *Ksauva* | [Or.11344/4] |
| Payment for cloth. Mura are owed, with interest. An official is accused of incompetence because he did not ask for money when he received vouchers, and did not clarify the entire transaction. Extra interest was then incurred on the money that he did not ask for. He is ordered to submit the account, note how much is owing, and to send the vouchers | *Ksauva* | [H: 3]; Skjærvø 2003 |
| (A list of names each with a quantity of cloth or *chau-pam*) | *Chau-pam* | [SI.P. 103.46] |
| One person is supposed to give a house, grain and *chau-pam* to another | *Chau-pam* | [SI.P. 103.49] |

**Table 43**
**Loans and deferred or delayed payments (often with interest)**

| Details | Repayment (with interest) | Reference |
|---|---|---|
| Grain and cloth to be received by a certain month | If they are not received, the interest for the five month period will be 1 *cha* of cloth | [Or.6392/2 (M.1)] |
| You have not delivered the cloths as promised. Now the two merchants who had paid 10,000 *mura* for 300 cloths are here asking for that money to be returned to them. They had paid the 10,000 *mura* in the form of 300 pieces of hemp cloth (worth 500) and I handed over from them 30 *cha* of cloth | When you hear this order, you must pay the *mura* and interest by the expiry date | [Or.6394/1 (M.9)] |
| You owe (unknown quantity of) *mura* per head and *mura* for payment for cloth for winter clothes. *Mura* are also owed to the Inner Fort and I asked for *mura* with interest from the Sogdian. Now the Sogdian has arrived. When you hear this order, bring the 1,370 *mura* with the interest here | If you do not bring the *mura* (including interest) within 5 days, you will face strong penalties | [Or.6394/2 (M.9)] |
| When you hear the order, and when they have paid for cloth in Gaysata, request 30 and give it to me . . . a record of debt (promissory note?) | – | [SI.P. 103.34] |
| The mura were sent to him. The total, with interest, came to 1,800 [*mura*] | Interest | [SI.M. 26] |
| One person was supposed to give grain to one official and a house, grain and *chau-pam* to another person. He could not give the grain, so the official gave it to him. He now gives the full payment of 2,000 *mura* for that grain, and sends a gift without interest. If his house is declining and he cannot give the *mura*, then he shall give 10 *mura* only as interest | (Difficulty in making payments) | [SI.P. 103.49] |
| For this (unknown quantity of) cloth he shall pay 1 cloth as interest | To pay cloth as interest | [Or.9615/2] |
| . . . with interest | With interest | [IOL Khot 40/3b] |
| The money collectors asked for a total of 20,000 *mura* and interest at 8 *mura* | Payment of *mura* with interest at 8 *mura* (= 80 per cent?) | [OIOC Photo 392/57 (T.O.34)]; Skjærvø 2003 |
| Requested: 2 pieces of cloth; to repay 4 in the autumn<br>Requested: 1 piece of cloth; to repay 2 in the autumn<br>Requested: 1 piece of cloth; to repay 2 in the autumn | Deferred payment: to repay double the advance | [SI.P. 103.22] |
| Promissory note: there are *mura* outstanding. Had promised to pay 6 or more people 125 *mura* each | If he cannot deliver the cloths he is to pay interest of 100 *mura* | [Or.6397/2 (M.3)] |
| Promised one . . . but had not delivered | . . . 10 *cha* | [Or.6401/1.2 (G.1)] |
| Promissory note: there are still *mura* to pay. Had promised to pay 6 or more people 125 *mura* each | If he cannot deliver the cloths he is to pay interest of 100 *mura* | [Or.6397/2 (M.3)] |
| One person delivered 1 piece of cloth and owes 300 [*mura*]<br>One person delivered 1 piece of cloth and owes 300 [*mura*]<br>One person delivered 1 piece of cloth and owes 200 [*mura*] | *Mura* owed | [Or.6401/1.4 (G.1)] |
| List of names owing barley and the quantities owed | – | [Or.8211/1474] |

for the child was 500 *mura* and 3 *cha* of white silk worth 200 *mura*. The total price was 700 *mura*, and this figure matches that of a woman and her son, sold for 700 *mura* seen in another document [WBH01] (Duan Qing and Wang Binghua 1997). As the total price for the adopted child was 700 *mura*, we may assume either that there were insufficient *mura* available at the time or that the white silk was an significant part of this transaction.

The sale of the woman and her son is particularly interesting as their original owner was a member of a monastery. The document suggests that he was not able to sell them himself and that he required an agent to do this. Skjærvø (2003) suggests that such an agent may have been from the monastery, yet it may be more appropriate to consider such agents as lay-people. The Tocharian documents (see Chapter 10) have already shown that certain lay-people played a signficant role in the economic management of the monasteries north of the Taklamakan and that the Buddhist clergy could engage in financial and economic affairs only with the help of groups of merchants and artisans who were loyal to the monastery.

***Other forms of money: textiles and grain***

The Khotanese documents indicate that coins (*mura*) were not the only form of money; textiles and grain were also used.

**Table 44**
**Contracts**

| Nature of contract | Details | Penalty clause | Reference |
|---|---|---|---|
| Purchase of water rights | One man purchased water rights for 2,500 *mura*, in order that he might profit from this | – | [Or.9268A]; Skjærvø 2003 |
| Purchase of land (782–3) | One man bought land. He received the land and 2 *thamga* of cotton. For a period of six autumns, if he has cultivated only one field, then the seller may buy back the land when he has sufficient grain and textiles to do so | Must cultivate the land as specified or be prepared to sell it back | [Or.6393/2 (M.9)] |
| Purchase of land (782) | One man bought 3 *kusem* of land for a period of four autumns at the price of 1,000 *mura*. If he has not sown *kira* on this land, then the seller may buy it back within the four-autumn period, but not after this period has expired | Must cultivate the land as specified or be prepared to sell it back | [Or.6397/1 (G.1) |
| Purchase of land | Seller can buy back land when he has sufficient *mura* to do so | – | [SI.P. 103.17] |
| Adoption of child | A man gave his son in adoption to the wife of his half-brother. The half-brother paid the desired price in full (500 *mura* and 3 *cha* of white silk worth 200 *mura*), and has received the child | Anyone wishing to change this agreement is to pay 200 *mura* to the court, to receive 50 strokes, and to give as *prahänaja* 1 *mura* and 5 (?) | [Or.9268B]; Skjærvø 2003 |
| Uncertain | Adoption or purchase (?) of a young woman | Anyone wishing to change this agreement is to pay (unknown quantity of) *mura* and to receive 30 strokes | [IOL Khot 3/1] |
| Sale of people (737?–746/7?) | The villagers of Birgamdara asked the official Visauna for 2,000 mura (to pay?) for felt. Later Visauna asked for the money back, but the villagers were unable to pay. It happened that there was a man, Bradyasai, who was unable to do his corvée work, so Visauna paid 2,500 *mura* to purchase this man. The villagers then did Bradyasai's corvée work and were paid for it. They were then able to repay 2,500 *mura* to Visauna. Bradyasai then sold his half-brother to Visauna for 2,500 *mura*. Bradyasai did not give any of this money to the villagers, so they sued him. The court ruled that Visauna would now own this man (Bradyasai?), and that when the brothers had earned 2,500 *mura*, Visauna will receive his money back [not fully understood] | – | [IOL Khot Wood 1]; Skjærvø 2003 |
| Notice of debt (to repay wheat) (746/7–756+) | The three brothers Bradyasai, Virsa and Briyaka sold their work capacity to Mamatti for 1,000 *mura*. The received the *mura* in full. Of these 1,000 *mura* they shall pay in 500 *mura*-worth of wheat with interest. 30 *kusa* and 500 *mura*-worth of wheat are to be placed in the public granary [not fully understood] | If they cannot deliver the wheat, then they may pay in *mura*. If they cannot pay, then Briyaka is to become the slave of Mamatti | [IOL Khot Wood 2]; Skjærvø 2003 |
| Sale of son | A man owes *mura*. When it is discovered that he is putting his son up for sale in order to make money, he is ordered to pay the *mura* owed or to hand over his son as payment instead | – | [SI.P. 142.1]; Skjærvø 2003 |
| Sale of son | A man sells his nephew for 2,000 *mura*. The buyer will profit from this as he will keep whatever the boy earns | Anyone violating this agreement will be punished with the stick | [Urumqi 1]; Skjærvø 2003 |
| Sale of woman and son | A member of the monastery seeks to sell a woman and her son, but is granted jurisdiction over them (until they are sold?). They are sold for 700 *mura*, this being the value of their work capacity. After the sale, they are to be under the jurisdiction of the new owner | – | [Urumqi 2]; Skjærvø 2003; [WBH01] (Duan Qing and Wang Binghua 1997) |

**Table 45**
**Payments in textiles or grain, with the value expressed in *mura***

| Reckoning | Reference |
|---|---|
| For each man textiles amounting to 1,640 *mura*, for five men textiles amounting to 8,200 [= 5 × 1,640]. According to the number of pieces of cloth, 14,310 *mura* [= 5 × 2,862] | [H: 13] |
| Cloth to the amount of 1,000 *mura* | [H:68] |
| One load of cloth worth 350 *mura*, One load of woollen cloth worth 1,000 *mura*, One bundle worth 50 *mura* | [SI.P. 98.7] |
| One person owed cloths worth 150 [*mura*] plus 2 *cha* of woollen cloth | [Or.6398/2 (G.1)] |
| 2 *samgha* (grain measurement), 1,000, I shall pay (as) interest | [IOL Khot 42/1] |
| Promised payment in grain for work (?) . . . delivery of grain | [Or.8211/1479] |

**Table 46**
**Payments made part in coin part in textiles**

| Part payments | Reference |
|---|---|
| Gave 3 [. . .] and 2,500 *mura* | [SI.P. 94.9] |
| List of people who gave cloth and *mura* | [SI.P. 103.19] |
| One person gave 1,000+ *mura*, thereafter 700 *mura* and 1 piece of woollen cloth, 1,000+ *mura*, 600 *mura*, 380 *mura* and 200 *mura*. He presented *trramcarra* skins and cloth . . . 10 . . . 2 and *mura* | [SI.P. 103.25] |
| Gave 2 cloths and 200 *mura* Gave 11 cloths, 1 sheep, 250 *mura*, 4 nanny goats, 4 sheep | [Or.6400/2.2 (G.1)] |
| Paid 1,000 *mura* and 53 pieces of cloth | [Or.11252/38] |
| Cloth and *mura* | [OIOC Photo 392/57 (T.O.20)] |

However, it was usually the case that the values or prices of these items were expressed in *mura* (see Table 45).

As in the adoption contract mentioned above [Or.9268B] some payments were made part in *mura* and part in textiles (see Table 46).

It is not clear from these examples of payments in a combination of *mura* and other goods whether there was a particular system or reason for this other than to make up the full amount in an acceptable way.

Wool, cotton, hemp, felt and silk are the main textiles mentioned. They were usually expressed in terms of numbers of cloths or in terms of length or width, and sometimes in both. The measurements for length or width are expressed in *cha* and *tsuna*, where 1 *cha* = 10 *tsuna*, corresponding with the Chinese *chi* [foot] and *cun* [inch], respectively (Bailey 1961 [*KT IV*: 53–4]). The term *mista thauna*, translated as 'great cloths', appears in two documents [Or.11252/30; Or.12637/23] but is not fully understood.[9]

Where payments were made part in textiles and part in *mura*, the textiles were usually expressed in quantities of cloths [*thauna* or *thaunaka*]: [SI.P. 103.19; SI.P. 103.25; SI.P. 94.23; SI.P. 95.12; SI.P. 98.2; SI.P. 98.7; Or.6394/1 (M.9); Or.6400/1.5 (G.1); Or.6400/2.2 (G.1); Or.6401/1.4 (G.1); Or.11252/23; Or.11344/14; Or.11252/30; Or.11252/38; Or/11344/15; IOL Khot 12; IOL Khot 31; OIOC Photo 392/57 (T.O.20); Or.12637/21.1a; Or.12637/23]. The terms *thauna* and *thaunaka* do not indicate the material of the cloth, nor do we know if the cloths were of a standard size. For now we can merely observe that, when the textiles are expressed as cloths, the number of cloths ranges from one to 80, with many examples of just one cloth. When expressed by measurement, the largest measurement is 40 *cha* [OIOC Photo 392/57 (T.O.20); H:1].[10]

As textiles are frequently mentioned in payments we might hope to find equivalent values between textiles and *mura*. Two records give the value of a woollen cloth (of unknown dimensions) at 1,200 *mura* and 1,000 *mura* [SI.P. 94.23 and SI.P. 98.7]; these are remarkably close to the unit of 1,000 *mura* (see above). Another document [IOL missing fragment 2: Godfrey 2: *KT II*, p. 76][11] is particularly useful for determining the values of hemp and cotton cloth:

> In the fifteenth regnal year, this much stuff was ordered for (each) half man in Gaysata: an amount of 606 *mura* per capita. And hemp cloth for winter clothing 9 *cha* 2 *tsuna*; for (a piece from) a 70-*cha* roll the *mura* become 616. And hemp cloth for summer clothing was ordered 8 *cha* 6 *tsuna*; for (a piece from) a 60-*cha* roll, the *mura* for it become 516. And cotton cloth for winter clothing was ordered 1 *cha* 5 *tsuna*, so for (a piece from) a 50-*cha* roll the *mura* become 225. And summer clothing, its amount was ordered (as) 170 *mura*. And for a half man, in total, 2133 *mura* (worth of stuff) was ordered, with the exception of the amount of 70 *cha* for the gracious lords.

In this case, the total amount ordered for each 'half man' was 2,133 *mura* [606 + 616 + 516 + 225 + 170 = 2,133]. A closer examination of this document (see Table 47) reveals that cotton cloth was more expensive than hemp cloth, indeed more than double the price; that hemp cloth was produced in at least two different sizes (60-*cha* and 70-*cha*) and that cotton was

**Table 47**
**The values of different textiles and different sizes of textiles**

| Type of textile | Size of roll | Length of cloth | Price (in *mura*) | Price per *cha* (in *mura*) |
|---|---|---|---|---|
| Hemp cloth (for winter clothing) | 70-*cha* | 9 *cha* 2 *tsuna* | 616 | 66.96 |
| Hemp cloth (for summer clothing) | 60-*cha* | 8 *cha* 6 *tsuna* | 516 | 60 |
| Cotton cloth (for winter clothing) | 50-*cha* | 1 *cha* 5 *tsuna* | 225 | 150 |
| Cotton cloth (for summer clothing) | [50-*cha*] | [1 *cha* 1–2 *tsuna*] | 170 | [150] |

available in at least one size. The rolls of textiles are expressed in three widths: 50, 60 and 70 *cha*. The values of the textiles determined above have come from a very small number of documents and need further corroboration before they can be confirmed as accurate in a more general sense.

### *Animals and skins*

Draught animals [Or.11252/11; Or.12637/60; Or.12637/78; IOL Khot 43/7; Or.11252/4], cattle/oxen [Or.6401/1.1 (G.1); Or.12637/2; Or.12637/71.3; IOL Khot 201/2; SI.P. 92.8; SI.P. 95.4; SI.P. 103.9; SI.O.77], camels [Or.6399/2.3 (G.1); IOL Khot Wood 8], horses [Or.11344/5; OIOC Photo 392/57 (T.O.34)], sheep [Or.11344/9; SI.P. 94.23; SI.P. 136.1] and goats [Or.6399/1.10 (G.1); SI.P. 95.12; SI.P. 103.19; SI.P. 103.27] appear frequently in transactions in the Khotanese documents. Normal prices or values of animals are difficult to determine; however, two documents may be useful in establishing the price or value of a goat: the first [SI.P. 95.12] mentions 23 goats worth 4,000-plus *mura*, in other words between 175–200 *mura* per goat. The other [SI.P. 103.27] mentions 1 goat worth 260 *mura*.

There are also frequent references to skins and hides being delivered or collected: [IOL Khot 23/14; SI.P. 103.45; SI.P. 94.9; Or.8212/162; SI.P. 103.25; IOL Khot Wood 62; SI.P. 95.3; SI.P. 96.5; SI.P. 96.9; SI.P. 103.7], in particular cow-hides [Or.12637/21.1a; IOL Khot Wood 2; SI.P. 95.7; SI.P. 103.6], 'goat cloth' [SI.P. 103.19; SI.P. 103.25], 'calf-hide' [SI.P. 103.25] and *trramcarra* skins [SI.P. 94.9; SI.P. 103.25; SI.P. 103.45]. Sheepskins are described as being for winter clothing [SI.P. 103.48; SI.P. 136.1]. Some skins or hides were used in payment, and some were deposited in the store at Gaysata. Occasionally animals and/or skins were used in part payments.

### *Tax payments*

The Khotanese word for tax is *thamga*. Many documents relate to tax payments and reveal that taxes were paid in *mura* and in kind. Emmerick and Vorob'ëva-Desyatovskaja (1995: 14) and Vorob'ëva-Desyatovskaja (1996) have noted that taxes were paid in *mura*, cloth, skins, cattle, sheep, wheat, barley, hemp and vegetable oil and suggested that many of the documents in the St Petersburg collection represent the records of tax payments. Two documents dated 779 and 784 suggest that there may have been tax payments at 1,000 *mura* per month: 5,000 for ten months [Or.6395/2 (M.9), dated 779] and '55 paying men . . . tax of 55,000 *mura*' [Or.6395/1 (M.10), dated 784]. There is also one document which lists tax payments by five wives [Or.8211/1477].

Labour, expressed as *ksirva kira* ('state work'), was also a form of tax. (Kumamoto 1996b: 49). One document [IOL Khot Wood 1; Skjærvø 2003] indicates that those unable or unwilling to do 'state work' could arrange to pay in coin instead. The bilingual Chinese-Khotanese document [Dx.18927] confirms that corvée obligations could be bought off with money (Kumamoto 2002: 5).[12]

## The documents from Domoko

The Domoko (= Damagou, Dumagu) site has yielded both Khotanese documents and bilingual Khotanese–Chinese documents which have corresponding texts. Seven bilingual Khotanese–Chinese documents have been found at Domoko, as well as Chinese documents dating from 755 to 790 (Stein 1907: Appendix A; Zhang and Rong 1993: 71–97). It is likely, therefore, that the Khotanese and bilingual Khotanese–Chinese documents from Domoko also date from the late seventh to eighth centuries. On his Fourth Expedition, Stein also found a bilingual Khotanese–Chinese document, which is similar to two of Ambolt's documents [H:15; H:16] (Wang Jiqing 1997, 1998). The contents of these documents are discussed below.

### *The Khotanese documents from Domoko*

Approximately half of the documents are written on paper and half on wooden tablets. They are official documents of an administrative and financial nature, and list personal and official names, quantities of money, textiles and grain, also debts with interest payments [H:2], collection of goods and redistribution. The documents are few and incomplete, yet it is possible to draw some conclusions from these documents of the late seventh and eighth centuries.

Two documents [H:16; H:19] express payments in units of 1,000. Fifteen documents (almost twenty per cent) list quantities in excess of 1,000 *mura*. Many documents record both textiles and *mura*. It is not always clear how the transactions worked, other than that textiles were collected in, and that their value was reckoned in *mura*; for example [H:13]:

> for 5 men, according to the number of pieces of cloth, the *mura* amount to 14,310 (= 5 × 2,862)
> for 5 men, according to the number of pieces of cloth, the *mura* amount to 8,200 (= 5 × 1,640)

The payment of 8,200 *mura* to five men is significant. If shared out equally, each man's quota would be 1,640, which matches two other quotas of 1,640 *mura* noted in another document [H:1].

In one document there appears to have been some kind of supplement which was payable with regard to the unidentified 'K'. If so, Bailey's cumbersome translation [H:33]:

> for one man the individual amount (for the man) 400 *mura*, and for the K. 9 *mura*, for the man 5 *mura*. Give at once 2,045. And the next

amount for the asses (for the animals?), for one man 260 *mura*. For the messengers (?) and the K. 5 *mura*, for a man 6 *mura*. Give at once 1,590. The order is thus issued for you [H:33]

can be clarified by the simple formula:

[individual amount] + [K's amount] = total
[400 *mura* × 5 men = 2,000 *mura*] + [9 *mura* × 5 men = 45 *mura*] = 2,045 *mura*
[260 *mura* × 6 men = 1,560 *mura*] + [5 *mura* × 6 men = 30 *mura*] = 1,590 *mura*

***The bilingual Khotanese–Chinese documents from Domoko***

There are several bilingual Khotanese–Chinese documents: [H:15, H:16, H:24] from Ambolt's expedition (Bailey 1961), [OIOC Photo 392/57; T.O.45/1+2] from Stein's Fourth Expedition (Wang Jiqing 1998; Skjærvø 2002), and a later find [1941–33–46/45/62] (Lin Meicun 1993). The bilingual documents are also being studied by Kumamoto (e.g. 2001). Many of these documents list the textiles brought from the Six Villages[13] for presentation at court, note the lengths of the textiles and state that a voucher or receipt was issued by the official (Khotanese *spata*; Chinese *sapo*). One document [H:16] specifies the use of coins in units of 1,000: the first five lines of the Khotanese text note that textiles were paid, and that their values were reckoned at 3,000 coins and 4,000 coins. This information is not repeated in the Chinese text.

**Chinese documents from the Khotan region**

The majority of Chinese documents relating to Khotan are those that survived at Dunhuang but which concern Khotan during the ninth and tenth centuries (Kumamoto 1996; Zhang Guangda and Rong Xinjiang 1993: 71–97) and are too late for this study. For the eighth century there is a small body of material from the Khotan region, most notably the eight Chinese loan contracts from Khotan and the 17 documents from the Dandan-Uiliq site (Stein 1907: Appendix A; Chavannes 1913; Maspéro 1953). A further 20 documents in the St Petersburg Collection have also been published recently (Zhang and Rong 2002).

The Chinese loan contracts from Khotan record loans of grain, coins and a donkey. One loan of 500 coins records the mortgaging of an ivory comb [Y&I:248]; two other loans are for 1,000 coins [Y&I:249], and 15,000 coins [Y&I:250; Y&I:251] (see Chapter 9).

Of the seventeen Chinese documents from Dandan-Uiliq, 14 were found in the 'modest residence of the monkish caretakers who looked after the outlying property of the Huguo Temple' (Stein 1907: 276). Eight of these were dated, covering the period 768–90. The other three were published by Hoernle (1899). One document from Dandan-Uiliq, dated 781, concerns the sale of a donkey for 6,000 coins. Ten months later, the payment has still not been made, and the letter asks for action to be taken [Stein D.v.6]. Many of the Chinese documents from Dandan-Uiliq were associated with the monastery there, and hint at the role of the monasteries in economic life south of the Tarim Basin. The similar role of the monasteries north of the Tarim Basin, as seen in the Tocharian documents, has been mentioned earlier (see Chapter 10).

Eight of the documents are private loan contracts. One, dated 786, concerns a loan of 15,000 coins. The conditions are similar to those seen in the Chinese documents from Turfan (see Chapter 9). The total is to be repaid, with a premium, within eight months, after which a monthly interest rate will be payable. If the debt is not repaid, then the value of the capital and interest will be extracted from his family assets, with his guarantors bearing ultimate responsibility. In 786, someone from Jiexie (= Gaysata) had paid back 10,000 coins of the loan [Hoernle 3]. These terms are similar to those found in Chinese contracts discussed earlier. Another loan contract, dated 782, concerns a loan of 1,000 coins from a monk of the Huguo Temple, with interest payable at the rate of 100 coins (10 per cent) per month [Stein D.vii.2]. The same monk also made a loan of grain that year, to be repaid within nine months [Stein D.vii.4]. Other loans are for 15,000 coins (AD 787) [Stein D.vii.3.d], 500 coins [Stein D.ii.3.a], several hundred coins [Stein D.vii.3.b], an unknown quantity of coins [Stein D.vii.4.b], and a donkey [Stein D.vii.3.c]. Stein found 17 Chinese coins, including wuzhu and Tang coin-types, at the Dandan-Uiliq site. The coins themselves, and the quantities measured in thousands, indicate that the coins mentioned in these documents are Chinese or local issues of Chinese-style coins.

Two documents relate to the affairs at the Chinese garrison of Jiexie. One, from the garrison to the civil magistrate, reports damage to the military equipment, and requests that replacements, including a supply of feathers for arrows, be sent immediately [Hoernle 2]. The second [Hoernle 1], dated 768, is a letter from the Chinese commandant of Jiexie to the king of Khotan. Having been attacked by brigands, many people of Jiexie had sought refuge in the capital of Khotan at Yutian, but were now obliged to pay taxes in grain to the king. However, the grain was still in Jiexie, and the Chinese commandant was therefore asking for the necessary administrative documents to be prepared so that the refugees could return to Jiexie and retrieve the grain needed to make the payments. The indigenous population of Jiexie did not speak Chinese, and the commandant noted that he had to have the correspondence translated. Chavannes (Stein 1907: 529, n.11) suggested that the Chinese commandant made this formal request in order to eliminate fraud and in order that the refugees should be forced to pay the grain transport costs themselves. The formal documents were drawn up in Chinese, probably for political reasons.

The twenty Chinese documents from Domoko in the St Petersburg Collection support these findings and throw more light on life in the region in the second half of the eighth century (see Table 49). The documents are dated from the 770s to 780s. They show that the words *qian* and *wen* indicated 'Chinese' coins. They record loans of 1,500-plus coins and 8,000 coins. Two of the documents record a situation and ask for action to be taken. There are tax payments in grain and wool, both measured by weight; payment for labour at 7,000 and 11,000 *wen*; combined payments made part in coins (*qian*) and part in textiles, and there are two records relating to ox-hides. The document recording the sale of the wild camel in 781 is particularly interesting: Zhang Guangda and Rong Xinjiang (2002: 233 n.4) have compared this example with prices of camels in Jiaohe (near Turfan) as seen in the Chinese historical text *Tang Liu dian*. This text gives the top, middle and lower prices for certain items. For a *bosi guofu* camel (the same type as the wild camel) the top and middle prices in Jiaohe in 743 were given as 33 and 30 *pi* of *dalian* silk; the lower price is not known.

**Table 48**
**Documents relating to tax payments**

| Details | Form of payment | Date | Reference |
|---|---|---|---|
| For the grain of the Chinese the tax of a man here is 5 . . . | Grain | – | [SI.P. 103.21] |
| The order has come for the tax of the Ttumjara month (autumn). Bring it here within five days | – | – | [SI.P. 103.42] |
| Send the tax with the hemp cloth | Hemp cloth (?) | – | [SI.M. 51] |
| (Taxation *mura* given as a gift, not as tax) | – | – | [SI.M. 53] |
| One person gave 550 *mura* in tax<br>One person gave 1 cloth and 250 *mura*<br>One person gave 1 cloth and 250 *mura*<br>One person gave 1 cloth and 250 *mura* | Cloth; *mura* | – | [SI.P. 103.33] |
| One man sends his brother as a tax payment of 500 *mura* . . . for tax . . . 5,000 for ten months | Man (= labour?) | 784 | [Or.6395/1 (M.10)] |
| Tax . . . 55 paying men . . . tax was 55,000 *mura* . . . 1,000 *mura* | *Mura* | 779 | [Or.6395/2 (M.9)] |
| Court tax<br>41 full-time workers to deliver 213 *mura* [total = 8,733?]<br>12 half-time workers to deliver 106 *mura* [total = 1,272?]<br>M had 18 full-time and 7 half-time, total 1,500<br>S had 23 full-time and 5 half-time, total 2,000 | *Mura* | – | [Or.6396/2 (G.G.M.1)] |
| Tax payments by women: 5 wives paid 100 *mura*, 204 *mura*, 212 *mura*, 100 *mura*, 55 *mura*, respectively | *Mura* | – | [Or.8211/1477] |

The same document gives the top, middle and lower prices per *pi* of *dalian* silk in coin as 470, 460 and 450 *wen*. Following the middle price, a *bosi guofu* camel at Turfan would cost 13,800 *wen* (= 30 × 460). The price for the wild camel (16,000 *wen*) nearly 40 years later in the Khotan region is significantly higher.

**Discussion**

The Khotanese, Chinese and bilingual Khotanese–Chinese documents from the Khotan region indicate that, in the late seventh century and eighth century, Chinese or Chinese-style coins served as the main form of money in this area, and that the value of most items was reckoned and expressed in terms of Chinese coins, known as *mura* in Khotanese and *qian* and *wen* in Chinese. Large quantities of *mura* are expressed in the Khotanese documents, many in units of a thousand or multiples of a thousand. These examples strongly suggest the use of a unit of 1,000 coins at Khotan, similar to the Chinese 'string' of coins, and the Tibetan *srang* of *dmar* (see Chapter 12). These results demonstrate the strength of the Chinese administration in the region and the widespread use of Chinese money at all levels of Khotanese society.

The Chinese and bilingual Khotanese–Chinese documents generally corroborate the findings in the Khotanese documents, and, as we might expect, throw more light upon relations between the Khotanese and the Chinese. They indicate for example that translation was necessary between Chinese and the language of the local people; and that high-level formal documents were drawn up in Chinese. The Khotanese documents confirm that the local Khotanese people identified themselves as being different from the Sogdians, Chinese and Tibetans: Sogdians [Or.6394/2 (M.9); Or.11252/38; Or.11344/4; Or.11344/16; Or.12637/23], Chinese [Or.6398/4 (M.3); SI.P. 103.35] and Tibetans [Or.11252/2; IOL Khot 27/10; IOL Khot Wood 31]. They suggest that most of the transactions recorded in the Khotanese documents concerned only the Khotanese people themselves.

The documents indicate that the *murahamgha* [money-collectors] played a pivotal role in the collection of money and liaison between the central administration and the localities. Previous studies have considered the roles of the *spata* (Chinese *sabao*, *safu*, *sabo*, *sahe*) and other officials in commercial affairs (e.g. Forte 2000: 186–90). The hierarchy of officialdom and the career progression of certain individuals whose names appear frequently in the Khotanese documents need further exploration. In particular, it would be useful to determine the relationship between the *spata*, the *murahamgha* and other officials in Khotan.

Vouchers or receipts were important for keeping records and balancing accounts, as expressed so vividly in the case of the incompetent official [H: 3]. They appear to have been used for recording payments of *mura* or goods into the stores, but it is not clear how the system worked, who handled the vouchers, and whether they could be used to recover goods deposited in the stores. It is tempting to think of the vouchers as a possible early form of paper money, similar to those seen in the Tibetan documents (see Chapter 12), but this requires further research.

The Chinese documents tell of tax payments in grain, and, if Chavannes is correct, hint at the added expense of transporting those payments, but it is only in the Khotanese documents that there is any suggestion that textiles may have played a role as money. Whilst the details of transactions involving textiles are not clear in many cases, there can be no doubt that there was an alternative to using coins in the Khotan area at this time. The Khotanese documents show that there were different forms of money in Khotan and that payments were made in *mura*, textiles, grain, animals and hides, and sometimes in a

**Table 49**
**Evidence of money in the Chinese documents from Khotan**

| Details | Date | Reference |
|---|---|---|
| Official purchase of 100 *jin* of wool (tax?) | *c.*782 | [Dx.18915] |
| 2 ox-hides for making drums | 780 | [Dx.18916] |
| Loan of 1,500+ coins (*qian*) making a total of 4,300 coins (*wen/qian*), and asking for action to be taken | 788 | [Dx.18917] |
| Tax | – | [Dx.18918] |
| 5 *shuo* of grain<br>500 coins (*wen*) | 782 | [Dx.18919] |
| Payment for labour: 7,000 coins (*wen*) and 11,000 coins (*wen*) | 779–80 | [Dx.18920] |
| – | 780 | [Dx.18921] |
| Payments in sheepskins:<br>3 people paid 10 sheepskins (3 × 10 = 30)<br>1 person paid 30 sheepskins<br>4 people paid 40 sheepskins<br>Total of 100 sheepskins paid | – | [Dx.18922] |
| Looking for a donkey, asking for action to be taken | *c.*785 | [Dx.18923] |
| Late payment of grain | – | [Dx.18924] |
| Loan of 8,000 coins (*wen*) | – | [Dx.18925] |
| Sale of a wild camel for 16,000 coins (*wen*) | 781 | [Dx.18926; SI.P. 93.22; Dx.18928], Kumamoto 2001 |
| Coins (*qian*) and cloth | Dali reign | [Dx.18929] |
| 1 ox-hide | – | [Dx.18930] |

combination of two or more money-objects. Taxes were collected in *mura* and in local produce. In most cases, it was normal for the values or prices of these goods to be reckoned and expressed in *mura*. The *murahamgha* were responsible for liaising between the central administration and their individual localities, and for collecting and delivering money in its various forms.

It is difficult to determine the equivalent values between textiles and *mura*. One document [IOL missing fragments; Godfrey 2: *KT II*, p. 76] confirms that rolls of hemp cloth were available in widths of 60-*cha* and 70-*cha*, and that cotton was available in rolls of 50-*cha*. The prices expressed in this document put hemp cloth at 60 to 70 *mura* per *cha*, and cotton cloth at 150 *mura* per *cha*, more than double the price of the hemp cloth. The prices given for woollen cloths are generally higher than this, but no dimensions are given. If we assume that the three materials – hemp, cotton and wool – were all local products, the extra labour (e.g. shepherding) required for producing wool might account for the higher price of the wool than for plant-based textiles such as hemp and cotton. However, if we consider that the main cotton centre in Eastern Central Asia was at Gaochang (see Chapter 9 n15), and that the cotton may have been brought to Khotan from Gaochang, the desirability and transport of the cotton may have contributed to its high price at Khotan.

It is also difficult to determine which money-objects were used in which contexts, and to determine whether payments were made part in *mura* and part in textiles owing to necessity (perhaps because of non-availability of *mura*) or out of preference, perhaps harking back to traditional customs in the region. A prime example of this is seen in the adoption of a child, where the desired price was expressed as 700 *mura*, comprising 500 *mura* and 3 *cha* of white silk worth 200 *mura*. There are few references to silk in the Khotanese documents, suggesting that silk was not generally used as a money-object, and that in this case the silk may have been a special payment. Payments generally concern money-objects that were locally available, in particular *mura* and local produce. Occasionally demands were made for products from groups of people, for example, the demand for a payment of one sack per ten men and one rope per ten men.

One document [Or.12637/12.1] is intriguing and may turn out to be important. It states that payments have been received in *mura* 'in multiples of thirteen' from ten people. The payments are listed as 426, 196, 100, 268, 200-plus, 117, 416, 108, 403 and elsewhere in this document we read that 2,977 *mura* are needed for 229 men. Four of these numbers are indeed multiples of thirteen: 117 (= 13 × 9), 416 (= 13 × 32), 403 (= 13 × 31), 2977 (= 13 × 229), but what is the significance of this? The recurrence of the number 13 is also seen in the earlier Chinese documents, where *da-huang-bu* were distributed in lots of 13, and where one salary payment had a total value of 14,443 coins (= 13 × 1,111) (see Chapter 7), as well as in the Kharoshthi documents, where 13 hands of *tavastaga* carpet were valued at 12 *muli* (see Chapter 8). Whether there was the equivalent of a 'baker's dozen' or whether these examples are coincidental and unrelated remains to be explored.

### Notes

1. For a history of the decipherment of the Khotanese language see Skjærvø (2002: lxix–lxxii). The study of Khotanese was advanced greatly by the work of H. W. Bailey and his publications, which include the series *Khotanese Texts* (1945–85) and his *Dictionary of Khotan Saka* (1979).

2. For details of the documents from Dunhuang see Kumamoto (1996a).
3. The documents collected by Ambolt during his investigations of Eastern Central Asia between 1929 and 1932 are housed as part of the Hedin collection in the National Museum of Ethnography, Stockholm. The documents were presumed to be from the Hedin collection until Rong Xinjiang checked the registers in the Museum of Ethnography in 1989, and found that most of them were, in fact, from Ambolt's investigations in Eastern Central Asia. Lin Meicun (1993) summarizes the work that has been done on these documents.
4. Bailey translated here as 14,000 *mura*; Skjærvø (private communication, May 2004) prefers 4,000 *mura*.
5. This translation is based on Emmerick and Vorob'ëva-Desjatovskaya (1995: 158–59), but with minor adjustments.
6. The Chinese name for Gaysata is Jiexie (see Skjærvø 2002: xlvii; Zhang Guangda and Rong Xinjiang 2002).
7. For the phonetic reconstructions see Pulleyblank 1991: 29–30.
8. The contracts were drawn and 'finger seals' [*hamgusti*] were taken from witnesses by drawing vertical lines separating the syllables of the person's name: for a clear example see [Or.6395/1]. I am grateful to Ursula Sims-Williams for showing this to me. It is not known if the 'finger seals' are related to the Chinese and Tibetan contracts, where the signature involved drawing lines from the finger joints.
9. Many documents include textiles followed by a quantity of *mura*. This is often translated as textiles 'and' followed by a quantity of *mura*. It is possible that some of these instances may be better translated as textiles 'with a value of' followed by quantity of *mura*. (Skjærvø, private communication, May 2004).
10. Skjærvø (in private communication, May 2004) suggests that this may refer literally to very big cloths, which were woven to a much larger width than normal. The function of these special cloths is not known.
11. There may be similarities here with the subcontracting out of tax obligations at Gaochang (see Chapter 9).
12. This document has now been located in the Bibliothèque Nationale, Paris. I am grateful to Ursula Sims-Williams for this correction.
13. There has been much debate over the identification of the 'Six Villages'; for a summary of the arguments see Kumamoto (1996: 43–50).

# 12 Tibetan documents, eighth and ninth centuries

The Stein collection of Tibetan manuscripts, now housed in the British Library, is the single largest source of such documents, comprising about 2,200 wooden tablets, and 702 paper fragments (Takeuchi 1997, 1998). Most are from the late eighth to the early ninth century, from the period of Tibetan control of southern Xinjiang and the Hexi Corridor in Gansu. They were acquired during Stein's second and third expeditions, from sites in Khotan (Mazar Tagh, Sampula, Domoko, Khadalik, Ile-dong, Balawaste, Keriya, Endere), Turfan (Kara-khoja, Toyuk, Hassar B) and Miran. Tibetan documents were also found by Chinese archaeologists in 1959, 1973 and 1974 (Wang Yao and Chen Jian 1986). The majority have come from the Tibetan sites at Mazar Tagh and Miran, where they were retrieved from refuse heaps (Francke 1921; Takeuchi 1997). Tibetan documents have also been found at Dunhuang, but these are of a later date, and are not considered here.

These documents offer first-hand evidence for money during Tibetan rule in the region. In particular, the wooden documents reveal details of tax collection, and the paper fragments include evidence of approximately eighty contracts.

**The wooden tablets**

By the third century wood slips were no longer in use in central China, but the practice of writing on wooden tablets continued among the Tibetan people. Many of the Tibetan wooden tablets are letters and letter covers bearing addresses, some of which were probably attached as labels to packages during transport. Other short wooden documents were used by tax collectors on their rounds to visit taxpayers, and again these bear little more than personal and local place names. Complete wooden documents are not so numerous: some relate to tax collection and others to supplies of military provisions. They are in two styles. The first consists of tablets about 30–40 cm long and square in section, with notches at the edges, marking the number of bushels of grain contributed by the taxpayers. Words such as 'barley', 'wheat', 'millet', 'grass', 'horse fodder' are written close to the notches, and personal names are written at the other end of the tablet. Most payments were made in grain. The second style of document consists of short wooden tablets, coloured red on the surface, with the lower right corner of the tablets cut out to mark them as special documents.[1] As before, they have notches at one end, and names at the other. A third style of document has a red band painted around the middle, in one instance in blood, but the function of these documents is unknown (Francke 1921).

The contents of the more complete wooden documents included lawsuits, inventories, distribution lists of provisions or gifts, demands for military assistance and provisions, guard duty, postal runners, complaints about late payment of wages and rewards, illness, prayers for medicine, accounts of debts and lists of transport of arms. It was also customary to address people in high positions with a small gift, which might include paper, flint-and-steel purses for firelighting and silk (Francke 1921; Thomas 1951).

The types of goods transported in trade, or taken as taxes or spoils of war, included various kinds of grain, fruit, fodder, spices, dried meat, butter or cheese, beer, clay-pots, *sida* (?), copper kettles, gold, silver, turquoise, pearls, coral, *snam* woollen cloth, *men-thri*-silk, *pha-thsa* coarse sackcloth, *thsos-bal* dyed wool, and *gtan/gdan* carpets. Francke suggested that *gtan/gdan* may refer to felt carpets, which would fit neatly if the linguistic assocation with Chinese *zhan* carpet can be established. One incomplete wooden document from the Mazar Tagh fort [M. Tagh.b.i,002] offers a partial glimpse at a large caravan, which carried 75 loads of barley, 1,000 *pi* [rolls] of silk, 900 *liang* [ounces] of silver, 600 *liang* [ounces] of gold, oil, medicinal flowers, and felt (Thomas 1951: 370).

Thomas (1951: 309) noted that, in contrast to the earlier Kharoshthi documents from Eastern Central Asia, the Tibetan documents were the work of foreigners administering an annexed country, with little interest in the local population. For example, during the Tibetan control of Khotan between 790 and *c.*850, the Tibetan officials resided in their own Tibetan fortress at Mazar Tagh, not in the Khotanese towns. They demanded supplies from the Khotanese and received them in bulk, but the general administration of Khotan was left in the hands of the king of Khotan.

**The paper documents**

The more fragile paper documents have not survived as well as the wooden tablets, and most appear to be only half of the original document (Takeuchi 1998). They were often reused. From the Tibetan documents in the Stein, Pelliot, Hedin, Kozlov, Oldenburg, Malov and Otani collections, Takeuchi (1995) has identified a total of 58 contracts: from Dunhuang (37), Miran fort (ten), Mazar Tagh (four), Domoko (four), Turfan (two) and Khadalik (one). The earliest are the contracts from Domoko, *c.*801. Those from Miran, Mazar Tagh and Turfan are probably from the early ninth century. Those from Dunhuang are from the first half of the ninth century. The formula of the Tibetan contracts is remarkably similar to that of the Chinese contracts of the seventh and eighth centuries, found at Turfan, except for the inclusion in the Tibetan contracts of an official penalty, usually whipping. This contrasts strongly with the Chinese contracts, which were strictly private transactions. Takeuchi (1995: 118) suggests that the Tibetans may have adopted the Chinese contract formula in Khotan – the earliest known Tibetan contracts are those found at Domoko, dated 796/808 and 801, a decade after the Tibetan conquest of Khotan. From then on, Tibetan contracts were drafted usually for non-Tibetan local inhabitants, as at Dunhuang.

There are three types of contract: sales (ten), loans (25) and hiring of labour (six). Another 17 contracts are very fragmented and offer limited evidence; and there are a further 20 documents of various contents which although incomplete are still of interest. These are presented in the tables later in this chapter, with the following abbreviations: T = Takeuchi (1995); P = Pelliot collection; VP = Louis de la Vallée Poussin; Ch. = Ch'ien-fo-tung/Qianfodong, Dunhuang (Stein collection); Hedin = Hedin collection; TLTD = Thomas (1955); SI/P = Serindia, Petrovsky collection, St Petersburg; Otani = Otani collection, Ryukoku University, Kyoto.

***Sales contracts (see Table 50)***

There are three categories of sales contracts: livestock (five), humans (two), land and property (three). The main purpose of these contracts was to state explicitly the post-sale conditions: usually the seller was responsible for the goods he sold, and, if a sale was problematic, the buyer could claim a full refund or replacement of similar quality. If either side breached the contract, the penalty was usually double the price, with an additional occasional official penalty of whipping.

Where prices were expressed, they were given in weights of *dmar* and grain. *Dmar* means red (Zhang Yisun 1985). Thomas (1951: 325) translated *dmar* simply as copper, as contrasted with Chinese coins, which are expressed in Tibetan as *dong-tse*, thought to be derived from the Chinese *tongzi* 銅子 meaning copper coin (Xiao Huaiyuan 1987: 2). However, it is likely that *dmar* may also refer to Chinese cash, though in the unit of 1 string (of 1,000 cash). The term *dmar* is usually found together with the term *srang*, a weight measure indicating the Chinese *liang*. Takeuchi (1995: 25–6) has shown how, in the Tibetan documents from the early ninth century, *srang* may indicate copper cash, taking into consideration the following evidence: (1) average prices in the early eighth century (cow at 2,200–4,200 cash, horse at 4,000–9,000 cash, slave at 4,200 cash); (2) the 4,500 *dong-tse* demanded for bail for releasing an accused Khotanese cook [T.58]; (3) loan contracts from Khotan: [T.46] (penalty of 4 *srang* of *dmar*); [T.48] (loan of 1 *srang* of *dmar*); [T.49] (loan of 100? *dong-tse*)] and Tibetan letters from Mazar Tagh [M. Tagh 0482; M. Tagh.a.vi.0065; M. Tagh.c.i.0065], which indicate that copper coins were used as money. In addition to this, there were, among the late eighth-century Chinese contracts found at Khotan (see Chapter 11), six for loans of cash, four of which were for 1,000 cash, which would match exactly the loan of 1 *srang* of *dmar* [T.48]. As the only coins found at the sites which yielded Tibetan documents were Chinese cash of the Tang dynasty (see Chapter 4), Takeuchi's argument appears acceptable.

Interpreting *dmar* and *srang* in this way, it appears that livestock and humans were reckoned in strings of cash, and land and property in grain.

***Loan contracts (see Table 51)***

The loan contracts are more numerous (25), and fall into two basic categories: items that were to be returned (as rental) (seven) [T.11–17], and items that might be consumed and replaced, e.g. grain and seeds (18) [T.12–35]. Items were sometimes deposited as security: for example, a door bolt and key as security for household items [T.16]; two doors as security for grain seeds [T.22]. The contracts specified the repayment date, the penalty for missing the deadline and the penalty for non-payment. The penalties were, respectively, doubling up the value of the loan and subsequent confiscation of family property up to the value of the amount owed. Family property is usually expressed as 'indoor treasures and outdoor cattle wealth' (*nang-nor phyi-phyug*). The interest rate was mentioned on only one loan contract, at 100 per cent [T.26].

Loans of grain and seeds were usually made from local residents and temples to commoners, to those belonging to monastic estates and to bondservants. Repayment was usually specified as the mid-autumn month, corresponding to the Chinese eighth month (as in the Chinese loan contracts) which was harvest-time. Some of the loans were made to groups of people rather than individuals, for example, the loan of grain to eight borrowers, who had failed to pay the grain tax and had been forced to borrow grain [T.26]. Some of the loans were in the form of ledgers, listing the amounts of grain borrowed by individuals in a group [T.26–32]; when the loans were repaid the entry was simply crossed out with a black line [T.25; T.27–32]. Three were in the form of receipts for repayment of loaned grain [T.33–5].

***Contracts of hiring labour (see Table 52)***

There are six contracts for hiring labour. Three are for substituting official, corvée or military duties, two are for agricultural labour and one is for hiring a personal servant. The employer hiring the servant for one year also took over responsibility for his employee's official duties during that period, and provided him with food. In the three cases of substitution for duty, the employee remained responsible for his own tax obligations, as well as for the good execution of any substitution work he took on. Payment, when specified, was in grain or food products, and in one case [T.36] in barley, millet and cotton cloth to a value of 14 *khal* of grain. The substitution work was paid in instalments. [T.36] was paid in two instalments, at the time of the contract, and on completion. [T.37] was for three months' work: the first month was paid according to the standard rate, but the second and third payments were not made, so a supplementary agreement was drawn up with repayment due at the end of the current month. [T.38] was payable upon completion of the duty.

***Fragments of contracts (see Table 53) and miscellaneous transactions (see Table 54)***

In addition to those documents that are clearly contracts, there are other Tibetan documents in the Stein collection, albeit mostly fragmentary, which also refer to money (Takeuchi 1998). Three of these relate to copper coins (*dong-tse*), and a fourth to *srang* of *dmar*, all probably associated with loans. One of these was to be repaid part in coin, part in silk. A further twelve documents refer to silk; in three of these it served as a means of payment, and a fourth may be a register noting loans of silk to various people. These documents indicate therefore that coins and silk were probably used together as money.

Furthermore, three documents indicate the use of silver (*dngul*) in measures of *srang*. The highest quantity is 27 *srang* of silver as the price for cattle. No document allows us to estimate directly the local exchange rate between Chinese copper coins and silver. However, Peng (1965: 327) noted that in China the price of silver was about 1,000 cash per *liang* throughout the

**Table 50**
**Contracts of sale (T. no. = Takeuchi 1995)**

| T. no | Object | Price | Conditions | Penalty for breach of contract | Form | Date | Location | Reference |
|---|---|---|---|---|---|---|---|---|
| 1 | Ox | 3 *srang* of *dmar* | Expresssed as barter. If problem, then repay the price | To pay penalty of 2 *srang* of *dmar*, also official penalty of whipping | – | 832 or 844 | Dunhuang | P1094 |
| 2 | Ox | – | If problem, then repay cow of similar age, or to the value of at least 1 cow and 1 calf | 4 *khal* of barley | – | 823+ | Dunhuang | P1095 |
| 3 | Cow | 3 *srang* of *dmar* | If problem, seller is responsible | – | – | 837 or 847 | Dunhuang | P1088/1 |
| 4 | Cow? | 1.5 *srang* of *dmar* | – | – | – | 829+ | Dunhuang | VP1435 |
| 5 | Horse | – | If problem, then repay horse of equal quality | 5 *srang* of *dmar* | – | 827 or 839 | Dunhuang | P1297/3 |
| 6 | Man (50-year-old Chinese bondservant) | 8 *srang* of *dmar* | – | – | – | – | Miran | Stein M. I.lxix.7 |
| 7 | Woman (seller's sister sold as wife to buyer) | 7 *srang* of *dmar* | Marriage sale; if problem, then repay double, or woman of same quality | – | – | 820+ | Dunhuang | Ch.frag.62 |
| 8 | House and land | 4 *sheg* of grain | – | – | Receipt | 831+ | Dunhuang | P1086 |
| 9 | House | 14 *sheg* of grain | Payment in instalments, document records the final payments | – | Receipt | 832+ | Dunhuang | P2220 |
| 10 | House | – | Names the seller and buyer | – | | 801 | Domoko | Hedin 1 |

ninth century. This may also turn out to be true for Eastern Central Asia. Four examples indicate the price of cattle: a single cow or ox at 3 *srang* of *dmar* [P1094, P1095, P1088], and an unknown number of cattle at 27 *srang* of silver [M.I.xxvii.21]. If, as proposed above, 1 *srang* of *dmar* indicated 1 string of 1,000 coins, which in turn was equivalent to 1 ounce (*liang*) of silver, then the value of 1 *srang* of coins and 1 *srang* of silver was the same. In this way, the price of 27 *srang* would indicate a purchase of nine cows. This neat equation suggests that the exchange rate in Eastern Central Asia may indeed have been 1 string of 1,000 copper coins to 1 *liang* of silver.

### Discussion

The paper contracts reveal that strings of cash and grain were the major forms of money for local sales, loans and hiring of labour. Strings of cash were used primarily for purchasing animals and humans. Grain was used in purchases of land and property, loans, and hiring of labour. The wooden documents also show the importance of grain in tax collection. Thomas (1951: 388, 255) concluded that:

> wages (rations, *tshal-ma* and *gla*) were usually reckoned in grain; where money payment was requisite, it was in the form of Chinese coins (*don-tse*) and copper *sran* [*srang*, ounce]. It will be realised that a sparse employment of coin entails a resort to orders or drafts convertible locally by travellers into supplies; and such seem, in fact, to be denoted by the expression *brygyags byan* ('provision-ticket'). We also have the expressions 'attested signature of the three times' (*dus-sum-gyi-dpan-gryá*),[2] which seems to be a bill payable at sight, and *bkah-rims-phye* 'circular flour order', which must be an order to levy flour at successive points along a route.

The early forms of drafts, bills and tickets noted by Thomas may be very important. Although some are clearly levies for supplies en route, others may be remittance notes. They appear to parallel the Tang dynasty remittance system known as 'flying cash' (*feiqian* 飛錢), from 806 to 811, whereby, having sold goods in the capital, merchants could deposit their cash with the government office representing their locality (*jinzouyuan* 進奏院), in exchange for a certificate, which would be

**Table 51**
**Contracts of loan (T. no. = Takeuchi 1995)**

| T. no | Object | Penalty for missing repayment deadline | Penalty for non-payment | Date | Form | Location | Reference |
|---|---|---|---|---|---|---|---|
| 11 | Paper (10 bolts) and cloth (for wrapping) | Double the value of loan | Confiscation of inkpot, handkerchief and other goods to the value of amount owed | 824+ | – | Dunhuang | Thomas TLTD 2: 66 (Ch.) |
| 12 | Knife | Double the value of loan | Confiscation of tools, handkerchief and other goods to the value of amount owed | 824+ | – | Dunhuang | P1166 |
| 13 | Paper (200 bolts) | – | Confiscation of family property, and official penalty of whipping | 824+ | – | Dunhuang | P1078 |
| 14 | Cotton | Double the value of loan | Confiscation of security deposit | 834+ | – | Dunhuang | P2127 |
| 15 | *Men-dri* silk | Double the value of loan | – | – | – | Domoko | Hedin 2 |
| 16 | 4 cups<br>3 *deb-tse* (?)<br>1 string of twisted cotton thread | Double the value of loan | Confiscation of security deposit (= door bolt and key). To redeem bolt and key, must pay 3.5 *chag* of cotton, 4 *bre* of barley | 829+ | – | Dunhuang | Ch.86.ii.v (VP1424) |
| 17 | Horse (pregnant mare) | Repay horse and foal, or pregnant mare | – | 822 or 834 | – | Dunhuang | P1297/5 |
| 18 | Grain seeds (8 *sheg*) | Repay by end of mid-autumn month, or double the value of loan | Confiscation of family property to the value of amount owed | 832 or 844? | – | Dunhuang | P1297/1a |
| 19 | Barley + wheat (3 *khal*) | Repay by end of mid-autumn month, or double the value of loan | Confiscation of family property to the value of amount owed | 832+ | – | Dunhuang | Ch.frag.82.v (VP1141) |
| 20 | Wheat (4 *khal*) | Double the value of loan | Confiscation of family property to the value of amount owed | 835 or 847 | – | Dunhuang | P1088 |
| 21 | Barley (2 *sheg*) | Repay by end of mid-autumn month, or double the value of loan | Confiscation of security (= vacant house and land), and other family property to the value of amount owed | 824+ | – | Dunhuang | Kozlov 4 |
| 22 | Grain seeds and beans | Repay by autumn | Confiscation of security (= 2 doors) | 825+ | – | Dunhuang | P1115 |
| 23 | Beans (10 *sheg*) | Repay by end of mid-autumn month, or double the value of loan | Confiscation of family property to the value of amount owed | 821 or 833 | – | Dunhuang | P1297 |
| 24 | Wheat and barley (9 *khal*) | Repay by 20th of mid-autumn month | Confiscation of family property to the value of amount owed | 825+ | – | Miran | Stein M.I.xvi.22 |
| 25 | Grain and barley | Repay by 15th of mid-autumn month, or double the value of loan | Confiscations of family property to the value of amount owed | – | – | Dunhuang | Stein Or.8210/S7133 |
| 26 | Grain (to 8 borrowers) | Repay by 15th of mid-autumn month, or double the value of loan | Confiscation of family property to the value of amount owed | 830+ | Ledger | Dunhuang | P1101 |

**Table 51**
**(*cont.*)**

| T. no | Object | Penalty for missing repayment deadline | Penalty for non-payment | Date | Form | Location | Reference |
|---|---|---|---|---|---|---|---|
| 27 | grain (4 x 10 *khal* of millet) (1 x 5 *khal* of millet) | Repay by 15th of mid-autumn month, or double the value of loan | Confiscation of family property to the value of amount owed | 830 or 842? | Ledger | Dunhuang | P1104 |
| 28 | Grain (9 loans) | Repay by 15th of mid-autumn month (or autumn), or double the value of loan | Confiscation of family property to the value of amount owed | 830 or 842? | Ledger | Dunhuang | P1203 |
| 29 | Barley (3 loans) | Repay by (15th of) winter month, or double the value of loan | Confiscation of family property to the value of amount owed | 828+ | Ledger | Dunhuang | P2124 |
| 30 | Barley (12 loans) | – | – | 828+ | Ledger | Dunhuang | P2125 |
| 31 | Millet (8 loans) | – | – | – | Ledger | Dunhuang | P1119 |
| 32 | Wheat (6 loans) | – | – | – | Ledger | Dunhuang | P1208 + P1221 |
| 33 | Wheat | – | – | 829+ | Receipt | Dunhuang | Stein Ch.80.v.1 (VP1412) |
| 34 | Wheat | – | – | 829+ | Receipt | Dunhuang | Stein Ch.79.xvi.7 (VP1477) |
| 35 | Wheat | – | – | 829+ | Receipt | Dunhuang | Stein Ch.77.xv.10 (VP1289) |

**Table 52**
**Contracts of hiring labour (T. no. – Takeuchi 1995)**

| T. no | Task | Payment | Date | Location | Reference |
|---|---|---|---|---|---|
| 36 | Official duty substitution: transportation of annual grain tribute | Barley, millet and cotton cloth, to total value of 14 *khal* of grain. Paid in instalments: at time of contract, and on completion | 820? | Dunhuang | P1098 |
| 37 | Corvée duty substitution: 3 months | 1st month paid according to standard rate, but non-payment of 2nd and 3rd months, so new deadline agreed for repayment at end of current month | 833+ | Dunhuang | P1162 |
| 38 | Military service substitution | 1 *dong* vessel containing 6 *sheq* of *gda* (?), and wine (?) to be paid on completion | 801 | Domoko | Hedin 3 |
| 39 | Reaping field of barley | Half of harvest | 834+ | Dunhuang | P1297/4 |
| 40 | Ploughing crop fields | Half of harvest | 830+ | Dunhuang | Stein Or.8212/194a |
| 41 | Working as servant for 1 year | Food; employer also took over corvée duties of employee | 796 or 808 | Domoko | SI.P/135 |

redeemed by the provincial authorities when they returned home (Kaplan 1995: 330; Twitchett 1970: 72–3).

The Tibetan contracts considered in this chapter are primarily of a local nature, and thus reflect circumstances at a local level. They indicate that there may have been a greater use of copper cash than previously suspected (Rhodes 1997: 184), particularly in the Khotan region. Thomas's (1951) impression that the Tibetans were content to let the prevailing local systems continue as far as possible appears to have applied also to the local currency systems.

However, these local documents contrast with the historical evidence which focuses on salt, silks, silver, and gold (including

**Table 53**
**Contracts – fragmentary and incomplete (T. no. = Takeuchi 1995)**

| T. no | Transaction | Object | Date | Location | Reference |
|---|---|---|---|---|---|
| 42 | Sale | Yaks | 825+ | Miran | M.I.xiv.109 |
| 43 | Sale | Sabre | 828+ | Mazar Tagh | M.Tagh.0506 |
| 44 | Sale | Cow | – | Miran | M.I.xxiii.0011 verso |
| 45 | Sale | Horse? | – | Mazar Tagh | M.Tagh.a.iv.00149 |
| 46 | Sale | – | – | Miran | M.I.xvi.1 |
| 47 | Loan | Cloth? | 832+? | Dunhuang | Or.8212/1946 |
| 48 | Loan? | *Dmar*? | 829+ | Mazar Tagh | M.Tagh.0509+0510 |
| 49 | Loan? | 900 copper coins (*dong-tse*) | – | Mazar Tagh | M.Tagh.c.iii.0086 |
| 50 | Loan | Grain | 818+ | Miran | M.I.xxiv.0029 |
| 51 | Loan | Grain? | 824+ | Miran | M.I.xiv.115 |
| 52 | Loan | Barley | – | Miran | M.I.xiv.113 |
| 53 | Loan | – | 823+ | Miran | M.I.xiv.24 |
| 54 | Loan | Barley | – | Miran | M.I.xxiii.0011 recto |
| 55 | Loan | Grain | 831+ | Dunhuang | Or.8210/S2228 |
| 56 | Loan? | Grain? | – | Turfan | Otani 60/2 |
| 57 | Loan? | – | – | Turfan | TBT 122, Berlin |
| 58 | Bail | Person / coins (*dong-tse*)? | 826+ | Khadalik | Khad.052 |

**Table 54**
**Miscellaneous fragments relating to payments and loans (Takeuchi 1998)**

| Transaction | Object | Date | Location | Reference |
|---|---|---|---|---|
| – | Copper coins (*dong-tse*) | – | Mazar Tagh | M.Tagh.0482 |
| Repayment of loan? | Repay in *dong-tse* and silk | – | Mazar Tagh | M.Tagh.a.vi.0065 |
| Loan | Copper coins (*dong-tse*) | – | Mazar Tagh | M.Tagh.c.i.0065 |
| Letter re wage increase | *Zho* (?) | – | Mazar Tagh | M.Tagh.b.i.00104 |
| Sale of cattle | Price 27 *srang* of silver | – | Miran | M.I.xxvii.21 |
| Buddhist text | *Srang* of silver, *srang* of gold | – | Miran | M.I.xxxii.5.h |
| Letter | *Srang* of *dmar* | – | Miran | M.I.xxxiv.11 |
| Inventory of property | Incl. 5 helmets, 40 *srang* of silver, 5 mares | – | Mazar Tagh | M.Tagh.0197 |
| Letter | 1 *srang* of silver | – | Mazar Tagh | M.Tagh.a.iv.00129 |
| Letter | Silk | – | Mazar Tagh | M.Tagh.0421 |
| – | Silk | – | Mazar Tagh | M.Tagh.a.ii.00105 |
| Demand for interest payment | 2 bolts of silk | – | Mazar Tagh | M.Tagh.a.iv.00121 |
| – | Glossed silk | – | Mazar Tagh | M.Tagh.a.iii.0071 |
| Letter re payment date | Silk | – | Mazar Tagh | M.Tagh.a.iv.00124 |
| Loan | Silk | – | Mazar Tagh | M.Tagh.a.iv.00130 |
| – | Silk | – | Mazar Tagh | M.Tagh.a.iv.00159 |
| Register of names and quantities of silk (loaned?) | Silk | – | Mazar Tagh | M.Tagh.a.vi.0063 & M.Tagh.b.i.00124 |
| Letter | 1 long bolt of *men-tri* silk | – | Mazar Tagh | M.Tagh.b.i.0098 |
| Letter | Silk and wool | – | Mazar Tagh | M.Tagh.c.i.0068 |
| Letter | About sending silk | – | Mazar Tagh | M.Tagh.c.ii.0064 |

gold dust) which were used in larger transactions, as suggested by Beckwith (1977: 103):

> Tibet's trade with Central Asia, the eastern Caliphate, and perhaps India, was conducted mainly in silver, and since southern China was a silver area too, it would appear that Tibet (with all its wealth of gold) should be included in a contiguous silver monetary area stetching from southern China to the central Caliphate and beyond.

Silk, silver and gold are indicated together in only one document [M.Tagh.b.i,002], recording the large caravan carrying 75 loads of barley, 1,000 *pi* [rolls] of silk, 900 *liang* of silver, 600 *liang* of gold, oil, medicinal flowers, and felt (Thomas 1951: 370). Francke (1921) noted that silver was probably counted in *dyam* (bars), whilst gold and jewels were counted in *zho* (one-tenth of an ounce) with ½ *zho* of gold equivalent in value to 3 *zho* of silver, i.e. a ratio of 1:6. This accords with Peng's (1965: 327) ratio of between 1:5 and 1:6.[3] However, the majority of the Tibetan documents from Eastern Central Asia suggest a somewhat bleaker picture, particularly in Dunhuang, of commoners having to borrow grain in order to pay their taxes.

## Notes

1. Compare these red-painted documents with the earlier Chinese wooden slips which were also painted red; see Chapter 4.
2. The 'attested signature of the three times' may refer to the 'drawing of finger-joints', which was a regular feature of Chinese contracts: the finger was placed on the document, and lines were drawn out at the finger joints; see Hansen (1995) for details. It may be also be a version of the 'measure of thumb' seen in the Tocharian documents (see Chapter 10).
3. I am grateful to Tsuguhito Takeuchi for confirming that this ratio can be confirmed by the Tibetan text (P1120) and that Kazushi Iwao plans to publish this text in the near future.

# Conclusion

The primary aim of this study was to examine the numismatic and documentary evidence found through archaeology in Eastern Central Asia and to attempt to establish a new framework for money in the region to *c*.800. To a degree, a broad historical framework of money in the region during this period has now been established. The details from the coins and the contexts in which they were found, and from the contemporary documents, allow us to focus in and out of particular places at particular times. It is, however, far more difficult to see the whole picture. To some extent this is owing to the complexity of the material used in this study, but it is also owing to the different dynamics – political, economic, social, cultural and religious – of those particular places at those particular times.

The new framework reflects the monetary changes that took place in Eastern Central Asia during much of the first millennium. It also proposes some general theoretical questions. Money does not only reflect changes, it also stimulates them, and can act as an 'incredibly powerful agent of profound social and cultural transformations' (Parry and Bloch 1989: 3). If Georg Simnel, author of *The Philosophy of Money*, saw money as the principal catalyst for the transformation of social life, and Marx saw money as the result of production for exchange, both associated money with the growth of individualism and the erosion of the traditional ways and structure of a community. A well-known illustration of such erosion can be seen in the anthropologist Mary Douglas's (1958) study of the money systems of the Lele people in the Belgian Congo, particularly the penetration of colonial coins into the exchange systems formerly associated with cloth money. In a seminal study, Paul Bohannan (1959) also demonstrated that, when Western money was first introduced to West Africa, the indigenous population accepted it, yet resisted its impact on their traditional systems. Can similar questions be asked of this study? How did the 'foreign money', or 'foreign coins', that came to Eastern Central Asia integrate with the indigenous systems of exchange? And to what degree did the arrival of that money affect those indigenous systems?

These are important questions, but ones that are difficult to answer. From the coins and documentary evidence we have been able to draw a number of conclusions. It has been possible to identify the various forms of money that were used in particular places at particular times. The key question now is how to establish the hierarchies of those forms, or to determine which forms of money were more highly valued. Value systems can be difficult to identify even in living societies, and most works on economic anthropology warn strongly against interpreting money from inappropriate perspectives, such as from a Eurocentric view (Plattner 1989; Gregory 1997). This is partly why it has proved so difficult to identify the physical money-objects represented by the units of account *muli* and *masa* in the Kharoshthi documents.

Although there is no evidence for the use of any coins in Eastern Central Asia before the arrival of the Chinese during the Western Han period, it is inconceivable that there was no exchange within and among the various kingdoms in the region. There must, at the very least, have been some exchange of goods, systems whereby goods could be exchanged, and probably an established hierarchy of those goods or identifiable media of exchange and units of account. Indeed, even after the arrival of Chinese and other coins, the local systems continued to work on a multi-faced basis. The documentary evidence from Eastern Central Asia provides many examples of natural produce and manufactured products in many different kinds of transactions involving payment or exchange, including purchases, loans, rent, and taxation.

If we take as our starting point the indigenous population of Eastern Central Asia, we must bear in mind that the various kingdoms, or polities, had their own political systems and traditions. How did these work? How did the local populations respond to the arrival of foreign money, especially coins, which were part of an external monetary system with practices different to their own? By what mechanisms or adjustments was it possible to integrate the established local practices with the newly arrived foreign practices?

The coins and documentary evidence from the Niya site provide a useful insight into this question. They show that the indigenous population had its own political system and traditions that were clearly different from those of the Chinese who dominated Eastern Central Asia. Barter was fairly commonplace, and there were established values of goods in relation to one another. In other words, there was a hierarchy of different forms of objects used in exchange. There were also procedures by which purchases could be made, objections could be raised and fines or penalties could be determined. Some coins have been found at the site, though all Chinese and in very small numbers. The only identifiable references to coins in the Kharoshthi documents are to Chinese coins and in each case the owner of the coins had external connections. The evidence suggests that the impact of Chinese money on the local population at the Niya site was minimal, and that the local traditions prevailed. Yet the documents also reveal that merchants passed through and that they brought goods such as silk. If coins were not used widely at the Niya site itself, then we must consider that other items were used in payment, perhaps along similar lines to exchange among the Niya people themselves. Yet some people from Niya also travelled to other centres such as Khotan and Loulan, where coins were widely used. They would have had to make some exchanges or adjustments in terms of the currency they were carrying in order to manage even a short stay.

Whilst we can make suppositions about adjustments and exchange at Niya, the Sino-Kharoshthi coins issued by the kings of Khotan provide an excellent example of a desire to integrate two very different currency systems: the Kushan coinage and the Chinese coinage. Both of these currencies were initially foreign to the indigenous population of Khotan. Khotan lay at the eastern extremity of the Kushan empire, and at the western extremity of the Chinese empire. The new bilingual, bicultural coinage reflects the use of both Kushan and Chinese currencies in Khotan, and shows that the impact of these currencies was sufficient to inspire the kings of Khotan to create their own new coinage. This conscious decision probably had a greater impact on the political structure than on local financial practices. However, it is difficult to assess the impact of this new coinage. Perhaps these practices had already been challenged by the arrival of the Kushan and Chinese currencies and it was a logical reaction to create a new coinage by and for the local population, rather than rely on coins issued by external authorities? The distribution of the new Sino-Kharoshthi coins was limited within the region of Khotan, and shows that such a new development was not appropriate throughout Eastern Central Asia at this time.

The impact of the Chinese monetary system on Eastern Central Asia was far-reaching. This can be explained partly by the Chinese authority over the region: the inhabitants of the Chinese military garrisons and farming settlements would have used Chinese coins in their everyday transactions. But at the same time, other goods, such as grain and textiles, were also being used in exchange. This appears to have been the case at Loulan, where coin finds are plentiful, and the documents show that there were exchanges between Loulan and the neighbouring indigenous settlements and that Chinese military leaders hired local soldiers when necessary. Some of these transactions were probably paid for in coin; some in other media. The Chinese documents found at the Juyan sites indicate that private commerce was probably quite widespread: if Chinese officials were able to hire private individuals for business purposes, this suggests that private commerce was widespread and that both officials and individuals could travel fairly freely. What we do not know is whether the cultural associations of Chinese money were also accepted by the local populations. The issuers of the Sino-Kharoshthi coins of Khotan, for example, chose to adopt the script indicating the value but not the form of Chinese coins. The issuers of the Qiuci coins followed the Chinese typology more closely. Whilst there is a wealth of philosophical discussion relating to coins and money in central China at this time, exemplified in Lu Bao's chilly criticism of money (see Chapter 2), there is none available to us from Eastern Central Asia. Instead, we see money, and the exchange system in which coins were just one part, as evidence of a flourishing market economy. Perhaps, owing to the particularity of the exchange systems of this region, now so readily associated with the concept of the 'Silk Road', the markets here were from the beginning very international. Payments at the markets were made in a variety of forms of money of differing values and cultural associations, often at the same time in the same place. How then can we understand the mechanisms of such transactions?

In this respect, it is extremely useful to consider the results of my study with the market intelligence acquired by the Russian army captain Chokan Valikhanov (1835–65) in Eastern Central Asia and the adjacent regions of Kazakhstan and Kyrgyzstan in the 1850s. Over a millennium later than the period I have studied, Valikhanov described how the Kyrgyz people did not go to trade in centres such as Kashgar and Yining. Instead, they set up temporary settlements (*aul*) each summer and winter to which caravans of merchants would bring goods from market centres such as Kashgar, Yining and Tacheng. At the *aul*, all goods were exchanged for sheep. But the prices in the market centres were expressed in terms of coins: for example, in Kashgar a sheep cost between 5 and 10 tangas, with an average price of 8 tangas. At the *aul*, merchants would exchange their goods for sheep, and reckon their profits in terms of tangas. Russian goods were also exchanged for sheep, but profits on these goods were reckoned in roubles. The sheep served as a kind of monetary unit equal to the silver rouble, where 1 sheep = 1 rouble; 1 lamb = 0.5 rouble; 1 sheep + 1 lamb = 1.5 roubles. The price in sheep of a cast-iron cauldron was calculated as follows: [circumference of the cauldron, measured in chetverts] – [3 chetverts] = price of cauldron in sheep. One chetvert measured 17.77 cm. A cauldron with a circumference of 11 chetvert would therefore cost 11 – 3 = 8 sheep. A Kyrgyz at the *aul* could also buy on credit: he could buy something for 1 lamb on one occasion, and pay back double (i.e. 1 sheep) at the next occasion. These are just a few of the hundreds of examples which Fedorov (2001) has compiled from nine reports by Valikhanov. The examples reveal how goods were moved around, and that there were different media of exchange and different units of account in different places. In the market centres of Kashgar, Yining and Tacheng, coins were an important unit of account. To the Kyrgyz traders at the *aul*, sheep were the most important form of money. To the merchants from the market centres, sheep were just one of many forms of money. The relative values of different media of exchange were understood and there were norms of exchange rates. The norms were subject to variation, and variations were the direct results of market changes. Valikhanov collected his data in the 1850s, a decade marked in China by the Taiping Rebellion, an uprising that threatened the Qing dynasty. The developments in central China, i.e. external developments at some distance, affected the market in Eastern Central Asia. Valikhanov wrote that by 1854 there was an accumulation of goods in Yining: the price of many goods fell, while the price of goods from China, especially silver and tea, rose dramatically.

Although the data collected by Valikhanov in the 1850s have a different temporal context from the evidence presented in this study, they offer a very real perspective from which to view money on the Silk Road in a much earlier period, and thereby lend support to the results of this study.

# Bibliography


Adams, D. Q., 1999. *A dictionary of Tocharian B*. Amsterdam: Rodolpi.

Adshead, S. A M, 1993. *Central Asia in world history*. Basingstoke: Macmillan.

Agnew, N. (ed.), 1997. *Conservation of ancient sites on the Silk Road: proceedings of an international conference on the conservation of grotto sites*. Los Angeles: Getty Conservation Institute.

Agrawala, R. C., 1952. 'Numismatic data in the Kharosthi documents from Chinese Turkestan', *Journal of the Numismatic Society of India* 14, 103–6.

Agrawala, R. C., 1954. 'Numismatic data in the Niya Kharosthi documents from Central Asia', *Journal of the Numismatic Society of India* 16, no. 2, 219–30.

Allan, J., 1936. *Catalogue of the coins of ancient India*. London: British Museum.

Anon., 1986, 'Wenwu jinghua xuanbian', *Xinjiang wenwu* 1986(2), 54–64.

Atwood, C., 1991. 'Life in third–fourth century Cadh'ota: a survey of information gathered from the Prakrit documents found north of Minfeng (Niyä)', *Central Asiatic Journal* 35: 161–99.

Bailey, H. W., 1945–85. *Indo–Scythian studies: being Khotanese Texts*, 7 vols. Cambridge: Cambridge University Press (esp. vol. 4, 1961).

Bailey, H. W., 1946. 'Gandhari', *Bulletin of the School of Oriental Studies* 11, 764–97.

Bailey H. W., 1949. 'Irano–Indica II', *Bulletin of the School of Oriental Studies* 13, 121–39.

Bailey, H. W., 1979. *Dictionary of Khotan Saka*. Cambridge: Cambridge University Press.

Bailey, H. W., 1982. *The culture of the Sakas in ancient Iranian Khotan*. Delmar, New York: Caravan Books (Columbia Lectures on Iranian Studies 1).

Beal, S., 1911. *The life of Hiuen-tsiang by the shaman Hwui Li with an introduction containing an account of the works of I-Tsing*. London: Kegan Paul, Trench, Trübener and Co. Ltd.

Beckwith, C. I., 1977. 'Tibet and the early medieval Florissance in Eurasia: a preliminary note on the economic history of the Tibetan empire', *Central Asiatic Journal* 21, 89–104.

Beckwith, C. I., 1987. *The Tibetan empire in Central Asia*. Princeton: Princeton University Press.

Benko, M., 1992–93. 'Burial masks of Eurasian mounted nomad peoples in the migration period (1st millennium AD)', *Acta Orientalia Academiae Scientiarum Hungaricae* 46, 113–31.

Bergman, F., 1935. 'Lou-lan wood-carvings and small finds discovered by Sven Hedin', *Bulletin of the Museum of Far Eastern Antiquities* 7, 71–144.

Bi Zongzheng, 1987. 'Xinjiang Qitai xian chutu de zhongyuan guqian', *Xinjiang wenwu* 1987(1), 52–55.

Bielenstein, H., 1954. 'The restoration of the Han dynasty, with prolegomena on the historiography of the Hou Han Shu', *Bulletin of the Museum of Far Eastern Antiquities* 26, 1–209.

Bielenstein, H., 1959. 'The restoration of the Han dynasty, 2, the civil war', *Bulletin of the Museum of Far Eastern Antiquities* 31, 1–287.

Bielenstein, H., 1967. 'The restoration of the Han dynasty, 3, the people', *Bulletin of the Museum of Far Eastern Antiquities* 39, 1–98.

Bielenstein, H., 1980. *The bureaucracy of Han times*. Cambridge: Cambridge University Press.

Bohannan, P., 1959. 'The impact of money on an African subsistence economy', *Journal of Economic History* 19, 491–503.

Bowman, A. K., 1998. *Life and letters from the Roman Frontier*. London: Routledge.

Boyer, A. M., 1911. 'Inscriptions de Miran', *Journal Asiatique*, Série X, Tome XVII (May–June), 412–30.

Boyer, Abbé A. M., Rapson, E. J. and Senart, M. E., 1920. *Kharosthi inscriptions discovered by Sir M. A. Stein in Chinese Turkestan*, part I. Oxford: Clarendon Press. [reprinted by New Delhi: Cosmo Publications 1997].

Boyer, Abbé A. M., Rapson, E. J. and Senart, M. E., 1927. *Kharosthi inscriptions discovered by Sir M. A. Stein in Chinese Turkestan*, part II. Oxford: Clarendon Press. [reprinted by New Delhi: Cosmo Publications 1997].

Bray, W. and Trump, D. H. (eds), 1982. *The Penguin dictionary of archaeology*. Harmondsworth: Penguin.

Brough, J., 1961. 'A Kharoshthi inscription from China', *Bulletin of the School of Oriental and African Studies* 24, 517–30.

Brough, J., 1965. 'Comments on third-century Shan-shan and the history of Buddhism', *Bulletin of the School of Oriental and African Studies* 28: 582–612.

Brysac, S. B., 1997. 'Last of the "Foreign Devils": Sir Aurel Stein's fourth foray into China was a humiliating failure. Who conspired to undermine the expedition and why?', *Archaeology* (November – December), 53–59.

Brysac, S., 2004. 'Sir Aurel Stein's fourth "American" expedition', in H. Wang (ed.) *Sir Aurel Stein. Proceedings of the British Museum study day, 23 March 2002*, 17–22. London: British Museum Occasional Paper 142.

Burnett, A., 1991. *Coins*. London: British Museum Press.

Burrow, T., 1937. *Language of the Kharosthi documents from Chinese Turkestan*, Cambridge: Cambridge University Press.

Burrow, T., 1939. 'Further Kharosthi documents from Niya', *Bulletin of the School of Oriental Studies* 9, 111–23.

Burrow, T., 1940. *A translation of the Kharoshthi documents from Chinese Turkestan*. London: Royal Asiatic Society (James G. Furlong Fund 20).

Bushell, S. W., 1886. 'Ancient Roman coins from Shansi', *Journal of the Peking Oriental Society* 1, 2, 17–28.

Cao–Wei, 1997, 1998 [= Cao–Wei wuzhu keti zu]. 'Cao–Wei wuzhu kao', *Zhongguo Qianbi* 1997(4), 3–7 [repr. in Zhongguo Qianbi Xuehui (ed.) *Zhongguo Qianbi Lunwenji 3 / A collection of Chinese numismatic theses* 3, 220–32. Beijing: Zhongguo jinrong chubanshe, 1998].

CASSIA, 1980 [= Chinese Academy of Social Sciences: Institute of Archaeology]. *Yinxu Fu Hao mu*. Beijing: Wenwu chubanshe.

CASSIA–Anyang, 1981 [= Chinese Academy of Social Sciences: Institute of Archaeology, Anyang team / Kaogu yanjiusuo Anyang gongzuodui]. 'Anyang Sui mu fajue baogao', *Kaogu xuebao*, 1981(3), 369–406.

Casey, J., and Reece, R. (eds), 1988. *Coins and the archaeologist*. London: Seaby.

Chavannes, E., 1913. *Les documents chinois découverts par Aurel Stein dans les sables du Turkestan oriental*. Oxford: Oxford University Press.

Chen Guocan, 1983a. 'Cong Tulufan chutu de "zhikuzhuan"' kan Tangdai de zhiku zhidu', in Wuhan daxue lishixi Wei Jin Nanbeichao Sui Tang shi yanjiushi (eds) *Dunhuang Tulufan chutu wenshu chutan*, 316–43. Wuhan: Wuhan daxue chubanshe.

Chen Guocan, 1983b. 'Tangdai de minjian jiedai – Tulufan deng di suochu Tangdai jiedai chiquan chutan', in Wuhan daxue lishixi Wei Jin Nanbeichao Sui Tang shi yanjiushi (eds) *Dunhuang Tulufan chutu wenshu chutan*, 217–44. Wuhan: Wuhan daxue chubanshe.

Chen Wunian, 1998. 'Liangzao xinquan de banbie ji qi duandai', *Zhongguo qianbi lunwenji 3 / A collection of Chinese numismatic theses 3*, 250–8. Beijing: Zhongguo jinrong chubanshe.

Chen Yuan, 1991. 'Sui Tang qianbi yu Sui Tang quandu', in Chen Yuan, Yao Shiduo and Jiang Qixiang (eds) *Zhongguo lidai huobi daxi 3: Sui Tang Wudai Shiguo huobi*, 551–64. Shanghai: Shanghai renmin chubanshe.

Chen Yuan and Sun Zhonghui, 1991, 'Zonglun', in Chen Yuan, Yao Shiduo and Jiang Qixiang (eds) *Zhongguo lidai huobi daxi 3: Sui Tang Wudai Shiguo huobi*: 9–29. Shanghai: Shanghai renmin chubanshe.

Conrady, A., 1920. *Die Chinesischen Handschriften und sonstigen Kleinfunde Sven Hedins in Loulan*. Stockholm: Generalstabens Litografiska Anstalt.

Coole, A. B., 1967. *A bibliography on Far Eastern numismatology and a coin index* (An encyclopaedia of Chinese coins, vol. 1). Mission, Kansas: Inter-Collegiate Press.

Cribb, J., 1978. 'Chinese lead ingots with barbarous Greek inscriptions', *Coin Hoards* 4, 76–8. (London: Royal Numismatic Society).

Cribb, J., 1979. 'An historical survey of the precious metal currencies of China', *Numismatic Chronicle*, 7th series, 19, 185–209.

Cribb, J., 1984. 'The Sino-Kharoshthi coins of Khotan – their attribution and relevance to Kushan chronology (Part 1)', *Numismatic Chronicle* 144, 128–52.

Cribb, J., 1985. 'The Sino-Kharoshthi coins of Khotan (Part 2)', *Numismatic Chronicle* 145, 136–49.

Cribb, J., 1986. *Money: from cowrie shells to credit cards*. London: British Museum Publications.

Cribb, J., 1987. *Money in the bank: an illustrated introduction to the money collection of the Hongkong and Shanghai Banking Corporation*. London: Spink & Son Ltd.

Crockett, A., 1979. *Money, theory, policy and institutions*. Sunbury on Thames: Nelson.

Cunningham, A., 1843. 'The ancient coinage of Kashmir, with chronological and historical notes, from the commencement of the Christian era to the conquest of the country by the Moguls', *Numismatic Chronicle and Journal of the Numismatic Society* 6, 1–38.

Cunningham, A., 1846. 'An attempt to explain some of the monograms found upon the Greek coins of Ariana and India', *Numismatic Chronicle* VIII, 175–97.

Cunningham, A., 1891. *Coins of ancient India from the earliest times down to the seventh century* AD. London: B. Quaritch.

Curiel, R., 1953. 'Le trésor du Tépé Maranjan', in R. Curiel and D. Schlumberger (eds) *Trésors monétaires d'Afghanistan*, 101–32. Paris: Imprimerie Nationale.

*Da Tang da ci en San Zang fa shi zhuan* (by Hui Li, annotated by Yan Zong). Beijing: Zhonghua shuju, 1983.

Dabbs, J. A., 1963. 'History of the discovery and exploration of Chinese Turkestan', *Central Asiatic Journal* 8: 1–255.

Dai Zhiqiang and Zhou Weirong, 1995. 'A study of bronze lumps used as primitive currency in ancient China', *Bulletin of the Metals Museum* 23. Sendai, Japan: Institute of Metals.

Dai Zhiqiang and Zhou Weirong, 1997. 'China', in C. Morrisson and B. Kluge (eds) *A survey of numismatic research 1990–1995*, 791–805. Berlin: International Association of Professional Numismatists Special Publication 13.

Dalton, G. (ed.), 1976. *Tribal and peasant economies: readings in economic anthropology*. Austin, Texas: University of Texas Press.

Dang Shunmin, 1994. 'Waiwen qianbing xin tan', *Kaogu yu wenwu* 1994(5), 84–9.

Dani, A. H., and Masson, V. M. (eds), 1978. *History of civilizations of Central Asia, vol. 1, the dawn of civilization: earliest times to 700* BC. Paris: UNESCO Publishing.

Daxi = Daxi series [= *Zhongguo lidai huobi daxi*, series editor Ma Feihai. Shanghai: Shanghai renmin chubanshe]. Daxi 1: (Wang Qingzheng and Ma Chengyuan, eds) *Xian-Qin huobi*, 1988. Daxi 3: (Chen Yuan, Yao Shiduo and Jiang Qixiang, eds) *Sui Tang Wudai Shiguo huobi*, 1991.

Debaine-Francfort, C., and Idriss, A., 2001. *Keriya, mémoires d'un fleuve*. Suilly-la-Tour: Ed. Findakly.

Deng Xiaonan, 1999. 'Women in Turfan during the sixth to eighth centuries: a look at their activities outside the home', *Journal of Asian Studies* 58, no.1, 85–103.

Deng Yanlin, 1958. *Zhongguo bianjiang tuji lu*. Shanghai: Shangwu yinshuguan.

Di Cosmo, N., 1994. 'Ancient Inner Asian nomads: their economic basis and its signficance in Chinese history', *The Journal of Asian Studies* 53, no. 4 (November), 1092–126.

Diamond, E., and Rogers, T. D., 1983. 'Catalogue of the papers of Sir (Marc) Aurel Stein (1862–1943)', Bodleian Library, Oxford (typescript catalogue).

Dien, A. E., 1995. 'Instructions for the grave: the case of Yan Zhitui', *Cahiers d'Extrême-Asie* 8, 41–58.

Ding Fubao, 1973. *Lidai guqian tushuo*. Taipei: Fangzhou chubanshe. [1st ed. publ. by Shanghai yixue shuju, 1940; revised ed., with annotations by Ma Dingxiang, publ. by Xinhua shudian, Shanghai, 1992].

Dong Qingxuan and Jiang Qixiang, 1991. *Xinjiang Qianbi / Xinjiang Numismatics*. Urumqi/Hong Kong: Xinjiang Art and Photo Press, and Hong Kong Educational and Cultural Press.

Douglas, M., 1958. 'Raffia cloth distribution in the Lele economy', *Africa* 28: 109–22. [Reprinted in G. Dalton (ed.) *Tribal and peasant economies: readings in economic anthropology*. Austin, Texas, 1976].

Dowson, J., 1863. 'On a newly discovered Bactrian Pali inscription; and other inscriptions in the Bactrian Pali character', *Journal of the Royal Asiatic Society* 20, 21–68.

Du Weisheng, 1992. *Sichou zhi lu guguo qianbi*. Shanghai: Shanghai Museum.

Duan Qing and Wang Binghua, 1997. 'Xinjiang xin chu Yuzhenwen mudu wenshu yanjiu', *Dunhuang Tulufan yanjiu, di er juan, 1996*, 1–12.

Duncan, G. L., 1993. *Coin circulation in the Danube and Balkan provinces of the Roman empire,* AD *294–578*. London: Royal Numismatic Society, Special Publication 26.

Duncan-Jones, R., 1994. *Money and government in the Roman empire*. Cambridge: Cambridge University Press.

Dunhuang xian wenhuaguan, 1984. 'Dunhuang Suyoutu Handai fengsui yizhi chutu de mujian', in Gansu wenwu gongzuodui and Gansu bowuguan [GS–WWGZD] (eds) *Han jian yanjiu wenji*, 1–14. Lanzhou: Gansu renmin chubanshe.

Eberhard, W., 1977. *A history of China*. London: Routledge and Kegan Paul.

Emmerick, R. E., 1979. *A guide to the literature of Khotan*. (Studia Philologia Buddhica Occasional Paper Series III). Tokyo: The Reiyukai Library.

Emmerick, R. E., 1996. 'Khotanese *murahamgha* and other *hamgha*' in Accademia Nazionale dei Lincei (ed.) (in collaboration with l'Istituto Italiano per il Medio de Estremo Oriente, international conference, 9–12 November 1994), *La Persia e l'Asia Centrale da Alessandro al X secolo*, 113–21. Rome: Accademia Nazionale dei Lincei.

Emmerick, R. E., 1985. 'Tibetan loanwords in Khotanese and Khotanese loanwords in Tibetan', in G. Gnoli and L. Lanciotti (eds), *Orientalia Iosephi Tucci Memoriae Dicata*, 301–17. Rome: Istituto Italiano per il Medio ed Estremo Oriente (Serie orientale Roma, vol. 56).

Emmerick, R. E. and Vorob'ëva-Desyatovskaja, M. I., *Corpus Inscriptionum Iranicarum. Part II Inscriptions of the Seleucid and Parthian periods and of Eastern Iran and Central Asia vol. 5 Saka. Saka Documents Text Volume III: the St. Petersburg collections*. London: Corpus Inscriptionum Iranicarum and the School of Oriental and African Studies.

Errington, E., and Cribb, J. (eds) with M. Claringbull, 1992. *The crossroads of Asia: transformation in image and symbol*. Cambridge: Ancient India and Iran Trust.

Falconer, J., Kartészi, Á., Kelecsényi, Á. and Russell-Smith, L., (ed. by É. Apor and H. Wang), 2002. *Catalogue of the collections of Sir Aurel Stein in the Library of the Hungarian Academy of Sciences*. Budapest: British Museum and Library of the Hungarian Academy of Sciences.

Falk, H., 2001. 'The yuga of Sphujiddhvaja and the era of the Kusanas', *Silk Road Art and Archaeology* 7: 121–36. Kamakura: Institute of Silk Road Studies.

Falkenhausen, L. von, 1992. 'Serials on Chinese archaeology published in the People's Republic of China: a bibliographical survey', *Ancient China* 17: 247–95.

Falkenhausen, L. von, 1993. 'On the historical orientation of Chinese archaeology', *Antiquity* 647: 839–49.

Fedorov, M., 2001. 'The works and archive of Chokan Valikhanov as a source of information about the trade and prices in East Turkestan and adjacent regions of Central Asia', *Central Asiatic Journal* 45, 232–42.

Filliozat, J., 1948. *Fragments de textes koutchéens de médecine et de magie. Texte, parallèles, sankrits et tibétains, traduction et glossaire*. Paris: Adrien-Maisonneuve.

Fletcher, J., 1978. 'Ch'ing Inner Asia', in J. K. Fairbank (ed.) *The Cambridge History of China, vol. 10, Late Ch'ing 1800–1911*. Cambridge: Cambridge University Press.

Forte, A., 2000. 'Iraniens en Chine. Buddhisme, masdéisme, bureaux de commerce', in J.-P. Drège (ed.) *La Sérinde, terre des échanges: art, religion, commerce du Ier au Xe siècle*, 181–90. Paris: XIVes Rencontres de l'Ecole du Louvre.

Francke, A. H., 1921. 'Notes on Sir Aurel Stein's collection of Tibetan documents from Chinese Turkestan', in M. A. Stein, *Serindia*

(Appendix G), 1461–6 [reprinted from *Journal of the Royal Asiatic Society*, 1914: 37–59].
Frank, A. G., 1992. *The centrality of Central Asia*. Amsterdam: VU University Press.
Frye, R. N., 1992. 'Sasanian–Central Asian Connections', in A. Harrack (ed.) *Contacts between cultures: West Asia and North Africa* 1, 271–3. Lampeter: Edwin Mellen Press.
Frye, R. N., 1995. 'Ancient Central Asian history notes', in B. G. Fragner et al. (eds) *Proceedings of the Second European Conference of Iranian Studies*, 189–90. Rome: Istituto Italiano per il Medio ed Estremo Oriente.
Gale, E. M., 1931. *Discourses on salt and iron*. Leiden: E. J. Brill.
Gan-bo-wen, 1972. 'Gansu Wuwei Leitai Dong Han mu qingli jianbao', *Wenwu* 1972(2), 16–19.
*Gao sen zhuan* (by Hui Xiao [6th century], annotated by Tang Yongtong). Beijing: Zhonghua shuju, 1992.
Gernet, J., 1956. *Les aspects économiques du bouddhisme dans la société chinoise du Ve au Xe siècle*. Saigon: Publications de l'Ecole Française de l'Extrême-Orient XXXIX [English translation by Franciscus Verellen, *Buddhism in Chinese society: an economic history from the fifth to the tenth centuries*. New York: Columbia University Press, 1995].
Giles, L., 1957. *Descriptive Catalogue of the Chinese Manuscripts from Tunhuang in the British Museum*. London: British Museum.
Göbl, R., 1983. 'Sasanian coins', in E. Yarshater (ed.), *The Cambridge History of Iran, vol. 3, The Seleucid, Parthian and Sasanian periods* (chapter 9), 322–36. Cambridge: Cambridge University Press.
Gregory, C. A., 1997. *Savage money. The anthropology and politics of commodity exchange*. Amsterdam: Harwood Academic Publishers.
Grierson, P., 1975. *Numismatics*. Oxford: Oxford University Press.
Grierson, P., 1982. *Byzantine coins*. London: Methuen & Co. Ltd; Berkeley and Los Angeles: University of California Press.
Griffiths, R. A., 1981. *The reign of King Henry VI*. London: Ernest Benn Ltd.
GS-Archaeology, 2000a [= Gansu sheng wenwu kaogu yanjiusuo]. 'Gansu Dunhuang Handai Xuanquan zhi yizhi fajue jianbao', *Wenwu* 2000(5): 4–20.
GS-Archaeology, 2000b [= Gansu sheng wenwu kaogu yanjiusuo]. 'Dunhuang Xuanquan Hanjian neirong gaishu', *Wenwu* 2000(5): 21–6.
GS-Archaeology, 2000c [= Gansu sheng wenwu kaogu yanjiusuo]. 'Dunhuang Xuanquan Han jian shiwen xuan', *Wenwu* 2000(5): 27–45.
GS-Archaeology et al., 1990 [= Gansu sheng wenwu kaogu yanjiusuo, Gansu sheng bowuguan, Wenhuabu gu wenxian yanjiushi and Zhongguo shehui kexue yuan lishi yanjiusuo (eds)]. *Juyan xinjian: Jiaqu houguan yu disi sui*. Beijing: Wenwu chubanshe.
GS-Juyan, 1978a [Gansu Juyan kaogudui]. 'Juyan Handai yizhi de fajue he xin chutu de jiance wenwu', *Wenwu* 1978(1), 1–25.
GS-Juyan, 1978b [= Gansu sheng Juyan kaogudui jiance zhengli xiaozu]. '"Jianwu san nian hou Li Jun suo ze Kou En shi" shiwen', *Wenwu* 1978(1), 30–1.
GS- Museum, 1960 [= Gansu sheng bowuguan]. 'Gansu Jiuquan Handai xiaohai mu qingli', *Kaogu* 1960(6), 16–17.
GS-Museum et al. 1981 [= Gansu sheng bowuguan, Dunhuang xian wenhuaguan]. 'Dunhuang Maquanwan Handai fengsui yizhi fajue jianbao', *Wenwu* 1981(10), 1–8.
GS-WWGZD, 1984 [= Gansu sheng wenwu gongzuodui and Gansu sheng bowuguan]. *Han jian yanjiu wenji*. Lanzhou: Gansu renmin chubanshe.
GSQBXH (ed.), 1989 [= Gansu qianbi xuehui]. *Gansu lishi huobi*. Lanzhou: Lanzhou daxue chubanshe.
Guo Ruoyu, 1998. *Gudai jixiang tuxiang shangxi*. Shanghai: Shanghai jiaoyu chubanshe.
Guo Yan, 1990. 'Shilun Sui Tang zhi ji Tulufan diqu de yinqian', *Zhongguo shi yanjiu*, 1990(4), 19–33.
Han Guopan (ed.), 1986. *Dunhuang Tulufan chutu jingji wenshu yanjiu*. Xiamen: Xiamen daxue chubanshe.
Han Xiang et al., 1988. *Niya kaogu ziliao*. Urumqi: Xinjiang shehui kexue yuan.
Hansen, V., 1995. *Negotiating daily life in traditional China: how ordinary people used contracts 600–1400*. New Haven: Yale University Press.
Hansen, V., 1997. 'Re-uniting Turfan's scattered treasures', *Circle for Inner Asian Art Newsletter* 6, 16.
Hansen, V., 1998a. 'Introduction: Turfan as a Silk Road community', *Asia Major*, 3rd series, XI, part 2, 1–11.
Hansen, V., 1998b. 'The path of Buddhism into China: the view from Turfan', *Asia Major*, 3rd series, XI, part 2, 37–66.
*Hanshu* (by Ban Gu, AD 32–92). Beijing: Zhonghua shuju, 1962.
Hao Benxing, 1980. 'Henan Fugou gucheng cun chutu de Chu jin yin bi', *Wenwu* 1980(10), 61–6.
Hao Benxing, 1985. 'Guanyu Zhoudai shiyong yinbi de tansuo', in Zhongguo Qianbi Xuehui (ed.), *Zhongguo qianbi lunwenji 1 / A collection of Chinese numismatic theses 1*, 103–8. Beijing: Zhongguo jinrong chubanshe.
Harmatta, J. (ed.), 1994. *History of civilizations of Central Asia, vol. II, The development of sedentary and nomadic civilizations, 700 BC – AD 250*. Paris: UNESCO Publishing.
He Shuangquan, 1989. '"Han jian – xiangli zhi" ji qi yanjiu', in Gansu wenwu kaogu suo (eds) *Qin Han jiandu lunwenji*, 145–235. Lanzhou: Gansu renmin chubanshe.
Hedin S. (with others), 1943–45. *History of the expedition in Asia 1927–1935*, 4 parts, especially parts 1 and 4. [*Part 4: General reports of travels and fieldwork* (by Folke Bergman, Gerhard Bexell, Birger Bohlin, Gösta Montell, trans. by Donal Burton).] Stockholm: Reports from the Scientific Expedition to the North-Western Provinces of China under the leadership of Dr Sven Hedin. The Sino–Swedish Expedition Publications 23 and 26.
HN–Museum, 1978 [= Henan sheng bowuguan] *Handai diezhu*. Beijing: Wenwu chubanshe.
Hoernle, A. R., 1899. 'A report on the British collection of antiquities from Central Asia, Part 1', extra no. to the *Journal of the Asiatic Society of Bengal* 68. Calcutta: Baptist Mission Press.
Hopkirk, P., 1980. *Foreign devils on the Silk Road: the search for the lost cities and treasures of Chinese Central Asia*. London: John Murray [repr. Oxford University Press, 1984, 1985, 1986, 1987, 1988, 1989, 1991].
Hou Can, 1982. 'Kaiping shiyi nian Wang Nian maituoqi ji qi shuoming de lishi wenti', *Kaogu yu wenwu* 1982(5), 104, 101.
Hou Can, 1988. 'Loulan xin faxian mujian zhi wenshu kaoshi', *Wenwu* 1998(7), 40–55.
Hou Ching-lang, 1975. *Monnaies d'offrande et la notion de la trésorerie dans la religion chinoise*. Paris: Collège de France.
*Hou Hanshu* (by Fan Yue, 398–445). Hong Kong: Zhonghua shuju, 1971.
Howgego, C., 1995. *Ancient history from coins*. London and New York: Routledge.
Hu Jichuang, 1988. *A concise history of Chinese economic thought*. Beijing: Foreign Languages Press.
Hu Pingsheng, 2000. *Jiandu wenwu lunji*, Taipei: Lantai chubanshe.
Hu Pingsheng and Zhang Defang (eds), 2001. *Dunhuang Xuanquan Han jian shicui*. Shanghai: Shanghai guji chubanshe.
Huang Liuchun, 1992. 'Qian tan Han Wei Xudu gucheng jiaocang tongqian', *Zhongguo Qianbi* 37, 1992(2): 30–5.
Huang Shengzhang, 1985. 'Guanyu matijin, linzhijin de dingming shidai yu yuanliu', in Zhongguo Qianbi Xuehui (ed.), *Zhongguo qianbi lunwenji 1 / A collection of Chinese numismatic theses 1*, 186–92. Beijing: Zhongguo jinrong chubanshe.
Huang Wenbi, 1948. *Luobuzhuo'er kaoguji*. Beijing: Board of Directors of the Mission of the Northwestern Expedition of China, and Institute of Historical Studies and Archaeology, National Academy of Peiping.
Huang Wenbi, 1954. *Tulufan kaogu ji*. Beijing: Zhongguo kexueyuan.
Huang Wenbi, 1958. *Talimu pendi kaogu ji*. Beijing: Kexue chubanshe.
Huang Wenbi, 1981. *Xibei shidi luncong*. Shanghai: Shanghai renmin chubanshe.
Huang Wenbi (ed.), 1983. *Xinjiang kaogu fajue jianbao (1957–1958)*. Beijing: Wenwu chubanshe.
Hucker, C. O., 1985. *A dictionary of official titles in imperial China*. Stanford: Stanford University Press.
Hudson, M., 2000. 'How interest rates were set, 2500 BC – 1000 AD: *máš, tokos* and *fœnus* as metapors for interest accruals', *Journal of the Economic and Social History of the Orient* vol. 43, no. 2, 132–61.
Hulsewé, A. F. P., 1955. *Remnants of Han law*. Leiden: E. J. Brill.
Hulsewé, A. F. P., 1978. 'The Ch'in documents discovered in Hupei in 1975', *T'oung Pao* 64, 175–217.
Hulsewé, A. F. P., 1979. *China in Central Asia, the early stage: 125 BC – AD 23. An annotated translation of chapters 61 and 96 of the history of the former Han dynasty*. Leiden: E. J. Brill.
Hulsewé, A. F. P., 1985. *Remnants of Ch'in law, an annotated translation of the Ch'in legal and administrative rules of the 3rd century BC, discovered in Yünmeng Prefecture, Hu-pei Province, in 1975*. Leiden: E. J. Brill.

Huntington, E., 1907. *The pulse of Asia: a journey in Central Asia illustrating the geographic basis of history*. Boston: Houghton Mifflin [repr. London: Constable, 1910].

ICOMON 2003 ( = ICOMON IX Organizing Committee, China Numismatic Museum [ed.]). *The 9th annual meeting of the International Committee of Money and Banking Museums (ICOMON). Money and banking: the varieties of the monetary experience. Beijing, China, October 14–18, 2002, Proceedings*. Beijing: China Numismatic Museum.

Isebart, L., 1980. 'De Indo-Iraanse Bestanddelen in de Tocharische Woordenschat' (unpublished thesis, Leuven).

Ivotchkina, N. V., 1975. 'Moneti Pervoi Vostochnoturkestanskoi Ekspeditzii S. F. Ol'denburga', in E. I. Lubo-Lesnichenko (ed.) *Kultura i iskusstvo Indii i stran Dal'nego Vostoka*, 27–38. Leningrad: Aurora.

Jiang Boqin, 1994. *Dunhuang Tulufan wenshu yu sichou zhi lu*, Beijing: Wenwu chubanshe.

Jiang Qixiang, 1990. 'Xinjiang gudai qianbi de faxian yu yanjiu', *Zhoushan Qianbi* 1990(1), 6–11; 1990(2), 3–10; 1990(3), 8–13; 1990(4), 3–11.

Jiang Qixiang, 1999. 'Xinjiang gudai qianbi', in Xinjiang weiwu'er zizhiqu wenwu shiye guanli ju (eds), *Xinjiang wenwu guji daguan*. Urumqi: Xinjiang meishu sheying chubanshe.

Jiang Ruoshi, 1989. 'Qin Han banliang qian fan duandai yanjiu', *Zhongguo Qianbi* 1989(4), 1–15.

Jiang Ruoshi, 1992. 'Xi Han wuzhu qianfan duandai yanjiu', in Zhongguo Qianbi Xuehui (ed.) *Zhongguo qianbi lunwenji 2 / A collection of Chinese numismatic theses* 2, 141–52. Beijing: Zhongguo jinrong chubanshe.

Jiang Ruoshi, 1993. 'Qin qian lun', in Cai Yunzhang and Li Yunxing (eds) *Luoyang qianbi*, 1–41. Beijing: Zhongguo shehui kexue chubanshe.

Jiang Ruoshi, 1994. 'Shaanxi, Luoyang suojian Qin Han jinshu mingqian shulüe', *Zhongguo Qianbi* 1994(2): 17–19.

Jie Yaohua (ed.), 1999. *Jiaohe gucheng baohu yu yanjiu*. Urumqi: Xinjiang renmin chubanshe.

*Jinshu* (by Fang Xuanling et al., 578–648). Beijing: Zhonghua shuju, 1974.

Kang Liushuo, 1991. 'Handai Gansu huobi jingji gailu', *Xinjiang Jinrong* (Quanguo di er ci sichou zhi lu huobi yantaohui wenji), 117–20.

Kang Liushuo, 1993. 'Gansu jingnei chutu de silu waiguo he xiyu qianbi zongshu', *Nei Menggu jinrong yanjiu – Qianbi zhuankan* 1993(4), 18–23.

Kang Liushuo, 1996. 'Tan Gansu chutu de qianbing', *Zhongguo Qianbi* 1996(4), 73.

Kaplan, E. H., 1993. *A monetary history of China* [= trans. of Peng Xinwei, *Zhongguo huobi shi*], 2 vols. Bellingham: Western Washington University.

Karlgren, B., 1957. 'Grammata serica recensa', *Bulletin of the Museum of Far Eastern Antiquities*, Stockholm, 29.

Keightley, D. (ed.), 1983. *The origins of Chinese Civilization*. Berkeley and London: University of California Press.

King, F. H. H., 1965. *Money and monetary policy in China 1845–1895*. Cambridge, Mass: Harvard University Press.

Konow, S., 1936. 'Note on Khotani Saka and the Central Asian Prakrit', *Acta Orientalia* 14, 231–40.

Kucha WGS, 1987 [= Kuche wenguansuo] 'Han-Qiu erti tongqian de faxian ji qi renshi', *Zhongguo Qianbi* 1987(1), 32–39.

Kumamoto Hiroshi, 1996a. 'The Khotanese in Dunhuang', in A. Cadonna and L. Lanciotti (eds) *Cina e Iran da Alessandro Magno alla dinastia Tang*. Florence: Leo S. Olschki Editore (Orientalia Venezlana V).

Kumamoto Hiroshi, 1996b. 'The Khotanese documents from the Khotan area', *Memoirs of the Toyo Bunko* 54, 27–64.

Kumamoto, Hiroshi, 2001. 'Sino-Hvatanica Petersburgensia, Part 1', *Manuscripta Orientalia*, vol. 7, no. 1 (March 2001), 3–9. [This paper was corrupted during publication; Kumamoto has posted an accurate version on http://www.gengo.l.u-tokyo.ac.jp/~hkum]

Lacouperie, T. de, 1892. *The British Museum catalogue of Chinese coins from the VIIth century BC to AD 621*. London: British Museum.

Lattimore, O., 1962. *Inner Asian Frontiers of China*. Boston: Beacon Press [repr. 1940].

Lattimore, O. and Lattimore E. F., 1973. *Silks, spices and Empire. Asia seen through the eyes of its discoverers*. London: Tandem.

Leslie, D. D. and Gardiner, K. H. J., 1996. *The Roman Empire in Chinese sources*. Rome: Pubblicati al Dipartimiento di Studio Orientali, 15.

Li Chaoquan, 1995. 'Kouhanwu xisu yanjiu', *Kaogu* 1995(8), 724–30.

Li Jiannong, 1963. *Wei Jin Nan Bei chao Sui Tang jingji shigao*. Beijing: Zhonghua shuju.

Li Junming, 1998. 'Han jian "kuaiji" kao', *Chutu wenxian yanjiu* 3, 119–238; 4, 31–43.

Li Junming and He Shuangquan, 1990. *Sanjian jiandu heji*. Beijing: Wenwu chubanshe.

Li Kai, 1991. 'Qiuciguo jingji yu Qiuci qianbi kao (tigang)', *Xinjiang Jinrong* (extra, no. 1), 39.

Li Peng, 2001. 'Xinjiang Moyu xian chutu jiaocang qianbi jianjie', *Xinjiang Qianbi* 2001(4), 30–2.

Li Shengwu, 1985. 'Shijiazhuang shi jiao faxian Tang dai jiaocang qianbi', *Kaogu* 1985(4), 382.

Li Shengwu, 1989. 'Shijiazhuang shi Huolu xian faxian guqian jiaocang', *Kaogu* 1989(2), 184.

Li Yinping, 1995. 'Xinjiang Luopu xian faxian changfang chuan qian qian', *Zhongguo Qianbi* 1995(1), 36.

Li Yinping, 1997. 'Xinjiang Luopu xian faxian de Quluwen yuanxing fangchuan xiao tongqian kaoshi', *Xinjiang Qianbi* 1997(4), 46–57.

Li Yinping, 1998. 'Xinjiang Luopu xian faxian Xiyu gu qianbi', *Zhongguo Qianbi* 1998(4), 50.

Li Yinping, 1999. 'Shuangmian luo, ma wen xiao tongqian', *Xinjiang Qianbi* 1999(4), 22.

Li Yinping, 2002. 'Guquan shiyi liangce', *Xinjiang Qianbi* 2002(1), 11–12.

Li Yuchun, 1959. 'Xinjiang Wuqia xian faxian jintiao he dapi Bosi yinbi', *Kaogu* 1959(9), 482–3.

Li Yuchun, 1981. 'Xinjiang Hetian xian Mailike'awati yizhi de diaocha he shijue', *Wenwu* 1981(1): 33–8.

Li Zheng, 1975. 'Xinjiang Asitana san zuo Tang mu chutu zhengui juanhua ji wenshu deng wenwu', *Wenwu* 1975(10), 89–90. [repr. in *Xinjiang Kaogu sanshi nian*, 1983, 106–8].

Lin Meicun, 1985. *Loulan Niya chutu wenshu*. Beijing: Wenwu chubanshe.

Lin Meicun, 1987. 'Zai lun Han-Qu erti qian', *Zhongguo Qianbi* 1987(4), 3–11, 20.

Lin Meicun, 1988. 'Loulan faxian de Dong Han Quluwen kaoshi', *Wenwu* 1988(8), 67–70.

Lin Meicun, 1988. *Shahai gujuan: Zhongguo suo chu Qulu wenshu: chu ji*. Beijing: Wenwu chubanshe.

Lin Meicun, 1989a. 'Xinjiang Niya faxian de Quluwen qiyue kaoshi', *Kaogu xuebao* 1989(1), 121–36.

Lin Meicun, 1989b. 'Yuzhen Hanwen qianbi kao', *Zhongguo Qianbi* 1989(3), 3–7.

Lin Meicun, 1990. 'A new Kharoshthi wooden tablet from China', *Bulletin of the School of Oriental and African Studies* 53, 283–91.

Lin Meicun, 1992. 'Zhongguo suochu Quluwen de liusan yu shoucang', *Kaogu* 1992(1), 76–9.

Lin Meicun, 1993. 'Xinjiang Hetian chutu Hanwen Yuzhenwen shuangyu wenshu', *Kaogu xuebao* 1993(1), 89–107.

Lin Meicun, 1996. 'Kharosthi bibliography: the collections from China (1897–1993)', *Central Asiatic Journal* 40/2, 188–220.

Lin Meicun and Li Jianming, 1984. *Shulehe liuyu chutu Han jian*. Beijing: Wenwu chubanshe.

Liu Jinwen, 1985. 'Bachu – Keping gu sidao diaocha', *Xinjiang Wenwu* 1985(1), 17–19.

Liu Jucheng, 1989. *Zhongguo guqian pu*. Beijing: Wenwu chubanshe.

Liu Songbai, 1991. 'Qiuci xiao tongqian chuyi', *Xinjiang Jinrong* (extra, no. 1), 29.

Liu Wensuo, 1991. 'Andi'er xin chu Han Qu erti qian kao', *Zhongguo Qianbi* 1991(3), 5.

Liu Wensuo, 1992a. 'Takelemagan shamo kaogu gaishu', *Xinjiang Wenwu* 1992(1), 48–51.

Liu Wensuo, 1992b. 'Niya kaogu yanjiu zongshu', *Xinjiang Wenwu* 1992(3), 75–82.

Liu Wensuo, 1993. 'Quluwen yiwu zai Xinjiang de kaogu faxian', *Xinjiang Wenwu* 1993(3), 75–84.

Liu Xuetang, 1999. 'Wu shiji zhongye yiqian Tulufan pendi kaogu, lishi shilun', in Jie Yaohua (ed.), *Jiaohe gucheng baohu yu yanjiu*, 423–60. Urumqi: Xinjiang renmin chubanshe.

Lockhart, J. H. S., 1907. *The currency of the Farther East – from the earliest times up to 1895, vol. I: a description of the Glover Collection*. Hong Kong: Noronha & Co.

Lockyear, K., 1997. *Multivariate money: a statistical analysis of Roman Republic coin hoards with special reference to material from Romania* (PhD thesis, University of London).

Loewe, M. A. N., 1967. *Records of Han administration*, 2 vols. Cambridge: Cambridge University Press.

Loewe, M. A. N. (ed.), 1993. *Early Chinese texts: a bibliographical guide*. Berkeley: Society for the Study of Early China, the Institute of East Asian Studies, University of California.

Long Fu, 1996. 'Hetian diqu wenguansuo can Han-Qu erti qian', *Zhongguo Qianbi* 1996(2), 56, 55.

Lüders, H., 1913. 'Die Sakas und die "nordarische" Sprache', *Sitzungsberichte der Preussischen Akademie der Wissenschaften*, phil.-hist. Kl., 406–27. Berlin.

Lüders, H., 1919. 'Die sakischen Mura', *Sitzungsberichte der Preussischen Akademie der Wissenschaften* 39, 734–66.

Lüders, H, 1936. *Textilien in alten Turkestan*. Berlin: Akademie der Wissenschaften [*Act. Or.* xviii], 39–43.

Luo Feng, 1993. 'Guanyu Xi'an suo chu Dong Luoma jinbi fangzhipin de taolun', *Zhongguo Qianbi* 1993(4), 17–19.

Ma Dazheng, Wang Rong and Yang Lian (eds), 1994. *Xiyu kaocha yu yanjiu (Explorations and studies in Central Asia)*, Urumqi: Xinjiang renmin chubanshe.

Ma Heng, 1997. 'Han–Tu wuzhu qian chutan', *Zhongguo Qianbi* 1997(2), 42–3.

Ma Yong, 1980. 'Gudai Shanshan, Yutian diqu Qulu wenzi ziliao zongkao', *Zhongguo minzu guwenzi yanjiu*. Beijing: Zhongguo shehui kexue chubanshe.

Ma Yong, 1990. *Xiyu shidi wenwu congkao*. Beijing: Wenwu chubanshe.

Ma Yong and Sun Yutang, 1994. 'The Western Regions under the Hsiung-nu and the Han', in J. Harmatta (ed.) *History of civilizations of Central Asia, vol. II, The development of sedentary and nomadic civilizations, 700 BC–AD 250*, 227–46. Paris: UNESCO Publishing.

Ma Yong and Wang Binghua, 1994. 'The culture of the Xinjiang region', in J. Harmatta (ed.) *History of civilizations of Central Asia, vol. II, The development of sedentary and nomadic civilizations, 700 BC–AD 250*, 209–25. Paris: UNESCO Publishing.

Ma Zengyi, 1996. 'Biepin Gaochang jili qian qiushi', *Xinjiang Qianbi* 1996(2), 48.

MacCormack, G., 1990. *Traditional Chinese penal law*. Edinburgh: Edinburgh University Press.

MacDowall, D. W., 1968. 'Numismatic evidence for the date of Kaniska', in A. L. Basham (ed.) *Papers on the date of Kaniska, submitted to the Conference on the date of Kaniska, London, 20–22 April 1960*, 134–49. Leiden: E. J. Brill.

Mair, V. H., n.d. 'Changes in the policies governing archaeological research in Xinjiang', http://www.lehigh.edu/~inmfl/ecn/mair.htm, accessed 3 February 2000.

Malek, H. M., 1993. 'Review article: a survey of research on Sasanian numismatics', *Numismatic Chronicle* 153, 227–51.

Maspéro, H., 1953. *Les documents chinois de la troisième expédition de Sir Aurel Stein en Asie Centrale*. London: British Museum.

Marx, K. (ed. by F. Engels), 1867. *Das Kapital*. Berlin [English translation: *Capital*, Chicago and London: Encyclopaedia Britannica, 1900].

Mei Jianjun, 2000. *Copper and bronze metallurgy in late Prehistoric Xinjiang: its cultural context and relationship with neighbouring regions*. Oxford: BAR S865.

Melitz, J., 1974. *Primitive and modern money: an interdisciplinary approach*. Reading, Mass.: Addison-Wesley Publishing Co.

Meng Fanren (1998). 'Preface', *Xiyu kaogu tuji*. Nanning: Guangxi shifan daxue chubanshe [repr. as 'Sitanyin "Xiyu kaogu tuji" Hanyiben qianyan', *Xinjiang kaogu yu shidi lunji*. Beijing: Kexue chubanshe, 2000, 193–6; published in English as 'Meng Fanren's Preface to the Chinese translation of Serindia', in H. Wang (ed.) *Sir Aurel Stein in The Times*, 2002, 147–51].

Miller, A. R., 1959. *Accounts of western nations in the history of the Northern Chou dynasty*. Berkeley: University of California Press.

Mirsky, J., 1977. *Sir Aurel Stein – archaeological explorer*. Chicago: Chicago University Press.

Monier-Williams, M., 1899. *A Sanskrit – English Dictionary etymologically and philologically arranged with special reference to cognate Indo-European languages*. Oxford: Clarendon Press.

Montell, G., 1936. 'Sven Hedin's archaeological collections from Khotan, 1', *Bulletin of the Museum of Far Eastern Antiquities* 7, 145–221.

Montell, G., 1938. 'Sven Hedin's archaeological collections from Khotan, 2', *Bulletin of the Museum of Far Eastern Antiquities* 10, 83–106.

Mu Shunying, 1987. *Shenmi de gucheng Loulan*. Urumqi: Xinjiang renmin chubanshe.

Mu Shunying, 1987. 'Cong kaogu cailiao kan Tang chao tongzhi xia de Xiyu jingji', *Xinjiang wenwu* 1987(3), 49–60.

Naert, P., 1965. 'Contacts lexicaus entre le tokharien et ses voisins non-indo-européens', *Orbis* 14, 528–45.

Needham, J. (ed.) 1954. *Science and civilization in China. Vol. 1. Introductory orientations*. Cambridge: Cambridge University Press.

Needham, J. (ed.), 1959. *Science and civilization in China. Vol. 3. Mathematics and the sciences of the heaven and the earth* (esp. 'Descriptions of southern regions and foreign countries, 510–14). Cambridge: Cambridge University Press.

Odani Nakao, 1990. 'Sizhe kou zhong han bi xisu – Han Tang muzang suo fanying de xifang yinsu', *Dunhuangxue jikan*, 1990(1), 129–42.

*OED* = *Oxford English Dictionary*, 1971.

Olsen, J. W., 1992. 'Archaeology in China today', *China Exchange News* 20/2, 3–6.

Parry, J. and Bloch, M., 1989. *Money and the morality of exchange*. Cambridge: Cambridge University Press.

Peng Jinzhang and Sha Wutian, 1998. 'Shilun Dunhuang Mogaoku beiqu chutu de Bosi yinbi he Xixia qianbi', *Wenwu* 1998(10), 22–7.

Peng Xinwei, 1965. *Zhongguo huobi shi*, Shanghai: Shanghai renmin chubanshe [1st ed. 1954, 2nd ed. 1962, revised 3rd ed. 1965. English translation: by E. H. Kaplan, *A monetary history of China*, 1993, Bellingham: Western Washington University].

Petrie, W. M. F., 1904. *Methods and aims in archaeology*. London: Macmillan & Co.

Pinault, G.-J., 1994. 'Aspects du bouddhisme pratiqué au nord du désert du Taklamakan, d'après les documents tokhariens', in F. Fumimasa and G. Fussman (eds) *Bouddhisme et cultures locales. Quelques cas de réciproques adaptations* (Actes du colloque franco–japonais de septembre 1991), 85–113. Paris: Ecole Française d'Extrême-Orient.

Pinault, G.-J., 1998. 'Economic and administrative documents in Tocharian B from the Berezovsky and Petrovsky collections', *Acta Orientalia* 4, no. 4, 3–20.

Plattner, S., 1989. *Economic anthropology*. Stanford: Stanford University Press.

Polanyi, K. (ed. by H. W. Pearson), 1977. *The livelihood of man*. New York and London: Academic Press.

Polanyi, K., Arensberg, C. M., and Pearson, H. W. (eds), 1957. *Trade and market in the early empires: economies in history and theory*. Glencoe: Free Press.

Porter, V., 1997. 'The Islamic coins collected by Stein in Chinese Central Asia', in K. Tanabe, J. Cribb and H. Wang (eds) *Studies in Silk Road coins and culture: papers in honour of Professor Ikuo Hirayama on his 65th birthday*, 201–20. Kamakura: Institute of Silk Road Studies.

Pulleyblank, E. G., 1991. *Lexicon of reconstructed pronunciation in Early Middle Chinese, Late Middle Chinese, and Early Mandarin*. Vancouver: University of British Columbia Press.

Qian Boquan, 1997. 'Qushi Gaochang wangguo tongxing de dong Luoma jinbi, Bosi yinbi ji wujia zhuangkuang', *Xinjiang Qianbi* 1997(3), 18–25.

Qian Boquan, 1998. 'Hezhen chutu de changfangchuan qian qian shiwen yanjiu', *Zhongguo Qianbi* 1998(4), 41–42.

Qian Boquan, 1999. 'Hetian diqu de xiao maqian yanjiu', *Xinjiang Qianbi* 1999(4), 4–5.

Qian Jiaju and Guo Yangang, 1982. *Zhongguo huobi fazhan jianshi he biaojie*. Beijing: Renmin chubanshe.

Qingyang diqu bowuguan and Huanxian bowuguan, 1991. 'Gansu Huanxian faxian yi chu Handai taoqianfan yizhi', *Kaogu* 1991(5), 479–80.

Rapson, E. J. and Noble, P. S., 1929. *Kharosthi inscriptions discovered by Sir Aurel Stein in Chinese Turkestan*. Oxford: Clarendon Press [reprinted New Delhi: Cosmo Publications, 1997].

Raschke, M. G., 1978. 'New studies in Roman commerce with the East', in H. Temporini (ed.), *Aufstieg und Niedergang der Römischen Welt: Geschichte und Kultur Roms im Spiegel der Neueren Forschung II*. Principat: Neunter Band (2. Halbband), 604–1361. Berlin and New York: Walter de Gruyter.

Raspopova, V., 1999. 'Gold coins and bracteates from Pendjikent', in M. Alram and D. Klimburg-Salter (eds), *Coins: art and chronology. Essays on the pre-Islamic history of the Indo–Iranian borderlands*, 453–60. Vienna: Verlag der Österreichischen Akademie der Wissenschaften.

Reece, R., 1987. *Coinage in Roman Britain*. London: Seaby.

Renfrew, C. and Bahn, P., 1991. *Archaeology: theories, method and practice*, London: Thames and Hudson [repr. 1996, 2000].

Rhodes, N., 1997. 'Tang dynasty coins made in Xinjiang', in K. Tanabe, J. Cribb and H. Wang (eds) *Studies in Silk Road coins and culture: papers in honour of Professor Ikuo Hirayama on his 65th birthday*, 181–6. Kamakura: Institute of Silk Road Studies.

Richthofen, Baron von, 1878. *Bemerkungen zu den Ergebnissen von Obersleutenant Przewalskis Reise nach dem Lopnur und Altyn-tagh*. Berlin.

Rickett, W. A., 1998. *Guanzi: political, economic and philosophical essays from early China*, vol. 2. Princeton: Princeton University Press.

Rong Xinjiang, 1996. *Haiwai Dunhuang Tulufan wenxian zhijian lu*. Nanchang: Jiangxi renmin chunbanshe.

Russell-Smith, L., 2002. 'Digitising Dunhuang: 21st century technology is making fragile Chinese paintings available worldwide', *British Museum Magazine* 42, 18–20.

Salomon, R. G., 1986a. 'A new Kharoshthi document from Central Asia', *Bulletin d'Etudes Indiennes* 4, 341–51.

Salomon, R. G., 1986b (Huang Shengzhuang trans.). 'Niya xin chu de yi jian Qulu wenshu', *Xinjiang shehui kexue* 4, 82–6.

Salomon, R. G., 1996. 'Brahmi and Kharosthi', in P. D. Daniels and W. Bright (eds) *The world's writing systems*, section 30, 373–83. Oxford: Oxford University Press.

Salomon, R. G., 1998a. *Indian epigraphy: a guide to the study of inscriptions in Sanskrit, Prakrit, and the other Indo–Aryan languages*. Austin, Texas: Center for Asian Studies & New York: Oxford University Press.

Salomon, R. G., 1988b. 'Two new Kharoshthi documents from Asia', *Central Asiatic Journal* 32, 98–108.

Sawara, K. 1995. 'Juyan Han jian yuefeng kao', in Liu Junwen (ed.) *Riben zhong qing nian xuezhe lun Zhongguo shi lunzhu xuanyi 3: Shang gu Qin Han juan*, 536–71. Beijing: Zhonghua shuju [first published in Japanese, in *Koshi hari-aku* 5, 1989].

Shaanxi Museum, 1972 [= Shaanxi sheng bowuguan wenguanhui ge weihui xiezuo xiaozu]. 'Xi'an nanjiao Hejiacun faxian Tangdai jiaocang wenwu', *Wenwu* 1972(1), 30–6.

Shaanxi-Coins (ed.), 2003 [= Shaanxi sheng qianbi xuehui]. *Shaanxi qianbi yanjiu wenji*. Xi'an: Shaanxi sheng qianbi xuehui. [pages 1–121 present the papers delivered at the conference devoted to *bai jin san pin*, held in Xi'an, 25 August 2003].

Sheng, A., 1998. 'Innovations in textile techniques on China's Northwest Frontier, 500–700 AD', *Asia Major*, 3rd series, XI, part 2, 117–60.

Shi Shuqing, 1960. 'Xinjiang wenwu diaocha suibi', *Wenwu* 1960(6), 22–31.

Shi Shuqing, 1962. 'Tan Xinjiang Minfeng Niya yizhi', *Wenwu* 1962(7/8), 20–7.

Shu Xue, 1978. 'Woguo gudai zhu mu jian faxian, chutu qingkuang', *Wenwu* 1978(1), 44.

*Shiji* (by Sima Qian, c.145–86 BC). Beijing: Zhonghua shuju, 1959.

Sichuan Museum et al., 1982 [= Sichuan sheng bowuguan and Qingchuan xian wenhuaguan]. 'Qingchuan xian chutu Qin gengxiu tianlü mudu – Sichuan Qingchuan xian Zhanguo mu fajue jianbao', *Wenwu* 1982(1), 1–21.

Sieg, E., 1950. 'Geschäftliche Aufzeichnungen in Tocharisch B aus der Berliner Sammlung', *Miscellanea Academica Berolinensia* II/2, Berlin, 208–23.

Sieg, E. and Siegling, W., 1921. *Tocharische Sprachreste. 1. Band, Die Texte*. Berlin: Vereinigung Wissenschaftlichen Verleger.

Sieg, E. and Siegling, W., 1953. *Tocharische Sprachreste: Sprache B*: *Heft 2*. Im Auftrag der Deutschen Akademie der Wissenschaften zu Berlin. Göttingen: Vandenhoeck und Ruprecht.

Simmel, G., 1990. *The philosophy of money* (trans. by Tom Bottomore and David Frisby) London: Routledge (*Philosophie des Geldes*, 1st ed. 1907).

Sinor, D., 1977. *Inner Asia and its contacts with medieval Europe*. London: Variorum Reprints.

Sinor, D. (ed.), 1990. *The Cambridge history of early Inner Asia*. Cambridge: Cambridge University Press.

Skaff, J. K., 1998. 'The silver Sasanian and Arab–Sasanian coins found at Turfan: their relationship to international trade and the local economy', *Asia Major*, 3rd series, XI, part 2, 67–115.

Skaff, J. K., 2003. 'The Sogdian trade diaspora in East Turkestan during the seventh and eighth centuries', *Journal of the Economic and Social History of the Orient* 46, part 4, 475–524.

Skjærvø, P. O., 2002. *Khotanese manuscripts from Chinese Turkestan in the British Library. A complete catalogue with texts and translations*. London: The British Library.

Skjærvø, P. O., 2004. 'Legal documents concerning ownership and sale from eighth-century Khotan', in L. Russell-Smith and M. Ghose (eds), *From Nisa to Niya: New discoveries in Central and Inner Asian art and archaeology*. London: Saffron Press (forthcoming).

Smirnova, O. I., 1981. *Svodnii Katalog Sogdiiskikh monet (bronza)*. Moscow: Nauka.

Smith, A., 1776. *An enquiry into the nature and causes of the wealth of nations*. London [5th edition, 1789].

Song Zhiyong, 1996. 'Bosi yinbi zai Xinjiang de you yi ci zhongda faxian – zhuiji 89 nian Tulufan chutu de yi pi zaoqi Bosi Sashan chao yinbi', *Xinjiang Qianbi* 1996(2), 36–9.

*Songshu* (by Sheng Yue, 441–513). Beijing: Zhonghua shuju, 1974.

Stein, M. A., 1887. 'Zoroastrian deities on Indo–Scythian coins', *Oriental and Babylonian Record*, London.

Stein, M. A., 1899. 'Notes on the monetary system of ancient Kasmir', *Numismatic Chronicle*, series 3, 19, 125–74.

Stein, M. A., 1900. *Kalhana's Rajatarangini, a chronicle of the kings of Kashmir*. London: Constable and Co.

Stein, M. A., 1907. *Ancient Khotan: detailed report of archaeological explorations in Chinese Turkestan*, 2 vols. Oxford: Clarendon Press [repr. New York: Hacker Art Books, Inc., 1975].

Stein, M. A., 1912. *Ruins of Desert Cathay – personal narrative of explorations in Central Asia and Westernmost China*. London: Macmillan & Co. Ltd [repr. New York: Dover Publications, Inc., 1987].

Stein, M. A., 1920. 'Central Asian relics of China's ancient silk trade', *T'oung Pao*, 2nd series, 20, 130–41.

Stein, M. A., 1921. *Serindia: detailed report of explorations in Central Asia and Westernmost China*, 5 vols. Oxford: Clarendon Press [repr. Delhi: Motilal Banarsidass, 1980; translated into Chinese and published as *Xiyu kaogu tuji*, Guangxi Normal University Press, 1998].

Stein, M. A., 1923. *Memoir on maps of Chinese Turkestan and Kansu from the surveys made during Sir Aurel Stein's explorations, 1900–1, 1906–8, 1913–15*. Dehra Dun: Trigonometrical Survey Office.

Stein, M. A., 1928. *Innermost Asia: detailed report of exploration in Central Asia, Kansu and Eastern Iran*, 4 vols. Oxford: Clarendon Press [repr. New Delhi: Cosmo Publications, 1981].

Stein, M. A., 1933. *On ancient Central Asian tracks*. London: Macmillan and Co. Ltd.

Su Qing, 1984. *Zhongguo gudai huobi shi*. Beijing: Renmin chubanshe.

*Suishu* (by Wei Zheng, 580–643, et al.). Beijing: Zhonghua shuju, 1973.

Sun Hao, 1994. 'Quluwen jiandu yu nifeng xiao yi', *Xinjiang Wenwu* 1994(3), 89.

Swann, N. L., 1950. *Food and money in ancient China: the earliest economic history of China to AD 25. Hanshu 24, with related texts, Hanshu 91 and Shiji 129, translated and annotated*. Princeton: Princeton University Press.

SXA, 1996 [= Institute of Archaeology of Shanxi Province]. *Art of the Houma foundry / Houma taofan yishu*. Princeton: Princeton University Press.

Takeuchi Tsuguhito, 1995. *Old Tibetan contracts from Central Asia*. Tokyo: Daizo Shuppan.

Takeuchi Tsuguhito, 1997. *Old Tibetan manuscripts from East Turkestan in the Stein collection of the British Library, vol. 1, plates*. Tokyo: The Centre for East Asian Cultural Studies for UNESCO, the Toyo Bunko, the British Library (Bibliotheca Codicum Asiaticorum 11).

Takeuchi Tsuguhito, 1998. *Old Tibetan manuscripts from East Turkestan in the Stein collection of the British Library, vol. 2, descriptive catalogue*. Tokyo: The Centre for East Asian Cultural Studies for UNESCO, the Toyo Bunko, the British Library (Bibliotheca Codicum Asiaticorum 11).

Talvio, T., 1999. 'The coins in the Mannerheim collection', in P. Koskikallio and A. Lehmuskallio (eds) *C. G. Mannerheim in Central Asia 1906–1908*, 117–21. Helsinki: National Board of Antiquities.

Tang Changru (ed.-in-chief), 1981–92 [= Guojia wenwuju gu wenxian yanjiusuo, Xinjiang weiwu'er zizhiqu bowuguan and Wuhan daxue lishi xi]. *Tulufan chutu wenshu*, 10 vols. Beijing: Wenwu chubanshe.

Tang Shifu, 1988. 'Han–Qiu erti wuzhu de zaoqi ziliao ji qita', *Zhongguo Qianbi* 1988(1), 73–6.

*TCW*, 1992 [= Tang Changru, ed.-in-chief] *Tulufan chutu wenshu*, 2 vols. Beijing: Wenwu chubanshe [first ed. by Guojia wenwuju guwenxian yanjiushi, Xinjiang weiwu'er zizhiqu bowuguan and Wuhan daxue lishixi (eds), without photographs, 10 vols, 1981].

Thierry, F., 1989. 'La chronologie des wuzhu: étude, analyse et propositions', *Revue Numismatique*, 6th series, 31, 223–47.

Thierry, F., 1992. *Monnaies de Chine*, Paris: Bibliothèque Nationale.
Thierry, F., 1993. 'Sur les monnaies sassanides trouvées en Chine', *Res Orientales* 5, 89–139.
Thierry, F., 1994. 'Le "trésor" de monnaies romaines de Lingshi (Shanxi, Chine)', *Bulletin de la Société Française de Numismatique*, 49th year, no. 4, 767–8.
Thierry, F., 1997a. 'On the Tang coins collected by Pelliot in Chinese Turkestan (1906–1909)', in K. Tanabe, J. Cribb and H. Wang (eds) *Studies in Silk Road coins and culture: papers in honour of Professor Ikuo Hirayama on his 65th birthday*, 149–79. Kamakura: Institute of Silk Road Studies.
Thierry, F., 1997b. *Monnaies chinoises: (I) L'antiquité préimpériale*. Paris: Bibliothèque Nationale de France.
Thierry, F., 1998. 'The origins and development of Chinese coins', in O. Bopearachchi and D. P. M. Weerakkody (eds) *Origin, evolution and circulation of foreign coins in the Indian Ocean*, 15–62. Manohar: Sri Lanka Society for Numismatic Studies and French Mission of Archaeological Co-operation in Sri Lanka.
Thierry, F., 1999. 'Sur les monnaies des Türgesh', in M. Alram and D. E. Klimberg-Salter (eds) *Coins, art and chronology: essays on the pre-Islamic history of the Indo-Iranian borderlands*, 321–49. Vienna: Verlag der Österreichische Akademie der Wissenschaften.
Thierry, F., 2000. 'Entre Iran et la China, la circulation monétaire en Sérinde du Ier au IXe siècle', in J.-P. Drège (ed.) *La Sérinde, terre des échanges: art, religion, commerce du Ier au Xe siècle*, 121–47. Paris: XIVes Rencontres de l'Ecole du Louvre.
Thierry, F., 2001. 'La fiduciarité idéale à l'épreuve des coûts de production: quelques éléments sur la contradiction fondamentale de la monnaie en Chine', *Revue Numismatique* 157, 131–52.
Thierry, F., and Morrisson, C., 1994. 'Sur les monnaies byzantines trouvées en Chine', *Revue Numismatique*, 6th series, 36, 109–45.
Thomas, F. W., 1924. 'Drakhme and stater in Khotan', *Journal of the Royal Asiatic Society*, 671–2.
Thomas, F. W., 1926. 'Greek *στατήρ* in Central Asia', *Journal of the Royal Asiatic Society*, 507.
Thomas, F. W., 1935. *Tibetan literary texts and documents concerning Chinese Turkestan, vol. I, literary texts*. London: Royal Asiatic Society (Oriental Translation Fund, new series, 32).
Thomas, F. W., 1946. 'Some notes on Central-Asian Kharosthi documents', *Bulletin of the School of Oriental Studies* 11, 513–49.
Thomas, F. W., 1951. *Tibetan literary texts and documents concerning Chinese Turkestan, vol. II, Documents*. London: Royal Asiatic Society (Oriental Translation Fund, new series, 37).
Thomas, F. W., 1955. *Tibetan literary texts and documents concerning Chinese Turkestan, vol. III, Addenda and corrigenda*. London: Royal Asiatic Society (Oriental Translation Fund, new series, 40).
*TNEB* = *The New Encylopaedia Britannica*, 1998, vol. 16.
*Tongdian* (by Du You, 734–812). Beijing: Zhonghua shuju, 1988.
Tomiya Itaru (ed.), 2001. *Ryusa shutsudo no moji shiryo: Roran, Niya bunsho o chushin ni / Written materials excavated from the sands*. Kyoto: Kyoto daigaku gakujutsu shuppankai.
Trombert, E., 1995. *Le crédit à Dunhuang: vie matérielle et société en Chine médiévale*, Paris: Collège de France, Institut des Hautes Etudes Chinoises.
Trombert, E., 1996. 'Une trajectoire d'ouest en est sur la route de la soie: la diffusion du coton dans l'Asie centrale sinisée (6$^{e}$–10$^{e}$ siècles)' in Accademia Nazionale dei Lincei (ed.) (in collaboration with l'Istituto Italiano per il Medio de Estremo Oriente, international conference, 9–12 November 1994), *La Persia e l'Asia Centrale da Alessandro al X secolo*, 205–27. Rome: Accademia Nazionale dei Lincei.
Trombert, E., 2000. 'Textiles et tissus sur la route de la soie. Eléments pour une géographie de la production et des échanges', in J.-P. Drège (ed.) *La Sérinde, terre des échanges: art, religion, commerce du Ier au Xe siècle*, 107–20. Paris: XIVes Rencontres de l'Ecole du Louvre.
Trombert, E., 2001. 'La vigne et le vin en Chine – misères et succès d'une tradition allogène', Premiere Partie: De la vigne au vin – un chemin difficile', *Journal Asiatique* 289.2, 285–327.
Trombert, E., 2002a. 'La vigne et le vin en Chine – misères et succès d'une tradition allogène, Deuxieme Partie: Vins, vignes et vignerons de Tourfan', *Journal Asiatique* 290.2, 485–563.
Trombert, E., 2002b. 'Les cycles de culture et l'organisation des terroirs à Tourfan aux VI$^{e}$-VIII$^{e}$ siècles', *Bulletin de l'Ecole Française de l'Extrême-Orient* 89, 203–35.
Trombert, E., 2003. 'Un sujet d'actualité: les Sogdiens en Chine des Han aux Tang, *Etudes chinoises* XXII, 231–41.
Tu Yanzhi, 2000. '"Quanzhi" banben yu yanjiu', *Zhongguo Qianbi* 2000(3): 13–15.
Turfan WGS, 1990 [= Tulufan diqu wenguansuo]. 'Tulufan Caikan gumuqun qingli jianbao', *Xinjiang wenwu* 1990(3), 1–7.
Turfan WGS, 1994 [= Tulufan diqu wenguansuo]. 'Tulufan Bei Liang Wuxuan wang Qu Qu Meng Xun furen Peng shi mu', *Wenwu* 1994(9), 75–82.
Turfan Museum (ed.), 1992. *Turfan Bowuguan / Turfan Museum*. Urumqi: Xinjiang Fine Arts and Photographic Publishing House.
Twitchett, D., 1970. *Financial administration under the T'ang dynasty*. Cambridge: Cambridge University Press [1st ed. 1963].
Van Heesch, J., forthcoming. 'Some aspects of wage payments and coinage in ancient Rome (1st–3rd century AD)', in J. Lucassen (ed.), *Wages and Currency*. Leiden: International Institute of Social History.
Vorob'ëva-Desyatovskaja, M. I., 1996. 'The toponym "Six Villages" according to Khotanese business documents', in Accademia Nazionale dei Lincei (ed.) (in collaboration with l'Istituto Italiano per il Medio de Estremo Oriente, international conference, 9–12 November 1994), *La Persia e l'Asia Centrale da Alessandro al X secolo*, 171–85. Rome: Accademia Nazionale dei Lincei.
Walker, A., 1995. *Aurel Stein, pioneer of the Silk Road*. London: John Murray.
Wang Binghua, 1991. '"Silu" kaogu xin shouhuo', *Xinjiang Wenwu* 1991(2), 21–41.
Wang Binghua, 1996. 'Silu "Xinjiang duan" kaogu xin shouhuo', in UNESCO and CASSIA (eds), *Land routes of the Silk Roads and the cultural exchanges between the East and West before the tenth century (Desert Route Expedition International Seminar in Urumqi, August 19–21, 1990)*, 305–34. Beijing: New World Press.
Wang Guichen, 2000. 'Hong Zun "Quanzhi" de xueshu jiazhi – jian tan gudai qianbi wenxian cunyi qingkuang', *Zhongguo Qianbi* 2000(3), 9–12.
Wang Guowei, 1984. *Shuijingzhu jiao*. Shanghai: Shanghai renmin chubanshe.
Wang, H., 1995. 'Le voyage d'études de Helen Wang, second lauréat de la bourse de la CIN / Report on the second INC Travelling Scholarship', *International Numismatic Report* 26, 3–5.
Wang, H., 1996. 'Archaeology on the Silk Road', in H. Coutts (ed.) *Gateway to the Silk Road. Relics from the Han to the Tang dynasties from Xi'an, China*, 7–12. Edinburgh: City of Edinburgh Museums and Galleries.
Wang, H., 1997. 'The Stein collection of coins from Chinese Central Asia', in K. Tanabe, J. Cribb and H. Wang (eds) *Studies in Silk Road coins and culture: papers in honour of Professor Ikuo Hirayama on his 65th birthday*, 187–99. Kamakura: Insitute of Silk Road Studies.
Wang, H., 1998. 'Stein's recording angel: Miss F. M. G. Lorimer', *Journal of the Royal Asiatic Society*, Series 3, 8, 2, 207–28.
Wang, H. (ed.), 1999. *Handbook to the Stein collections in the UK*. London: British Museum Occasional Paper 129.
Wang, H., 2000. 'Money on the Eastern Silk Road in the pre-Islamic period', in B. Kluge and B. Weisser (eds) *XII Internationaler Numismatischer Kongress, Berlin 1977, Proceedings II*, 1350–64. Berlin: International Numismatic Congress.
Wang, H. (ed.), 2002. *Sir Aurel Stein in The Times*. London: Saffron Books.
Wang, H. (ed.), 2004. *Sir Aurel Stein. Proceedings of the British Museum study day, 23 March 2002*. London: British Museum Occasional Paper 142.
Wang, H., Cowell, M., Cribb, J., and Bowman, S. (eds), 2004. *Metallurgical analysis of Chinese coins at the British Museum*. London: British Museum Occasional Paper 147.
Wang Jiqing, 1993. 'Aulai'er Sidanyin de di si ci Zhongyang Yaxiya kaocha', *Dunhuangxue jikan*, 1993(1), no. 23, 98–110.
Wang Jiqing, 1994. 'Zhong Ying guanyu Sidanyin di si ci Zhongya kaocha suohuo wenwu de jiaoshe neimu', *Jindaishi yanjiu*, 1994(4): 242–57.
Wang Jiqing, 1998. 'Photographs in the British Library of the documents and manuscripts from Sir Aurel Stein's fourth Central Asian expedition', *The British Library Journal*, vol. 24, no. 1, spring, 23–74. [Published in Chinese as 'Sitanyin di si ci Zhongya kaocha suohuo Hanwen wenshu', *Dunhuang Tulufan yanjiu* 3 (1998), 259–90].

Wang Lin, 1987. 'Lushun bowuguan cang Xinjiang chutu qianbi', *Zhongguo qianbi* 1987(2), 26–9.

Wang Pikao, 1962. 'Qinghai Xining Bosi Sashan chao yinbi chutu qingkuang', *Kaogu*, 1962(9), 492.

Wang Su, 1998. *Gaochang shigao*. Beijing: Wenwu chubanshe.

Wang Tao, 1997. 'Establishing the Chinese archaeological school: Su Bingqi and contemporary Chinese archaeology', *Antiquity* 71, 31–9.

Wang Tao, 2000. 'Letter from Beijing. China's "Dead Sea scrolls"', *Archaeology* 54(4) July/August, 62–3.

Wang Yao and Chen Jian, 1986. *Tufan jiandu zonglu*. Beijing: Wenwu chubanshe.

Wang Yongsheng, 1993. 'Han–Qu erti qian zhong de zhenpin', *Zhongguo Qianbi* 1993(4), 49.

Wang Yongsheng, 1995. 'Dali yuanbao, Jianzhong tongbao zhudi kao – jianlun Shangyuan yuannian (760 nian) hou Tang dui Xiyu de jianshou', *Xinjiang Qianbi* 1995(2), 1–14.

Wang Yongsheng, 1996, 1998. 'Dali yuanbao, Jianzhong tongbao zhudi kao – jian lun Shangyuan yuan nian yihou Tang dui Xiyu de jianshou', *Zhongguo Qianbi* 1996(3), 3–11. [repr. in Zhongguo Qianbi Xuehui (ed.), *Zhongguo qianbi lunwenji* 3, 1998, 295–305. Beijing: Zhongguo jinrong chubanshe].

Watters, T., 1904. *On Yuan Chwang's travels in India 629–645 AD*. Oriental Translation Fund, new series, vol. IV. London: Royal Asiatic Society.

Weatherford, J., 1997. *The history of man*. New York: Three Rivers Press.

*Weishu* (by Wei Shou, 506–72). Beijing: Zhonghua shuju, 1974.

Wenwu baohu, 1982 [= Wenwu baohu kexue jishu yanjiusuo tan shisi shiyanshi]. 'Tan shisi niandai ceding baogao 4', *Wenwu* 1982(4), 88–93.

Whitfield, R., 1982–83. *The art of Central Asia. The Stein collection in the British Museum, vol. 3: textiles, sculpture and other arts*. Tokyo: Kodansha International in co-operation with the Trustees of the British Museum.

Whitfield, S., 1997. 'The future of the Stein collection in the British Library', in K. Tanabe, J. Cribb and H. Wang (eds) *Studies in Silk Road coins and culture: papers in honour of Professor Ikuo Hirayama on his 65th birthday*, 229–42. Kamakura: Institute of Silk Road Studies.

Wicks, R. S., 1992. *Money, markets and trade in early Southeast Asia: the development of indigenous monetary systems to AD 1400*. New York: Cornell South East Asia Program.

Wiesehöfer, J., 1998. *Ancient Persia: from 550 BC to 650 AD*. London: I. B. Tauris Ltd.

Wilkinson, E. P., 2000. *Chinese history: A manual*. Cambridge, Mass. and London: Harvard University Press. (Harvard-Yenching Institute monograph series 52).

Williams, J. (ed.), with Cribb, J., and Errington, E., 1997. *Money: a history*. London: British Museum.

Wood, F., 1997. 'From Central Asia to London: the Stein collection of manuscripts in the British Library', in K. Tanabe, J. Cribb and H. Wang (eds) *Studies in Silk Road coins and culture: papers in honour of Professor Ikuo Hirayama on his 65th birthday*, 221–7. Kamakura: Institute of Silk Road Studies.

Woolley, L., 1958. *History unearthed: a survey of eighteen archaeological sites throughout the world*. London: Ernest Benn Ltd.

Wu Rongzeng, 1988. 'Liang Han wuzhu qian yanjiu zhong de jige wenti', in Wenwu chubanshe bianjibu (eds) *Wenwu chubanshe chengli sanshi zhounian jinian – wenwu yu kaogu lunji / The thirtieth anniversary of the Cultural Relics Publishing House – treatises on archaeology and cultural relics*, 286–96. Beijing: Wenwu chubanshe.

Wu Rongzeng, 1995, 1998. 'Eyan qian kaolüe', *Zhongguo Qianbi* 1995(2), 42–5 [repr. in Zhongguo qianbi xuehui (eds) *Zhongguo qianbi lunwenji 3 / A collection of Chinese numismatic theses 3*, 205–9. Beijing: Zhongguo jinrong chubanshe, 1998].

Wu Zhenfeng, 1985. 'Banliang qian ji qi xiangguan de wenti', in Zhongguo Qianbi Xuehui (eds) *Zhongguo qianbi lunwenji 1 / A collection of Chinese numismatic theses 1*, 166–85. Beijing: Zhongguo jinrong chubanshe.

Wuhan, 1983 [Wuhan daxue lishi xi – Wei Jin nanbei chao Sui Tang shi yanjiushi]. *Dunhuang Tulufan wenshu chutan*. Wuhan: Wuhan daxue chubanshe.

Xia Nai, 1957. 'Zhongguo zuijin faxian de Bosi Sashan chao yinbi', *Kaogu xuebao* 1957(2), 49–60. [repr. in Zhongguo kexueyuan kaogu yanjiusuo (ed.), *Kaoguxue lunwenji*, 1961, 118–21, 170–1, pl. 30. Beijing: Kexue chubanshe, and in Xinjiang shehui kexueyuan kaogu yanjiusuo (ed.) *Xinjiang kaogu sanshi nian*, 470–80. Urumqi: Xinjiang renmin chubanshe].

Xia Nai, 1958, 1961. 'Qinghai Xining chutu de Bosi Sashan chao yinbi', *Kaogu xuebao* 1958(1), 105–10. [repr. in Zhongguo kexueyuan kaogu yanjiusuo (ed.), *Kaoguxue lunwenji*, 1961, 129–34, 171–72. Beijing: Kexue chubanshe, and in Xinjiang shehui kexueyuan kaogu yanjiusuo (ed.) *Xinjiang kaogu sanshi nian*, 495–9. Urumqi: Xinjiang renmin chubanshe].

Xia Nai, 1962. '"Hezhen maqian" kao', *Wenwu* 1962(7–8). [reprinted in Xinjiang shehui kexueyuan kaogu yanjiusuo (ed.) *Xinjiang kaogu sanshi nian*, 466–70. Urumqi: Xinjiang renmin chubanshe].

Xia Nai, 1966. 'Xinjiang Tulufan zuijin chutu de Bosi Sashan chao yinbi', *Kaogu* 1966(4), 211–16.

Xia Nai, 1974. 'Zongshu Zhongguo chutu de Bosi Sashan chao yinbi', *Kaogu xuebao* 1974(1), 91–112. [reprinted in Xinjiang shehui kexueyuan kaogu yanjiusuo (ed.) *Xinjiang kaogu sanshi nian*, 480–95. Urumqi: Xinjiang renmin chubanshe].

Xia Nai, 1977. 'Zanhuang Li Xizong mu chutu de Baizhanting jinbi', *Kaogu* 1977(6), 403–6.

Xiang Da, 1983. 'Xinjiang kaogu gaikuang', in Xinjiang shehui kexueyuan kaogu yanjiusuo (ed.) *Xinjiang kaogu sanshi nian*, 175–81. Urumqi: Xinjiang renmin chubanshe.

Xiao Huaiyuan, 1987. *Xizang difang huobi shi / The history of Tibetan money*. Beijing: Minzu chubanshe.

Xiao Kangda, 1978. '"Li Jun suo ze Kou En shi" jiance lüe kao', *Wenwu* 1978(1), 32–4.

Xie Guihua, Li Junming and Zhu Guozhao, 1987. *Juyan hanjian shiwen hexiao*, 2 vols. Beijing: Wenwu chubanshe.

Xie Shiping, 1986. 'Anyang chutu Nanbeichao guqian jiaocang', *Zhongyuan wenwu* 1986(3), 36–41.

XJ–Archaeology, 1983 [= Xinjiang shehui kexue yuan kaogu yanjiusuo]. *Xinjiang kaogu sanshi nian*. Urumqi: Xinjiang renmin chubanshe.

XJ–Archaeology, 1985 [= Xinjiang shehui kexue yuan kaogu yanjiusuo]. *Xinjiang gudai minzu wenwu*. Beijing: Wenwu chubanshe.

XJ–Archaeology, 1991 [= Xinjiang wenwu kaogu yanjiusuo]. 'Xinjiang wenwu kaogu gongzuo de xin fazhan', in Wenwu bianji weiyuanhui (ed.) *Wenwu kaogu gongzuo shi nian 1979–1989*, 343–51. Beijing: Wenwu chubanshe.

XJ–Conservation (ed), 1991 [= Zizhiqu wenhuating wenwu baohu weixiu bangongshi]. '1989 nian Kesun'er qianfodong ku qian qingli jianbao', *Xinjiang wenwu* 1991(3), 1–35.

XJ–History, 1987 [= Xinjiang shehui kexueyuan lishi yanjiusuo]. *Xinjiang difang lishi ziliao xuanji*. Beijing: Renmin chubanshe.

XJ–Loulan, 1988 [= Xinjiang Loulan Kaogudui]. 'Loulan gucheng zhi diaocha yu shijue jianbao', *Wenwu* 1988(7), 1–39.

XJ–Museum, 1960, 1983 [= Xinjiang Weiwu'er zizhiqu bowuguan]. 'Xinjiang Minfeng xian bei da shamo zhong gu yizhi muzangqu dong Han hezangmu qingli jianbao', *Wenwu* 1960(6), 9–12, [repr. in Xinjiang shehui kexue yuan kaogu yanjiusuo (eds) *Xinjiang kaogu sanshi nian*, 1983, 64–68. Urumqi: Xinjiang renmin chubanshe].

XJ–Museum, 1960 [= Xinjiang weiwu'er zizhiqu bowuguan]. 'Xinjiang Tulufan Asitana beiqu muzang fajue jianbao', *Wenwu* 1960(6), 13–21.

XJ–Museum, 1961 [= Xinjiang Weiwu'er zizhiqu bowuguan]. 'Xinjiang Minfeng dashamo zhong de gudai yizhi', *Kaogu* 1961(3), 119–22, 126.

XJ–Museum, 1972 [= Xinjiang weiwu'er zizhiqu bowuguan]. 'Tulufan xian Asitana – Halahezhuo gu muqun qingli jianbao', *Wenwu* 1972(1), 8–21.

XJ–Museum, 1975 [= Xinjiang weiwu'er zizhiqu bowuguan]. *Xinjiang chutu wenwu*. Beijing: Wenwu chubanshe.

XJ–Museum, 1991 [= Xinjiang weiwu'er zizhiqu bowuguan]. *Xinjiang Weiwu'er Zizhiqu Bowuguan* (Zhongguo bowuguan congshu 9). Beijing: Wenwu chubanshe.

XJ–Museum–Archaeology, 1978 [= Xinjiang bowuguan kaogudui]. 'Tulufan Asitana – Halahezhuo gu muqun fajue jianbao', *Wenwu* 1978(6), 1–14 [repr. in Xinjiang shehui kexue yuan kaogu yanjiusuo (eds) *Xinjiang kaogu sanshi nian*, 1983, 117–18. Urumqi: Xinjiang renmin chubanshe].

XJ–Museum et al., 1975 [= Xinjiang weiwu'er zizhiqu bowuguan and Xibei daxue lishi xi kaogu zhuanye]. '1973 Tulufan Asitana gu muqun fajue jianbao', *Wenwu* 1975(7), 8–26.

XJ–Relics, 1999 [ = Xinjiang wenwu shiye guanli ju]. *Xinjiang wenwu gujin daguan*. Urumqi: Xinjiang meishu sheying chubanshe.
XJ–Survey, 1993 [ = Xinjiang weiwu'er zizhiqu puchadui]. 'Baiyingeleng Menggu zizhiqu pucha ziliao', *Xinjiang Wenwu* 1993(1), 1–94.
Xu Diankui, 1991. 'Shilun Tang Kaiyuan tongbao de fenqi', *Kaogu* 1991(6), 555–60.
Xu Pingfang, 1978. 'Juyan kaogu fajue de xin shouhuo', *Wenwu* 1978(1), 26–9, 34.
Xu Pingfang, 1995. 'Kaoguxue shang suojian Zhongguo jing nei de Sichou zhi lu', *Yanjing xuebao/Yenching Journal of Chinese Studies*, di yi qi / new number 1, 291–344.
Xu Shen, 1963. *Shuowen jiezi*. Beijing: Zhonghua shuju.
Xu Yueyao, 1989. 'Juyan Han jian suo jian de shi', in Gansu wenwu kaogusuo (eds) *Qin Han jiandu lunwenji*, 49–69. Lanzhou: Gansu renmin chubanshe.
Xuan Zang, 1997 *Da Tang xiyuji / Xuan Zang juan*, annotated by Zhang Xun. Shanghai: Shanghai renmin chubanshe.
Xue Li (ed.-in-chief), 1994. *Zhongguo sichou zhilu cidian*, Urumqi: Xinjiang renmin chubanshe.
Xue Zongzheng, 1987. 'Xinjiang Luntai xian chutu de Zhongyuan guqian', *Xinjiang Wenwu* 1987(1), 52–55.
Yamamoto Tatsuro and Ikeda On, 1987. *Tun-huang and Turfan documents concerning social and economic history, Part III: Contracts (A) Introduction and Texts*. Tokyo: Toyo Bunko.
Yang Jiping, 1997. 'Dunhuang Tulufan chutu gugongqi yanjiu', *Dunhuang Tulufan yanjiu* 2, 215–30.
Yang Jixian and Yu Tingming, 1991. 'Shaan, Gan chutu faxian de waiguo mingwen qianbing xintan', *Xinjiang Jinrong* (Quanguo di er ci sichou zhi lu huobi yantaohui wenji), 80–85.
Yang Lien-sheng, 1952. *Money and credit in China: a short history*. Cambridge, Mass.: Harvard University Press.
Yang Weisheng, 2000. 'Guanyu Hong Zun de shiji yu zhushu', *Zhongguo Qianbi* 2000(3): 16–19.
Yu Taishan (ed.), 1996. *Xiyu tongshu*. Zhengzhou: Zhongzhou guji chubanshe.
Yü Ying-shih, 1967. *Trade and expansion in Han China: a study in the structure of Sino–barbarian economic relations*. Berkeley: University of California Press.
Yü Ying-shih, 1986. 'Han foreign relations', in D. Twitchett and M. Loewe (eds) *Cambridge History of China, vol. I, The Ch'in and Han Empires*. Cambridge: Cambridge University Press.
Zeymal, E. V., 1992. 'Eastern (Chinese) Turkestan on the Silk Road – first millennium AD numismatic evidence', *Silk Road Art and Archaeology* 2, 137–77.
Zeymal, E. V., 1994. 'The circulation of coins in Central Asia during the early medieval period (fifth–eighth centuries AD)', *Bulletin of the Asia Institute* 8, 245–67.
Zhang Feng, 1931. *Han Jin xichui mujian huibian*, Shanghai: Shanghai youzheng shuju.
Zhang Guangda and Rong Xinjiang, 1993. *Yutian shi congkao*. Shanghai: Shanghai shudian.
Zhang Guangda and Rong Xinjiang, 1998. 'A concise history of the Turfan oasis and its exploration', *Asia Major*, 3rd series, XI, part 2, 13–26.
Zhang Guangda and Rong Xinjiang, 2002. 'Shengpidebao cang Hetian chutu Hanwen wenshu kaoshi', *Dunhuang Tulufan yanjiu, di liu juan*, 221–41.
Zhang Junmin, 1989. '"Jianwu san nian hou su jun suo zhai Kou En shi" ce jingji kaolüe', in Gansu wenwu kaogusuo (eds) *Qin Han jiandu lunwenji*, 136–44. Lanzhou: Gansu renmin chubanshe.
Zhang Ping, 1987a. 'Han–Qiu erti qian ji qi youguan wenti', *Zhongguo Qianbi* 1987(1), 26–31.
Zhang Ping 1987b. 'Xinjiang Luntai xian chutu de Han-Qiu erti wuzhu', *Xinjiang wenwu* 1987(1), 56–61.
Zhang Ping, 1988. 'Xinjiang Luntai xian chutu de Han-Qiu erti wuzhu', *Kaogu* 1988(7), 666–8.
Zhang Ping, 1989. 'Xinjiang kaogu faxian de Qiuci qianfan', *Zhongguo Qianbi* 1989(3), 38–40.
Zhang Ping, 1991. 'Qiuci difang zhubi de kaogu faxian yu yanjiu', *Xinjiang Jinrong: quanguo di er ci silu huobi yantaohui wenji*, 1991(2), 135–47.
Zhang Tian'en, 1991. 'Dong Zhou lieguo bei hua de kaocha', *Zhongguo Qianbi* 1991(2), 33, 27–33/7.
Zhang Yisun, 1985. *Zang Han dacidian*, 3 vols. Beijing: Minzu chubanshe.
Zhang Zhongshan, 1991. 'On coin "Liang zao xin quan" excavated in Wuwei, a well-known city on the Silk Road', in *Abstracts of papers from the XIth International Numismatic Congress, Brussels* (printed for attendees at the XIth INC).
Zhang Zhongshan, 1999. *Zhongguo sichou zhilu huobi*. Lanzhou: Lanzhou daxue chubanshe.
Zheng Ming and Huai Sheng, 1988. 'Shandong Gaotang xian chutu Tangdai huobi', *Kaogu* 1988(1), 94.
Zheng Xuemeng, 1986. 'Shiliuguo zhi Qu shi wangchao shiqi Gaochang shiyong yinqian de qingkuang yanjiu', in Han Guopan (ed.) *Dunhuang Tulufan chutu jingji wenshu yanjiu*, 293–318. Xiamen: Xiamen daxue chubanshe.
ZGQBDCD, 1998 [ = Zhongguo Qianbi Dacidian bianzhuan weiyuanhui]. *Zhongguo qianbi dacidian – Qin Han bian*. Beijing: Zhonghua shuju.
ZGQBXH (ed.), 1992 [ = Zhongguo qianbi xuehui]. *Zhongguo qianbi xuehui chengli shi zhounian – jinian wenji*. Beijing: Zhongguo jinrong chubanshe.
ZGQBXH–SR, 1993 [ = Zhongguo qianbi xuehui silu huobi kaochadui]. 'Sichou zhi lu (Xinjiang duan) lishi huobi kaocha baogao', *Nei Menggu jinrong yanjiu – Qianbi zhuankan* 1993(4), 9–17, contd p. 3.
ZGQBXH–SR, 1995 [ = Zhongguo qianbi xuehui sichou zhilu kaochadui]. 'Sichou zhilu Xinjiang duan, lishi huobi kaocha jiyao', *Zhongguo Qianbi* 1995(1), 20–3.
ZGKXY–ARC, 1963 [ = Zhongguo kexueyuan kaogu yanjiusuo Luoyang fajuedui]. 'Luoyang xijiao Han mu fajue baogao', *Kaogu xuebao*, 1963(2), 1–58.
ZWJ (ed), 1992 [ = Zhongguo wenwuju] (trans. by M. Lai). 'Regulations for foreign participation in archaeological work in China, promulgated February 22, 1991', *China Exchange News*: 20–1.
Zhong Changfa, 1996. 'Gansu Wuwei shiliuguo jiaozang chutu Liang zao xinquan', *Zhongguo Qianbi* 1996(1), 45–7.
Zhong-Ri, 1996 [ = Zhong-Ri gongtong Niya yizhi xueshu diaocha dui]. *Zhong-Ri gongtong Niya yizhi xueshu diaocha baogao shu, di yi juan*. Tokyo: Nakamura insatsu kabushiki kaisha.
Zhong-Ri, 1999 [ = Zhong-Ri gongtong Niya yizhi xueshu diaocha dui]. *Zhong-Ri gongtong Niya yizhi xueshu diaocha baogaoshu, di er juan*, three vols (text volume in Japanese, text volume in Chinese, volume of plates). Tokyo: Nakamura insatsu kabushiki kaisha.
*Zhoushu* (by Linghu Defen et al., 583–661). Beijing: Zhonghua shuju, 1971.
Zhou Shirong, 1985. 'Changsha Hengyang chutu Xi Han huobi yanjiu', in Zhongguo Qianbi Xuehui (ed.) *Zhongguo qianbi lunwenji 1 / A collection of Chinese numismatic theses 1*, 193–208. Beijing: Zhongguo jinrong chubanshe.
Zhu Huo, 1992. 'Xin huo gu xue lun', in Zhongguo Qianbi Xuehui (eds) *Zhongguo Qianbi lunwenji 2 / A collection of Chinese numismatic theses 2*, 188–93. Beijing: Zhongguo jinrong chubanshe.
Zhu Shulin, 1988. 'Lanchengzi chutu de Jianzhong tongbao he Dali yuanbao', *Shaanxi jinrong: Qianbi zhuankan* 1988(9).
Zou Zhiliang, 2000. 'Lun "Gu Xuan Qianpu" dui Zhongguo qianbixue de gongxian', *Zhongguo Qianbi* 2000(3), 5–8.
Zürcher, E., 1990. 'Han Buddhism and the Western Region', in W. L. Idema and E. Zürcher (eds) *Thought and law in Qin and Han China: studies dedicated to Anthony Hulsewé on the occasion of his eightieth birthday*, 158–82. Leiden: E. J. Brill.

# Catalogue of the Stein Collection of coins from Eastern Central Asia

# Part 1 The coins

## Contents

This catalogue includes all the coins collected by Sir Aurel Stein during his three expeditions to Eastern Central Asia (1900–1, 1906–8, 1914–16) that are now housed in the Department of Coins and Medals, British Museum. They total over four thousand specimens.

## Arrangement

The arrangement of the catalogue follows the three Lists of Coins which Stein included as Appendices to his detailed reports of the three expeditions: *Ancient Khotan*, *Serindia*, *Innermost Asia*. See p. 244 for a summary of the coin lists. The coins themselves are arranged in this order in the Museum. For the sake of convenience and completeness, all the coins are listed in this order, including a small number of non-coin pieces (e.g. buckles, buttons) that are also housed with the coins. However, details are given only for the coins relevant to this study. For those coins which postdate this study, as well as for the non-coin material, only the minimum of information is given.

## Catalogue entries

Details of the individual coins are presented in table form, in seven columns:

1. **BM no.** refers to the numbering of the coins in the British Museum. It follows Stein's Lists of Coins, and gives each coin an individual identification code. For example, the identification number [IA.IV.a.1] indicates the Sino-Kharoshthi coin, which is in the **I**nnermost **A**sia List of Coins, in batch **IV**, group **a**, no. 1.
2. **Identification** refers to my identification of the coins after conservation and cleaning. It corrects any errors in Stein's Lists of Coins, and where appropriate gives additional details of identification. Romanization of Chinese coin-names is in pinyin.

   'Missing' or 'Extra' indicates a discrepancy with the number of coins in Stein's Lists. Although Stein's principle (S: 1342 n1) was that 'in the record of coins found or excavated at sites, fragments of coins, when belonging to distinct specimens, have been counted as one coin', this is not always watertight. Furthermore, some coins previously corroded together became separated during cleaning in 1993, and this has slightly increased the number of coins. It is also possible that some of the coins marked 'missing' or 'extra' may have been misplaced in the trays.

   For those Chinese coins where the inscription is not secure, any illegible or missing characters are indicated by 'x'.
3. **Weight**, in grams, is given for each coin and fragment where possible.
4. **Diameter**, in millimetres, is given for each coin and fragment where possible.
5. **Notes** indicates the physical conditions of the coin: for example, if the piece is a fragment rather than a full coin, if several fragments fit together to make one coin (e.g. 3 frags = 1 coin), or if the casting sprues are still visible. The measurement of the central square hole (**H:**) is given for the wuzhu coins only.
6. **Acquisition** indicates concisely how the coins were acquired: found (**F**), found at site (**FAS**), purchased (**p**), purchased at site (**pas**), gift (**g**), gift at site (**gas**).

   Stein's consistent attention to detail and provenance makes it very clear which coins have an archaeological context (those found at site, and, less precisely, those which were gifts or purchased at site), and those which have no archaeological context (those which were gifts or purchased, say, in bazaars).
7. **Acquisition/archaeological context** indicates the contexts of the acquisitions. Further details are presented in Part 2 of the catalogue. Here, as in Part 2, Stein's imperial measurements have not been adjusted.

**Imperial to Metric Conversions**

| | |
|---|---|
| 1 mile = 1.61 km | 1 square mile = 2.59 km$^2$ |
| 1 yard = 0.91 m | 1 square yard = 0.84 m$^2$ |
| 1 foot = 30.48 cm | 1 square foot = 929 cm$^2$ |
| 1 inch = 2.54 cm | |

## ANCIENT KHOTAN

### AK.I: COINS FROM TOGUJAI, MOJI

| BM no. | Identification | Wt | Diam. | Notes | Acqn | Acquisition/Archaeological context |
|---|---|---|---|---|---|---|
| AK I.a.1–78 | Islamic | – | – | – | pas | Allegedly from Togujai (Moji) site |
| AK I.b.1–9 | Islamic | – | – | – | pas | Allegedly from Togujai (Moji) site |
| AK I.c.1–3 | Islamic | – | – | – | pas | Allegedly from Togujai (Moji) site |
| AK I.d.1–29 | Islamic | – | – | – | pas | Allegedly from Togujai (Moji) site |
| AK I.e.1 | Qianyuan zhongbao – small | 2.24 | 22 | – | pas | Allegedly from Togujai (Moji) site |
| AK.I.e.2 | Qianyuan zhongbao – small | 2.31 | 21 | – | pas | Allegedly from Togujai (Moji) site |
| AK.I.e.3 | Qianyuan zhongbao – small | 1.80 | 22 | misaligned, forced hole | pas | Allegedly from Togujai (Moji) site |
| AK.I.e.4 | Qianyuan zhongbao – small | 1.76 | 22 | – | pas | Allegedly from Togujai (Moji) site |
| AK.I.e.5 | Qianyuan zhongbao – small | 2.60 | 22 | – | pas | Allegedly from Togujai (Moji) site |
| AK.I.e.6 | Qianyuan zhongbao – small | 2.47 | 22 | forced hole | pas | Allegedly from Togujai (Moji) site |
| AK.I.e.7 | Qianyuan zhongbao – small | 1.99 | 22 | misaligned, forced hole | pas | Allegedly from Togujai (Moji) site |
| AK.I.e.8 | Qianyuan zhongbao – small | 1.37 | 21 | frag., misaligned, forced hole | pas | Allegedly from Togujai (Moji) site |
| AK.I.e.9 | Qianyuan zhongbao – small | 2.48 | 22 | – | pas | Allegedly from Togujai (Moji) site |
| AK.I.e.10 | Qianyuan zhongbao – small | 1.53 | 22 | 3 frags restored | pas | Allegedly from Togujai (Moji) site |
| AK.I.e.11 | Qianyuan zhongbao – small | 2.23 | 22 | – | pas | Allegedly from Togujai (Moji) site |
| AK.I.e.12 | Qianyuan zhongbao – small | 1.88 | 22 | – | pas | Allegedly from Togujai (Moji) site |
| AK.I.e.13 | Qianyuan zhongbao – small | 2.16 | 22 | – | pas | Allegedly from Togujai (Moji) site |
| AK.I.e.14 | Qianyuan zhongbao – small | 2.36 | 22.5 | misaligned | pas | Allegedly from Togujai (Moji) site |
| AK.I.e.15 | Qianyuan zhongbao – small | 1.92 | 21.5 | – | pas | Allegedly from Togujai (Moji) site |
| AK.I.e.16 | [Qian] yuan zhongbao – small | 1.24 | 22 | frag. | pas | Allegedly from Togujai (Moji) site |
| AK.I.e.17 | Dali yuanbao – large | 3.22 | 23 | encrusted with earth | pas | Allegedly from Togujai (Moji) site |
| AK.I.e.18 | Dali yuanbao – small | 2.22 | 22 | 2 frags restored | pas | Allegedly from Togujai (Moji) site |
| AK.I.e.19 | Dali yuanbao – small | 2.33 | 21 | – | pas | Allegedly from Togujai (Moji) site |
| AK.I.e.20 | 'Wuzhu' – illegible | 1.42 | 24 | (H: 10) thin, very worn | pas | Allegedly from Togujai (Moji) site |
| AK.I.f.1 | Qianyuan zhongbao – large | 6.69 | 27 | – | pas | Allegedly from Togujai (Moji) site |
| AK.I.f.2 | Qianyuan zhongbao – large | 5.74 | 28 | – | pas | Allegedly from Togujai (Moji) site |
| AK.I.f.3 | Chinese coin – illegible, prob. Tang dynasty | 4.84 | 25 | corroded | pas | Allegedly from Togujai (Moji) site |
| AK.I.f.4 | Chinese coin – illegible, prob. Tang dynasty | 2.60 | 25 | frag., corroded | pas | Allegedly from Togujai (Moji) site |
| AK I.g.1–12 | Islamic coins; button | – | – | – | pas | Allegedly from Togujai (Moji) site |

## AK.II: COINS PURCHASED AT YOTKAN

| BM no. | Identification | Wt | Diam. | Notes | Acqn | Acquisition/Archaeological context |
|---|---|---|---|---|---|---|
| AK.II.a.1 | Kushan coin of Wima Takhto (bull & lion type) | 3.02 | 26 | – | pas | Allegedly from Yotkan site |
| AK.II.a.2 | Kushan coin of Kanishka I – drachm | 4.02 | 18 | attempted piercing at centre | pas | Allegedly from Yotkan site |
| AK.II.a.3 | Kushan coin of Kanishka I – drachm | 3.00 | 17 | – | pas | Allegedly from Yotkan site |
| AK.II.a.4 | Chinese-style lead coin of Khotan | 5.45 | 24 | – | pas | Allegedly from Yotkan site |
| AK.II.a.5 | Huoquan | 3.31 | 23 | – | pas | Allegedly from Yotkan site |
| AK.II.a.6–8 | 3 wuzhu corroded together | 5.51 | 25 | – | pas | Allegedly from Yotkan site |
| AK.II.a.9 | Qianyuan zhongbao – large | 6.72 | 29 | – | pas | Allegedly from Yotkan site |
| AK.II.a.10 | Qianyuan zhongbao – large | 7.33 | 29 | – | pas | Allegedly from Yotkan site |
| AK.II.a.11 | Qianyuan zhongbao – large | 7.36 | 29 | – | pas | Allegedly from Yotkan site |
| AK.II.a.12 | Qianyuan zhongbao – large | 4.31 | 28 | – | pas | Allegedly from Yotkan site |
| AK.II.a.13 | Qianyuan zhongbao – large | 5.09 | 28 | – | pas | Allegedly from Yotkan site |
| AK.II.a.14 | Qianyuan zhongbao – large | 6.75 | 28 | – | pas | Allegedly from Yotkan site |
| AK.II.a.15 | Qianyuan zhongbao – large | 5.85 | 28 | – | pas | Allegedly from Yotkan site |
| AK.II.a.16 | Qianyuan zhongbao – small | 1.70 | 22 | forced hole | pas | Allegedly from Yotkan site |
| AK.II.a.17 | Qianyuan zhongbao – small | 2.50 | 22 | – | pas | Allegedly from Yotkan site |
| AK.II.a.18 | Qianyuan zhongbao – small | 2.22 | 22 | forced hole | pas | Allegedly from Yotkan site |
| AK.II.a.19 | Qianyuan zhongbao – small | 2.44 | 22 | forced hole | pas | Allegedly from Yotkan site |
| AK.II.a.20 | Qianyuan zhongbao – small | 2.23 | 22 | – | pas | Allegedly from Yotkan site |
| AK.II.a.21 | Qianyuan zhongbao – small | 1.96 | 22 | – | pas | Allegedly from Yotkan site |
| AK.II.a.22 | Qianyuan zhongbao – small | 2.69 | 21.5 | – | pas | Allegedly from Yotkan site |
| AK.II.a.23 | Qianyuan zhongbao – small | 2.88 | 22 | – | pas | Allegedly from Yotkan site |
| AK.II.a.24 | Qianyuan zhongbao – small | 2.10 | 22 | – | pas | Allegedly from Yotkan site |
| AK.II.a.25 | Qianyuan zhongbao – small | 1.89 | 22 | misaligned | pas | Allegedly from Yotkan site |
| AK.II.a.26 | Qianyuan zhongbao – small | 2.73 | 22 | – | pas | Allegedly from Yotkan site |
| AK.II.a.27 | Qianyuan zhongbao – small | 1.96 | 22 | – | pas | Allegedly from Yotkan site |
| AK.II.a.28 | Qianyuan zhongbao – small | 1.70 | 21 | – | pas | Allegedly from Yotkan site |
| AK.II.a.29 | Qianyuan zhongbao – small | 2.70 | 21 | misaligned | pas | Allegedly from Yotkan site |
| AK.II.a.30 | Qianyuan zhongabo – small | 2.95 | 22 | forced hole | pas | Allegedly from Yotkan site |
| AK.II.a.31 | Dali yuanbao – small | 2.71 | 22 | – | pas | Allegedly from Yotkan site |
| AK.II.a.32 | Qianyuan zhongbao – small | 2.06 | 21.5 | – | pas | Allegedly from Yotkan site |
| AK.II.a.33 | Qianyuan zhongbao – small | 1.74 | 22 | misaligned | pas | Allegedly from Yotkan site |
| AK.II.a.34 | [Dali] yuanbao – small | 0.81 | 22 | frag. | pas | Allegedly from Yotkan site |
| AK.II.a.35 | Dali yuanbao – small | 1.92 | 22 | misaligned | pas | Allegedly from Yotkan site |
| AK.II.a.36 | Dali yuanbao – large | 3.07 | 23.5 | – | pas | Allegedly from Yotkan site |
| AK.II.a.37 | Dali yuanbao – small | 2.19 | 22 | – | pas | Allegedly from Yotkan site |
| AK.II.a.38 | Dali yuanbao – small | 1.83 | 21.5 | – | pas | Allegedly from Yotkan site |
| AK.II.a.39 | Dali yuanbao – large | 2.52 | 23.5 | misaligned | pas | Allegedly from Yotkan site |
| AK.II.a.40 | Sino-Kharoshthi coin (Cribb 3) | 0.82 | 17 | – | pas | Allegedly from Yotkan site |
| AK.II.a.41 | Sino-Kharoshthi coin (Cribb 1–6) | 1.86 | 17 | – | pas | Allegedly from Yotkan site |
| AK.II.a.42 | Sino-Kharoshthi coin (Cribb 1–6) | 1.63 | 19 | – | pas | Allegedly from Yotkan site |
| AK.II.a.43 | Sino-Kharoshthi coin (Cribb 2) | 2.67 | 18.5 | – | pas | Allegedly from Yotkan site |
| AK.II.a.44 | Sino-Kharoshthi coin (Cribb 2) | 1.87 | 18.5 | – | pas | Allegedly from Yotkan site |
| AK.II.a.45 | Sino-Kharoshthi coin (Cribb 1–6) | 2.27 | 17 | – | pas | Allegedly from Yotkan site |

| BM no. | Identification | Wt | Diam. | Notes | Acqn | Acquisition/Archaeological context |
|---|---|---|---|---|---|---|
| AK.II.a.46 | Sino-Kharoshthi coin (Cribb 1–6) | 1.95 | 18.5 | – | pas | Allegedly from Yotkan site |
| AK.II.a.47 | Sino-Kharoshthi coin (Cribb 2) | 1.98 | 19.5 | – | pas | Allegedly from Yotkan site |
| AK.II.a.48 | Sino-Kharoshthi coin (Cribb 2) | 2.63 | 20 | – | pas | Allegedly from Yotkan site |
| AK.II.a.49 | Sino-Kharoshthi coin (Cribb 5) | 3.22 | 17.5 | – | pas | Allegedly from Yotkan site |
| AK.II.a.50 | Coin of Indo-Scythian King Azes II (bull & lion type) | 7.42 | 26 | – | pas | Allegedly from Yotkan site |
| AK.II.a.51 | Sino-Kharoshthi coin (Cribb 6) | 2.66 | 18 | – | pas | Allegedly from Yotkan site |
| AK.II.a.52 | Sino-Kharoshthi coin (Cribb 6) | 1.42 | 18 | – | pas | Allegedly from Yotkan site |
| AK.II.a.53 | Sino-Kharoshthi coin (Cribb 1–6) | 2.16 | 17 | – | pas | Allegedly from Yotkan site |
| AK.II.a.54 | Sino-Kharoshthi coin (Cribb 2) | 2.46 | 18 | – | pas | Allegedly from Yotkan site |
| AK.II.a.55 | Sino-Kharoshthi coin (Cribb 1–6) | 0.82 | 8 | – | pas | Allegedly from Yotkan site |
| AK.II.a.56 | (button) | – | – | – | pas | Allegedly from Yotkan site |
| AK.II.a.57–58 | (misc. holed piece) | – | – | – | pas | Allegedly from Yotkan site |
| AK.II.a.59 | Türgesh coin (Type II) | 1.60 | 24 | frag. | pas | Allegedly from Yotkan site |
| AK.II.a.60 | Chinese coin – illegible | 2.09 | 23.5 | corroded | pas | Allegedly from Yotkan site |
| AK.II.a.61 | Chinese coin – illegible, Tang dynasty | 2.68 | 25.5 | 5 frags restored | pas | Allegedly from Yotkan site |
| AK.II.a.62 | Qianyuan zhongbao – small | 1.75 | 22 | misaligned | pas | Allegedly from Yotkan site |
| AK.II.a.63 | Qianyuan zhongbao – small | 2.55 | 22 | forced hole | pas | Allegedly from Yotkan site |
| AK.II.a.64 | Qianyuan zhongbao – small | 2.15 | 22 | – | pas | Allegedly from Yotkan site |
| AK II.a.65 | 'small wuzhu' without inscription | 0.29 | 9.5 | – | pas | Allegedly from Yotkan site |
| AK.II.a.66 | Sino-Kharoshthi coin (Cribb 1–6) | 2.00 | 17 | – | pas | Allegedly from Yotkan site |
| AK.II.a.67 | (button) | – | – | – | pas | Allegedly from Yotkan site |
| AK.II.a.68 | Sino-Kharoshthi coin (Cribb 1–6) | 1.08 | 16 | – | pas | Allegedly from Yotkan site |
| AK.II.a.69 | Sino-Kharoshthi coin (Cribb 2) | 2.37 | 17.5 | – | pas | Allegedly from Yotkan site |
| AK.II.a.70 | (button) | – | – | – | pas | Allegedly from Yotkan site |
| AK.II.a.71 | Sino-Kharoshthi coin (Cribb 1–6) | 2.25 | 20.5 | – | pas | Allegedly from Yotkan site |
| AK.II.a.72 | (not coin) | – | – | – | pas | Allegedly from Yotkan site |
| AK.II.a.73 | Sino-Kharoshthi coin (Cribb 2) | 2.39 | 18.5 | – | pas | Allegedly from Yotkan site |
| AK.II.a.74 | Sino-Kharoshthi coin (Cribb 13) | 1.11 | 10.5 | – | pas | Allegedly from Yotkan site |
| AK.II.a.75 | (clay – with impressions) | – | – | – | pas | Allegedly from Yotkan site |
| AK.II.a.76 | Chinese coin – illegible | 2.34 | 24 | corroded | pas | Allegedly from Yotkan site |
| AK.II.a.77 | Qianyuan zhongbao – small | 2.19 | 21.5 | crude, misaligned | pas | Allegedly from Yotkan site |
| AK.II.a.78 | Chinese coin – illegible | 1.20 | – | frag., corroded | pas | Allegedly from Yotkan site |
| AK.II.a.79 | Chinese coin – illegible | 0.78 | – | frag., corroded | pas | Allegedly from Yotkan site |
| AK.II.a.80 | Chinese coin – illegible | 0.98 | – | frag., corroded | pas | Allegedly from Yotkan site |

| | | | | | | |
|---|---|---|---|---|---|---|
| AK.II.b.1 | Sino-Kharoshthi coin (Cribb 2) | 3.52 | 20 | – | pas | Allegedly from Yotkan site |

| BM no. | Identification | Wt | Diam. | Notes | Acqn | Acquisition/Archaeological context |
|---|---|---|---|---|---|---|
| AK.II.b.2 | Sino-Kharoshthi coin (Cribb 1–2) | 2.57 | 15.5 | – | pas | Allegedly from Yotkan site |
| AK.II.b.3 | Wuzhu | 4.22 | 25.5 | – | pas | Allegedly from Yotkan site |
| AK.II.b.4 | Qianyuan zhongbao – large | 7.27 | 29 | – | pas | Allegedly from Yotkan site |
| AK.II.b.5 | Qianyuan zhongbao – large | 7.56 | 30 | – | pas | Allegedly from Yotkan site |
| AK.II.b.6 | Qianyuan zhongbao – large | 5.72 | 29 | misaligned | pas | Allegedly from Yotkan site |
| AK.II.b.7 | Qianyuan zhongbao – large | 6.57 | 28.5 | forced hole | pas | Allegedly from Yotkan site |
| AK.II.b.8 | Qianyuan zhongbao – large | 5.54 | 28 | – | pas | Allegedly from Yotkan site |
| AK.II.b.9 | Qianyuan zhongbao – large | 6.88 | 29.5 | – | pas | Allegedly from Yotkan site |
| AK.II.b.10 | Qianyuan zhongbao – large | 4.25 | 29.5 | thin; weak rev.; forced hole | pas | Allegedly from Yotkan site |
| AK.II.b.11 | Qianyuan zhongbao – large | 5.12 | 30 | 3 frags restored | pas | Allegedly from Yotkan site |
| AK.II.b.12 | [missing: Qianyuan zhongbao – large] | – | – | – | pas | Allegedly from Yotkan site |
| AK.II.b.13 | Qianyuan zhongbao – small | 1.91 | 21.5 | – | pas | Allegedly from Yotkan site |
| AK.II.b.14 | Qianyuan zhongbao – small | 1.44 | 22 | – | pas | Allegedly from Yotkan site |
| AK.II.b.15 | Qianyuan zhongbao – small | 2.02 | 21.5 | – | pas | Allegedly from Yotkan site |
| AK.II.b.16 | Qianyuan zhongbao – small | 1.26 | 21.5 | crude | pas | Allegedly from Yotkan site |
| AK.II.b.17 | Dali yuanbao – small | 2.33 | 21.5 | – | pas | Allegedly from Yotkan site |
| AK.II.b.18 | Chinese coin – illegible, Tang dynasty | 3.37 | 23 | – | pas | Allegedly from Yotkan site |
| AK.II.b.19 | [missing: Chinese] | – | – | – | pas | Allegedly from Yotkan site |
| AK.II.b.20–23 | Chinese – Song dynasty | – | – | – | pas | Allegedly from Yotkan site |
| AK.II.b.24 | Islamic | – | – | – | pas | Allegedly from Yotkan site |
| AK.II.b.25 | Sino-Kharoshthi coin (Cribb 1–6) | 1.73 | 17 | – | pas | Allegedly from Yotkan site |
| AK.II.b.26 | Sino-Kharoshthi coin (Cribb 1–6) | 1.87 | 17.5 | – | pas | Allegedly from Yotkan site |
| AK.II.b.27 | Kushan coin of Kanishka I – hemi-drachm | 0.79 | 13 | – | pas | Allegedly from Yotkan site |
| AK.II.b.28 | [uncertain – 19th c. non-Chinese coins?] | 2.81 | 12.5 | – | pas | Allegedly from Yotkan site |
| AK.II.b.29 | [uncertain – 19th c. non-Chinese coins?] | 1.26 | 10.5 | – | pas | Allegedly from Yotkan site |
| AK.II.b.30 | [uncertain – 19th c. non-Chinese coins?] | 1.21 | 9.5 | – | pas | Allegedly from Yotkan site |
| AK.II.b.31 | [missing: non-Chinese coin) | – | – | – | pas | Allegedly from Yotkan site |
| AK.II.b.32–35 | [extra: 4 wuzhu corroded together] | 32.35 | 7.49 | corroded | pas | Allegedly from Yotkan site |

| | | | | | | |
|---|---|---|---|---|---|---|
| AK.II.c.1 | Kai[yuan] tongbao | 2.69 | 25.5 | frag., misaligned | pas | Allegedly from Yotkan site |
| AK.II.c.2 | Qianyuan zhongbao – small | 2.15 | 21.5 | – | pas | Allegedly from Yotkan site |
| AK.II.c.3 | Qianyuan zhongbao – small | 1.87 | 21 | – | pas | Allegedly from Yotkan site |
| AK.II.c.4 | Qianyuan zhongbao – small | 2.14 | 22 | forced hole | pas | Allegedly from Yotkan site |
| AK.II.c.5 | Dali yuanbao – small | 2.60 | 22 | – | pas | Allegedly from Yotkan site |
| AK.II.c.6 | Qianyuan zhongbao – small | 2.69 | 21.5 | – | pas | Allegedly from Yotkan site |
| AK.II.c.7 | Qianyuan zhongbao – small | 2.43 | 21 | – | pas | Allegedly from Yotkan site |
| AK.II.c.8 | Qianyuan zhongbao – small | 1.45 | 22 | frag. | pas | Allegedly from Yotkan site |
| AK.II.c.9 | Qianyuan zhongbao – small | 2.33 | 22 | forced hole | pas | Allegedly from Yotkan site |
| AK.II.c.10 | Qianyuan zhongbao – small | 1.68 | 22 | – | pas | Allegedly from Yotkan site |
| AK.II.c.11 | Qianyuan zhongbao – small | 2.00 | 21.5 | forced hole | pas | Allegedly from Yotkan site |
| AK.II.c.12 | Jianzhong tongbao – small | 1.32 | 21 | forced hole | pas | Allegedly from Yotkan site |
| AK.II.c.13 | Qianyuan zhongbao – small | 1.19 | 21 | forced hole | pas | Allegedly from Yotkan site |
| AK.II.c.14 | Qianyuan zhongbao – small | 1.57 | 22 | 4 frags restored | pas | Allegedly from Yotkan site |

| BM no. | Identification | Wt | Diam. | Notes | Acqn | Acquisition/Archaeological context |
|---|---|---|---|---|---|---|
| AK.II.c.15 | Qian [yuan] zhong [bao] | 0.89 | – | frag. (half-coin with c.18?) | pas | Allegedly from Yotkan site |
| AK.II.c.16 | [Qian] yuan [zhong] bao | 0.72 | – | frag. | pas | Allegedly from Yotkan site |
| AK.II.c.17 | Qian [yuan] zhong [bao] | 0.80 | – | frag. | pas | Allegedly from Yotkan site |
| AK.II.c.18 | [Qian] yuan [zhong] bao | 1.28 | – | frag. (half-coin with c.15?) | pas | Allegedly from Yotkan site |
| AK.II.c.19 | [Qian] yuan zhong [bao] | 1.23 | – | frag. | pas | Allegedly from Yotkan site |
| AK.II.c.20 | Dali yuanbao – large | 2.01 | 24 | frag., forced hole | pas | Allegedly from Yotkan site |
| AK.II.c.21 | Dali yuanbao – large | 3.16 | 24 | – | pas | Allegedly from Yotkan site |
| AK.II.c.22 | [missing: Dali yuanbao] | – | – | – | pas | Allegedly from Yotkan site |
| AK.II.c.23 | Kaiyuan tongbao | 4.62 | 25 | bubbled surface | pas | Allegedly from Yotkan site |
| AK.II.c.24 | Chinese coin – illegible, Tang dynasty | 2.34 | 23 | corroded, damaged | pas | Allegedly from Yotkan site |
| AK.II.c.25 | Non-Chinese coin, illegible | 0.90 | 13 | – | pas | Allegedly from Yotkan site |

| | | | | | | |
|---|---|---|---|---|---|---|
| AK.II.d.1 (OR.0400) | Sino-Kharoshthi coin (Cribb 4) | 4.12 | 20×19 | – | pas | Allegedly from Yotkan site |
| AK.II.d.2 (OR.0427) | Sino-Kharoshthi coin (Cribb 5) | 2.94 | 19×17 | – | pas | Allegedly from Yotkan site |
| AK.II.d.3 (OR.0411) | Sino-Kharoshthi coin (Cribb 2) | 2.40 | 19 | – | pas | Allegedly from Yotkan site |
| AK.II.d.4 | Sino-Kharoshthi coin (Cribb 2) | 1.97 | 19 | – | pas | Allegedly from Yotkan site |
| AK.II.d.5 | Sino-Kharoshthi coin (Cribb 3) | 2.63 | 18 | – | pas | Allegedly from Yotkan site |
| AK.II.d.6 | Non-Chinese coin – illegible | 1.04 | 22 | – | pas | Allegedly from Yotkan site |
| AK.II.d.7 | Kushan coin of Kanishka I – hemi-drachm | 1.74 | 12 | – | pas | Allegedly from Yotkan site |
| AK.II.d.8 | 'Wuzhu' – without inscription | 1.17 | 17 | (H: 7) | pas | Allegedly from Yotkan site |
| AK.II.d.9 | 'Wuzhu' – without inscription | 1.68 | 21 | (H: 9) | pas | Allegedly from Yotkan site |
| AK.II.d.10 | 'Wuzhu' – without inscription | 1.14 | 17.5 | (H: 9) | pas | Allegedly from Yotkan site |
| AK.II.d.11 | Qianyuan zhongbao – large | 7.55 | 30 | – | pas | Allegedly from Yotkan site |
| AK.II.d.12 | Qianyuan zhongbao – large | 7.05 | 28.5 | – | pas | Allegedly from Yotkan site |
| AK.II.d.13 | Qianyuan zhongbao – small | 2.05 | 22 | misaligned | pas | Allegedly from Yotkan site |
| AK.II.d.14 | Qianyuan zhongbao – small | 2.46 | 22 | corroded | pas | Allegedly from Yotkan site |
| AK.II.d.15 | Qianyuan zhongbao – small | 2.60 | 21.5 | – | pas | Allegedly from Yotkan site |
| AK.II.d.16 | Qianyuan zhongbao – small | 1.46 | 22 | forced hole | pas | Allegedly from Yotkan site |
| AK.II.d.17 | [extra: Sino-Kharoshthi coin (Cribb 2)] | 3.01 | 20 | – | pas | Allegedly from Yotkan site |
| AK.II.d.18 | Kushan coin of Kanishka I – hemi-drachm | 1.40 | 14 | – | pas | Allegedly from Yotkan site |
| AK.II.d.19 | Islamic | – | – | – | pas | Allegedly from Yotkan site |
| AK.II.d.20 | Chinese coin – illegible | 4.64 | – | 2 frags, corroded | pas | Allegedly from Yotkan site |
| AK.II.d.21 | Qianyuan zhongbao – small | 1.73 | 20.5 | – | pas | Allegedly from Yotkan site |
| AK.II.d.22 | Chinese coin – illegible | 3.45 | 22 | corroded | pas | Allegedly from Yotkan site |

## AK.III: COINS PURCHASED AT KHOTAN (MOST OF THEM PROBABLY FROM YOTKAN)

| BM no. | Identification | Wt | Diam. | Notes | Acqn | Acquisition/Archaeological context |
|---|---|---|---|---|---|---|
| AK III.a.1 (OR.0386) | Sino-Kharoshthi coin (Cribb 8) | 14.47 | 27×26 | – | p | Probably from Yotkan site, purchased at Khotan |
| AK.III.a.2 (OR.0388) | Sino-Kharoshthi coin (Cribb 8) | 11.97 | 26×24 | – | p | Probably from Yotkan site, purchased at Khotan |
| AK III.a.3 | Sino-Kharoshthi coin (Cribb 1–6) | 2.28 | 19 | – | p | Probably from Yotkan site, purchased at Khotan |

| | | | | | | |
|---|---|---|---|---|---|---|
| AK III.b.1 (OR.0381) | Sino-Kharoshthi coin (Cribb 8) | 11.97 | 28×26 | | p | Probably from Yotkan site, purchased at Khotan |
| AK.III.b.2 | [missing: Sino-Kharoshthi coin] | – | – | – | p | Probably from Yotkan site, purchased at Khotan |

| | | | | | | |
|---|---|---|---|---|---|---|
| AK III.c.1 | [missing: Sino-Kharoshthi coin] | – | – | – | p | Probably from Yotkan site, purchased at Khotan |
| AK.III.c.2 | [missing: Sino-Kharoshthi coin] | – | – | – | p | Probably from Yotkan site, purchased at Khotan |

| | | | | | | |
|---|---|---|---|---|---|---|
| AK III.d.1 (OR.0392) | Sino-Kharoshthi coin (Cribb 8) | 9.27 | 26×24 | – | p | Probably from Yotkan site, purchased at Khotan |
| AK.III.d.2 | [missing: Sino-Kharoshthi coin] | – | – | – | p | Probably from Yotkan site, purchased at Khotan |
| AK III.d.3 | Sino-Kharoshthi coin (Cribb 3) | 2.05 | 16 | – | p | Probably from Yotkan site, purchased at Khotan |
| AK.III.d.4–6 | [missing: Sino-Kharoshthi coins] | – | – | – | p | Probably from Yotkan site, purchased at Khotan |
| AK III.d.7–8 | Islamic | – | – | – | p | Probably from Yotkan site, purchased at Khotan |

| | | | | | | |
|---|---|---|---|---|---|---|
| AK III.e.1 (OR.0390) | Sino-Kharoshthi coin (Cribb 8) | 14.95 | 25×24 | – | p | Probably from Yotkan site, purchased at Khotan |
| AK III.e.2 | Sino-Kharoshthi coin (Cribb 2) | 2.38 | 17 | – | p | Probably from Yotkan site, purchased at Khotan |
| AK III.e.3 (OR.0407) | Sino-Kharoshthi coin (Cribb 2) | 4.78 | – | – | p | Probably from Yotkan site, purchased at Khotan |
| AK III.e.4 (OR.0428) | Sino-Kharoshthi coin (Cribb 5) | 3.47 | 19 | – | p | Probably from Yotkan site, purchased at Khotan |
| AK III.e.5 (OR.0435) | Sino-Kharoshthi coin (Cribb 10) | 1.34 | 18 | – | p | Probably from Yotkan site, purchased at Khotan |
| AK III.e.6 (OR.0420) | Sino-Kharoshthi coin (Cribb 1) | 2.51 | 27 | – | p | Probably from Yotkan site, purchased at Khotan |
| AK.II.e.7–15 | [missing: Sino-Kharoshthi coins] | – | – | – | p | Probably from Yotkan site, purchased at Khotan |

| | | | | | | |
|---|---|---|---|---|---|---|
| AK III.f.1 | Sino-Kharoshthi coin (Cribb 4) | 3.43 | 18 | – | p | Probably from Yotkan site, purchased at Khotan |
| AK.III.f.2 (OR.0389) | Sino-Kharoshthi coin (Cribb 8) | 14.64 | 24×23 | – | p | Probably from Yotkan site, purchased at Khotan |
| AK.III.f.3 (OR.0396) | Sino-Kharoshthi coin (Cribb 4) | 3.02 | 19×18 | – | p | Probably from Yotkan site, purchased at Khotan |
| AK.III.f.4 (OR.0415) | Sino-Kharoshthi coin (Cribb 2) | 3.85 | 19.5×18 | – | p | Probably from Yotkan site, purchased at Khotan |

| BM no. | Identification | Wt | Diam. | Notes | Acqn | Acquisition/Archaeological context |
|---|---|---|---|---|---|---|
| AK.III.f.5–6 | [missing: Sino-Kharoshthi coins] | – | – | – | p | Probably from Yotkan site, purchased at Khotan |
| AK.III.g.1 | Sino-Kharoshthi coin (Cribb 2) | 2.75 | 18 | – | p | Probably from Yotkan site, purchased at Khotan |
| AK.III.g.2 (OR.0413) | Sino-Kharoshthi coin (Cribb 2) | 2.62 | 21.5 | – | p | Probably from Yotkan site, purchased at Khotan |
| AK.III.g.3 (OR.0399) | Sino-Kharoshthi coin (Cribb 4) | 3.22 | 20×19 | – | p | Probably from Yotkan site, purchased at Khotan |
| AK.III.g.4 | Kushan coin of Kanishka I – hemi-drachm | 1.27 | 14 | – | p | Probably from Yotkan site, purchased at Khotan |
| AK III.h.1 | Kushan coin of Kanishka I – drachm | 3.68 | 17 | – | p | Probably from Yotkan site, purchased at Khotan |
| AK.III.h.2 | Islamic | – | – | – | p | Probably from Yotkan site, purchased at Khotan |
| AK III.i.1 | Qianyuan zhongbao – large | 4.96 | 29 | misaligned | p | Probably from Yotkan site, purchased at Khotan |
| AK.III.i.2 | Qianyuan zhongbao – large | 5.94 | 28 | – | p | Probably from Yotkan site, purchased at Khotan |
| AK.III.i.3–4 | Chinese – Song dynasty | – | – | – | p | Probably from Yotkan site, purchased at Khotan |
| AK III.k.1 (OR.0381) | Sino-Kharoshthi coin (Cribb 8) | 16.35 | 28×26 | – | p | Probably from Yotkan site, purchased at Khotan |
| AK.III.k.2 (OR.0403) | Sino-Kharoshthi coin (Cribb 3) | 2.99 | 27 | – | p | Probably from Yotkan site, purchased at Khotan |
| AK III.k.3–5 | Chinese – Song dynasty | – | – | – | p | Probably from Yotkan site, purchased at Khotan |
| AK III.k.6–16 | Islamic | – | – | – | p | Probably from Yotkan site, purchased at Khotan |
| AK III.l.1–5 | Islamic | – | – | – | p | Probably from Yotkan site, purchased at Khotan |
| AK III.m.1 | coins? – unidentified | 5.64 | – | coins corroded together? | p | Allegedly from Halal-bagh, purchased in Khotan |
| AK III.m.2 | coins? – unidentified | 6.10 | – | coins corroded together? | p | Probably from Yotkan site, purchased at Khotan |
| AK III.m.3 | coin? – unidentified | 4.05 | 21.5 | corroded | p | Probably from Yotkan site, purchased at Khotan |
| AK III.m.4 | coin? – unidentified | 4.24 | 21 | corroded | p | Probably from Yotkan site, purchased at Khotan |
| AK III.m.5 | coin? – unidentified | 6.54 | – | corroded | p | Probably from Yotkan site, purchased at Khotan |
| AK III.m.6 | coin? – unidentified | 7.54 | – | corroded | p | Probably from Yotkan site, purchased at Khotan |
| AK III.m.7 | coin? – unidentified | 7.03 | – | corroded | p | Probably from Yotkan site, purchased at Khotan |
| AK III.m.8 | Chinese coin? – unidentified | 4.61 | – | corroded | p | Probably from Yotkan site, purchased at Khotan |
| AK III.m.9 | Chinese coin – illegible, Tang dynasty | 3.45 | 23 | corroded | p | Probably from Yotkan site, purchased at Khotan |

| BM no. | Identification | Wt | Diam. | Notes | Acqn | Acquisition/Archaeological context |
|---|---|---|---|---|---|---|
| AK III.m.10 | coin? – unidentified | 3.64 | – | corroded | p | Probably from Yotkan site, purchased at Khotan |
| AK III.m.11 | coin? – unidentified | 3.54 | 22 | corroded | p | Probably from Yotkan site, purchased at Khotan |
| AK III.m.12 | coin? – unidentified | 2.75 | 21 | corroded | p | Probably from Yotkan site, purchased at Khotan |
| AK III.m.13 | coin? – unidentified | 3.84 | 19 | corroded | p | Probably from Yotkan site, purchased at Khotan |

## AK.IV: COINS SAID TO HAVE BEEN FOUND AT CHALMA-KAZAN

| BM no. | Identification | Wt | Diam. | Notes | Acqn | Acquisition/Archaeological context |
|---|---|---|---|---|---|---|
| AK IV.a.1 | Kaiyuan tongbao – rev.: line above hole | 2.70 | 23.5 | misaligned | g | Allegedly from Chalma-kazan; gift of Wang Daloi |
| AK.IV.a.2 | Kaiyuan tongbao – rev.: crescent above hole | 3.29 | 25 | – | g | Allegedly from Chalma-kazan; gift of Wang Daloi |
| AK.IV.a.3 | Qianyuan zhongbao – large | 5.71 | 29 | – | g | Allegedly from Chalma-kazan; gift of Wang Daloi |
| AK.IV.a.4 | Qianyuan zhongbao – large | 6.15 | 30 | – | g | Allegedly from Chalma-kazan; gift of Wang Daloi |
| AK.IV.a.5 | Qianyuan zhongbao – large | 7.46 | 29 | – | g | Allegedly from Chalma-kazan; gift of Wang Daloi |
| AK.IV.a.6 | Dali yuanbao – large | 2.25 | 24 | – | g | Allegedly from Chalma-kazan; gift of Wang Daloi |
| AK.IV.a.7 | Dali yuanbao – large | 3.05 | 24 | misaligned | g | Allegedly from Chalma-kazan; gift of Wang Daloi |
| AK.IV.a.8 | Jianzhong tongbao – large | 3.65 | 22.5 | faint reverse | g | Allegedly from Chalma-kazan; gift of Wang Daloi |
| AK.IV.a.9 | Chinese – Song dynasty | – | – | – | g | Allegedly from Chalma-kazan; gift of Wang Daloi |

| | | | | | | |
|---|---|---|---|---|---|---|
| AK.IV.b.1–4 | [missing: Sino-Kharoshthi coin] | – | – | – | p | Allegedly from Chalma-kazan |
| AK.IV.b.5 | Sino-Kharoshthi coin (Cribb 12) | 3.20 | 19 | – | p | Allegedly from Chalma-kazan |
| AK.IV.b.6–7 | [missing: Sino-Kharoshthi coin] | – | – | – | p | Allegedly from Chalma-kazan |
| AK.IV.b.8–10 | Islamic | – | – | – | p | Allegedly from Chalma-kazan |

## AK.V: COINS FROM DANDAN-UILIQ

| BM no. | Identification | Wt | Diam. | Notes | Acqn | Acquisition/Archaeological context |
|---|---|---|---|---|---|---|
| AK.V.a.1 | Wuzhu – full size | 1.66 | 26 | (H: 9.5) | (p) | Brought from Dandan-Uiliq site by Turdi |
| AK.V.a.2 | Wuzhu – full size | 2.42 | 26 | (H: 9.5) | (p) | Brought from Dandan-Uiliq site by Turdi |
| AK.V.a.3 | Wuzhu – full size | 2.68 | 25.5 | (H: 9.5) | (p) | Brought from Dandan-Uiliq site by Turdi |
| AK.V.a.4 | 'Wuzhu' – illegible | 0.82 | 23 | (H: 9.5) thin, worn | (p) | Brought from Dandan-Uiliq site by Turdi |
| AK.V.a.5 | Wuzhu – clipped, cutting through inscription | 0.92 | 17 | (H: 8.5) | (p) | Brought from Dandan-Uiliq site by Turdi |

| BM no. | Identification | Wt | Diam. | Notes | Acqn | Acquisition/Archaeological context |
|---|---|---|---|---|---|---|
| AK.V.a.6 | Wuzhu – full size | 0.96 | 20 | (H: 9.5) thin, worn | (p) | Brought from Dandan-Uiliq site by Turdi |
| AK.V.a.7 | Wuzhu – clipped, cutting through inscription | 0.82 | 17 | (H: 8.5) | (p) | Brought from Dandan-Uiliq site by Turdi |
| AK.V.a.8 | 'Wuzhu' – without inscription, but with rim | 0.82 | 15.5 | (H: 8) | (p) | Brought from Dandan-Uiliq site by Turdi |
| AK.V.a.9 | Qian [yuan zhong] bao – large | 3.39 | 29 | frag. | (p) | Brought from Dandan-Uiliq site by Turdi |

| | | | | | | |
|---|---|---|---|---|---|---|
| AK.V.b.1 | Wuzhu – clipped, cutting through inscription | 1.47 | 18 | (H: 8.5) worn | FAS | Found at site |
| AK.V.b.2 | Kaiyuan tongbao | 4.63 | 25 | – | FAS | Found on ground near ruined buildings |
| AK.V.b.3 | Kaiyuan tongbao | 3.69 | 24.5 | misaligned; forced hole | FAS | Found 150 yd SW of ruined dwelling D.v |
| AK.V.b.4 | Wuzhu – clipped, cutting through inscription | 0.87 | 16.5 | (H: 8.5) red, faint | FAS | Found 150 yd SW of ruined dwelling D.v |
| AK.V.b.5 | Wuzhu – clipped, cutting through inscription | 1.20 | 20.5 | (H: 9.5) red, faint | FAS | Found 150 yd SW of ruined dwelling D.v |
| AK.V.b.6 | Wuzhu – full size | 1.19 | 24 | (H: 10) red, faint, thin | FAS | Found 150 yd SW of ruined dwelling D.v |
| AK.V.b.7 | Wuzhu – clipped, cutting through inscription | 1.32 | 21 | (H: 9.5) red, faint | FAS | Found 150 yd SW of ruined dwelling D.v |
| AK.V.b.8 | Wuzhu – full size (with small frags attached) | 2.39 | 25 | (H: 10) red, faint | FAS | Found 150 yd SW of ruined dwelling D.v |
| AK.V.b.9 | 'Wuzhu' – without inscription or rim | 1.10 | 23 | (H: 9.5) red, thin | FAS | Found 150 yd SW of ruined dwelling D.v |
| AK.V.b.10 | Wu[zhu] – full size, with rim | 1.24 | – | frag. (H: 9), red | FAS | Found 150 yd SW of ruined dwelling D.v |
| AK.V.b.11 | Kaiyuan tongbao – rev.: crescent above hole | 4.45 | 25 | red | FAS | Found 150 yd SW of ruined dwelling D.v |
| AK.V.b.12 | Kaiyuan tongbao | 3.90 | 24.5 | damaged, red | FAS | Found 150 yd SW of ruined dwelling D.v |
| AK.V.b.13 | Kaiyuan tongbao | 2.53 | 23 | red | FAS | Found 150 yd SW of ruined dwelling D.v |
| AK.V.b.14 | Kaiyuan tongbao | 4.94 | 23 | red, misaligned | FAS | Found 150 yd SW of ruined dwelling D.v |
| AK.V.b.15 | Qianyuan zhongbao – large, rev.: crescent above hole | 5.81 | 29.5 | misaligned | FAS | Found 150 yd SW of ruined dwelling D.v |
| AK.V.b.16 | Qianyuan zhongbao – small | 3.28 | 22 | – | FAS | Found 150 yd SW of ruined dwelling D.v |
| AK.V.b.17 | Qianyuan zhongbao – large, rev.: line at NW corner of hole | 8.08 | 30 | – | FAS | Found 150 yd SW of ruined dwelling D.v |
| AK.V.b.18 | [extra: Qianyuan zhongbao – small] | 2.28 | 22 | misaligned | FAS | Found 150 yd SW of ruined dwelling D.v |
| AK.V.b.19 | [extra: 'Wuzhu' – without inscription? but with pronounced rim round hole on rev.] | 0.68 | 15 | (H: 8) damaged | FAS | Found 150 yd SW of ruined dwelling D.v |
| AK.V.b.20 | [extra: Qian [yuan] zhong [bao] – small] | 0.67 | 22 | 2 frags, pierced at top | FAS | Found 150 yd SW of ruined dwelling D.v |

### AK.VI: COPPER COINS FOUND AT RAWAK BEYOND DANDAN-UILIQ

| BM no. | Identification | Wt | Diam. | Notes | Acqn | Acquisition/Archaeological context |
|---|---|---|---|---|---|---|
| AK.VI.a.1 | 'Wuzhu' – without inscription | 0.25 | 9.5 | (H: 4.5) 2 frags (= 1 coin) | FAS | Found near ruins |
| AK.VI.a.2 | Wuzhu – clipped, cutting through inscription | 1.14 | 20 | (H: 9.5) red | FAS | Found near ruins |
| AK.VI.a.3 | Wuzhu – clipped, cutting through inscription | 0.92 | 18 | (H: 9.5) | FAS | Found near ruins |
| AK.VI.a.4 | Wuzhu – zhu without metal radical | 0.94 | 17.5 | (H: 9) | FAS | Found near ruins |
| AK.VI.a.5 | Wuzhu – small, thin wu | 0.96 | 18 | (H: 8.5) | FAS | Found near ruins |
| AK.VI.a.6 | Kaiyuan tongbao | 2.65 | 24.5 | damaged, red | FAS | Found near ruins |

### AK.VII: COPPER COINS FOUND AT NIYA SITE

| BM no. | Identification | Wt | Diam. | Notes | Acqn | Acquisition/Archaeological context |
|---|---|---|---|---|---|---|
| AK.VII.a.1 | Wuzhu – full size; rev.: mark above hole | 1.45 | 24.5 | (H: 9.5) red, thin, faint | FAS | Found near stupa |
| AK.VII.b.1 | Wuzhu – full size | 1.87 | 24.5 | (H: 9.5) red, faint | FAS | Found W of stupa |
| AK.VII.c.1 | 'Wuzhu' – illegible | 1.06 | 17 | (H: 9) 3 frags, corroded | FAS | Found near ruin N.v |
| AK.VII.c.2 | 'Wuzhu' illegible, with pronounced rim round hole on rev. | 1.67 | 18 | (H: 8) corroded | FAS | Found near ruin N.v |
| AK.VII.c.3 | Huoquan | 2.08 | 23 | red | FAS | Found near ruin N.v |
| AK.VII.c.4 | 'Wuzhu' – illegible | 1.20 | 20.5 | (H: 9.5) frag. | FAS | Found near ruin N.v |
| AK.VII.c.5 | Wuzhu – small, thin wu, zhu without metal radical | 0.94 | 17 | (H: 8) red, damaged | FAS | Found near ruin N.v |
| AK.VII.c.6 | Wuzhu – clipped, cutting into inscription | 1.30 | 22 | (H: 9) red | FAS | Found near ruin N.v |
| AK.VII.c.7 | Wuzhu – with rim touching character | 1.10 | – | frag., red | FAS | Found near ruin N.v |
| AK.VII.c.8 | Wuzhu – full size | 1.62 | 26 | damaged | FAS | Found near ruin N.v |
| AK.VII.d.1 | [missing: Qianyuan zhongbao] | – | – | – | F on road | Found by Turdi Khwaja, on road from Imam Ja'far Sadiq; no association with Niya site |
| AK.VII.e.1 | Wuzhu – with small inscription?; rim round hole on rev. | 0.79 | 15 | (H: 8.5) red, faint | FAS | Found near ruin N.viii |
| AK.VII.e.2 | 'Wuzhu' – without inscription, with rim | 0.45 | 12 | (H: 3) flat on one side | FAS | Found near ruin N.viii |
| AK.VII.e.3 | Wuzhu – full size | 2.85 | 26 | (H: 9.5) | FAS | Found near ruin N.viii |
| AK.VII.e.4 | Wuzhu – full size | 2.60 | 25 | (H: 9.5) | FAS | Found near ruin N.viii |
| AK.VII.f.1 | Wuzhu | 2.19 | 25 | (H: 9.5) | FAS | Found by Hassan Akhun, *c.*3 miles N of stupa |
| AK.VII.f.2 | Wuzhu: line above hole on obv. | 3.11 | 25 | (H: 10) faint rev. | FAS | Found by Hassan Akhun, *c.*3 miles N of stupa |
| AK.VII.g.1 | 'Wuzhu' – illegible, full size | 1.71 | – | frag. | – | Not known |
| AK.VII.g.2–3 | 'Wuzhu' – illegible | 2.10 | 23 | (H: 9.5) red, 2 frags (= 1 coin) | – | Not known |
| AK.VII.g.4 | Chinese coin – illegible | 2.76 | 25 | frag., corroded | – | Not known |

### AK.VIII: COPPER COINS FOUND AT ENDERE SITE

| BM no. | Identification | Wt | Diam. | Notes | Acqn | Acquisition/Archaeological context |
|---|---|---|---|---|---|---|
| AK.VIII.a.1 | 'Wuzhu' – without inscription, without rim | 1.31 | – | 2 frags | FAS | Found inside Endere Fort |
| AK.VIII.a.2 | 'Wuzhu' – illegible | 1.66 | – | 2 frags, red | FAS | Found inside Endere Fort |
| AK.VIII.a.3 | 'Wuzhu' – illegible, rim round hole on rev. | 1.14 | 19 | 2 frags (H: 8) | FAS | Found inside Endere Fort |
| AK.VIII.a.4 | Wuzhu – full size | 2.68 | 25 | damaged | FAS | Found inside Endere Fort |
| AK.VIII.b.1 | 'Wuzhu' – without inscription, without rim | 0.91 | 19.5 | (H: 10) red, thin | FAS | Found near Endere Fort |
| AK.VIII.b.2 | 'Wuzhu' – with rim | 0.44 | – | frag., red | FAS | Found near Endere Fort |
| AK.VIII.b.3 | 'Wuzhu' – with rim | 0.42 | – | frag., red | FAS | Found near Endere Fort |
| AK.VIII.b.4 | Wu [zhu] – with rim | 0.65 | – | frag., red | FAS | Found near Endere Fort |

### AK.IX: COPPER COINS FOUND AT KARA-DONG SITE

| BM no. | Identification | Wt | Diam. | Notes | Acqn | Acquisition/Archaeological context |
|---|---|---|---|---|---|---|
| AK.IX.a.1 | [Wu] zhu – clipped, cutting through inscription | 0.44 | – | frag. (H: 5) | FAS | Found within ruined quadrangle |
| AK.IX.a.2 | Wuzhu – with rim | 0.35 | – | frag., red | FAS | Found within ruined quadrangle |
| AK.IX.a.3 | 'Wuzhu' – illegible | 0.67 | – | 2 frags, red | FAS | Found within ruined quadrangle |
| AK.IX.a.4 | Wuzhu – clipped, cutting through inscription | 1.45 | 21 | (H: 9.5), faint | FAS | Found within ruined quadrangle |
| AK.IX.a.5 | Wuzhu – small wu, clipped, cutting through inscription, pronounced rim on rev. | 1.56 | 21 | (H: 9.5) | FAS | Found within ruined quadrangle |
| AK.IX.b.1 | 'Wuzhu' – faint rim round hole | 1.34 | 18 | (H: 9.5) | FAS | Found near Kara-dong ruin |
| AK.IX.b.2 | 'Wuzhu' – faint rim round hole | 1.18 | 19 | (H: 8) | FAS | Found near Kara-dong ruin |
| AK.IX.b.3 | 'Wuzhu' – without inscription | 0.83 | 20 | (H: 10) thin | FAS | Found near Kara-dong ruin |
| AK.IX.b.4 | Wuzhu – faint zhu without metal radical; rim on rev. | 0.94 | 17 | (H: 9.5) | FAS | Found near Kara-dong ruin |
| AK.IX.b.5 | Wuzhu – full size | 2.34 | 25 | (H: 10) faint | FAS | Found near Kara-dong ruin |
| AK.IX.b.6 | Wuzhu – clipped, cutting into inscription; faint rim round hole on rev. | 0.98 | 17 | (H: 8) faint | FAS | Found near Kara-dong ruin |
| AK.IX.b.7 | Wuzhu – clipped, cutting into inscription | 1.00 | 19 | (H: 10) faint | FAS | Found near Kara-dong ruin |
| AK.IX.b.8 | Wuzhu | 0.65 | – | frag. | FAS | Found near Kara-dong ruin |
| AK.IX.b.9 | Wuzhu – zhu without metal radical; rim round hole on rev. | 0.89 | 16.5 | (H: 9) | FAS | Found near Kara-dong ruin |
| AK.IX.c.1 | Wuzhu – small, thin wuzhu; clipped, cutting into inscription | 0.89 | 17.5 | 2 frags (= 1 coin) (H: 9.5), flat rev. | – | Not known |
| AK.IX.c.2 | 'Wuzhu' – illegible | 2.00 | – | 5 frags restored | – | Not known |

### AK.X: COPPER COINS FOUND AT UZUN TATI SITE

| BM no. | Identification | Wt | Diam. | Notes | Acqn | Acquisition/Archaeological context |
|---|---|---|---|---|---|---|
| AK.X.a.1 | Chinese – Song dynasty | – | – | – | FAS | Found at Uzun Tati site |
| AK.X.a.2 | Islamic | – | – | – | FAS | Found at Uzun Tati site |

### AK.XI: COPPER COINS FROM HANGUYA SITE

| BM no. | Identification | Wt | Diam. | Notes | Acqn | Acquisition/Archaeological context |
|---|---|---|---|---|---|---|
| AK.XI.a.1 | 'Wuzhu' – illegible | 0.93 | 17 | (H: 8) flat rev. | FAS | Found near Hanguya stupa ruin |

| | | | | | | |
|---|---|---|---|---|---|---|
| AK.XI.b.1 | Sino-Kharoshthi coin (Cribb 8) | 11.99 | 24 | frag. | p | Allegedly from Hanguya Tati, purchased at Khotan |
| AK.XI.b.2 | Sino-Kharoshthi coin (Cribb 1–6) | 0.65 | 14 | – | p | Allegedly from Hanguya Tati, purchased at Khotan |
| AK.XI.b.3 | Sino-Kharoshthi coin (Cribb 1–6) | 1.67 | 16 | – | p | Allegedly from Hanguya Tati, purchased at Khotan |
| AK.XI.b.4 | Sino-Kharoshthi coin (Cribb 2) | 2.24 | 18 | – | p | Allegedly from Hanguya Tati, purchased at Khotan |
| AK.XI.b.5 | Sino-Kharoshthi coin (Cribb 2) | 2.33 | 18 | – | p | Allegedly from Hanguya Tati, purchased at Khotan |
| AK.XI.b.6 | Sino-Kharoshthi coin (Cribb 2) | 2.54 | 17 | – | p | Allegedly from Hanguya Tati, purchased at Khotan |
| AK.XI.b.7 | Sino-Kharoshthi coin (Cribb 2) | 2.42 | 19 | – | p | Allegedly from Hanguya Tati, purchased at Khotan |
| AK.XI.b.8 | Sino-Kharoshthi coin (Cribb 2–4) | 0.82 | 16 | – | p | Allegedly from Hanguya Tati, purchased at Khotan |
| AK.XI.b.9 | Sino-Kharoshthi coin (Cribb 2) | 2.27 | 18 | – | p | Allegedly from Hanguya Tati, purchased at Khotan |
| AK.XI.b.10 | Sino-Kharoshthi coin (Cribb 2) | 1.88 | 17 | – | p | Allegedly from Hanguya Tati, purchased at Khotan |
| AK.XI.b.11 | Sino-Kharoshthi coin (Cribb 1–6) | 2.73 | 18 | – | p | Allegedly from Hanguya Tati, purchased at Khotan |
| AK.XI.b.12 | Sino-Kharoshthi coin (Cribb 1–6) | 1.46 | 16 | – | p | Allegedly from Hanguya Tati, purchased at Khotan |
| AK.XI.b.13 | Sino-Kharoshthi coin (Cribb 3–4) | 2.30 | 18 | – | p | Allegedly from Hanguya Tati, purchased at Khotan |
| AK.XI.b.14 | Sino-Kharoshthi coin (Cribb 1–6) | 1.95 | 17 | – | p | Allegedly from Hanguya Tati, purchased at Khotan |
| AK.XI.b.15 | Sino-Kharoshthi coin (Cribb 1–6) | 0.89 | 14 | – | p | Allegedly from Hanguya Tati, purchased at Khotan |
| AK.XI.b.16 | Sino-Kharoshthi coin (Cribb 1–6) | 0.68 | 16 | frag. | p | Allegedly from Hanguya Tati, purchased at Khotan |
| AK.XI.b.17–21 | [missing: Sino-Kharoshthi coins] | – | – | – | p | Allegedly from Hanguya Tati, purchased at Khotan |
| AK.XI.b.22 | [lead spinning whorl] | – | 27 | (H: 7) round hole | p | Allegedly from Hanguya Tati, purchased at Khotan |
| AK.XI.b.23 | [disk with round hole in centre] | 0.95 | 11 | (H: 2.5) round hole | p | Allegedly from Hanguya Tati, purchased at Khotan |
| AK.XI.b.24–26 | Islamic | – | – | – | p | Allegedly from Hanguya Tati, purchased at Khotan |
| AK.XI.b.27 | 'Wuzhu' – without inscription | 0.34 | 10 | (H: 7×5), flat rev. | p | Allegedly from Hanguya Tati, purchased at Khotan |

| BM no. | Identification | Wt | Diam. | Notes | Acqn | Acquisition/Archaeological context |
|---|---|---|---|---|---|---|
| AK.XI.b.28 | [Wu] zhu – with rim, full size | 0.51 | – | frag., red | p | Allegedly from Hanguya Tati, purchased at Khotan |
| AK.XI.b.29 | Islamic | 4.20 | 25 | – | p | Allegedly from Hanguya Tati, purchased at Khotan |
| AK.XI.b.30 | Qianyuan zhongbao – small | 3.19 | 22.5 | – | p | Allegedly from Hanguya Tati, purchased at Khotan |
| AK.XI.b.31 | Lead piece with horse design and tamgha | 12.88 | 23 | – | p | Allegedly from Hanguya Tati, purchased at Khotan |
| AK.XI.b.32–37 | [missing: unidentified] | – | – | – | p | Allegedly from Hanguya Tati, purchased at Khotan |
| AK.XI.b.38 | Qianyuan zhongbao – large | 2.53 | 29 | frags restored, damaged | p | Allegedly from Hanguya Tati, purchased at Khotan |

**AK.XII: COPPER COINS FROM TAM-ÖGHIL**

| BM no. | Identification | Wt | Diam. | Notes | Acqn | Acquisition/Archaeological context |
|---|---|---|---|---|---|---|
| AK.XII.a.1 | 'Wuzhu' – illegible | 0.62 | 14 | (H: 7.5) flat on one side | pas | Purchased from Tam-Öghil villager |
| AK.XII.b.1–4 | Chinese – Song dynasty | – | – | – | p | Allegedly from Tam-Öghil, purchased at Yurung-kash |
| AK.XII.c.1 | Islamic | – | – | – | – | Not known |

**AK.XIII: COPPER COINS FROM AK-SIPIL SITE**

| BM no. | Identification | Wt | Diam. | Notes | Acqn | Acquisition/Archaeological context |
|---|---|---|---|---|---|---|
| AK.XIII.a.1 | Wuzhu – clipped, cutting through inscription | 1.37 | 20 | (H: 10) red | FAS | Found on remains of Ak-sipil rampart |
| AK.XIII.b.1 | Wuzhu – full size | 1.86 | 25 | (H: 9) red | p | Allegedly from near Ak-sipil, purchased at Khotan |
| AK.XIII.b.2 | Qianyuan zhongbao – small | 2.24 | 21 | misaligned | p | Allegedly from near Ak-sipil, purchased at Khotan |
| AK.XIII.b.3 | Qianyuan zhongbao – small | 1.51 | 21 | – | p | Allegedly from near Ak-sipil, purchased at Khotan |
| AK.XIII.b.4 | Qianyuan zhongbao – large | 7.74 | 28 | – | p | Allegedly from near Ak-sipil, purchased at Khotan |
| AK.XIII.c.1 | Sino-Kharoshthi coin (Cribb 5–6) | 3.08 | 16 | – | p | Allegedly from near Ak-sipil, purchased at Khotan |
| AK.XIII.c.2 | Qianyuan zhongbao – large | 6.45 | 18 | misaligned | p | Allegedly from near Ak-sipil, purchased at Khotan |
| AK.XIII.c.3–4 | Chinese – Song dynasty | – | – | – | p | Allegedly from near Ak-sipil, purchased at Khotan |
| AK.XIII.c.5–8 | Islamic | – | – | – | p | Allegedly from near Ak-sipil, purchased at Khotan |
| AK.XIII.d.1 | Islamic | – | – | – | – | Not known |
| AK.XIII.d.2 | Chinese coin – illegible, Tang dynasty | 2.52 | 21 | – | – | Not known |
| AK.XIII.d.3 | Qianyuan zhongbao – small | 2.98 | 21 | – | – | Not known |

## AK.XIV: COPPER COINS FROM RAWAK STUPA AND VICINITY

| BM no. | Identification | Wt | Diam. | Notes | Acqn | Acquisition/Archaeological context |
|---|---|---|---|---|---|---|
| AK.XIV.a.1 | Wuzhu – clipped, cutting through inscription | 1.60 | 20 | (H: 9.5) red | FAS | Found at SE foot of stupa base |
| AK.XIV.a.2 | Wuzhu – without rim | 1.70 | 23 | (H: 9) faint | FAS | Found at SE foot of stupa base |
| AK.XIV.a.3 | Wuzhu – full size | 2.03 | 25 | frags restored (H: 10) red | FAS | Found at SE foot of stupa base |
| AK.XIV.a.4 | Wuzhu – small, thin wuzhu, zhu without metal radical; clipped, cutting through inscription | 1.32 | 18 | (H: 8) | FAS | Found at SE foot of stupa base |
| AK.XIV.b.1 | Wuzhu – full size | 1.86 | 26 | 2 frags (H: 9.5) | FAS | Found below relief R.xi |
| AK.XIV.b.2 | Wuzhu – full size | 1.69 | 25 | (H: 9) | FAS | Found below relief R.xi |
| AK.XIV.c.1 | Wuzhu – full size | 2.49 | 25 | (H: 9) | FAS | Found behind relief R.xxviii |
| AK.XIV.d.1 | Wuzhu – full size | 1.89 | 25 | (H: 9.5) | FAS | Found in wall on N side of gateway, Rawak Stupa court |
| AK.XIV.e.1 | Wuzhu – full size | 2.93 | 26 | (H: 9.5) | FAS | Found at foot of statue R.lxiv |
| AK.XIV.f.1 | Wuzhu – full size | 1.89 | 25 | (H: 10) faint | FAS | Found on S side of small stupa base |
| AK.XIV.f.2 | Wuzhu – full size | 3.38 | 26 | (H: 10) | FAS | Found on S side of small stupa base |
| AK.XIV.f.3 | Wuzhu – without rim | 1.88 | 24 | (H: 9.5) faint | FAS | Found on S side of small stupa base |
| AK.XIV.f.4 | Wuzhu – full size | 1.91 | 25 | 2 frags (H: 9.5) red | FAS | Found on S side of small stupa base |
| AK.XIV.f.5 | Wuzhu – full size | 2.10 | – | 5 frags | FAS | Found on S side of small stupa base |
| AK.XIV.f.6 | Wuzhu – full size | 2.09 | 25.5 | (H: 10) | FAS | Found on S side of small stupa base |
| AK.XIV.f.7 | Wuzhu – without rim | 1.42 | 23 | 3 frags (H: 10) faint | FAS | Found on S side of small stupa base |
| AK.XIV.f.8 | Wuzhu – full size | 2.05 | 26 | (H: 9.5) | FAS | Found on S side of small stupa base |
| AK.XIV.f.9 | Wuzhu – full size | 2.10 | 25 | (H: 10) | FAS | Found on S side of small stupa base |
| AK.XIV.f.10 | Wuzhu – without rim | 1.53 | 22 | (H: 9.5) | FAS | Found on S side of small stupa base |
| AK.XIV.f.11 | Wuzhu – full size | 2.95 | 25.5 | (H: 9.5) | FAS | Found on S side of small stupa base |
| AK.XIV.f.12 | 'Wuzhu' – without inscription | 0.96 | 22 | restored (H: 9.5), thin | FAS | Found on S side of small stupa base |
| AK.XIV.f.13 | [Wu] zhu – without rim | 1.20 | 23 | frag. (H: 9.5) | FAS | Found on S side of small stupa base |
| AK.XIV.f.14 | [Wu] zhu – without rim | 1.26 | 23 | frag. (H: 9.5) | FAS | Found on S side of small stupa base |
| AK.XIV.f.15 | 'Wuzhu' – illegible | 1.07 | – | frag. | FAS | Found on S side of small stupa base |
| AK.XIV.f.16 | Wu [zhu] | 0.54 | – | frag. | FAS | Found on S side of small stupa base |
| AK.XIV.f.17 | [Wu] zhu | 0.89 | – | frag. | FAS | Found on S side of small stupa base |

| BM no. | Identification | Wt | Diam. | Notes | Acqn | Acquisition/Archaeological context |
|---|---|---|---|---|---|---|
| AK.XIV.f.18 | [Wu] zhu | 1.60 | 25 | frag. (H: 9) faint | FAS | Found on S side of small stupa base |
| AK.XIV.f.19 | 'Wuzhu' – illegible | 0.43 | – | frag. | FAS | Found on S side of small stupa base |
| AK.XIV.f.20 | 'Wuzhu' – illegible | 0.35 | – | frag. | FAS | Found on S side of small stupa base |
| AK.XIV.f.21 | 'Wuzhu' – illegible | 1.62 | – | frags | FAS | Found on S side of small stupa base |
| AK.XIV.f.22 | 'Wuzhu' – illegible | 2.10 | – | 3 frags corroded together | FAS | Found on S side of small stupa base |

| | | | | | | |
|---|---|---|---|---|---|---|
| AK.XIV.g.1 | Wuzhu – full size | 1.95 | 25 | (H: 9.5) red, faint | FAS | Found on E side of small stupa base |
| AK.XIV.g.2 | Wuzhu – full size | 2.26 | (25) | frags restored | FAS | Found on E side of small stupa base |
| AK.XIV.g.3 | Wuzhu – full size | 2.93 | 25.5 | (H: 9.5) | FAS | Found on E side of small stupa base |
| AK.XIV.g.4 | Wuzhu – full size | 1.93 | 25.5 | (H: 9.5) | FAS | Found on E side of small stupa base |
| AK.XIV.g.5 | Wuzhu – full size | 1.92 | 25 | (H: 9.5) faint | FAS | Found on E side of small stupa base |
| AK.XIV.g.6 | Wuzhu – full size | 2.50 | 25 | (H: 9.5) red | FAS | Found on E side of small stupa base |
| AK.XIV.g.7 | Wuzhu – full size | 2.16 | 25 | (H: 9.5) | FAS | Found on E side of small stupa base |
| AK.XIV.g.8 | Wuzhu – full size | 3.19 | 27 | (H: 9) | FAS | Found on E side of small stupa base |
| AK.XIV.g.9 | Wuzhu – full size | 2.57 | 26 | (H: 9.5) pierced twice | FAS | Found on E side of small stupa base |
| AK.XIV.g.10 | Wuzhu – without rim | 1.79 | 23.5 | (H: 9.5) red, faint | FAS | Found on E side of small stupa base |
| AK.XIV.g.11 | Wuzhu – without rim | 1.62 | 23 | (H: 9) red, faint | FAS | Found on E side of small stupa base |
| AK.XIV.g.12 | Wuzhu – full size | 2.62 | 25.5 | (H: 9.5) red | FAS | Found on E side of small stupa base |
| AK.XIV.g.13 | Wuzhu – full size, with frag. attached | 2.36 | 25 | (H: 9.5) red, + frag. | FAS | Found on E side of small stupa base |
| AK.XIV.g.14 | Wuzhu – clipped, cutting through inscription | 1.41 | 20 | (H: 9.5) faint | FAS | Found on E side of small stupa base |
| AK.XIV.g.15 | [Wu] zhu – full size | 1.30 | – | frag. (H: 9.5) | FAS | Found on E side of small stupa base |
| AK.XIV.g.16 | [Wu] zhu – full size | 1.12 | – | frag. | FAS | Found on E side of small stupa base |
| AK.XIV.g.17 | [Wu] zhu | 0.66 | – | frag., red | FAS | Found on E side of small stupa base |
| AK.XIV.g.18 | Wu [zhu] – full size | 1.15 | – | frag., red | FAS | Found on E side of small stupa base |
| AK.XIV.g.19 | 'Wuzhu' – illegible | 0.77 | – | frag. | FAS | Found on E side of small stupa base |
| AK.XIV.g.20 | Wu [zhu] | 0.81 | – | frag., faint | FAS | Found on E side of small stupa base |

| BM no. | Identification | Wt | Diam. | Notes | Acqn | Acquisition/Archaeological context |
|---|---|---|---|---|---|---|
| AK.XIV.h.1 | Wuzhu – full size | 2.03 | 26 | (H: 10) red | FAS | Found on N side of small stupa base |
| AK.XIV.h.2 | Wuzhu – full size | 1.72 | 25 | (H: 10) red | FAS | Found on N side of small stupa base |
| AK.XIV.h.3 | Wuzhu – full size | 2.11 | 25 | (H: 10) red | FAS | Found on N side of small stupa base |
| AK.XIV.h.4 | Wuzhu | 1.50 | 24 | (H: 9.5) | FAS | Found on N side of small stupa base |
| AK.XIV.h.5 | Wuzhu | 0.64 | – | 2 frags corroded together | FAS | Found on N side of small stupa base |
| AK.XIV.h.6 | Wuzhu | 1.82 | 25.5 | (H: 9.5) damaged | FAS | Found on N side of small stupa base |
| AK.XIV.h.7 | Wuzhu – full size | 2.69 | 25 | (H: 9.5) | FAS | Found on N side of small stupa base |
| AK.XIV.h.8 | Wuzhu – full size | 2.14 | 25 | (H: 9.5) | FAS | Found on N side of small stupa base |
| AK.XIV.h.9 | Wuzhu – full size | 2.28 | 26 | (H: 9) red | FAS | Found on N side of small stupa base |
| AK.XIV.h.10 | 'Wuzhu' – illegible, without rim | 1.27 | 23 | (H: 9.5) red | FAS | Found on N side of small stupa base |
| AK.XIV.h.11 | Wuzhu – full size | 1.72 | 26 | (H: 9.5) red, worn | FAS | Found on N side of small stupa base |
| AK.XIV.h.12 | 'Wuzhu' – illegible | 0.14 | – | frag. | FAS | Found on N side of small stupa base |
| AK.XIV.i group | (Many of the coins in this group were corroded together before cleaning, and came apart during cleaning, 1993) | | | | | |
| AK.XIV.i.1 | Wuzhu – full size | 3.65 | 25.5 | (H: 10) | FAS | Found on W side of small stupa base |
| AK.XIV.i.2 | Wuzhu – full size | 2.85 | 26 | (H: 9) red | FAS | Found on W side of small stupa base |
| AK.XIV.i.3 | Wuzhu – full size | 3.06 | 27 | (H: 9.5) red, damaged | FAS | Found on W side of small stupa base |
| AK.XIV.i.4 | Wuzhu – full size | 2.17 | 26 | restored (H: 9.5) | FAS | Found on W side of small stupa base |
| AK.XIV.i.5 | Wuzhu – full size | – | 26 | restored (H: 10) | FAS | Found on W side of small stupa base |
| AK.XIV.i.6 | Wuzhu – full size | 2.13 | 26 | frags restored (H: 9.5) red | FAS | Found on W side of small stupa base |
| AK.XIV.i.7 | Wuzhu – full size | 2.05 | 26 | (H: 9.5) red | FAS | Found on W side of small stupa base |
| AK.XIV.i.8 | 'Wuzhu' – illegible, without rim | 2.00 | 24.5 | restored (H: 9.5) red | FAS | Found on W side of small stupa base |
| AK.XIV.i.9 | Wuzhu – without rim | 1.33 | 23 | (H: 9.5) | FAS | Found on W side of small stupa base |
| AK.XIV.i.10 | Wuzhu – without rim | 1.41 | 23 | restored (H: 9.5) red | FAS | Found on W side of small stupa base |
| AK.XIV.i.11 | Wuzhu – full size | 2.72 | 26 | (H: 9.5) red | FAS | Found on W side of small stupa base |
| AK.XIV.i.12 | Wuzhu – full size | 2.82 | 26 | (H: 9.5) red | FAS | Found on W side of small stupa base |
| AK.XIV.i.13 | Wuzhu – full size | 2.33 | 25 | (H: 10) red | FAS | Found on W side of small stupa base |

| BM no. | Identification | Wt | Diam. | Notes | Acqn | Acquisition/Archaeological context |
|---|---|---|---|---|---|---|
| AK.XIV.i.14 | Wuzhu – without rim | 1.96 | 24 | (H: 9) red | FAS | Found on W side of small stupa base |
| AK.XIV.i.15 | Wuzhu – full size | 2.89 | 26 | (H: 9.5) red, + frag. | FAS | Found on W side of small stupa base |
| AK.XIV.i.16 | Wuzhu – full size | 2.28 | 26 | (H: 9) red, damaged | FAS | Found on W side of small stupa base |
| AK.XIV.i.17 | Wuzhu – full size | 2.67 | 27 | restored, damaged (H: 9) | FAS | Found on W side of small stupa base |
| AK.XIV.i.18–20 | Wuzhu – full size (coin + frags) | 5.93 | – | 1 coin + 2 frags, red | FAS | Found on W side of small stupa base |
| AK.XIV.i.21 | Wuzhu – full size (2 coins) | 2.76 | (26?) | 2 coins corroded, red | FAS | Found on W side of small stupa base |
| AK.XIV.i.22 | Wuzhu – without rim | 1.71 | 23 | (H: 10) red | FAS | Found on W side of small stupa base |
| AK.XIV.i.23 | [Wu] zhu – full size | 0.82 | – | frag. (H: 10) red | FAS | Found on W side of small stupa base |
| AK.XIV.i.24 | [Wu] zhu – full size | 0.65 | – | frag. (H: 9.5) | FAS | Found on W side of small stupa base |
| AK.XIV.i.25 | Wu [zhu] – full size | 0.99 | – | 2 frags | FAS | Found on W side of small stupa base |
| AK.XIV.i.26a | Wu [zhu] – full size | 0.75 | – | frag., red | FAS | Found on W side of small stupa base |
| AK.XIV.i.26b | Wu [zhu] – full size | 0.99 | – | frag. | FAS | Found on W side of small stupa base |
| AK.XIV.i.27 | Wu [zhu] – without rim | 0.46 | – | 2 frags | FAS | Found on W side of small stupa base |
| AK.XIV.i.28 | Wu [zhu] – full size | 2.53 | – | 8 frags, red | FAS | Found on W side of small stupa base |
| AK.XIV.j.1 | 'Wuzhu' – small, without inscription, square | 0.51 | 12 | (H: 4.5) flat on one side | FAS | Found between dunes near Rawak Stupa |
| AK.XIV.j.2 | 'Wuzhu' – small, without inscription, square | 0.61 | 14 | (H: 5) flat on one side | FAS | Found between dunes near Rawak Stupa |
| AK.XIV.j.3 | 'Wuzhu' – small, without inscription, square | 0.26 | 10 | (H: 4) flat on one side | FAS | Found between dunes near Rawak Stupa |
| AK.XIV.j.4 | 'Wuzhu' – small, without inscription | 0.49 | 13 | (H: 7.5) | FAS | Found between dunes near Rawak Stupa |
| AK.XIV.j.5 | 'Wuzhu' – small, without inscription, square | 0.35 | 12 | (H: 4.5) flat on one side | FAS | Found between dunes near Rawak Stupa |
| AK.XIV.j.6 | 'Wuzhu' – small, without inscription | 0.62 | 15 | (H: 8.5) | FAS | Found between dunes near Rawak Stupa |
| AK.XIV.j.7–8 | [missing: Wuzhu] | – | – | – | FAS | Found between dunes near Rawak Stupa |
| AK.XIV.k.1–10 | cluster of wuzhu coins + frags – various sizes | 8.96 | – | >8 coin frags corroded, red | F | Found by labourers near Rawak camp |
| AK.XIV.k.1–10 | 1 coin and 2 frags – various sizes | 3.87 | – | 1 coin + frags, corroded, red | F | Found by labourers near Rawak camp |
| AK.XIV.l.1 | Wuzhu | 2.75 | 25 | – | p | From Rawak Stupa hoard, purchased at Khotan |
| AK.XIV.l.2 | Wuzhu | 1.55 | 20 | – | p | From Rawak Stupa hoard, purchased at Khotan |
| AK.XIV.l.3 | Wuzhu – full size | 3.18 | 25.5 | (H: 9.5) | p | From Rawak Stupa hoard, purchased at Khotan |

| BM no. | Identification | Wt | Diam. | Notes | Acqn | Acquisition/Archaeological context |
|---|---|---|---|---|---|---|
| AK.XIV.l.4 | Wuzhu – without full rim | 1.82 | 24 | (H: 9.5), thin, worn | p | From Rawak Stupa hoard, purchased at Khotan |
| AK.XIV.l.5 | Wuzhu – full size | 2.23 | 25.5 | (H: 9.5) | p | From Rawak Stupa hoard, purchased at Khotan |
| AK.XIV.l.6 | Wuzhu – without rim | 2.46 | 24 | (H: 9.5) | p | From Rawak Stupa hoard, purchased at Khotan |
| AK.XIV.l.7 | Wuzhu – full size | 2.28 | 25 | (H: 9.5) | p | From Rawak Stupa hoard, purchased at Khotan |
| AK.XIV.l.8 | Wuzhu – without rim | 2.28 | 23 | (H: 9.5) | p | From Rawak Stupa hoard, purchased at Khotan |
| AK.XIV.l.9 | Wuzhu – without rim | 1.72 | 23 | (H: 10) | p | From Rawak Stupa hoard, purchased at Khotan |
| AK.XIV.l.10 | Wuzhu – smaller than full size | 2.26 | 24 | (H: 9.5) | p | From Rawak Stupa hoard, purchased at Khotan |
| AK.XIV.l.11 | Wuzhu – without rim | 1.63 | 24 | (H: 9.5) | p | From Rawak Stupa hoard, purchased at Khotan |
| AK.XIV.l.12 | Wuzhu – without rim | 1.58 | 23 | (H: 9) | p | From Rawak Stupa hoard, purchased at Khotan |
| AK.XIV.l.13 | Wuzhu – clipped, cutting through inscription | 1.66 | 21 | (H: 9.5) faint | p | From Rawak Stupa hoard, purchased at Khotan |
| AK.XIV.l.14 | Wuzhu – clipped, cutting through inscription | 1.38 | 20 | (H: 9.5) faint | p | From Rawak Stupa hoard, purchased at Khotan |
| AK.XIV.l.15 | Wuzhu – clipped, cutting through inscription | 1.53 | 22 | (H: 10) faint | p | From Rawak Stupa hoard, purchased at Khotan |
| AK.XIV.l.16 | Wuzhu – without rim | 1.87 | 23.5 | (H: 9) | p | From Rawak Stupa hoard, purchased at Khotan |
| AK.XIV.l.17 | Wuzhu – clipped, cutting through inscription | 1.28 | 21.5 | (H: 9.5) | p | From Rawak Stupa hoard, purchased at Khotan |
| AK.XIV.l.18 | Wuzhu – clipped, cutting through inscription | 1.20 | 22 | (H: 10) | p | From Rawak Stupa hoard, purchased at Khotan |
| AK.XIV.l.19 | 'Wuzhu' – without inscription | 1.21 | 21 | (H: 10.5) flat | p | From Rawak Stupa hoard, purchased at Khotan |
| AK.XIV.l.20 | Wuzhu – clipped, cutting through inscription | 1.06 | 21 | (H: 9.5) | p | From Rawak Stupa hoard, purchased at Khotan |
| AK.XIV.l.21 | Wuzhu – clipped, cutting through inscription | 1.44 | 22 | (H: 10) | p | From Rawak Stupa hoard, purchased at Khotan |
| AK.XIV.l.22 | Wuzhu – clipped, cutting through inscription | 1.65 | 22 | (H: 10) | p | From Rawak Stupa hoard, purchased at Khotan |
| AK.XIV.l.23 | Wuzhu – clipped, cutting through inscription | 1.43 | 22 | (H: 9.5) flat | p | From Rawak Stupa hoard, purchased at Khotan |

| | | | | | | |
|---|---|---|---|---|---|---|
| AK.XIV.m.1 | Wuzhu – full size | 2.75 | 25.5 | (H: 10) | p | Purchased from Rawak Stupa hoard |
| AK.XIV.m.2 | Wuzhu – full size | 2.44 | 25.5 | (H: 9.5) | p | Purchased from Rawak Stupa hoard |
| AK.XIV.m.3 | Wuzhu – full size | 3.87 | 26 | (H: 9) | p | Purchased from Rawak Stupa hoard |
| AK.XIV.m.4 | Wuzhu – full size | 2.10 | 26 | (H: 9.5) | p | Purchased from Rawak Stupa hoard |
| AK.XIV.m.5 | Wizhu – without rim | 1.84 | 24 | (H: 9.5) | p | Purchased from Rawak Stupa hoard |
| AK.XIV.m.6 | Wuzhu – full size | 2.52 | 25.5 | (H: 9.5) | p | Purchased from Rawak Stupa hoard |

| BM no. | Identification | Wt | Diam. | Notes | Acqn | Acquisition/Archaeological context |
|---|---|---|---|---|---|---|
| AK.XIV.n.1 | Wuzhu – without rim | 1.58 | 24 | (H: 9.5) | p | Allegedly from Ak-sipil, Rawak and Jumbe-kum, purchased at Yurung-kash |
| AK.XIV.n.2 | Wuzhu – without full rim | 1.95 | 24 | (H: 9.5) red, faint | p | Allegedly from Ak-sipil, Rawak and Jumbe-kum, purchased at Yurung-kash |
| AK.XIV.n.3 | Wuzhu – full size | 2.41 | 25 | (H: 9) faint | p | Allegedly from Ak-sipil, Rawak and Jumbe-kum, purchased at Yurung-kash |
| AK.XIV.n.4 | Wuzhu – without rim | 1.95 | 23.5 | (H: 9.5) faint | p | Allegedly from Ak-sipil, Rawak and Jumbe-kum, purchased at Yurung-kash |
| AK.XIV.n.5 | Wuzhu – clipped, cutting through inscription | 1.98 | 22.5 | (H: 10) | p | Allegedly from Ak-sipil, Rawak and Jumbe-kum, purchased at Yurung-kash |
| AK.XIV.n.6 | Wuzhu – clipped, cutting through inscription | 1.52 | 23 | (H: 9.5) faint | p | Allegedly from Ak-sipil, Rawak and Jumbe-kum, purchased at Yurung-kash |
| AK.XIV.n.7 | Wuzhu – without rim | 1.69 | 23.5 | (H: 9.5) faint | p | Allegedly from Ak-sipil, Rawak and Jumbe-kum, purchased at Yurung-kash |
| AK.XIV.n.8 | Wuzhu – clipped, cutting through inscription | 1.78 | 22 | (H: 9.5) faint | p | Allegedly from Ak-sipil, Rawak and Jumbe-kum, purchased at Yurung-kash |
| AK.XIV.n.9 | Wuzhu – clipped, cutting through inscription | 1.48 | 22.5 | (H: 9.5) faint | p | Allegedly from Ak-sipil, Rawak and Jumbe-kum, purchased at Yurung-kash |
| AK.XIV.n.10 | Wuzhu – without rim | 1.59 | 23.5 | (H: 9.5) faint, thin | p | Allegedly from Ak-sipil, Rawak and Jumbe-kum, purchased at Yurung-kash |
| AK.XIV.n.11 | Wuzhu – without rim | 2.40 | 24 | (H: 9) faint | p | Allegedly from Ak-sipil, Rawak and Jumbe-kum, purchased at Yurung-kash |
| AK.XIV.n.12 | Wuzhu – without rim | 1.87 | 24 | (H: 9.5) | p | Allegedly from Ak-sipil, Rawak and Jumbe-kum, purchased at Yurung-kash |
| AK.XIV.n.13 | Wuzhu – without rim | 1.94 | 23 | (H: 9) | p | Allegedly from Ak-sipil, Rawak and Jumbe-kum, purchased at Yurung-kash |
| AK.XIV.n.14 | Wuzhu – without rim | 1.69 | 23 | (H: 9.5) | p | Allegedly from Ak-sipil, Rawak and Jumbe-kum, purchased at Yurung-kash |
| AK.XIV.n.15 | Wuzhu – without rim | 1.67 | 23 | (H: 9.5) | p | Allegedly from Ak-sipil, Rawak and Jumbe-kum, purchased at Yurung-kash |
| AK.XIV.n.16 | Wuzhu – without rim | 1.69 | 23 | (H: 9.5) faint | p | Allegedly from Ak-sipil, Rawak and Jumbe-kum, purchased at Yurung-kash |
| AK.XIV.n.17 | Wuzhu – clipped, cutting through inscription | 1.51 | 21 | (H: 9.5) | p | Allegedly from Ak-sipil, Rawak and Jumbe-kum, purchased at Yurung-kash |
| AK.XIV.n.18 | Wuzhu – clipped, cutting through inscription | 1.42 | 21.5 | (H: 10) red | p | Allegedly from Ak-sipil, Rawak and Jumbe-kum, purchased at Yurung-kash |

| BM no. | Identification | Wt | Diam. | Notes | Acqn | Acquisition/Archaeological context |
|---|---|---|---|---|---|---|
| AK.XIV.n.19 | Wuzhu – clipped, cutting through inscription | 0.98 | 19.5 | (H: 9.5) | p | Allegedly from Ak-sipil, Rawak and Jumbe-kum, purchased at Yurung-kash |
| AK.XIV.n.20 | Wuzhu – smaller than full size, without rim | 2.72 | 21 | (H: 9.5) red | p | Allegedly from Ak-sipil, Rawak and Jumbe-kum, purchased at Yurung-kash |
| AK.XIV.n.21 | 'Wuzhu' – illegible; (3 dots on rev.?) | 1.53 | 22 | (H: 9.5) | p | Allegedly from Ak-sipil, Rawak and Jumbe-kum, purchased at Yurung-kash |
| AK.XIV.n.22 | Wuzhu – clipped, cutting through inscription | 1.55 | 21 | (H: 9.5) red, faint | p | Allegedly from Ak-sipil, Rawak and Jumbe-kum, purchased at Yurung-kash |
| AK.XIV.n.23 | Wuzhu – inscription reversed (mirror image) – clipped, cutting through inscription | 1.93 | 22 | (H: 9) red | p | Allegedly from Ak-sipil, Rawak and Jumbe-kum, purchased at Yurung-kash |
| AK.XIV.n.24 | Wuzhu – clipped, cutting through inscription | 1.74 | 21.5 | (H: 9) | p | Allegedly from Ak-sipil, Rawak and Jumbe-kum, purchased at Yurung-kash |
| AK.XIV.n.25 | Wuzhu – clipped, cutting through inscription | 1.24 | 20 | (H: 10) | p | Allegedly from Ak-sipil, Rawak and Jumbe-kum, purchased at Yurung-kash |
| AK.XIV.n.26 | Wuzhu – clipped, cutting through inscription | 1.93 | 23 | (H: 9.5) | p | Allegedly from Ak-sipil, Rawak and Jumbe-kum, purchased at Yurung-kash |
| AK.XIV.n.27 | Wuzhu – clipped, cutting through inscription | 1.24 | 20 | (H: 9.5) | p | Allegedly from Ak-sipil, Rawak and Jumbe-kum, purchased at Yurung-kash |
| AK.XIV.n.28 | 'Wuzhu' – illegible | 1.12 | 21 | (H: 9.5) | p | Allegedly from Ak-sipil, Rawak and Jumbe-kum, purchased at Yurung-kash |
| AK.XIV.n.29 | Wuzhu – clipped, cutting through inscription | 1.09 | 18 | (H: 9.5) | p | Allegedly from Ak-sipil, Rawak and Jumbe-kum, purchased at Yurung-kash |
| AK.XIV.n.30 | Wuzhu – clipped, cutting through inscription | 1.07 | 20 | (H: 9.5) | p | Allegedly from Ak-sipil, Rawak and Jumbe-kum, purchased at Yurung-kash |
| AK.XIV.n.31 | 'Wuzhu' – illegible | 1.26 | 21.5 | (H: 9.5) | p | Allegedly from Ak-sipil, Rawak and Jumbe-kum, purchased at Yurung-kash |
| AK.XIV.n.32 | Wuzhu – small wu; zhu without metal radical | 0.85 | 18.5 | (H: 9.5) | p | Allegedly from Ak-sipil, Rawak and Jumbe-kum, purchased at Yurung-kash |
| AK.XIV.n.33 | Wuzhu – tall, thin wu, without rim | 1.96 | 21 | (H: 9) | p | Allegedly from Ak-sipil, Rawak and Jumbe-kum, purchased at Yurung-kash |
| AK.XIV.n.34 | Wuzhu – clipped, cutting through inscription | 1.03 | 19 | (H. 9.5) | p | Allegedly from Ak-sipil, Rawak and Jumbe-kum, purchased at Yurung-kash |
| AK.XIV.n.35 | Huoquan | 1.25 | (22?) | frag. (H: 8) red, faint | p | Allegedly from Ak-sipil, Rawak and Jumbe-kum, purchased at Yurung-kash |
| AK.XIV.n.36 | 'Wuzhu' – illegible | 1.54 | 23 | (H: 10) | p | Allegedly from Ak-sipil, Rawak and Jumbe-kum, purchased at Yurung-kash |

| BM no. | Identification | Wt | Diam. | Notes | Acqn | Acquisition/Archaeological context |
|---|---|---|---|---|---|---|
| AK.XIV.n.37 | 'Wuzhu' – illegible | 1.42 | 23.5 | (H: 9.5) | p | Allegedly from Ak-sipil, Rawak and Jumbe-kum, purchased at Yurung-kash |
| AK.XIV.n.38 | 'Wuzhu' – illegible | 1.45 | 21 | (H: 9.5) | p | Allegedly from Ak-sipil, Rawak and Jumbe-kum, purchased at Yurung-kash |
| AK.XIV.n.39 | Wuzhu – clipped, cutting through inscription | 1.38 | 21 | (H: 10) | p | Allegedly from Ak-sipil, Rawak and Jumbe-kum, purchased at Yurung-kash |
| AK.XIV.n.40 | Wuzhu – clipped, cutting through inscription | 1.25 | 20.5 | (H: 10) | p | Allegedly from Ak-sipil, Rawak and Jumbe-kum, purchased at Yurung-kash |
| AK.XIV.n.41 | Wuzhu – clipped, cutting through inscription | 1.14 | 20.5 | (H: 10) | p | Allegedly from Ak-sipil, Rawak and Jumbe-kum, purchased at Yurung-kash |
| AK.XIV.n.42 | 'Wuzhu' – illegible | 1.16 | 20 | (H: 9.5) | p | Allegedly from Ak-sipil, Rawak and Jumbe-kum, purchased at Yurung-kash |
| AK.XIV.n.43 | Wuzhu – clipped, cutting through inscription | 1.00 | 20.5 | (H: 9.5) | p | Allegedly from Ak-sipil, Rawak and Jumbe-kum, purchased at Yurung-kash |
| AK.XIV.n.44 | Wuzhu – clipped, cutting through inscription | 1.52 | 22 | (H: 9.5) | p | Allegedly from Ak-sipil, Rawak and Jumbe-kum, purchased at Yurung-kash |
| AK.XIV.n.45 | Wuzhu – crude inscription, without rim | 1.61 | 23 | (H: 9.5) | p | Allegedly from Ak-sipil, Rawak and Jumbe-kum, purchased at Yurung-kash |
| AK.XIV.n.46 | 'Wuzhu' – illegible | 1.26 | 23 | (H: 9.5) | p | Allegedly from Ak-sipil, Rawak and Jumbe-kum, purchased at Yurung-kash |
| AK.XIV.n.47 | Wuzhu – without rim | 1.54 | 23.5 | (H: 9.5) faint | p | Allegedly from Ak-sipil, Rawak and Jumbe-kum, purchased at Yurung-kash |
| AK.XIV.n.48 | Wuzhu – tall, thin wu, cut through zhu | 1.69 | 20.5 | (H: 9.5) | p | Allegedly from Ak-sipil, Rawak and Jumbe-kum, purchased at Yurung-kash |
| AK.XIV.n.49 | 'Wuzhu' – illegible | 1.29 | 20 | (H: 9.5) red | p | Allegedly from Ak-sipil, Rawak and Jumbe-kum, purchased at Yurung-kash |
| AK.XIV.n.50 | Wuzhu – clipped, cutting through inscription | 1.53 | 21 | (H: 9.5) faint | p | Allegedly from Ak-sipil, Rawak and Jumbe-kum, purchased at Yurung-kash |
| AK.XIV.n.51 | Wuzhu – without rim | 1.60 | 23 | (H: 10) faint | p | Allegedly from Ak-sipil, Rawak and Jumbe-kum, purchased at Yurung-kash |
| AK.XIV.n.52 | 'Wuzhu' – illegible | 0.97 | 20 | (H: 9.5) | p | Allegedly from Ak-sipil, Rawak and Jumbe-kum, purchased at Yurung-kash |
| AK.XIV.n.53 | 'Wuzhu' – without inscription | 1.40 | 23 | (H: 9.5) | p | Allegedly from Ak-sipil, Rawak and Jumbe-kum, purchased at Yurung-kash |
| AK.XIV.n.54 | Wuzhu – clipped, cutting through inscription | 1.10 | 21.5 | (H: 9.5) faint | p | Allegedly from Ak-sipil, Rawak and Jumbe-kum, purchased at Yurung-kash |

| BM no. | Identification | Wt | Diam. | Notes | Acqn | Acquisition/Archaeological context |
|---|---|---|---|---|---|---|
| AK.XIV.n.55 | 'Wuzhu' – small, without inscription, square | 0.31 | 12 | (H: 6) flat on one side | p | Allegedly from Ak-sipil, Rawak and Jumbe-kum, purchased at Yurung-kash |
| AK.XIV.n.56 | 'Wuzhu' – small, without inscription, square | 0.38 | 11 | (H: 5) flat on one side | p | Allegedly from Ak-sipil, Rawak and Jumbe-kum, purchased at Yurung-kash |
| AK.XIV.n.57 | 'Wuzhu' – small, without inscription, round | 0.66 | 14 | (H: 6) flat on one side | p | Allegedly from Ak-sipil, Rawak and Jumbe-kum, purchased at Yurung-kash |
| AK.XIV.n.58 | 'Wuzhu' – small, without inscription, round | 0.56 | 13 | (H: 7.5) flat on one side | p | Allegedly from Ak-sipil, Rawak and Jumbe-kum, purchased at Yurung-kash |
| AK.XIV.n.59 | 'Wuzhu' – small, without inscription, square | 0.29 | 11 | (H: 4) flat on one side | p | Allegedly from Ak-sipil, Rawak and Jumbe-kum, purchased at Yurung-kash |

| | | | | | | |
|---|---|---|---|---|---|---|
| AK.XIV.o group | (During cleaning in 1993, 5 clusters were separated, making a total of 29 wuzhu and 1 non-coin/Islamic? coin) | | | | | Label in coin-tray reads 'circ. 45 much corroded coins, purchased from Muhammad Sharif. Rawak find. One clearly Wu-tchu. Groups of 11, 7, 4 sticking together' |
| AK.XIV.o.1 | Wuzhu – full size | 2.39 | 26 | (H: 10) | p | Rawak find, purchased from Muhammad Sharif |
| AK.XIV.o.2 | Wuzhu – without full rim | 2.07 | 24.5 | (H: 10) red, faint | p | Rawak find, purchased from Muhammad Sharif |
| AK.XIV.o.3 | Wuzhu – full size | 2.05 | 25.5 | (H: 10.5) red | p | Rawak find, purchased from Muhammad Sharif |
| AK.XIV.o.4 | Wuzhu – full size | 1.93 | 26 | (H: 10) red | p | Rawak find, purchased from Muhammad Sharif |
| AK.XIV.o.5 | Wuzhu – full size | 3.31 | 25.5 | (H: 9.5) red | p | Rawak find, purchased from Muhammad Sharif |
| AK.XIV.o.6 | Wuzhu – full size | 2.45 | 25.5 | (H: 10) red | p | Rawak find, purchased from Muhammad Sharif |
| AK.XIV.o.7 | Wuzhu – full size | 3.44 | 25.5 | (H: 9.5) red | p | Rawak find, purchased from Muhammad Sharif |
| AK.XIV.o.8 | Wuzhu – full size | 1.91 | 25.5 | (H: 9.5) red | p | Rawak find, purchased from Muhammad Sharif |
| AK.XIV.o.9 | Wuzhu – full size | 2.62 | 26 | (H: 9.5) red | p | Rawak find, purchased from Muhammad Sharif |
| AK.XIV.o.10 | Wuzhu – full size | 2.29 | 25.5 | (H: 9.5) red | p | Rawak find, purchased from Muhammad Sharif |
| AK.XIV.o.11 | Wuzhu – full size | 3.26 | 25.5 | (H: 10) red | p | Rawak find, purchased from Muhammad Sharif |
| AK.XIV.o.12 | 'Wuzhu' – without inscription | 1.23 | 23 | (H: 9.5) red | p | Rawak find, purchased from Muhammad Sharif |
| AK.XIV.o.13 | 'Wuzhu' – illegible | 0.92 | 20.5 | (H: 10.5) red | p | Rawak find, purchased from Muhammad Sharif |
| AK.XIV.o.14 | Wuzhu – full size | 2.22 | 25.5 | (H: 10) red | p | Rawak find, purchased from Muhammad Sharif |
| AK.XIV.o.15 | Wuzhu – full size | 2.33 | 25 | (H: 10) red | p | Rawak find, purchased from Muhammad Sharif |
| AK.XIV.o.16 | Wuzhu – full size | 1.84 | 25 | (H: 9.5) red | p | Rawak find, purchased from Muhammad Sharif |

| BM no. | Identification | Wt | Diam. | Notes | Acqn | Acquisition/Archaeological context |
|---|---|---|---|---|---|---|
| AK.XIV.o.17 | Wuzhu – without full rim | 2.22 | 24 | (H: 9.5) red | p | Rawak find, purchased from Muhammad Sharif |
| AK.XIV.o.18 | Wuzhu – full size | 1.73 | 25 | (H: 9.5) red | p | Rawak find, purchased from Muhammad Sharif |
| AK.XIV.o.19 | Wuzhu – full size | 2.45 | 26 | (H: 10.5) | p | Rawak find, purchased from Muhammad Sharif |
| AK.XIV.o.20 | Wuzhu – full size | 2.13 | 26 | (H: 10.5) | p | Rawak find, purchased from Muhammad Sharif |
| AK.XIV.o.21 | Wuzhu – without full rim | 1.79 | 24 | (H: 9) red, faint | p | Rawak find, purchased from Muhammad Sharif |
| AK.XIV.o.22 | Wuzhu – without rim | 2.07 | 23.5 | (H: 9.5) red | p | Rawak find, purchased from Muhammad Sharif |
| AK.XIV.o.23 | Wuzhu – full size | 1.99 | 26 | (H: 9.5) | p | Rawak find, purchased from Muhammad Sharif |
| AK.XIV.o.24 | Wuzhu – without rim | 1.87 | 22.5 | (H: 9.5) red | p | Rawak find, purchased from Muhammad Sharif |
| AK.XIV.o.25 | Wuzhu – clipped, cutting through inscription | 1.24 | 21 | restored (H: 10) | p | Rawak find, purchased from Muhammad Sharif |
| AK.XIV.o.26 | Wuzhu – clipped, cutting through inscription | 1.50 | 21 | (H: 10) faint | p | Rawak find, purchased from Muhammad Sharif |
| AK.XIV.o.26a | [extra: Wuzhu: zhu without metal radical; clipped, cutting through inscription] | 1.00 | 17 | (H: 8.5) | p | Rawak find, purchased from Muhammad Sharif |
| AK.XIV.o.26b | [extra: Wuzhu – Cao–Wei type?] | 1.29 | 20.5 | (H: 10) | p | Rawak find, purchased from Muhammad Sharif |
| AK.XIV.o.26c | [extra: 'Wuzhu' – illegible | 1.03 | 20.5 | (H: 10) | p | Rawak find, purchased from Muhammad Sharif |
| AK.XIV.o.26d | [extra: non-Chinese coin – Islamic?] | 1.22 | 11 | red | p | Rawak find, purchased from Muhammad Sharif |
| AK.XIV.o.27–31 | (After cleaning, 1993, this cluster yielded 7 separate coins and 2 coins stuck together) | | | | | |
| AK.XIV.o.27 | Wuzhu – full size | 2.46 | 25.5 | (H: 10) red | p | Rawak find, purchased from Muhammad Sharif |
| AK.XIV.o.28 | Wuzhu – full size | 2.26 | 25.5 | (H: 10) red, faint | p | Rawak find, purchased from Muhammad Sharif |
| AK.XIV.o.29 | Wuzhu – full size | 2.13 | 25 | (H: 9.5) red | p | Rawak find, purchased from Muhammad Sharif |
| AK.XIV.o.30 | Wuzhu – full size | 1.99 | 29 | (H: 10) red | p | Rawak find, purchased from Muhammad Sharif |
| AK.XIV.o.31a | Wuzhu – full size | 3.85 | 25.5 | 2 coins, (H: 10) red | p | Rawak find, purchased from Muhammad Sharif |
| AK.XIV.o.31b | Wuzhu – clipped, cutting through inscription | 1.26 | 21 | (H: 10) red | p | Rawak find, purchased from Muhammad Sharif |
| AK.XIV.o.31c | Wuzhu – clipped, cutting through inscription | 0.88 | 18.5 | (H: 10) red | p | Rawak find, purchased from Muhammad Sharif |
| AK.XIV.o.31d | Wuzhu – clipped, cutting through inscription | 0.56 | 17 | (H: 9) red, faint | p | Rawak find, purchased from Muhammad Sharif |
| AK.XIV.o.32–45 | cluster of *c.*16 coins of differing sizes – not cleaned, unidentified | 31.28 | 17 | – | p | Rawak find, purchased from Muhammad Sharif |

## AK.XV: COPPER COINS FOUND AT JUMBE-KUM SITE

| BM no. | Identification | Wt | Diam. | Notes | Acqn | Acquisition/Archaeological context |
|---|---|---|---|---|---|---|
| AK.XV.a.1 | Wuzhu – small, without inscription, square | 0.27 | 11 | (H: 5) flat on one side | FAS | Found near structure |
| AK.XV.a.2 | Wuzhu – small, without inscription, square | 0.27 | 10 | (H: 4.5) flat on one side, with sprue | FAS | Found near structure |
| AK.XV.a.3 | Wuzhu – small, without inscription, round | 0.40 | 12 | (H: 5) flat on one side | FAS | Found near structure |
| AK.XV.a.4 | 'Wuzhu' – illegible | 1.27 | 19 | (H: 8.5) | FAS | Found near structure |
| AK.XV.a.5 | Wuzhu – clipped, cutting through inscription | 2.03 | 21.5 | (H: 9.5 mm) faint | FAS | Found halfway between structure and small stupa |

## AK.XVI: COPPER COINS FOUND NEAR KARA-DÖBE

| BM no. | Identification | Wt | Diam. | Notes | Acqn | Acquisition/Archaeological context |
|---|---|---|---|---|---|---|
| AK.XVI.a.1 | 'Wuzhu' – illegible (clipped or small coin) | 0.60 | – | frag., red | FAS | Found near stupa at Kara-döbe site |
| AK.XVI.a.2 | [Wu] zhu – full size | 0.91 | – | frag., red | FAS | Found near stupa at Kara-döbe site |

## AK.XVII: COPPER COINS SAID TO COME FROM MAZAR TAGH (NEAR LOWER YURUNG-KASH); PURCHASED AT KHOTAN

| BM no. | Identification | Wt | Diam. | Notes | Acqn | Acquisition/Archaeological context |
|---|---|---|---|---|---|---|
| AK.XVII.a.1 | Sino-Kharoshthi coin (Cribb 2) | 2.40 | 11 | – | p | Allegedly from 'Mazar Tagh', near lower Yurung-kash River; purchased at Khotan |
| AK.XVII.a.2 | Qianyuan zhongbao – large | 7.66 | 29 | – | p | Allegedly from 'Mazar Tagh', near lower Yurung-kash River; purchased at Khotan |
| AK.XVII.a.3 | Qianyuan zhongbao – large | 8.52 | 29 | – | p | Allegedly from 'Mazar Tagh', near lower Yurung-kash River; purchased at Khotan |
| AK.XVII.a.4 | [missing: Qianyuan zhongbao] | – | – | – | p | Allegedly from 'Mazar Tagh', near lower Yurung-kash River; purchased at Khotan |
| AK.XVII.a.5 | Qianyuan zhongbao – small | 2.24 | 22 | red | p | Allegedly from 'Mazar Tagh', near lower Yurung-kash River; purchased at Khotan |
| AK.XVII.a.6 | Qianyuan zhongbao – small | 2.04 | 21.5 | forced hole, red | p | Allegedly from 'Mazar Tagh', near lower Yurung-kash River; purchased at Khotan |
| AK.XVII.a.7 | Qianyuan zhongbao – small | 2.75 | 22 | red | p | Allegedly from 'Mazar Tagh', near lower Yurung-kash River; purchased at Khotan |

| BM no. | Identification | Wt | Diam. | Notes | Acqn | Acquisition/Archaeological context |
|---|---|---|---|---|---|---|
| AK.XVII.a.8 | Qianyuan zhongbao – small | 1.40 | 21.5 | forced hole | p | Allegedly from 'Mazar Tagh', near lower Yurung-kash River; purchased at Khotan |
| AK.XVII.a.9 | Qianyuan zhongbao – small | 1.88 | 22 | – | p | Allegedly from 'Mazar Tagh', near lower Yurung-kash River; purchased at Khotan |
| AK.XVII.a.10 | Qianyuan zhongbao – small | 1.72 | 22 | – | p | Allegedly from 'Mazar Tagh', near lower Yurung-kash River; purchased at Khotan |
| AK.XVII.a.11 | Qianyuan zhongbao – small | 1.97 | 22 | – | p | Allegedly from 'Mazar Tagh', near lower Yurung-kash River; purchased at Khotan |
| AK.XVII.a.12 | Qianyuan zhongbao – small | 1.83 | 21.5 | – | p | Allegedly from 'Mazar Tagh', near lower Yurung-kash River; purchased at Khotan |
| AK.XVII.a.13 | Dali yuanbao – small | 1.46 | 21.5 | red | p | Allegedly from 'Mazar Tagh', near lower Yurung-kash River; purchased at Khotan |
| AK.XVII.a.14 | Dali yuanbao – small | 2.87 | 22 | red | p | Allegedly from 'Mazar Tagh', near lower Yurung-kash River; purchased at Khotan |
| AK.XVII.a.15–21 | Chinese – Song dynasty | – | – | – | p | Allegedly from 'Mazar Tagh', near lower Yurung-kash River; purchased at Khotan |
| AK.XVII.a.22 | Wuzhu – without rims | 1.09 | 22 | (H: 10) red, faint | p | Allegedly from 'Mazar Tagh', near lower Yurung-kash River; purchased at Khotan |
| AK.XVII.a.23 | Wuzhu – full size coin | 2.30 | 25 | (H: 10) red, faint | p | Allegedly from 'Mazar Tagh', near lower Yurung-kash River; purchased at Khotan |
| AK.XVII.a.24 | Chinese – unidentified – not cleaned | 1.10 | – | frag. | p | Allegedly from 'Mazar Tagh', near lower Yurung-kash River; purchased at Khotan |
| AK.XVII.a.25 | Qianyuan zhongbao – small | 2.15 | 22 | red | p | Allegedly from 'Mazar Tagh', near lower Yurung-kash River; purchased at Khotan |
| AK.XVII.a.26 | [missing: Chinese coin – unidentified] | – | – | – | p | Allegedly from 'Mazar Tagh', near lower Yurung-kash River; purchased at Khotan |
| AK XVII.a.27–28 | [extra: not coins] | – | – | – | p | Allegedly from 'Mazar Tagh', near lower Yurung-kash River; purchased at Khotan |

### Kh.002: PURCHASED AT KHOTAN, 16 OCT. 1900, BUT NOT INCLUDED IN LIST OF COINS

| BM no. | Identification | Wt | Diam. | Notes | Acqn | Acquisition/Archaeological context |
|---|---|---|---|---|---|---|
| Kh.002: | Sino-Kharoshthi coin (Cribb 3) | 2.90 | 18 | overstruck on Hermaius imitation | p | Purchased at Khotan |
| Kh.002.B | Sino-Kharoshthi coin (Cribb 3–4) | 3.28 | 20×18 | – | p | Purchased at Khotan |
| Kh.002.B.ii | Sino-Kharoshthi coin (Cribb 2) | 3.48 | 19 | – | p | Purchased at Khotan |
| Kh.002.B.ii | Sino-Kharoshthi coin (Cribb 4) | 3.40 | 18 | – | p | Purchased at Khotan |
| Kh.002.B | Sino-Kharoshthi coin (Cribb 4) | 3.29 | 19×18 | – | p | Purchased at Khotan |
| Kh.002.C | Sino-Kharoshthi coin (Cribb 2) | 3.01 | 20×19.5 | – | p | Purchased at Khotan |
| Kh.002.C | Sino-Kharoshthi coin (Cribb 3) | 4.14 | 21×19.5 | – | p | Purchased at Khotan |
| Kh.002.C | Sino-Kharoshthi coin (Cribb 4) | 3.10 | 18×17 | – | p | Purchased at Khotan |
| Kh.002.D | Sino-Kharoshthi coin (Cribb 1) | 3.47 | 20×19 | – | p | Purchased at Khotan |
| Kh.002.D | Sino-Kharoshthi coin (Cribb 1) | 3.42 | 19×17.5 | – | p | Purchased at Khotan |
| Kh.002.E | Sino-Kharoshthi coin (Cribb 6) | 4.52 | 20×19 | – | p | Purchased at Khotan |
| Kh.002.E | Sino-Kharoshthi coin (Cribb 6) | 3.80 | 20.5×20 | – | p | Purchased at Khotan |
| Kh.002.E | Sino-Kharoshthi coin (Cribb 6) | 4.39 | 21×20 | – | p | Purchased at Khotan |
| Kh.002.E | Sino-Kharoshthi coin (Cribb 6) | 2.70 | 21×19 | – | p | Purchased at Khotan |
| Kh.002.E | Sino-Kharoshthi coin (Cribb 6) | 2.94 | 21×20 | – | p | Purchased at Khotan |
| Kh.002.A | Sino-Kharoshthi (Cribb 8) | 15.35 | 28×26 | – | p | Purchased at Khotan |
| Kh.002.A | Sino-Kharoshthi (Cribb 8) | 17.15 | 28×25 | – | p | Purchased at Khotan |
| Kh.002.A | Sino-Kharoshthi (Cribb 8) | 15.38 | 28×27 | – | p | Purchased at Khotan |
| Kh.002.A | Sino-Kharoshthi (Cribb 8) | 12.67 | 23×22.5 | – | p | Purchased at Khotan |
| Kh.002.A | Sino-Kharoshthi (Cribb 8) | 13.10 | 27×26 | – | p | Purchased at Khotan |
| Kh.002.F | Sino-Kharoshthi (Cribb 9) | 14.40 | 26 | – | p | Purchased at Khotan |
| Kh.002 (OR.0647) | Sino-Kharoshthi coin (Cribb 10) | 3.04 | 20×19 | – | p | Purchased at Khotan |
| – | 1 Dali yuanbao | 3.94 | 24 | – | – | – |

## SERINDIA

### S.I: COINS OBTAINED AT YARKAND

| BM no. | Identification | Wt | Diam. | Notes | Acqn | Acquisition/Archaeological context |
|---|---|---|---|---|---|---|
| S.I.a.1 | Kaiyuan tongbao | 3.44 | 25 | – | g | From a local find, presented by Pên Ta-jên, Amban of Yarkand |
| S.I.a.2–10 | Chinese – Song dynasty | – | – | – | g | From a local find, presented by Pên Ta-jên, Amban of Yarkand |
| S.I.b.1 (OR.0424) | Sino-Kharoshthi coin (Cribb 5) | 4.08 | 20.5×18 | – | p | Purchased at Yarkand |

### S.II: COINS PURCHASED AT KARGHALIK

| BM no. | Identification | Wt | Diam. | Notes | Acqn | Acquisition/Archaeological context |
|---|---|---|---|---|---|---|
| S.II.1 | Parthian drachm of Phraates III (c.70–57 BC), Ecbatana or Rhagae Mint | 3.75 | 17 | – | p | Purchased at Karghalik |
| S.II.2 | Parthian drachm of Mithridates II (c.123–88 BC), Rhagae Mint | 3.41 | 19 | – | p | Purchased at Karghalik |
| S.II.3 | Indian coin (Hermaius?) | 7.87 | 22 | – | p | Purchased at Karghalik |
| S.II.4 | Roman coin of Constantine II (RIC 87: Period II, Antioch Mint AD 330–35) | 2.73 | 17 | – | p | Purchased at Karghalik |
| S.II.5 | Roman coin of Constantius II (RIC18: Alexandria Mint AD 340) | 1.90 | 15 | – | p | Purchased at Karghalik |

### S.III: COINS COLLECTED FROM TOGUJAI, MOJI

| BM no. | Identification | Wt | Diam. | Notes | Acqn | Acquisition/Archaeological context |
|---|---|---|---|---|---|---|
| S.III.a.1–32 | Islamic | – | – | – | p | Purchased from villagers, at Togujai, Moji |

### S.IV: COINS COLLECTED WITHIN THE KHOTAN OASIS

### S.IV.A: COINS PURCHASED AT OR FROM YOTKAN SITE

| BM no. | Identification | Wt | Diam. | Notes | Acqn | Acquisition/Archaeological context |
|---|---|---|---|---|---|---|
| S.IV.A.a.1 | Sino-Kharoshthi coin (Cribb 7–8) | 12.88 | 36 | – | pas | Purchased at Yotkan site |
| S.IV.A.a.2 | Sino-Kharoshthi coin (Cribb 1–6) | 0.93 | 16 | – | pas | Purchased at Yotkan site |
| S.IV.A.a.3 (OR.0382) | Sino-Kharoshthi coin (Cribb 7) | 12.95 | 27 | – | pas | Purchased at Yotkan site |
| S.IV.A.a.4 (OR.0391) | Sino-Kharoshthi coin (Cribb 8) | 16.52 | 27×25 | – | pas | Purchased at Yotkan site |
| S.IV.A.a.5 | Sino-Kharoshthi coin (Cribb 1–6) | 2.20 | 18.5 | – | pas | Purchased at Yotkan site |
| S.IV.A.a.6 | Sino-Kharoshthi coin (Cribb 1–6) | 1.58 | 18 | – | pas | Purchased at Yotkan site |
| S.IV.A.a.7 | Sino-Kharoshthi coin (Cribb 1–6) | 1.86 | 15.5 | – | pas | Purchased at Yotkan site |
| S.IV.A.a.8 | Kushan coin of Kanishka I – hemi-drachm | 1.58 | 13 | – | pas | Purchased at Yotkan site |
| S.IV.A.a.9 | Wuzhu – full size | 3.66 | 25 | (H: 9.5) corroded | pas | Purchased at Yotkan site |
| S.IV.A.a.10 | Wuzhu – small inscription, inscription reversed, no rim | 1.31 | 21 | (H: 10) flat | pas | Purchased at Yotkan site |
| S.IV.A.a.11 | Wuzhu – full size | 2.21 | 25 | (H: 10) damaged | pas | Purchased at Yotkan site |
| S.IV.A.a.12 | Wuzhu – full size | 1.43 | 24.5 | (H: 9.5) red, flat | pas | Purchased at Yotkan site |
| S.IV.A.a.13 | 'Wuzhu' – without inscription | 1.07 | 21 | (H: 9.5) flat | pas | Purchased at Yotkan site |
| S.IV.A.a.14 | 'Wuzhu' – illegible | 1.79 | 24 | (H: 9.5) red, with sprue, faint | pas | Purchased at Yotkan site |
| S.IV.A.a.15 | Wuzhu – without rim | 1.40 | 24 | (H: 9.5) red, faint, thin | pas | Purchased at Yotkan site |
| S.IV.A.a.16 | Wuzhu – full size | 2.40 | 25 | (H: 9.5) corroded | pas | Purchased at Yotkan site |
| S.IV.A.a.17 | Wuzhu – without rim | 1.91 | 23 | (H: 9.5) red, faint | pas | Purchased at Yotkan site |
| S.IV.A.a.18 | 'Wuzhu' – illegible, small | 1.36 | 21 | (H: 9.5) red, misaligned | pas | Purchased at Yotkan site |
| S.IV.A.a.19 | Wuzhu – without rim | 1.50 | 23 | (H: 9.5) red, faint, thin | pas | Purchased at Yotkan site |
| S.IV.A.a.20 | 'Wuzhu' – illegible, small | 1.21 | 20.5 | (H: 9.5) red, misaligned | pas | Purchased at Yotkan site |
| S.IV.A.a.21 | 'Wuzhu' – illegible, without rim | 1.72 | 24 | (H: 9.5), red, crude | pas | Purchased at Yotkan site |
| S.IV.A.a.22 | Wuzhu | 1.20 | – | frag. (H: 9.5) red, crude | pas | Purchased at Yotkan site |
| S.IV.A.a.23 | Qianyuan zhongbao – small | 1.42 | 22 | – | pas | Purchased at Yotkan site |
| S.IV.A.a.24 | Qianyuan zhongbao – small | 1.88 | 21.5 | damaged | pas | Purchased at Yotkan site |
| S.IV.A.a.25 | Qianyuan zhongbao – small | 1.66 | 22 | forced hole | pas | Purchased at Yotkan site |
| S.IV.A.a.26 | Qianyuan zhongbao – small | 2.37 | 21.5 | – | pas | Purchased at Yotkan site |
| S.IV.A.a.27 | Qianyuan zhongbao – small | 1.79 | 21.5 | forced hole | pas | Purchased at Yotkan site |
| S.IV.A.a.28 | Qianyuan zhongbao – small | 2.80 | 22 | damaged | pas | Purchased at Yotkan site |
| S.IV.A.a.29 | Qianyuan zhongbao – medium | 2.80 | 24.5 | – | pas | Purchased at Yotkan site |
| S.IV.A.a.30 | Qianyuan zhongbao – small | 1.85 | 21 | – | pas | Purchased at Yotkan site |
| S.IV.A.a.31 | Qianyuan zhongbao – small | 1.92 | 22 | damaged | pas | Purchased at Yotkan site |
| S.IV.A.a.32 | Qianyuan zhongbao – small | 2.06 | 21.5 | – | pas | Purchased at Yotkan site |

| BM no. | Identification | Wt | Diam. | Notes | Acqn | Acquisition/Archaeological context |
|---|---|---|---|---|---|---|
| S.IV.A.a.33 | Qianyuan zhongbao – small | 1.90 | 22 | – | pas | Purchased at Yotkan site |
| S.IV.A.a.34 | Qianyuan zhongbao – small | 2.81 | 21.5 | – | pas | Purchased at Yotkan site |
| S.IV.A.a.35 | Qianyuan zhongbao – small | 1.85 | 22 | – | pas | Purchased at Yotkan site |
| S.IV.A.a.36 | Qianyuan zhongbao – small | 2.72 | 20 | – | pas | Purchased at Yotkan site |
| S.IV.A.a.37 | Qianyuan zhongbao – small | 2.16 | 22 | damaged | pas | Purchased at Yotkan site |
| S.IV.A.a.38 | Qianyuan zhongbao – small | 2.17 | 22 | damaged | pas | Purchased at Yotkan site |
| S.IV.A.a.39 | Qianyuan zhongbao – small | 2.55 | 22 | – | pas | Purchased at Yotkan site |
| S.IV.A.a.40 | Qianyuan zhongbao – small | 2.63 | 21.5 | forced hole | pas | Purchased at Yotkan site |
| S.IV.A.a.41 | Qianyuan zhongbao – small | 2.13 | 22.5 | forced hole | pas | Purchased at Yotkan site |
| S.IV.A.a.42 | Qianyuan zhongbao – small | 1.90 | 22 | faint | pas | Purchased at Yotkan site |
| S.IV.A.a.43 | Qianyuan zhongbao – small | 1.78 | 22 | forced hole, damaged | pas | Purchased at Yotkan site |
| S.IV.A.a.44 | Qianyuan zhongbao – small | 2.14 | 21.5 | – | pas | Purchased at Yotkan site |
| S.IV.A.a.45 | Qianyuan zhongbao – small | 2.86 | 21.5 | faint | pas | Purchased at Yotkan site |
| S.IV.A.a.46 | Qianyuan zhongbao – small | 1.81 | 21.5 | – | pas | Purchased at Yotkan site |
| S.IV.A.a.47 | Qianyuan zhongbao – small | 1.45 | 20 | damaged | pas | Purchased at Yotkan site |
| S.IV.A.a.48 | Qianyuan zhongbao – small | 2.53 | 21.5 | faint | pas | Purchased at Yotkan site |
| S.IV.A.a.49 | Chinese – unidentified, Tang dynasty | 1.38 | 21.5 | frag. | pas | Purchased at Yotkan site |
| S.IV.A.a.50 | Qian [yuan zhong] bao | 0.80 | – | frag. | pas | Purchased at Yotkan site |
| S.IV.A.a.51 | Qianyuan zhong [bao] – small | 1.50 | 22 | frag. | pas | Purchased at Yotkan site |
| S.IV.A.a.52–53, 58–59 | Chinese – unidentified, Tang dynasty? | 1.87 | 22 | 4 frags (= 1 coin) | pas | Purchased at Yotkan site |
| S.IV.A.a.54 | Chinese – unidentified, Tang dynasty? | 0.74 | – | frag. | pas | Purchased at Yotkan site |
| S.IV.A.a.55 | Chinese – unidentified, Tang dynasty? | 0.86 | – | frag. | pas | Purchased at Yotkan site |
| S.IV.A.a.56 | Chinese – unidentified, Tang dynasty? | 0.95 | – | frag. | pas | Purchased at Yotkan site |
| S.IV.A.a.57 | Chinese – unidentified, Tang dynasty? | 0.44 | – | frag. | pas | Purchased at Yotkan site |
| S.IV.A.a.60 | Chinese – unidentified | 0.55 | – | frag. | pas | Purchased at Yotkan site |
| S.IV.A.a.61 | Chinese – unidentified | 0.31 | – | frag. | pas | Purchased at Yotkan site |
| S.IV.A.a.62 | Unidentified | 0.06 | – | frag. | pas | Purchased at Yotkan site |
| S.IV.A.a.63 | Unidentified | 0.09 | – | frag. | pas | Purchased at Yotkan site |
| S.IV.A.a.64 | Chinese – unidentified | 0.33 | – | frag. | pas | Purchased at Yotkan site |
| S.IV.A.a.65 | Dali yuanbao – small | 2.42 | 22.5 | – | pas | Purchased at Yotkan site |
| S.IV.A.a.66 | Dali yuanbao – small | 2.35 | 22 | – | pas | Purchased at Yotkan site |
| S.IV.A.a.67 | Dali yuanbao – small | 1.64 | 22 | – | pas | Purchased at Yotkan site |
| S.IV.A.a.68 | Dali yuanbao – small | 1.83 | 22 | – | pas | Purchased at Yotkan site |
| S.IV.A.a.69 | Dali yuanbao – small | 1.88 | 22 | – | pas | Purchased at Yotkan site |
| S.IV.A.a.70–72 | [missing: Dali yuanbao] | | | | pas | Purchased at Yotkan site |
| S.IV.A.a.73 | Chinese – unidentified, Tang dynasty? | 2.01 | 21 | 2 frags (= 1 coin) | pas | Purchased at Yotkan site |
| S.IV.A.a.74 | Qianyuan zhongbao – small | 1.80 | 22 | damaged | pas | Purchased at Yotkan site |
| S.IV.A.a.75 | Qianyuan zhongbao – small | 2.42 | 22 | damaged | pas | Purchased at Yotkan site |
| S.IV.A.a.76 | Chinese – unidentified | 2.13 | 19 | with sprue | pas | Purchased at Yotkan site |
| S.IV.A.a.77–78 | [extra: non-coins] | – | – | – | pas | Purchased at Yotkan site |
| S.IV.A.b.1 | Qianyuan zhongbao – small | 2.42 | 22 | – | pas | Purchased at Yotkan site |
| S.IV.A.b.2 | Qianyuan zhongbao – small | 2.54 | 22 | – | pas | Purchased at Yotkan site |
| S.IV.A.b.3 | Qianyuan zhongbao – small | 1.85 | 21 | 2 frags (= 1 coin) | pas | Purchased at Yotkan site |
| S.IV.A.b.4 | Dali yuanbao – large | 2.67 | 23 | – | pas | Purchased at Yotkan site |
| S.IV.A.b.5 | Chinese coin – illegible – corroded | 3.43 | 22 | – | pas | Purchased at Yotkan site |
| S.IV.A.b.6 | [missing: Dali yuanbao] | – | – | – | pas | Purchased at Yotkan site |

| BM no. | Identification | Wt | Diam. | Notes | Acqn | Acquisition/Archaeological context |
|---|---|---|---|---|---|---|
| S.IV.A.c.1 | Qianyuan zhongbao – small | 6.21 | 28.5 | rev. flat | gas | Presented by Khuda-berdi, Yuz-bashi of Yotkan |
| S.IV.A.c.2 | Qianyuan zhongbao – small | 7.72 | 29 | rev. flat | gas | Presented by Khuda-berdi, Yuz-bashi of Yotkan |
| S.IV.A.c.3 | Qianyuan zhongbao – small | 6.54 | 29 | – | gas | Presented by Khuda-berdi, Yuz-bashi of Yotkan |
| S.IV.A.c.4 | [missing: Qianyuan zhongbao] | – | – | – | gas | Presented by Khuda-berdi, Yuz-bashi of Yotkan |
| S.IV.A.c.5 | [extra: Chinese – Song dynasty] | – | – | – | gas | Presented by Khuda-berdi, Yuz-bashi of Yotkan |

| | | | | | | |
|---|---|---|---|---|---|---|
| S.IV.A.d.1 | Kushan coin of Kanishka I – drachm | 4.72 | 18 | – | pas | Purchased at Yotkan |
| S.IV.A.d.2–8 | [missing: Qianyuan zhongbao] | – | – | – | pas | Purchased at Yotkan |
| S.IV.A.d.9–10 | Islamic | – | – | – | pas | Purchased at Yotkan |

| | | | | | | |
|---|---|---|---|---|---|---|
| S.IV.A.e.1 | 'Wuzhu' – full size, illegible | 1.84 | 25 | (H: 10) damaged | pas | From hoard of copper coins, purchased at Yotkan |
| S.IV.A.e.2 | Wuzhu – full size | 1.53 | 25.5 | (H: 10.5) damaged, faint | pas | From hoard of copper coins, purchased at Yotkan |
| S.IV.A.e.3 | Wuzhu – full size | 1.89 | 25 | (H: 10) red, damaged | pas | From hoard of copper coins, purchased at Yotkan |
| S.IV.A.e.4 | Wuzhu – full size | 2.36 | 26 | (H: 9.5) red | pas | From hoard of copper coins, purchased at Yotkan |
| S.IV.A.e.5 | Wuzhu – full size | 2.20 | 25.5 | (H: 9.5) damaged | pas | From hoard of copper coins, purchased at Yotkan |
| S.IV.A.e.6 | Wuzhu – full size | 1.47 | 25.5 | (H: 9.5) red, damaged, thin | pas | From hoard of copper coins, purchased at Yotkan |
| S.IV.A.e.7 | Wuzhu – without rim | 2.81 | 23 | (H: 9.5) red, thick | pas | From hoard of copper coins, purchased at Yotkan |
| S.IV.A.e.8 | 'Wuzhu' – illegible | 1.15 | 25 | (H: 10.5) red, damaged | pas | From hoard of copper coins, purchased at Yotkan |
| S.IV.A.e.9 | Wuzhu – without rim | 1.76 | 24 | (H: 9.5) red, faint | pas | From hoard of copper coins, purchased at Yotkan |
| S.IV.A.e.10 | 'Wuzhu' – illegible | 1.50 | 24 | (H: 10) | pas | From hoard of copper coins, purchased at Yotkan |
| S.IV.A.e.11 | 'Wuzhu' – illegible | 1.40 | 23.5 | (H: 10.5) red | pas | From hoard of copper coins, purchased at Yotkan |
| S.IV.A.e.12 | Wuzhu – without rim, lines on rev. | 2.33 | 23.5 | (H: 10) red | pas | From hoard of copper coins, purchased at Yotkan |
| S.IV.A.e.13 | Wuzhu – without rim | 1.23 | 23 | (H: 10) red, faint | pas | From hoard of copper coins, purchased at Yotkan |
| S.IV.A.e.14 | Wuzhu – without rim | 1.77 | 23 | (H: 9.5) red, faint | pas | From hoard of copper coins, purchased at Yotkan |
| S.IV.A.e.15 | 'Wuzhu' – illegible | 1.32 | 23 | (H: 9.5) thin | pas | From hoard of copper coins, purchased at Yotkan |
| S.IV.A.e.16 | Wuzhu – clipped, cuts through inscription | 1.33 | 22 | (H: 9.5) red, faint | pas | From hoard of copper coins, purchased at Yotkan |
| S.IV.A.e.17 | 'Wuzhu' – illegible, lines on rev. | 1.99 | 23 | (H: 9.5) | pas | From hoard of copper coins, purchased at Yotkan |
| S.IV.A.e.18 | 'Wuzhu' – illegible | 1.42 | 23 | (H: 10) red | pas | From hoard of copper coins, purchased at Yotkan |
| S.IV.A.e.19 | 'Wuzhu' – illegible | 1.30 | 22.5 | (H: 9.5) red | pas | From hoard of copper coins, purchased at Yotkan |
| S.IV.A.e.20 | 'Wuzhu' – illegible | 1.28 | 22.5 | (H: 10) red | pas | From hoard of copper coins, purchased at Yotkan |

| BM no. | Identification | Wt | Diam. | Notes | Acqn | Acquisition/Archaeological context |
|---|---|---|---|---|---|---|
| S.IV.A.e.21 | 'Wuzhu' – illegible | 1.27 | 23 | (H: 9.5) | pas | From hoard of copper coins, purchased at Yotkan |
| S.IV.A.e.22 | 'Wuzhu' – illegible | 1.48 | 23 | (H: 10) red | pas | From hoard of copper coins, purchased at Yotkan |
| S.IV.A.e.23 | Wuzhu – clipped, cuts through inscription | 1.47 | 22 | (H: 10) red, bent | pas | From hoard of copper coins, purchased at Yotkan |
| S.IV.A.e.24 | Wuzhu – clipped, cuts through inscription | 1.00 | 22 | (H: 9.5) red | pas | From hoard of copper coins, purchased at Yotkan |
| S.IV.A.e.25 | 'Wuzhu' – illegible | 0.93 | 21 | (H: 9.5) red, damaged | pas | From hoard of copper coins, purchased at Yotkan |
| S.IV.A.e.26 | 'Wuzhu' – illegible | 1.06 | 21 | (H: 9.5) red | pas | From hoard of copper coins, purchased at Yotkan |
| S.IV.A.e.27 | 'Wuzhu' – illegible | 1.07 | 21 | (H: 10) red | pas | From hoard of copper coins, purchased at Yotkan |
| S.IV.A.e.28 | 'Wuzhu' – illegible | 1.13 | 20.5 | (H: 9.5) red | pas | From hoard of copper coins, purchased at Yotkan |
| S.IV.A.e.29 | 'Wuzhu' – illegible | 1.32 | 21 | (H: 10) red | pas | From hoard of copper coins, purchased at Yotkan |
| S.IV.A.e.30 | 'Wuzhu' – illegible | 1.10 | 22 | (H: 9.5) red | pas | From hoard of copper coins, purchased at Yotkan |
| S.IV.A.e.31 | Wuzhu – clipped, cuts through inscription | 1.34 | 21 | (H: 9.5) red, faint | pas | From hoard of copper coins, purchased at Yotkan |
| S.IV.A.e.32 | 'Wuzhu' – illegible | 0.95 | 21.5 | (H: 9.5) red | pas | From hoard of copper coins, purchased at Yotkan |
| S.IV.A.e.33 | 'Wuzhu' – illegible | 1.03 | 20.5 | (H: 9.5) red | pas | From hoard of copper coins, purchased at Yotkan |
| S.IV.A.e.34 | 'Wuzhu' – illegible | 0.81 | 20 | (H: 10) red | pas | From hoard of copper coins, purchased at Yotkan |
| S.IV.A.e.35 | 'Wuzhu' – illegible | 0.92 | 21.5 | (H: 10.5) red, damaged | pas | From hoard of copper coins, purchased at Yotkan |
| S.IV.A.e.36 | Wuzhu – clipped, cuts through inscription | 1.21 | 21 | (H: 9) | pas | From hoard of copper coins, purchased at Yotkan |
| S.IV.A.e.37 | 'Wuzhu' – illegible | 1.63 | 21.5 | (H: 10) red | pas | From hoard of copper coins, purchased at Yotkan |
| S.IV.A.e.38 | 'Wuzhu' – illegible | 1.24 | 20.5 | (H: 10) red | pas | From hoard of copper coins, purchased at Yotkan |
| S.IV.A.e.39 | 'Wuzhu' – illegible | 1.18 | 21.5 | (H: 9.5) | pas | From hoard of copper coins, purchased at Yotkan |
| S.IV.A.e.40 | 'Wuzhu' – illegible | 1.09 | 20.5 | (H: 9.5) | pas | From hoard of copper coins, purchased at Yotkan |
| S.IV.A.e.41 | 'Wuzhu' – illegible | 1.00 | 20.5 | (H: 10) | pas | From hoard of copper coins, purchased at Yotkan |
| S.IV.A.e.42 | 'Wuzhu' – illegible | 1.12 | 25 | (H: 10) | pas | From hoard of copper coins, purchased at Yotkan |
| S.IV.A.e.43 | 'Wuzhu' – illegible | 0.65 | 20 | (H: 10) thin | pas | From hoard of copper coins, purchased at Yotkan |
| S.IV.A.e.44 | Wuzhu – clipped, cuts through inscription | 0.68 | 18 | (H: 10) red | pas | From hoard of copper coins, purchased at Yotkan |
| S.IV.A.e.45 | 'Wuzhu' – illegible | 0.66 | 18.5 | (H: 10) red | pas | From hoard of copper coins, purchased at Yotkan |
| S.IV.A.e.46 | 'Wuzhu' – illegible | 0.88 | 20 | (H: 10.5) | pas | From hoard of copper coins, purchased at Yotkan |
| S.IV.A.e.47 | Wuzhu – clipped, cuts through rim | 0.80 | 20 | (H: 9.5) red, faint | pas | From hoard of copper coins, purchased at Yotkan |
| S.IV.A.e.48 | 'Wuzhu' – illegible | 0.77 | 20.5 | (H: 10) red | pas | From hoard of copper coins, purchased at Yotkan |

## S.IV.B: PURCHASED AT KHOTAN, MOST PROBABLY BROUGHT FROM YOTKAN

| BM no. | Identification | Wt | Diam. | Notes | Acqn | Acquisition/Archaeological context |
|---|---|---|---|---|---|---|
| S.IV.B.a.1 | Wuzhu | 2.48 | 25.5 | (H: 10) red, scyphate | p | Probably from Yotkan site, purchased at Khotan |
| S.IV.B.a.2–4 | [mising: Wuzhu] | – | – | – | p | Probably from Yotkan site, purchased at Khotan |
| S.IV.B.a.5 | Chinese coin – tin – unidentified | 0.46 | 19 | elongated hole? | p | Probably from Yotkan site, purchased at Khotan |
| S.IV.B.a.6 | Lead – unidentified, pierced (non-coin?) | 9.77 | 21 | corroded | p | Probably from Yotkan site, purchased at Khotan |
| S.IV.B.a.7 | (non–coin) | – | – | – | p | Probably from Yotkan site, purchased at Khotan |
| S.IV.B.a.8 | Qianyuan zhongbao – small | 1.84 | 22 | damaged | p | Probably from Yotkan site, purchased at Khotan |
| S.IV.B.a.9 | Qianyuan zhongbao – medium | 2.78 | 24.5 | – | p | Probably from Yotkan site, purchased at Khotan |
| S.IV.B.a.10 | Qianyuan zhongbao – small | 1.90 | 22 | – | p | Probably from Yotkan site, purchased at Khotan |
| S.IV.B.a.11 | Qianyuan zhongbao – small | 2.01 | 22 | – | p | Probably from Yotkan site, purchased at Khotan |
| S.IV.B.a.12 | Chinese – unidentified, Tang dynasty? | 2.40 | 22 | – | p | Probably from Yotkan site, purchased at Khotan |
| S.IV.B.a.13 | Jianzhong tongbao – small | 1.55 | 21.5 | – | p | Probably from Yotkan site, purchased at Khotan |
| S.IV.B.a.14 | [missing: Qianyuan zhongbao] | – | – | – | p | Probably from Yotkan site, purchased at Khotan |
| S.IV.B.a.15 | Dali yuanbao | 1.52 | 22 | frag. | p | Probably from Yotkan site, purchased at Khotan |

| | | | | | | |
|---|---|---|---|---|---|---|
| S.IV.B.b.1 | Sino-Kharoshthi coin (Cribb 1–6) | 1.54 | 20 | – | p | Probably from Yotkan site, purchased at Khotan |
| S.IV.B.b.2 | Sino-Kharoshthi coin (Cribb 1–6) | 1.86 | 16 | – | p | Probably from Yotkan site, purchased at Khotan |
| S.IV.B.b.3 (OR.0429) | Sino-Kharoshthi coin (Cribb 6) | 2.77 | 21×19 | overstruck on Hermaius imitation | p | Probably from Yotkan site, purchased at Khotan |
| S.IV.B.b.4 (OR.0394) | Sino-Kharoshthi coin (Cribb 7–8) | 11.69 | 25 | – | p | Probably from Yotkan site, purchased at Khotan |
| S.IV.B.b.5 (OR.0436) | Sino-Kharoshthi coin (Cribb 10) | 1.71 | 21×18 | – | p | Probably from Yotkan site, purchased at Khotan |
| S.IV.B.b.6 (OR.0439) | Sino-Kharoshthi coin (Cribb 12) | 1.25 | 17 | – | p | Probably from Yotkan site, purchased at Khotan |
| S.IV.B.b.7 | Kaiyuan tongbao | 2.82 | 25 | serrated edge | p | Probably from Yotkan site, purchased at Khotan |
| S.IV.B.b.8 | Qianyuan zhongbao – large | 6.21 | 29 | red, corroded | p | Probably from Yotkan site, purchased at Khotan |
| S.IV.B.b.9 | Qianyuan zhongbao – small | 1.66 | 21 | forced hole | p | Probably from Yotkan site, purchased at Khotan |
| S.IV.B.b.10 | Qianyuan zhongbao – small | 1.64 | 22.5 | red | p | Probably from Yotkan site, purchased at Khotan |

| | | | | | | |
|---|---|---|---|---|---|---|
| S.IV.B.c.1 | Sino-Kharoshthi coin (Cribb 2) | 3.28 | 19 | – | p | Probably from Yotkan site, purchased at Khotan |
| S.IV.B.c.2 (OR.0440) | Sino-Kharoshthi coin (Cribb 12) | 5.47 | 18 | – | p | Probably from Yotkan site, purchased at Khotan |

| BM no. | Identification | Wt | Diam. | Notes | Acqn | Acquisition/Archaeological context |
|---|---|---|---|---|---|---|
| S.IV.B.c.3 (OR.0438) | Sino-Kharoshthi coin (Cribb 12) | 1.17 | 17×16 | – | p | Probably from Yotkan site, purchased at Khotan |
| S.IV.B.c.4 (OR.0412) | Sino-Kharoshthi coin (Cribb 2) | 3.08 | 19×18.5 | – | p | Probably from Yotkan site, purchased at Khotan |
| S.IV.B.c.5 (OR.0417) | Sino-Kharoshthi coin (Cribb 2) | 3.16 | 19 | – | p | Probably from Yotkan site, purchased at Khotan |
| S.IV.B.c.6 | Wuzhu – without rim, dot above wu | 2.52 | 22 | (H: 9.5) | p | Probably from Yotkan site, purchased at Khotan |
| S.IV.B.c.7 | Wuzhu – full size | 2.06 | 26 | (H: 10) | p | Probably from Yotkan site, purchased at Khotan |
| S.IV.B.c.8 | Wuzhu – full size | 2.35 | 25.5 | (H: 9.5) | p | Probably from Yotkan site, purchased at Khotan |
| S.IV.B.c.9 | Wuzhu – full size (small characters) | 2.73 | 26 | (H: 9.5) | p | Probably from Yotkan site, purchased at Khotan |
| S.IV.B.c.10 | Wuzhu – full size | 1.99 | 25 | (H: 9.5) | p | Probably from Yotkan site, purchased at Khotan |
| S.IV.B.c.11 | Wuzhu – full size | 1.98 | 25.5 | (H: 10.5) | p | Probably from Yotkan site, purchased at Khotan |
| S.IV.B.c.12 | Wuzhu – without inscription | 1.41 | 23 | (H: 9.5) | p | Probably from Yotkan site, purchased at Khotan |
| S.IV.B.c.13 | Wuzhu – full size | 2.27 | 25.5 | (H: 10) | p | Probably from Yotkan site, purchased at Khotan |
| S.IV.B.c.14 | Wuzhu – no inscription | 2.07 | 23.5 | (H: 9.5) | p | Probably from Yotkan site, purchased at Khotan |
| S.IV.B.c.15 | Wuzhu – without rim, incised + on rev. | 1.77 | 24.5 | (H: 9.5) | p | Probably from Yotkan site, purchased at Khotan |
| S.IV.B.c.16 | Wuzhu – clipped, cuts through inscription | 1.27 | 20 | (H: 9.5) faint | p | Probably from Yotkan site, purchased at Khotan |
| S.IV.B.c.17 | Wuzhu – clipped, cuts through inscription | 1.18 | 23 | (H: 10.5) forced hole, faint | p | Probably from Yotkan site, purchased at Khotan |
| S.IV.B.c.18 | Wuzhu – clipped, cuts through inscription | 1.51 | 22 | (H: 9.5) | p | Probably from Yotkan site, purchased at Khotan |
| S.IV.B.c.19 | Wuzhu – without full rim | 1.81 | 25 | (H: 10.5) | p | Probably from Yotkan site, purchased at Khotan |
| S.IV.B.c.20 | Wuzhu – small, small characters | 1.84 | 22 | (H: 7.5) | p | Probably from Yotkan site, purchased at Khotan |
| S.IV.B.c.21 | Wuzhu – without rim | 2.22 | 23 | (H: 9) | p | Probably from Yotkan site, purchased at Khotan |
| S.IV.B.c.22 | Wuzhu – without rim | 2.12 | 23 | (H: 9.5) | p | Probably from Yotkan site, purchased at Khotan |
| S.IV.B.c.23 | Wuzhu – clipped, cuts through rim | 1.17 | 21 | (H: 9.5) | p | Probably from Yotkan site, purchased at Khotan |
| S.IV.B.c.24 | Wuzhu – clipped, cuts through rim | 0.93 | 17 | (H: 9) | p | Probably from Yotkan site, purchased at Khotan |
| S.IV.B.c.25 | Wuzhu – without rim | 1.87 | 23 | (H: 9) | p | Probably from Yotkan site, purchased at Khotan |
| S.IV.B.c.26 | Wuzhu – without rim | 1.68 | 24 | (H: 9) | p | Probably from Yotkan site, purchased at Khotan |
| S.IV.B.c.27 | Wuzhu – without rim | 1.31 | 22.5 | (H: 10) damaged | p | Probably from Yotkan site, purchased at Khotan |
| S.IV.B.c.28 | Qianyuan zhongbao – large | 7.21 | 28.5 | – | p | Probably from Yotkan site, purchased at Khotan |
| S.IV.B.c.29 | Qianyuan zhongbao – medium | 5.36 | 26.5 | misaligned | p | Probably from Yotkan site, purchased at Khotan |

| BM no. | Identification | Wt | Diam. | Notes | Acqn | Acquisition/Archaeological context |
|---|---|---|---|---|---|---|
| S.IV.B.c.30 | Qianyuan zhongbao – medium | 3.36 | 24.5 | – | p | Probably from Yotkan site, purchased at Khotan |
| S.IV.B.c.31 | Qianyuan zhongbao – small | 2.40 | 22 | forced hole | p | Probably from Yotkan site, purchased at Khotan |
| S.IV.B.c.32 | Qianyuan zhongbao – small | 2.06 | 22 | – | p | Probably from Yotkan site, purchased at Khotan |
| S.IV.B.c.33 | Qianyuan zhongbao – small | 2.29 | 21.5 | – | p | Probably from Yotkan site, purchased at Khotan |
| S.IV.B.c.34 | Qianyuan zhongbao – small | 1.68 | 21.5 | misaligned | p | Probably from Yotkan site, purchased at Khotan |
| S.IV.B.c.35 | Qianyuan zhongbao – small | 2.68 | 22 | – | p | Probably from Yotkan site, purchased at Khotan |
| S.IV.B.c.36 | Qianyuan zhongbao – small | 1.97 | 21.5 | misaligned | p | Probably from Yotkan site, purchased at Khotan |
| S.IV.B.c.37 | Chinese coin – unidentified, Tang dynasty? | 2.14 | 21.5 | – | p | Probably from Yotkan site, purchased at Khotan |
| S.IV.B.c.38 | [missing: Qianyuan zhongbao] | – | – | – | p | Probably from Yotkan site, purchased at Khotan |
| S.IV.B.c.39 | Dali yuanbao – small | 2.25 | 22 | – | p | Probably from Yotkan site, purchased at Khotan |
| S.IV.B.c.40 | [extra: Dali yuanbao – small] | 2.58 | 22 | damaged rim | p | Probably from Yotkan site, purchased at Khotan |
| S.IV.B.c.41–52 | Islamic | – | – | – | p | Probably from Yotkan site, purchased at Khotan |
| S.IV.B.c.53 | [extra: Qianyuan zhongbao – large] | 9.07 | 30 | corroded | p | Probably from Yotkan site, purchased at Khotan |
| S.IV.B.c.54 | [extra: Chinese coin – unidentified] | 10.46 | 31 | corroded | p | Probably from Yotkan site, purchased at Khotan |

| | | | | | | |
|---|---|---|---|---|---|---|
| S.IV.B.d.1 | Sino-Kharoshthi coin (Cribb 3) | 2.44 | 18 | – | p | Probably from Yotkan site, purchased at Khotan |
| S.IV.B.d.2 | Sino-Kharoshthi coin (Cribb 4) | 3.35 | 18 | – | p | Probably from Yotkan site, purchased at Khotan |
| S.IV.B.d.3 | Sino-Kharoshthi coin (Cribb 4) | 2.12 | 18 | – | p | Probably from Yotkan site, purchased at Khotan |
| S.IV.B.d.4 | Kushan coin of Kanishka – drachm | 3.31 | 16 | – | p | Probably from Yotkan site, purchased at Khotan |
| S.IV.B.d.5 (OR.0432) | Sino-Kharoshthi coin (Cribb 10) | 2.81 | 21×20 | – | p | Probably from Yotkan site, purchased at Khotan |
| S.IV.B.d.6 (OR.0425) | Sino-Kharoshthi coin (Cribb 5) | 2.89 | 19×18 | – | p | Probably from Yotkan site, purchased at Khotan |
| S.IV.B.d.7 (OR.0423) | Sino-Kharoshthi coin (Cribb 1) | 1.39 | 17 | – | p | Probably from Yotkan site, purchased at Khotan |
| S.IV.B.d.8 (OR.0395) | Sino-Kharoshthi coin (Cribb 4) | 2.74 | 21×19 | – | p | Probably from Yotkan site, purchased at Khotan |
| S.IV.B.d.9 (OR.0397) | Sino-Kharoshthi coin (Cribb 4) | 3.37 | 19 | – | p | Probably from Yotkan site, purchased at Khotan |
| S.IV.B.d.10 (OR.0404) | Sino-Kharoshthi coin (Cribb 2) | 3.00 | 18 | – | p | Probably from Yotkan site, purchased at Khotan |
| S.IV.B.d.11 (OR.0409) | Sino-Kharoshthi coin (Cribb 2) | 3.77 | 19×18 | – | p | Probably from Yotkan site, purchased at Khotan |
| S.IV.B.d.12 (OR.0414) | Sino-Kharoshthi coin (Cribb 2) | 2.95 | 20×19 | – | p | Probably from Yotkan site, purchased at Khotan |
| S.IV.B.d.13 (OR.0433) | Sino-Kharoshthi coin (Cribb 10) | 2.66 | 20 | – | p | Probably from Yotkan site, purchased at Khotan |

| BM no. | Identification | Wt | Diam. | Notes | Acqn | Acquisition/Archaeological context |
|---|---|---|---|---|---|---|
| S.IV.B.d.14 (OR.0434) | Sino-Kharoshthi coin (Cribb 10) | 2.45 | 19×18 | – | p | Probably from Yotkan site, purchased at Khotan |
| S.IV.B.d.15 | Kaiyuan tongbao | 3.40 | 25 | – | p | Probably from Yotkan site, purchased at Khotan |
| S.IV.B.d.16 | Qianyuan zhongbao – medium | 2.37 | 24 | – | p | Probably from Yotkan site, purchased at Khotan |
| S.IV.B.d.17 | Dali yuanbao – small | 2.86 | 23 | – | p | Probably from Yotkan site, purchased at Khotan |
| S.IV.B.d.18 | Dali yuanbao – large | 2.93 | 24 | – | p | Probably from Yotkan site, purchased at Khotan |
| S.IV.B.d.19 | Dali yuanbao – large | 3.13 | 24 | – | p | Probably from Yotkan site, purchased at Khotan |
| S.IV.B.d.20–21 | Chinese – Song dynasty | – | – | – | p | Probably from Yotkan site, purchased at Khotan |
| S.IV.B.d.22–23 | Islamic | – | – | – | p | Probably from Yotkan site, purchased at Khotan |
| S.IV.B.e.1 | (non–coin) | – | – | – | p | Probably from Yotkan site, purchased at Khotan |
| S.IV.B.e.2 | Qianyuan zhongbao – large | 6.26 | 29 | – | p | Probably from Yotkan site, purchased at Khotan |
| S.IV.B.e.3 | Qianyuan zhongbao – small | 1.97 | 22 | – | p | Probably from Yotkan site, purchased at Khotan |
| S.IV.B.e.4 | Qianyuan zhongbao – small | 2.08 | 21 | – | p | Probably from Yotkan site, purchased at Khotan |
| S.IV.B.e.5–6 | [missing: Qianyuan zhongbao] | – | – | – | p | Probably from Yotkan site, purchased at Khotan |
| S.IV.B.e.7 | Kaiyuan tongbao | 2.65 | 24.5 | damaged, misaligned | p | Probably from Yotkan site, purchased at Khotan |
| S.IV.B.e.8 | Chinese coin – Qing dynasty | – | – | – | p | Probably from Yotkan site, purchased at Khotan |
| S.IV.B.e.9–13 | [extra: Islamic] | – | – | – | p | Probably from Yotkan site, purchased at Khotan |
| S.IV.B.e.14 | [extra: coin? – unidentified] | 0.58 | – | frag. | p | Probably from Yotkan site, purchased at Khotan |
| S.IV.B.e.15 | [extra: Wu[zhu]] | 0.22 | – | frag. | p | Probably from Yotkan site, purchased at Khotan |
| S.IV.B.e.16 | [extra: Islamic?] | – | – | – | p | Probably from Yotkan site, purchased at Khotan |
| S.IV.B.f.1 | 'Wuzhu' – illegible | 0.47 | – | frag. | p | Probably from Yotkan site, purchased at Khotan |
| S.IV.B.f.2 | 'Wuzhu' – illegible | 0.48 | – | frag. | p | Probably from Yotkan site, purchased at Khotan |
| S.IV.B.f.3 | (impression in clay casing around coin?) | 2.61 | – | 6 frags | p | Probably from Yotkan site, purchased at Khotan |
| S.IV.B.f.4 | Qianyuan zhongbao – small | 1.49 | 21.5 | 2 frags (= 1 coin) | p | Probably from Yotkan site, purchased at Khotan |
| S.IV.B.f.5 | Chinese coin – unidentified | 6.53 | 28 | corroded | p | Probably from Yotkan site, purchased at Khotan |
| S.IV.B.f.6–7 | Islamic | – | – | – | p | Probably from Yotkan site, purchased at Khotan |

| BM no. | Identification | Wt | Diam. | Notes | Acqn | Acquisition/Archaeological context |
|---|---|---|---|---|---|---|
| S.IV.B.g.1 | [missing: Sino-Kharoshthi coin] | – | – | – | p | Probably from Yotkan site, purchased at Khotan |
| S.IV.B.g.2 | 'Wuzhu' – illegible | 1.23 | 20 | (H: 9.5) uncleaned | p | Probably from Yotkan site, purchased at Khotan |
| S.IV.B.g.3 | 'Wuzhu' – illegible | 1.30 | 23 | (H: 9.5) uncleaned | p | Probably from Yotkan site, purchased at Khotan |
| S.IV.B.g.4 | 'Wuzhu' – illegible | 1.95 | 23 | (H: 8.5) uncleaned | p | Probably from Yotkan site, purchased at Khotan |
| S.IV.B.g.5 | Qianyuan zhongbao – large | 6.15 | 29 | misaligned, uncleaned | p | Probably from Yotkan site, purchased at Khotan |
| S.IV.B.g.6 | Qianyuan zhongbao – small | 2.12 | 21 | uncleaned | p | Probably from Yotkan site, purchased at Khotan |
| S.IV.B.g.7 | Qianyuan zhongbao – small | 3.04 | 21 | uncleaned | p | Probably from Yotkan site, purchased at Khotan |
| S.IV.B.g.8 | Qianyuan zhongbao – small | 2.17 | 22 | forced hole, uncleaned | p | Probably from Yotkan site, purchased at Khotan |
| S.IV.B.g.9 | Qianyuan zhongbao – small | 1.67 | 22 | frag., uncleaned | p | Probably from Yotkan site, purchased at Khotan |
| S.IV.B.g.10 | Qianyuan zhongbao – small | 2.20 | 22 | forced hole, uncleaned | p | Probably from Yotkan site, purchased at Khotan |
| S.IV.B.g.11 | Qianyuan zhongbao – small | 1.99 | 21 | uncleaned | p | Probably from Yotkan site, purchased at Khotan |
| S.IV.B.g.12 | Qianyuan zhongbao – small | 2.38 | 21 | uncleaned | p | Probably from Yotkan site, purchased at Khotan |
| S.IV.B.g.13 | Qianyuan zhongbao – small | 2.65 | 22 | red, uncleaned | p | Probably from Yotkan site, purchased at Khotan |
| S.IV.B.g.14 | Qianyuan zhongbao – small | 2.93 | 22 | uncleaned | p | Probably from Yotkan site, purchased at Khotan |
| S.IV.B.g.15 | Qianyuan zhongbao – small | 2.17 | 22 | uncleaned | p | Probably from Yotkan site, purchased at Khotan |
| S.IV.B.g.16 | Qianyuan zhongbao – small | 2.99 | 21 | uncleaned | p | Probably from Yotkan site, purchased at Khotan |
| S.IV.B.g.17 | Qianyuan zhongbao – small | 2.54 | 21 | uncleaned | p | Probably from Yotkan site, purchased at Khotan |
| S.IV.B.g.18 | Qianyuan zhongbao – small | 1.96 | 21 | uncleaned | p | Probably from Yotkan site, purchased at Khotan |
| S.IV.B.g.19 | Chinese coin – unidentified, Tang dynasty? | 3.05 | 22 | uncleaned | p | Probably from Yotkan site, purchased at Khotan |
| S.IV.B.g.20 | Chinese coin – unidentified, Tang dynasty? | 2.26 | 21 | uncleaned | p | Probably from Yotkan site, purchased at Khotan |
| S.IV.B.g.21 | Qianyuan zhongbao – small | 2.19 | 21 | uncleaned | p | Probably from Yotkan site, purchased at Khotan |
| S.IV.B.g.22 | Chinese coin – unidentified, Tang dynasty? | 3.17 | 22 | uncleaned | p | Probably from Yotkan site, purchased at Khotan |
| S.IV.B.g.23 | Chinese coin– unidentified | 3.54 | 26 | 3 frags (= 1 coin) | p | Probably from Yotkan site, purchased at Khotan |
| S.IV.B.g.24–25 | [missing: Qianyuan zhongbao] | – | – | – | p | Probably from Yotkan site, purchased at Khotan |
| S.IV.B.g.26 | Dali yuanbao – small | 2.25 | 22 | – | p | Probably from Yotkan site, purchased at Khotan |
| S.IV.B.g.27 | Dali yuanbao – small | 2.78 | 22 | – | p | Probably from Yotkan site, purchased at Khotan |
| S.IV.B.g.28 | Dali yuanbao – small | 2.62 | 19 | forced hole | p | Probably from Yotkan site, purchased at Khotan |

| BM no. | Identification | Wt | Diam. | Notes | Acqn | Acquisition/Archaeological context |
|---|---|---|---|---|---|---|
| S.IV.B.g.29 | Chinese coin – Song dynasty | – | – | – | p | Probably from Yotkan site, purchased at Khotan |
| S.IV.B.g.30 | [extra: uncertain] | 1.45 | 14 | – | p | – |
| S.IV.B.g.31 | [extra: uncertain] | 0.91 | 15 | frag. | p | – |
| S.IV.B.g.32 | [extra: Chinese coin – unidentified] | 4.29 | 25 | corroded | p | – |

| | | | | | | |
|---|---|---|---|---|---|---|
| S.IV.B.h.1 (OR.0422) | Sino-Kharoshthi coin (Cribb 1) | 3.59 | 20×19 | – | p | Probably from Yotkan site, purchased at Khotan |
| S.IV.B.h.2–3 | [missing: Sino-Kharoshthi coin] | – | – | – | p | Probably from Yotkan site, purchased at Khotan |
| S.IV.B.h.4 | Qianyuan zhongbao – small | 2.95 | 21 | misaligned | p | Probably from Yotkan site, purchased at Khotan |
| S.IV.B.h.5 | Dali yuanbao – small | 2.73 | 21.5 | red | p | Probably from Yotkan site, purchased at Khotan |
| S.IV.B.h.6 | [extra: Chinese coin – unidentified | 1.65 | 18 | red, corroded | p | Probably from Yotkan site, purchased at Khotan |

| | | | | | | |
|---|---|---|---|---|---|---|
| S.IV.B.i.1 | [uncertain] | 2.03 | – | frag., pierced | p | Probably from Yotkan site, purchased at Khotan |
| S.IV.B.i.2 | Kushan coin of Kanishka I – drachm | 3.38 | 17 | – | p | Probably from Yotkan site, purchased at Khotan |
| S.IV.B.i.3 | Wuzhu – full size | 2.19 | 26 | (H: 9.5) red | p | Probably from Yotkan site, purchased at Khotan |
| S.IV.B.i.4 | Wuzhu – full size | 2.13 | 25 | (H: 9.5) red, damaged | p | Probably from Yotkan site, purchased at Khotan |
| S.IV.B.i.5 | Wuzhu – full size | 2.21 | 25 | (H: 9.5) red | p | Probably from Yotkan site, purchased at Khotan |
| S.IV.B.i.6 | Wuzhu – full size | 2.03 | 25 | (H: 9.5) red, damaged | p | Probably from Yotkan site, purchased at Khotan |
| S.IV.B.i.7 | Wuzhu – full size | 1.85 | 25 | (H: 9.5) red | p | Probably from Yotkan site, purchased at Khotan |
| S.IV.B.i.8 | Wuzhu – full size | 1.30 | 25 | (H: 9.5) red, damaged | p | Probably from Yotkan site, purchased at Khotan |
| S.IV.B.i.9 | Wuzhu – full size | 1.99 | 26 | (H: 10.5) red | p | Probably from Yotkan site, purchased at Khotan |
| S.IV.B.i.10 | 'Wuzhu' – illegible, without full rim | 1.91 | 24.5 | (H: 9.5) red | p | Probably from Yotkan site, purchased at Khotan |
| S.IV.B.i.11 | Wuzhu – full size | 2.10 | 25.5 | (H: 10) red | p | Probably from Yotkan site, purchased at Khotan |
| S.IV.B.i.12 | 'Wuzhu' – illegible | 1.08 | 22 | (H: 8.5) corroded | p | Probably from Yotkan site, purchased at Khotan |
| S.IV.B.i.13 | 'Wuzhu' – illegible | 1.28 | 22 | (H: 10.5) red | p | Probably from Yotkan site, purchased at Khotan |
| S.IV.B.i.14 | Wuzhu – Northern Wei? | 1.78 | 23 | restored (H: 8.5) | p | Probably from Yotkan site, purchased at Khotan |
| S.IV.B.i.15 | Kaiyuan tongbao | 2.61 | 24.5 | – | p | Probably from Yotkan site, purchased at Khotan |
| S.IV.B.i.16 | Qianyuan zhongbao – large | 9.03 | 30 | – | p | Probably from Yotkan site, purchased at Khotan |
| S.IV.B.i.17 | Qianyuan zhongbao – large | 7.01 | 29 | – | p | Probably from Yotkan site, purchased at Khotan |
| S.IV.B.i.18 | Qianyuan zhongbao – large | 6.42 | 29 | – | p | Probably from Yotkan site, purchased at Khotan |
| S.IV.B.i.19 | Qianyuan zhongbao – large | 6.39 | 29 | – | p | Probably from Yotkan site, purchased at Khotan |

| BM no. | Identification | Wt | Diam. | Notes | Acqn | Acquisition/Archaeological context |
|---|---|---|---|---|---|---|
| S.IV.B.i.20 | Qianyuan zhongbao – large | 6.38 | 28.5 | misaligned, forced hole | p | Probably from Yotkan site, purchased at Khotan |
| S.IV.B.i.21 | Qianyuan zhongbao – large | 5.95 | 28.5 | misaligned | p | Probably from Yotkan site, purchased at Khotan |
| S.IV.B.i.22 | Qianyuan zhongbao – large | 6.21 | 29 | – | p | Probably from Yotkan site, purchased at Khotan |
| S.IV.B.i.23 | Qianyuan zhongbao – large | 6.05 | 28.5 | – | p | Probably from Yotkan site, purchased at Khotan |
| S.IV.B.i.24 | Qianyuan zhongbao – large | 4.78 | 29 | – | p | Probably from Yotkan site, purchased at Khotan |
| S.IV.B.i.25 | Qianyuan zhongbao – large | 6.09 | 28.5 | – | p | Probably from Yotkan site, purchased at Khotan |
| S.IV.B.i.26 | Qianyuan zhongbao – large | 4.74 | 28.5 | – | p | Probably from Yotkan site, purchased at Khotan |
| S.IV.B.i.27 | Qianyuan zhongbao – small | 2.33 | 22 | forced hole | p | Probably from Yotkan site, purchased at Khotan |
| S.IV.B.i.28 | Qianyuan zhongbao – small | 1.74 | 22 | – | p | Probably from Yotkan site, purchased at Khotan |
| S.IV.B.i.29 | Qianyuan zhongbao – small | 2.30 | 21.5 | – | p | Probably from Yotkan site, purchased at Khotan |
| S.IV.B.i.30 | Qianyuan zhongbao – small | 1.73 | 21.5 | misaligned | p | Probably from Yotkan site, purchased at Khotan |
| S.IV.B.i.31 | Qianyuan zhongbao – small | 1.96 | 20 | – | p | Probably from Yotkan site, purchased at Khotan |
| S.IV.B.i.32 | Chinese – unidentified, Tang dynasty? | 2.38 | 21.5 | misaligned | p | Probably from Yotkan site, purchased at Khotan |
| S.IV.B.i.33 | Wuzhu – clipped, cuts through inscription | 1.34 | 16.5 | (H: 10) | p | Probably from Yotkan site, purchased at Khotan |
| S.IV.B.i.34 | Huoquan | 0.64 | 22 | (H: 6.5) | p | Probably from Yotkan site, purchased at Khotan |
| S.IV.B.i.35 | Dali yuanbao – large | 3.42 | 23 | misaligned, forced hole | p | Probably from Yotkan site, purchased at Khotan |
| S.IV.B.i.36–40 | Islamic | – | – | – | p | Probably from Yotkan site, purchased at Khotan |
| S.IV.B.i.41–42 | Chinese – Qing dynasty | – | – | – | p | Probably from Yotkan site, purchased at Khotan |
| S.IV.B.i.43–45 | [extra: Chinese – Song dynasty] | – | – | – | p | Probably from Yotkan site, purchased at Khotan |
| S.IV.B.i.46 | [extra: Islamic] | – | – | – | p | Probably from Yotkan site, purchased at Khotan |

| | | | | | | |
|---|---|---|---|---|---|---|
| S.IV.B.j.1 (OR.0393) | Sino-Kharoshthi coin (Cribb 7–8) | 14.17 | 26×24 | – | p | Probably from Yotkan site, purchased at Khotan |
| S.IV.B.j.2 (OR.0383) | Sino-Kharoshthi coin (Cribb 7) | 10.24 | 25 | – | p | Probably from Yotkan site, purchased at Khotan |
| S.IV.B.j.3 (OR.0385) | Sino-Kharoshthi coin (Cribb 7) | 15.54 | 28 | – | p | Probably from Yotkan site, purchased at Khotan |
| S.IV.B.j.4 | Sino-Kharoshthi coin (Cribb 5–6) | 3.71 | 17 | – | p | Probably from Yotkan site, purchased at Khotan |
| S.IV.B.j.5 | Sino-Kharoshthi coin (Cribb 4) | 3.48 | 20 | – | p | Probably from Yotkan site, purchased at Khotan |
| S.IV.B.j.6 | Sino-Kharoshthi coin (Cribb 2) | 1.97 | 16 | – | p | Probably from Yotkan site, purchased at Khotan |
| S.IV.B.j.7 | Wuzhu – full size | 2.59 | 25.5 | (H: 10) red | p | Probably from Yotkan site, purchased at Khotan |

| BM no. | Identification | Wt | Diam. | Notes | Acqn | Acquisition/Archaeological context |
|---|---|---|---|---|---|---|
| S.IV.B.j.8 | Wuzhu – full size | 2.95 | 25 | (H: 9.5) red | p | Probably from Yotkan site, purchased at Khotan |
| S.IV.B.j.9 | Qianyuan zhongbao – large | 4.02 | 29 | misaligned | p | Probably from Yotkan site, purchased at Khotan |
| S.IV.B.j.10 | Qianyuan zhongbao – small | 1.97 | 22 | – | p | Probably from Yotkan site, purchased at Khotan |
| S.IV.B.j.11 | Qianyuan zhongbao – small | 1.85 | 21.5 | – | p | Probably from Yotkan site, purchased at Khotan |
| S.IV.B.j.12 | Qianyuan zhongbao – small | 2.11 | 21.5 | misaligned | p | Probably from Yotkan site, purchased at Khotan |
| S.IV.B.j.13 | Qianyuan zhongbao – small | 1.88 | 21.5 | – | p | Probably from Yotkan site, purchased at Khotan |
| S.IV.B.j.14 | Qianyuan zhongbao – small | 1.35 | 20 | misaligned | p | Probably from Yotkan site, purchased at Khotan |
| S.IV.B.j.15 | Qianyuan zhongbao – small | 2.54 | 21.5 | – | p | Probably from Yotkan site, purchased at Khotan |
| S.IV.B.j.16 | Dali yuanbao – small | 1.70 | 23 | – | p | Probably from Yotkan site, purchased at Khotan |
| S.IV.B.j.17 | Dali yuanbao – small | 1.85 | 22 | – | p | Probably from Yotkan site, purchased at Khotan |
| S.IV.B.j.18 | Dali yuanbao – small | 1.71 | 21.5 | – | p | Probably from Yotkan site, purchased at Khotan |
| S.IV.B.j.19 | Dali yuanbao – small | 1.88 | 22 | – | p | Probably from Yotkan site, purchased at Khotan |
| S.IV.B.j.20 | Dali yuanbao – small | 1.19 | 22 | restored, damaged | p | Probably from Yotkan site, purchased at Khotan |
| S.IV.B.j.21 | [missing: Dali yuanbao] | – | – | – | p | Probably from Yotkan site, purchased at Khotan |
| S.IV.B.j.22 | [extra: Islamic coin] | – | – | – | p | Probably from Yotkan site, purchased at Khotan |
| S.IV.B.j.23 | [extra: Islamic coin] | – | – | – | p | Probably from Yotkan site, purchased at Khotan |
| S.IV.B.j.24 | [extra: Chinese coin – unidentified] | 3.32 | 23 | corroded | p | Probably from Yotkan site, purchased at Khotan |
| S.IV.B.j.25 | [extra: Chinese coin – unidentified] | 3.72 | 25 | corroded | p | Probably from Yotkan site, purchased at Khotan |

| | | | | | | |
|---|---|---|---|---|---|---|
| S.IV.B.k.1–2 | [extra: Islamic coins] | – | | | – | – |

| | | | | | | |
|---|---|---|---|---|---|---|
| S.IV.B.l.1 | [extra: unidentified] | 5.28 | 29 | corroded, uncleaned | – | Not in List of Coins |
| S.IV.B.l.2 | [extra: unidentified] | 4.40 | 25 | corroded, uncleaned | – | Not in List of Coins |
| S.IV.B.l.3 | [extra: unidentified] | 5.06 | 25 | corroded, uncleaned | – | Not in List of Coins |
| S.IV.B.l.4 | [extra: unidentified] | 3.63 | 24 | corroded, uncleaned | – | Not in List of Coins |
| S.IV.B.l.5 | [extra: unidentified] | 5.13 | 26 | corroded, uncleaned | – | Not in List of Coins |
| S.IV.B.l.6 | [extra: unidentified, Chinese – Tang dynasty?] | 2.82 | 22 | frag., uncleaned | – | Not in List of Coins |
| S.IV.B.l.7 | [extra: unidentified, Chinese – Tang dynasty?] | 1.54 | 21 | restored, uncleaned | – | Not in List of Coins |
| S.IV.B.l.8 | [extra: unidentified, Chinese – Tang dynasty?] | 4.04 | 22 | uncleaned | – | Not in List of Coins |

| BM no. | Identification | Wt | Diam. | Notes | Acqn | Acquisition/Archaeological context |
|---|---|---|---|---|---|---|
| S.IV.B.l.9 | [extra: Qian [yuan zhong] bao – large] | 2.58 | 27 | frag., uncleaned | – | Not in List of Coins |
| S.IV.B.l.10 | [extra: [x x] yuan bao] | 1.34 | – | frag., uncleaned | – | Not in List of Coins |
| S.IV.B.l.11 | [extra: clay casing of Chinese coin] | 1.98 | – | frag. | – | Not in List of Coins |
| S.IV.B.l.12 | [extra: Qianyuan [zhong] bao] | 1.65 | 22 | frag., uncleaned | – | Not in List of Coins |
| S.IV.B.l.13 | [extra: Chinese coin – unidentified] | 0.39 | – | frag., uncleaned | – | Not in List of Coins |
| S.IV.B.l.14 | [extra: Islamic coin] | – | – | – | – | Not in List of Coins |
| S.IV.B.l.15 | [extra: Sino-Kharoshthi coin (Cribb 3)] | 4.06 | 18 | – | – | Not in List of Coins |
| S.IV.B.l.16 | [extra: Sino-Kharoshthi coin (Cribb 1–6)] | 2.29 | 18 | – | – | Not in List of Coins |
| S.IV.B.l.17 | [extra: Sino-Kharoshthi coin (Cribb 1)] | 2.11 | 19 | – | – | Not in List of Coins |
| S.IV.B.l.18 | [extra: Sino-Kharoshthi coin (Cribb 1–6)] | 1.31 | 19 | – | – | Not in List of Coins |
| S.IV.B.l.19–32 | [extra: Islamic coin] | – | – | – | – | Not in List of Coins |

## S.IV.C: COINS OF MISCELLANEOUS ORIGIN PURCHASED AT KHOTAN

| BM no. | Identification | Wt | Diam. | Notes | Acqn | Acquisition/Archaeological context |
|---|---|---|---|---|---|---|
| S.IV.C.a.1 | Kaiyuan tongbao | 4.68 | 24 | misaligned | p | Purchased at Khotan |
| S.IV.C.a.2 | Qianyuan zhongbao – large | 5.64 | 28 | – | p | Purchased at Khotan |
| S.IV.C.a.3 | Qianyuan zhongbao – large | 6.32 | 29 | – | p | Purchased at Khotan |
| S.IV.C.a.4 | Qianyuan zhongbao – large; crescent on rev. | 5.89 | 29 | forced hole | p | Purchased at Khotan |
| S.IV.C.a.5 | Qianyuan zhongbao – large | 5.01 | 29 | – | p | Purchased at Khotan |
| S.IV.C.a.6 | Qianyuan zhongbao – medium | 2.97 | 26 | – | p | Purchased at Khotan |
| S.IV.C.a.7 | Qianyuan zhongbao – large | 6.40 | 28.5 | forced hole | p | Purchased at Khotan |
| S.IV.C.a.8 | Qianyuan zhongbao – large; crescent on rev. | 6.82 | 29 | misaligned | p | Purchased at Khotan |
| S.IV.C.a.9 | Qianyuan zhongbao – medium | 2.73 | 26.5 | 2 frags (= 1 coin) | p | Purchased at Khotan |
| S.IV.C.a.10 | Wuzhu | 2.05 | 25.5 | (H: 10) | p | Purchased at Khotan |
| S.IV.C.a.11 | Dali yuanbao – large | 2.88 | 23 | – | p | Purchased at Khotan |
| S.IV.C.a.12–14 | Chinese coins – Song dynasty | – | – | – | p | Purchased at Khotan |
| S.IV.C.b.1 | Qianyuan zhongbao – large | 7.07 | 28 | misaligned | p | Purchased at Khotan |
| S.IV.C.b.2 | Qianyuan zhongbao – medium | 3.36 | 23 | misaligned | p | Purchased at Khotan |
| S.IV.C.b.3 | [missing: Qianyuan zhongbao] | – | – | – | p | Purchased at Khotan |
| S.IV.C.b.4–22 | Chinese coins– Song dynasty | – | – | – | p | Purchased at Khotan |
| S.IV.C.b.23–24 | [extra: Chinese coins – Song dynasty) | – | – | – | p | Purchased at Khotan |
| S.IV.C.c.1–2 | [missing: Sino-Kharoshthi coin] | – | – | – | p | Purchased at Khotan |
| S.IV.C.c.3 | [missing: Qianyuan zhongbao] | – | – | – | p | Purchased at Khotan |
| S.IV.C.c.4–5 | Islamic coins | – | – | – | p | Purchased at Khotan |
| S.IV.C.d.1 (OR.0421) | Sino-Kharoshthi coin (Cribb 1) | 1.61 | 18×16 | – | p | Purchased at Khotan |
| S.IV.C.d.2 (OR.0431) | Sino-Kharoshthi coin (Cribb 10) | 2.63 | 19 | – | p | Purchased at Khotan |
| S.IV.C.d.3 (OR.0398) | Sino-Kharoshthi coin (Cribb 4) | 2.63 | 16 | – | p | Purchased at Khotan |
| S.IV.C.d.4 | Sino-Kharoshthi coin (Cribb 3) | 2.99 | 22 | – | p | Purchased at Khotan |
| S.IV.C.d.5 | Sino-Kharoshthi coin (Cribb1–6) | 2.77 | 18 | – | p | Purchased at Khotan |

| BM no. | Identification | Wt | Diam. | Notes | Acqn | Acquisition/Archaeological context |
|---|---|---|---|---|---|---|
| S.IV.C.d.6 | Kushan coin of Kanishka I – hemi-drachm? | 1.03 | 13 | pierced | p | Purchased at Khotan |
| S.IV.C.d.7 | Sino-Kharoshthi coin (Cribb 1–6) | 1.18 | 15 | – | p | Purchased at Khotan |
| S.IV.C.d.8(OR.4013) | Sino-Kharoshthi coin (Cribb 2) | 3.39 | 20×19 | – | p | Purchased at Khotan |
| S.IV.C.d.9 | Wuzhu – full size | 2.67 | 26 | (H: 9) red | p | Purchased at Khotan |
| S.IV.C.d.10 | Wuzhu – full size | 2.23 | 25 | (H: 9.5) red | p | Purchased at Khotan |
| S.IV.C.d.11 | Wuzhu – full size | 1.48 | 24 | (H: 9.5) red, faint | p | Purchased at Khotan |
| S.IV.C.d.12 | Wuzhu – without full rim, lines on rev. | 1.66 | 24 | (H: 9.5) red | p | Purchased at Khotan |
| S.IV.C.d.13 | 'Wuzhu' – illegible | 1.35 | 22.5 | (H: 9.5) red | p | Purchased at Khotan |
| S.IV.C.d.14 | Wuzhu – small. small characters | 1.48 | 22 | (H: 10.5) red | p | Purchased at Khotan |
| S.IV.C.d.15 | Wuzhu – clipped, cuts through inscription | 1.78 | 22.5 | (H: 9.5) red | p | Purchased at Khotan |
| S.IV.C.d.16 | Wuzhu – clipped, cuts through inscription | 0.85 | 19.5 | (H: 9.5) red | p | Purchased at Khotan |
| S.IV.C.d.17 | Wuzhu – clipped, cuts through inscription | 0.90 | 20 | (H: 10) faint | p | Purchased at Khotan |
| S.IV.C.d.18 | 'Wuzhu' – illegible | 0.96 | 19.5 | (H: 9.5) | p | Purchased at Khotan |
| S.IV.C.d.19 | 'Wuzhu' – illegible | 0.68 | 21.5 | frag., red | p | Purchased at Khotan |
| S.IV.C.d.20 | Chinese coin – unidentified, Wuzhu? | 2.65 | 24 | corroded (H: 9.5) | p | Purchased at Khotan |
| S.IV.C.d.21 | [Qian] yuan zhongbao – medium | 2.98 | 25 | frag., uncleaned | p | Purchased at Khotan |
| S.IV.C.d.22 | Qianyuan zhongbao – small | 2.44 | 21 | uncleaned | p | Purchased at Khotan |
| S.IV.C.d.23 | Dali yuanbao | 1.49 | 19 | uncleaned | p | Purchased at Khotan |
| S.IV.C.d.24–27 | Islamic coins | – | – | – | p | Purchased at Khotan |
| S.IV.C.e.1–2 | Islamic coins | – | – | – | p | Purchased at Khotan |
| S.IV.C.f.1–2 | Chinese coins – Song dynasty | – | – | – | p | Purchased at Khotan |
| S.IV.C.f.3 | [extra: Chinese coin – unidentified] | 12.44 | 35 | corroded | p | Purchased at Khotan |
| S.IV.C.f.4 | [extra: Chinese coin – unidentified] | 10.13 | 33 | corroded | p | Purchased at Khotan |
| S.IV.C.f.5 | [extra: Chinese coin – unidentified] | 11.31 | 31 | corroded | p | Purchased at Khotan |
| S.IV.C.g.1 | Islamic coin | – | – | – | p | Purchased at Khotan |
| S.IV.C.h.1 | 'Wuzhu' – illegible | 0.96 | 20 | (H: 10) misaligned | p | Allegedly from Halal-bagh, purchased at Khotan |
| S.IV.C.h.2 | Wuzhu – clipped, cuts through inscription | 0.83 | 20 | (H: 10) misaligned | p | Allegedly from Halal-bagh, purchased at Khotan |
| S.IV.C.h.3 | 'Wuzhu' – illegible | 1.15 | 21 | (H: 9.5) misaligned | p | Allegedly from Halal-bagh, purchased at Khotan |
| S.IV.C.h.4 | Wuzhu – clipped, cuts through inscription | 1.13 | 20.5 | (H: 9.5) | p | Allegedly from Halal-bagh, purchased at Khotan |
| S.IV.C.h.5 | Wuzhu – clipped, cuts through inscription | 1.27 | 20.5 | (H: 10.5) | p | Allegedly from Halal-bagh, purchased at Khotan |
| S.IV.C.h.6 | 'Wuzhu' – illegible | 1.07 | 20.5 | (H: 9.5) | p | Allegedly from Halal-bagh, purchased at Khotan |
| S.IV.C.h.7 | Wuzhu – clipped, cuts through inscription | 1.66 | 23 | (H: 10.5) damaged | p | Allegedly from Halal-bagh, purchased at Khotan |
| S.IV.C.h.8 | 'Wuzhu' – illegible | 1.05 | 21 | (H: 9.5) | p | Allegedly from Halal-bagh, purchased at Khotan |
| S.IV.C.h.9 | Wu [zhu] – full size | 0.85 | (26) | frag. | p | Allegedly from Halal-bagh, purchased at Khotan |
| S.IV.C.h.10 | 'Wuzhu' – illegible | 1.02 | 19.5 | (H: 9) frag. | p | Allegedly from Halal-bagh, purchased at Khotan |

| BM no. | Identification | Wt | Diam. | Notes | Acqn | Acquisition/Archaeological context |
|---|---|---|---|---|---|---|
| S.IV.C.h.11 | 'Wuzhu' – illegible | 1.02 | 20 | (H: 9.5) | p | Allegedly from Halal-bagh, purchased at Khotan |
| S.IV.C.h.12 | Wuzhu – without full rim | 1.99 | 23.5 | (H: 9.5) | p | Allegedly from Halal-bagh, purchased at Khotan |
| S.IV.C.h.13 | Wuzhu – clipped, cuts through inscription | 1.31 | 23 | (H: 11) | p | Allegedly from Halal-bagh, purchased at Khotan |
| S.IV.C.h.14 | Wuzhu – without full rim | 1.57 | 23.5 | (H: 9.5) | p | Allegedly from Halal-bagh, purchased at Khotan |
| S.IV.C.h.15 | 'Wuzhu' – illegible | 1.33 | 23.5 | (H: 10) | p | Allegedly from Halal-bagh, purchased at Khotan |
| S.IV.C.h.16 | Wuzhu – full size | 2.21 | 24.5 | (H: 9.5) | p | Allegedly from Halal-bagh, purchased at Khotan |
| S.IV.C.h.17 | Wuzhu – without full rim | 1.75 | 24 | (H: 9.5) | p | Allegedly from Halal-bagh, purchased at Khotan |
| S.IV.C.h.18 | Wuzhu – clipped, cuts through inscription | 1.38 | 21 | (H: 10) | p | Allegedly from Halal-bagh, purchased at Khotan |
| S.IV.C.h.19 | Wuzhu – without rim | 1.46 | 22 | (H: 9.5) | p | Allegedly from Halal-bagh, purchased at Khotan |
| S.IV.C.h.20 | 'Wuzhu' – illegible | 1.65 | 22 | (H: 10) | p | Allegedly from Halal-bagh, purchased at Khotan |
| S.IV.C.h.21 | Wuzhu – without rim | 1.91 | 24 | (H: 9.5) | p | Allegedly from Halal-bagh, purchased at Khotan |
| S.IV.C.h.22 | 'Wuzhu' – illegible | 1.52 | 24 | (H: 9.5) | p | Allegedly from Halal-bagh, purchased at Khotan |
| S.IV.C.h.23 | Wuzhu – full size | 2.01 | 25.5 | (H: 9.5) | p | Allegedly from Halal-bagh, purchased at Khotan |
| S.IV.C.h.24 | Wuzhu – without full rim | 1.76 | 24.5 | (H: 9.5) | p | Allegedly from Halal-bagh, purchased at Khotan |
| S.IV.C.h.25 | Wuzhu – clipped, cuts through inscription | 1.54 | 22 | (H: 10) | p | Allegedly from Halal-bagh, purchased at Khotan |
| S.IV.C.h.26 | Wuzhu – without full rim | 1.82 | 23.5 | (H: 9) | p | Allegedly from Halal-bagh, purchased at Khotan |
| S.IV.C.h.27 | Wuzhu – without inscription | 1.63 | 24 | (H: 9.5) | p | Allegedly from Halal-bagh, purchased at Khotan |
| S.IV.C.h.28 | Wuzhu – without full rim | 1.63 | 24 | (H: 9.5) | p | Allegedly from Halal-bagh, purchased at Khotan |
| S.IV.C.h.29 | Wuzhu – full size | 1.94 | 25 | (H: 10) damaged | p | Allegedly from Halal-bagh, purchased at Khotan |
| S.IV.C.h.30 | Wuzhu – full size | 1.49 | 26 | (H: 9.5) damaged | p | Allegedly from Halal-bagh, purchased at Khotan |
| S.IV.C.h.31 | Wuzhu – without full rim | 1.45 | 24 | (H: 9.5) | p | Allegedly from Halal-bagh, purchased at Khotan |
| S.IV.C.h.32 | Wuzhu – clipped, cuts through inscription | 1.74 | 22 | (H: 9.5) scyphate | p | Allegedly from Halal-bagh, purchased at Khotan |
| S.IV.C.h.33 | Wuzhu – tall, thin wu touching rim | 1.58 | 22 | (H: 10.5) | p | Allegedly from Halal-bagh, purchased at Khotan |
| S.IV.C.h.34 | Wuzhu – clipped, cuts through inscription | 2.30 | 22 | (H: 9.5) crack in rev. mould | p | Allegedly from Halal-bagh, purchased at Khotan |
| S.IV.C.h.35 | 'Wuzhu' – illegible | 0.18 | – | frag. | p | Allegedly from Halal-bagh, purchased at Khotan |
| S.IV.C.h.36 | 'Wuzhu' – illegible | 0.25 | – | frag. | p | Allegedly from Halal-bagh, purchased at Khotan |

| BM no. | Identification | Wt | Diam. | Notes | Acqn | Acquisition/Archaeological context |
|---|---|---|---|---|---|---|
| S.IV.C.i.1 | Qianyuan zhongbao – large | 7.04 | 29 | – | p | From hoard at Kum-bagh, purchased at Khotan |
| S.IV.C.i.2 | Qianyuan zhongbao – large | 5.69 | 28 | – | p | From hoard at Kum-bagh, purchased at Khotan |
| S.IV.C.i.3 | Qianyuan zhongbao – large | 7.32 | 27.5 | – | p | From hoard at Kum-bagh, purchased at Khotan |
| S.IV.C.i.4 | Qianyuan zhongbao – large | 5.61 | 29 | – | p | From hoard at Kum-bagh, purchased at Khotan |
| S.IV.C.i.5 | Qianyuan zhongbao – large | 7.34 | 29.5 | – | p | From hoard at Kum-bagh, purchased at Khotan |
| S.IV.C.i.6 | Qianyuan zhongbao – large | 5.45 | 30 | – | p | From hoard at Kum-bagh, purchased at Khotan |
| S.IV.C.i.7 | Qianyuan zhongbao – medium | 3.53 | 26 | crack in rev. mould | p | From hoard at Kum-bagh, purchased at Khotan |
| S.IV.C.i.8 | Qianyuan zhongbao – large; crescent on rev. | 7.33 | 29.5 | – | p | From hoard at Kum-bagh, purchased at Khotan |
| S.IV.C.i.9 | Qianyuan zhongbao – large | 7.91 | 28.5 | – | p | From hoard at Kum-bagh, purchased at Khotan |
| S.IV.C.i.10 | Qianyuan zhongbao – large | 7.49 | 29.5 | – | p | From hoard at Kum-bagh, purchased at Khotan |

| | | | | | | |
|---|---|---|---|---|---|---|
| S.IV.C.k.1–36 | Islamic coins | – | – | – | p | From S of Tar-bogaz, purchased at Khotan |
| S.IV.C.k.37 | [extra: Chinese coin – unidentified] | 0.64 | – | frag., uncleaned | – | – |
| S.IV.C.k.38 | [extra: Qianyuan zhong (bao) – small] | 1.52 | 21 | frag., uncleaned | – | – |

| | | | | | | |
|---|---|---|---|---|---|---|
| K.Y.1 | [extra: Sino-Kharoshthi coin (Cribb 1–6)] | 2.47 | 16 | – | – | Not in List of Coins |
| K.Y.2 | [extra: Kushan coin of Kanishka I – hemi-drachm?] | 2.01 | 16 | – | – | Not in List of Coins |
| K.Y.3 | [extra: Sino-Kharoshthi coin (Cribb 2)] | 1.47 | 17 | – | – | Not in List of Coins |
| K.Y.4 | [extra: Sino-Kharoshthi coin (Cribb 1–6)] | 1.62 | 18 | | | Not in List of Coins |
| K.Y.5 | [extra: Sino-Kharoshthi coin (Cribb 1–6)] | 1.12 | 18 | – | – | Not in List of Coins |
| K.Y.6 | [extra: Sino-Kharoshthi coin (Cribb 2–4)] | 2.51 | 17 | – | – | Not in List of Coins |
| K.Y.7 | [extra: Sino-Kharoshthi coin (Cribb 1–6)] | 1.90 | 14 | – | – | Not in List of Coins |
| K.Y.8 | [extra: Sino-Kharoshthi coin (Cribb 1–6)] | 1.19 | 14 | – | – | Not in List of Coins |
| K.Y.9 | [extra: Sino-Kharoshthi coin (Cribb 1–6)] | 2.77 | 18 | – | – | Not in List of Coins |
| K.Y.10 | [extra: Sino-Kharoshthi coin (Cribb 1–6)] | 0.30 | 10 | – | – | Not in List of Coins |
| K.Y.11 | [extra: unidentified] | 2.01 | – | frags | – | Not in List of Coins |
| K.Y.12 | [extra: non–coin] | – | – | – | – | Not in List of Coins |
| K.Y.13 (OR.0419) | [extra: Sino-Kharoshthi coin (Cribb 1)] | 3.08 | 19×17.5 | 4 frags | – | Not in List of Coins |
| K.Y.14 | Kushan coin of Kanishka I – hemi-drachm | 1.04 | 13 | – | – | Not in List of Coins |
| K.Y.15 | Qianyuan zhongbao – large | 6.23 | 28 | – | – | Not in List of Coins |
| K.Y.16 | Unidentified: round with hole | 1.07 | 12 | – | – | Not in List of Coins |

| BM no. | Identification | Wt | Diam. | Notes | Acqn | Acquisition/Archaeological context |
|---|---|---|---|---|---|---|
| K.Y.17 | Sino-Kharoshthi coin (Cribb 2) | 2.62 | 18 | – | – | Not in List of Coins |
| K.Y.18 | Sino-Kharoshthi coin (Cribb 2–4) | 1.91 | 17 | – | – | Not in List of Coins |
| K.Y.19 | 'Wuzhu' – illegible | 0.69 | – | – | – | Not in List of Coins |
| K.Y.20 | Dali yuanbao – large | 3.07 | 24 | 3 frags | – | Not in List of Coins |
| K.Y.21 | Qianyuan zhongbao – small | 2.64 | 22 | forced hole | – | Not in List of Coins |
| K.Y.22 | Qianyuan zhongbao – small | 2.69 | 23 | – | – | Not in List of Coins |
| K.Y.23 | Chinese coin – unidentified, Tang dynasty? | 3.24 | 23 | – | – | Not in List of Coins |
| K.Y.24 | Qianyuan zhongbao – small | 1.96 | 23 | – | – | Not in List of Coins |
| K.Y.25 | Qianyuan zhongbao – small | 2.12 | 21.5 | – | – | Not in List of Coins |
| K.Y.26 | Chinese coin – unidentified, Tang dynasty? | 3.15 | 21.5 | corroded | – | Not in List of Coins |
| K.Y.27 | Qianyuan zhongbao – small | 2.41 | 22 | central hole not cut, rough rim | – | Not in List of Coins |
| K.Y.28 | Unidentified, clay casing of coin | 0.20 | – | frag. | – | Not in List of Coins |
| K.Y.29–37 | [extra: Islamic] | – | – | – | – | Not in List of Coins |
| K.Y.38 | 'Wuzhu' – illegible | 1.07 | 19.5 | (H: 9.5) red | – | Not in List of Coins |
| K.Y.39 | Dali yuanbao – large | 2.35 | 23.5 | – | – | Not in List of Coins |

## S.IV.D: COPPER COINS BROUGHT TO KHOTAN FROM TATI SITES EAST OF YURUNG KASH

| BM no. | Identification | Wt | Diam. | Notes | Acqn | Acquisition/Archaeological context |
|---|---|---|---|---|---|---|
| S.IV.D.a.1 (OR.0387) | Sino-Kharoshthi coin (Cribb 8) | 15.67 | 26 | – | p | Allegedly from Tati sites E of Yurung Kash, collected by 'treasure-seekers' of Tam-Öghil |
| S.IV.D.a.2 (OR.0416) | Sino-Kharoshthi coin (Cribb 2) | 3.91 | 20×19 | – | p | Allegedly from Tati sites E of Yurung Kash, collected by 'treasure-seekers' of Tam-Öghil |
| S.IV.D.a.3 (OR.0408) | Sino-Kharoshthi coin (Cribb 2) | 2.66 | 20 | – | p | Allegedly from Tati sites E of Yurung Kash, collected by 'treasure-seekers' of Tam-Öghil |
| S.IV.D.a.4 (OR.0402) | Sino-Kharoshthi coin (Cribb 4) | 6.57 | 22×21 | – | p | Allegedly from Tati sites E of Yurung Kash, collected by 'treasure-seekers' of Tam-Öghil |
| S.IV.D.a.5 | Sino-Kharoshthi coin (Cribb 1–6) | 2.59 | 19 | – | p | Allegedly from Tati sites E of Yurung Kash, collected by 'treasure-seekers' of Tam-Öghil |
| S.IV.D.a.6 | Sino-Kharoshthi coin (Cribb 1–6) | 2.25 | 18 | – | p | Allegedly from Tati sites E of Yurung Kash, collected by 'treasure-seekers' of Tam-Öghil |
| S.IV.D.a.7–9 | [missing: Sino-Kharoshthi coin] | – | – | – | p | Allegedly from Tati sites E of Yurung Kash, collected by 'treasure-seekers' of Tam-Öghil |
| S.IV.D.a.10 | Huoquan | 2.17 | 23 | – | p | Allegedly from Tati sites E of Yurung Kash, collected by 'treasure-seekers' of Tam-Öghil |
| S.IV.D.a.11 | Wuzhu – full size | 2.41 | 25.5 | (H: 10.5) | p | Allegedly from Tati sites E of Yurung Kash, collected by 'treasure-seekers' of Tam-Öghil |

| BM no. | Identification | Wt | Diam. | Notes | Acqn | Acquisition/Archaeological context |
|---|---|---|---|---|---|---|
| S.IV.D.a.12 | Wuzhu – without full rim | 1.56 | 25 | (H: 10) bent | p | Allegedly from Tati sites E of Yurung Kash, collected by 'treasure-seekers' of Tam-Öghil |
| S.IV.D.a.13 | Wuzhu – without rim | 1.37 | 23 | (H: 10) | p | Allegedly from Tati sites E of Yurung Kash, collected by 'treasure-seekers' of Tam-Öghil |
| S.IV.D.a.14 | Wuzhu – clipped, cuts through inscription | 1.03 | 21.5 | (H: 9) misaligned, faint | p | Allegedly from Tati sites E of Yurung Kash, collected by 'treasure-seekers' of Tam-Öghil |
| S.IV.D.a.15 | 'Wuzhu' – illegible | 0.79 | 16.5 | (H: 8) | p | Allegedly from Tati sites E of Yurung Kash, collected by 'treasure-seekers' of Tam-Öghil |
| S.IV.D.a.16 | 'Wuzhu' – illegible | 0.99 | 20 | (H: 10) | p | Allegedly from Tati sites E of Yurung Kash, collected by 'treasure-seekers' of Tam-Öghil |
| S.IV.D.a.17 | Wuzhu – clipped, cuts through inscription | 1.52 | 23 | (H: 10) corroded | p | Allegedly from Tati sites E of Yurung Kash, collected by 'treasure-seekers' of Tam-Öghil |
| S.IV.D.a.18 | 'Wuzhu' – illegible | 0.99 | 18.5 | (H: 9) with sprue | p | Allegedly from Tati sites E of Yurung Kash, collected by 'treasure-seekers' of Tam-Öghil |
| S.IV.D.a.19 | 'Wuzhu' – illegible | 1.03 | 20 | (H: 9.5) corroded, misaligned | p | Allegedly from Tati sites E of Yurung Kash, collected by 'treasure-seekers' of Tam-Öghil |
| S.IV.D.a.20 | Wuzhu – clipped, cuts through inscription | 1.34 | 16.5 | (H: 8.5) crack in rev. mould | p | Allegedly from Tati sites E of Yurung Kash, collected by 'treasure-seekers' of Tam-Öghil |
| S.IV.D.a.21 | 'Wuzhu' – illegible | 0.90 | 15 | (H: 9.5) damaged | p | Allegedly from Tati sites E of Yurung Kash, collected by 'treasure-seekers' of Tam-Öghil |
| S.IV.D.a.22 | 'Wuzhu' – illegible | 0.90 | 21.5 | (H: 8) | p | Allegedly from Tati sites E of Yurung Kash, collected by 'treasure-seekers' of Tam-Öghil |
| S.IV.D.a.23 | 'Wuzhu' – illegible | 0.63 | 15 | (H: 7.5) | p | Allegedly from Tati sites E of Yurung Kash, collected by 'treasure-seekers' of Tam-Öghil |
| S.IV.D.a.24 | Wuzhu – clipped, cuts through inscription | 1.65 | 21.5 | (H: 9.5) damaged | p | Allegedly from Tati sites E of Yurung Kash, collected by 'treasure-seekers' of Tam-Öghil |
| S.IV.D.a.25 | Wuzhu – clipped, cuts through inscription | 1.47 | 21.5 | (H: 9.5) red | p | Allegedly from Tati sites E of Yurung Kash, collected by 'treasure-seekers' of Tam-Öghil |
| S.IV.D.a.26 | 'Wuzhu' – illegible | 1.08 | 21 | (H: 10) | p | Allegedly from Tati sites E of Yurung Kash, collected by 'treasure-seekers' of Tam-Öghil |
| S.IV.D.a.27 | Wuzhu – without rim | 2.39 | 23 | (H: 9) red | p | Allegedly from Tati sites E of Yurung Kash, collected by 'treasure-seekers' of Tam-Öghil |
| S.IV.D.a.27.a | Wu [zhu] – full size | 0.92 | – | frag. | p | Allegedly from Tati sites E of Yurung Kash, collected by 'treasure-seekers' of Tam-Öghil |
| S.IV.D.a.27.b | Wuzhu – clipped, cuts through inscription; line below hole | 0.79 | 19 | frag. (H: 9.5) | p | Allegedly from Tati sites E of Yurung Kash, collected by 'treasure-seekers' of Tam-Öghil |

| BM no. | Identification | Wt | Diam. | Notes | Acqn | Acquisition/Archaeological context |
|---|---|---|---|---|---|---|
| S.IV.D.a.27.c | [Wu] zhu full size | 0.52 | – | frag. | p | Allegedly from Tati sites E of Yurung Kash, collected by 'treasure-seekers' of Tam-Öghil |
| S.IV.D.a.28 | Wuzhu – clipped, cuts through inscription | 1.30 | 21 | (H: 10) red | p | Allegedly from Tati sites E of Yurung Kash, collected by 'treasure-seekers' of Tam-Öghil |
| S.IV.D.a.29 | 'Wuzhu' – illegible | 0.68 | 20 | (H: 9.5) red | p | Allegedly from Tati sites E of Yurung Kash, collected by 'treasure-seekers' of Tam-Öghil |
| S.IV.D.a.30 | 'Wuzhu' – illegible | 1.12 | 20.5 | (H: 10) red | p | Allegedly from Tati sites E of Yurung Kash, collected by 'treasure-seekers' of Tam-Öghil |
| S.IV.D.a.31 | Wuzhu – clipped, cuts through inscription | 1.20 | 19.5 | (H: 9.5) red | p | Allegedly from Tati sites E of Yurung Kash, collected by 'treasure-seekers' of Tam-Öghil |
| S.IV.D.a.32 | Wuzhu – clipped, cuts through inscription | 1.41 | 22 | (H: 9.5) red | p | Allegedly from Tati sites E of Yurung Kash, collected by 'treasure-seekers' of Tam-Öghil |
| S.IV.D.a.33 | Wuzhu – clipped, cuts through inscription | 0.90 | 21.5 | (H: 10) red | p | Allegedly from Tati sites E of Yurung Kash, collected by 'treasure-seekers' of Tam-Öghil |
| S.IV.D.a.34 | Wuzhu – crude | 1.11 | 20 | (H: 10) red, crude | p | Allegedly from Tati sites E of Yurung Kash, collected by 'treasure-seekers' of Tam-Öghil |
| S.IV.D.a.35 | Wuzhu – full size | 1.83 | 25.5 | (H: 9.5) | p | Allegedly from Tati sites E of Yurung Kash, collected by 'treasure-seekers' of Tam-Öghil |
| S.IV.D.a.36 | Wuzhu – clipped, cuts through inscription | 1.88 | 21.5 | (H: 9) | p | Allegedly from Tati sites E of Yurung Kash, collected by 'treasure-seekers' of Tam-Öghil |
| S.IV.D.a.37 | 'Wuzhu' – illegible | 1.10 | 19 | (H: 9) red | p | Allegedly from Tati sites E of Yurung Kash, collected by 'treasure-seekers' of Tam-Öghil |
| S.IV.D.a.38 | Wuzhu – small, thin wu | 1.09 | 17.5 | (H: 8) red | p | Allegedly from Tati sites E of Yurung Kash, collected by 'treasure-seekers' of Tam-Öghil |
| S.IV.D.a.39 | 'Wuzhu' – illegible | 1.04 | 18 | (H: 9.5) | p | Allegedly from Tati sites E of Yurung Kash, collected by 'treasure-seekers' of Tam-Öghil |
| S.IV.D.a.40 | Wuzhu – without rim | 1.80 | 23 | (H: 9.5) red | p | Allegedly from Tati sites E of Yurung Kash, collected by 'treasure-seekers' of Tam-Öghil |
| S.IV.D.a.41 | Wuzhu – clipped, cuts through inscription | 1.38 | 18 | (H: 8) red | p | Allegedly from Tati sites E of Yurung Kash, collected by 'treasure-seekers' of Tam-Öghil |
| S.IV.D.a.42 | Wuzhu – clipped, cuts through inscription | 0.54 | 18 | (H: 10) | p | Allegedly from Tati sites E of Yurung Kash, collected by 'treasure-seekers' of Tam-Öghil |
| S.IV.D.a.43 | Wuzhu – clipped, cuts through inscription | 1.50 | 20 | (H: 9.5) red | p | Allegedly from Tati sites E of Yurung Kash, collected by 'treasure-seekers' of Tam-Öghil |
| S.IV.D.a.44 | Wuzhu – clipped, cuts through inscription | 0.86 | 18 | (H: 9) damaged | p | Allegedly from Tati sites E of Yurung Kash, collected by 'treasure-seekers' of Tam-Öghil |

| BM no. | Identification | Wt | Diam. | Notes | Acqn | Acquisition/Archaeological context |
|---|---|---|---|---|---|---|
| S.IV.D.a.45 | Kaiyuan tongbao | 2.87 | 25.5 | 2 frags restored | p | Allegedly from Tati sites E of Yurung Kash, collected by 'treasure-seekers' of Tam-Öghil |
| S.IV.D.a.46 | Qianyuan zhongbao – medium | 4.15 | 25 | – | p | Allegedly from Tati sites E of Yurung Kash, collected by 'treasure-seekers' of Tam-Öghil |
| S.IV.D.a.47 | Qianyuan zhongbao – small | 2.27 | 21.5 | – | p | Allegedly from Tati sites E of Yurung Kash, collected by 'treasure-seekers' of Tam-Öghil |
| S.IV.D.a.48 | Qianyuan zhongbao – small | 2.31 | 21.5 | – | p | Allegedly from Tati sites E of Yurung Kash, collected by 'treasure-seekers' of Tam-Öghil |
| S.IV.D.a.49 | Qianyuan zhongbao – small | 2.38 | 22 | – | p | Allegedly from Tati sites E of Yurung Kash, collected by 'treasure-seekers' of Tam-Öghil |
| S.IV.D.a.50 | [Qian] yuan zhong [bao] – medium | 1.47 | – | frag. | p | Allegedly from Tati sites E of Yurung Kash, collected by 'treasure-seekers' of Tam-Öghil |
| S.IV.D.a.51 | Qianyuan zhongbao – small | 2.51 | 22 | – | p | Allegedly from Tati sites E of Yurung Kash, collected by 'treasure-seekers' of Tam-Öghil |
| S.IV.D.a.52 | Qianyuan zhongbao – small | 1.90 | 21 | – | p | Allegedly from Tati sites E of Yurung Kash, collected by 'treasure-seekers' of Tam-Öghil |
| S.IV.D.a.53 | Chinese – [Qian] yuan [zhong] bao – large? | 3.45 | – | frag. | p | Allegedly from Tati sites E of Yurung Kash, collected by 'treasure-seekers' of Tam-Öghil |
| S.IV.D.a.54 | [Kai] yuan tong [bao] | 1.44 | 25 | frag. | p | Allegedly from Tati sites E of Yurung Kash, collected by 'treasure-seekers' of Tam-Öghil |
| S.IV.D.a.55 | 3 Chinese coins corroded together | 3.23 | 23 | corroded | p | Allegedly from Tati sites E of Yurung Kash, collected by 'treasure-seekers' of Tam-Öghil |
| S.IV.D.a.56 | Chinese coin – (Qianyuan zhongbao?) | – | 32 | 6 frags, corroded | p | Allegedly from Tati sites E of Yurung Kash, collected by 'treasure-seekers' of Tam-Öghil |
| S.IV.D.a.57 | Qianyuan zhongbao – large | 9.00 | 31 | corroded | p | Allegedly from Tati sites E of Yurung Kash, collected by 'treasure-seekers' of Tam-Öghil |
| S.IV.D.a.58 | Qianyuan zhongbao – large | 9.37 | 31 | corroded | p | Allegedly from Tati sites E of Yurung Kash, collected by 'treasure-seekers' of Tam-Öghil |
| S.IV.D.a.59 | Qianyuan zhongbao – large | 9.39 | 30.5 | corroded | p | Allegedly from Tati sites E of Yurung Kash, collected by 'treasure-seekers' of Tam-Öghil |
| S.IV.D.a.60 | Qian [yuan zhongbao] | 0.84 | – | frag. | p | Allegedly from Tati sites E of Yurung Kash, collected by 'treasure-seekers' of Tam-Öghil |
| S.IV.D.a.61 | [Kai] yuan tong [bao] | 0.96 | 24 | frag., red | p | Allegedly from Tati sites E of Yurung Kash, collected by 'treasure-seekers' of Tam-Öghil |
| S.IV.D.a.62 | Chinese coin – unidentified | 1.49 | 22 | frag., corroded | p | Allegedly from Tati sites E of Yurung Kash, collected by 'treasure-seekers' of Tam-Öghil |

| BM no. | Identification | Wt | Diam. | Notes | Acqn | Acquisition/Archaeological context |
|---|---|---|---|---|---|---|
| S.IV.D.a.63 | Qianyuan zhongbao – small | 2.79 | 22 | – | p | Allegedly from Tati sites E of Yurung Kash, collected by 'treasure-seekers' of Tam-Öghil |
| S.IV.D.a.64 | Dali yuanbao – small | 2.72 | 22 | corroded | p | Allegedly from Tati sites E of Yurung Kash, collected by 'treasure-seekers' of Tam-Öghil |
| S.IV.D.a.65 | [Da] li yuan [bao] – small | 1.43 | – | misaligned, frag. | p | Allegedly from Tati sites E of Yurung Kash, collected by 'treasure-seekers' of Tam-Öghil |
| S.IV.D.a.66–83 | Chinese coins – Song dynasty | – | – | – | p | Allegedly from Tati sites E of Yurung Kash, collected by 'treasure-seekers' of Tam-Öghil |
| S.IV.D.a.84–89 | [extra: Chinese coins – Song dynasty] | – | – | – | p | Allegedly from Tati sites E of Yurung Kash, collected by 'treasure-seekers' of Tam-Öghil |
| S.IV.D.a.90–107 | Islamic coins | – | – | – | p | Allegedly from Tati sites E of Yurung Kash, collected by 'treasure-seekers' of Tam-Öghil |
| S.IV.D.a.108–22 | [extra: Islamic coins] | – | – | – | p | Allegedly from Tati sites E of Yurung Kash, collected by 'treasure-seekers' of Tam-Öghil |
| S.IV.D.a.123–25 | Islamic coins | – | – | – | p | Allegedly from Tati sites E of Yurung Kash, collected by 'treasure-seekers' of Tam-Öghil |
| S.IV.D.a.126–36 | [extra: Islamic coins] | – | – | – | p | Allegedly from Tati sites E of Yurung Kash, collected by 'treasure-seekers' of Tam-Öghil |
| S.IV.D.a.137–39 | Islamic coins | – | – | – | p | Allegedly from Tati sites E of Yurung Kash, collected by 'treasure-seekers' of Tam-Öghil |
| S.IV.D.a.140–42 | [extra: Islamic coins] | – | – | – | p | Allegedly from Tati sites E of Yurung Kash, collected by 'treasure-seekers' of Tam-Öghil |
| S.IV.D.b.1 | 'Wuzhu' – illegible | 1.34 | 21.5 | (H: 9.5) | p | Allegedly from N of Jiya and Suya |
| S.IV.D.b.2 | 'Wuzhu' – illegible | 1.57 | 22.5 | (H: 9.5) misaligned | p | Allegedly from N of Jiya and Suya |
| S.IV.D.b.3 | Chinese coin – unidentified | 2.01 | 24 | (H: 9) corroded | p | Allegedly from N of Jiya and Suya |
| S.IV.D.b.4–5 | 'Wuzhu' – illegible | 3.91 | – | 2 frags corroded together | p | Allegedly from N of Jiya and Suya |
| S.IV.D.b.6 | [Wu] zhu – full size | 1.26 | 25.5 | frag. | p | Allegedly from N of Jiya and Suya |
| S.IV.D.b.7 | 'Wuzhu' – without inscription, rim round hole | 0.53 | 11 | (H: 5.5) | p | Allegedly from N of Jiya and Suya |
| S.IV.D.b.8 | 'Wuzhu' – illegible | 0.91 | 13 | (H: 4.5) corroded | p | Allegedly from N of Jiya and Suya |
| S.IV.D.b.9 | Qianyuan zhongbao – large | 7.39 | 28.5 | misaligned | p | Allegedly from N of Jiya and Suya |
| S.IV.D.b.10 | Qianyuan zhongbao – medium | 3.76 | 25.5 | misaligned | p | Allegedly from N of Jiya and Suya |
| S.IV.D.b.11 | Qianyuan zhongbao – small | 1.75 | 21 | damaged | p | Allegedly from N of Jiya and Suya |
| S.IV.D.b.12 | Qianyuan zhongbao – small | 3.27 | 22 | misaligned | p | Allegedly from N of Jiya and Suya |
| S.IV.D.b.13 | [missing: Qianyuan zhongbao] | – | – | – | p | Allegedly from N of Jiya and Suya |
| S.IV.D.b.14 | Dali yuanbao – large | 3.76 | 24 | – | p | Allegedly from N of Jiya and Suya |
| S.IV.D.b.15–17 | Chinese coins – Song dynasty | – | – | – | p | Allegedly from N of Jiya and Suya |
| S.IV.D.b.18–19 | [extra: Chinese coins – Song dynasty] | – | – | – | p | Allegedly from N of Jiya and Suya |

| BM no. | Identification | Wt | Diam. | Notes | Acqn | Acquisition/Archaeological context |
|---|---|---|---|---|---|---|
| S.IV.D.c.1 | Wuzhu – without rim | 2.00 | 24 | (H: 9) | p | Allegedly from site S of Sampula |

| | | | | | | |
|---|---|---|---|---|---|---|
| S.IV.D.d.1 (OR.0418) | Sino-Kharoshthi coin (Cribb 2) | 3.20 | 20 | – | p | Allegedly found at, or near, Kine-tokmak |
| S.IV.D.d.2 (OR.0405) | Sino-Kharoshthi coin (Cribb 2) | 3.54 | 22 | – | p | Allegedly found at, or near, Kine-tokmak |
| S.IV.D.d.3 | [missing: Sino-Kharoshthi coin] | – | – | – | p | Allegedly found at, or near, Kine-tokmak |
| S.IV.D.d.4 | [missing: Sino-Kharoshthi coin] | – | – | – | p | Allegedly found at, or near, Kine-tokmak |
| S.IV.D.d.5 | Wuzhu – full size | 1.93 | 25.5 | (H: 10) red | p | Allegedly found at, or near, Kine-tokmak |
| S.IV.D.d.6 | Qianyuan zhongbao – small | 2.14 | 22 | – | p | Allegedly found at, or near, Kine-tokmak |
| S.IV.D.d.7 | Qianyuan zhongbao – small | 2.74 | 22 | misaligned | p | Allegedly found at, or near, Kine-tokmak |
| S.IV.D.d.8 | [Qian]yuan zhong [bao] – large | 2.69 | – | frag. | p | Allegedly found at, or near, Kine-tokmak |
| S.IV.D.d.9–10 | Chinese coins – Song dynasty | – | – | – | p | Allegedly found at, or near, Kine-tokmak |
| S.IV.D.d.11–18 | Islamic coins | – | – | – | p | Allegedly found at, or near, Kine-tokmak |

| | | | | | | |
|---|---|---|---|---|---|---|
| S.IV.D.e.1–15 | (In this group, during cleaning 2 coins previously stuck together came apart) | | | | | |
| S.IV.D.e.1 | 'Wuzhu' – illegible | 0.70 | 18 | (H: 10) | p | Allegedly from Ak-terek Tatis |
| S.IV.D.e.2.a | 'Wuzhu' – illegible | 0.62 | 19.5 | (H: 9.5) | p | Allegedly from Ak-terek Tatis |
| S.IV.D.e.2.b | 'Wuzhu' – illegible | 1.30 | 18.5 | (H: 8) | p | Allegedly from Ak-terek Tatis |
| S.IV.D.e.3 | 'Wuzhu' – illegible | 1.53 | 21.5 | (H: 10) | p | Allegedly from Ak-terek Tatis |
| S.IV.D.e.4 | 'Wuzhu' – illegible | 1.29 | 24 | (H: 9.5) | p | Allegedly from Ak-terek Tatis |
| S.IV.D.e.5 | Chinese coin – unidentified | 1.43 | 18 | (H: 5.5) corroded | p | Allegedly from Ak-terek Tatis |
| S.IV.D.e.6 | Wuzhu – without full rim | 1.75 | 23.5 | (H: 9.5) | p | Allegedly from Ak-terek Tatis |
| S.IV.D.e.7 | Wuzhu – clipped, cuts through inscription | 1.75 | 23.5 | (H: 9.5) | p | Allegedly from Ak-terek Tatis |
| S.IV.D.e.8 | Wuzhu – crude inscription | 2.30 | 23 | (H: 9) corroded | p | Allegedly from Ak-terek Tatis |
| S.IV.D.e.9 | Unidentified, pierced disk | 1.21 | 14.5 | – | p | Allegedly from Ak-terek Tatis |
| S.IV.D.e.10 | Wuzhu – crude inscription | 1.02 | 20.5 | (H: 9) crude | p | Allegedly from Ak-terek Tatis |
| S.IV.D.e.11 | Clay casing for Chinese coin | 0.64 | – | – | p | Allegedly from Ak-terek Tatis |
| S.IV.D.e.12 | 'Wuzhu' – illegible | 0.08 | 24 | restored | p | Allegedly from Ak-terek Tatis |
| S.IV.D.e.13 | Chinese coin – unidentified | 0.87 | – | 2 frags | p | Allegedly from Ak-terek Tatis |
| S.IV.D.e.14 | 'Wuzhu' – illegible | 0.95 | 15.5 | (H: 8) misaligned | p | Allegedly from Ak-terek Tatis |
| S.IV.D.e.15 | Chinese coin – unidentified | 0.24 | – | frag. | p | Allegedly from Ak-terek Tatis |
| S.IV.D.e.16 | Chinese coin – unidentified | 3.65 | 24 | corroded | p | Allegedly from Ak-terek Tatis |
| S.IV.D.e.17 | Chinese coin – unidentified | 2.29 | 21 | packed in clay, uncleaned | p | Allegedly from Ak-terek Tatis |
| S.IV.D.e.18 | Qianyuan zhongbao – small | 2.41 | 22 | – | p | Allegedly from Ak-terek Tatis |
| S.IV.D.e.19 | Qianyuan zhongbao – medium | 1.76 | 23.5 | – | p | Allegedly from Ak-terek Tatis |
| S.IV.D.e.20 | Chinese coin – unidentified | 2.45 | 23 | corroded | p | Allegedly from Ak-terek Tatis |
| S.IV.D.e.21 | Qianyuan zhongbao – small | 2.06 | 21.5 | – | p | Allegedly from Ak-terek Tatis |
| S.IV.D.e.22 | Qianyuan zhongbao – small | 1.56 | 21.5 | – | p | Allegedly from Ak-terek Tatis |
| S.IV.D.e.23 | Qianyuan zhongbao – small | 2.17 | 22 | – | p | Allegedly from Ak-terek Tatis |
| S.IV.D.e.24 | Chinese coin – unidentified | 3.06 | 22 | packed in clay, uncleaned | p | Allegedly from Ak-terek Tatis |

| BM no. | Identification | Wt | Diam. | Notes | Acqn | Acquisition/Archaeological context |
|---|---|---|---|---|---|---|
| S.IV.D.e.25 | Qianyuan zhongbao – small | 2.47 | 22.5 | – | p | Allegedly from Ak-terek Tatis |
| S.IV.D.e.26 | Qianyuan zhongbao – small | 2.09 | 22 | forced hole, uncleaned | p | Allegedly from Ak-terek Tatis |
| S.IV.D.e.27 | Qianyuan zhongbao – small | 2.38 | 21.5 | misaligned | p | Allegedly from Ak-terek Tatis |
| S.IV.D.e.28 | Qianyuan zhongbao – small | 1.11 | 21.5 | restored | p | Allegedly from Ak-terek Tatis |
| S.IV.D.e.29 | Qianyuan zhongbao – small | 2.30 | 21.5 | – | p | Allegedly from Ak-terek Tatis |
| S.IV.D.e.30 | Qianyuan zhongbao – small | 1.98 | 22 | – | p | Allegedly from Ak-terek Tatis |
| S.IV.D.e.31 | Qianyuan zhongbao – small | 2.74 | 21 | – | p | Allegedly from Ak-terek Tatis |
| S.IV.D.e.32 | Qianyuan zhongbao – small | 2.27 | 21 | – | p | Allegedly from Ak-terek Tatis |
| S.IV.D.e.33 | Qianyuan zhongbao – small | 2.01 | 21 | misaligned | p | Allegedly from Ak-terek Tatis |
| S.IV.D.e.34 | Qianyuan zhongbao – small | 2.40 | 21 | – | p | Allegedly from Ak-terek Tatis |
| S.IV.D.e.35 | Qianyuan zhongbao – small | 2.33 | 21 | – | p | Allegedly from Ak-terek Tatis |
| S.IV.D.e.36 | Qianyuan zhongbao – small | 2.18 | 22 | – | p | Allegedly from Ak-terek Tatis |
| S.IV.D.e.37 | Qianyuan zhongbao – small | 1.91 | 22 | misaligned, forced hole | p | Allegedly from Ak-terek Tatis |
| S.IV.D.e.38 | Qianyuan zhongbao – small | 1.48 | 21 | – | p | Allegedly from Ak-terek Tatis |
| S.IV.D.e.39 | Qianyuan zhongbao – small | 1.47 | 21.5 | – | p | Allegedly from Ak-terek Tatis |
| S.IV.D.e.40 | Qianyuan zhongbao – small | 1.69 | 21.5 | misaligned, damaged | p | Allegedly from Ak-terek Tatis |
| S.IV.D.e.41 | Dali yuanbao – small | 2.18 | 21.5 | misaligned | p | Allegedly from Ak-terek Tatis |
| S.IV.D.e.42 | Dali yuanbao – large | 2.39 | 23.5 | forced hole | p | Allegedly from Ak-terek Tatis |
| S.IV.D.e.43 | Dali yuanbao – small | 1.77 | 22 | – | p | Allegedly from Ak-terek Tatis |
| S.IV.D.e.44 | Dali yuanbao – small | 2.71 | 20 | crude | p | Allegedly from Ak-terek Tatis |
| S.IV.D.e.45–51 | Islamic coins | – | – | – | p | Allegedly from Ak-terek Tatis |
| S.IV.D.e.52 | Chinese coin – Song dynasty | – | – | – | p | Allegedly from Ak-terek Tatis |

## S.V: COPPER COINS FOUND AT DESERT SITES NORTH OF JIYA

| BM no. | Identification | Wt | Diam. | Notes | Acqn | Acquisition/Archaeological context |
|---|---|---|---|---|---|---|
| S.V.a.1 | 'Wuzhu' – illegible | 1.78 | 20 | (H: 9) uncleaned | FAS | Found at Kök-kumarish site |
| S.V.a.2 | Wuzhu – small, without rim | 1.10 | 19 | (H: 9) uncleaned | FAS | Found at Kök-kumarish site |
| S.V.a.3 | 'Wuzhu' – illegible | 0.83 | 15 | (H: 7.5) uncleaned, with sprue | FAS | Found at Kök-kumarish site |

| | | | | | | |
|---|---|---|---|---|---|---|
| S.V.b.1 | 'Wuzhu' – illegible | 1.51 | 16 | (H: 7.5) red, uncleaned | FAS | Found at Kine-tokmak site |
| S.V.b.2 | 'Wuzhu' – small, illegible | 0.49 | 11 | (H: 2.5) corroded | FAS | Found at Kine-tokmak site |

### S.VI: COPPER COINS FOUND AT AK-TEREK SITE

| BM no. | Identification | Wt | Diam. | Notes | Acqn | Acquisition/Archaeological context |
|---|---|---|---|---|---|---|
| S.VI.a.1 | Chinese coins – Song dynasty | – | – | – | F | Found between Ak-terek and Siyelik |
| S.VI.b.1 | Wuzhu – clipped, cuts through inscription | 0.87 | 20 | (H: 10) faint | FAS | Found by Stein's guides on Ak-terek Tatis |
| S.VI.b.2 | 'Wuzhu' – illegible | 1.14 | 20 | (H: 9.5) | FAS | Found by Stein's guides on Ak-terek Tatis |
| S.VI.b.3 | 'Wuzhu' – illegible | 0.99 | 21 | (H: 9.5) misaligned | FAS | Found by Stein's guides on Ak-terek Tatis |
| S.VI.b.4 | Wuzhu – small wu, without rim | 1.24 | 21 | (H: 9) | FAS | Found by Stein's guides on Ak-terek Tatis |
| S.VI.b.5 | Wuzhu – clipped, cuts through inscription | 1.21 | 21 | (H: 9.5) faint | FAS | Found by Stein's guides on Ak-terek Tatis |
| S.VI.b.6 | Wuzhu – clipped, cuts through inscription | 1.23 | 20.5 | (H: 9) | FAS | Found by Stein's guides on Ak-terek Tatis |
| S.VI.b.7 | Wuzhu – clipped, cuts through inscription | 0.88 | 17 | (H: 9) | FAS | Found by Stein's guides on Ak-terek Tatis |
| S.VI.b.8 | Wuzhu – clipped, cuts through inscription | 0.96 | 17.5 | (H: 8) misaligned | FAS | Found by Stein's guides on Ak-terek Tatis |
| S.VI.b.9 | 'Wuzhu' – illegible | 0.62 | 17 | (H: 9) | FAS | Found by Stein's guides on Ak-terek Tatis |
| S.VI.b.10 | 'Wuzhu' – illegible | 0.58 | 14 | (H: 8) flat on one side | FAS | Found by Stein's guides on Ak-terek Tatis |
| S.VI.b.11 | 'Wuzhu' – illegible | 0.47 | 14.5 | (H: 7) | FAS | Found by Stein's guides on Ak-terek Tatis |
| S.VI.b.12 | 'Wuzhu' – illegible | 0.43 | 13 | (H: 6) | FAS | Found by Stein's guides on Ak-terek Tatis |
| S.VI.b.13 | 'Wuzhu' – illegible | 0.66 | 17.5 | frag. (H: 8.5) | FAS | Found by Stein's guides on Ak-terek Tatis |
| S.VI.b.14 | Kai [yuan tong] bao | 1.71 | – | frag., misaligned | FAS | Found by Stein's guides on Ak-terek Tatis |
| S.VI.b.15 | Qianyuan zhongbao – small | 3.25 | 22 | misaligned | FAS | Found by Stein's guides on Ak-terek Tatis |
| S.VI.b.16–17 | Chinese coins – Song dynasty | – | – | – | FAS | Found by Stein's guides on Ak-terek Tatis |
| S.VI.b.18–26 | Islamic coins | – | – | – | FAS | Found by Stein's guides on Ak-terek Tatis |
| S.VI.b.27 | [Wu] zhu – full size | 0.75 | – | frag., red | FAS | Found by Stein's guides on Ak-terek Tatis |
| S.VI.b.28 | Wuzhu – full size | 1.82 | 25.5 | frag., red | FAS | Found by Stein's guides on Ak-terek Tatis |
| S.VI.b.29 | Chinese coin – unidentified, xx yuan bao | 1.91 | – | frags, red | FAS | Found by Stein's guides on Ak-terek Tatis |
| S.VI.b.30–40 | Islamic coins | – | – | red | FAS | Found by Stein's guides on Ak-terek Tatis |
| S.VI.b.41–43 | Chinese coins – unidentified | – | – | frags, corroded | FAS | Found by Stein's guides on Ak-terek Tatis |

## S.VII: COPPER COINS FOUND AT KHADALIK AND NEIGHBOURING SITES

| BM no. | Identification | Wt | Diam. | Notes | Acqn | Acquisition/Archaeological context |
|---|---|---|---|---|---|---|
| S.VII.a.1–87 | Two strings of coins found in NW corner of cella at Khadalik (Kha.ii) | | | | | |
| S.XII.a.1–33 | First string (including 13 coins found detached) | | | | | |
| S.VII.a.1 | Wuzhu – full size | 1.53 | 25 | (H: 9.5) | FAS | From first string of coins found in cella Kha.ii |
| S.VII.a.2 | Wuzhu – without full rim | 1.24 | 23 | (H: 9.5) | FAS | From first string of coins found in cella Kha.ii |
| S.VII.a.3 | Kaiyuan tongbao | 4.97 | 26 | 3 frags (= 1 coin) | FAS | From first string of coins found in cella Kha.ii |
| S.VII.a.4 | Qianyuan zhongbao – small | 2.64 | 22 | misaligned | FAS | From first string of coins found in cella Kha.ii |
| S.VII.a.5 | Qianyuan zhongbao – small | 3.15 | 21.5 | misaligned | FAS | From first string of coins found in cella Kha.ii |
| S.VII.a.6 | Qianyuan zhongbao – small | 3.21 | 22 | misaligned | FAS | From first string of coins found in cella Kha.ii |
| S.VII.a.7 | Qianyuan zhongbao – small | 3.36 | 22 | misaligned | FAS | From first string of coins found in cella Kha.ii |
| S.VII.a.8 | Qianyuan zhongbao – small | 3.08 | 21.5 | with sprue | FAS | From first string of coins found in cella Kha.ii |
| S.VII.a.9 | Qianyuan zhongbao – small | 2.81 | 22.5 | – | FAS | From first string of coins found in cella Kha.ii |
| S.VII.a.10 | Qianyuan zhongbao – small | 2.71 | 22 | damaged | FAS | From first string of coins found in cella Kha.ii |
| S.VII.a.11 | Qianyuan zhongbao – small | 2.78 | 23 | misaligned | FAS | From first string of coins found in cella Kha.ii |
| S.VII.a.12 | Qianyuan zhongbao – small | 2.80 | 22 | – | FAS | From first string of coins found in cella Kha.ii |
| S.VII.a.13 | Qianyuan zhongbao – small | 1.39 | 20.5 | – | FAS | From first string of coins found in cella Kha.ii |
| S.VII.a.14 | Qianyuan zhongbao – small | 2.43 | 22 | misaligned, damaged | FAS | From first string of coins found in cella Kha.ii |
| S.VII.a.15 | Qianyuan zhongbao – small | 2.20 | 22 | misaligned | FAS | From first string of coins found in cella Kha.ii |
| S.VII.a.16 | Qianyuan zhongbao – small | 2.14 | 21 | misaligned | FAS | From first string of coins found in cella Kha.ii |
| S.VII.a.17 | Qianyuan zhongbao – small | 2.68 | 22 | – | FAS | From first string of coins found in cella Kha.ii |
| S.VII.a.18 | Qianyuan zhongbao – small | 2.28 | 21 | misaligned | FAS | From first string of coins found in cella Kha.ii |
| S.VII.a.19 | Qianyuan zhongbao – small | 2.62 | 22 | misaligned, forced hole | FAS | From first string of coins found in cella Kha.ii |
| S.VII.a.20 | Qianyuan zhongbao – small | 2.29 | 21.5 | misaligned, damaged | FAS | From first string of coins found in cella Kha.ii |
| S.VII.a.21 | Qianyuan zhongbao – small | 3.30 | 22 | – | FAS | From first string of coins found in cella Kha.ii |
| S.VII.a.22 | Qianyuan zhongbao – small | 3.21 | 22 | misaligned, forced hole | FAS | From first string of coins found in cella Kha.ii |
| S.VII.a.23 | Qianyuan zhongbao – small | 2.41 | 21 | misaligned | FAS | From first string of coins found in cella Kha.ii |
| S.VII.a.24 | Qianyuan zhongbao – small | 3.18 | 21.5 | misaligned | FAS | From first string of coins found in cella Kha.ii |
| S.VII.a.25 | Qianyuan zhongbao – medium | 3.02 | 23.5 | misaligned | FAS | From first string of coins found in cella Kha.ii |

| BM no. | Identification | Wt | Diam. | Notes | Acqn | Acquisition/Archaeological context |
|---|---|---|---|---|---|---|
| S.VII.a.26 | Qianyuan zhongbao – small | 2.14 | 22 | – | FAS | From first string of coins found in cella Kha.ii |
| S.VII.a.27 | Qianyuan zhongbao – large | 6.51 | 29 | – | FAS | From first string of coins found in cella Kha.ii |
| S.VII.a.28 | Qianyuan zhongbao – large | 7.44 | 28.5 | misaligned | FAS | From first string of coins found in cella Kha.ii |
| S.VII.a.29 | Dali yuanbao – small | 2.27 | 22 | crack in rev. mould, damaged | FAS | From first string of coins found in cella Kha.ii |
| S.VII.a.30 | Dali yuanbao – large | 4.10 | 24 | damaged | FAS | From first string of coins found in cella Kha.ii |
| S.VII.a.31 | Dali yuanbao – small | 3.25 | 22 | – | FAS | From first string of coins found in cella Kha.ii |
| S.VII.a.32 | Dali yuanbao – small | 2.57 | 22.5 | – | FAS | From first string of coins found in cella Kha.ii |
| S.VII.a.33 | Dali yuanbao – small | 1.71 | 22 | – | FAS | From first string of coins found in cella Kha.ii |
| S,VII.a.34–87 | Second string | | | | | |
| S.VII.a.34 | Wuzhu – without rim | 1.20 | 23.5 | (H: 10) faint | FAS | From second string of coins found in cella Kha.ii |
| S.VII.a.35 | 'Wuzhu' – illegible | 1.30 | 23 | (H: 9.5) | FAS | From second string of coins found in cella Kha.ii |
| S.VII.a.36 | Kaiyuan tongbao | 3.80 | 24 | – | FAS | From second string of coins found in cella Kha.ii |
| S.VII.a.37 | Kaiyuan tongbao | 4.09 | 24.5 | misaligned | FAS | From second string of coins found in cella Kha.ii |
| S.VII.a.38 | Qianyuan zhongbao – medium | 3.36 | 25.5 | – | FAS | From second string of coins found in cella Kha.ii |
| S.VII.a.39 | Qianyuan zhongbao – medium | 3.86 | 24.5 | misaligned | FAS | From second string of coins found in cella Kha.ii |
| S.VII.a.40 | Qianyuan zhongbao – medium | 4.17 | 25 | – | FAS | From second string of coins found in cella Kha.ii |
| S.VII.a.41 | Qianyuan zhongbao – medium | 3.91 | 24.5 | – | FAS | From second string of coins found in cella Kha.ii |
| S.VII.a.42 | Qianyuan zhongbao – medium | 3.68 | 25 | misaligned | FAS | From second string of coins found in cella Kha.ii |
| S.VII.a.43 | Qianyuan zhongbao – small | 2.71 | 22 | – | FAS | From second string of coins found in cella Kha.ii |
| S.VII.a.44 | Qianyuan zhongbao – small | 2.18 | 22 | – | FAS | From second string of coins found in cella Kha.ii |
| S.VII.a.45 | Qianyuan zhongbao – small | 2.23 | 21 | crack in rev. mould | FAS | From second string of coins found in cella Kha.ii |
| S.VII.a.46 | Qianyuan zhongbao – small | 3.09 | 22 | misaligned | FAS | From second string of coins found in cella Kha.ii |
| S.VII.a.47 | Qianyuan zhongbao – small | 2.73 | 21.5 | misaligned | FAS | From second string of coins found in cella Kha.ii |
| S.VII.a.48 | Qianyuan zhongbao – small, four dots on flan | 2.89 | 22 | – | FAS | From second string of coins found in cella Kha.ii |
| S.VII.a.49 | Qianyuan zhongbao – small | 3.28 | 22 | – | FAS | From second string of coins found in cella Kha.ii |
| S.VII.a.50 | Qianyuan zhongbao – small | 2.52 | 22 | – | FAS | From second string of coins found in cella Kha.ii |
| S.VII.a.51 | Qianyuan zhongbao – small | 2.83 | 22 | misaligned | FAS | From second string of coins found in cella Kha.ii |
| S.VII.a.52 | Qianyuan zhongbao – small | 2.58 | 22 | misaligned | FAS | From second string of coins found in cella Kha.ii |

| BM no. | Identification | Wt | Diam. | Notes | Acqn | Acquisition/Archaeological context |
|---|---|---|---|---|---|---|
| S.VII.a.53 | Qianyuan zhongbao – small | 2.69 | 21 | misaligned | FAS | From second string of coins found in cella Kha.ii |
| S.VII.a.54 | Qianyuan zhongbao – small | 2.70 | 22 | misaligned | FAS | From second string of coins found in cella Kha.ii |
| S.VII.a.55 | Qianyuan zhongbao – small | 2.63 | 22 | misaligned | FAS | From second string of coins found in cella Kha.ii |
| S.VII.a.56 | Qianyuan zhongbao – small | 2.64 | 21 | – | FAS | From second string of coins found in cella Kha.ii |
| S.VII.a.57 | Qianyuan zhongbao – small | 2.26 | 21 | – | FAS | From second string of coins found in cella Kha.ii |
| S.VII.a.58 | Qianyuan zhongbao – small | 2.39 | 20.5 | – | FAS | From second string of coins found in cella Kha.ii |
| S.VII.a.59 | Qianyuan zhongbao – small | 2.26 | 22 | – | FAS | From second string of coins found in cella Kha.ii |
| S.VII.a.60 | Qianyuan zhongbao – small | 2.20 | 21.5 | misaligned, forced hole | FAS | From second string of coins found in cella Kha.ii |
| S.VII.a.61 | Qianyuan zhongbao – small | 3.33 | 22 | with sprue | FAS | From second string of coins found in cella Kha.ii |
| S.VII.a.62 | Qianyuan zhongbao – small | 2.10 | 21 | – | FAS | From second string of coins found in cella Kha.ii |
| S.VII.a.63 | Qianyuan zhongbao – small | 2.50 | 21.5 | – | FAS | From second string of coins found in cella Kha.ii |
| S.VII.a.64 | Qianyuan zhongbao – small | 2.19 | 21 | misaligned | FAS | From second string of coins found in cella Kha.ii |
| S.VII.a.65 | Qianyuan zhongbao – small | 2.91 | 22 | – | FAS | From second string of coins found in cella Kha.ii |
| S.VII.a.66 | Qianyuan zhongbao – small | 2.50 | 21 | misaligned, forced hole | FAS | From second string of coins found in cella Kha.ii |
| S.VII.a.67 | Qianyuan zhongbao – small | 2.61 | 21 | – | FAS | From second string of coins found in cella Kha.ii |
| S.VII.a.68 | Qianyuan zhongbao – small | 3.03 | 22 | misaligned | FAS | From second string of coins found in cella Kha.ii |
| S.VII.a.69 | Qianyuan zhongbao – small | 3.36 | 22 | misaligned, forced hole | FAS | From second string of coins found in cella Kha.ii |
| S.VII.a.70 | Qianyuan zhongbao – small | 1.75 | 21 | misaligned | FAS | From second string of coins found in cella Kha.ii |
| S.VII.a.71 | Qianyuan zhongbao – small | 2.85 | 22 | misaligned | FAS | From second string of coins found in cella Kha.ii |
| S.VII.a.72 | Qianyuan zhongbao – small | 2.32 | 22 | misaligned, forced hole | FAS | From second string of coins found in cella Kha.ii |
| S.VII.a.73 | Qianyuan zhongbao – small | 2.19 | 21.5 | damaged | FAS | From second string of coins found in cella Kha.ii |
| S.VII.a.74 | Qianyuan zhongbao – small | 3.09 | 22 | misaligned, forced hole | FAS | From second string of coins found in cella Kha.ii |
| S.VII.a.75 | Qianyuan zhongbao – small | 1.98 | 20 | misaligned | FAS | From second string of coins found in cella Kha.ii |
| S.VII.a.76 | Qianyuan zhongbao – small | 1.89 | 21 | misaligned, damaged | FAS | From second string of coins found in cella Kha.ii |
| S.VII.a.77 | Qianyuan zhongbao – small | 1.87 | 21.5 | damaged | FAS | From second string of coins found in cella Kha.ii |
| S.VII.a.78 | Qianyuan zhongbao – small | 2.36 | 22 | misaligned, forced hole | FAS | From second string of coins found in cella Kha.ii |
| S.VII.a.79 | Qianyuan zhongbao – small | 1.77 | 22 | frag., misaligned, forced hole | FAS | From second string of coins found in cella Kha.ii |

| BM no. | Identification | Wt | Diam. | Notes | Acqn | Acquisition/Archaeological context |
|---|---|---|---|---|---|---|
| S.VII.a.80 | Dali yuanbao – small | 3.37 | 22 | misaligned | FAS | From second string of coins found in cella Kha.ii |
| S.VII.a.81 | Dali yuanbao – small | 2.84 | 22 | forced hole | FAS | From second string of coins found in cella Kha.ii |
| S.VII.a.82 | Dali yuanbao – large | 3.97 | 24 | misaligned | FAS | From second string of coins found in cella Kha.ii |
| S.VII.a.83 | Dali yuanbao – small | 2.83 | 22 | misaligned | FAS | From second string of coins found in cella Kha.ii |
| S.VII.a.84 | Dali yuanbao – small | 3.31 | 22 | – | FAS | From second string of coins found in cella Kha.ii |
| S.VII.a.85 | Dali yuanbao – large | 3.22 | 24 | – | FAS | From second string of coins found in cella Kha.ii |
| S.VII.a.86 | Dali yuanbao – large | 3.43 | 24 | – | FAS | From second string of coins found in cella Kha.ii |
| S.VII.a.87 | Dali yuanbao – large | 3.58 | 24 | misaligned | FAS | From second string of coins found in cella Kha.ii |

| | | | | | | |
|---|---|---|---|---|---|---|
| S.VII.b.1 | 'Wuzhu' – illegible | 1.02 | 22.5 | (H: 10) | FAS | Found outside W wall of cella Kha.ii. |
| S.VII.b.2 | Qianyuan zhongbao – small | 3.20 | 22 | – | FAS | Found outside W wall of cella Kha.ii. |
| S.VII.b.3 | Qianyuan zhongbao – small | 2.66 | 22.5 | misaligned, forced hole | FAS | Found outside W wall of cella Kha.ii. |
| S.VII.b.4 | Qianyuan zhongbao – small | 2.33 | 22.5 | misaligned, forced hole | FAS | Found outside W wall of cella Kha.ii. |
| S.VII.b.5 | Qianyuan zhongbao – small | 5.08 | 22 | – | FAS | Found outside W wall of cella Kha.ii. |
| S.VII.b.6 | Qianyuan zhongbao – small | 2.83 | 22 | cracks on rev. mould | FAS | Found outside W wall of cella Kha.ii. |
| S.VII.b.7 | Qianyuan zhongbao – small | 2.79 | 23 | misaligned | FAS | Found outside W wall of cella Kha.ii. |
| S.VII.b.8 | Qianyuan zhongbao – small | 2.38 | 21.5 | – | FAS | Found outside W wall of cella Kha.ii. |
| S.VII.b.9 | Qianyuan zhongbao – small | 2.14 | 21 | misaligned | FAS | Found outside W wall of cella Kha.ii. |
| S.VII.b.10 | Qianyuan zhongbao – small | 2.74 | 22 | misaligned | FAS | Found outside W wall of cella Kha.ii. |
| S.VII.b.11 | [extra: Qianyuan zhongbao – small] | 3.57 | 21 | – | FAS | Found outside W wall of cella Kha.ii. |
| S.VII.b.12 | Dali yuanbao – small | 2.47 | 22 | – | FAS | Found outside W wall of cella Kha.II. |
| S.VII.b.13–14 | [missing: Dali yuanbao] | – | – | – | FAS | Found outside W wall of cella Kha.ii. |

| | | | | | | |
|---|---|---|---|---|---|---|
| S.VII.c.1 | Kaiyuan tongbao | 3.71 | 24.5 | – | FAS | Found in shrine Kha.vi |

| | | | | | | |
|---|---|---|---|---|---|---|
| S.VII.d.1 | 'Wuzhu' – illegible | 0.79 | 19 | (H: 9.5) | FAS | Found at Kighillik, E of Khadalik |
| S.VII.d.2 | Qianyuan zhongbao – small | 2.37 | 21.5 | scyphate | FAS | Found at Kighillik, E of Khadalik |

| | | | | | | |
|---|---|---|---|---|---|---|
| S.VII.e.1 | 'Wuzhu' – illegible | 1.25 | 23.5 | (H: 10) | F | Allegedly found near Khadalik, received from Mullah Khwaja |

| BM no. | Identification | Wt | Diam. | Notes | Acqn | Acquisition/Archaeological context |
|---|---|---|---|---|---|---|
| S.VII.e.2 | Qianyuan zhongbao – small | 2.07 | 22 | – | F | Allegedly found near Khadalik, received from Mullah Khwaja |
| S.VII.e.3 | Jianzhong tongbao – small | 1.97 | 21.5 | – | F | Allegedly found near Khadalik, received from Mullah Khwaja |

| | | | | | | |
|---|---|---|---|---|---|---|
| S.VII.f.1 | 'Wuzhu' – illegible | 1.15 | 22 | (H: 9) | FAS | Found at Balawaste |

| | | | | | | |
|---|---|---|---|---|---|---|
| S.VII.g.1 | 'Wuzhu' – illegible | 1.24 | 23 | (H: 9.5) | FAS | Found at Mazar-toghrak |

## S.VIII: COPPER COINS FOUND AT NIYA SITE

| BM no. | Identification | Wt | Diam. | Notes | Acqn | Acquisition/Archaeological context |
|---|---|---|---|---|---|---|
| S.VIII.a.1 | Huoquan, inscription repeated on rev. | 4.32 | 22 | – | FAS | Found near ruin N.XII |
| S.VIII.a.2 | Wuzhu – without full rim | 2.76 | 24.5 | (H: 9) | FAS | Found near ruin N.XII |

| | | | | | | |
|---|---|---|---|---|---|---|
| S.VIII.b.1 | Huoquan | 1.77 | 21.5 | damaged | FAS | Found near ruin N.XIV |

| | | | | | | |
|---|---|---|---|---|---|---|
| S.VIII.c.1 | Wuzhu – full size | 2.53 | 26 | (H: 10) | FAS | Found near ruin N.XXIV |
| S.VIII.c.2 | Wuzhu – full size | 1.47 | 26 | 2 frags | FAS | Found near ruin N.XXIV |
| S.VIII.c.3 | Wuzhu – clipped, cuts through inscription | 0.70 | 18 | (H: 10) | FAS | Found near ruin N.XXIV |

| | | | | | | |
|---|---|---|---|---|---|---|
| S.VIII.d.1 | 'Wuzhu' – illegible | 0.62 | – | frag. | FAS | Found in N part of site |
| S.VIII.d.2 | Wuzhu – full size | 2.36 | 26 | (H: 9.5) | FAS | Found in N part of site |
| S.VIII.d.3 | Wuzhu – full size | 2.17 | 26 | (H: 10) corroded | FAS | Found in N part of site |

| | | | | | | |
|---|---|---|---|---|---|---|
| S.VIII.e.1 | Wuzhu – clipped, cuts through inscription | 1.29 | 20.5 | (H: 10) | FAS | Found near SE ruins of site |
| S.VIII.e.2 | 'Wuzhu' – illegible | 0.89 | 18.5 | (H: 9.5) | FAS | Found near SE ruins of site |

## S.IX: COPPER COINS FOUND AT ENDERE SITE

| BM no. | Identification | Wt | Diam. | Notes | Acqn | Acquisition/Archaeological context |
|---|---|---|---|---|---|---|
| S.IX.a.1 | Wuzhu – full size | 2.11 | 26 | (H: 9.5) | FAS | Found near stupa |
| S.IX.a.2 | Wuzhu – clipped, cuts through inscription | 1.03 | 18.5 | (H: 9) | FAS | Found near stupa |
| S.IX.a.3 | Wuzhu – small wu | 0.99 | – | frag. | FAS | Found near stupa |
| S.IX.a.4 | Wuzhu – small wu | 0.41 | – | frag. | FAS | Found near stupa |
| S.IX.a.5 | 'Wuzhu' – illegible | 0.94 | 15.5 | (H: 8) | FAS | Found near stupa |

| | | | | | | |
|---|---|---|---|---|---|---|
| S.IX.b.1 | 'Wuzhu' – illegible | 1.48 | 21.5 | (H: 9.5) crack on rev. mould | FAS | Found between stupa and Tang fort |
| S.IX.b.2 | Wuzhu – without rim | 1.64 | 23.5 | frag. (H: 9) | FAS | Found between stupa and Tang fort |
| S.IX.b.3 | Wuzhu – small, without inscription, square | 0.23 | 9.5 | (H: 6) | FAS | Found between stupa and Tang fort |

| | | | | | | |
|---|---|---|---|---|---|---|
| S.IX.c.1 | 'Wuzhu' – illegible | 1.04 | 18 | 2 frags (= 1 coin) (H: 8.5) | FAS | Found W of ruin E.vii |

| BM no. | Identification | Wt | Diam. | Notes | Acqn | Acquisition/Archaeological context |
|---|---|---|---|---|---|---|
| S.IX.d.1 | Wuzhu – without rim | 1.19 | – | frags | FAS | Found near Tang fort |
| S.IX.d.2 | 'Wuzhu' – illegible, small | 0.56 | 19 | (H: 7.5) | FAS | Found near Tang fort |
| S.IX.d.3 | 'Wuzhu' – illegible | 0.98 | 20.5 | (H: 9) 2 frags | FAS | Found near Tang fort |
| S.IX.d.4 | Unidentified | 0.98 | – | frag. | FAS | Found near Tang fort |
| S.IX.d.5 | 'Wuzhu' – illegible | 0.53 | – | frag. | FAS | Found near Tang fort |
| S.IX.d.6 | [Wu] zhu – full size | 0.41 | – | frag. | FAS | Found near Tang fort |
| S.IX.d.7 | [extra: Kai (yuan tong) bao] | 1.24 | – | frag. | – | – |

## S.X: COPPER COINS COLLECTED AT VASH–SHAHRI SITE

| BM no. | Identification | Wt | Diam. | Notes | Acqn | Acquisition/Archaeological context |
|---|---|---|---|---|---|---|
| S.X.a.1 | Kaiyuan tongbao | 3.57 | 25.5 | – | FAS | Found at Vash-shahri site |
| S.X.a.2 | Kaiyuan tongbao | 4.33 | 25 | – | FAS | Found at Vash-shahri site |
| S.X.a.3 | Kaiyuan tongbao | 3.20 | 25.5 | – | FAS | Found at Vash-shahri site |
| S.X.a.4–7 | Chinese coins – Song dynasty | – | – | – | FAS | Found at Vash-shahri site |
| S.X.a.8 | Chinese coin – unidentified, Tang dynasty? | 1.71 | 23.5 | frag. | FAS | Found at Vash-shahri site |
| S.X.a.9–10 | [extra: Chinese – Song dynasty] | – | – | – | – | – |
| S.X.a.11–12 | [extra: Kai (yuan) tong (bao)] | 1.90 | – | 2 frags | – | – |

## S.XI: COPPER COINS FOUND AT LOULAN SITES

### S.XI.A: COINS FROM LOULAN STATION, L.A.

| BM no. | Identification | Wt | Diam. | Notes | Acqn | Acquisition/Archaeological context |
|---|---|---|---|---|---|---|
| S.XI.A.a.1 | Wuzhu – clipped, cuts through inscription | 0.99 | 10.5 | frag | FAS | Found 9 miles N of Camp 122 |

| | | | | | | |
|---|---|---|---|---|---|---|
| S.XI.A.b.1 | Huoquan – without rim | 1.39 | 20 | red | FAS | Found W. of L.A. site |
| S.XI.A.b.2 | 'Wuzhu' – without inscription, small | 0.29 | 18 | (H: 7.5) red | FAS | Found W. of L.A. site |
| S.XI.A.b.3 | Unidentified, coin or perforated disk | 1.52 | 15 | (H: 6.5) | FAS | Found W. of L.A. site |
| S.XI.A.b.4 | [extra: Wuzhu – full size – thin wu] | 2.85 | 25.5 | (H: 10.5) | FAS | Found W. of L.A. site |

| | | | | | | |
|---|---|---|---|---|---|---|
| S.XI.A.c.1 | Xiaoquan zhiyi | 1.11 | 14.5 | 2 holes in flan | FAS | Found on wind-eroded ground near station L.A. |
| S.XI.A.c.2 | Huoquan | 2.18 | 22.5 | – | FAS | Found on wind-eroded ground near station L.A. |
| S.XI.A.c.3 | Huoquan | 2.03 | 23 | – | FAS | Found on wind-eroded ground near station L.A. |
| S.XI.A.c.4 | Huoquan | 1.17 | – | frag. | FAS | Found on wind-eroded ground near station L.A. |
| S.XI.A.c.5 | [extra: Huoquan – clipped, cuts through inscription] | 1.20 | 19.5 | – | FAS | Found on wind-eroded ground near station L.A. |
| S.XI.A.c.6a | Wu [zhu] –clipped, cuts through inscription | 0.72 | – | frag. | FAS | Found on wind-eroded ground near station L.A. |
| S.XI.A.c.6b | Wu [zhu] – with line below hole | 0.60 | – | frag. | FAS | Found on wind-eroded ground near station L.A. |
| S.XI.A.c.7 | Wuzhu – full size | 4.23 | 27.5 | (H: 10) corroded | FAS | Found on wind-eroded ground near station L.A. |

| BM no. | Identification | Wt | Diam. | Notes | Acqn | Acquisition/Archaeological context |
|---|---|---|---|---|---|---|
| S.XI.A.c.8 | Wuzhu – clipped, cuts through inscription | 1.31 | 21 | (H: 9.5) | FAS | Found on wind-eroded ground near station L.A. |
| S.XI.A.c.9 | 'Wuzhu' – illegible | 1.95 | 24 | (H: 9) corroded | FAS | Found on wind-eroded ground near station L.A. |
| S.XI.A.c.10 | Wuzhu – full size | 2.46 | 26 | (H: 9) | FAS | Found on wind-eroded ground near station L.A. |
| S.XI.A.c.11 | 'Wuzhu' – illegible | 1.74 | 22 | (H: 9) | FAS | Found on wind-eroded ground near station L.A. |
| S.XI.A.c.12 | Wuzhu – clipped, cuts through inscription | 1.30 | 17.5 | (H: 7.5) | FAS | Found on wind-eroded ground near station L.A. |
| S.XI.A.c.13 | 'Wuzhu' – illegible | 1.52 | 21 | (H: 9) | FAS | Found on wind-eroded ground near station L.A. |
| S.XI.A.c.14 | Wuzhu – without full rim | 1.49 | 24.5 | (H: 9.5) | FAS | Found on wind-eroded ground near station L.A. |
| S.XI.A.c.15 | Wuzhu – without rim | 2.14 | 23.5 | (H: 9.5) | FAS | Found on wind-eroded ground near station L.A. |
| S.XI.A.c.16 | Wuzhu – without rim | 1.63 | 23.5 | (H: 9) forced hole | FAS | Found on wind-eroded ground near station L.A. |
| S.XI.A.c.17 | Wuzhu – clipped, cuts through inscription | 1.70 | 21 | (H: 9) damaged | FAS | Found on wind-eroded ground near station L.A. |
| S.XI.A.c.18 | Wuzhu – full size | 2.42 | 26 | (H: 10.5) | FAS | Found on wind-eroded ground near station L.A. |
| S.XI.A.c.19 | Wuzhu – without rim | 2.87 | 24.5 | (H: 10) | FAS | Found on wind-eroded ground near station L.A. |
| S.XI.A.c.20 | Wuzhu – full size | 2.02 | 26 | (H: 9) | FAS | Found on wind-eroded ground near station L.A. |
| S.XI.A.c.21 | Wuzhu – full size | 3.14 | 25 | (H: 9.5) | FAS | Found on wind-eroded ground near station L.A. |
| S.XI.A.c.22 | Wuzhu – without rim | 2.21 | 24.5 | (H: 10) | FAS | Found on wind-eroded ground near station L.A. |
| S.XI.A.c.23 | 'Wuzhu' – illegible | 1.29 | 18 | (H: 7.5) corroded | FAS | Found on wind-eroded ground near station L.A. |
| S.XI.A.c.24 | Wuzhu – full size | 2.68 | 26 | (H: 10.5) | FAS | Found on wind-eroded ground near station L.A. |
| S.XI.A.c.25 | Wuzhu – clipped, cuts through inscription | 1.36 | 22.5 | (H: 9.5) red | FAS | Found on wind-eroded ground near station L.A. |
| S.XI.A.c.26 | 'Wuzhu' – illegible | 1.14 | 20 | (H: 9.5) | FAS | Found on wind-eroded ground near station L.A. |
| S.XI.A.c.27 | 'Wuzhu' – illegible, without rim | 1.17 | 23.5 | (H: 9.5) | FAS | Found on wind-eroded ground near station L.A. |
| S.XI.A.c.28 | Wuzhu – full size | 2.23 | 25 | (H: 10) | FAS | Found on wind-eroded ground near station L.A. |
| S.XI.A.c.29 | Wuzhu – clipped, cuts through inscription | 1.90 | 23 | (H: 10) | FAS | Found on wind-eroded ground near station L.A. |
| S.XI.A.c.30 | 'Wuzhu' – illegible | 2.01 | 21 | (H: 9.5) misaligned, damaged | FAS | Found on wind-eroded ground near station L.A. |
| S.XI.A.c.31 | Wuzhu – without rim | 1.44 | 23 | (H: 10) | FAS | Found on wind-eroded ground near station L.A. |
| S.XI.A.c.32 | Banliang | 1.74 | 23 | – | FAS | Found on wind-eroded ground near station L.A. |
| S.XI.A.c.33 | Wuzhu – full size | 2.35 | 25.5 | (H: 10.5) | FAS | Found on wind-eroded ground near station L.A. |
| S.XI.A.c.34 | Chinese coin – unidentified | 4.58 | 26 | corroded | FAS | Found on wind-eroded ground near station L.A. |

| BM no. | Identification | Wt | Diam. | Notes | Acqn | Acquisition/Archaeological context |
|---|---|---|---|---|---|---|
| S.XI.A.c.35 | 'Wuzhu' – illegible | 1.08 | 22 | (H: 9.5) red, damaged | FAS | Found on wind-eroded ground near station L.A. |
| S.XI.A.c.36 | Wuzhu – full size | 2.53 | 26 | (H: 10) | FAS | Found on wind-eroded ground near station L.A. |
| S.XI.A.c.37 | Wu [zhu] – full size | 1.29 | 26.5 | frag. | FAS | Found on wind-eroded ground near station L.A. |
| S.XI.A.c.38 | [Wu] zhu – full size | 1.04 | – | frag. | FAS | Found on wind-eroded ground near station L.A. |
| S.XI.A.c.39 | [Wu] zhu – full size | 1.25 | – | frag. | FAS | Found on wind-eroded ground near station L.A. |
| S.XI.A.c.40 | Wu [zhu] – thin wu | 1.14 | – | frag. | FAS | Found on wind-eroded ground near station L.A. |
| S.XI.A.c.41 | [Wu]zhu – clipped, cuts through inscription | 0.71 | 22 | (H: 10) frag. | FAS | Found on wind-eroded ground near station L.A. |
| S.XI.A.c.42 | [Wuzhu] – frag. has no inscription | 0.66 | – | frag. | FAS | Found on wind-eroded ground near station L.A. |
| S.XI.A.c.43 | [Wu] zhu – full size | 0.79 | – | frag. | FAS | Found on wind-eroded ground near station L.A. |
| S.XI.A.c.44 | [Wu] zhu – dot below hole on obv. | 1.86 | 26 | (H: 9) frag. | FAS | Found on wind-eroded ground near station L.A. |
| S.XI.A.c.45 | [Wu] zhu | 0.78 | – | frag. | FAS | Found on wind-eroded ground near station L.A. |
| S.XI.A.c.46 | Wu [zhu] – full size | 0.84 | – | frag. | FAS | Found on wind-eroded ground near station L.A. |
| S.XI.A.c.47 | Wu [zhu] – full size | 0.87 | – | (H: 9) frag. | FAS | Found on wind-eroded ground near station L.A. |
| S.XI.A.c.48 | Wu [zhu] – full size | 0.99 | – | frag. | FAS | Found on wind-eroded ground near station L.A. |
| S.XI.A.c.49 | Wu [zhu] – full size | 1.28 | 25.5 | (H: 10) frag. | FAS | Found on wind-eroded ground near station L.A. |
| S.XI.A.c.50 | Wu [zhu] – full size | 0.78 | – | frag. | FAS | Found on wind-eroded ground near station L.A. |
| S.XI.A.c.51 | [Wu] zhu – clipped, cuts through inscription | 0.64 | – | frag. | FAS | Found on wind-eroded ground near station L.A. |
| S.XI.A.c.52 | Wu[zhu] – clipped, cuts through inscription | 0.56 | – | frag. | FAS | Found on wind-eroded ground near station L.A. |
| S.XI.A.c.53 | Daquan wushi – incomplete rim | 2.42 | 24 | faint | FAS | Found on wind-eroded ground near station L.A. |
| S.XI.A.c.54 | Huoquan | 1.50 | 22.5 | faint, damaged | FAS | Found on wind-eroded ground near station L.A. |
| S.XI.A.c.55 | Wuzhu – clipped, cuts through inscription | 1.56 | 19 | (H: 8.5) | FAS | Found on wind-eroded ground near station L.A. |
| S.XI.A.c.56 | Wuzhu – clipped, cuts through inscription | 1.51 | 21 | (H: 9.5) | FAS | Found on wind-eroded ground near station L.A. |
| S.XI.A.c.57 | 'Wuzhu' – illegible | 1.01 | 18 | (H: 8) corroded | FAS | Found on wind-eroded ground near station L.A. |
| S.XI.A.c.58 | Wuzhu – without inscription, square | 0.77 | 16 | (H: 9) flat rev. | FAS | Found on wind-eroded ground near station L.A. |
| S.XI.A.c.59 | Wuzhu – without inscription, square | 0.76 | 14 | (H: 8) flat rev. | FAS | Found on wind-eroded ground near station L.A. |
| S.XI.A.c.60 | 'Wuzhu' – illegible | 0.94 | 24.5 | (H: 10.5) | FAS | Found on wind-eroded ground near station L.A. |
| S.XI.A.c.61 | 'Wuzhu' – illegible, small coin | 1.26 | 20 | (H: 9) | FAS | Found on wind-eroded ground near station L.A. |

| BM no. | Identification | Wt | Diam. | Notes | Acqn | Acquisition/Archaeological context |
|---|---|---|---|---|---|---|
| S.XI.A.c.62 | 'Wuzhu' – illegible | 1.03 | 18 | (H: 9) damaged | FAS | Found on wind-eroded ground near station L.A. |
| S.XI.A.c.63 | Wuzhu – clipped, cuts through inscription | 1.19 | 20.5 | (H: 9.5) | FAS | Found on wind-eroded ground near station L.A. |
| S.XI.A.c.64 | Wuzhu – clipped, cuts through inscription | 0.86 | 18.5 | (H: 9.5) | FAS | Found on wind-eroded ground near station L.A. |
| S.XI.A.c.65 | Wuzhu – clipped, cuts through inscription, square | 0.84 | 16 | (H: 9.5) | FAS | Found on wind-eroded ground near station L.A. |
| S.XI.A.c.66 | 'Wuzhu' – illegible, square | 0.55 | 15 | (H: 9.5) | FAS | Found on wind-eroded ground near station L.A. |
| S.XI.A.c.67 | Wuzhu – small characters, without rim | 0.98 | 15 | (H: 8) flat rev. | FAS | Found on wind-eroded ground near station L.A. |
| S.XI.A.c.68 | 'Wuzhu' – illegible | 0.58 | 15 | (H: 8) bent | FAS | Found on wind-eroded ground near station L.A. |
| S.XI.A.c.69 | Wuzhu – clipped, cuts through inscription | 1.17 | 20.5 | (H: 9.5) | FAS | Found on wind-eroded ground near station L.A. |
| S.XI.A.c.70 | Wuzhu – zhu with metal radical | 1.09 | 17.5 | (H: 8) red, faint | FAS | Found on wind-eroded ground near station L.A. |
| S.XI.A.c.71 | 'Wuzhu' – illegible | 0.70 | 16.5 | (H: 8) | FAS | Found on wind-eroded ground near station L.A. |
| S.XI.A.c.72 | 'Wuzhu' – illegible | 0.69 | 17 | (H: 7.5) corroded | FAS | Found on wind-eroded ground near station L.A. |
| S.XI.A.c.73 | 'Wuzhu' – illegible | 0.61 | 14.5 | (H: 8) flat rev. | FAS | Found on wind-eroded ground near station L.A. |
| S.XI.A.c.74.a | Wuzhu – clipped, cuts through inscription | 1.11 | 17.5 | (H: 10) misaligned | FAS | Found on wind-eroded ground near station L.A. |
| S.XI.A.c.74.b | 'Wuzhu' – illegible | 0.40 | – | frag. | FAS | Found on wind-eroded ground near station L.A. |
| S.XI.A.c.75 | 'Wuzhu' – illegible | 0.22 | – | frag. | FAS | Found on wind-eroded ground near station L.A. |
| S.XI.A.c.76 | 'Wuzhu' – illegible | 0.43 | – | frag. | FAS | Found on wind-eroded ground near station L.A. |
| S.XI.A.c.77 | 'Wuzhu' – illegible | 1.26 | 21 | (H: 9.5) frag. | FAS | Found on wind-eroded ground near station L.A. |
| S.XI.A.c.78 | [Wu]zhu – clipped, cuts through inscription | 0.48 | – | frag. | FAS | Found on wind-eroded ground near station L.A. |
| S.XI.A.c.79 | 'Wuzhu' – illegible | 0.59 | – | (H: 9.5) frag. | FAS | Found on wind-eroded ground near station L.A. |
| S.XI.A.c.80 | 'Wuzhu' – illegible | 0.69 | 18 | (H: 9.5) frag. | FAS | Found on wind-eroded ground near station L.A. |
| S.XI.A.c.81 | 'Wuzhu' – illegible | 0.64 | – | frag. | FAS | Found on wind-eroded ground near station L.A. |
| S.XI.A.c.82 | 'Wuzhu' – illegible | 0.51 | – | frag. | FAS | Found on wind-eroded ground near station L.A. |
| S.XI.A.c.83 | 'Wuzhu' – illegible | 0.43 | – | frag. | FAS | Found on wind-eroded ground near station L.A. |
| S.XI.A.c.84 | 'Wuzhu' – illegible | 0.83 | – | frag. | FAS | Found on wind-eroded ground near station L.A. |
| S.XI.A.c.85 | 'Wuzhu' – illegible, small | 0.48 | 13 | (H: 6.5) | FAS | Found on wind-eroded ground near station L.A. |
| S.XI.A.c.86 | 'Wuzhu' – illegible, small | 0.47 | 12 | (H: 5.5) flat rev. | FAS | Found on wind-eroded ground near station L.A. |
| S.XI.A.c.87 | 'Wuzhu' – illegible, small, square | 0.54 | 10.5 | (H: 4) with sprue | FAS | Found on wind-eroded ground near station L.A. |

| BM no. | Identification | Wt | Diam. | Notes | Acqn | Acquisition/Archaeological context |
|---|---|---|---|---|---|---|
| S.XI.A.c.88 | 'Wuzhu' – illegible, small | 0.40 | 12.5 | (H: 6) flat rev. | FAS | Found on wind-eroded ground near station L.A. |
| S.XI.A.c.89 | 'Wuzhu' – illegible, small, square | 0.38 | 12 | (H: 6.5) flat rev. | FAS | Found on wind-eroded ground near station L.A. |
| S.XI.A.c.90 | 'Wuzhu' – illegible, small, rim round hole | 0.55 | 12.5 | (H: 7) | FAS | Found on wind-eroded ground near station L.A. |
| S.XI.A.c.91 | 'Wuzhu' – illegible, small, square | 0.32 | 10.5 | (H: 6) with sprue, flat rev. | FAS | Found on wind-eroded ground near station L.A. |
| S.XI.A.c.92 | 'Wuzhu' – illegible, small, square | 0.56 | 10.5 | (H: 4) with sprue, flat rev. | FAS | Found on wind-eroded ground near station L.A. |
| S.XI.A.c.93 | 'Wuzhu' – illegible, small | 0.26 | 10 | (H: 3.5) | FAS | Found on wind-eroded ground near station L.A. |
| S.XI.A.c.94 | 'Wuzhu' – illegible, small, square | 0.59 | 10 | (H: 4) with sprue, flat rev. | FAS | Found on wind-eroded ground near station L.A. |
| S.XI.A.c.95 | 'Wuzhu' – illegible, small, square | 0.35 | 10 | (H: 5) flat rev. | FAS | Found on wind-eroded ground near station L.A. |
| S.XI.A.c.96 | 'Wuzhu' – illegible, small, square | 0.41 | 10.5 | (H: 5) flat rev. | FAS | Found on wind-eroded ground near station L.A. |
| S.XI.A.c.97 | 'Wuzhu' – illegible, small | 0.38 | 10 | (H: 4) with sprue, flat rev. | FAS | Found on wind-eroded ground near station L.A. |
| S.XI.A.c.98 | Wuzhu – coin, with clipped inscription? | 0.46 | 12.5 | (H: 6.5) flat rev. | FAS | Found on wind-eroded ground near station L.A. |
| S.XI.A.c.99 | 'Wuzhu' – illegible, small | 0.57 | 16 | (H: 7) | FAS | Found on wind-eroded ground near station L.A. |
| S.XI.A.c.100 | 'Wuzhu' – illegible, small | 0.55 | 12 | (H: 5) flat rev., damaged | FAS | Found on wind-eroded ground near station L.A. |
| S.XI.A.c.101 | 'Wuzhu' – illegible, small, square | 0.44 | 12 | (H: 6.5) flat rev. | FAS | Found on wind-eroded ground near station L.A. |
| S.XI.A.c.102 | 'Wuzhu' – illegible, small, square | 0.38 | 12.5 | (H: 7) flat rev. | FAS | Found on wind-eroded ground near station L.A. |
| S.XI.A.c.103 | 'Wuzhu' – illegible, small, rim round hole | 0.39 | 12.5 | (H: 7.5) flat rev. | FAS | Found on wind-eroded ground near station L.A. |
| S.XI.A.c.104 | 'Wuzhu' – illegible, small, square | 0.45 | 12 | (H: 6) red, with sprue | FAS | Found on wind-eroded ground near station L.A. |
| S.XI.A.c.105 | 'Wuzhu' – illegible, small | 0.54 | 13 | (H: 6.5) red | FAS | Found on wind-eroded ground near station L.A. |
| S.XI.A.c.106 | 'Wuzhu' – illegible, small, rim round hole | 0.49 | 13 | (H: 6.5) | FAS | Found on wind-eroded ground near station L.A. |
| S.XI.A.c.107 | 'Wuzhu' – illegible, small | 0.48 | 11 | (H: 5) with sprue | FAS | Found on wind-eroded ground near station L.A. |
| S.XI.A.c.108 | 'Wuzhu' – illegible, small, square | 0.25 | 9 | (H: 4.5) frag., red | FAS | Found on wind-eroded ground near station L.A. |
| S.XI.A.c.109 | 'Wuzhu' – illegible, small | 0.46 | 10 | (H: 4) with sprue, flat rev. | FAS | Found on wind-eroded ground near station L.A. |
| S.XI.A.c.110 | 'Wuzhu' – illegible, small, square | 0.37 | 11 | (H: 6) flat rev. | FAS | Found on wind-eroded ground near station L.A. |
| S.XI.A.c.111 | 'Wuzhu' – illegible, small | 0.14 | 7 | (H: 3) | FAS | Found on wind-eroded ground near station L.A. |
| S.XI.A.c.112 | 'Wuzhu' – illegible, small | 0.36 | 10 | (H: 5) corroded | FAS | Found on wind-eroded ground near station L.A. |
| S.XI.A.c.113 | 'Wuzhu' – illegible, small, square | 0.18 | 7 | (H: 3) with sprue | FAS | Found on wind-eroded ground near station L.A. |
| S.XI.A.c.114 | 'Wuzhu' – illegible, small, square | 0.35 | 10 | (H: 5) flat rev. | FAS | Found on wind-eroded ground near station L.A. |

| BM no. | Identification | Wt | Diam. | Notes | Acqn | Acquisition/Archaeological context |
|---|---|---|---|---|---|---|
| S.XI.A.c.115 | 'Wuzhu' – illegible, small | 0.24 | 10 | (H: 5) | FAS | Found on wind-eroded ground near station L.A. |
| S.XI.A.c.116 | 'Wuzhu' – illegible, small, square | 0.23 | 10 | (H: 5) corrroded | FAS | Found on wind-eroded ground near station L.A. |
| S.XI.A.c.117 | 'Wuzhu' – illegible, small | 0.53 | 13 | (H: 8) red | FAS | Found on wind-eroded ground near station L.A. |
| S.XI.A.c.118 | 'Wuzhu' – illegible, small, square | 0.33 | 10 | (H: 5.5) red, flat rev. | FAS | Found on wind-eroded ground near station L.A. |
| S.XI.A.c.119 | 'Wuzhu' – illegible, small | 0.18 | 9 | (H: 5.5) red | FAS | Found on wind-eroded ground near station L.A. |
| S.XI.A.c.120 | Unidentified, round disk with perforation | 0.78 | 14 | red | FAS | Found on wind-eroded ground near station L.A. |
| S.XI.A.c.121 | Unidentified, round disk with perforation | 3.22 | 18 | lead | FAS | Found on wind-eroded ground near station L.A. |
| S.XI.A.c.122 | Unidentified, round disk with perforation | 1.73 | – | red, frag. | FAS | Found on wind-eroded ground near station L.A. |
| S.XI.A.c.123 | 'Wuzhu' – illegible | 0.58 | – | frag. | FAS | Found on wind-eroded ground near station L.A. |
| S.XI.A.c.124 | 'Wuzhu' – illegible | 0.41 | – | 2 frags | FAS | Found on wind-eroded ground near station L.A. |
| S.XI.A.c.125 | Unidentified, round disk with perforation | 3.42 | 25.5 | – | FAS | Found on wind-eroded ground near station L.A. |

| | | | | | | |
|---|---|---|---|---|---|---|
| S.XI.A.d.1 | Wuzhu – full size | 2.59 | 26 | (H: 9.5) damaged | FAS | Found at ruin L.A.I |
| S.XI.A.d.2 | Wuzhu – full size | 2.23 | 26 | (H: 9.5) | FAS | Found at ruin L.A.I |
| S.XI.A.d.3 | Wuzhu – full size, tall thin wu | 3.15 | 25.5 | (H: 9) | FAS | Found at ruin L.A.I |
| S.XI.A.d.4 | Wuzhu – full size, line above hole on obv. | 3.35 | 25 | (H: 9.5) | FAS | Found at ruin L.A.I |
| S.XI.A.d.5 | Wuzhu – full size | 2.74 | 26.5 | (H: 10) | FAS | Found at ruin L.A.I |
| S.XI.A.d.6 | 'Wuzhu' – illegible | 1.42 | 24 | (H: 10.5) 2 frags (= 1 coin) | FAS | Found at ruin L.A.I |
| S.XI.A.d.7 | 'Wuzhu' – illegible | 2.67 | 23 | (H: 9) corroded | FAS | Found at ruin L.A.I |

| | | | | | | |
|---|---|---|---|---|---|---|
| S.XI.A.e.1 | 'Wuzhu' – illegible | 1.04 | 21 | (H: 9.5) | FAS | Found within, or close to, ruin L.A.II |
| S.XI.A.e.2 | Wuzhu – clipped, cuts through inscription | 1.18 | 21.5 | (H: 9.5) | FAS | Found within, or close to, ruin L.A.II |
| S.XI.A.e.3 | 'Wuzhu' – illegible | 0.97 | 21 | (H: 9.5) frag. | FAS | Found within, or close to, ruin L.A.II |
| S.XI.A.e.4 | Wuzhu – clipped, cuts through inscription | 1.30 | 21 | (H: 9.5) | FAS | Found within, or close to, ruin L.A.II |
| S.XI.A.e.5 | 'Wuzhu' – illegible | 1.17 | 18 | (H: 9) damaged | FAS | Found within, or close to, ruin L.A.II |
| S.XI.A.e.6 | Wuzhu – without inscription | 1.45 | 17 | (H: 7.5) red, flat rev. | FAS | Found within, or close to, ruin L.A.II |
| S.XI.A.e.7 | 'Wuzhu' – illegible, small | 0.55 | 12.5 | (H: 7) red | FAS | Found within, or close to, ruin L.A.II |

| | | | | | | |
|---|---|---|---|---|---|---|
| S.XI.A.f.1 | Wuzhu – clipped, cuts through inscription, with rim | 1.67 | 23 | (H: 9.5) red | FAS | Found in ruin L.A.III.ii |

| | | | | | | |
|---|---|---|---|---|---|---|
| S.XI.A.g.1 | Huoquan | 0.98 | 20.5 | – | FAS | Found within, or close to, ruins L.A.IV–VI |
| S.XI.A.g.2 | Wuzhu – full size | 2.49 | 25.5 | (H: 9.5) | FAS | Found within, or close to, ruins L.A.IV–VI |

| BM no. | Identification | Wt | Diam. | Notes | Acqn | Acquisition/Archaeological context |
|---|---|---|---|---|---|---|
| S.XI.A.g.3 | Wuzhu – full size | 3.02 | 26 | (H: 10) | FAS | Found within, or close to, ruins L.A.IV–VI |
| S.XI.A.g.4 | Wuzhu – full size | 2.36 | 25 | (H: 9) | FAS | Found within, or close to, ruins L.A.IV–VI |
| S.XI.A.g.5 | Wuzhu – full size | 3.18 | 25 | (H: 10) | FAS | Found within, or close to, ruins L.A.IV–VI |
| S.XI.A.g.6 | 'Wuzhu' – illegible | 1.60 | 26 | (H: 11) | FAS | Found within, or close to, ruins L.A.IV–VI |
| S.XI.A.g.7 | [Wu] zhu – without full rim | 1.06 | – | frag. | FAS | Found within, or close to, ruins L.A.IV–VI |
| S.XI.A.g.8 | Wu [zhu] – full size | 1.90 | 26 | frag. | FAS | Found within, or close to, ruins L.A.IV–VI |
| S.XI.A.g.9 | [Wu] zhu – full size | 1.09 | – | frag. | FAS | Found within, or close to, ruins L.A.IV–VI |
| S.XI.A.g.10 | Bu [quan] | 0.84 | – | frag. | FAS | Found within, or close to, ruins L.A.IV–VI |
| S.XI.A.g.11 | 'Wuzhu' – illegible, small | 0.21 | 10 | (H: 4) flat rev. | FAS | Found within, or close to, ruins L.A.IV–VI |
| S.XI.A.g.12 | 'Wuzhu' – illegible, small | 0.29 | – | 4 frags | FAS | Found within, or close to, ruins L.A.IV–VI |
| S.XI.A.g.13 | 'Wuzhu' – illegible, small | 0.62 | 10.5 | (H: 4) with sprue | FAS | Found within, or close to, ruins L.A.IV–VI |
| S.XI.A.g.14 | 'Wuzhu' – illegible, small | 0.29 | 11 | (H: 6) | FAS | Found within, or close to, ruins L.A.IV–VI |
| S.XI.A.g.15 | 'Wuzhu' – illegible, small, square | 0.27 | 10.5 | (H: 5.5) | FAS | Found within, or close to, ruins L.A.IV–VI |
| S.XI.A.g.16 | 'Wuzhu' – illegible, small, square | 0.46 | 10.5 | (H: 6) | FAS | Found within, or close to, ruins L.A.IV–VI |
| S.XI.A.g.17 | 'Wuzhu' – illegible | 0.88 | 18.5 | (H: 8.5) | FAS | Found within, or close to, ruins L.A.IV–VI |
| S.XI.A.g.18 | 'Wuzhu' – illegible | 0.43 | 12 | (H: 3.5) | FAS | Found within, or close to, ruins L.A.IV–VI |
| S.XI.A.g.19 | 'Wuzhu' – illegible, rim round hole | 0.55 | 16.5 | (H: 9) | FAS | Found within, or close to, ruins L.A.IV–VI |
| S.XI.A.g.20 | 'Wuzhu' – illegible, small | 0.43 | 13 | (H: 7) | FAS | Found within, or close to, ruins L.A.IV–VI |
| S.XI.A.g.21 | 'Wuzhu' – illegible | 1.20 | 20 | (H: 9.5) | FAS | Found within, or close to, ruins L.A.IV–VI |
| S.XI.A.g.22 | Wuzhu – clipped, cuts through inscription | 1.28 | 22 | (H: 10.5) | FAS | Found within, or close to, ruins L.A.IV–VI |
| S.XI.A.g.23–24 | Wuzhu – clipped, cuts through inscription | 0.81 | 20.5 | (H: 10) 2 frags | FAS | Found within, or close to, ruins L.A.IV–VI |
| S.XI.A.g.25 | 'Wuzhu' – illegible | 0.60 | – | frag., bent | FAS | Found within, or close to, ruins L.A.IV–VI |
| S.XI.A.g.26–29 | [missing: Wuzhu] | – | – | – | FAS | Found within, or close to, ruins L.A.IV–VI |

| | | | | | | |
|---|---|---|---|---|---|---|
| S.XI.A.h.1–3 | [missing: Wuzhu] | – | – | – | FAS | Found in refuse heap L.A.VI.ii |

| | | | | | | |
|---|---|---|---|---|---|---|
| S.XI.A.i.1 | Huoquan | 1.91 | 21.5 | – | FAS | Found at ruin L.A.VII |
| S.XI.A.i.2 | Wuzhu – full size | 2.60 | 26.5 | (H: 9.5) | FAS | Found at ruin L.A.VII |
| S.XI.A.i.3 | Wuzhu – without full rim | 1.82 | 24.5 | (H: 9) forced hole | FAS | Found at ruin L.A.VII |

| BM no. | Identification | Wt | Diam. | Notes | Acqn | Acquisition/Archaeological context |
|---|---|---|---|---|---|---|
| S.XI.A.i.4 | Wuzhu – clipped, cuts through inscription | 1.71 | 22 | (H: 9) | FAS | Found at ruin L.A.VII |
| S.XI.A.i.5–8 | Wuzhu – various sizes | 4.23 | – | 4 coins corroded together | FAS | Found at ruin L.A.VII |
| S.XI.A.i.9 | 'Wuzhu' – illegible | 0.88 | 17 | (H: 9.5) | FAS | Found at ruin L.A.VII |
| S.XI.A.i.10 | Wuzhu – clipped, cuts through inscription | 1.14 | 17 | (H: 8) | FAS | Found at ruin L.A.VII |
| S.XI.A.i.11 | 'Wuzhu' – illegible, small, square | 0.28 | 9 | (H: 3.5) | FAS | Found at ruin L.A.VII |
| S.XI.A.i.12 | Wuzhu – clipped, cuts through inscription | 1.06 | 18 | (H: 9.5) | FAS | Found at ruin L.A.VII |
| S.XI.A.i.13 | 'Wuzhu' – illegible, rim round hole | 0.78 | 14 | (H: 7.5) | FAS | Found at ruin L.A.VII |
| S.XI.A.i.14 | 'Wuzhu' – illegible, rim round hole | 0.60 | 14 | (H: 8) | FAS | Found at ruin L.A.VII |
| S.XI.A.i.15 | 'Wuzhu' – illegible, small, rim round hole | 0.44 | 13 | (H: 7.5) | FAS | Found at ruin L.A.VII |
| S.XI.A.i.16 | 'Wuzhu' – illegible, small, rim round hole | 0.46 | 12 | (H: 7.5) | FAS | Found at ruin L.A.VII |
| S.XI.A.i.17 | 'Wuzhu' – illegible, small, rim round hole | 0.67 | 13 | (H: 7) 1 coin + frags | FAS | Found at ruin L.A.VII |
| S.XI.A.i.18 | 'Wuzhu' – illegible, small | 0.25 | 10 | (H: 5) | FAS | Found at ruin L.A.VII |
| S.XI.A.i.19 | 'Wuzhu' – illegible, small | 0.31 | – | 2 frags | FAS | Found at ruin L.A.VII |
| S.XI.A.i.20 | 'Wuzhu' – illegible, small | 0.26 | 11 | (H: 6) | FAS | Found at ruin L.A.VII |
| S.XI.A.j.1 | Wuzhu – full size | 3.02 | 25.5 | (H: 9.5) | FAS | Found near ruins L.A.VIII–IX |
| S.XI.A.j.2 | 'Wuzhu' – illegible | 2.02 | 23.5 | (H: 9) | FAS | Found near ruins L.A.VIII–IX |
| S.XI.A.j.3 | Wuzhu – full size | 2.46 | 26.5 | (H: 10.5) 2 frags (= 1 coin) | FAS | Found near ruins L.A.VIII–IX |
| S.XI.A.j.4 | Wuzhu – without full rim | 2.15 | 24 | (H: 9.5) | FAS | Found near ruins L.A.VIII–IX |
| S.XI.A.j.5 | 'Wuzhu' – illegible | 1.71 | 22.5 | (H: 9.5) | FAS | Found near ruins L.A.VIII–IX |
| S.XI.A.j.6 | Wuzhu – full size | 1.36 | 26.5 | frag. | FAS | Found near ruins L.A.VIII–IX |
| S.XI.A.j.7 | [missing: Wuzhu] | – | – | – | FAS | Found near ruins L.A.VIII–IX |
| S.XI.A.j.8 | 'Wuzhu' – illegible, square | 1.09 | 17 | (H: 9.5) | FAS | Found near ruins L.A.VIII–IX |
| S.XI.A.j.9 | 'Wuzhu' – illegible, small | 0.72 | 13 | (H: 7.5) misaligned | FAS | Found near ruins L.A.VIII–IX |
| S.XI.A.j.10 | 'Wuzhu' – illegible | 1.16 | 20.5 | (H: 9.5) red | FAS | Found near ruins L.A.VIII–IX |
| S.XI.A.j.11 | Wuzhu – clipped, cuts through inscription | 1.23 | 20 | (H: 10) red | FAS | Found near ruins L.A.VIII–IX |
| S.XI.A.j.12 | 'Wuzhu' – illegible | 2.26 | 18 | corroded | FAS | Found near ruins L.A.VIII–IX |
| S.XI.A.j.13 | 'Wuzhu' – illegible | 1.13 | 20 | (H: 9.5) | FAS | Found near ruins L.A.VIII–IX |
| S.XI.A.j.14 | 'Wuzhu' – illegible | 1.34 | 21 | (H: 9.5) frag. | FAS | Found near ruins L.A.VIII–IX |
| S.XI.A.j.15 | 'Wuzhu' – illegible, small | 0.36 | 11 | (H: 9.5) | FAS | Found near ruins L.A.VIII–IX |
| S.XI.A.j.16 | 'Wuzhu' – illegible, small, square | 0.48 | 11 | (H: 5.5) with sprue | FAS | Found near ruins L.A.VIII–IX |
| S.XI.A.j.17 | 'Wuzhu' – illegible, small, square | 0.47 | 10.5 | (H: 6) frag., with sprue | FAS | Found near ruins L.A.VIII–IX |

### S.XI.B: COINS FROM RUINED SITE L.B.

| BM no. | Identification | Wt | Diam. | Notes | Acqn | Acquisition/Archaeological context |
|---|---|---|---|---|---|---|
| S.XI.B.a.1 | Wuzhu – full size | 2.68 | 25.5 | (H: 10.5) | FAS | Found near L.B. |
| S.XI.B.a.2 | Wuzhu – clipped, cuts through inscription | 1.04 | 20 | (H: 10.5) red | FAS | Found near L.B. |
| S.XI.B.a.3 | Wuzhu – clipped, cuts through inscription | 1.51 | 20.5 | (H: 10) | FAS | Found near L.B. |

| | | | | | | |
|---|---|---|---|---|---|---|
| S.XI.B.b.1 | Huoquan | 2.48 | 22 | – | FAS | Found at, or near, ruins L.B.I–III |
| S.XI.B.b.2 | Wuzhu – full size | 1.85 | 25.5 | (H: 10) | FAS | Found at, or near, ruins L.B.I–III |
| S.XI.B.b.3 | Wuzhu – clipped, cuts through inscription | 0.85 | 17.5 | (H: 9.5) | FAS | Found at, or near, ruins L.B.I–III |
| S.XI.B.b.4 | 'Wuzhu' – illegible | 1.54 | 21.5 | (H: 9) | FAS | Found at, or near, ruins L.B.I–III |
| S.XI.B.b.5 | 'Wuzhu' – illegible | 1.05 | 18 | (H: 9) | FAS | Found at, or near, ruins L.B.I–III |
| S.XI.B.b.6 | Wuzhu – clipped, cuts through inscription | 0.63 | 18 | (H: 10) | FAS | Found at, or near, ruins L.B.I–III |

| | | | | | | |
|---|---|---|---|---|---|---|
| S.XI.B.c.1 | Wuzhu – full size | 2.56 | 27 | (H: 9.5) | FAS | Found at ruins L.B.IV–V |
| S.XI.B.c.2–3 | Wuzhu – without rim | 1.61 | 24 | 2 frags (= 1 coin) (H: 10) | FAS | Found at ruins L.B.IV–V |
| S.XI.B.c.4 | Wuzhu – full size | 3.11 | 25 | (H: 9.5) | FAS | Found at ruins L.B.IV–V |
| S.XI.B.c.5 | Wuzhu – clipped, cuts through inscription | 1.46 | 20.5 | (H: 9.5) | FAS | Found at ruins L.B.IV–V |

| | | | | | | |
|---|---|---|---|---|---|---|
| S.XI.B.d.1 | 'Wuzhu' – illegible | 1.67 | 21.5 | (H: 9) | F | Found 1 mile WSW of Camp 126 |

### S.XII: COPPER COINS FOUND AT MERDEK TIM

| BM no. | Identification | Wt | Diam. | Notes | Acqn | Acquisition/Archaeological context |
|---|---|---|---|---|---|---|
| S.XII.a.1–2 | [missing: Huoquan] | – | – | – | FAS | Found on rampart of ancient fort |
| S.XII.a.3–6 | [missing: Wuzhu] | – | – | – | FAS | Found on rampart of ancient fort |

### S.XIII: COPPER COINS FOUND AT MIRAN SITE

| BM no. | Identification | Wt | Diam. | Notes | Acqn | Acquisition/Archaeological context |
|---|---|---|---|---|---|---|
| S.XIII.a.1 | Wuzhu | 1.44 | 25.5 | frag. | FAS | Found to N of ruined shrine M.III |

| | | | | | | |
|---|---|---|---|---|---|---|
| S.XIII.b.1 | Kaiyuan tongbao | 3.30 | 24.5 | red | FAS | Found on eroded ground N of ruined fort |
| S.XIII.b.2 | Kaiyuan tongbao | 4.23 | 25 | red | FAS | Found on eroded ground N of ruined fort |
| S.XIII.b.3 | Kaiyuan tongbao – crescent above hole on rev. | 3.59 | 25 | red | FAS | Found on eroded ground N of ruined fort |
| S.XIII.b.4 | Kaiyuan tongbao | 2.72 | 23.5 | red, misaligned | FAS | Found on eroded ground N of ruined fort |

| BM no. | Identification | Wt | Diam. | Notes | Acqn | Acquisition/Archaeological context |
|---|---|---|---|---|---|---|
| S.XIII.b.5 | Kaiyuan tongbao | 3.13 | 24 | red | FAS | Found on eroded ground N of ruined fort |
| S.XIII.b.6–7 | Kaiyuan tongbao | 3.03 | 25 | 2 frags (= 1 coin) red | FAS | Found on eroded ground N of ruined fort |

| | | | | | | |
|---|---|---|---|---|---|---|
| S.XIII.c.1 | Chinese coin – Song dynasty | – | – | – | FAS | Found on surface within ruined fort, M.I |
| S.XIII.c.2 | Chinese coin – Qing dynasty | – | – | – | FAS | Found on surface within ruined fort, M.I |

| | | | | | | |
|---|---|---|---|---|---|---|
| S.XIII.d.1 | [extra: Wuzhu] | 1.14 | 24 | (H: 8.5) frag., corroded | – | Not known |

## S.XIV: COPPER COINS FOUND OR COLLECTED AT NANHU

| BM no. | Identification | Wt | Diam. | Notes | Acqn | Acquisition/Archaeological context |
|---|---|---|---|---|---|---|
| S.XIV.a.1 | 'Wuzhu' – illegible | 1.24 | 21 | (H: 9) frag., corroded | FAS | Excavated within ruined town |
| S.XIV.a.2 | 'Wuzhu' – illegible | 0.50 | 14 | (H: 7.5) corroded | FAS | Excavated within ruined town |
| S.XIV.a.3 | Chinese coin – uncertain [x x] tongbao | 1.29 | – | frag. | FAS | Excavated within ruined town |
| S.XIV.a.4 | Kai [yuan tong] bao | 2.08 | – | frag. | FAS | Excavated within ruined town |

| | | | | | | |
|---|---|---|---|---|---|---|
| S.XIV.b.1 | Banliang | 2.27 | 24.5 | – | FAS | Found on eroded site E and NE of ruined town |
| S.XIV.b.2 | Huoquan | 2.43 | 23 | – | FAS | Found on eroded site E and NE of ruined town |
| S.XIV.b.3 | Huoquan | 2.53 | 23 | – | FAS | Found on eroded site E and NE of ruined town |
| S.XIV.b.4 | Huoquan | 2.06 | 23 | – | FAS | Found on eroded site E and NE of ruined town |
| S.XIV.b.5 | Wuzhu – full size | 2.90 | 26 | (H: 10.5) | FAS | Found on eroded site E and NE of ruined town |
| S.XIV.b.6 | Wuzhu – full size | 2.63 | 25.5 | (H: 9.5) | FAS | Found on eroded site E and NE of ruined town |
| S.XIV.b.7 | Wuzhu – full size | 3.37 | 26 | (H: 10) | FAS | Found on eroded site E and NE of ruined town |
| S.XIV.b.8 | Wuzhu – full size | 2.43 | 26 | (H: 10) | FAS | Found on eroded site E and NE of ruined town |
| S.XIV.b.9 | Wuzhu – Sui? | 2.41 | 23.5 | (H: 8) | FAS | Found on eroded site E and NE of ruined town |
| S.XIV.b.10 | Wuzhu – full size | 0.44 | – | frag. | FAS | Found on eroded site E and NE of ruined town |
| S.XIV.b.11 | Wuzhu – full size | 0.52 | – | frag. | FAS | Found on eroded site E and NE of ruined town |
| S.XIV.b.12 | Kaiyuan tongbao | 3.41 | 25 | – | FAS | Found on eroded site E and NE of ruined town |
| S.XIV.b.13 | Kaiyuan tongbao | 3.20 | 24.5 | – | FAS | Found on eroded site E and NE of ruined town |
| S.XIV.b.14 | Kaiyuan tongbao | 2.71 | 24 | – | FAS | Found on eroded site E and NE of ruined town |

| BM no. | Identification | Wt | Diam. | Notes | Acqn | Acquisition/Archaeological context |
|---|---|---|---|---|---|---|
| S.XIV.b.15 | [Kai] yuan tongbao | 2.79 | 24 | frag. | FAS | Found on eroded site E and NE of ruined town |
| S.XIV.b.16 | [Kaiyuan] tong [bao] | 0.90 | 26 | frag. | FAS | Found on eroded site E and NE of ruined town |
| S.XIV.b.17 | [Kai] yuan [tongbao] | 1.09 | – | frag. | FAS | Found on eroded site E and NE of ruined town |
| S.XIV.b.18 | [Kai] yuan [tong] bao | 0.88 | – | frag. | FAS | Found on eroded site E and NE of ruined town |
| S.XIV.b.19 | [Kai] yuan [tong] bao | 0.81 | – | frag. | FAS | Found on eroded site E and NE of ruined town |
| S.XIV.b.20 | [Kaiyuan] tong [bao] | 0.65 | – | frag. | FAS | Found on eroded site E and NE of ruined town |
| S.XIV.b.21 | Chinese coin – Song dynasty | – | – | – | FAS | Found on eroded site E and NE of ruined town |

| | | | | | | |
|---|---|---|---|---|---|---|
| S.XIV.c.1 | Wuzhu – full size, line above hole on obv. | 1.85 | 23.5 | (H: 10) frag. | p | From vicinity of ruined town, collected at Nanhu |
| S.XIV.c.2 | Wuzhu – without full rim | 2.16 | 24 | (H: 10) | p | From vicinity of ruined town, collected at Nanhu |
| S.XIV.c.3 | [Wu] zhu | 1.05 | – | frag. | p | From vicinity of ruined town, collected at Nanhu |
| S.XIV.c.4 | [Wu] zhu – line above hole on obv. | 1.70 | – | frag. | p | From vicinity of ruined town, collected at Nanhu |
| S.XIV.c.5–6 | Wu [zhu] – Northern Wei? | 1.22 | – | 2 frags | p | From vicinity of ruined town, collected at Nanhu |
| S.XIV.c.7 | Wu [zhu] | 0.62 | – | frag. | p | From vicinity of ruined town, collected at Nanhu |
| S.XIV.c.8 | [Wu] zhu | 0.57 | – | frag. | p | From vicinity of ruined town, collected at Nanhu |
| S.XIV.c.9 | 'Wuzhu' – illegible, small | 0.43 | 14.5 | frag. (H: 7) | p | From vicinity of ruined town, collected at Nanhu |
| S.XIV.c.10 | 'Wuzhu' – illegible, small | 0.57 | 11 | (H: 4) corroded | p | From vicinity of ruined town, collected at Nanhu |
| S.XIV.c.11 | 'Wuzhu' – illegible, small | 0.39 | 11.5 | (H: 6) | p | From vicinity of ruined town, collected at Nanhu |
| S.XIV.c.12 | [extra: 'Wuzhu' – illegible, small, square] | 0.40 | 11 | (H: 5) with sprue | p | From vicinity of ruined town, collected at Nanhu |
| S.XIV.c.13 | [extra: 'Wuzhu' – illegible, small, rim round hole] | 0.57 | 11.5 | (H: 5.5) frag. | p | From vicinity of ruined town, collected at Nanhu |
| S.XIV.c.14 | [extra: 2 Wuzhu frags] | 0.16<br>0.35 | – | 2 frags | p | From vicinity of ruined town, collected at Nanhu |
| S.XIV.c.15–16 | Chinese coins – Song dynasty | – | | – | p | From vicinity of ruined town, collected at Nanhu |

| | | | | | | |
|---|---|---|---|---|---|---|
| S.XIV.d.1 | Chinese coin – Song dynasty | – | – | – | FAS | Found at abandoned site of Kuan-tsou (Guanzhou) |
| S.XIV.d.2–6 | Chinese coins – Qing dynasty | – | – | – | FAS | Found at abandoned site of Kuan-tsou (Guanzhou) |

| | | | | | | |
|---|---|---|---|---|---|---|
| S.XIV.e.1–11 | [extra: Chinese xxx bao] | 0.95 | – | frag. | – | Not known |
| S.XIV.e.2 | [extra: unidentified] | 0.83 | – | frag. | – | Not known |
| S.XIV.e.3 | [extra: 'Wuzhu' – illegible] | 0.47 | – | frag. | – | Not known |
| S.XIV.e.4 | [extra: (Wu) zhu – full size] | 0.52 | – | frag. | – | Not known |
| S.XIV.e.5 | [extra: 'Wuzhu' – illegible] | 0.61 | – | frag. | – | Not known |

| BM no. | Identification | Wt | Diam. | Notes | Acqn | Acquisition/Archaeological context |
|---|---|---|---|---|---|---|
| S.XIV.e.6 | [extra: (wu) zhu – full size] | 0.87 | – | frag. | – | Not known |
| S.XIV.e.7 | [extra: Wu (zhu) – thin wu] | 1.17 | – | frag. | – | Not known |
| S.XIV.e.8 | [extra: 'Wuzhu' – illegible] | 0.29 | – | frag. | – | Not known |
| S.XIV.e.9 | [extra: non–coin] | 1.07 | – | frag. | – | Not known |
| S.XIV.e.10 | [extra: metal frags] | – | – | 3 frags | – | Not known |
| S.XIV.e.11 | [extra: Chinese coin – unidentified] | 2.73 | 26 | 2 frags restored, corroded | – | Not known |
| S.XIV.e.12 | [extra: Kaiyuan tongbao – crescent above hole] | 3.75 | 25.5 | – | – | Not known |

## S.XV: COPPER COINS FOUND ALONG ANCIENT *LIMES* OF TUN–HUANG (DUNHUANG)

| BM no. | Identification | Wt | Diam. | Notes | Acqn | Acquisition/Archaeological context |
|---|---|---|---|---|---|---|
| S.XV.a.1 | 'Wuzhu' – illegible, small | 0.52 | 11.5 | (H: 6) corroded | FAS | Found at watch-tower T.IV.c |
| S.XV.b.1 | Wuzhu – full size | 3.70 | 26 | (H: 9.5) corroded, not cleaned | FAS | Found near watch-station T.VI.b |
| S.XV.c.1 | Wuzhu – full size, line above hole on obv. | 3.52 | 25 | (H: 10) | FAS | Found on top of watch-tower T.VI.c |
| S.XV.d.1 | 'Wuzhu' – illegible | 1.14 | 20.5 | (H: 9.5) | FAS | Found at ruin T.XI.iii |
| S.XV.e.1 | Wuzhu – full size | 3.79 | 26 | (H: 9.5) red | FAS | Found in refuse on slopes of T.XIV |
| S.XV.e.2 | Wuzhu – full size | 1.56 | (26) | 2 frags | FAS | Found in refuse on slopes of T.XIV |
| S.XV.f.1 | Wuzhu – full size | 2.42 | 25 | (H: 9.5) | FAS | Found in bowl below ruined shrine T.XIV.v |
| S.XV.f.2 | Wuzhu – full size | 4.10 | 25.5 | (H: 9.5) | FAS | Found in bowl below ruined shrine T.XIV.v |
| S.XV.f.3 | Kaiyuan tongbao | 3.80 | 24.5 | – | FAS | Found in bowl below ruined shrine T.XIV.v |
| S.XV.f.4 | Kaiyuan tongbao | 3.15 | 24.5 | – | FAS | Found in bowl below ruined shrine T.XIV.v |
| S.XV.f.5 | Kaiyuan tongbao | 3.46 | 24 | – | FAS | Found in bowl below ruined shrine T.XIV.v |
| S.XV.f.6 | Kaiyuan tongbao | 3.41 | 24.5 | – | FAS | Found in bowl below ruined shrine T.XIV.v |
| S.XV.f.7 | Kaiyuan tongbao | 4.27 | 24.5 | – | FAS | Found in bowl below ruined shrine T.XIV.v |
| S.XV.f.8 | Kaiyuan tongbao | 4.25 | 24.5 | – | FAS | Found in bowl below ruined shrine T.XIV.v |
| S.XV.f.9 | Kaiyuan tongbao | 3.93 | 24.5 | – | FAS | Found in bowl below ruined shrine T.XIV.v |
| S.XV.f.10 | Kaiyuan tongbao | 3.28 | 24 | – | FAS | Found in bowl below ruined shrine T.XIV.v |
| S.XV.f.11 | Kaiyuan tongbao | 4.03 | 24.5 | misaligned | FAS | Found in bowl below ruined shrine T.XIV.v |

| BM no. | Identification | Wt | Diam. | Notes | Acqn | Acquisition/Archaeological context |
|---|---|---|---|---|---|---|
| S.XV.f.12 | Kaiyuan tongbao | 3.46 | 24.5 | – | FAS | Found in bowl below ruined shrine T.XIV.v |
| S.XV.f.13 | Kaiyuan tongbao | 4.12 | 25 | – | FAS | Found in bowl below ruined shrine T.XIV.v |
| S.XV.f.14 | Kaiyuan tongbao | 4.16 | 25 | – | FAS | Found in bowl below ruined shrine T.XIV.v |
| S.XV.f.15 | Kaiyuan tongbao | 4.41 | 25 | – | FAS | Found in bowl below ruined shrine T.XIV.v |
| S.XV.f.16 | Kaiyuan tongbao | 3.60 | 24 | – | FAS | Found in bowl below ruined shrine T.XIV.v |
| S.XV.f.17 | Kaiyuan tongbao | 3.97 | 24.5 | – | FAS | Found in bowl below ruined shrine T.XIV.v |
| S.XV.f.18 | Kaiyuan tongbao | 4.16 | 24.5 | – | FAS | Found in bowl below ruined shrine T.XIV.v |
| S.XV.f.19 | Kaiyuan tongbao | 3.89 | 24.5 | – | FAS | Found in bowl below ruined shrine T.XIV.v |
| S.XV.f.20 | Kaiyuan tongbao | 3.50 | 25 | misaligned | FAS | Found in bowl below ruined shrine T.XIV.v |
| S.XV.f.21 | Kaiyuan tongbao | 3.88 | 24.5 | – | FAS | Found in bowl below ruined shrine T.XIV.v |
| S.XV.f.22 | Kaiyuan tongbao | 3.57 | 24.5 | misaligned, forced hole | FAS | Found in bowl below ruined shrine T.XIV.v |
| S.XV.f.23 | Kaiyuan tongbao | 4.12 | 25.5 | – | FAS | Found in bowl below ruined shrine T.XIV.v |
| S.XV.f.24 | Kaiyuan tongbao | 3.87 | 24.5 | – | FAS | Found in bowl below ruined shrine T.XIV.v |
| S.XV.f.25 | Kaiyuan tongbao | 4.23 | 24.5 | – | FAS | Found in bowl below ruined shrine T.XIV.v |
| S.XV.f.26 | Kaiyuan tongbao – 'nail mark' on rev. | 4.17 | 25 | – | FAS | Found in bowl below ruined shrine T.XIV.v |
| S.XV.f.27 | Kaiyuan tongbao | 4.29 | 25 | – | FAS | Found in bowl below ruined shrine T.XIV.v |
| S.XV.f.28 | Kaiyuan tongbao | 4.25 | 25 | – | FAS | Found in bowl below ruined shrine T.XIV.v |
| S.XV.f.29 | Kaiyuan tongbao | 4.08 | 25 | – | FAS | Found in bowl below ruined shrine T.XIV.v |
| S.XV.f.30 | Kaiyuan tongbao | 4.65 | 25.5 | – | FAS | Found in bowl below ruined shrine T.XIV.v |
| S.XV.f.31 | Kaiyuan tongbao | 3.38 | 24.5 | – | FAS | Found in bowl below ruined shrine T.XIV.v |
| S.XV.f.32 | Kaiyuan tongbao | 3.45 | 24.5 | – | FAS | Found in bowl below ruined shrine T.XIV.v |
| S.XV.f.33 | Kaiyuan tongbao | 4.18 | 25 | misaligned | FAS | Found in bowl below ruined shrine T.XIV.v |
| S.XV.f.34 | Kaiyuan tongbao | 3.19 | 23.5 | – | FAS | Found in bowl below ruined shrine T.XIV.v |
| S.XV.f.35 | Kaiyuan tongbao | 3.56 | 24.5 | – | FAS | Found in bowl below ruined shrine T.XIV.v |
| S.XV.f.36 | Kaiyuan tongbao | 3.58 | 24 | misaligned | FAS | Found in bowl below ruined shrine T.XIV.v |
| S.XV.f.37 | Kaiyuan tongbao | 4.45 | 25 | – | FAS | Found in bowl below ruined shrine T.XIV.v |
| S.XV.f.38 | Kaiyuan tongbao | 3.85 | 25 | – | FAS | Found in bowl below ruined shrine T.XIV.v |

| BM no. | Identification | Wt | Diam. | Notes | Acqn | Acquisition/Archaeological context |
|---|---|---|---|---|---|---|
| S.XV.f.39 | Kaiyuan tongbao | 3.72 | 24.5 | misaligned | FAS | Found in bowl below ruined shrine T.XIV.v |
| S.XV.f.40 | Kaiyuan tongbao | 4.28 | 24 | – | FAS | Found in bowl below ruined shrine T.XIV.v |
| S.XV.f.41 | Kaiyuan tongbao | 4.09 | 25 | – | FAS | Found in bowl below ruined shrine T.XIV.v |
| S.XV.f.42 | Kaiyuan tongbao | 4.08 | 25.5 | – | FAS | Found in bowl below ruined shrine T.XIV.v |
| S.XV.f.43 | Kaiyuan tongbao | 3.41 | 24.5 | – | FAS | Found in bowl below ruined shrine T.XIV.v |
| S.XV.f.44 | Kaiyuan tongbao | 3.61 | 24.5 | – | FAS | Found in bowl below ruined shrine T.XIV.v |
| S.XV.f.45 | Kaiyuan tongbao | 4.60 | 25 | – | FAS | Found in bowl below ruined shrine T.XIV.v |
| S.XV.f.46 | Kaiyuan tongbao | 4.92 | 25 | misaligned | FAS | Found in bowl below ruined shrine T.XIV.v |
| S.XV.f.47 | Kaiyuan tongbao | 4.25 | 25 | – | FAS | Found in bowl below ruined shrine T.XIV.v |
| S.XV.f.48 | Kaiyuan tongbao | 4.17 | 25 | – | FAS | Found in bowl below ruined shrine T.XIV.v |
| S.XV.f.49 | Kaiyuan tongbao | 2.89 | 23.5 | – | FAS | Found in bowl below ruined shrine T.XIV.v |
| S.XV.f.50 | Kaiyuan tongbao | 3.46 | 24.5 | – | FAS | Found in bowl below ruined shrine T.XIV.v |
| S.XV.f.51 | Kaiyuan tongbao | 3.73 | 23.5 | – | FAS | Found in bowl below ruined shrine T.XIV.v |
| S.XV.f.52 | Kaiyuan tongbao | 4.49 | 25 | – | FAS | Found in bowl below ruined shrine T.XIV.v |
| S.XV.f.53 | Kaiyuan tongbao | 3.43 | 24 | – | FAS | Found in bowl below ruined shrine T.XIV.v |
| S.XV.f.54 | Kaiyuan tongbao | 3.84 | 24 | misaligned | FAS | Found in bowl below ruined shrine T.XIV.v |
| S.XV.f.55 | Kaiyuan tongbao | 3.37 | 24 | – | FAS | Found in bowl below ruined shrine T.XIV.v |
| S.XV.f.56 | Kaiyuan tongbao | 4.41 | 25 | – | FAS | Found in bowl below ruined shrine T.XIV.v |
| S.XV.f.57 | Kaiyuan tongbao | 3.86 | 25 | misaligned | FAS | Found in bowl below ruined shrine T.XIV.v |
| S.XV.f.58 | Kaiyuan tongbao | 4.78 | 25 | misaligned | FAS | Found in bowl below ruined shrine T.XIV.v |
| S.XV.f.59 | Kaiyuan tongbao | 4.13 | 24 | – | FAS | Found in bowl below ruined shrine T.XIV.v |
| S.XV.f.60 | Kaiyuan tongbao | 3.45 | 24 | misaligned, forced hole | FAS | Found in bowl below ruined shrine T.XIV.v |
| S.XV.f.61 | Kaiyuan tongbao | 4.02 | 24.5 | misaligned | FAS | Found in bowl below ruined shrine T.XIV.v |
| S.XV.f.62 | Kaiyuan tongbao | 3.87 | 25 | – | FAS | Found in bowl below ruined shrine T.XIV.v |
| S.XV.f.63 | Kaiyuan tongbao | 3.84 | 24 | misaligned | FAS | Found in bowl below ruined shrine T.XIV.v |
| S.XV.f.64 | Kaiyuan tongbao | 4.33 | 25 | – | FAS | Found in bowl below ruined shrine T.XIV.v |
| S.XV.f.65 | Kaiyuan tongbao | 3.24 | 24 | – | FAS | Found in bowl below ruined shrine T.XIV.v |

| BM no. | Identification | Wt | Diam. | Notes | Acqn | Acquisition/Archaeological context |
|---|---|---|---|---|---|---|
| S.XV.f.66 | Kaiyuan tongbao | 3.57 | 24.5 | – | FAS | Found in bowl below ruined shrine T.XIV.v |
| S.XV.f.67 | Kaiyuan tongbao | 4.54 | 25 | – | FAS | Found in bowl below ruined shrine T.XIV.v |
| S.XV.f.68 | Kaiyuan tongbao | 3.72 | 24.5 | – | FAS | Found in bowl below ruined shrine T.XIV.v |
| S.XV.f.69 | Kaiyuan tongbao | 3.87 | 24.5 | – | FAS | Found in bowl below ruined shrine T.XIV.v |
| S.XV.f.70 | Kaiyuan tongbao | 4.63 | 25 | misaligned | FAS | Found in bowl below ruined shrine T.XIV.v |
| S.XV.f.71 | Kaiyuan tongbao | 3.62 | 24.5 | – | FAS | Found in bowl below ruined shrine T.XIV.v |
| S.XV.f.72 | Kaiyuan tongbao | 4.11 | 25 | – | FAS | Found in bowl below ruined shrine T.XIV.v |
| S.XV.f.73 | Kaiyuan tongbao | 3.41 | 24 | misaligned | FAS | Found in bowl below ruined shrine T.XIV.v |
| S.XV.f.74 | Kaiyuan tongbao | 4.41 | 24.5 | – | FAS | Found in bowl below ruined shrine T.XIV.v |
| S.XV.f.75 | Kaiyuan tongbao | 3.68 | 24.5 | – | FAS | Found in bowl below ruined shrine T.XIV.v |
| S.XV.f.76 | Kaiyuan tongbao | 3.98 | 24 | – | FAS | Found in bowl below ruined shrine T.XIV.v |
| S.XV.f.77 | Kaiyuan tongbao | 2.97 | 23 | misaligned | FAS | Found in bowl below ruined shrine T.XIV.v |
| S.XV.f.78 | Kaiyuan tongbao | 3.88 | 25 | – | FAS | Found in bowl below ruined shrine T.XIV.v |
| S.XV.f.79 | Kaiyuan tongbao | 3.08 | 24 | – | FAS | Found in bowl below ruined shrine T.XIV.v |
| S.XV.f.80 | Kaiyuan tongbao | 3.98 | 24.5 | – | FAS | Found in bowl below ruined shrine T.XIV.v |

| | | | | | | |
|---|---|---|---|---|---|---|
| S.XV.g.1 | Wuzhu – full size | 3.36 | 26.5 | (H: 9) damaged | FAS | Found at ruined military magazine/stores T.XVIII.iii |

| | | | | | | |
|---|---|---|---|---|---|---|
| S.XV.h.1 | Wuzhu – full size | 3.76 | 26.5 | (H: 9) | FAS | Found on slope below watch-tower T.XX |

| | | | | | | |
|---|---|---|---|---|---|---|
| S.XV.i.1 | Daquan wushi | 1.39 | 22 | frag. (H: 10.5) red | FAS | Found W of watch-tower T.XXVI |
| S.XV.i.2 | Daquan wushi | 1.94 | 21.5 | 5 frags (= 1 coin), corroded | FAS | Found W of watch-tower T.XXVI |

| | | | | | | |
|---|---|---|---|---|---|---|
| S.XV.j.1 | Wuzhu – full size, dot on baseline of hole | 3.20 | 25.5 | (H: 9.5) | FAS | Found between watch-towers T.XXVII–XXVIII |

| | | | | | | |
|---|---|---|---|---|---|---|
| S.XV.k.1 | Wuzhu – full size | 3.13 | 25.5 | (H: 9.5) | FAS | Found in refuse heap of watch-tower T.XXVIII |
| S.XV.k.2 | Wu [zhu] – full size | 1.14 | – | frag. | FAS | Found in refuse heap of watch-tower T.XXVIII |

| | | | | | | |
|---|---|---|---|---|---|---|
| S.XV.l.1 | 'Wuzhu' – illegible | 1.18 | – | frag. | FAS | Found on eroded ground near watch-tower T.XXVIII |
| S.XV.l.2 | 'Wuzhu' – illegible | 0.85 | 22 | frag., corroded | FAS | Found on eroded ground near watch-tower T.XXVIII |

| BM no. | Identification | Wt | Diam. | Notes | Acqn | Acquisition/Archaeological context |
|---|---|---|---|---|---|---|
| S.XV.l.3 | Chinese coin – Qing dynasty | – | – | – | FAS | Found on eroded ground near watch-tower T.XXVIII |
| S.XV.m.1 | Wuzhu – full size | 4.09 | 26.5 | (H: 9) corroded | FAS | Found near watch-tower T.XXIV |
| S.XV.n.1 | Chinese coin – Qing dynasty | – | – | – | FAS | Found at graziers' hut near Camp 171 |
| S.XV.o.1 | [extra: 'Wuzhu' – illegible] | 0.84 | – | frag. | – | – |
| S.XV.o.2 | [extra: 'Wuzhu' – illegible] | 0.88 | – | frag. corroded | – | – |
| S.XV.o.3 | [extra: Chinese coin – unidentified] | 2.03 | 25 | frag., corroded | – | – |

## S.XVI: COPPER COINS FOUND AT SO-YANG-CH'ÊNG SITE

| BM no. | Identification | Wt | Diam. | Notes | Acqn | Acquisition/Archaeological context |
|---|---|---|---|---|---|---|
| S.XVI.a.1 | Wuzhu – full size | 3.08 | 25.5 | (H: 9.5) | FAS | Found at So-yang-ch'êng site |
| S.XVI.a.2 | Wuzhu – Northern Wei | 1.93 | 23 | (H: 8.5) | FAS | Found at So-yang-ch'êng site |
| S.XVI.a.3 | Wu [zhu] – full size, small thin wu | 2.52 | 25.5 | (H: 9.5) frag. | FAS | Found at So-yang-ch'êng site |
| S.XVI.a.4 | 'Wuzhu' – illegible | 0.87 | – | frag. | FAS | Found at So-yang-ch'êng site |
| S.XVI.a.5 | 'Wuzhu' – illegible | 0.61 | – | frag. | FAS | Found at So-yang-ch'êng site |
| S.XVI.a.6 | Wu [zhu] – full size | 0.62 | – | frag. | FAS | Found at So-yang-ch'êng site |
| S.XVI.a.7 | Wuzhu – clipped, cuts through inscription | 1.53 | 22 | (H: 9.5) red, bent | FAS | Found at So-yang-ch'êng site |
| S.XVI.a.8 | (Unidentified: non–coin?) | 0.91 | – | frag. | FAS | Found at So-yang-ch'êng site |
| S.XVI.a.9 | 'Wuzhu' – illegible | 1.00 | 17.5 | (H: 5.5) red, with sprue | FAS | Found at So-yang-ch'êng site |
| S.XVI.a.10 | 'Wuzhu' – illegible | 1.20 | 17.5 | (H: 6) with sprue | FAS | Found at So-yang-ch'êng site |
| S.XVI.a.11 | Kaiyuan tongbao | 3.62 | 24.5 | misaligned | FAS | Found at So-yang-ch'êng site |
| S.XVI.a.12 | Kaiyuan tongbao | 2.86 | 24.5 | – | FAS | Found at So-yang-ch'êng site |
| S.XVI.a.13 | Kaiyuan tongbao | 2.29 | 23.5 | – | FAS | Found at So-yang-ch'êng site |
| S.XVI.a.14 | Kaiyuan tongbao | 3.01 | 25 | – | FAS | Found at So-yang-ch'êng site |
| S.XVI.a.15 | Kaiyuan tongbao | 3.84 | 25 | – | FAS | Found at So-yang-ch'êng site |
| S.XVI.a.16 | Kaiyuan tongbao | 3.31 | 24.5 | misaligned | FAS | Found at So-yang-ch'êng site |
| S.XVI.a.17 | Kaiyuan tongbao | 3.62 | 25 | – | FAS | Found at So-yang-ch'êng site |
| S.XVI.a.18 | Kaiyuan tongbao | 3.15 | 25 | misaligned | FAS | Found at So-yang-ch'êng site |
| S.XVI.a.19 | Kaiyuan tongbao | 1.90 | 24.5 | pierced twice, corroded | FAS | Found at So-yang-ch'êng site |
| S.XVI.a.20 | Kaiyuan tongbao | 4.13 | 25 | – | FAS | Found at So-yang-ch'êng site |
| S.XVI.a.21 | Kaiyuan tongbao | 2.99 | 24.5 | misaligned | FAS | Found at So-yang-ch'êng site |
| S.XVI.a.22 | [Kaiyuan] tong [bao] | 0.23 | – | frag. | FAS | Found at So-yang-ch'êng site |
| S.XVI.a.23 | [Kaiyuan tong] bao | 1.20 | – | frag. | FAS | Found at So-yang-ch'êng site |
| S.XVI.a.24 | [Kaiyuan] tong [bao] | 0.58 | – | frag. | FAS | Found at So-yang-ch'êng site |
| S.XVI.a.25 | [Kaiyuan] tong [bao] | 1.07 | – | frag. | FAS | Found at So-yang-ch'êng site |
| S.XVI.a.26 | [Kaiyuan] tong [bao] | 1.32 | – | frag. | FAS | Found at So-yang-ch'êng site |
| S.XVI.a.27 | [Kaiyuan] tong [bao] | 0.38 | – | frag. | FAS | Found at So-yang-ch'êng site |
| S.XVI.a.28 | Kai [yuan tongbao] | 1.10 | – | frag. | FAS | Found at So-yang-ch'êng site |
| S.XVI.a.29 | Kai [yuan tongbao] | 0.53 | – | frag. | FAS | Found at So-yang-ch'êng site |
| S.XVI.a.30 | [Kai] yuan [tongbao] | 1.59 | – | frag. | FAS | Found at So-yang-ch'êng site |
| S.XVI.a.31 | [Kai] yuan [tong] bao | 1.02 | – | frag. | FAS | Found at So-yang-ch'êng site |

| BM no. | Identification | Wt | Diam. | Notes | Acqn | Acquisition/Archaeological context |
|---|---|---|---|---|---|---|
| S.XVI.a.32 | Kai [yuan tongbao] | 0.73 | – | frag. | FAS | Found at So-yang-ch'êng site |
| S.XVI.a.33 | Chinese – unidentified | 0.52 | – | 2 frags | FAS | Found at So-yang-ch'êng site |
| S.XVI.a.34 | [Kaiyuan] tong [bao] | 0.45 | – | frag. | FAS | Found at So-yang-ch'êng site |
| S.XVI.a.35 | Chinese coin – unidentified | 0.24 | – | frag. | FAS | Found at So-yang-ch'êng site |
| S.XVI.a.36 | Qianyuan zhongbao – small | 1.99 | 21 | forced hole | FAS | Found at So-yang-ch'êng site |
| S.XVI.a.37 | Chinese coin – Song dynasty | – | – | – | FAS | Found at So-yang-ch'êng site |
| S.XVI.a.38 | Chinese coin – Jin dynasty (1127–1234) | – | – | – | FAS | Found at So-yang-ch'êng site |
| S.XVI.a.39 | [extra: (Qian) yuan zhong (bao) – large] | 4.07 | – | frag. | – | – |
| S.XVI.a.40–42 | [extra: non–coins] | – | – | – | – | – |

**S.XVII: COPPER COIN FOUND AT HEI-SHUI-KUO SITE, WEST OF KANCHOU**

| BM no. | Identification | Wt | Diam. | Notes | Acqn | Acquisition/Archaeological context |
|---|---|---|---|---|---|---|
| S.XVII.a.1 | Chinese coin – unidentified | 2.66 | 22 | corroded | FAS | Found at Hei-shui-kuo site, W of Kanchou (Ganzhou) |

**S.XVIII: COPPER COIN FOUND EAST OF CHONG HASSAR, TURFAN**

| BM no. | Identification | Wt | Diam. | Notes | Acqn | Acquisition/Archaeological context |
|---|---|---|---|---|---|---|
| S.XVIII.a.1 | Kaiyuan tongbao – 'nail mark' on rev. | 3.93 | 25 | 2 frags (= 1 coin) misaligned | F | Found E of Chong Hassar, Turfan |

**S.XIX: COPPER COINS FOUND AT YAR-KHOTO, TURFAN**

| BM no. | Identification | Wt | Diam. | Notes | Acqn | Acquisition/Archaeological context |
|---|---|---|---|---|---|---|
| S.XIX.a.1 | 'Wuzhu' – Illegible | 1.59 | 22 | (H: 9) corroded | FAS | Found in ruined dwelling Y.K.i |
| S.XIX.a.2 | Kaiyuan tongbao | 3.58 | 24.5 | misaligned | FAS | Found in ruined dwelling Y.K.i |
| S.XIX.a.3 | Kaiyuan tongbao | 1.57 | 22.5 | – | FAS | Found in ruined dwelling Y.K.i |
| S.XIX.a.4 | Kaiyuan tongbao | 2.95 | 23.5 | – | FAS | Found in ruined dwelling Y.K.i |
| S.XIX.a.5 | Kaiyuan tongbao | 4.07 | 26 | misaligned | FAS | Found in ruined dwelling Y.K.i |
| S.XIX.a.6 | Kaiyuan tongbao | 3.21 | 25 | – | FAS | Found in ruined dwelling Y.K.i |
| S.XIX.a.7 | Kaiyuan tongbao | 3.84 | 24.5 | – | FAS | Found in ruined dwelling Y.K.i |
| S.XIX.a.8 | Kaiyuan tongbao | 3.82 | 25.5 | – | FAS | Found in ruined dwelling Y.K.i |
| S.XIX.a.9 | Kaiyuan tongbao | 3.25 | 25 | – | FAS | Found in ruined dwelling Y.K.i |
| S.XIX.a.10 | Kaiyuan tongbao | 3.58 | 24.5 | – | FAS | Found in ruined dwelling Y.K.i |
| S.XIX.a.11 | Kaiyuan tongbao | 4.12 | 25.5 | – | FAS | Found in ruined dwelling Y.K.i |
| S.XIX.a.12 | Kaiyuan tongbao | 3.29 | 24.5 | – | FAS | Found in ruined dwelling Y.K.i |
| S.XIX.a.13 | Kaiyuan tongbao | 3.76 | 25.5 | – | FAS | Found in ruined dwelling Y.K.i |
| S.XIX.a.14 | Kaiyuan tongbao | 3.62 | 24 | misaligned | FAS | Found in ruined dwelling Y.K.i |
| S.XIX.a.15 | Kaiyuan tongbao | 4.59 | 25.5 | – | FAS | Found in ruined dwelling Y.K.i |
| S.XIX.a.16 | Kaiyuan tongbao | 3.28 | 24 | misaligned | FAS | Found in ruined dwelling Y.K.i |
| S.XIX.a.17 | Kaiyuan tongbao | 4.01 | 24.5 | misaligned | FAS | Found in ruined dwelling Y.K.i |
| S.XIX.a.18 | Kaiyuan tongbao – 'nail mark' on rev. | 4.07 | 25 | – | FAS | Found in ruined dwelling Y.K.i |
| S.XIX.a.19 | Kaiyuan tongbao | 4.21 | 25.5 | misaligned | FAS | Found in ruined dwelling Y.K.i |

| BM no. | Identification | Wt | Diam. | Notes | Acqn | Acquisition/Archaeological context |
|---|---|---|---|---|---|---|
| S.XIX.a.20 | Kaiyuan tongbao | 4.17 | 24.5 | – | FAS | Found in ruined dwelling Y.K.i |
| S.XIX.a.21 | Kaiyuan tongbao | 2.32 | 24 | misaligned | FAS | Found in ruined dwelling Y.K.i |
| S.XIX.a.22 | Kaiyuan tongbao | 3.81 | 24.5 | misaligned | FAS | Found in ruined dwelling Y.K.i |
| S.XIX.a.23 | Kaiyuan tongbao | 3.03 | 24.5 | – | FAS | Found in ruined dwelling Y.K.i |
| S.XIX.a.24 | Kaiyuan tongbao | 3.84 | 25 | misaligned | FAS | Found in ruined dwelling Y.K.i |
| S.XIX.a.25 | Kaiyuan tongbao | 3.91 | 25 | – | FAS | Found in ruined dwelling Y.K.i |
| S.XIX.a.26 | Kaiyuan tongbao | 3.76 | 25.5 | – | FAS | Found in ruined dwelling Y.K.i |
| S.XIX.a.27 | Kaiyuan tongbao | 2.92 | 24.5 | misaligned | FAS | Found in ruined dwelling Y.K.i |
| S.XIX.a.28 | Kaiyuan tongbao | 3.72 | 24.5 | pierced at top | FAS | Found in ruined dwelling Y.K.i |
| S.XIX.a.29 | Kaiyuan tongbao – crescent above hole on rev. | 4.00 | 25.5 | forced hole | FAS | Found in ruined dwelling Y.K.i |
| S.XIX.a.30 | Kaiyuan tongbao – crescent above hole on rev. | 4.00 | 25 | – | FAS | Found in ruined dwelling Y.K.i |
| S.XIX.a.31 | Kaiyuan tongbao | 2.41 | 24.5 | – | FAS | Found in ruined dwelling Y.K.i |
| S.XIX.a.32 | Kaiyuan tongbao | 3.58 | 24.5 | misaligned | FAS | Found in ruined dwelling Y.K.i |
| S.XIX.a.33 | Kaiyuan tongbao – crescent above hole on rev. | 3.87 | 25 | – | FAS | Found in ruined dwelling Y.K.i |
| S.XIX.a.34 | Kaiyuan tongbao – crescent above hole on rev. | 4.24 | 25.5 | – | FAS | Found in ruined dwelling Y.K.i |
| S.XIX.a.35 | Kaiyuan tongbao – crescent below hole on rev. | 4.00 | 25.5 | – | FAS | Found in ruined dwelling Y.K.i |
| S.XIX.a.36 | Kaiyuan tongbao | 2.37 | 22.5 | – | FAS | Found in ruined dwelling Y.K.i |
| S.XIX.a.37 | Kaiyuan tongbao – crescent above hole on rev. | 3.64 | 25.5 | – | FAS | Found in ruined dwelling Y.K.i |
| S.XIX.a.38 | Kaiyuan tongbao – crescent above hole on rev. | 4.14 | 25.5 | – | FAS | Found in ruined dwelling Y.K.i |
| S.XIX.a.39 | Kaiyuan tongbao | 3.13 | 24.5 | – | FAS | Found in ruined dwelling Y.K.i |
| S.XIX.a.40 | Kaiyuan tongbao | 3.16 | 24.5 | – | FAS | Found in ruined dwelling Y.K.i |
| S.XIX.a.41 | Kaiyuan tongbao | 2.05 | 22 | – | FAS | Found in ruined dwelling Y.K.i |
| S.XIX.a.42 | Kaiyuan tongbao – crescent above hole on rev. | 4.08 | 25 | – | FAS | Found in ruined dwelling Y.K.i |
| S.XIX.a.43 | Kaiyuan tongbao | 4.72 | 26 | misaligned | FAS | Found in ruined dwelling Y.K.i |
| S.XIX.a.44 | Kaiyuan tongbao | 3.02 | 24.5 | – | FAS | Found in ruined dwelling Y.K.i |
| S.XIX.a.45 | Kaiyuan tongbao | 3.64 | 24.5 | – | FAS | Found in ruined dwelling Y.K.i |
| S.XIX.a.46 | Kaiyuan tongbao | 3.33 | 24 | – | FAS | Found in ruined dwelling Y.K.i |
| S.XIX.a.47 | Kaiyuan tongbao | 3.69 | 25.5 | corroded | FAS | Found in ruined dwelling Y.K.i |
| S.XIX.a.48 | Kaiyuan tongbao | 2.05 | 23.5 | 3 frags restored, damaged | FAS | Found in ruined dwelling Y.K.i |
| S.XIX.a.49 | Kaiyuan tongbao | 2.05 | 23 | frag. | FAS | Found in ruined dwelling Y.K.i |
| S.XIX.a.50 | Kaiyuan tongbao | 3.04 | 24 | misaligned | FAS | Found in ruined dwelling Y.K.i |
| S.XIX.a.51 | Kaiyuan tongbao | 3.82 | 25.5 | – | FAS | Found in ruined dwelling Y.K.i |
| S.XIX.a.52 | Kaiyuan tongbao | 3.25 | 23.5 | – | FAS | Found in ruined dwelling Y.K.i |
| S.XIX.a.53 | Kaiyuan tongbao | 2.78 | 25.5 | misaligned | FAS | Found in ruined dwelling Y.K.i |
| S.XIX.a.54 | Kaiyuan tongbao | 4.13 | 25 | misaligned | FAS | Found in ruined dwelling Y.K.i |
| S.XIX.a.55 | Kaiyuan tongbao | 4.55 | 24.5 | – | FAS | Found in ruined dwelling Y.K.i |
| S.XIX.a.56 | Kaiyuan tongbao | 3.79 | 25.5 | – | FAS | Found in ruined dwelling Y.K.i |
| S.XIX.a.57 | Kaiyuan tongbao – crescent below hole on rev. | 4.03 | 25 | – | FAS | Found in ruined dwelling Y.K.i |
| S.XIX.a.58 | Kaiyuan tongbao – crescent above hole on rev. | 4.29 | 25.5 | – | FAS | Found in ruined dwelling Y.K.i |
| S.XIX.a.59 | Kaiyuan tongbao | 3.17 | 25.5 | – | FAS | Found in ruined dwelling Y.K.i |
| S.XIX.a.60 | Kaiyuan tongbao | 3.48 | 24.5 | – | FAS | Found in ruined dwelling Y.K.i |
| S.XIX.a.61 | Kaiyuan tongbao | 4.05 | 24.5 | – | FAS | Found in ruined dwelling Y.K.i |
| S.XIX.a.62 | Kaiyuan tongbao | 3.56 | 25 | – | FAS | Found in ruined dwelling Y.K.i |
| S.XIX.a.63 | Kaiyuan tongbao | 2.74 | 24 | – | FAS | Found in ruined dwelling Y.K.i |

| BM no. | Identification | Wt | Diam. | Notes | Acqn | Acquisition/Archaeological context |
|---|---|---|---|---|---|---|
| S.XIX.a.64 | Kaiyuan tongbao – crescent above hole on rev. | 3.86 | 25 | – | FAS | Found in ruined dwelling Y.K.i |
| S.XIX.a.65 | Kaiyuan tongbao – crescent above hole on rev. | 3.71 | 25.5 | – | FAS | Found in ruined dwelling Y.K.i |
| S.XIX.a.66 | Kaiyuan tongbao | 2.71 | 24 | misaligned | FAS | Found in ruined dwelling Y.K.i |
| S.XIX.a.67 | Kaiyuan tongbao | 3.27 | 24.5 | – | FAS | Found in ruined dwelling Y.K.i |
| S.XIX.a.68 | Kaiyuan tongbao | 2.21 | 24 | – | FAS | Found in ruined dwelling Y.K.i |
| S.XIX.a.69 | Kaiyuan tongbao | 3.86 | 25 | – | FAS | Found in ruined dwelling Y.K.i |
| S.XIX.a.70 | Kaiyuan tongbao | 3.62 | 25 | – | FAS | Found in ruined dwelling Y.K.i |
| S.XIX.a.71 | Kaiyuan tongbao – crescent above hole on rev. | 3.46 | 25 | – | FAS | Found in ruined dwelling Y.K.i |
| S.XIX.a.72 | Kaiyuan tongbao | 3.68 | 24 | – | FAS | Found in ruined dwelling Y.K.i |
| S.XIX.a.73 | Kaiyuan tongbao | 1.67 | 22.5 | – | FAS | Found in ruined dwelling Y.K.i |
| S.XIX.a.74 | Kaiyuan tongbao | 3.32 | 24.5 | misaligned | FAS | Found in ruined dwelling Y.K.i |
| S.XIX.a.75 | Kaiyuan tongbao | 2.71 | 22.5 | misaligned | FAS | Found in ruined dwelling Y.K.i |
| S.XIX.a.76 | Kaiyuan tongbao | 4.53 | 25 | – | FAS | Found in ruined dwelling Y.K.i |
| S.XIX.a.77 | Kaiyuan tongbao | 4.48 | 24.5 | – | FAS | Found in ruined dwelling Y.K.i |
| S.XIX.a.78 | Kaiyuan tongbao | 4.16 | 25 | – | FAS | Found in ruined dwelling Y.K.i |
| S.XIX.a.79 | Kaiyuan tongbao | 3.08 | 24 | misaligned | FAS | Found in ruined dwelling Y.K.i |
| S.XIX.a.80 | Kaiyuan tongbao | 2.75 | 25 | – | FAS | Found in ruined dwelling Y.K.i |
| S.XIX.a.81 | Kaiyuan tongbao | 3.34 | 24.5 | – | FAS | Found in ruined dwelling Y.K.i |
| S.XIX.a.82 | Kaiyuan tongbao | 4.35 | 25 | – | FAS | Found in ruined dwelling Y.K.i |
| S.XIX.a.83 | Kaiyuan tongbao | 3.63 | 25.5 | misaligned, corroded | FAS | Found in ruined dwelling Y.K.i |
| S.XIX.a.84 | Kaiyuan tongbao | 2.71 | 25.5 | damaged | FAS | Found in ruined dwelling Y.K.i |
| S.XIX.a.85 | Kaiyuan tongbao | 1.96 | 23 | – | FAS | Found in ruined dwelling Y.K.i |
| S.XIX.a.86 | Kaiyuan tongbao | 4.22 | 25.5 | – | FAS | Found in ruined dwelling Y.K.i |
| S.XIX.a.87 | Kaiyuan tongbao – crescent below hole on rev. | 3.90 | 25.5 | – | FAS | Found in ruined dwelling Y.K.i |
| S.XIX.a.88 | Kaiyuan tongbao – crescent above hole on rev. | 4.27 | – | 4 frags | FAS | Found in ruined dwelling Y.K.i |
| S.XIX.a.89 | Kaiyuan tongbao | – |  | 3 frags (= 1 coin) | FAS | Found in ruined dwelling Y.K.i |
| S.XIX.a.90 | Kaiyuan tongbao (3 frags, 2 frags = 1 coin?) | – | – | 3 frags (= 1 coin) | FAS | Found in ruined dwelling Y.K.i |
| S.XIX.a.91 | Kaiyuan tongbao | 2.74 | – | 4 frags (= 1 coin) | FAS | Found in ruined dwelling Y.K.i |
| S.XIX.a.92 | Kaiyuan tongbao | 3.80 | 25 | – | FAS | Found in ruined dwelling Y.K.i |
| S.XIX.a.93 | Kaiyuan tongbao | 1.70 | 24 | – | FAS | Found in ruined dwelling Y.K.i |
| S.XIX.a.94 | Kaiyuan tongbao | 1.60 | 25 | 2 frags (= 1 coin) | FAS | Found in ruined dwelling Y.K.i |
| S.XIX.a.95 | Qianyuan zhongbao – small | 2.57 | 23 | misaligned | FAS | Found in ruined dwelling Y.K.i |
| S.XIX.a.96 | Qianyuan zhongbao – large | 4.47 | 26 | – | FAS | Found in ruined dwelling Y.K.i |
| S.XIX.a.97 | [missing: Kaiyuan tongbao] |  | – | – | FAS | Found in ruined dwelling Y.K.i |
| S.XIX.a.98 | [missing: Kaiyuan tongbao] | – | – | – | FAS | Found in ruined dwelling Y.K.I |
| S.XIX.a.99 | Qianyuan zhongbao – large | 4.16 | 26 | misaligned | FAS | Found in ruined dwelling Y.K.i |
| S.XIX.a.100 | Qianyuan zhongbao – small | 2.23 | 21.5 | with sprue | FAS | Found in ruined dwelling Y.K.i |
| S.XIX.a.101 | Qianyuan zhongbao – large | 3.53 | 26 | misaligned | FAS | Found in ruined dwelling Y.K.i |
| S.XIX.a.102 | [extra: Wuzhu – without rim] | 1.67 | 24 | (H: 9.5) | FAS | Found in ruined dwelling Y.K.i |
| S.XIX.a.103 | [extra: 'Wuzhu' – illegible] | 1.13 | 23.5 | (H: 9.5) | FAS | Found in ruined dwelling Y.K.i |
| S.XIX.a.104 | [extra: 'Wuzhu' – illegible] | 0.59 | 17 | (H: 8.5) | FAS | Found in ruined dwelling Y.K.i |
| S.XIX.a.105 | [extra: Chinese – Qing dynasty] | – | – | – | FAS | Found in ruined dwelling Y.K.i |

| | | | | | | |
|---|---|---|---|---|---|---|
| S.XIX.b.1 | Kaiyuan tongbao | 3.56 | 24 | – | FAS | Found in ruined shrine Y.K.iii |
| S.XIX.b.2 | Jianzhong tongbao – small | 2.47 | 21.5 | – | FAS | Found in ruined shrine Y.K.iii |

| | | | | | | |
|---|---|---|---|---|---|---|
| S.XIX.c.1 | Qianyuan zhongbao – small | 2.10 | 21 | – | FAS | Found at Yar-khoto, Khotan |

## S.XX: COPPER COIN FOUND ON RAMPART OF RUINED FORT NEAR USHAK-TAL, KARA-SHAHR

| BM no. | Identification | Wt | Diam. | Notes | Acqn | Acquisition/Archaeological context |
|---|---|---|---|---|---|---|
| S.XX.a.1 | Qianyuan zhongbao – large | 7.16 | 29 | misaligned | FAS | Found on rampart of ruined fort near Ushak-tal |

## S.XXI: COPPER COIN FOUND AT BAGHDAD–SHAHRI SITE, KARA–SHAHR

| BM no. | Identification | Wt | Diam. | Notes | Acqn | Acquisition/Archaeological context |
|---|---|---|---|---|---|---|
| S.XXI.a.1 | [Jian] zhong [tongbao] | 0.77 | – | frag. | FAS | Found at Baghdad-shahri site, Kara-shahr |

## S.XXII: COPPER COINS EXCAVATED AT MING-OI SITE, NORTH OF SHOR-CHUK

| BM no. | Identification | Wt | Diam. | Notes | Acqn | Acquisition/Archaeological context |
|---|---|---|---|---|---|---|
| S.XXII.a.1 | Kaiyuan tongbao – crescent above hole on rev. | 4.29 | 25.5 | – | FAS | Found before image base in shrine Mi.i |
| S.XXII.a.2 | Kaiyuan tongbao – crescent above hole on rev. | 3.55 | 25 | – | FAS | Found before image base in shrine Mi.i |
| S.XXII.a.3 | Dali yuanbao – small | 2.46 | 22 | misaligned | FAS | Found before image base in shrine Mi.i |
| S.XXII.a.4 | Dali yuanbao – large | 3.13 | 24 | misaligned | FAS | Found before image base in shrine Mi.i |

| | | | | | | |
|---|---|---|---|---|---|---|
| S.XXII.b.1 | Coin with single character zhong | 1.44 | 21 | forced hole | FAS | Found in ante-chapel Mi.x |
| S.XXII.b.2 | Wuzhu | 1.44 | 22 | 2 frags (= 1 coin) | FAS | Found in ante-chapel Mi.x |
| S.XXII.b.3 | Coin with single character yuan | 1.72 | 20.5 | – | FAS | Found in ante-chapel Mi.x |
| S.XXII.b.4 | Chinese coin – unidentified | 1.18 | – | 6 frags (= 1 coin) | FAS | Found in ante-chapel Mi.x |
| S.XXII.b.5 | Chinese coin – unidentified | 3.05 | 22.5 | 2 frags (= 1 coin) corroded | FAS | Found in ante-chapel Mi.x |
| S.XXII.b.6 | Kaiyuan tongbao | 3.58 | 25.5 | – | FAS | Found in ante-chapel Mi.x |
| S.XXII.b.7 | Dali yuanbao – small | 2.43 | 22 | misaligned | FAS | Found in ante-chapel Mi.x |
| S.XXII.b.8 | Jianzhong tongbao – small | 1.85 | 21 | misaligned | FAS | Found in ante-chapel Mi.x |
| S.XXII.b.9 | Jianzhong tongbao – small | 2.21 | 21.5 | – | FAS | Found in ante-chapel Mi.x |
| S.XXII.b.10 | Jianzhong tongbao – small | 2.32 | 21 | misaligned | FAS | Found in ante-chapel Mi.x |
| S.XXII.b.11 | Jianzhong tongbao – large | 3.31 | 22.5 | – | FAS | Found in ante-chapel Mi.x |
| S.XXII.b.12 | Jianzhong tongbao – large | 2.59 | 22.5 | damaged | FAS | Found in ante-chapel Mi.x |
| S.XXII.b.13 | Chinese coin – unidentified | 2.34 | 22 | corroded | FAS | Found in ante-chapel Mi.x |
| S.XXII.b.14 | Jianzhong tongbao – large | 3.34 | 25 | corroded | FAS | Found in ante-chapel Mi.x |

| | | | | | | |
|---|---|---|---|---|---|---|
| S.XXII.c.1 | Kaiyuan tongbao | 5.29 | 25 | – | FAS | Found in temple cella Mi.xi |
| S.XXII.c.2 | Jianzhong tongbao – large | 3.33 | 22 | scyphate | FAS | Found in temple cella Mi.xi |
| S.XXII.c.3 | Jianzhong tongbao – large | 3.25 | 23.5 | – | FAS | Found in temple cella Mi.xi |

| | | | | | | |
|---|---|---|---|---|---|---|
| S.XXII.d.1 | Huoquan | 1.99 | 22.5 | bent | FAS | Found at image bases in temple passage Mi.xii |
| S.XXII.d.2 | Kaiyuan zhongbao | 2.57 | 23 | – | FAS | Found at image bases in temple passage Mi.xii |
| S.XXII.d.3 | Dali yuanbao – small | 2.32 | 22 | – | FAS | Found at image bases in temple passage Mi.xii |

| BM no. | Identification | Wt | Diam. | Notes | Acqn | Acquisition/Archaeological context |
|---|---|---|---|---|---|---|
| S.XXII.d.4 | Dali yuanbao – small | 3.02 | 22 | – | FAS | Found at image bases in temple passage Mi.xii |
| S.XXII.d.5 | Dali yuanbao – small | 3.49 | 22 | forced hole, scyphate | FAS | Found at image bases in temple passage Mi.xii |
| S.XXII.d.6 | Jianzhong tongbao – small | 2.52 | 20.5 | – | FAS | Found at image bases in temple passage Mi.xii |
| S.XXII.d.7 | Jianzhong tongbao – large | 3.45 | 23 | – | FAS | Found at image bases in temple passage Mi.xii |
| S.XXII.e.1 | Kaiyuan tongbao | 3.11 | 24 | misaligned | FAS | Found in shrine Mi.xiv |
| S.XXII.e.2 | Chinese coin – unidentified | 2.63 | 21.5 | corroded | FAS | Found in shrine Mi.xiv |
| S.XXII.f.1 | Jianzhong tongbao – small | 2.18 | 20.5 | – | FAS | Found before entrance to shrine Mi.xvii |
| S.XXII.g.1 | Kaiyuan tongbao | 2.74 | 23 | misaligned | FAS | Found among SE group of ruins |
| S.XXII.g.2 | Jianzhong tongbao – small | 2.32 | 21 | red | FAS | Found among SE group of ruins |

### S.XXIII: COPPER COINS FOUND NEAR RUIN KA.I, KARADONG

| BM no. | Identification | Wt | Diam. | Notes | Acqn | Acquisition/Archaeological context |
|---|---|---|---|---|---|---|
| S.XXIII.a.1 | 'Wuzhu' – illegible | 0.96 | 16 | (H: 8) | FAS | Found near ruin Ka.I |
| S.XXIII.a.2 | 'Wuzhu' – illegible | 1.68 | 24.5 | (H: 10.5) damaged | FAS | Found near ruin Ka.I |

### S.XXIV: COPPER COINS FOUND AT FARHAD-BEG-YAILAKI SITE

| BM no. | Identification | Wt | Diam. | Notes | Acqn | Acquisition/Archaeological context |
|---|---|---|---|---|---|---|
| S.XXIV.a.1 | 'Wuzhu' – illegible | 1.18 | 20 | (H: 9.5) forced hole | FAS | Found near ruin F.I |
| S.XXIV.a.2 | Wuzhu – small, clipped, cuts through inscription | 1.72 | 22.5 | (H: 9) red | FAS | Found near ruin F.I |
| S.XXIV.a.3 | 'Wuzhu' – illegible, small | 0.56 | – | frag. | FAS | Found near ruin F.I |
| S.XXIV.a.4 | 'Wuzhu' – illegible | 0.75 | 18 | (H: 8) | FAS | Found near ruin F.I |
| S.XXIV.b.1 | 'Wuzhu' – illegible, small, rim on rev. | 1.00 | 18 | (H: 9) sprue | FAS | Found near ruin F.II |
| S.XXIV.b.2 | 'Wuzhu' – Illegible, small | 0.43 | – | frags, corroded | FAS | Found near ruin F.II |
| S.XXIV.b.3 | Wuzhu | 0.41 | 18 | (H. 7) frag., red | FAS | Found near ruin F.II |
| S.XXIV.c.1 | Wuzhu – clipped, cuts through inscription | 1.00 | 21 | (H: 10) red | FAS | Found in cella F.III.i |
| S.XXIV.d.1 | Wuzhu – clipped, cuts through inscription, small wu | 1.17 | 19.5 | (H: 10) red | FAS | Found near ruin F.V |

## S.XXV: COPPER COIN FOUND IN RUINED SHRINE, KARA YANTAK

| BM no. | Identification | Wt | Diam. | Notes | Acqn | Acquisition/Archaeological context |
|---|---|---|---|---|---|---|
| S.XXV.a.1 | Qianyuan zhongbao – large | 7.31 | 29.5 | misaligned, forced hole | FAS | Found in ruined shrine, Kara Yantak |

## S.XXVI: WEST LACH [NOT INCLUDED IN LIST OF COINS]

| BM no. | Identification | Wt | Diam. | Notes | Acqn | Acquisition/Archaeological context |
|---|---|---|---|---|---|---|
| S.XXVI.1 | Chinese coin – Song dynasty | – | – | – | – | – |
| S.XXVI.2 | Islamic coin | – | – | – | – | – |

## S.XXVI: COPPER COINS FOUND AT, OR BROUGHT FROM, TATI SITES, NORTHWEST OF DOMOKO

| BM no. | Identification | Wt | Diam. | Notes | Acqn | Acquisition/Archaeological context |
|---|---|---|---|---|---|---|
| S.XXVI.a.1 | Unidentified (Sino-Kharoshthi?) | 4.54 | 22×21 | – | FAS | Found at sites near Ulugh-mazar |
| S.XXVI.a.2 | Wuzhu – full size | 1.50 | 25 | (H: 9.5) damaged | FAS | Found at sites near Ulugh-mazar |
| S.XXVI.a.3 | 'Wuzhu' – illegible | 1.33 | 23 | (H: 9.5) damaged | FAS | Found at sites near Ulugh-mazar |
| S.XXVI.a.4 | 'Wuzhu' – illegible | 0.83 | – | frag. | FAS | Found at sites near Ulugh-mazar |
| S.XXVI.a.5 | 'Wuzhu' – illegible | 0.44 | 19 | (H: 9) frag. | FAS | Found at sites near Ulugh-mazar |
| S.XXVI.a.6 | Chinese coin – Song dynasty | – | – | – | FAS | Found at sites near Ulugh-mazar |
| S.XXVI.b.1 | 'Wuzhu' – illegible | 0.74 | 20 | (H: 9.5) frag. | p | Allegedly from sites NW of Domoko |
| S.XXVI.b.2 | Wuzhu – small wu, clipped, cuts through inscription | 0.86 | 17.5 | (H: 8.5) | p | Allegedly from sites NW of Domoko |
| S.XXVI.b.3 | 'Wuzhu' – illegible | 0.69 | 17.5 | (H: 9) | p | Allegedly from sites NW of Domoko |
| S.XXVI.b.4 | 'Wuzhu' – illegible | 1.30 | 22.5 | (H: 10.5) | p | Allegedly from sites NW of Domoko |
| S.XXVI.b.5 | Wuzhu | 1.23 | 20 | (H: 10) | p | Allegedly from sites NW of Domoko |
| S.XXVI.b.6 | Kaiyuan tongbao | 4.14 | 25 | – | p | Allegedly from sites NW of Domoko |
| S.XXVI.b.7 | Kaiyuan tongbao | 3.34 | 24 | corroded | p | Allegedly from sites NW of Domoko |
| S.XXVI.b.8 | Chinese coin – unidentified | 2.11 | 22.5 | corroded | p | Allegedly from sites NW of Domoko |
| S.XXVI.b.9 | Qianyuan zhongbao – small | 3.00 | 22 | – | p | Allegedly from sites NW of Domoko |
| S.XXVI.b.10–13 | Chinese coins – Song dynasty | 1.44 | – | 2 frags | p | Allegedly from sites NW of Domoko |
| S.XXVI.b.14 | Islamic coin | – | – | – | p | Allegedly from sites NW of Domoko |

## S.XXVII: COPPER COINS BROUGHT AS FROM CHALMA-KAZAN

| BM no. | Identification | Wt | Diam. | Notes | Acqn | Acquisition/Archaeological context |
|---|---|---|---|---|---|---|
| S.XXVII.a.1 | Sino-Kharoshthi coin (Cribb 1–6) | 0.94 | 16×9 | – | p | Allegedly from Chalma-kazan |
| S.XXVII.a.2 | Sino-Kharoshthi coin (Cribb 1–6) | 1.11 | 16 | – | p | Allegedly from Chalma-kazan |
| S.XXVII.a.3 | Sino-Kharoshthi coin (Cribb 1–6) | 1.59 | 15 | – | p | Allegedly from Chalma-kazan |
| S.XXVII.a.4 | Sino-Kharoshthi coin (Cribb 1–6) | 0.60 | 15 | – | p | Allegedly from Chalma-kazan |
| S.XXVII.a.5 | Sino-Kharoshthi coin (contemporary copy?) | 0.71 | 14 | – | p | Allegedly from Chalma-kazan |
| S.XXVII.a.6 (OR.0384) | Sino-Kharoshthi coin (Cribb 7) | 11.33 | 26 | – | p | Allegedly from Chalma-kazan |
| S.XXVII.a.7 | 'Wuzhu' –illegible | 2.24 | 25 | (H: 10.5) damaged | p | Allegedly from Chalma-kazan |
| S.XXVII.a.8 | 'Wuzhu' –illegible | 1.32 | 19 | (H: 8.5) corroded | p | Allegedly from Chalma-kazan |
| S.XXVII.a.9 | Qianyuan zhongbao – large | 5.05 | 28.5 | misaligned | p | Allegedly from Chalma-kazan |
| S.XXVII.a.10 | Qianyuan zhongbao – large | 5.43 | 28 | pierced | p | Allegedly from Chalma-kazan |
| S.XXVII.a.11 | Qianyuan zhongbao – small | 2.06 | 21.5 | – | p | Allegedly from Chalma-kazan |
| S.XXVII.a.12 | Qianyuan zhongbao – small | 2.09 | 21.5 | – | p | Allegedly from Chalma-kazan |
| S.XXVII.a.13 | Qianyuan zhongbao – small | 1.78 | 21.5 | forced hole | p | Allegedly from Chalma-kazan |
| S.XXVII.a.14 | Qianyuan zhongbao – small | 3.01 | 21.5 | – | p | Allegedly from Chalma-kazan |
| S.XXVII.a.15 | Dali yuanbao – small | 2.18 | 21.5 | – | p | Allegedly from Chalma-kazan |
| S.XXVII.a.16 | Dali yuanbao – small | 3.14 | 21.5 | – | p | Allegedly from Chalma-kazan |
| S.XXVII.a.17 | Dali yuanbao – small | 3.25 | 23 | corroded | p | Allegedly from Chalma-kazan |

## S.XXVIII: COPPER COIN FOUND AT KARA-SAI SITE

| BM no. | Identification | Wt | Diam. | Notes | Acqn | Acquisition/Archaeological context |
|---|---|---|---|---|---|---|
| S.XXVIII.a.1 | [missing: Chinese – 'Wuzhu'] | – | – | – | FAS | Found at Kara-sai site |

## S.XXIX: COINS FOUND AT, OR NEAR, TARISHLAK SITE

| BM no. | Identification | Wt | Diam. | Notes | Acqn | Acquisition/Archaeological context |
|---|---|---|---|---|---|---|
| S.XXIX.a.1 | 'Wuzhu' – illegible | 1.18 | – | 2 frags | FAS | Found within ruin Ta.i, ii |
| S.XXIX.a.2 | 'Wuzhu' – illegible, small | 0.44 | 11 | (H: 5.5) corroded | FAS | Found within ruin Ta.i, ii |
| S.XXIX.b.1 | Wuzhu – clipped, cuts through inscription | 1.08 | 17.5 | (H: 8) corroded | FAS | Collected from Tati S of site |
| S.XXIX.b.2 | 'Wuzhu' – illegible, small | 0.48 | 10.5 | (H: 3.5) corroded | FAS | Collected from Tati S of site |
| S.XXIX.b.3 | 'Wuzhu' – illegible, small | 0.42 | 12.5 | (H: 7) | FAS | Collected from Tati S of site |
| S.XXIX.b.4 | 'Wuzhu' – illegible, small, square | 0.31 | 12.5 | (H: 7) | FAS | Collected from Tati S of site |
| S.XXIX.b.5 | 'Wuzhu' – illegible, small, square | 0.33 | 12.5 | (H: 7) | FAS | Collected from Tati S of site |
| S.XXIX.b.6 | 'Wuzhu' – illegible, small, square | 0.26 | 10 | (H: 5) | FAS | Collected from Tati S of site |
| S.XXIX.b.7 | 'Wuzhu' – illegible, small, square | 0.42 | 11 | (H: 5) corroded | FAS | Collected from Tati S of site |
| S.XXIX.b.8 | 'Wuzhu' – illegible | 1.30 | 19 | (H: 9) corroded | FAS | Collected from Tati S of site |

### S.XXX: COPPER COINS FOUND AT, OR BROUGHT FROM, MAZAR TAGH SITE

| BM no. | Identification | Wt | Diam. | Notes | Acqn | Acquisition/Archaeological context |
|---|---|---|---|---|---|---|
| S.XXX.a.1 | Qianyuan zhongbao – small | 2.53 | 21.5 | – | FAS | Found within ruined fort |
| S.XXX.a.2 | Qianyuan zhongbao – small | 2.65 | 22 | – | FAS | Found within ruined fort |
| S.XXX.a.3 | Qianyuan zhongbao – small | 2.32 | 22 | – | FAS | Found within ruined fort |
| S.XXX.a.4 | [extra: Qianyuan zhongbao – small] | 2.60 | 22 | misaligned | FAS | Found within ruined fort |
| S.XXX.b.1 | Qianyuan zhongbao – small | 2.79 | 22 | – | FAS | Found on path leading to fort |
| S.XXX.c.1 | [missing: Kaiyuan zhongbao] | – | – | – | FAS | Found in refuse layers below fort |
| S.XXX.c.2 | Qianyuan zhongbao – small | 2.86 | 22 | misaligned | FAS | Found in refuse layers below fort |
| S.XXX.c.3 | Qianyuan zhongbao – small | 2.55 | 22 | – | FAS | Found in refuse layers below fort |
| S.XXX.c.4 | Qianyuan zhongbao – small | 2.38 | 22 | damaged | FAS | Found in refuse layers below fort |
| S.XXX.c.5 | Dali yuanbao – small | 2.66 | 22 | – | FAS | Found in refuse layers below fort |
| S.XXX.d.1 | 'Wuzhu' – illegible, small, square | 0.39 | 11.5 | (H: 5) | p | Brought from Mazar Tagh site |
| S.XXX.d.2 | 'Wuzhu' – illegible | 0.93 | 20 | (H: 10) | p | Brought from Mazar Tagh site |
| S.XXX.d.3 | Wuzhu – clipped, cuts through inscription | 0.95 | 18.5 | (H: 10) | p | Brought from Mazar Tagh site |
| S.XXX.d.4 | Wuzhu – clipped, cuts through inscription | 1.79 | 23.5 | (H: 9.5) | p | Brought from Mazar Tagh site |
| S.XXX.d.5 | 'Chinese' coin with non–Chinese inscription | 1.41 | 16 | (H: 5.5) inscr. on side with rim | p | Brought from Mazar Tagh site |
| S.XXX.d.6 | 'Wuzhu' – illegible, small, square | 0.35 | 12.5 | (H: 7) | p | Brought from Mazar Tagh site |
| S.XXX.d.7 | 'Wuzhu' – illegible, small, square | 0.19 | 9 | (H: 4) with sprue, flat rev. | p | Brought from Mazar Tagh site |
| S.XXX.d.8 | 'Wuzhu' – illegible, small | 0.31 | 8 | (H: 2) corroded | p | Brought from Mazar Tagh site |
| S.XXX.d.9 | 'Wuzhu' – illegible, small | 0.32 | 12 | (H: 7) frag. | p | Brought from Mazar Tagh site |
| S.XXX.d.10 | 'Wuzhu' – illegible, small, square | 0.26 | 9 | (H: 4) | p | Brought from Mazar Tagh site |
| S.XXX.d.11 | 'Wuzhu' – illegible, small | 0.21 | 10.5 | (H: 4) frag. | p | Brought from Mazar Tagh site |
| S.XXX.d.12 | 'Wuzhu' – illegible, small | 0.47 | 13 | (H: 8.5) | p | Brought from Mazar Tagh site |

### S.XXXI: COPPER COINS FOUND AT, OR BROUGHT FROM, DESERT SITES SOUTH OF KELPIN

| BM no. | Identification | Wt | Diam. | Notes | Acqn | Acquisition/Archaeological context |
|---|---|---|---|---|---|---|
| S.XXXI.a.1 | 'Wuzhu' – illegible | 1.36 | 20.5 | (H: 9.5) | FAS | Found close to fort at Chong-tim site |
| S.XXXI.a.2 | 'Wuzhu' – illegible | 0.98 | 16.5 | (H: 8) flat rev. | FAS | Found close to fort at Chong-tim site |
| S.XXXI.a.3 | Wuzhu – clipped, cuts through inscription | 0.59 | 16 | (H: 9) | FAS | Found close to fort at Chong-tim site |
| S.XXXI.a.4 | 'Wuzhu' – illegible, small | 0.64 | 15 | (H: 7.5) | FAS | Found close to fort at Chong-tim site |
| S.XXXI.a.5 | 'Wuzhu' – illegible, small | 0.58 | 14 | (H: 8) | FAS | Found close to fort at Chong-tim site |
| S.XXXI.a.6 | 'Wuzhu' – illegible, small, square | 0.22 | 11 | (H: 5) | FAS | Found close to fort at Chong-tim site |

| BM no. | Identification | Wt | Diam. | Notes | Acqn | Acquisition/Archaeological context |
|---|---|---|---|---|---|---|
| S.XXXI.a.7 | 'Wuzhu' – illegible, small, square | 0.23 | 11 | (H: 6) | FAS | Found close to fort at Chong-tim site |
| S.XXXI.a.8 | 'Wuzhu' – illegible, small, square | 0.32 | 10.5 | (H: 4.5) flat rev. | FAS | Found close to fort at Chong-tim site |
| S.XXXI.a.9 | 'Wuzhu' – illegible, small, square | 0.24 | 10 | (H: 6.5) frag. | FAS | Found close to fort at Chong-tim site |
| S.XXXI.a.10 | 'Wuzhu' – illegible, small | 0.22 | 12.5 | (H: 8.5) 2 frags (= 1 coin) | FAS | Found close to fort at Chong-tim site |
| S.XXXI.a.11 | 'Wuzhu' – illegible, small | 0.26 | 12 | (H: 7.5) 3 frags (= 1 coin) | FAS | Found close to fort at Chong-tim site |
| S.XXXI.a.12 | 'Wuzhu' – illegible | 1.46 | 24.5 | (H: 10) | FAS | Found at Chong-tim site |
| S.XXXI.a.13 | 'Wuzhu' – illegible | 1.22 | 24.5 | (H: 9) frag. | FAS | Found at Chong-tim site |
| S.XXXI.a.14 | 'Wuzhu' – illegible | 0.90 | 22 | (H: 9.5) frag. | FAS | Found at Chong-tim site |
| S.XXXI.a.15 | Kaiyuan tongbao | 4.33 | 25 | – | FAS | Found at Chong-tim site |
| S.XXXI.a.16–18 | Chinese coins – Qing dynasty | – | – | – | FAS | Found at Chong-tim site |
| S.XXXI.b.1 | Wuzhu – full size | 1.53 | 25.5 | (H: 9.5) frag. | FAS | Found on Tati S of Chong-tim |
| S.XXXI.b.2 | Kaiyuan tongbao | 4.01 | 25 | red | FAS | Found on Tati S of Chong-tim |
| S.XXXI.b.3 | Kaiyuan tongbao – crescent above hole on rev. | 3.81 | 25 | – | FAS | Found on Tati S of Chong-tim |
| S.XXXI.b.4 | Kaiyuan tongbao | 3.79 | 24.5 | misaligned | FAS | Found on Tati S of Chong-tim |
| S.XXXI.b.5 | Chinese coin – unidentified | – | – | corroded, now disintegrated | FAS | Found on Tati S of Chong-tim |
| S.XXXI.b.6 | [extra: Chinese coin – Qing dynasty] | – | – | – | – | – |
| S.XXXI.c.1 | Huoquan | 2.61 | 23 | – | p | Allegedly from Chong-tim site, purchased at Kelpin |
| S.XXXI.c.2 | Kaiyuan tongbao | 3.56 | 25.5 | – | p | Allegedly from Chong-tim site, purchased at Kelpin |
| S.XXXI.c.3 | Kaiyuan tongbao | 3.63 | 24.5 | misaligned | p | Allegedly from Chong-tim site, purchased at Kelpin |
| S.XXXI.c.4 | Kaiyuan tongbao | 3.05 | 24.5 | misaligned | p | Allegedly from Chong-tim site, purchased at Kelpin |
| S.XXXI.c.5 | Kaiyuan tongbao – crescent above hole on rev. | 3.66 | 25 | – | p | Allegedly from Chong-tim site, purchased at Kelpin |
| S.XXXI.c.6 | Kaiyuan tongbao | 3.44 | 25 | misaligned | p | Allegedly from Chong-tim site, purchased at Kelpin |
| S.XXXI.c.7 | Kaiyuan tongbao – crescent below hole on rev. | 4.04 | 25 | misaligned | p | Allegedly from Chong-tim site, purchased at Kelpin |
| S.XXXI.c.8 | Kaiyuan tongbao | 4.06 | 25.5 | – | p | Allegedly from Chong-tim site, purchased at Kelpin |
| S.XXXI.c.9 | Dali yuanbao – large | 3.28 | 23.5 | – | p | Allegedly from Chong-tim site, purchased at Kelpin |
| S.XXXI.c.10 | Dali yuanbao – large | 3.57 | 24 | misaligned | p | Allegedly from Chong-tim site, purchased at Kelpin |
| S.XXXI.c.11 | Dali yuanbao – large | 3.56 | 24 | misaligned | p | Allegedly from Chong-tim site, purchased at Kelpin |
| S.XXXI.c.12 | Dali yuanbao – large | 3.32 | 24.5 | misaligned | p | Allegedly from Chong-tim site, purchased at Kelpin |
| S.XXXI.c.13 | Dali yuanbao – large | 3.18 | 24 | – | p | Allegedly from Chong-tim site, purchased at Kelpin |

| BM no. | Identification | Wt | Diam. | Notes | Acqn | Acquisition/Archaeological context |
|---|---|---|---|---|---|---|
| S.XXXI.d.1 | 'Wuzhu' – illegible | 1.46 | 23 | (H: 9.5) | p | From various sites, also from W of Kudughun, purchased at Kelpin |
| S.XXXI.d.2 | 'Wuzhu' – illegible | 1.96 | 24.5 | (H: 10) | p | From various sites, also from W of Kudughun, purchased at Kelpin |
| S.XXXI.d.3 | 'Wuzhu' – illegible | 1.49 | 18 | (H: 7) corroded | p | From various sites, also from W of Kudughun, purchased at Kelpin |
| S.XXXI.d.4 | 'Wuzhu' – illegible | 1.81 | 23 | (H: 9.5) red | p | From various sites, also from W of Kudughun, purchased at Kelpin |
| S.XXXI.d.5 | Wuzhu – clipped, cuts through inscription | 1.87 | 22 | (H: 9) damaged | p | From various sites, also from W of Kudughun, purchased at Kelpin |
| S.XXXI.d.6 | 'Wuzhu' – illegible | 1.79 | 20.5 | (H: 9) | p | From various sites, also from W of Kudughun, purchased at Kelpin |
| S.XXXI.d.7 | 'Wuzhu' – illegible, small, square | 0.42 | 10 | (H: 4.5) flat rev. | p | From various sites, also from W of Kudughun, purchased at Kelpin |
| S.XXXI.d.8 | 'Wuzhu' – illegible, small, square | 0.22 | – | frag. | p | From various sites, also from W of Kudughun, purchased at Kelpin |
| S.XXXI.d.9 | 'Wuzhu' – illegible, small, square | 0.43 | 10.5 | (H: 5) corroded | p | From various sites, also from W of Kudughun, purchased at Kelpin |
| S.XXXI.d.10 | 'Wuzhu' – illegible, small, square | 0.31 | 9 | (H: 5) | p | From various sites, also from W of Kudughun, purchased at Kelpin |
| S.XXXI.d.11 | 'Wuzhu' – illegible, small | 0.39 | 12 | (H: 6) flat rev. | p | From various sites, also from W of Kudughun, purchased at Kelpin |
| S.XXXI.d.12 | 'Wuzhu' – illegible, small, square | 0.53 | 11 | (H: 4) corroded | p | From various sites, also from W of Kudughun, purchased at Kelpin |
| S.XXXI.d.13 | 'Wuzhu' – illegible | 0.21 | – | frag. | p | From various sites, also from W of Kudughun, purchased at Kelpin |
| S.XXXI.d.14 | 'Wuzhu' – illegible, small, square | 0.27 | 9 | (H: 4.5) flat rev. | p | From various sites, also from W of Kudughun, purchased at Kelpin |
| S.XXXI.d.15 | (non–coin?) | 1.28 | – | – | p | From various sites, also from W of Kudughun, purchased at Kelpin |
| S.XXXI.d.16 | 'Wuzhu' – illegible, small, square | 0.43 | 10 | (H: 4) | p | From various sites, also from W of Kudughun, purchased at Kelpin |
| S.XXXI.d.17 | 'Wuzhu' – illegible, small, square | 0.49 | 11 | (H: 5.5) with sprues | p | From various sites, also from W of Kudughun, purchased at Kelpin |

| BM no. | Identification | Wt | Diam. | Notes | Acqn | Acquisition/Archaeological context |
|---|---|---|---|---|---|---|
| S.XXXI.d.18 | 'Wuzhu' – illegible, small, square | 0.61 | 13.5 | (H: 6) | p | From various sites, also from W of Kudughun, purchased at Kelpin |
| S.XXXI.d.19 | 'Wuzhu' – illegible, small | 0.87 | 14 | (H: 7.5) corroded | p | From various sites, also from W of Kudughun, purchased at Kelpin |
| S.XXXI.d.20 | 'Wuzhu' – illegible, small, square | 0.41 | 11 | (H: 5) corroded | p | From various sites, also from W of Kudughun, purchased at Kelpin |
| S.XXXI.d.21 | 'Wuzhu' – illegible, small, square | 0.47 | 10 | (H: 5) + frag. | p | From various sites, also from W of Kudughun, purchased at Kelpin |
| S.XXXI.d.22 | 'Wuzhu' – illegible, small, square | 0.70 | 12 | (H: 5.5) with sprue | p | From various sites, also from W of Kudughun, purchased at Kelpin |
| S.XXXI.d.23 | 'Wuzhu' – illegible, small, square | 0.25 | 10 | (H: 5.5) flat rev. | p | From various sites, also from W of Kudughun, purchased at Kelpin |
| S.XXXI.d.24 | 'Wuzhu' – illegible, small, square | 0.26 | 11.5 | (H: 5.5) flat rev. | p | From various sites, also from W of Kudughun, purchased at Kelpin |
| S.XXXI.d.25 | Türgesh coin (Thierry 1999, Type II) | 5.22 | 25 | – | p | From various sites, also from W of Kudughun, purchased at Kelpin |
| S.XXXI.d.26 | Unidentified corroded frags of coin | – | – | corroded, now disintegrated | p | From various sites, also from W of Kudughun, purchased at Kelpin |
| S.XXXI.d.27 | Kaiyuan tongbao | 3.73 | 24.5 | – | p | From various sites, also from W of Kudughun, purchased at Kelpin |
| S.XXXI.d.28 | Kaiyuan tongbao | 2.41 | 23.5 | – | p | From various sites, also from W of Kudughun, purchased at Kelpin |
| S.XXXI.d.29 | Kaiyuan tongbao – crescent above hole on rev. | 3.43 | 25 | – | p | From various sites, also from W of Kudughun, purchased at Kelpin |
| S.XXXI.d.30 | Kaiyuan tongbao – crescent above hole on rev. | 3.59 | 25 | misaligned | p | From various sites, also from W of Kudughun, purchased at Kelpin |
| S.XXXI.d.31 | [mising: Kaiyuan tongbao] | – | – | – | p | From various sites, also from W of Kudughun, purchased at Kelpin |
| S.XXXI.d.32 | Dali yuanbao – large | 3.19 | 24.5 | misaligned | p | From various sites, also from W of Kudughun, purchased at Kelpin |
| S.XXXI.d.33 | [extra: Qianyuan zhongbao – small] | 2.82 | 23 | misaligned | p | From various sites, also from W of Kudughun, purchased at Kelpin |
| S.XXXI.d.34 | [extra: non–coin] | – | – | – | p | From various sites, also from W of Kudughun, purchased at Kelpin |

### S.XXXII: COPPER AND SILVER COINS FOUND ON TATIS NORTH OF TUMSHUK

| BM no. | Identification | Wt | Diam. | Notes | Acqn | Acquisition/Archaeological context |
|---|---|---|---|---|---|---|
| S.XXXII.a.1 | Kaiyuan tongbao – nail mark below hole on rev. | 3.43 | 25 | notchings on rim, damaged | F | Found on Tatis N of Tumshuk |
| S.XXXII.a.2 | Kaiyuan tongbao – crescent above hole on rev. | 3.31 | 25 | misaligned, forced hole | F | Found on Tatis N of Tumshuk |
| S.XXXII.a.3–4 | Chinese coins – Song dynasty | – | – | – | F | Found on Tatis N of Tumshuk |
| S.XXXII.a.5 | Islamic coin | – | – | – | F | Found on Tatis N of Tumshuk |

### S.XXXIII: COPPER COINS BROUGHT FROM TOKUZ–SARAI RUINS, TUMSHUK

| BM no. | Identification | Wt | Diam. | Notes | Acqn | Acquisition/Archaeological context |
|---|---|---|---|---|---|---|
| S.XXXIII.a.1–16 | Islamic coins | – | – | – | p | Brought from Tokuz-sarai ruins, Tumshuk |

### EXTRA – NOT INCLUDED IN LIST

| BM no. | Identification | Wt | Diam. | Notes | Acqn | Acquisition/Archaeological context |
|---|---|---|---|---|---|---|
| | [extra: 'Wuzhu' – illegible, small, square] | 0.26 | 10 | (H: 3.5) corroded, with sprue | – | Not in List of Coins |
| | [extra: Indian? coin] | 1.55 | 11 | – | – | Not in List of Coins |
| | [extra: Kushan coin] | 3.75 | 18 | – | – | Not in List of Coins |

## INNERMOST ASIA

### IA.I: COINS FOUND AT OR BROUGHT FROM SITES BETWEEN KASHGAR AND MARAL-BASHI

| BM no. | Identification | Wt | Diam. | Notes | Acqn | Acquisition/Archaeological context |
|---|---|---|---|---|---|---|
| IA.I.a.1–2 | Islamic coins | – | – | – | – | From sites between Kashgar and Maral-bashi |
| IA.I.b.1–3 | Islamic coins | – | – | – | – | From sites between Kashgar and Maral-bashi |
| IA.I.c.1–3 | Islamic coins | – | – | – | – | From sites between Kashgar and Maral-bashi |
| IA.I.d.1–5 | Islamic coins | – | – | – | – | From sites between Kashgar and Maral-bashi |
| IA.I.e.1 | Islamic coin | – | – | – | – | From sites between Kashgar and Maral-bashi |

### IA.II: COINS BROUGHT FROM MAZAR TAGH SITE

| BM no. | Identification | Wt | Diam. | Notes | Acqn | Acquisition/Archaeological context |
|---|---|---|---|---|---|---|
| IA.II.a.1 | Wuzhu | 0.58 | 13 | (H: 6) small | p | Brought from Mazar Tagh site |
| IA.II.a.2 | Qianyuan zhongbao – small | 3.36 | 22 | – | p | Brought from Mazar Tagh site |

## IA.III: COINS COLLECTED AT OR FROM KHOTAN

### IA.III.A: COINS OF MISCELLANEOUS ORIGIN

| BM no. | Identification | Wt | Diam. | Notes | Acqn | Acquisition/Archaeological context |
|---|---|---|---|---|---|---|
| IA.III.A.a.1–2 | Chinese coin – Song dynasty | – | – | – | p | Purchased in Khotan |
| IA.III.A.a.3–9 | Chinese coin – Qing dynasty | – | – | – | p | Purchased in Khotan |
| IA.III.A.b.1 | Huobu spade (Wang Mang, AD 10) | 15.71 | 22×57 | damaged | g | Presented by Li Ssü-yeh |
| IA.III.A.b.2 | [missing: Huobu spade] | – | – | – | g | Presented by Li Ssü-yeh |
| IA.III.A.c.1 (OR.0426) | Sino-Kharoshthi coin (Cribb 5) | 2.69 | 18.5×17 | – | g | Presented by Mr Moldovack |
| IA.III.A.c.2 (OR.0406) | Sino-Kharoshthi coin (Cribb 2) | 2.74 | 17 | – | g | Presented by Mr Moldovack |
| IA.III.A.c.3 | Sino-Kharoshthi coin (Cribb 7–8) | 9.60 | 24 | damaged | g | Presented by Mr Moldovack |
| IA.III.A.c.4 | Sino-Kharoshthi coin (Cribb 1) | 2.35 | 28 | – | g | Presented by Mr Moldovack |
| IA.III.A.c.5 | Sino-Kharoshthi coin (Cribb 5) | 4.35 | 28 | – | g | Presented by Mr Moldovack |
| IA.III.A.c.6 | Sino-Kharoshthi coin (Cribb 2) | 2.82 | 19 | – | g | Presented by Mr Moldovack |
| IA.III.A.c.7 | Sino-Kharoshthi coin (Cribb 2) | 1.94 | 17 | – | g | Presented by Mr Moldovack |
| IA.III.A.c.8 | Sino-Kharoshthi coin (Cribb 2) | 2.99 | 19 | – | g | Presented by Mr Moldovack |
| IA.III.A.c.9 | [missing: Kushan coin of Kanishka] | – | – | – | g | Presented by Mr Moldovack |
| IA.III.A.c.10 | Islamic coin | – | – | – | g | Presented by Mr Moldovack |
| IA.III.A.d.1–10 | Islamic coin | – | – | – | p | Allegedly from Arka-kuduk and Kumat |
| IA.III.A.e.1 | 'Wuzhu' – illegible | 0.53 | – | frag. | p | Allegedly from Jigda-kuduk |
| IA.III.A.e.2 | 'Wuzhu' – illegible | 0.86 | 23.5 | (H: 9.5) frag. | p | Allegedly from Jigda-kuduk |
| IA.III.A.e.3 | Wuzhu – full size | 1.34 | 25 | (H: 10.5) frag. | p | Allegedly from Jigda-kuduk |
| IA.III.A.e.4 | 'Wuzhu' – illegible | 1.15 | 22.5 | (H: 9) 2 frags | p | Allegedly from Jigda-kuduk |
| IA.III.A.e.5 | Wuzhu – full size | 1.47 | 25 | (H: 9.5) frag. | p | Allegedly from Jigda-kuduk |
| IA.III.A.e.6 | 'Wuzhu' – illegible | 0.39 | – | 3 frags | p | Allegedly from Jigda-kuduk |
| IA.III.A.e.7 | Wuzhu | 1.43 | 24.5 | (H: 10.5) frag. | p | Allegedly from Jigda-kuduk |
| IA.III.A.e.8 | 'Wuzhu' – illegible | 0.53 | – | (H: 10.5) frag. | p | Allegedly from Jigda-kuduk |
| IA.III.A.e.9 | 'Wuzhu' – illegible, small | 1.28 | 18 | (H: 8) corroded | p | Allegedly from Jigda-kuduk |
| IA.III.A.e.10a | Wuzhu – without full rim | 1.62 | 23.5 | (H: 9.5) misaligned | p | Allegedly from Jigda-kuduk |
| IA.III.A.e.10b | Wuzhu – without full rim | 1.36 | 23.5 | (H: 9.5) | p | Allegedly from Jigda-kuduk |
| IA.III.A.e.11 | 'Wuzhu' – illegible | 1.14 | 20.5 | (H: 9.5) corroded | p | Allegedly from Jigda-kuduk |
| IA.III.A.e.12 | 'Wuzhu' – illegible | 1.15 | 20.5 | (H: 9) | p | Allegedly from Jigda-kuduk |
| IA.III.A.e.13a | 'Wuzhu' – illegible | 0.86 | 22 | (H: 9.5) frag. | p | Allegedly from Jigda-kuduk |
| IA.III.A.e.13b | 'Wuzhu' – illegible, rim on reverse | 0.88 | 17.5 | (H: 8) corroded | p | Allegedly from Jigda-kuduk |
| IA.III.A.e.14 | 'Wuzhu' – illegible | 0.81 | – | frag. | p | Allegedly from Jigda-kuduk |
| IA.III.A.e.15 | 'Wuzhu' – illegible | 1.42 | 22 | (H: 9.5) corroded | p | Allegedly from Jigda-kuduk |
| IA.III.A.e.16a | 'Wuzhu' – illegible | 1.04 | 22.5 | (H: 9.5) 2 frags (= 1 coin) | p | Allegedly from Jigda-kuduk |
| IA.III.A.e.16b | 'Wuzhu' – illegible | 1.64 | 22.5 | (H: 9.5) corroded | p | Allegedly from Jigda-kuduk |
| IA.III.A.e.17a | 'Wuzhu' – illegible | 1.46 | 22 | (H: 10) 4 frags restored | p | Allegedly from Jigda-kuduk |
| IA.III.A.e.17b | 'Wuzhu' – illegible | 1.81 | 23 | (H: 9) | p | Allegedly from Jigda-kuduk |
| IA.III.A.e.17c | 'Wuzhu' – illegible | 1.54 | 22 | (H: 9.5) | p | Allegedly from Jigda-kuduk |
| IA.III.A.e.17d | 'Wuzhu' – illegible | 1.68 | 23 | (H: 9.5) | p | Allegedly from Jigda-kuduk |
| IA.III.A.e.18 | [extra: Wuzhu – full size] | 2.55 | 25.5 | crude inscription | p | Allegedly from Jigda-kuduk |
| IA.III.A.e.19 | Qianyuan zhongbao – large, crescent below hole on rev. | 7.35 | 29.5 | misaligned | p | Allegedly from Jigda-kuduk |
| IA.III.A.e.20–22 | Chinese coins – Song dynasty | – | – | – | p | Allegedly from Jigda-kuduk |

| BM no. | Identification | Wt | Diam. | Notes | Acqn | Acquisition/Archaeological context |
|---|---|---|---|---|---|---|
| IA.III.A.f.1 | 'Wuzhu' – illegible, full size | 2.31 | 27 | (H: 9.5) damaged | p | Allegedly from Lachin-ata |
| IA.III.A.f.2 | 'Wuzhu' – illegible | 1.11 | 21.5 | (H: 10) damaged | p | Allegedly from Lachin-ata |
| IA.III.A.f.3 | 'Wuzhu' – illegible, small | 0.55 | 14 | (H: 8) | p | Allegedly from Lachin-ata |
| IA.III.A.f.4 | 'Wuzhu' – illegible, small | 0.66 | 17 | (H: 8) frag. | p | Allegedly from Lachin-ata |
| IA.III.A.f.5.a–c | 'Wuzhu' – illegible, 3 coins corroded together | 2.25 | – | corroded | p | Allegedly from Lachin-ata |
| IA.III.A.f.6.a–c | 'Wuzhu' – illegible, 3 coins corroded together | 6.90 | – | corroded | p | Allegedly from Lachin-ata |
| IA.III.A.f.7 | Non-Chinese inscription, small | 0.62 | 14 | (H: 5.5) red | p | Allegedly from Lachin-ata |
| IA.III.A.f.8 | 'Wuzhu' – illegible | 0.96 | 21.5 | (H: 10) frag. | p | Allegedly from Lachin-ata |
| IA.III.A.f.9 | Kaiyuan tongbao – crescent above hole on rev. | 2.73 | 25.5 | misaligned | p | Allegedly from Lachin-ata |
| IA.III.A.f.10–12 | Islamic coin | – | – | – | p | Allegedly from Lachin-ata |

| | | | | | | |
|---|---|---|---|---|---|---|
| IA.III.A.g.1 | Qianyuan zhongbao – large | 8.53 | 28.5 | misaligned | p | Allegedly from Kalalik |
| IA.III.A.g.2 | Qianyuan zhongbao – large | 8.48 | 30 | – | p | Allegedly from Kalalik |
| IA.III.A.g.3 | Qianyuan zhongbao – large | 7.23 | 29.5 | misaligned | p | Allegedly from Kalalik |
| IA.III.A.g.4 | Qianyuan zhongbao – medium | 5.30 | 25.5 | misaligned | p | Allegedly from Kalalik |
| IA.III.A.g.5 | Qianyuan zhongbao – medium | 3.08 | 26 | thin | p | Allegedly from Kalalik |
| IA.III.A.g.6 | Qianyuan zhongbao – small | 2.16 | 22 | – | p | Allegedly from Kalalik |
| IA.III.A.g.7 | Qianyuan zhongbao – small | 1.96 | 22 | forced hole, misaligned | p | Allegedly from Kalalik |
| IA.III.A.g.8 | Qianyuan zhongbao – medium | 2.89 | 26 | frag., misaligned | p | Allegedly from Kalalik |
| IA.III.A.g.9 | [Dali] yuanbao (bottom–left) – small | 1.07 | 20.5 | misaligned | p | Allegedly from Kalalik |
| IA.III.A.g.10 | Chinese coin – Song dynasty | – | – | – | p | Allegedly from Kalalik |

| | | | | | | |
|---|---|---|---|---|---|---|
| IA.III.A.h.1 | 'Wuzhu' – illegible | 1.52 | 23 | (H: 9.5) red | p | Allegedly from Bash-kumat |
| IA.III.A.h.2 | Wuzhu – full-size | 1.77 | 26 | (H: 10) | p | Allegedly from Bash-kumat |
| IA.III.A.h.3 | 'Wuzhu' – illegible | 1.15 | 22 | (H: 9.5) | p | Allegedly from Bash-kumat |
| IA.III.A.h.4 | Wuzhu | 1.73 | 23.5 | (H: 9.5) corroded | p | Allegedly from Bash-kumat |
| IA.III.A.h.5 | 'Wuzhu' – illegible (coin + frags) | 2.44 | 23 | (H: 9) corroded | p | Allegedly from Bash-kumat |
| IA.III.A.h.6 | Wuzhu | 1.47 | 23 | (H: 10) faint | p | Allegedly from Bash-kumat |
| IA.III.A.h.7 | 'Wuzhu' – illegible | 1.66 | 22 | (H: 9.5) corroded | p | Allegedly from Bash-kumat |
| IA.III.A.h.8 | 'Wuzhu' – illegible | 1.16 | 22.5 | (H: 9.5) frag. | p | Allegedly from Bash-kumat |
| IA.III.A.h.9 | 'Wuzhu' – illegible | 0.99 | 20 | (H: 8.5) | p | Allegedly from Bash-kumat |
| IA.III.A.h.10 | Wuzhu – clipped, cutting through inscription | 0.87 | 20 | (H: 10) clipped square | p | Allegedly from Bash-kumat |
| IA.III.A.h.11 | 'Wuzhu' – small | 0.37 | – | frag. | p | Allegedly from Bash-kumat |
| IA.III.A.h.12 | [extra: Wuzhu – small, without inscription, square] | 0.33 | 11 | (H: 5) flat on rev. | p | Allegedly from Bash-kumat |
| IA.III.A.h.13 | Chinese coin – Song dynasty | – | – | – | p | Allegedly from Bash-kumat |
| IA.III.A.h.14–23 | Islamic coins | – | – | – | p | Allegedly from Bash-kumat |

| | | | | | | |
|---|---|---|---|---|---|---|
| IA.III.A.i.1 | [missing: Sino-Kharoshthi coin] | – | – | – | p | Allegedly from Kizil-yar |
| IA.III.A.i.2–21 | Islamic coin | – | – | – | p | Allegedly from Kizil-yar |

| | | | | | | |
|---|---|---|---|---|---|---|
| IA.III.A.j.1 | 'Wuzhu' – without inscription | 1.65 | 21 | (H: 9.5) | p | Brought from Karim Akhun |
| IA.III.A.j.2 | 'Wuzhu' – illegible | 2.14 | 24 | (H: 10) corroded | p | Brought from Karim Akhun |
| IA.III.A.j.3 | [missing: Wuzhu] | – | – | – | p | Brought from Karim Akhun |
| IA.III.A.j.4 | Qianyuan zhongbao – small | 2.11 | 20.5 | – | p | Brought from Karim Akhun |
| IA.III.A.j.5 | Qianyuan zhongbao – small | 1.51 | 21 | forced hole | p | Brought from Karim Akhun |
| IA.III.A.j.6 | Dali yuanbao | 1.52 | – | 6 frags | p | Brought from Karim Akhun |

| BM no. | Identification | Wt | Diam. | Notes | Acqn | Acquisition/Archaeological context |
|---|---|---|---|---|---|---|
| IA.III.A.j.7 | Chinese coin – unidentified | 3.18 | 24 | corroded, 3 frags | p | Brought from Karim Akhun |
| IA.III.A.j.8 | Chinese coin – unidentified | 2.75 | – | corroded, 5 frags | p | Brought from Karim Akhun |
| IA.III.A.j.9.a–c | Chinese coins – 3 coins corroded together | 11.64 | – | corroded | p | Brought from Karim Akhun |
| IA.III.A.j.10 | Chinese coin – unidentified | 3.14 | 24 | corroded | p | Brought from Karim Akhun |
| IA.III.A.j.11 | Chinese coin – unidentified | 3.56 | 24 | corroded | p | Brought from Karim Akhun |
| IA.III.A.j.12 | Chinese coin – unidentified | 3.71 | 24 | corroded, 2 frags | p | Brought from Karim Akhun |
| IA.III.A.j.13 | Chinese coin – unidentified | 3.20 | 24 | corroded, 3 frags | p | Brought from Karim Akhun |
| IA.III.A.j.14 | Chinese coin – unidentified | 3.32 | 25 | corroded, 2 frags | p | Brought from Karim Akhun |
| IA.III.A.j.15 | Chinese coin – unidentified | 2.72 | – | corroded, frags | p | Brought from Karim Akhun |
| IA.III.A.j.16 | Chinese coin – unidentified | 3.27 | – | corroded, frags | p | Brought from Karim Akhun |
| IA.III.A.j.17 | Chinese coin – unidentified | 3.17 | 24 | corroded | p | Brought from Karim Akhun |
| IA.III.A.j.18 | Chinese coin – unidentified | 2.65 | 24 | corroded | p | Brought from Karim Akhun |
| IA.III.A.j.19 | Chinese coin – unidentified | 1.46 | 22.5 | corroded, 5 frags | p | Brought from Karim Akhun |
| IA.III.A.j.20 | Chinese coin – unidentified | 1.97 | – | corroded, 4 frags | p | Brought from Karim Akhun |
| IA.III.A.j.21 | Chinese coin – unidentified | 3.01 | – | corroded, numerous frags | p | Brought from Karim Akhun |
| IA.III.A.j.22 | Chinese coin – unidentified | 1.84 | – | corroded, 4 frags | p | Brought from Karim Akhun |
| IA.III.A.j.23 | Chinese coin – unidentified (> 1 coin?) | 4.47 | – | corroded, numerous frags | p | Brought from Karim Akhun |
| IA.III.A.j.24 | Chinese coin – unidentified (> 1 coin?) | 4.32 | – | corroded, numerous frags | p | Brought from Karim Akhun |
| IA.III.A.k.1 | Wuzhu – full size | 2.37 | 26 | (H: 9.5) damaged | p | Allegedly from Khotan Tatis, brought by Abbas |
| IA.III.A.k.2 | 'Wuzhu' – illegible | 2.15 | 22 | (H: 9.5×10) | p | Allegedly from Khotan Tatis, brought by Abbas |
| IA.III.A.k.3 | Wuzhu – without full rim, rev.: line above hole | 1.86 | 23.5 | (H: 9.5) faint | p | Allegedly from Khotan Tatis, brought by Abbas |
| IA.III.A.k.4 | Wuzhu | 2.23 | 24.5 | (H: 9.5) red | p | Allegedly from Khotan Tatis, brought by Abbas |
| IA.III.A.k.5 | 'Wuzhu' – illegible | 0.80 | 20 | (H. 10) corroded, damaged | p | Allegedly from Khotan Tatis, brought by Abbas |
| IA.III.A.k.6 | 'Wuzhu' – illegible | 1.24 | 21 | (H: 10) | p | Allegedly from Khotan Tatis, brought by Abbas |
| IA.III.A.k.7 | Wuzhu – without full rim | 1.52 | 24 | (H: 10.5) damaged, worn | p | Allegedly from Khotan Tatis, brought by Abbas |
| IA.III.A.k.8 | Wuzhu – without full rim | 1.50 | 24 | (H: 9.5) damaged, worn | p | Allegedly from Khotan Tatis, brought by Abbas |
| IA.III.A.k.9 | 'Wuzhu' – illegible | 1.03 | 20.5 | (H: 9.5) | p | Allegedly from Khotan Tatis, brought by Abbas |
| IA.III.A.k.10 | 'Wuzhu' – illegible | 1.24 | 22.5 | (H: 9.5) | p | Allegedly from Khotan Tatis, brought by Abbas |
| IA.III.A.k.11 | 'Wuzhu' – illegible | 0.91 | 21 | (H: 9.5) | p | Allegedly from Khotan Tatis, brought by Abbas |
| IA.III.A.k.12 | Qianyuan zhongbao – small | 1.86 | 21 | – | p | Allegedly from Khotan Tatis, brought by Abbas |
| IA.III.A.l.1–54 | Islamic coins | – | – | – | p | Brought by Muhammad Sharif |
| IA.III.A.l.55 | [extra: Qianyuan zhongbao – medium] | 4.94 | 24 | heavy, misaligned | – | – |
| IA.III.A.l.56 | [extra: pierced lead disk] | 1.81 | 14.5 | – | – | – |
| IA.III.A.l.57–58 | [extra: Islamic coins] | – | – | – | – | – |

| BM no. | Identification | Wt | Diam. | Notes | Acqn | Acquisition/Archaeological context |
|---|---|---|---|---|---|---|
| IA.III.A.m.1–300 | [missing: 300-plus Chinese coins, corroded in lumps, prob. all Wuzhu] | – | – | – | p | Allegedly from Yotkan |
| IA.III.A.m.301 | Qianyuan zhongbao – small | 1.93 | 20.5 | damaged, corroded | p | Allegedly from Yotkan |
| IA.III.A.m.302 | Dali yuanbao – small | 2.08 | 21.5 | – | p | Allegedly from Yotkan |

| | | | | | | |
|---|---|---|---|---|---|---|
| IA.III.A.n.1 | Wuzhu | 1.78 | 23 | (H: 9.5) lop-sided, faint | p | Allegedly from Yotkan, received from Muhammad Sharif |
| IA.III.A.n.2 | Wuzhu – full-size | 1.68 | 25 | (H: 10×11) | p | Allegedly from Yotkan, received from Muhammad Sharif |
| IA.III.A.n.3 | Wuzhu – full-size | 1.41 | 25 | (H: 10.5) damaged, faint | p | Allegedly from Yotkan, received from Muhammad Sharif |
| IA.III.A.n.4 | Wuzhu – without full rim | 0.98 | 24 | (H: 9.5) damaged, thin | p | Allegedly from Yotkan, received from Muhammad Sharif |
| IA.III.A.n.5 | Wuzhu | 1.36 | 22.5 | (H: 10) lop-sided, faint | p | Allegedly from Yotkan, received from Muhammad Sharif |
| IA.III.A.n.6 | Wuzhu – without full rim | 1.66 | 23 | (H: 9.5) | p | Allegedly from Yotkan, received from Muhammad Sharif |
| IA.III.A.n.7 | 'Wuzhu' – illegible (2 coins) | 2.85 | – | (H: 11 + 9) corroded together | p | Allegedly from Yotkan, received from Muhammad Sharif |
| IA.III.A.n.8 | 'Wuzhu' – illegible, full-size | 1.43 | 24 | (H: 11) | p | Allegedly from Yotkan, received from Muhammad Sharif |
| IA.III.A.n.9 | Wuzhu | 0.83 | – | frag. | p | Allegedly from Yotkan, received from Muhammad Sharif |
| IA.III.A.n.10 | Wuzhu | 0.89 | – | (H: 10.5) frag. | p | Allegedly from Yotkan, received from Muhammad Sharif |
| IA.III.A.n.11 | Qianyuan zhongbao – small | 2.24 | 22 | 2 frags = 1 coin | p | Allegedly from Yotkan, received from Muhammad Sharif |
| IA.III.A.n.12 | Qianyuan zhongbao – small | 2.23 | 22 | red | p | Allegedly from Yotkan, received from Muhammad Sharif |
| IA.III.A.n.13 | Qianyuan zhongbao – small | 1.10 | 20.5 | frag. | p | Allegedly from Yotkan, received from Muhammad Sharif |
| IA.III.A.n.14 | Dali yuanbao – small | 1.42 | 21.5 | red | p | Allegedly from Yotkan, received from Muhammad Sharif |

| | | | | | | |
|---|---|---|---|---|---|---|
| IA.III.A.o.1 | Kushan coin | 3.63 | 17.5 | pierced | p | Allegedly from Tatis near Hanguya, Arkalik, brought by Toktha Akhun |
| IA.III.A.o.2 | Wuzhu – without full rim | 2.01 | 22.5 | (H: 9) | p | Allegedly from Tatis near Hanguya, Arkalik, brought by Toktha Akhun |
| IA.III.A.o.3 | Kaiyuan tongbao | 2.88 | 26 | corroded | p | Allegedly from Tatis near Hanguya, Arkalik, brought by Toktha Akhun |
| IA.III.A.o.4 | Qianyuan zhongbao – small | 2.41 | 21 | misaligned | p | Allegedly from Tatis near Hanguya, Arkalik, brought by Toktha Akhun |
| IA.III.A.o.5 | [extra: Qianyuan zhongbao] | 2.19 | 22 | misaligned | p | Allegedly from Tatis near Hanguya, Arkalik, brought by Toktha Akhun |
| IA.III.A.o.6–28 | Islamic coins | – | – | – | p | Allegedly from Tatis near Hanguya, Arkalik, brought by Toktha Akhun |
| IA.III.A.o.29 | [extra: Chinese coin frag. – illegible] | 0.52 | – | frag. | – | – |

| BM no. | Identification | Wt | Diam. | Notes | Acqn | Acquisition/Archaeological context |
|---|---|---|---|---|---|---|
| IA.III.A.p. 1 | Qianyuan zhongbao – large | 5.79 | 28.5 | – | p | Allegedly from Chalma-kazan |
| IA.III.A.p. 2 | Qianyuan zhongbao – large | 2.78 | 27 | 5 frags | P | Allegedly from Chalma-kazan |
| IA.III.A.p. 3 | Chinese coin – Song dynasty | – | – | – | p | Allegedly from Chalma-kazan |
| IA.III.A.q.1 | [extra: Chinese coin – Qing dynasty] | – | – | – | – | – |
| IA.III.A.q.2–3 | [extra: Islamic coins] | – | – | – | – | – |

### IA.III.B: COINS PURCHASED FROM BADRUDDIN KHAN

| BM no. | Identification | Wt | Diam. | Notes | Acqn | Acquisition/Archaeological context |
|---|---|---|---|---|---|---|
| IA.III.B.a.1 | Wuzhu – full size, narrow wu | 3.07 | 26 | (H: 10) hole in flan | p | Purchased from Badruddin Khan |
| IA.III.B.a.2 | 'Wuzhu' – illegible, small | 0.43 | 12.5 | (H: 6×5.5) corroded | p | Purchased from Badruddin Khan |
| IA.III.B.a.3 | 'Wuzhu' – illegible | 1.16 | 19.5 | (H: 9.5) corroded | p | Purchased from Badruddin Khan |
| IA.III.B.a.4 | 'Wuzhu' – illegible | 0.71 | – | 2 frags | p | Purchased from Badruddin Khan |
| IA.III.B.a.5 | Kaiyuan tongbao | 2.95 | 25 | – | p | Purchased from Badruddin Khan |
| IA.III.B.a.6 | Qianyuan zhongbao – small | 3.20 | 22 | heavy | p | Purchased from Badruddin Khan |
| IA.III.B.a.7 | Qianyuan zhongbao – small | 3.13 | 22 | – | p | Purchased from Badruddin Khan |
| IA.III.B.a.8 | Dali yuanbao – large | 3.17 | 23 | heavy, misaligned, damaged | p | Purchased from Badruddin Khan |
| IA.III.B.a.9 | Dali yuanbao – large | 2.42 | 22.5 | misaligned | p | Purchased from Badruddin Khan |
| IA.III.B.a.10 | Chinese coin – Song dynasty | | – | – | p | Purchased from Badruddin Khan |
| IA.III.B.a.11 | Yongtong wanguo (AD 580–581) | 5.87 | 28.5 | pierced twice, as ornament | p | Purchased from Badruddin Khan |
| IA.III.B.a.12–18 | Islamic coins | – | – | – | p | Purchased from Badruddin Khan |
| IA.III.B.b.1 | Kushan coin of Wima Kadphises | 16.72 | 26 | – | p | Purchased from Badruddin Khan |
| IA.III.B.b.2 (OR.0437) | Sino-Kharoshthi coin (Cribb 11) | 16.05 | 27 | | p | Purchased from Badruddin Khan |
| IA.III.B.b.3 | Sino-Kharoshthi coin (Cribb 5) | 1.90 | 19 | – | p | Purchased from Badruddin Khan |
| IA.III.B.b.4 | [extra: Sino-Kharoshthi coin (Cribb 1–6) | 1.05 | 27 | – | p | Purchased from Badruddin Khan |
| IA.III.B.c.1 | Qianyuan zhongbao – small | 2.67 | 21.5 | misaligned | p | Allegedly from Hanguya Tatis (Badruddin Khan) |
| IA.III.B.c.2 | 'Wuzhu' – illegible | 0.70 | 21.5 | (H: 10) frag., lop-sided | p | Allegedly from Hanguya Tatis (Badruddin Khan) |

| BM no. | Identification | Wt | Diam. | Notes | Acqn | Acquisition/Archaeological context |
|---|---|---|---|---|---|---|
| IA.III.B.c.3 | Wuzhu – small, wu without radical | 1.82 | 21 | (H: 8.5×9) faint, flat on rev. | p | Allegedly from Hanguya Tatis (Badruddin Khan) |
| IA.III.B.c.4 | 'Wuzhu' – illegible, small | 0.71 | 14.5 | (H: 8) flat rev. | p | Allegedly from Hanguya Tatis (Badruddin Khan) |
| IA.III.B.c.5 | 'Wuzhu' – illegible | 0.90 | 18 | (H: 9) | p | Allegedly from Hanguya Tatis (Badruddin Khan) |
| IA.III.B.c.6 | Wuzhu – narrow wu | 1.11 | 20 | (H: 9.5) faint | p | Allegedly from Hanguya Tatis (Badruddin Khan) |
| IA.III.B.c.7 | Wuzhu – without rim | 1.67 | 23 | (H: 10) | p | Allegedly from Hanguya Tatis (Badruddin Khan) |
| IA.III.B.c.8 | 'Wuzhu' – illegible | 1.15 | 21 | bent double | p | Allegedly from Hanguya Tatis (Badruddin Khan) |
| IA.III.B.c.9 | Wuzhu – without rim | 1.57 | 23 | (H: 10) | p | Allegedly from Hanguya Tatis (Badruddin Khan) |
| IA.III.B.c.10 | Wuzhu – clipped, cutting through inscription | 0.89 | 18 | (H: 9.5) | p | Allegedly from Hanguya Tatis (Badruddin Khan) |
| IA.III.B.c.11 | Wuzhu – clipped, cutting through inscription | 0.86 | 17 | (H: 8.5) | p | Allegedly from Hanguya Tatis (Badruddin Khan) |
| IA.III.B.c.12 | Wuzhu – small (inscription?) | 0.47 | 14 | (H: 7) diamond-shaped | p | Allegedly from Hanguya Tatis (Badruddin Khan) |
| IA.III.B.c.13 | 'Wuzhu' – illegible | 0.35 | – | frag. | p | Allegedly from Hanguya Tatis (Badruddin Khan) |
| IA.III.B.c.14 | 'Wuzhu' – illegible | 0.26 | 12 | (H: 7) frag. | p | Allegedly from Hanguya Tatis (Badruddin Khan) |
| IA.III.B.c.15 | [Wu]zhu – without rim | 0.56 | 21 | (H: 10) frag. | p | Allegedly from Hanguya Tatis (Badruddin Khan) |
| IA.III.B.c.16 | [Wu]zhu – without full rim | 0.76 | – | frag. | p | Allegedly from Hanguya Tatis (Badruddin Khan) |
| IA.III.B.c.17 | 'Wuzhu' – illegible | 0.45 | – | frag. | p | Allegedly from Hanguya Tatis (Badruddin Khan) |
| IA.III.B.c.18 | 'Wuzhu' – illegible | 0.81 | – | frag. | p | Allegedly from Hanguya Tatis (Badruddin Khan) |
| IA.III.B.c.19 | [Wu]zhu | 0.64 | – | frag. | p | Allegedly from Hanguya Tatis (Badruddin Khan) |
| IA.III.B.c.20 | Wu[zhu] | 0.62 | – | frag. | p | Allegedly from Hanguya Tatis (Badruddin Khan) |
| IA.III.B.c.21 | Wu[zhu] | 0.39 | – | frag. | p | Allegedly from Hanguya Tatis (Badruddin Khan) |
| IA.III.B.c.22 | 'Wuzhu' – illegible | 0.98 | – | 3 frags | p | Allegedly from Hanguya Tatis (Badruddin Khan) |
| IA.III.B.c.23 | Wu[zhu] | 0.26 | – | frag. | p | Allegedly from Hanguya Tatis (Badruddin Khan) |
| IA.III.B.c.24 | 'Wuzhu' – illegible | 0.32 | – | 2 frags | p | Allegedly from Hanguya Tatis (Badruddin Khan) |
| IA.III.B.c.25 | 'Wuzhu' – illegible, small | 0.36 | 10×12 | (H: 4.5) square, corroded | p | Allegedly from Hanguya Tatis (Badruddin Khan) |
| IA.III.B.c.26 | 'Wuzhu' – illegible, small | 0.30 | 9×10 | (H: 3) corroded, with sprue | p | Allegedly from Hanguya Tatis (Badruddin Khan) |
| IA.III.B.c.27 | 'Wuzhu' – illegible, small | 0.42 | 11 | (H: 5.5) corroded, with sprue | p | Allegedly from Hanguya Tatis (Badruddin Khan) |
| IA.III.B.c.28 | 'Wuzhu' – illegible, small | 0.20 | 8×10 | (H: 3) corroded, with sprue | p | Allegedly from Hanguya Tatis (Badruddin Khan) |
| IA.III.B.c.29 | 'Wuzhu' – illegible, small | 0.34 | 9×10 | (H: 3.5) corroded, with sprue | p | Allegedly from Hanguya Tatis (Badruddin Khan) |

| BM no. | Identification | Wt | Diam. | Notes | Acqn | Acquisition/Archaeological context |
|---|---|---|---|---|---|---|
| IA.III.B.c.30 | 'Wuzhu' – illegible, small | 0.33 | 8×10 | (H: 3) corroded, with sprue | p | Allegedly from Hanguya Tatis (Badruddin Khan) |
| IA.III.B.c.31 | 'Wuzhu' – illegible, small | 0.22 | 8×9 | (H: 3) corroded, with sprue | p | Allegedly from Hanguya Tatis (Badruddin Khan) |
| IA.III.B.c.32 | 'Wuzhu' – illegible, small | 0.21 | 8×10 | (H: 4) corroded | p | Allegedly from Hanguya Tatis (Badruddin Khan) |
| IA.III.B.c.33 | 'Wuzhu' – illegible, small | 0.20 | 8×10 | (H: 5×6) with sprue | p | Allegedly from Hanguya Tatis (Badruddin Khan) |
| IA.III.B.c.34 | 'Wuzhu' – illegible, small | 0.29 | 10×11 | (H: 5×7) corroded | p | Allegedly from Hanguya Tatis (Badruddin Khan) |
| IA.III.B.c.35 | 'Wuzhu' – illegible, small | 0.78 | 11×13 | (H: 4) corroded, with sprue | p | Allegedly from Hanguya Tatis (Badruddin Khan) |
| IA.III.B.c.36 | Qianyuan zhongbao – small | 2.36 | 22 | misaligned, forced hole | p | Allegedly from Hanguya Tatis (Badruddin Khan) |
| IA.III.B.c.37 | Qianyuan zhongbao – small | 2.44 | 22 | misaligned | p | Allegedly from Hanguya Tatis (Badruddin Khan) |
| IA.III.B.c.38 | Qianyuan zhongbao – small | 2.64 | 22 | misaligned, damaged | p | Allegedly from Hanguya Tatis (Badruddin Khan) |
| IA.III.B.c.39 | Qianyuan zhongbao – small | 2.18 | 22 | – | p | Allegedly from Hanguya Tatis (Badruddin Khan) |
| IA.III.B.c.40–43 | Chinese coins – Song dynasty | – | – | – | p | Allegedly from Hanguya Tatis (Badruddin Khan) |
| IA.III.B.c.44–45 | Islamic coins | – | – | – | p | Allegedly from Hanguya Tatis (Badruddin Khan) |
| IA.III.B.c.46–63 | | | | | p | Allegedly from Hanguya Tatis (Badruddin Khan) |
| IA.III.B.c.46 | [extra: Wuzhu – clipped, cutting through inscription] | 0.86 | 17 | (H: 8.5) | p | Allegedly from Hanguya Tatis (Badruddin Khan) |
| IA.III.B.c.47 | [extra: 'Wuzhu' – illegible, small] | 0.96 | 14 | (H: 7) | p | Allegedly from Hanguya Tatis (Badruddin Khan) |
| IA.III.B.c.48 | [extra: Wuzhu – clipped, cutting through inscription] | 0.60 | 17 | (H: 9) | p | Allegedly from Hanguya Tatis (Badruddin Khan) |
| IA.III.B.c.49 | [extra: 'Wuzhu' – illegible, small] | 0.46 | 13×14 | (H: 6) | p | Allegedly from Hanguya Tatis (Badruddin Khan) |
| IA.III.B.c.50 | [extra: 'Wuzhu' – illegible, small, with rim] | 0.68 | 14 | (H: 7×9) with sprue | p | Allegedly from Hanguya Tatis (Badruddin Khan) |
| IA.III.B.c.51 | [extra: 'Wuzhu' – illegible, small] | 0.45 | 14 | (H: 7) square | p | Allegedly from Hanguya Tatis (Badruddin Khan) |
| IA.III.B.c.52 | [extra: 'Wuzhu' – illegible, small] | 0.39 | 15 | damaged | p | Allegedly from Hanguya Tatis (Badruddin Khan) |
| IA.III.B.c.53 | [extra: 'Wuzhu' – illegible, small] | 0.53 | 11.5 | (H: 6) | p | Allegedly from Hanguya Tatis (Badruddin Khan) |
| IA.III.B.c.54 | [extra: 'Wuzhu' – illegible, small] | 0.32 | 12 | (H: 7) | p | Allegedly from Hanguya Tatis (Badruddin Khan) |
| IA.III.B.c.55 | [extra: 'Wuzhu' – illegible, small] | 0.44 | 10 | (H: 4) square | p | Allegedly from Hanguya Tatis (Badruddin Khan) |
| IA.III.B.c.56 | [extra: 'Wuzhu' – illegible, small] | 0.42 | 11×13 | (H: 6×7) | p | Allegedly from Hanguya Tatis (Badruddin Khan) |
| IA.III.B.c.57 | [extra: 'Wuzhu' – illegible, small, with rim] | 0.32 | – | frag. | p | Allegedly from Hanguya Tatis (Badruddin Khan) |
| IA.III.B.c.58 | [extra: 'Wuzhu' – illegible, small] | 0.26 | 10.5 | (H: 3.5) | p | Allegedly from Hanguya Tatis (Badruddin Khan) |
| IA.III.B.c.59 | [extra: 'Wuzhu' – illegible, small] | 0.21 | 11 | (H: 5) | p | Allegedly from Hanguya Tatis (Badruddin Khan) |

| BM no. | Identification | Wt | Diam. | Notes | Acqn | Acquisition/Archaeological context |
|---|---|---|---|---|---|---|
| IA.III.B.c.60 | [extra: 'Wuzhu' – illegible, small] | 0.23 | 10×12 | (H: 5) | p | Allegedly from Hanguya Tatis (Badruddin Khan) |
| IA.III.B.c.61 | [extra: 'Wuzhu' – illegible, small] | 0.37 | 11×13 | (H: 6×7) | p | Allegedly from Hanguya Tatis (Badruddin Khan) |
| IA.III.B.c.62 | [extra: 'Wuzhu' – illegible, small] | 0.40 | 11×12 | (H: 4.5×5.5) | p | Allegedly from Hanguya Tatis (Badruddin Khan) |
| IA.III.B.c.63 | [extra: 'Wuzhu' – illegible, small] | 0.56 | 13 | (H: 6.5) | p | Allegedly from Hanguya Tatis (Badruddin Khan) |
| IA.III.B.c.64 | [extra: Wuzhu – illegible] | 1.12 | 20 | (H: 10) | p | Allegedly from Hanguya Tatis (Badruddin Khan) |
| IA.III.B.c.65 | [extra: [Wu]zhu – clipped, cutting through inscription] | 0.62 | – | frag. | p | Allegedly from Hanguya Tatis (Badruddin Khan) |
| IA.III.B.c.66 | [extra: Wuzhu – full size] | 1.70 | 25 | (H: 9) | p | Allegedly from Hanguya Tatis (Badruddin Khan) |
| IA.III.B.c.67 | [extra: 'Wuzhu' – illegible] | 0.91 | 21 | (H: 10.5) | p | Allegedly from Hanguya Tatis (Badruddin Khan) |
| IA.III.B.c.68 | [extra: Wuzhu] | 1.10 | 24 | (H: 10) 2 frags | p | Allegedly from Hanguya Tatis (Badruddin Khan) |
| IA.III.B.c.69 | [extra: 'Wuzhu' – illegible] | 0.54 | 15 | (H: 9) 2 frags, corroded, square | p | Allegedly from Hanguya Tatis (Badruddin Khan) |
| IA.III.B.c.70 | [extra: 'Wuzhu' – illegible] | 1.16 | 18 | (H: 7.5) 2 frags | p | Allegedly from Hanguya Tatis (Badruddin Khan) |
| IA.III.B.c.71 | [extra: 'Wuzhu' – illegible] | 1.47 | 22 | (H: 10) 4 frags | p | Allegedly from Hanguya Tatis (Badruddin Khan) |

| | | | | | | |
|---|---|---|---|---|---|---|
| IA.III.B.d.1 | 'Wuzhu' – illegible | 0.97 | 22 | (H: 10) | p | Allegedly from Yotkan (Badruddin Khan) |
| IA.III.B.d.2 | Wuzhu | 1.20 | 20 | (H: 9.5) faint | p | Allegedly from Yotkan (Badruddin Khan) |
| IA.III.B.d.3 | 'Wuzhu' – illegible | 0.91 | 21.5 | (H: 9.5) damaged | p | Allegedly from Yotkan (Badruddin Khan) |
| IA.III.B.d.4 | 'Wuzhu' – illegible | 1.24 | 21 | (H: 10) | p | Allegedly from Yotkan (Badruddin Khan) |
| IA.III.B.d.5 | 'Wuzhu' – illegible | 1.22 | 20 | (H: 9) | p | Allegedly from Yotkan (Badruddin Khan) |
| IA.III.B.d.6 | 'Wuzhu' – illegible | 0.85 | 19 | (H: 10) | p | Allegedly from Yotkan (Badruddin Khan) |
| IA.III.B.d.7 | 'Wuzhu' – illegible | 1.31 | 22 | (H: 9.5) | p | Allegedly from Yotkan (Badruddin Khan) |
| IA.III.B.d.8 | Wuzhu – full size | 1.42 | 24 | (H: 10) | p | Allegedly from Yotkan (Badruddin Khan) |
| IA.III.B.d.9 | Wuzhu | 1.32 | 22 | (H: 9.5) faint | p | Allegedly from Yotkan (Badruddin Khan) |
| IA.III.B.d.10 | 'Wuzhu' – illegible | 1.19 | 23 | (H: 9.5) | p | Allegedly from Yotkan (Badruddin Khan) |
| IA.III.B.d.11 | Wuzhu – full size | 1.13 | 24.5 | (H: 9.5) damaged | p | Allegedly from Yotkan (Badruddin Khan) |
| IA.III.B.d.12 | 'Wuzhu' – illegible | 1.07 | 20 | (H: 10.5) | p | Allegedly from Yotkan (Badruddin Khan) |
| IA.III.B.d.13 | 'Wuzhu' – illegible | 0.67 | 20 | (H: 9.5) | p | Allegedly from Yotkan (Badruddin Khan) |
| IA.III.B.d.14 | 'Wuzhu' – illegible | 1.28 | 20.5 | (H: 10) | p | Allegedly from Yotkan (Badruddin Khan) |
| IA.III.B.d.15 | 'Wuzhu' – illegible | 1.14 | 22.5 | (H: 10) | p | Allegedly from Yotkan (Badruddin Khan) |

| BM no. | Identification | Wt | Diam. | Notes | Acqn | Acquisition/Archaeological context |
|---|---|---|---|---|---|---|
| IA.III.B.d.16 | 'Wuzhu' – illegible | 0.86 | 18 | (H: 9) | p | Allegedly from Yotkan (Badruddin Khan) |
| IA.III.B.d.17 | Wuzhu | 1.14 | 22 | (H: 9.5) faint | p | Allegedly from Yotkan (Badruddin Khan) |
| IA.III.B.d.18 | 'Wuzhu' – illegible | 0.75 | 17.5 | (H: 9) | p | Allegedly from Yotkan (Badruddin Khan) |
| IA.III.B.d.19 | 'Wuzhu' – illegible | 0.93 | 18 | (H: 8×8.5) | p | Allegedly from Yotkan (Badruddin Khan) |
| IA.III.B.d.20 | 'Wuzhu' – illegible | 1.06 | 20 | (H: 9.5) | p | Allegedly from Yotkan (Badruddin Khan) |
| IA.III.B.d.21 | 'Wuzhu' – illegible | 0.83 | 21 | (H: 10) damaged | p | Allegedly from Yotkan (Badruddin Khan) |
| IA.III.B.d.22 | 'Wuzhu' – illegible | 0.99 | 21 | (H: 10) lop-sided | p | Allegedly from Yotkan (Badruddin Khan) |
| IA.III.B.d.23 | 'Wuzhu' – illegible | 1.62 | 24 | (H: 9.5) damaged | p | Allegedly from Yotkan (Badruddin Khan) |
| IA.III.B.d.24 | Wuzhu | 1.34 | 25 | (H: 10) damaged | p | Allegedly from Yotkan (Badruddin Khan) |
| IA.III.B.d.25 | Wuzhu – clipped, cutting through inscription, small wu | 1.25 | 21 | (H: 10) | p | Allegedly from Yotkan (Badruddin Khan) |
| IA.III.B.d.26 | Wuzhu | 1.19 | 23×24 | (H: 9.5) damaged | p | Allegedly from Yotkan (Badruddin Khan) |
| IA.III.B.d.27 | Wuzhu – small wu | 0.92 | 20×21 | (H: 10) | p | Allegedly from Yotkan (Badruddin Khan) |
| IA.III.B.d.28 | 'Wuzhu' – illegible | 1.10 | 20 | (H: 8.5×9) damaged | p | Allegedly from Yotkan (Badruddin Khan) |
| IA.III.B.d.29 | 'Wuzhu' – illegible | 1.02 | 20.5 | (H: 9.5) damaged | p | Allegedly from Yotkan (Badruddin Khan) |
| IA.III.B.d.30 | 'Wuzhu' – illegible | 1.31 | 22.5 | (H: 10) | p | Allegedly from Yotkan (Badruddin Khan) |
| IA.III.B.d.31 | Wuzhu – full size | 1.88 | 26 | (H: 10) frag. | p | Allegedly from Yotkan (Badruddin Khan) |
| IA.III.B.d.32 | 'Wuzhu' – illegible | 0.74 | 19.5 | (H: 10) | p | Allegedly from Yotkan (Badruddin Khan) |
| IA.III.B.d.33 | Wuzhu – clipped, cutting through inscription small wu | 1.20 | 21×22 | (H: 10) | p | Allegedly from Yotkan (Badruddin Khan) |
| IA.III.B.d.34 | 'Wuzhu' – illegible | 0.78 | 20 | (H: 9×10) damaged | p | Allegedly from Yotkan (Badruddin Khan) |
| IA.III.B.d.35 | 'Wuzhu' – illegible | 1.63 | 23 | (H: 9) | p | Allegedly from Yotkan (Badruddin Khan) |
| IA.III.B.d.36 | 'Wuzhu' – illegible | 1.50 | 23 | (H: 9.5) | p | Allegedly from Yotkan (Badruddin Khan) |
| IA.III.B.d.37 | 'Wuzhu' – illegible | 0.86 | 18 | (H: 9) | p | Allegedly from Yotkan (Badruddin Khan) |
| IA.III.B.d.38 | Wuzhu – full size | 2.16 | 25.5 | (H: 10) damaged | p | Allegedly from Yotkan (Badruddin Khan) |
| IA.III.B.d.39 | 'Wuzhu' – illegible | 1.42 | 20 | (H: 10) misaligned | p | Allegedly from Yotkan (Badruddin Khan) |
| IA.III.B.d.40 | Wuzhu – clipped, cutting through inscription | 0.86 | 17.5 | (H: 8.5) | p | Allegedly from Yotkan (Badruddin Khan) |
| IA.III.B.d.41 | Wuzhu – clipped, cutting through inscription | 1.02 | 19 | (H: 9) | p | Allegedly from Yotkan (Badruddin Khan) |
| IA.III.B.d.42–43 | 'Wuzhu' – illegible (2 coins) | 1.77 | 21 | (H: 10 + 11) 2 coins | p | Allegedly from Yotkan (Badruddin Khan) |

| BM no. | Identification | Wt | Diam. | Notes | Acqn | Acquisition/Archaeological context |
|---|---|---|---|---|---|---|
| IA.III.B.d.44–45 | 'Wuzhu' – illegible (1 coin + frags) | 2.50 | – | 1 coin + frags | p | Allegedly from Yotkan (Badruddin Khan) |
| IA.III.B.d.46 | Kaiyuan tongbao | 2.72 | 25 | misaligned, hole in flan | p | Allegedly from Yotkan (Badruddin Khan) |
| IA.III.B.d.47–49 | Chinese coins – Song dynasty | – | – | – | p | Allegedly from Yotkan (Badruddin Khan) |
| IA.III.B.d.50 | [extra: Chinese coin – Song dynasty] | – | – | – | p | Allegedly from Yotkan (Badruddin Khan) |
| IA.III.B.d.51 | [extra: Qianyuan zhongbao – small] | 2.81 | 22.5 | not cleaned, corroded | p | Allegedly from Yotkan (Badruddin Khan) |
| IA.III.B.e.1 | Kaiyuan tongbao | 2.17 | 24.5 | – | p | Allegedly from Ak-tiken (Badruddin Khan) |
| IA.III.B.e.2 | Wuzhu | 1.11 | 22 | (H: 9.5 × 10) faint | p | Allegedly from Ak-tiken (Badruddin Khan) |
| IA.III.B.e.3 | Wuzhu | 1.29 | 23.5 | (H: 10) damaged | p | Allegedly from Ak-tiken (Badruddin Khan) |
| IA.III.B.e.4 | Wuzhu | 1.35 | 23 | (H: 9.5 × 10) faint | p | Allegedly from Ak-tiken (Badruddin Khan) |
| IA.III.B.e.5 | Wuzhu | 0.98 | 20.5 | (H: 9.5) damaged | p | Allegedly from Ak-tiken (Badruddin Khan) |
| IA.III.B.e.6 | 'Wuzhu' – illegible | 1.47 | 23 | (H: 9) damaged | p | Allegedly from Ak-tiken (Badruddin Khan) |
| IA.III.B.e.7 | 'Wuzhu' – illegible | 0.70 | 21 | (H: 10) damaged | p | Allegedly from Ak-tiken (Badruddin Khan) |
| IA.III.B.e.8 | Wuzhu | 1.04 | 22.5 | (H: 9.5) lop-sided | p | Allegedly from Ak-tiken (Badruddin Khan) |
| IA.III.B.e.9 | Wuzhu – narrow wu | 1.37 | 21 | (H: 9.5) | p | Allegedly from Ak-tiken (Badruddin Khan) |
| IA.III.B.e.10 | Wuzhu – clipped, cutting through inscription | 1.02 | 22 | (H: 10.5) | p | Allegedly from Ak-tiken (Badruddin Khan) |
| IA.III.B.e.11 | Wuzhu – clipped, cutting through inscription | 0.94 | 21 | (H: 9.5) faint | p | Allegedly from Ak-tiken (Badruddin Khan) |
| IA.III.B.e.12 | Wuzhu – clipped, cutting through inscription | 1.53 | 23 | (H: 10) damaged | p | Allegedly from Ak-tiken (Badruddin Khan) |
| IA.III.B.e.13 | Wuzhu – clipped, cutting through inscription | 1.05 | 21 | (H: 9.5) | p | Allegedly from Ak-tiken (Badruddin Khan) |
| IA.III.B.e.14 | 'Wuzhu' – illegible | 1.53 | 24.5 | (H: 9.5) damaged | p | Allegedly from Ak-tiken (Badruddin Khan) |
| IA.III.B.e.15 | Wuzhu | 1.42 | 24 | (H: 9.5) damaged, faint | p | Allegedly from Ak-tiken (Badruddin Khan) |
| IA.III.B.e.16 | 'Wuzhu' – illegible | 0.81 | 22 | (H: 10) damaged | p | Allegedly from Ak-tiken (Badruddin Khan) |
| IA.III.B.e.17 | Wuzhu | 1.00 | 23 | (H: 9.5) damaged | p | Allegedly from Ak-tiken (Badruddin Khan) |
| IA.III.B.e.18 | Wuzhu – clipped, cutting through inscription | 0.81 | 21 | (H: 10) | p | Allegedly from Ak-tiken (Badruddin Khan) |
| IA.III.B.e.19 | 'Wuzhu' – illegible | 0.87 | 19 | (H: 9.5) (octagonal) | p | Allegedly from Ak-tiken (Badruddin Khan) |
| IA.III.B.e.20 | Wuzhu – clipped, cutting through inscription; wuzhu on obverse, and on reverse | 0.92 | 17 | (H: 9) | p | Allegedly from Ak-tiken (Badruddin Khan) |
| IA.III.B.e.21 | Wuzhu – clipped, cutting through inscription | 1.17 | 18.5 | (H: 9) damaged | p | Allegedly from Ak-tiken (Badruddin Khan) |

| BM no. | Identification | Wt | Diam. | Notes | Acqn | Acquisition/Archaeological context |
|---|---|---|---|---|---|---|
| IA.III.B.e.22 | 'Wuzhu' – illegible, rim on rev. | 0.29 | 12 | (H: 7.5) | p | Allegedly from Ak-tiken (Badruddin Khan) |
| IA.III.B.e.23 | 'Wuzhu' – illegible, rim on rev. | 0.43 | 12.5 | (H: 7) | p | Allegedly from Ak-tiken (Badruddin Khan) |
| IA.III.B.e.24 | Wuzhu – clipped, cutting through inscription | 0.75 | 18.5 | (H: 10) frag. | p | Allegedly from Ak-tiken (Badruddin Khan) |
| IA.III.B.e.25 | Wuzhu – full size | 1.15 | 24.5 | (H: 10) frag. | p | Allegedly from Ak-tiken (Badruddin Khan) |
| IA.III.B.e.26 | 'Wuzhu' – illegible | 0.50 | 19.5 | (H: 10) frag. | p | Allegedly from Ak-tiken (Badruddin Khan) |
| IA.III.B.e.27 | 'Wuzhu' – illegible | 0.73 | – | 3 frags | p | Allegedly from Ak-tiken (Badruddin Khan) |
| IA.III.B.e.28 | 'Wuzhu' – illegible | 0.56 | – | 5 frags | p | Allegedly from Ak-tiken (Badruddin Khan) |
| IA.III.B.e.29 | 'Wuzhu' – illegible | 0.90 | – | 3 frags | p | Allegedly from Ak-tiken (Badruddin Khan) |
| IA.III.B.e.30 | 'Wuzhu' – illegible | 1.18 | 25 | (H: 9.5) 2 frags | p | Allegedly from Ak-tiken (Badruddin Khan) |
| IA.III.B.e.31 | 'Wuzhu' – illegible | 1.04 | – | 4 frags | p | Allegedly from Ak-tiken (Badruddin Khan) |
| IA.III.B.e.32 | Wuzhu – clipped, cutting through inscription | 1.63 | 23 | (H: 10) 1 coin + 1 frag. | p | Allegedly from Ak-tiken (Badruddin Khan) |
| IA.III.B.e.33–35 | Wuzhu – clipped, cutting through inscription | 2.62 | 23 | (H: 10) 1 coin + 2 frags | p | Allegedly from Ak-tiken (Badruddin Khan) |
| IA.III.B.e.36–37 | Wuzhu – clipped, cutting through inscription | 2.69 | 23 | (H: 10) 2 coins + 1 frag. | p | Allegedly from Ak-tiken (Badruddin Khan) |
| IA.III.B.e.38 | Kai [yuan] tong [bao] | 1.20 | 24 | frag. | p | Allegedly from Ak-tiken (Badruddin Khan) |
| IA.III.B.e.39 | Kai [yuan] tong [bao] | 1.27 | 23 | frag. | p | Allegedly from Ak-tiken (Badruddin Khan) |
| IA.III.B.e.40 | Kai [yuan] tong [bao] | 1.45 | 23 | frag. | p | Allegedly from Ak-tiken (Badruddin Khan) |
| IA.III.B.e.41 | Qianyuan zhongbao – small | 2.55 | 22 | forced hole | p | Allegedly from Ak-tiken (Badruddin Khan) |
| IA.III.B.e.42 | Qianyuan zhongbao – small | 3.26 | 22 | plain rev. | p | Allegedly from Ak-tiken (Badruddin Khan) |
| IA.III.B.e.43 | Qianyuan zhongbao – large | 7.60 | 30 | – | p | Allegedly from Ak-tiken (Badruddin Khan) |
| IA.III.B.e.44 | Qianyuan zhongbao – large, crescent on rev. | 8.50 | 30 | – | p | Allegedly from Ak-tiken (Badruddin Khan) |
| IA.III.B.e.45–56 | Chinese coins – Song dynasty | – | – | – | p | Allegedly from Ak-tiken (Badruddin Khan) |
| IA.III.B.e.57 | Chinese coin – Jin dynasty (1127–1234) | – | – | – | p | Allegedly from Ak-tiken (Badruddin Khan) |
| IA.III.B.e.58–59 | Islamic coins | – | – | – | p | Allegedly from Ak-tiken (Badruddin Khan) |
| IA.III.B.e.60–62 | [extra: Chinese coins – Song dynasty] | – | – | – | p | Allegedly from Ak-tiken (Badruddin Khan) |
| IA.III.B.e.63 | [extra: Chinese coin – unidentified] | 0.38 | – | frag. | p | Allegedly from Ak-tiken (Badruddin Khan) |
| IA.III.B.e.64 | [extra: Chinese coin – unidentified] | 1.15 | – | frag. | p | Allegedly from Ak-tiken (Badruddin Khan) |

| BM no. | Identification | Wt | Diam. | Notes | Acqn | Acquisition/Archaeological context |
|---|---|---|---|---|---|---|
| IA.III.B.f.1 | 'Wuzhu' – illegible, small | 0.87 | 16 | (H: 8) | p | Purchased from Badruddin Khan |
| IA.III.B.f.2 | 'Wuzhu' – illegible, small | 0.66 | 15 | (H: 9) | p | Purchased from Badruddin Khan |
| IA.III.B.f.3 | 'Wuzhu' – illegible, small | 0.95 | 18 | (H: 9) | p | Purchased from Badruddin Khan |
| IA.III.B.f.4 | 'Wuzhu' – illegible | 1.38 | 18 | (H: 7.5) | p | Purchased from Badruddin Khan |
| IA.III.B.f.5 | 'Wuzhu' – illegible | 0.94 | 17.5 | (H: 8) corroded | p | Purchased from Badruddin Khan |
| IA.III.B.f.6 | 'Wuzhu' – illegible | 0.81 | 17 | (H: 9) | p | Purchased from Badruddin Khan |
| IA.III.B.f.7 | 'Wuzhu' – illegible | 1.21 | 19 | (H: 8.5) corroded, square | p | Purchased from Badruddin Khan |
| IA.III.B.f.8 | 'Wuzhu' – illegible | 0.98 | 17 | (H: 7) corroded, diamond-shaped | p | Purchased from Badruddin Khan |
| IA.III.B.f.9 | 'Wuzhu' – illegible, small | 0.65 | 15 | (H: 7) corroded | p | Purchased from Badruddin Khan |
| IA.III.B.f.10 | 'Wuzhu' – illegible, small | 0.51 | 14 | (H: 5) corroded | p | Purchased from Badruddin Khan |
| IA.III.B.f.11 | 'Wuzhu' – illegible, small | 0.49 | 13 | (H: 6) corroded | p | Purchased from Badruddin Khan |
| IA.III.B.f.12 | 'Wuzhu' – illegible, small | 0.59 | 13.5 | (H: 6) corroded | p | Purchased from Badruddin Khan |
| IA.III.B.f.13 | 'Wuzhu' – illegible, small | 0.53 | 12.5 | (H: 5×6) corroded | p | Purchased from Badruddin Khan |
| IA.III.B.f.14 | 'Wuzhu' – illegible, small | 0.42 | 12 | (H: 5) corroded | p | Purchased from Badruddin Khan |
| IA.III.B.f.15 | 'Wuzhu' – illegible, small | 0.34 | 10.5 | (H: 4×6) corroded | p | Purchased from Badruddin Khan |
| IA.III.B.f.16 | 'Wuzhu' – illegible, small | 0.31 | 10 | (H: 5) corroded, with sprue | p | Purchased from Badruddin Khan |
| IA.III.B.f.17 | Kaiyuan tongbao | 2.73 | 25 | – | p | Purchased from Badruddin Khan |
| IA.III.B.f.18 | Qianyuan zhongbao – large | 4.58 | 27 | corroded | p | Purchased from Badruddin Khan |
| IA.III.B.f.19 | Qianyuan zhongbao – small | 3.17 | 22 | misaligned | p | Purchased from Badruddin Khan |
| IA.III.B.f.20 | Qianyuan zhongbao – small | 2.69 | 22 | – | p | Purchased from Badruddin Khan |
| IA.III.B.f.21 | Qianyuan zhongbao – medium | 4.77 | 26 | red, misaligned | p | Purchased from Badruddin Khan |
| IA.III.B.f.22 | Qianyuan zhongbao – small | 2.35 | 23 | red, misaligned | p | Purchased from Badruddin Khan |
| IA.III.B.f.23 | Qianyuan zhongbao – small | 2.32 | 22 | misaligned | p | Purchased from Badruddin Khan |
| IA.III.B.f.24 | Qianyuan zhongbao – small | 2.51 | 22.5 | misaligned | p | Purchased from Badruddin Khan |
| IA.III.B.f.25 | Qianyuan zhongbao – small | 1.96 | 22.5 | – | p | Purchased from Badruddin Khan |
| IA.III.B.f.26–27 | Chinese coins – Song dynasty | – | – | – | p | Purchased from Badruddin Khan |
| IA.III.B.f.28 | [extra: Chinese coin – unidentified] | 0.57 | – | frag. | p | Purchased from Badruddin Khan |
| IA.III.B.f.29 | [extra: Chinese coin – unidentified] | 0.64 | – | 3 frags | p | Purchased from Badruddin Khan |

| BM no. | Identification | Wt | Diam. | Notes | Acqn | Acquisition/Archaeological context |
|---|---|---|---|---|---|---|
| IA.III.B.g.1 | 'Wuzhu' – illegible (1 coin + 4 frags) | 2.97 | – | (1 coin + 4 frags) | p | Allegedly from Arkalik (Badruddin Khan) |
| IA.III.B.g.2 | Wuzhu – full size | 2.31 | 26 | (H: 9.5) | p | Allegedly from Arkalik (Badruddin Khan) |
| IA.III.B.g.3 | Wuzhu – full size | 2.10 | 26 | (H: 10.5) | p | Allegedly from Arkalik (Badruddin Khan) |
| IA.III.B.g.4 | 'Wuzhu' – illegible | 1.75 | 22.5 | (H: 9.5) | p | Allegedly from Arkalik (Badruddin Khan) |
| IA.III.B.g.5 | Wuzhu – clipped, cutting through inscription | 1.83 | 22.5 | (H: 9.5) faint | p | Allegedly from Arkalik (Badruddin Khan) |
| IA.III.B.g.6 | Wuzhu | 1.15 | 24 | (H: 10) corroded | p | Allegedly from Arkalik (Badruddin Khan) |
| IA.III.B.g.7 | 'Wuzhu' – illegible | 1.21 | 23 | (H: 10) lop-sided | p | Allegedly from Arkalik (Badruddin Khan) |
| IA.III.B.g.8 | Wuzhu | 1.54 | 22.5 | (H: 9) faint | p | Allegedly from Arkalik (Badruddin Khan) |
| IA.III.B.g.9 | 'Wuzhu' – illegible | 1.18 | 22.5 | (H: 9) | p | Allegedly from Arkalik (Badruddin Khan) |
| IA.III.B.g.10 | Wuzhu | 1.62 | 23 | (H: 10) faint | p | Allegedly from Arkalik (Badruddin Khan) |
| IA.III.B.g.11 | 'Wuzhu' – illegible | 1.36 | 23 | (H: 10.5) | p | Allegedly from Arkalik (Badruddin Khan) |
| IA.III.B.g.12 | Wuzhu | 1.55 | 23 | (H: 9×10) scyphate | p | Allegedly from Arkalik (Badruddin Khan) |
| IA.III.B.g.13 | Wuzhu | 1.56 | 21.5 | (H: 9) | p | Allegedly from Arkalik (Badruddin Khan) |
| IA.III.B.g.14 | Wuzhu | 1.15 | 21 | (H: 10) | p | Allegedly from Arkalik (Badruddin Khan) |
| IA.III.B.g.15 | 'Wuzhu' – illegible | 0.71 | 22.5 | (H: 10) frag. | p | Allegedly from Arkalik (Badruddin Khan) |
| IA.III.B.g.16 | Wu[zhu] | 0.98 | – | frag. | p | Allegedly from Arkalik (Badruddin Khan) |
| IA.III.B.g.17 | 'Wuzhu' – illegible | 0.53 | 16 | (H: 9) frag. | p | Allegedly from Arkalik (Badruddin Khan) |
| IA.III.B.g.18 | 'Wuzhu' – illegible | 0.64 | 22 | (H: 9.5) frag. | p | Allegedly from Arkalik (Badruddin Khan) |
| IA.III.B.g.19 | 'Wuzhu' – illegible, rim round hole | 0.57 | 17 | (H: 8) frag. | p | Allegedly from Arkalik (Badruddin Khan) |
| IA.III.B.g.20 | 'Wuzhu' – illegible | 0.52 | – | frag. | p | Allegedly from Arkalik (Badruddin Khan) |
| IA.III.B.g.21 | 'Wuzhu' – illegible | 0.51 | – | frag. | p | Allegedly from Arkalik (Badruddin Khan) |
| IA.III.B.g.22 | 'Wuzhu' – illegible | 0.21 | – | frag. | p | Allegedly from Arkalik (Badruddin Khan) |
| IA.III.B.g.23 | 'Wuzhu' – illegible | 0.35 | – | frag. | p | Allegedly from Arkalik (Badruddin Khan) |
| IA.III.B.g.24 | 'Wuzhu' – illegible | 0.38 | – | frag. | p | Allegedly from Arkalik (Badruddin Khan) |
| IA.III.B.g.25 | 'Wuzhu' – illegible | 0.79 | – | frag. | p | Allegedly from Arkalik (Badruddin Khan) |
| IA.III.B.g.26 | 'Wuzhu' – illegible | 0.27 | – | frag. | p | Allegedly from Arkalik (Badruddin Khan) |
| IA.III.B.g.27 | 'Wuzhu' – illegible | 0.64 | – | frag. | p | Allegedly from Arkalik (Badruddin Khan) |

| BM no. | Identification | Wt | Diam. | Notes | Acqn | Acquisition/Archaeological context |
|---|---|---|---|---|---|---|
| IA.III.B.g.28 | 'Wuzhu' – illegible | 0.33 | – | frag. | p | Allegedly from Arkalik (Badruddin Khan) |
| IA.III.B.g.29 | Wu[zhu] | 0.50 | – | frag. | p | Allegedly from Arkalik (Badruddin Khan) |
| IA.III.B.g.30 | 'Wuzhu' – illegible | 0.36 | – | frag. | p | Allegedly from Arkalik (Badruddin Khan) |
| IA.III.B.g.31 | 'Wuzhu' – illegible | 0.79 | – | 3 frags | p | Allegedly from Arkalik (Badruddin Khan) |
| IA.III.B.g.32 | 'Wuzhu' – illegible | 0.82 | – | 3 frags | p | Allegedly from Arkalik (Badruddin Khan) |
| IA.III.B.g.33–35 | [missing: Wuzhu] | – | – | – | p | Allegedly from Arkalik (Badruddin Khan) |
| IA.III.B.g.36 | Kaiyuan zhongbao | 2.32 | 23 | – | p | Allegedly from Arkalik (Badruddin Khan) |
| IA.III.B.g.37 | Qianyuan zhongbao – small | 2.82 | 22 | red, misaligned | p | Allegedly from Arkalik (Badruddin Khan) |
| IA.III.B.g.38 | Dali yuanbao – small, without rim | 1.69 | 20 | red, misaligned | p | Allegedly from Arkalik (Badruddin Khan) |
| IA.III.B.g.39–40 | Chinese coins – Song dynasty | – | – | – | p | Allegedly from Arkalik (Badruddin Khan) |
| IA.III.B.g.41 | Islamic coin | – | – | – | p | Allegedly from Arkalik (Badruddin Khan) |
| IA.III.B.g.42 | [extra: [Kaiyuan] tong [bao] | 0.89 | – | frag. | p | Allegedly from Arkalik (Badruddin Khan) |
| IA.III.B.g.43 | [extra: [Kaiyuan] tong [bao] | 1.14 | – | frag. | p | Allegedly from Arkalik (Badruddin Khan) |
| IA.III.B.g.44 | [extra: Islamic coin] | – | – | – | p | Allegedly from Arkalik (Badruddin Khan) |

| | | | | | | |
|---|---|---|---|---|---|---|
| IA.III.B.h.1 | Huoquan | 1.34 | 21 | (H: 7.5) damaged | p | Purchased from Badruddin Khan |
| IA.III.B.h.2 | Wuzhu | 2.37 | 24 | (H: 9) | p | Purchased from Badruddin Khan |
| IA.III.B.h.3 | Wuzhu | 1.96 | 25 | (H: 9.5) | p | Purchased from Badruddin Khan |
| IA.III.B.h.4 | Wuzhu – full size | 2.16 | 26 | (H: 9.5) | p | Purchased from Badruddin Khan |
| IA.III.B.h.5 | Wuzhu – full size | 2.72 | 25 | (H: 9.5) restored | p | Purchased from Badruddin Khan |
| IA.III.B.h.6 | Wuzhu – full size | 1.90 | 25 | (H: 10.5) hole in flan | p | Purchased from Badruddin Khan |
| IA.III.B.h.7 | Wuzhu – full size | 2.65 | 25 | (H: 9.5) | p | Purchased from Badruddin Khan |
| IA.III.B.h.8 | Wuzhu – full size | 2.34 | 25 | (H: 9.5) hole in flan | p | Purchased from Badruddin Khan |
| IA.III.B.h.9 | Wuzhu – full size | 1.20 | 24 | (H: 10) damaged | p | Purchased from Badruddin Khan |
| IA.III.B.h.10 | Wuzhu – clipped, cutting through inscription | 1.57 | 23 | (H: 9.5 × 10) | p | Purchased from Badruddin Khan |
| IA.III.B.h.11 | Wuzhu | 1.15 | 23 | (H: 9.5) damaged | p | Purchased from Badruddin Khan |
| IA.III.B.h.12 | Wuzhu – clipped, cutting through inscription, narrow wu | 1.80 | 22 | (H: 10) misaligned | p | Purchased from Badruddin Khan |
| IA.III.B.h.13 | Wuzhu – narrow wu | 1.34 | 23 | (H: 10) | p | Purchased from Badruddin Khan |

| BM no. | Identification | Wt | Diam. | Notes | Acqn | Acquisition/Archaeological context |
|---|---|---|---|---|---|---|
| IA.III.B.h.14 | Wuzhu – clipped, cutting through inscription | 1.86 | 22 | (H: 9.5) scyphate | p | Purchased from Badruddin Khan |
| IA.III.B.h.15 | Wuzhu – clipped, cutting through inscription | 1.75 | 23 | (H: 10) | p | Purchased from Badruddin Khan |
| IA.III.B.h.16 | Wuzhu – clipped, cutting through inscription | 1.15 | 22 | (H: 10) | p | Purchased from Badruddin Khan |
| IA.III.B.h.17 | Wuzhu – clipped, cutting through inscription | 1.31 | 22 | (H: 10) scyphate | p | Purchased from Badruddin Khan |
| IA.III.B.h.18 | Wuzhu | 1.58 | 22 | (H: 9.5) damaged | p | Purchased from Badruddin Khan |
| IA.III.B.h.19 | 'Wuzhu' – illegible | 2.19 | 20 | (H: 8) damaged | p | Purchased from Badruddin Khan |
| IA.III.B.h.20 | 'Wuzhu' – illegible | 0.91 | 21 | (H: 10.5) damaged | p | Purchased from Badruddin Khan |
| IA.III.B.h.21 | 'Wuzhu' – illegible | 1.06 | 21 | (H: 9.5) | p | Purchased from Badruddin Khan |
| IA.III.B.h.22 | 'Wuzhu' – illegible | 0.97 | 21 | (H: 10) | p | Purchased from Badruddin Khan |
| IA.III.B.h.23 | 'Wuzhu' – illegible | 1.32 | 19.5 | (H: 9.5) misaligned | p | Purchased from Badruddin Khan |
| IA.III.B.h.24 | Wuzhu | 0.94 | 20 | (H: 10) faint | p | Purchased from Badruddin Khan |
| IA.III.B.h.25 | 'Wuzhu' – illegible | 1.08 | 21 | (H: 9.5) | p | Purchased from Badruddin Khan |
| IA.III.B.h.26 | 'Wuzhu' – illegible | 0.89 | 18 | (H: 9) | p | Purchased from Badruddin Khan |
| IA.III.B.h.27 | 'Wuzhu' – illegible | 0.72 | 21 | (H: 9×10) | p | Purchased from Badruddin Khan |
| IA.III.B.h.28 | Wuzhu – clipped, cutting through inscription | 0.98 | 19 | (H: 9.5) | p | Purchased from Badruddin Khan |
| IA.III.B.h.29 | 'Wuzhu' – illegible | 0.91 | 18 | (H: 10) | p | Purchased from Badruddin Khan |
| IA.III.B.h.30 | 'Wuzhu' – illegible | 0.96 | 20 | (H: 10) | p | Purchased from Badruddin Khan |
| IA.III.B.h.31 | 'Wuzhu' – illegible | 0.87 | 19 | (H: 9) frag. | p | Purchased from Badruddin Khan |
| IA.III.B.h.32 | Wuzhu – clipped, cutting through inscription | 0.89 | 18 | (H: 9) | p | Purchased from Badruddin Khan |
| IA.III.B.h.33 | 'Wuzhu' – illegible | 0.97 | 20 | (H: 9) | p | Purchased from Badruddin Khan |
| IA.III.B.h.34 | 'Wuzhu' – illegible | 0.82 | 17 | (H: 9) | p | Purchased from Badruddin Khan |
| IA.III.B.h.35 | Wuzhu – clipped, cutting through inscription | 1.04 | 18 | (H: 8.5) faint | p | Purchased from Badruddin Khan |
| IA.III.B.h.36 | Wuzhu – clipped, cutting through inscription | 0.88 | 19 | (H: 10) lop-sided | p | Purchased from Badruddin Khan |
| IA.III.B.h.37 | Wuzhu – clipped, cutting through inscription | 0.85 | 18 | (H: 9) faint | p | Purchased from Badruddin Khan |
| IA.III.B.h.38 | Wuzhu – clipped, cutting through inscription | 0.75 | 17 | (H: 9) | p | Purchased from Badruddin Khan |
| IA.III.B.h.39 | Wuzhu – clipped, cutting through inscription | 0.92 | 18 | (H: 9) | p | Purchased from Badruddin Khan |
| IA.III.B.h.40 | 'Wuzhu' – illegible | 0.39 | – | frag. | p | Purchased from Badruddin Khan |

| BM no. | Identification | Wt | Diam. | Notes | Acqn | Acquisition/Archaeological context |
|---|---|---|---|---|---|---|
| IA.III.B.h.41 | 'Wuzhu' – illegible | – | – | 1 coin frag., and 2 other frags | p | Purchased from Badruddin Khan |
| IA.III.B.h.42 | 'Wuzhu' – illegible | 0.17 | 7×9 | (H: 3) corroded, with sprue | p | Purchased from Badruddin Khan |
| IA.III.B.h.43 | 'Wuzhu' – illegible, with rim round hole | 0.49 | 12 | (H: 6) | p | Purchased from Badruddin Khan |
| IA.III.B.h.44 | 'Wuzhu' – illegible | 0.24 | 9×11 | (H: 3.5×5) octagonal | p | Purchased from Badruddin Khan |
| IA.III.B.h.45 | 'Wuzhu' – illegible, with rim round hole | 0.44 | 11×13 | (H: 4.5) octagonal | p | Purchased from Badruddin Khan |
| IA.III.B.h.46 | 'Wuzhu' – illegible | 0.70 | 11×14 | (H: 5.5) with casting remains | p | Purchased from Badruddin Khan |
| IA.III.B.h.47 | 'Wuzhu' – illegible (or faint inscription?) | 0.51 | 13 | (H: 6) flat rev. | p | Purchased from Badruddin Khan |
| IA.III.B.h.48 | 'Wuzhu' – illegible, with rim round hole | 0.31 | 9×12 | (H: 5) diamond–shaped | p | Purchased from Badruddin Khan |
| IA.III.B.h.49 | 'Wuzhu' – illegible | 0.33 | 12 | (H: 7.5) | p | Purchased from Badruddin Khan |
| IA.III.B.h.50 | Wuzhu – full size | 1.95 | 25 | (H: 9.5) | p | Purchased from Badruddin Khan |
| IA.III.B.h.51 | Kaiyuan tongbao, crescent above hole on rev. | 2.50 | 25 | – | p | Purchased from Badruddin Khan |
| IA.III.B.h.52 | Kaiyuan tongbao, crescent above hole on rev. | 4.67 | 25 | – | p | Purchased from Badruddin Khan |
| IA.III.B.h.53 | Kaiyuan tongbao | 3.51 | 24 | red | p | Purchased from Badruddin Khan |
| IA.III.B.h.54 | Qianyuan zhongbao – small | 2.72 | 23 | misaligned | p | Purchased from Badruddin Khan |
| IA.III.B.h.55 | Qianyuan zhongbao – small | 1.60 | 21 | bent | p | Purchased from Badruddin Khan |
| IA.III.B.h.56–140 | Chinese coins – Song dynasty | – | – | – | p | Purchased from Badruddin Khan |
| IA.III.B.h.141–145 | [extra: Chinese coins – Song dynasty] | – | – | – | p | Purchased from Badruddin Khan |
| IA.III.B.h.146 | Sino-Kharoshthi coin (Cribb 1–6) | 1.79 | 18.5 | – | p | Purchased from Badruddin Khan |
| IA.III.B.h.147 | [extra: Sino-Kharoshthi coin (Cribb 2)] | 3.21 | 21 | – | p | Purchased from Badruddin Khan |
| IA.III.B.h.148–167 | Islamic coins | – | – | – | p | Purchased from Badruddin Khan |

| | | | | | | |
|---|---|---|---|---|---|---|
| IA.III.B.j.1 | [extra: lead coin] | 5.59 | 23 | rectangular hole | p | Purchased from Badruddin Khan |
| IA.III.B.j.2 | [extra: lead coin] | 3.93 | 21×24 | rectangular hole, misaligned | p | Purchased from Badruddin Khan |

## IA.IV: COINS COLLECTED FROM OR NEAR DOMOKO

| BM no. | Identification | Wt | Diam. | Notes | Acqn | Acquisition/Archaeological context |
|---|---|---|---|---|---|---|
| IA.IV.a.1 | Sino-Kharoshthi coin (Cribb 1–6) | 2.70 | 17.5 | – | | From/near Domoko, obtained by Badruddin Khan |
| IA.IV.a.2 | Wuzhu – clipped, cutting through inscription | 1.66 | 23 | (H: 10.5) red | | From/near Domoko, obtained by Badruddin Khan |
| IA.IV.a.3 | Wuzhu – clipped, cutting through inscription | 1.79 | 23 | (H: 9.5) | | From/near Domoko, obtained by Badruddin Khan |
| IA.IV.a.4 | Wuzhu – clipped, cutting through inscription | 1.30 | 22.5 | (H: 10) | | From/near Domoko, obtained by Badruddin Khan |
| IA.IV.a.5 | 'Wuzhu' – illegible | 0.71 | 21 | (H: 9.5) | | From/near Domoko, obtained by Badruddin Khan |
| IA.IV.a.6 | 'Wuzhu' – illegible | 0.82 | 21 | (H: 9.5) lop-sided | | From/near Domoko, obtained by Badruddin Khan |
| IA.IV.a.7 | Wuzhu – clipped, cutting through inscription | 0.91 | 19 | (H: 9.5) red | | From/near Domoko, obtained by Badruddin Khan |
| IA.IV.a.8 | Kaiyuan tongbao (rev.: ping) | 2.96 | 24 | – | | From/near Domoko, obtained by Badruddin Khan |
| IA.IV.a.9 | Qianyuan zhongbao – small | 2.68 | 21 | misaligned | | From/near Domoko, obtained by Badruddin Khan |
| IA.IV.a.10 | Qianyuan zhongbao – small | 2.58 | 21 | – | | From/near Domoko, obtained by Badruddin Khan |
| IA.IV.a.11 | Qianyuan zhongbao – small | 2.21 | 22 | misaligned, damaged | | From/near Domoko, obtained by Badruddin Khan |
| IA.IV.a.12 | Qianyuan zhongbao – small | 2.23 | 22 | – | | From/near Domoko, obtained by Badruddin Khan |
| IA.IV.a.13 | Qianyuan zhongbao – small | 2.11 | 21.5 | – | | From/near Domoko, obtained by Badruddin Khan |
| IA.IV.a.14 | Qianyuan zhongbao – small | 2.29 | 21.5 | – | | From/near Domoko, obtained by Badruddin Khan |
| IA.IV.a.15–38 | Chinese coins – Song dynasty | – | – | – | | From/near Domoko, obtained by Badruddin Khan |
| IA.IV.a.39 | [extra: Chinese coin – Song dynasty] | – | – | – | | From/near Domoko, obtained by Badruddin Khan |
| IA.IV.a.40–50 | Islamic coins | – | – | – | | From/near Domoko, obtained by Badruddin Khan |
| IA.IV.a.51–56 | [extra: Islamic coins] | – | – | – | | From/near Domoko, obtained by Badruddin Khan |
| IA.IV.a.57–63 | [extra: Islamic coins] | – | – | – | | From/near Domoko, obtained by Badruddin Khan |

| | | | | | | |
|---|---|---|---|---|---|---|
| IA.IV.b.1 | 'Wuzhu' – illegible, with outer rim, small | 0.90 | 21 | (H: 10) red | | From/near Domoko, allegedly from Uzun Tati |
| IA.IV.b.2 | 'Wuzhu' – illegible | 1.29 | 22.5 | (H: 9) damaged | | From/near Domoko, allegedly from Uzun Tati |
| IA.IV.b.3 | 'Wuzhu' – illegible, with rim round hole | 0.93 | 17.5 | (H: 8.5) | | From/near Domoko, allegedly from Uzun Tati |
| IA.IV.b.4 | 'Wuzhu' – illegible | 0.89 | 18 | (H: 8.5) lop-sided | | From/near Domoko, allegedly from Uzun Tati |
| IA.IV.b.5 | 'Wuzhu' – illegible | 0.83 | 19.5 | (H: 10) | | From/near Domoko, allegedly from Uzun Tati |
| IA.IV.b.6 | 'Wuzhu' – illegible | 0.99 | 16 | (H: 8.5) | | From/near Domoko, allegedly from Uzun Tati |
| IA.IV.b.7 | Wuzhu – clipped, cutting through inscription | 0.68 | 18 | (H: 8.5×9.5) faint, lop-sided | | From/near Domoko, allegedly from Uzun Tati |

| BM no. | Identification | Wt | Diam. | Notes | Acqn | Acquisition/Archaeological context |
|---|---|---|---|---|---|---|
| IA.IV.b.8 | 'Wuzhu' – illegible, with rim round hole | 0.48 | 15 | (H: 9.5) | | From/near Domoko, allegedly from Uzun Tati |
| IA.IV.b.9 | 'Wuzhu' – illegible | 0.74 | 17 | (H: 8) | | From/near Domoko, allegedly from Uzun Tati |
| IA.IV.b.10 | 'Wuzhu' – illegible | 0.34 | 13 | (H: 7) lop-sided | | From/near Domoko, allegedly from Uzun Tati |
| IA.IV.b.11 | 'Wuzhu' – illegible | 0.54 | 14 | (H: 8) | | From/near Domoko, allegedly from Uzun Tati |
| IA.IV.b.12–13 | Wuzhu – clipped, cutting through inscription | 1.09 | 21 | (H: 9) 2 frags | | From/near Domoko, allegedly from Uzun Tati |
| IA.IV.b.14 | Qianyuan zhongbao – small | 2.85 | 22 | – | | From/near Domoko, allegedly from Uzun Tati |
| IA.IV.b.15 | Qianyuan zhongbao – large | 7.50 | 30 | – | | From/near Domoko, allegedly from Uzun Tati |
| IA.IV.b.16–17 | Chinese coins – Song dynasty | – | – | – | | From/near Domoko, allegedly from Uzun Tati |
| IA.IV.b.18–23 | Islamic coins | – | – | – | | From/near Domoko, allegedly from Uzun Tati |

| | | | | | | |
|---|---|---|---|---|---|---|
| IA.IV.c.1 | 'Wuzhu' – illegible | 0.83 | 16 | (H: 7) flat rev. | p | Allegedly from Domoko Tatis, purchased at Achma |
| IA.IV.c.2–43 | Islamic coins | – | – | – | p | Allegedly from Domoko Tatis, purchased at Achma |

### IA.V: COPPER COINS FROM NIYA, CHARCHAN AND VASH-SHAHRI

| BM no. | Identification | Wt | Diam. | Notes | Acqn | Acquisition/Archaeological context |
|---|---|---|---|---|---|---|
| IA.V.a.1 | Wuzhu | 2.37 | 23 | (H: 9) corroded, faint | FAS | Found near stupa |
| IA.V.a.2 | Chinese coin – Song dynasty | – | – | – | p | Allegedly found near Yalghu-tagh, purchased at Charchan |
| IA.V.a.3 | Chinese coin – Song dynasty | – | – | – | p | Obtained from Vash-shahri site |

### IA.VI: COPPER COINS FOUND AT LOP DESERT SITES A–F

### IA.VI.A: COINS FROM RUINED SITES L.K. (RUINED FORT) AND L.M. (SETTLEMENT SITE SUPPORTING L.K. FORT)

| BM no. | Identification | Wt | Diam. | Notes | Acqn | Acquisition/Archaeological context |
|---|---|---|---|---|---|---|
| IA.VI.A.a.1–3 | [missing: Wuzhu] | – | – | – | FAS | Found near L.K. fort |
| IA.VI.A.a.4 | Wu[zhu] – small wu (Shu–Han?), outer and inner rims on both sides | 0.95 | 21 | frag. | FAS | Found near L.K. fort |
| IA.VI.A.a.5 | Wuzhu | 1.05 | 18 | (H: 10) red, misaligned | FAS | Found near L.K. fort |
| IA.VI.A.a.6 | [missing: Wuzhu] | – | – | – | FAS | Found near L.K. fort |
| IA.VI.A.a.7 | [missing: Huoquan] | – | – | – | FAS | Found near L.K. fort |

| | | | | | | |
|---|---|---|---|---|---|---|
| IA.VI.A.b.1 | Wuzhu – full size | 1.87 | 25 | (H: 10) frag. | FAS | Found at L.M. site |
| IA.VI.A.b.2 | (non-coin?) | 0.46 | – | | FAS | Found at L.M. site |
| IA.VI.A.b.3 | 'Wuzhu' – illegible | 1.89 | 24 | (H: 10.5) | FAS | Found at L.M. site |
| IA.VI.A.b.4 | Wuzhu – full size | 1.81 | 25 | (H: 10) damaged | FAS | Found at L.M. site |
| IA.VI.A.b.5–6 | [missing: Wuzhu] | – | – | – | FAS | Found at L.M. site |

## IA.VI.B: COINS FROM LOULAN STATION L.A. OR ITS VICINITY

### IA.VI.B.a: COINS FOUND 8½ MILES BEYOND CAMP C.xciii

| BM no. | Identification | Wt | Diam. | Notes | Acqn | Acquisition/Archaeological context |
|---|---|---|---|---|---|---|
| IA.VI.B.a.1 | Wuzhu – full size | 1.99 | 26 | (H: 9.5) frag. | FAS | Found 8½ miles beyond C.xciii |
| IA.VI.B.a.2 | Wuzhu – clipped, cutting through inscription | 1.46 | 19 | (H: 9.5) | FAS | Found 8½ miles beyond C.xciii |
| IA.VI.B.a.3 | Huoquan – clipped | 0.71 | 15.5 | (H: 8) red, lop-sided | FAS | Found 8½ miles beyond C.xciii |

### IA.VI.B.b: COINS FOUND AT OR CLOSE TO WALLED STATION L.A.

| BM no. | Identification | Wt | Diam. | Notes | Acqn | Acquisition/Archaeological context |
|---|---|---|---|---|---|---|
| IA.VI.B.b.1 | 'Wuzhu' – illegible, with rim round hole | 0.61 | 15 | (H: 9) red | FAS | Found at, or close to, walled station L.A |
| IA.VI.B.b.2 | 'Wuzhu' – illegible, small | 0.78 | 15 | (H: 8) | FAS | Found at, or close to, walled station L.A |
| IA.VI.B.b.3 | 'Wuzhu' – illegible, small | 0.43 | 11.5 | (H: 6) with sprue | FAS | Found at, or close to, walled station L.A |
| IA.VI.B.b.4 | 'Wuzhu' – illegible | 0.77 | 19 | (H: 9.5) misaligned | FAS | Found at, or close to, walled station L.A |
| IA.VI.B.b.5 | 'Wuzhu' – illegible | 0.59 | – | 2 frags | FAS | Found at, or close to, walled station L.A |
| IA.VI.B.b.6 | 'Wuzhu' – illegible | 0.96 | – | (H: 10) 3 frags | FAS | Found at, or close to, walled station L.A |
| IA.VI.B.b.7 | Wuzhu – clipped, cutting through inscription | 0.68 | 19 | (H: 10.5) | FAS | Found at, or close to, walled station L.A |
| IA.VI.B.b.8 | 'Wuzhu' – illegible, small | 0.60 | 12 | (H: 4) corroded | FAS | Found at, or close to, walled station L.A |
| IA.VI.B.b.9 | 'Wuzhu' – illegible, with rim round hole | 0.89 | 15 | (H: 7.5) | FAS | Found at, or close to, walled station L.A |
| IA.VI.B.b.10 | Wuzhu – clipped, cutting through inscription | 0.89 | 21 | (H: 10) 2 frags (= 1 coin) | FAS | Found at, or close to, walled station L.A |
| IA.VI.B.b.11 | 'Wuzhu' – illegible | 0.36 | 12×13 | (H: 6×7.5) lop-sided | FAS | Found at, or close to, walled station L.A |
| IA.VI.B.b.12 | 'Wuzhu' – illegible | 1.78 | 24.5 | (H: 9.5) | FAS | Found at, or close to, walled station L.A |
| IA.VI.B.b.13 | 'Wuzhu' – illegible, (+ above hole on rev.?) | 2.19 | 26 | (H: 10) red | FAS | Found at, or close to, walled station L.A |
| IA.VI.B.b.14 | Wuzhu – without full rim | 2.26 | 25 | (H: 9.5) damaged | FAS | Found at, or close to, walled station L.A |
| IA.VI.B.b.15 | Wuzhu – full size | 2.73 | 26 | (H: 9.5) | FAS | Found at, or close to, walled station L.A |
| IA.VI.B.b.16 | Wuzhu – clipped, cutting through inscription | 1.64 | 21 | (H: 10) red | FAS | Found at, or close to, walled station L.A |
| IA.VI.B.b.17 | [Wu]zhu – full size | 1.14 | – | frag. | FAS | Found at, or close to, walled station L.A |
| IA.VI.B.b.18 | Wu[zhu] – full size | 1.28 | 27 | frag. | FAS | Found at, or close to, walled station L.A |
| IA.VI.B.b.19 | Wuzhu – full size | 2.75 | 26.5 | (H: 11) | FAS | Found at, or close to, walled station L.A |
| IA.VI.B.b.20 | 'Wuzhu' – illegible | 0.65 | – | frag. | FAS | Found at, or close to, walled station L.A |

| BM no. | Identification | Wt | Diam. | Notes | Acqn | Acquisition/Archaeological context |
|---|---|---|---|---|---|---|
| IA.VI.B.b.21 | [Wu]zhu – without full rim | 0.92 | 23 | frag. | FAS | Found at, or close to, walled station L.A |
| IA.VI.B.b.22 | Wu[zhu] | 1.14 | – | frag. | FAS | Found at, or close to, walled station L.A |
| IA.VI.B.b.23 | Wuzhu – clipped, cutting through inscription | 1.18 | 17 | (H: 8.5) | FAS | Found at, or close to, walled station L.A |
| IA.VI.B.b.24 | Wu[zhu] | 2.34 | 26 | (H: 10) frag., pierced twice | FAS | Found at, or close to, walled station L.A |
| IA.VI.B.b.25 | [Wu]zhu | 1.20 | 24.5 | (H: 10) frag. | FAS | Found at, or close to, walled station L.A |
| IA.VI.B.b.26 | Wu[zhu] | 1.01 | – | 2 frags | FAS | Found at, or close to, walled station L.A |
| IA.VI.B.b.27 | Wuzhu – clipped, cutting through inscription | 1.46 | 22 | (H: 9) lop-sided | FAS | Found at, or close to, walled station L.A |
| IA.VI.B.b.28 | 'Wuzhu' – illegible, with rim round hole | 0.74 | 16 | (H: 8.5) | FAS | Found at, or close to, walled station L.A |
| IA.VI.B.b.29 | 'Wuzhu' – illegible | 1.95 | 21 | (H: 9) misaligned | FAS | Found at, or close to, walled station L.A |
| IA.VI.B.b.30 | Wuzhu – full size | 3.07 | 25 | (H: 9.5) not cleaned, corroded | FAS | Found in ruin L.A.I |
| IA.VI.B.b.31 | Wuzhu – without full rim | 1.88 | 24 | (H: 9.5) | FAS | Found in refuse heap L.A.VI.ii |
| IA.VI.B.b.32 | [Wu]zhu | 0.93 | – | frag. | FAS | Found in refuse heap L.A.VI.ii |
| IA.VI.B.b.33 | Wuzhu – full size | 2.33 | 26 | (H: 10) damaged | FAS | Found at, or close to, walled station L.A |
| IA.VI.B.b.34 | 'Wuzhu' – illegible | 1.03 | – | frag., red | FAS | Found at, or close to, walled station L.A |
| IA.VI.B.b.35 | Wuzhu – clipped, cutting through inscription | 1.70 | 20.5 | (H: 10) red | FAS | Found at, or close to, walled station L.A |
| IA.VI.B.b.36 | 'Wuzhu' – illegible, with rim round hole | 0.44 | 11 | (H: 4×5) | FAS | Found at, or close to, walled station L.A |
| IA.VI.B.b.37 | 'Wuzhu' – illegible, small | 0.28 | 11.5 | (H: 5) with sprues | FAS | Found at, or close to, walled station L.A |
| IA.VI.B.b.38 | 'Wuzhu' – illegible, small | 0.36 | 11 | (H: 5) diamond–shaped, red | FAS | Found at, or close to, walled station L.A |
| IA.VI.B.b.39 | 'Wuzhu' – illegible, small, with rim round hole | 0.40 | 11 | (H: 4.5) | FAS | Found at, or close to, walled station L.A |
| IA.VI.B.b.40 | 'Wuzhu' – illegible, small, with rim round hole | 0.46 | 13 | (H: 6.5) with sprues | FAS | Found at, or close to, walled station L.A |
| IA.VI.B.b.41 | 'Wuzhu' – illegible, small | 0.32 | 11 | (H: 6) diamond–shaped, red | FAS | Found at, or close to, walled station L.A |
| IA.VI.B.b.42 | 'Wuzhu' – illegible, small, with rim round hole | 0.52 | 11 | (H: 6) with sprues | FAS | Found at, or close to, walled station L.A |
| IA.VI.B.b.43 | 'Wuzhu' – illegible | 0.38 | 17 | frag., red | FAS | Found at, or close to, walled station L.A |
| IA.VI.B.b.44 | 'Wuzhu' – illegible, small | 0.21 | 11 | (H: 5) frag. | FAS | Found at, or close to, walled station L.A |
| IA.VI.B.b.45 | 'Wuzhu' – illegible | 0.56 | 18 | (H: 9.5) frag., red | FAS | Found at, or close to, walled station L.A |
| IA.VI.B.b.46 | Wuzhu – without full rim | 2.20 | 25 | (H: 10) 4 frags (= 1 coin) | FAS | Found at, or close to, walled station L.A |
| IA.VI.B.b.47 | Wuzhu – full size | 2.63 | 25 | (H: 9.5) red | FAS | Found at, or close to, walled station L.A |

| BM no. | Identification | Wt | Diam. | Notes | Acqn | Acquisition/Archaeological context |
|---|---|---|---|---|---|---|
| IA.VI.B.b.48 | 'Wuzhu' – illegible | 1.54 | 23.5 | (H: 9) frag. | FAS | Found at, or close to, walled station L.A |
| IA.VI.B.b.49 | Wuzhu – full size | 2.90 | 25.5 | (H: 9.5) frag., corroded | FAS | Found at, or close to, walled station L.A |
| IA.VI.B.b.50 | 'Wuzhu' – illegible, small | 0.36 | 12 | (H: 7.5) red, with sprue | FAS | Found at, or close to, walled station L.A |
| IA.VI.B.b.51 | Wuzhu – full size | 1.68 | 25 | frag. | FAS | Found at, or close to, walled station L.A |
| IA.VI.B.b.52 | 'Wuzhu' – illegible, with rim round hole | 0.54 | 13 | (H: 7) corroded | FAS | Found at, or close to, walled station L.A |
| IA.VI.B.b.53 | 'Wuzhu' – illegible, with rim round hole | 0.65 | 12 | (H: 5) square, corroded | FAS | Found at, or close to, walled station L.A |
| IA.VI.B.b.54 | 'Wuzhu' – illegible, small | 0.32 | 11 | (H: 5.5) octagonal | FAS | Found at, or close to, walled station L.A |
| IA.VI.B.b.55 | Huoquan | 2.30 | 22 | (H: 7) | FAS | Found at, or close to, walled station L.A |
| IA.VI.B.b.56 | Huoquan | 2.39 | 22 | (H: 7) | FAS | Found at, or close to, walled station L.A |
| IA.VI.B.b.57 | Huoquan – very large characters | 2.82 | 23 | (H: 7) | FAS | Found at, or close to, walled station L.A |

## IA.VI.C: COINS FROM CEMETERY L.C. AND ITS VICINITY

| BM no. | Identification | Wt | Diam. | Notes | Acqn | Acquisition/Archaeological context |
|---|---|---|---|---|---|---|
| IA.VI.C.a.1 | [missing: Wuzhu] | – | – | – | FAS | Found in grave-pits |
| IA.VI.C.a.2 | [missing: Chinese coin – unidentified] | – | – | – | FAS | Found in grave-pits |
| IA.VI.C.b.1–4 | [missing: Wuzhu] | – | – | – | FAS | Found near L.C. and on way to L.E. |
| IA.VI.C.b.5 | [missing: Chinese coin – unidentified] | – | – | – | FAS | Found near L.C. and on way to L.E. |

## IA.VI.D: COINS FROM L.E. CASTRUM AND MESA L.F.

| BM no. | Identification | Wt | Diam. | Notes | Acqn | Acquisition/Archaeological context |
|---|---|---|---|---|---|---|
| IA.VI.D.a.1 | [missing: Wuzhu] | – | – | – | FAS | Found near circumvallation of L.E. |
| IA.VI.D.b.1 | [missing: Wuzhu] | – | – | – | FAS | Found in room L.F.iii |
| IA.VI.D.b.2–6 | [missing: Wuzhu] | – | – | – | FAS | Found at foot of Mesa L.F. |
| IA.VI.D.b.7–10 | [missing: Wuzhu] | – | – | – | FAS | Found at foot of Mesa L.F. |

## IA.VI.E: COINS FROM MINOR SITES, L.D., L.G., L.I., L.J., L.Q.

### IA.VI.E.a: COINS FOUND AT RUIN L.D.

| BM no. | Identification | Wt | Diam. | Notes | Acqn | Acquisition/Archaeological context |
|---|---|---|---|---|---|---|
| IA.VI.E.a.1 | 'Wuzhu' – illegible | 0.95 | 21 | (H: 10) | FAS | Found at ruin L.D. |
| IA.VI.E.a.2 | Wu[zhu] – without full rim | 1.36 | 25 | (H: 9.5) frag. | FAS | Found at ruin L.D. |
| IA.VI.E.a.3 | 'Wuzhu' – illegible | 1.02 | – | 2 frags stuck together | FAS | Found at ruin L.D. |
| IA.VI.E.a.4 | Wu[zhu] | 0.90 | 23.5 | (H: 9.5) frag. | FAS | Found at ruin L.D. |
| IA.VI.E.a.5 | Wu[zhu] – small, small wu | 1.12 | 21 | (H: 7.5) red | FAS | Found at ruin L.D. |
| IA.VI.E.a.6 | 'Wuzhu' – illegible | 0.54 | – | frag., square | FAS | Found at ruin L.D. |
| IA.VI.E.a.7 | Wu[zhu] | 0.88 | – | 2 frags | FAS | Found at ruin L.D. |
| IA.VI.E.a.8 | Wuzhu – clipped., cutting through inscription | 1.36 | 18 | (H: 9.5) | FAS | Found at ruin L.D. |
| IA.VI.E.a.9 | 'Wuzhu' – illegible | 0.47 | 18 | (H: 8) | FAS | Found at ruin L.D. |
| IA.VI.E.a.10 | 'Wuzhu' – illegible, with rim round hole | 0.52 | 13 | (H: 7) | FAS | Found at ruin L.D. |
| IA.VI.E.a.11 | 'Wuzhu' – illegible, with rim round hole | 0.42 | 12.5 | (H: 7.5) red | FAS | Found at ruin L.D. |
| IA.VI.E.a.12 | coin weight | 52.43 | 13×23×36 | | FAS | Found at ruin L.D. |
| IA.VI.E.a.13–21 | [missing: Wuzhu] | – | – | – | FAS | Found at ruin L.D. |

### IA.VI.E.b: COINS FOUND NEAR RUIN L.G.

| BM no. | Identification | Wt | Diam. | Notes | Acqn | Acquisition/Archaeological context |
|---|---|---|---|---|---|---|
| IA.VI.E.b.1 | Wu[zhu] – full size | 1.54 | *26.5* | (H: 9.5) frag. | FAS | Found at or near ruin L.G. |
| IA.VI.E.b.2 | Wu[zhu] | 0.84 | – | frag. | FAS | Found at or near ruin L.G. |
| IA.VI.E.b.3 | 'Wuzhu' – illegible | 0.68 | – | frag. | FAS | Found at or near ruin L.G. |
| IA.VI.E.b.4–7 | [missing: Wuzhu] | – | – | – | FAS | Found at or near ruin L.G. |
| IA.VI.E.b.8 | Huoquan | 1.28 | 20 | (H: 7.5) 2 frags (= 1 coin) | FAS | Found at or near ruin L.G. |
| IA.VI.E.b.9–11 | [missing: Chinese coins – unidentified | – | – | – | FAS | Found at or near ruin L.G. |
| IA.VI.E.b.12–15 | [missing: Wuzhu] | – | – | – | FAS | Found at or near ruin L.G. |

### IA.VI.E.c: COINS FOUND NE OF L.I.

| BM no. | Identification | Wt | Diam. | Notes | Acqn | Acquisition/Archaeological context |
|---|---|---|---|---|---|---|
| IA.VI.E.c.1 | Wuzhu – Shaodi type (86–74 BC) – line above hole on obv. | 2.38 | 24 | (H: 10) | FAS | Found NE of L.I. |
| IA.VI.E.c.2 | Wuzhu – Shaodi type (86–74 BC) – line above hole on obv. | 3.52 | 25 | (H: 10) red | FAS | Found NE of L.I. |

## IA.VI.E.d: COINS FOUND ENE OF L.J. ON ANCIENT ROUTE LINE

| BM no. | Identification | Wt | Diam. | Notes | Acqn | Acquisition/Archaeological context |
|---|---|---|---|---|---|---|
| IA.VI.E.d.1 | Wuzhu – full size | 2.74 | 25 | (H: 11) red | FAS | Found ENE of L.J. on ancient route |
| IA.VI.E.d.2 | Wuzhu – Shaodi type (86–74 BC) – line above hole on obv. | 2.58 | 25 | (H: 11) red | FAS | Found ENE of L.J. on ancient route |
| IA.VI.E.d.3 | Wuzhu – Shaodi type (86–74 BC) – line above hole on obv. | 2.25 | 25 | (H: 10) | FAS | Found ENE of L.J. on ancient route |
| IA.VI.E.d.4 | Wuzhu – Xuandi–Yuandi type – dot below hole on obv. | 2.54 | 25 | (H: 10) | FAS | Found ENE of L.J. on ancient route |
| IA.VI.E.d.5 | Wuzhu – full size (Aidi type?) – line above hole on obv. | 2.34 | 25 | (H: 10.5) | FAS | Found ENE of L.J. on ancient route |
| IA.VI.E.d.6 | Wuzhu – full size | 1.83 | 25 | (H: 11) | FAS | Found ENE of L.J. on ancient route |
| IA.VI.E.d.7 | Wuzhu – full size | 2.47 | 25 | (H: 10.5) | FAS | Found ENE of L.J. on ancient route |
| IA.VI.E.d.8 | Wuzhu – full size | 3.11 | 25 | (H: 10.5) | FAS | Found ENE of L.J. on ancient route |
| IA.VI.E.d.9 | Wuzhu – full size (Aidi type?) dot below hole on obv. | 2.35 | 25 | (H: 10.5) | FAS | Found ENE of L.J. on ancient route |
| IA.VI.E.d.10 | Wuzhu – full size, line above hole on obv. | 3.04 | 25 | (H: 10) | FAS | Found ENE of L.J. on ancient route |
| IA.VI.E.d.11 | Wuzhu – full size, line above hole on obv. | 2.18 | 24 | (H: 11) | FAS | Found ENE of L.J. on ancient route |
| IA.VI.E.d.12 | Wuzhu – full size, line above hole on obv. | 2.73 | 25 | (H: 10) | FAS | Found ENE of L.J. on ancient route |
| IA.VI.E.d.13 | Wuzhu – full size, dot below hole on obv. | 2.59 | 25 | (H: 10.5) | FAS | Found ENE of L.J. on ancient route |
| IA.VI.E.d.14 | Wuzhu – full size, dot below hole on obv. | 2.92 | 25.5 | (H: 10) | FAS | Found ENE of L.J. on ancient route |
| IA.VI.E.d.15 | Wuzhu – full size, line above hole on obv. | 3.22 | 25 | (H: 10) | FAS | Found ENE of L.J. on ancient route |
| IA.VI.E.d.16 | Wuzhu – full size, line above hole on obv. | 2.03 | 25 | (H: 11) | FAS | Found ENE of L.J. on ancient route |
| IA.VI.E.d.17 | Wuzhu – full size, line above hole on obv. | 2.31 | 25 | (H: 10) | FAS | Found ENE of L.J. on ancient route |
| IA.VI.E.d.18 | Wuzhu – full size, line above hole on obv. | 3.51 | 25 | (H: 10) | FAS | Found ENE of L.J. on ancient route |
| IA.VI.E.d.19 | Wuzhu – full size, dot below hole on obv. | 2.54 | 25 | (H: 10.5) | FAS | Found ENE of L.J. on ancient route |
| IA.VI.E.d.20 | Wuzhu – full size, dot below hole on obv. | 3.00 | 25 | (H: 10) | FAS | Found ENE of L.J. on ancient route |
| IA.VI.E.d.21 | Wuzhu – full size, dot below hole on obv. | 2.91 | 25 | (H: 10) | FAS | Found ENE of L.J. on ancient route |
| IA.VI.E.d.22 | Wuzhu – full size, dot below hole on obv. | 2.61 | 25 | (H: 10) | FAS | Found ENE of L.J. on ancient route |
| IA.VI.E.d.23 | Wuzhu – full size | 2.51 | 25.5 | (H: 10.5) | FAS | Found ENE of L.J. on ancient route |
| IA.VI.E.d.24 | Wuzhu – full size, dot below hole on obv. | 2.50 | 25.5 | (H: 10.5) | FAS | Found ENE of L.J. on ancient route |
| IA.VI.E.d.25 | Wuzhu – full size, dot below hole on obv. | 3.13 | 25 | (H: 10) | FAS | Found ENE of L.J. on ancient route |
| IA.VI.E.d.26 | Wuzhu – full size | 2.98 | 25 | (H: 10) | FAS | Found ENE of L.J. on ancient route |

| BM no. | Identification | Wt | Diam. | Notes | Acqn | Acquisition/Archaeological context |
|---|---|---|---|---|---|---|
| IA.VI.E.d.27 | Wuzhu – full size, dot below hole on obv. | 3.05 | 25 | (H: 10) | FAS | Found ENE of L.J. on ancient route |
| IA.VI.E.d.28 | Wuzhu – full size, line above hole on obv. | 2.41 | 25 | (H: 10) | FAS | Found ENE of L.J. on ancient route |
| IA.VI.E.d.29 | Wuzhu – full size, line above hole on obv. | 3.84 | 25 | (H: 10) | FAS | Found ENE of L.J. on ancient route |
| IA.VI.E.d.30 | Wuzhu – full size, dot below hole on obv. | 2.79 | 25 | (H: 10.5) | FAS | Found ENE of L.J. on ancient route |
| IA.VI.E.d.31 | Wuzhu – full size, dot below hole on obv. | 2.93 | 25 | (H: 10.5) | FAS | Found ENE of L.J. on ancient route |
| IA.VI.E.d.32 | Wuzhu – full size, line above hole on obv. | 2.75 | 25 | (H: 10.5) | FAS | Found ENE of L.J. on ancient route |
| IA.VI.E.d.33 | Wuzhu – full size, dot below hole on obv. | 2.27 | 25 | (H: 11) damaged | FAS | Found ENE of L.J. on ancient route |
| IA.VI.E.d.34 | Wuzhu – full size, dot below hole on obv. | 2.66 | 25 | (H: 10.5) | FAS | Found ENE of L.J. on ancient route |
| IA.VI.E.d.35 | Wuzhu – full size, dot below hole on obv. | 2.53 | 25 | (H: 10.5) | FAS | Found ENE of L.J. on ancient route |
| IA.VI.E.d.36 | Wuzhu – full size | 2.68 | 25.5 | (H: 10.5) | FAS | Found ENE of L.J. on ancient route |
| IA.VI.E.d.37 | Wuzhu – full size, dot below hole on obv. | 2.36 | 25 | (H: 10) | FAS | Found ENE of L.J. on ancient route |
| IA.VI.E.d.38 | Wuzhu – full size, line above hole on obv. | 4.11 | 25 | (H: 10) | FAS | Found ENE of L.J. on ancient route |
| IA.VI.E.d.39 | Wuzhu – full size, line above hole on obv. | 2.61 | 25 | (H: 10.5) | FAS | Found ENE of L.J. on ancient route |
| IA.VI.E.d.40 | Wuzhu – full size | 2.18 | 25 | (H: 10.5) | FAS | Found ENE of L.J. on ancient route |
| IA.VI.E.d.41 | Wuzhu – full size, dot below hole on obv. | 3.33 | 25 | (H: 10) | FAS | Found ENE of L.J. on ancient route |
| IA.VI.E.d.42 | Wuzhu – full size, dot below hole on obv. | 3.23 | 25 | (H: 10) | FAS | Found ENE of L.J. on ancient route |
| IA.VI.E.d.43 | Wuzhu – full size, dot below hole on obv. | 3.10 | 25 | (H: 10) | FAS | Found ENE of L.J. on ancient route |
| IA.VI.E.d.44 | Wuzhu – full size, dot below hole on obv. | 3.93 | 25 | (H: 10) | FAS | Found ENE of L.J. on ancient route |
| IA.VI.E.d.45 | Wuzhu – full size, dot below hole on obv. | 2.00 | 25 | (H: 10.5) | FAS | Found ENE of L.J. on ancient route |
| IA.VI.E.d.46 | Wuzhu – full size | 1.81 | 25 | (H: 10) | FAS | Found ENE of L.J. on ancient route |
| IA.VI.E.d.47 | Wuzhu – full size, dot below hole on obv. | 2.58 | 25 | (H: 10) | FAS | Found ENE of L.J. on ancient route |
| IA.VI.E.d.48 | Wuzhu – full size, dot below hole on obv. | 3.62 | 25 | (H: 10) | FAS | Found ENE of L.J. on ancient route |
| IA.VI.E.d.49 | Wuzhu – full size, dot below hole on obv. | 3.34 | 25 | (H: 10.5) | FAS | Found ENE of L.J. on ancient route |
| IA.VI.E.d.50 | Wuzhu – full size | 2.27 | 25.5 | (H: 10.5) | FAS | Found ENE of L.J. on ancient route |
| IA.VI.E.d.51–161 | [missing: Wuzhu] | – | – | – | FAS | Found ENE of L.J. on ancient route |

| | | | | | | |
|---|---|---|---|---|---|---|
| IA.VI.E.e.1 | Wuzhu – full size | 2.48 | 24.5 | (H: 11) red | FAS | Found NNW of L.Q. |

## IA.VI.F: COINS FOUND ON LOP DESERT MARCHES

| BM no. | Identification | Wt | Diam. | Notes | Acqn | Acquisition/Archaeological context |
|---|---|---|---|---|---|---|
| IA.VI.F.a.1 | Wuzhu – clipped, cutting through inscription | 1.66 | 21 | (H: 9.5) red | FAS | Found near C.xcvi (NW of L.A.01) |
| IA.VI.F.a.2 | Wuzhu – clipped, cutting through inscription | 1.08 | 18.5 | (H: 9.5) | FAS | Found near C.xcvi (NW of L.A.01) |
| IA.VI.F.a.3 | [extra: (Wu)zhu] | 0.27 | – | 2 frags | FAS | Found near C.xcvi (NW of L.A.01) |
| IA.VI.F.b.1 | [missing: Wuzhu] | – | – | – | FAS | Found S of C.xcix |
| IA.VI.F.c.1 | Wuzhu – full size | 2.87 | 25 | (H: 10) corroded | FAS | Found ½ mile E of C.ci |
| IA.VI.F.d.1 | Wuzhu – full size | 2.34 | 25 | (H: 11) | FAS | Found on Mesa, 6 miles E of C.ci |
| IA.VI.F.d.2 | [missing: Wuzhu] | – | – | – | FAS | Found on Mesa, 6 miles E of C.ci |
| IA.VI.F.d.3 | Wuzhu – full size, line above hole on obv. | 1.94 | 25 | (H: 11) | FAS | Found on Mesa, 6 miles E of C.ci |
| IA.VI.F.d.4 | Wuzhu – full size, dot below hole on obv. | 2.09 | 25 | (H: 10) | FAS | Found on Mesa, 6 miles E of C.ci |
| IA.VI.F.d.5 | Wuzhu – full size, dot below hole on obv. | 2.41 | 24.5 | (H: 11) | FAS | Found on Mesa, 6 miles E of C.ci |
| IA.VI.F.e.1 | Wuzhu – full size, dot below hole on obv. | 2.16 | 25.5 | (H: 10.5) | FAS | Found 13 miles SE of C.ciii |
| IA.VI.F.e.2 | Wuzhu – full size, dot below hole on obv. | 3.10 | 25.5 | (H: 10) | FAS | Found 14½ miles SE of C.ciii |
| IA.VI.F.f.1 | 'Wuzhu' – illegible | 2.89 | 26 | (H: 10) 3 frags | FAS | Found NW of C.ccxlix.a |
| IA.VI.F.g.1 | Wuzhu – full size, line above hole on obv. | 1.96 | 25 | (H: 10) | FAS | Found SW of Toghrak-bulak |

## IA.VII: COPPER COINS FOUND ALONG ANCIENT HAN *LIMES*

| BM no. | Identification | Wt | Diam. | Notes | Acqn | Acquisition/Archaeological context |
|---|---|---|---|---|---|---|
| IA.VII.a.1 | 'Wuzhu' – illegible | 0.48 | 12 | (H: 5.5) corroded | FAS | Found at watch-tower T.XXII.d |
| IA.VII.b.1 | Wuzhu | 0.40 | 20.5 | (H: 10.5) frag., red | FAS | Found in watch-station T.XXIII.b |
| IA.VII.b.2 | [extra: (Wu)zhu – full size] | 2.02 | 26 | (H: 9.5) frag. | FAS | Found in watch-station T.XXIII.b |
| IA.VII.c.1 | Wuzhu – without full rim | 2.26 | 24.5 | (H: 10) red | FAS | Found at watch-station T.XXIII.f |
| IA.VII.d.1 | Wuzhu – full size | 3.50 | 25.5 | (H: 9.5) red | FAS | Found at watch-station T.XL.b |
| IA.VII.e.1 | [Wu]zhu | 1.37 | – | frag. | FAS | Found at watch-station T.XLI.c |
| IA.VII.f.1 | 'Wuzhu' – illegible | 0.49 | 14 | (H: 7.5) frag. | FAS | Found at watch-tower T.XLI.d |
| IA.VII.g.1 | Wu[zhu] | 1.77 | – | 2 frags | FAS | Found at watch-station T.XLI.e |
| IA.VII.h.1 | Daquan [wu] shi | 1.20 | 21 | 3 frags | FAS | Found below watch-tower T.XLI.f |
| IA.VII.h.2–3 | Chinese coins – Qing dynasty | – | – | – | FAS | Found near T.XLI.f |

| BM no. | Identification | Wt | Diam. | Notes | Acqn | Acquisition/Archaeological context |
|---|---|---|---|---|---|---|
| IA.VII.i.1 | Chinese coin – Qing dynasty | – | – | – | FAS | Found at ruin T.XLI.g |
| IA.VII.j.1 | Wuzhu – full size | 2.94 | 25 | (H: 10.5) | FAS | Found at watch-post T.XLI.k |
| IA.VII.k.1 | Wuzhu – full size | 2.89 | 25 | frags restored, corroded | FAS | Found at station T.XLI.1 |
| IA.VII.l.1 | Wuzhu – full size, line above hole on obv. | 4.40 | 25 | (H: 9.5) | FAS | Found at watch-tower T.XLI.r |
| IA.VII.m.1 | Wuzhu – full size | 3.83 | 26 | (H: 10) corroded | FAS | Found at watch-tower T.XLIII.a |
| IA.VII.n.1 | [Wu]zhu | 1.39 | 26 | (H: 9) frag., red | FAS | Found at watch-tower T.XLIII.g |
| IA.VII.o.1 | [Daquan wu] shi | 0.44 | – | frag. | FAS | Found at station T.XLIII.h |
| IA.VII.p. 1 | Wuzhu – full size, dot below hole on obv. | 2.46 | 25.5 | (H: 10.5) | FAS | Found at tower T.XLIII.i |
| IA.VII.q.1 | Wu[zhu] | 0.26 | – | frag. | FAS | Found at tower T.XLIV.a |
| IA.VII.r.1 | Wuzhu – full size, dot below hole on obv. | 3.69 | 25 | (H: 9.5) | FAS | Found at watch-tower T.XLIV.c |
| IA.VII.r.2 | Huoquan | 1.36 | 21 | (H: 8) 3 holes in flan | FAS | Found at watch-tower T.XLIV.c |
| IA.VII.s.1 | Chinese coin – Qing dynasty | – | – | – | FAS | Found near watch-tower T.XLIV.d |

**IA.VIII: COPPER COINS FOUND AT OR NEAR KHARAKHOTO**

**IA.VIII.A: COINS FROM RUINED TOWN OF KHARAKHOTO**

| BM no. | Identification | Wt | Diam. | Notes | Acqn | Acquisition/Archaeological context |
|---|---|---|---|---|---|---|
| IA.VIII.A.a.1 | Chinese coin – Song dynasty | – | – | – | FAS | Found below image in shrine K.K.i |
| IA.VIII.A.b.1 | Chinese coin – Song dynasty | – | – | – | FAS | Found in NW corner of walled area |
| IA.VIII.A.c.1 | Wuzhu – full size | 2.71 | 26 | (H: 10.5) | FAS | Found within, or outside, walled town |
| IA.VIII.A.c.2 | Kaiyuan tongbao | 2.36 | 24 | round hole | FAS | Found within, or outside, walled town |
| IA.VIII.A.c.3 | Kaiyuan tongbao | 3.08 | 25 | – | FAS | Found within, or outside, walled town |
| IA.VIII.A.c.4 | Kaiyuan tongbao | 3.30 | 24 | misaligned, forced hole | FAS | Found within, or outside, walled town |
| IA.VIII.A.c.5–20 | Chinese coins – Song dynasty | – | – | – | FAS | Found within, or outside, walled town |
| IA.VIII.A.c.21 | Chinese coin – Jin dynasty (1127–1234) | – | – | – | FAS | Found within, or outside, walled town |
| IA.VIII.A.c.22 | Chinese coin – Yuan dynasty | – | – | – | FAS | Found within, or outside, walled town |
| IA.VIII.A.c.23–25 | [extra: Chinese coins – Song dynasty] | – | – | – | FAS | Found within, or outside, walled town |

### IA.VIII.B: COINS FROM RUINED SETTLEMENTS E OF KHARAKHOTO

| BM no. | Identification | Wt | Diam. | Notes | Acqn | Acquisition/Archaeological context |
|---|---|---|---|---|---|---|
| IA.VIII.B.a.1 | Chinese coin – Song dynasty | – | – | – | FAS | Found at ruin K.E.VI |

| | | | | | | |
|---|---|---|---|---|---|---|
| IA.VIII.B.b.1 | Wu[zhu] | 1.19 | – | frag. | FAS | Found at ruins K.E.IX–X |
| IA.VIII.B.b.2 | Round 'coin' with square hole, ring of dots around flan | 0.78 | 15×16 | (H: 5×6) | FAS | Found at ruins K.E.IX–X |
| IA.VIII.B.b.3 | Kaiyuan tongbao, crescent above hole on rev. | 3.31 | 24 | misaligned | FAS | Found at ruins K.E.IX–X |
| IA.VIII.B.b.4–7 | Chinese coins – Song dynasty | – | – | – | FAS | Found at ruins K.E.IX–X |
| IA.VIII.B.b.8 | Chinese coin – Qing dynasty | – | – | – | FAS | Found at ruins K.E.IX–X |

| | | | | | | |
|---|---|---|---|---|---|---|
| IA.VIII.B.c.1 | Kai [yuan tongbao] | 0.83 | – | frag. | FAS | Found at ruins K.E.XIV–XIX |
| IA.VIII.B.c.2–7 | Chinese coins – Song dynasty | – | – | – | FAS | Found at ruins K.E.XIV–XIX |
| IA.VIII.B.c.8 | Mongol coin | – | – | – | FAS | Found at ruins K.E.XIV–XIX |

### IA.VIII.C: COINS FROM RUINED FORT OF ADUNA-KORA

| BM no. | Identification | Wt | Diam. | Notes | Acqn | Acquisition/Archaeological context |
|---|---|---|---|---|---|---|
| IA.VIII.C.a.1 | Kaiyuan tongbao | 3.65 | 24.5 | – | FAS | Found close to outer eastern wall of fort |
| IA.VIII.C.a.2 | Kaiyuan tongbao, small | 1.72 | 22 | damaged | FAS | Found close to outer eastern wall of fort |
| IA.VIII.C.a.3 | Kaiyuan tongbao | 2.54 | 25 | – | FAS | Found close to outer eastern wall of fort |
| IA.VIII.C.a.4 | Kaiyuan tong [bao] | 2.06 | 24 | frag. | FAS | Found close to outer eastern wall of fort |
| IA.VIII.C.a.5 | Chinese coin – Song dynasty | – | – | – | FAS | Found close to outer eastern wall of fort |

### IA.IX: COPPER COINS OF MANCHU DYNASTY FOUND AT LUOTUOCHENG AND BEITING

| BM no. | Identification | Wt | Diam. | Notes | Acqn | Acquisition/Archaeological context |
|---|---|---|---|---|---|---|
| IA.IX.a.1–85 | Chinese coins – Qing dynasty | – | | | FAS | Found at Luotuocheng |
| IA.IX.a.86 | Chinese coins – Qing dynasty | – | – | – | FAS | From ruined temple, Beiting |

### IA.X: COINS EXCAVATED OR PURCHASED AT KARA KHOJA

| BM no. | Identification | Wt | Diam. | Notes | Acqn | Acquisition/Archaeological context |
|---|---|---|---|---|---|---|
| IA.X.a.1 | Kaiyuan tongbao, crescent above hole on rev. | 3.93 | 25 | misaligned | FAS | Found in ruin Kao.I |
| IA.X.a.2 | Kaiyuan tongbao | 4.28 | 26 | misaligned | FAS | Found in ruin Kao.I |
| IA.X.a.3 | Kaiyuan tongbao | 4.27 | 25 | misaligned | FAS | Found in ruin Kao.I |
| IA.X.a.4 | Kaiyuan tongbao | 2.94 | 24 | – | FAS | Found in ruin Kao.I |
| IA.X.a.5 | Kaiyuan tongbao | 5.10 | 25 | – | FAS | Found in ruin Kao.I |

| BM no. | Identification | Wt | Diam. | Notes | Acqn | Acquisition/Archaeological context |
|---|---|---|---|---|---|---|
| IA.X.b.1 | Kaiyuan tongbao | 2.43 | 23.5 | – | FAS | Found near ruin Kao.I |
| IA.X.b.2 | Jianzhong tongbao | 2.49 | 21 | – | FAS | Found near ruin Kao.I |
| IA.X.b.3 | Chinese coin – Song dynasty | – | – | – | FAS | Found near ruin Kao.I |
| IA.X.c.1 | Kaiyuan tongbao | 2.98 | 24 | – | FAS | Hoard of coins found in ruin Kao.III |
| IA.X.c.2 | Kaiyuan tongbao | 3.81 | 25.5 | – | FAS | Hoard of coins found in ruin Kao.III |
| IA.X.c.3 | Kaiyuan tongbao | 3.44 | 24 | – | FAS | Hoard of coins found in ruin Kao.III |
| IA.X.c.4 | Kaiyuan tongbao | 3.42 | 24.5 | – | FAS | Hoard of coins found in ruin Kao.III |
| IA.X.c.5 | Kaiyuan tongbao | 3.24 | 24.5 | – | FAS | Hoard of coins found in ruin Kao.III |
| IA.X.c.6 | Kaiyuan tongbao | 3.05 | 23 | – | FAS | Hoard of coins found in ruin Kao.III |
| IA.X.c.7 | Kaiyuan tongbao | 4.64 | 23 | – | FAS | Hoard of coins found in ruin Kao.III |
| IA.X.c.8 | Kaiyuan tongbao | 2.97 | 24 | misaligned | FAS | Hoard of coins found in ruin Kao.III |
| IA.X.c.9 | Kaiyuan tongbao | 2.76 | 24 | hole in flan, worn | FAS | Hoard of coins found in ruin Kao.III |
| IA.X.c.10 | Kaiyuan tongbao | 3.92 | 25 | – | FAS | Hoard of coins found in ruin Kao.III |
| IA.X.c.11 | Kaiyuan tongbao | 3.56 | 24 | – | FAS | Hoard of coins found in ruin Kao.III |
| IA.X.c.12 | Kaiyuan tongbao | 3.42 | 25 | misaligned | FAS | Hoard of coins found in ruin Kao.III |
| IA.X.c.13 | Kaiyuan tongbao | 3.47 | 24 | – | FAS | Hoard of coins found in ruin Kao.III |
| IA.X.c.14 | Kaiyuan tongbao | 3.92 | 25 | – | FAS | Hoard of coins found in ruin Kao.III |
| IA.X.c.15 | Kaiyuan tongbao | 2.72 | 23.5 | – | FAS | Hoard of coins found in ruin Kao.III |
| IA.X.c.16–27 | [missing: Kaiyuan tongbao] | – | – | – | FAS | Hoard of coins found in ruin Kao.III |
| IA.X.c.28–32 | [missing: Qianyuan zhongbao] | – | – | – | FAS | Hoard of coins found in ruin Kao.III |
| IA.X.c.33 | Jianzhong tongbao – small | 1.93 | 21 | red | FAS | Hoard of coins found in ruin Kao.III |
| IA.X.c.34–39 | [missing: Tang dynasty] | – | – | – | FAS | Hoard of coins found in ruin Kao.III |
| IA.X.c.40–61 | Chinese coins – Song dynasty | – | – | – | FAS | Hoard of coins found in ruin Kao.III |
| IA.X.d.1 | Sasanian drachm of Ohrmazd IV, AD 584 | 2.32 | 25×24 | – | pas | Purchased at Kara-khoja |
| IA.X.d.2 | Kaiyuan tongbao | 3.52 | 25 | misaligned | pas | Purchased at Kara-khoja |
| IA.X.d.3 | Kaiyuan tongbao | 2.52 | 23.5 | – | pas | Purchased at Kara-khoja |
| IA.X.d.4 | Gaochang jili | 10.24 | 2.55 | worn surface | pas | Purchased at Kara-khoja |
| IA.X.d.5–11 | Mongol coins | – | – | – | pas | Purchased at Kara-khoja |

### IA.XI: COPPER COINS PURCHASED AT TOYUK

| BM no. | Identification | Wt | Diam. | Notes | Acqn | Acquisition/Archaeological context |
|---|---|---|---|---|---|---|
| IA.XI.a.1 | Kaiyuan tongbao | 4.05 | 25.5 | – | p | Purchased at Toyuk |
| IA.XI.a.2 | Kaiyuan tongbao | 3.61 | 24.5 | – | p | Purchased at Toyuk |
| IA.XI.a.3 | Kaiyuan tongbao, small | 1.81 | 22 | – | p | Purchased at Toyuk |
| IA.XI.a.4 | Kaiyuan tongbao | 4.70 | 25 | – | p | Purchased at Toyuk |
| IA.XI.a.5 | Kaiyuan tongbao, small | 2.36 | 23 | holes in flan | p | Purchased at Toyuk |
| IA.XI.a.6 | Kaiyuan tongbao | 3.09 | 25 | – | p | Purchased at Toyuk |
| IA.XI.a.7 | Kaiyuan tongbao | 4.11 | 24.5 | corroded | p | Purchased at Toyuk |
| IA.XI.a.8 | Kaiyuan tongbao | 3.11 | 24.5 | – | p | Purchased at Toyuk |
| IA.XI.a.9 | Kaiyuan tongbao | 4.45 | 25 | – | p | Purchased at Toyuk |
| IA.XI.a.10 | Kaiyuan tongbao | 3.97 | 25 | – | p | Purchased at Toyuk |
| IA.XI.a.11 | Qianyuan zhongbao – large | 6.26 | 28 | hole in flan, misaligned | p | Purchased at Toyuk |
| IA.XI.a.12 | [missing: Qianyuan zhongbao] | – | – | – | p | Purchased at Toyuk |
| IA.XI.a.13–18 | Chinese coins – Song dynasty | – | – | – | p | Purchased at Toyuk |
| IA.XI.a.19–32 | [extra: Chinese coins – Qing dynasty] | – | – | – | p | Purchased at Toyuk |

### IA.XII: COINS FROM TOMBS AT ASTANA

| BM no. | Identification | Wt | Diam. | Notes | Acqn | Acquisition/Archaeological context |
|---|---|---|---|---|---|---|
| IA.XII.a.1 | imitation of Byzantine coin | 0.48 | 11 | pierced at top | FAS | Found in mouth of body in Tomb Ast.i.3 |
| IA.XII.a.2 | Sasanian coin of Ohrmazd IV of Nahr Tire (Khuzistan) or Narmashir (Kirman) mint, AD 588 | 1.84 | 29×28 | light | FAS | Found over eyes of body in Tomb Ast.i.3 |
| IA.XII.a.3 | imitation/fantasy based on Sasanian coin | 2.95 | 31x30 | – | FAS | Found over eyes of body in Tomb Ast.i.3 |
| IA.XII.a.4 | Changping wuzhu (issued from AD 553) | 2.45 | 23.5 | – | FAS | Found in Tomb Ast.i.3 |
| IA.XII.b.1 | Imitation of Byzantine coin, 5–6th c. | 0.59 | 16.5 | hole in flan | FAS | Found in mouth of male in Tomb Ast.i.5 |
| IA.XII.c.1 | imitation of Byzantine coin, 5–6th c. | 0.85 | 16 | uniface | FAS | Found in mouth of female in Tomb Ast.i.6 |
| IA.XII.c.2 | Wuzhu – Sui or N. Wei | 2.92 | 23.5 | (H: 8.5) | FAS | Found near head of female in Tomb Ast.i.6 |
| IA.XII.c.3 | Wuzhu – Sui or N. Wei | 2.33 | 23 | (H: 8.5) | FAS | Found near head of female in Tomb Ast.i.6 |
| IA.XII.d.1 | Kaiyuan tongbao, small | 2.48 | 22.5 | – | FAS | Found at entrance to Tomb Ast.iii.2 |
| IA.XII.e.1 | [missing: Sasanian fragments] | – | – | – | FAS | Found in mouth of body in Tomb Ast.v.2 |
| IA.XII.f.1–3 | [extra: 3 imitation Chinese coins – round with square hole, each pierced twice, gold plated] | 0.80<br>0.62<br>0.65 | 20<br>20.5<br>20 | (H: 7) pierced twice<br>(H: 5.5×7) pierced twice<br>(H: 7.5) pierced twice | FAS | Found in tomb Ast.i.3.06 at the Astana cemetery. Not in List of Coins |

### IA.XIII: COPPER COINS FOUND AT YINGPAN SITE

| BM no. | Identification | Wt | Diam. | Notes | Acqn | Acquisition/Archaeological context |
|---|---|---|---|---|---|---|
| IA.XIII.a.1 | Wuzhu, small | 2.21 | 21 | (H: 7) | FAS | Found near main Stupa, Ying.I |
| IA.XIII.a.2 | Wuzhu, small | 1.70 | 22 | (H: 7.5) | FAS | Found on Tati E of Ying.II |
| IA.XIII.a.3 | Chinese – lead 'coin' | 6.51 | 22.5 | corroded | FAS | Found near shrine, Ying.II |

### A.XIV: COPPER COIN FOUND AT WATCH-STATION Y.i (KURGHAN)

| BM no. | Identification | Wt | Diam. | Notes | Acqn | Acquisition/Archaeological context |
|---|---|---|---|---|---|---|
| IA.XIV.a.1 | Kai[yuan] tongbao | 1.63 | – | 2 frags | FAS | Found at watch-station Y.i (Kurghan) |

### IA.XV: COPPER COINS OBTAINED AT KUCHA

| BM no. | Identification | Wt | Diam. | Notes | Acqn | Acquisition/Archaeological context |
|---|---|---|---|---|---|---|
| IA.XV.a.1 | Sino-Kharoshthi coin (Cribb 2) | 3.74 | 22 | – | F or p | Obtained at Kucha |
| IA.XV.a.2 | Sino-Kharoshthi coin (Cribb 2) | 4.33 | 17 | – | F or p | Obtained at Kucha |
| IA.XV.a.3 | Sino-Kharoshthi coin (Cribb 1–6) | 3.12 | 20×21 | pierced at centre | F or p | Obtained at Kucha |
| IA.XV.a.4 | Sino-Kharoshthi coin (Cribb 2) | 3.54 | 20 | – | F or p | Obtained at Kucha |
| IA.XV.a.5 | Sino-Kharoshthi coin (Cribb 2) | 4.66 | 21 | – | F or p | Obtained at Kucha |
| IA.XV.a.6 | Sino-Kharoshthi coin (Cribb 5–6) | 5.32 | 21×22 | – | F or p | Obtained at Kucha |
| IA.XV.a.7 | [missing: Sino-Kharoshthi coin] | – | – | – | F or p | Obtained at Kucha |
| IA.XV.a.8 | [missing: Chinese] | – | – | – | F or p | Obtained at Kucha |
| IA.XV.a.9 | Wuzhu – full size | 1.65 | 26 | (H: 10) frag. | F or p | Obtained at Kucha |
| IA.XV.a.10 | Wuzhu – full size | 2.89 | 26 | (H: 9.5) | F or p | Obtained at Kucha |
| IA.XV.a.11 | Wuzhu – full size | 1.88 | 25 | (H: 9.5) 2 frags | F or p | Obtained at Kucha |
| IA.XV.a.12 | Wuzhu | 2.73 | 26 | (H: 9) | F or p | Obtained at Kucha |
| IA.XV.a.13 | 'Wuzhu' – illegible | 1.18 | 17 | (H: 8.5) | F or p | Obtained at Kucha |
| IA.XV.a.14 | Wuzhu | 1.63 | 19 | (H: 9) coin + frag. together | F or p | Obtained at Kucha |
| IA.XV.a.15 | [missing: Wuzhu] | – | – | – | F or p | Obtained at Kucha |
| IA.XV.a.16 | Qiuci wuzhu – Qiuci script only | 1.01 | 16 | (H: 6) | F or p | Obtained at Kucha |
| IA.XV.a.17 | Qiuci wuzhu – Qiuci script only | 0.77 | 14 | (H: 6) | F or p | Obtained at Kucha |
| IA.XV.a.18 | Qiuci wuzhu – Qiuci script only | 2.13 | 20.5 | (H: 8.5) | F or p | Obtained at Kucha |
| IA.XV.a.19 | Kaiyuan tongbao, crescent above hole on rev. | 3.64 | 24.5 | misaligned | F or p | Obtained at Kucha |
| IA.XV.a.20 | Qianyuan zhongbao – large | 7.01 | 30 | forced hole | F or p | Obtained at Kucha |
| IA.XV.a.21 | Qianyuan zhongbao – large | 7.45 | 28 | – | F or p | Obtained at Kucha |
| IA.XV.a.22 | Qianyuan zhongbao – large | 6.67 | 29.5 | damaged | F or p | Obtained at Kucha |
| IA.XV.a.23 | Jianzhong tongbao, large | 2.41 | 22 | – | F or p | Obtained at Kucha |
| IA.XV.a.24 | Chinese coin – Song dynasty | – | – | – | F or p | Obtained at Kucha |

| | | | | | | |
|---|---|---|---|---|---|---|
| IA.XV.b.1–5 | Islamic coins | – | – | – | p | Allegedly from S of Yulduz-bagh |

| | | | | | | |
|---|---|---|---|---|---|---|
| IA.XV.c.1 | Sino-Kharoshthi coin (Cribb 2) | 4.16 | 20 | – | p | Allegedly from Yulduz-bagh sites |
| IA.XV.c.2 | Sino-Kharoshthi coin (Cribb 1–6) | 1.89 | 17 | 1 | p | Allegedly from Yulduz-bagh sites |
| IA.XV.c.3.a–b | Sino-Kharoshthi coin (Cribb 2–6) | 3.76 | 21 | 2 coins + frag. together | p | Allegedly from Yulduz-bagh sites |
| IA.XV.c.4 | Wuzhu – full size | 2.21 | 21 | (H: 10.5) | p | Allegedly from Yulduz-bagh sites |

| BM no. | Identification | Wt | Diam. | Notes | Acqn | Acquisition/Archaeological context |
|---|---|---|---|---|---|---|
| IA.XV.c.5 | Wuzhu – full size | 1.45 | 26 | damaged, red | p | Allegedly from Yulduz-bagh sites |
| IA.XV.c.6 | Wuzhu – full size | 1.73 | 21 | (H: 8.5) | p | Allegedly from Yulduz-bagh sites |
| IA.XV.c.7 | Wuzhu – small | 2.03 | 24.5 | (H: 9.5) | p | Allegedly from Yulduz-bagh sites |
| IA.XV.c.8 | Wuzhu – without full rim | 1.52 | 25 | (H: 9.5) damaged, holes in flan | p | Allegedly from Yulduz-bagh sites |
| IA.XV.c.9 | Wuzhu – full size | 3.26 | 26 | (H: 9) | p | Allegedly from Yulduz-bagh sites |
| IA.XV.c.10 | Wuzhu – clipped, cutting through inscription | 1.28 | 23 | (H: 9.5) faint | p | Allegedly from Yulduz-bagh sites |
| IA.XV.c.11 | Wuzhu – clipped, cutting through inscription | 1.07 | 22.5 | (H: 9.5) red | p | Allegedly from Yulduz-bagh sites |
| IA.XV.c.12 | Wuzhu | 2.44 | 24 | (H: 10) 2 frags, damaged edges | p | Allegedly from Yulduz-bagh sites |
| IA.XV.c.13 | 'Wuzhu' – illegible | 2.18 | 23 | (H: 9.5) 3 frags (= 1 coin) | p | Allegedly from Yulduz-bagh sites |
| IA.XV.c.14–15 | [missing: Wuzhu] | – | – | – | p | Allegedly from Yulduz-bagh sites |
| IA.XV.c.16 | 'Wuzhu' – illegible | 1.23 | 20 | (H: 9) 2 frags (= 1 coin) | p | Allegedly from Yulduz-bagh sites |
| IA.XV.c.17 | Wuzhu – clipped, cutting through inscription | 1.12 | 22 | (H: 8.5) red | p | Allegedly from Yulduz-bagh sites |
| IA.XV.c.18 | Qiuci wuzhu – Chinese + Qiuci script on obv. | 1.48 | 20 | (H: 7.5) red | p | Allegedly from Yulduz-bagh sites |
| IA.XV.c.19 | Wuzhu – clipped, cutting through inscription | 1.34 | 19 | (H: 8.5) red, faint | p | Allegedly from Yulduz-bagh sites |
| IA.XV.c.20 | 'Wuzhu' – illegible | 1.32 | 18 | (H: 8.5) red, corroded | p | Allegedly from Yulduz-bagh sites |
| IA.XV.c.21 | Wuzhu | 1.07 | 17 | (H: 8.5) red, corroded | p | Allegedly from Yulduz-bagh sites |
| IA.XV.c.22–24 | [missing: Wuzhu] | – | – | – | p | Allegedly from Yulduz-bagh sites |

| | | | | | | |
|---|---|---|---|---|---|---|
| IA.XV.d.1–2 | [missing: Wuzhu] | – | – | – | p | Allegedly from Dawan kum Tati sites |
| IA.XV.d.3–12 | [missing: Wuzhu] | – | | | p | Allegedly from Dawan kum Tati sites |
| IA.XV.d.13 | [missing: Chinese coin – Qing dynasty | – | | | p | Allegedly from Dawan kum Tati sites |

## IA.XVI: COPPER COINS FOUND AT SITES WEST OF KUCHA

| BM no. | Identification | Wt | Diam. | Notes | Acqn | Acquisition/Archaeological context |
|---|---|---|---|---|---|---|
| IA.XVI.a.1 | Wu[zhu] | 0.60 | – | frag. | FAS | Found at Tajik |
| IA.XVI.a.2 | 'Wuzhu' – illegible | 1.08 | 20 | (H: 9.5) lop-sided, red | FAS | Found at Tajik |
| IA.XVI.a.3 | Wuzhu – full size | 1.66 | 25 | (H: 10) faint | FAS | Found at Tajik |

| | | | | | | |
|---|---|---|---|---|---|---|
| IA.XVI.b.1 | Dali yuanbao – small | 2.24 | 22 | – | FAS | Found at ruin T.A.I, Toghrak-akin site |

| | | | | | | |
|---|---|---|---|---|---|---|
| IA.XVI.c.1 | 'Wuzhu'– illegible | 0.96 | 17 | (H: 8) corroded | FAS | Found at Cave T.A.IV, Toghrak-akin site |
| IA.XVI.c.2 | Kaiyuan tongbao, crescent above hole on rev. | 4.37 | 26 | – | FAS | Found at Cave T.A.IV, Toghrak-akin site |

| BM no. | Identification | Wt | Diam. | Notes | Acqn | Acquisition/Archaeological context |
|---|---|---|---|---|---|---|
| IA.XVI.c.3 | Dali yuanbao | 2.98 | 22 | – | FAS | Found at Cave T.A.IV, Toghrak-akin site |
| IA.XVI.c.4 | [extra: Dali yuanbao] | 2.76 | 22 | holes in flan | FAS | Found at Cave T.A.IV, Toghrak-akin site |
| IA.XVI.c.5 | Jianzhong tongbao | 2.95 | 21.5 | misaligned | FAS | Found at Cave T.A.IV, Toghrak-akin site |
| IA.XVI.c.6 | Jianzhong tongbao | 2.00 | 21 | misaligned | FAS | Found at Cave T.A.IV, Toghrak-akin site |
| IA.XVI.c.7 | Jianzhong tongbao | 2.69 | 21 | forced hole | FAS | Found at Cave T.A.IV, Toghrak-akin site |
| IA.XVI.c.8 | Jianzhong tongbao | 2.43 | 21.5 | – | FAS | Found at Cave T.A.IV, Toghrak-akin site |
| IA.XVI.c.9 | Jianzhong tongbao | 3.62 | 21 | – | FAS | Found at Cave T.A.IV, Toghrak-akin site |
| IA.XVI.c.10 | Jianzhong tongbao | 3.17 | 23 | – | FAS | Found at Cave T.A.IV, Toghrak-akin site |
| IA.XVI.c.11 | Jianzhong tongbao | 2.30 | 21 | – | FAS | Found at Cave T.A.IV, Toghrak-akin site |
| IA.XVI.c.12 | Jianzhong tongbao | 1.99 | 21.5 | misaligned | FAS | Found at Cave T.A.IV, Toghrak-akin site |
| IA.XVI.c.13 | Jianzhong tongbao | 2.22 | 21.5 | – | FAS | Found at Cave T.A.IV, Toghrak-akin site |
| IA.XVI.c.14 | Jianzhong tongbao | 2.14 | 21 | misaligned | FAS | Found at Cave T.A.IV, Toghrak-akin site |
| IA.XVI.c.15 | Jianzhong tongbao | 2.62 | 22.5 | misaligned, damaged | FAS | Found at Cave T.A.IV, Toghrak-akin site |
| IA.XVI.c.16 | Jianzhong tongbao | 2.13 | 21 | – | FAS | Found at Cave T.A.IV, Toghrak-akin site |
| IA.XVI.c.17 | Coin with single character 'zhong' | 1.65 | 20.5 | – | FAS | Found at Cave T.A.IV, Toghrak-akin site |
| IA.XVI.c.18 | Jianzhong tongbao | 2.46 | 21 | – | FAS | Found at Cave T.A.IV, Toghrak-akin site |
| IA.XVI.c.19 | [extra: Jianzhong tongbao] | 2.24 | 21 | misaligned | FAS | Found at Cave T.A.IV, Toghrak-akin site |
| IA.XVI.c.20 | [extra: Jianzhong tongbao] | 2.62 | 21 | – | FAS | Found at Cave T.A.IV, Toghrak-akin site |
| IA.XVI.c.21 | Coin with single character 'yuan' | 1.96 | 20 | damaged | FAS | Found at Cave T.A.IV, Toghrak-akin site |
| IA.XVI.c.22 | Jianzhong tongbao | 2.08 | 21 | hole in flan | FAS | Found at Cave T.A.IV, Toghrak-akin site |
| IA.XVI.c.23 | Coin with single character 'zhong' | 1.93 | 21 | – | FAS | Found at Cave T.A.IV, Toghrak-akin site |
| IA.XVI.c.24 | Coin with single character 'yuan' | 2.01 | 21 | – | FAS | Found at Cave T.A.IV, Toghrak-akin site |
| IA.XVI.c.25 | Coin with single character 'zhong' | 2.89 | 21 | – | FAS | Found at Cave T.A.IV, Toghrak-akin site |
| IA.XVI.c.26 | Coin with single character 'yuan' | 1.94 | 20 | – | FAS | Found at Cave T.A.IV, Toghrak-akin site |
| IA.XVI.c.27 | Wuzhu | 1.20 | 22.5 | (H: 9.5) red, damaged | FAS | Found at Cave T.A.IV, Toghrak-akin site |
| IA.XVI.d.1 | [missing: Kaiyuan tongbao] | – | – | – | FAS | Found at Dawan kum Tati |

### IA.XVII: COINS FOUND AT SISTAN SITES, PERSIA

| BM no. | Identification | Wt | Diam. | Notes | Acqn | Acquisition/Archaeological context |
|---|---|---|---|---|---|---|
| IA.XVII.a.1 | Sasanian drachm of Queen Boran, AD 630 | – | – | – | FAS | Found at foot of rotunda, Pai-kash-i-Rustam |

| | | | | | | |
|---|---|---|---|---|---|---|
| IA.XVII.b.1–2 | Islamic coins | – | – | – | FAS | Found at Machi site |

| | | | | | | |
|---|---|---|---|---|---|---|
| IA.XVII.c.1–13 | Islamic coins | – | – | – | FAS | Found at Machi site |

### IA.XVIII: MERDEK-SHAHRI (KORLA)

| BM no. | Identification | Wt | Diam. | Notes | Acqn | Acquisition/Archaeological context |
|---|---|---|---|---|---|---|
| IA.XVIII.a.1 | [extra: Wuzhu – full size] | 2.38 | 25 | (H: 9.5) | p | Allegedly from Merdek-Shahri, purchased at Korla |

### THE FOLLOWING COINS WERE NOT INCLUDED IN THE LIST OF COINS

| BM no. | Identification | Wt | Diam. | Notes | Acqn | Acquisition/Archaeological context |
|---|---|---|---|---|---|---|
| IA.x.1–29 | [extra: Islamic coins] | – | – | – | – | (x.1– 42) found in metal tin marked [Har.1]. |
| IA.x.30 | [extra: Sino-Kharoshthi coin] | 2.23 | 20×18 | – | – | (x.1– 42) found in metal tin marked [Har.1]. |
| IA.x.31 | [extra: 'Wuzhu' – illegible] | 1.13 | 20×21 | (H: 9.5) corroded, lop-sided | – | (x.1– 42) found in metal tin marked [Har.1]. |
| IA.x.32 | [extra: Qianyuan zhongbao – small] | 2.76 | 21.5 | – | – | (x.1– 42) found in metal tin marked [Har.1]. |
| IA.x.33–41 | [extra: Chinese coins – Song dynasty] | – | – | – | – | (x.1– 42) found in metal tin marked [Har.1]. |
| IA.x.42 | [extra: 1 furniture lock] | – | – | | – | (x.1– 42) found in metal tin marked [Har.1]. |

**Label: 'These 4 items found loose – no number'**

| BM no. | Identification | Wt | Diam. | Notes | Acqn | Acquisition/Archaeological context |
|---|---|---|---|---|---|---|
| IA.x.43–45 | Islamic coins | – | – | | – | – |
| IA.x.46 | Chinese coin – Song dynasty | – | – | – | – | – |

**Label: 'The following 4 coins were given an x. classif. (origin unknown) by Stein?'**

| BM no. | Identification | Wt | Diam. | Notes | Acqn | Acquisition/Archaeological context |
|---|---|---|---|---|---|---|
| IA.x.05–08 | Chinese coins – Song dynasty | – | – | – | – | Not known |

**Label: Other**

| BM no. | Identification | Wt | Diam. | Notes | Acqn | Acquisition/Archaeological context |
|---|---|---|---|---|---|---|
| – | Dali yuanbao – large | 3.94 | 24 | misaligned | – | Not known |

## SUMMARY OF STEIN'S LISTS OF COINS

### *ANCIENT KHOTAN*

AK.I Coins from Togujai, Moji
AK.II Coins purchased at Yotkan
AK.III Coins purchased at Khotan, most of them probably from Yotkan
AK.IV Coins said to have been found at Chalma-kazan
AK.V Coins from Dandan-Uiliq
AK.VI Copper coins found at Rawak beyond Dandan-Uiliq
AK.VII Copper coins found at Niya site
AK.VIII Copper coins found at Endere site
AK.IX Copper coins found at Kara-dong site
AK.X Copper coins found at Uzun Tati site
AK.XI Copper coins from Hanguya site
AK.XII Copper coins from Tam-Öghil
AK.XIII Copper coins from Ak-sipil site
AK.XIV Copper coins from Rawak stupa and vicinity
AK.XV Copper coins found at Jumbe-kum site
AK.XVI Copper coins found near Kara-döbe
AK.XVII Copper coins said to come from Mazar Tagh, near lower Yurung-kash
Kh.002 Purchased in Khotan

### *SERINDIA*

S.I Coins obtained at Yarkand
S.II Coins purchased at Karghalik
S.III Coins collected from Togujai, Moji
S.IV Coins collected within Khotan oasis
S.IV.A Coins purchased at or from Yotkan site
S.IV.B Purchased at Khotan, most probably brought from Yotkan
S.IV.C Coins of miscellaneous origin purchased at Khotan
S.IV.D Copper coins brought to Khotan from tati sites east of Yurung-kash
S.V Copper coins found at desert sites north of Jiya
S.VI Copper coins found at Ak-terek site
S.VII Copper coins found at Khadalik and neighbouring sites
S.VII.a–c Khadalik
S.VII.d Kighillik
S.VII.e Khadalik
S.VII.f Balawaste
S.VII.g Mazar-toghrak
S.VIII Copper coins found at Niya site
S.IX Copper coins found at Endere site
S.X Copper coins collected at Vash-shahri site
S.XI Copper coins found at Loulan sites
S.XI.A Coins from Loulan station L.A.
S.XI.B Coins from ruined site L.B.
S.XII Copper coins found at Merdek-tim site
S.XIII Copper coins found at Miran site
S.XIV Copper coins found or collected at Nanhu
S.XV Copper coins found along ancient *limes* of Tun-huang
S.XVI Copper coins found at So-yang-ch'êng site
S.XVII Copper coin found at Hei-shui-kuo site, west of Kan-chou (Ganzhou)
S.XVIII Copper coin found east of Chong Hassar, Turfan
S.XIX Copper coins found at Yar-khoto, Turfan
S.XX Copper coin found on rampart of ruined fort near Ushak-tal, Kara-shahr
S.XXI Copper coin found at Baghdad-shahri site, Kara-shahr
S.XXII Copper coins excavated at Ming-oi site, north of Shor-chuk
S.XXIII Copper coins found near ruin KA.I, Karadong
S.XXIV Copper coins found at Farhad-beg-Yailaki site
S.XXV Copper coin found in ruined shrine, Kara Yantak
S.XXVI West Lach
S.XXVI Copper coins found at, or brought from, tati sites, northwest of Domoko
S.XXVII Copper coins brought as from Chalma-kazan
S.XXVIII Copper coin found at Kara-sai site
S.XXIX Coins found at, or near, Tarishlak site
S.XXX Copper coins found at, or brought from, Mazar Tagh site
S.XXXI Copper coins found at, or brought from, desert sites south of Kelpin
S.XXXII Copper and silver coins found on tatis north of Tumshuk
S.XXXIII Copper coins brought from Tokuz-sarai ruins, Tumshuk

### *INNERMOST ASIA*

IA.I Coins found at, or brought from, sites between Kashgar and Maral-bashi
IA.II Coins brought from Mazar Tagh site
IA.III Coins collected at or from Khotan
IA.IV Coins of miscellaneous origin
IA.IV.A Coins acquired at Khotan town
IA.IV.B Coins purchased from Badruddin Khan
IA.IV Coins collected from or near Domoko
IA.V Copper coins from Niya site, Charchan and Vash-shahri
IA.VI Copper coins found at Lop Desert sites A–F
IA.VI.A Coins from ruined sites L.K. (ruined fort) and L.M. (settlement site supporting L.K. fort)
IA.VI.B Coins from Loulan station L.A. or vicinity
IA.VI.C Coins from cemetery L.C. and its vicinity
IA.VI.D Coins from L.E. castrum and mesa L.F.
IA.VI.E Coins from minor sites L.D., L.G., L.I., L.J., L.Q.
IA.VI.F Coins found on Lop Desert marches
IA.VII Copper coins found along ancient Han *limes*
IA.VIII Copper coins found at or near Kharakhoto
IA.VIII.A Coins from ruined town of Kharakhoto
IA.VIII.B Coins from ruined settlements east of Kharakhoto
IA.VIII.C Coins from ruined fort of Aduna-kora
IA.IX Copper coins of Manchu dynasty found at Luotuocheng and Beiting
IA.X Coins excavated or purchased at Kara-khoja
IA.XI Copper coins purchased at Toyuk
IA.XII Coins from tombs at Astana
IA.XIII Copper coins found at Yingpan site
IA.XIV Copper coin found at watch-station Y.i (Kurghan)
IA.XV Copper coins obtained at Kucha
IA.XVI Copper coins found at sites west of Kucha
IA.XVII Coins found at Sistan sites, Persia
[IA.XVIII Merdek Shahri (Korla)]

# Part 2 The contexts of the coin-finds and Stein's interpretation of the numismatic evidence

Stein's Lists of Coins present the contexts of the finds in extremely concise form, and, of course, refer back to his detailed reports. Part 2 expands on the contexts in which Stein found, or otherwise acquired, the coins, and presents his comments on the numismatic evidence. It considers only the evidence, information and comments supplied by Stein in *Ancient Khotan*, *Serindia* and *Innermost Asia*. It follows the order of the Catalogue (which follows the order of the Lists of Coins) and is intended for use alongside Part 1. Here, as in Part 1, Stein's imperial measurements have not been adjusted.

#### ARRANGEMENT

Each entry has a maximum of two components:

1. **Site** gives very brief details of each site, and the key locations relevant to the coin finds. Full details of the sites, as described by Stein, can be found in his reports.
2. **Acquisition/archaeological context** refers specifically to the numismatic evidence, gives details of where the coins were found, or otherwise acquired, and presents Stein's interpretation of the numismatic evidence.

## ANCIENT KHOTAN

### *AK.I: COINS FROM TOGUJAI, MOJI (AK: 110–11, 113)*

**Site:** Stein described the Togujai site as lying three-quarters of a mile north of Guma Bazar, Khotan, 'an area of bare loess ground extending over about ¼ sq mile furrowed by the broad channels of a flood-water bed, and the banks thus formed covered with pottery débris'.

**Acquisition/archaeological context:** Coins purchased at site by Stein from the local beg and village headmen, who brought him bags full of coins, metal seals and bronze ornaments they had found there.

### *AK.II: COINS PURCHASED AT YOTKAN (AK: 191–2, 203–6)*

**Site:** Yotkan is the collective name for a group of hamlets lying *c.*5 miles west of Yangi-shahr, Khotan. A ravine ('the Yotkan Yar') passes through the village lands, cutting deep into the loess soil. The Yotkan site lies just south of the northernmost hamlet, Khalche. The location of the site matches the description of Yutian, the ancient capital of the Khotan kingdom, given in the *Beishi*.

Stein described the site as 'a large depressed area sunk from 20–30 ft below the level of the surrounding ground, forming an irregular oblong with sides each about half a mile in length. Except where the Yotkan-Yar enters and leaves it, this depression proved to be bordered everywhere by steep banks cut into what at first seemed natural loess, but which on closer examination showed, besides pure soil, layers full of pottery débris, ashes, decayed wood, and other decomposed matter.'

Villagers had been digging into the banks, and deeply embedded layers in search of gold, jade and other ornaments, since the 1860s, when little bits of gold started appearing in flood-water, and the Khotanese Governor Niaz Hakim Beg sent large parties of men to wash and dig for gold at Yotkan. 'No coins or solid ornaments of gold and silver were admitted to be found now, though the discovery of such precious articles was readily acknowledged for the early years of the working.' The purchase of all gold produced in Khotan and Keriya was a monopoly of the Chinese administration, which paid diggers 110 tangas per *ser* of gold, significantly below the market value of 138 tangas. Consequently, any finds of value would disappear on to the black market.

**Acquisition/archaeological context:**

**AK.II.a:** Purchased at Yotkan site, 16 Oct 1900.

**AK.II.b:** Purchased at Yotkan site, 27 Nov 1900.

**AK.II.c:** Purchased at Yotkan site, 28 Apr 1901.

**AK.II.d:** Purchased at Yotkan site, 29 Apr 1901.

### *AK.III: COINS PURCHASED AT KHOTAN, MOST OF THEM PROBABLY FROM YOTKAN (AK: 203–6, 233)*

**Site:** See AK.II.

**Acquisition/archaeological context:** 'I purchased through Munshi Badruddin, the Ak-sakal or headman of the Afghan traders at Khotan, and some other agents, whatever antiques were traceable in the Bazars of Khotan. It is certain that the latter receive by far the greater part of their supply in antiques such as ancient coins, cut stones, ornamented pottery, directly from the diggings of Yotkan, and relatively little from those professional "treasure-seekers" who annually in the winter months visit the old sites in the desert around the [Khotan] oasis, or else from chance finds elsewhere . . . But full certainty can never be obtained about the find-place of any objects which have once found their way into a Turkestan Bazar, and consequently it would not be safe to base far-reaching arguments on any individual article procured through such channels. The distinctive marking of all batches of antiques purchased by me either at Yotkan or in Khotan town will render this exercise of critical caution easy.'

**AK.III.g:** Presented by Wang Daloi, 23 Nov 1900, as coming from Yotkan. Stein noted that Wang Daloi, a jade-trader serving as his guide, had mixed up the Tang dynasty coins he found at the Jamada site with those he had collected at Yotkan and elsewhere.

**AK.III.m:** Said to come from Halal-bagh.

### *AK.IV: COINS SAID TO HAVE BEEN FOUND AT CHALMA-KAZAN (AK: 233–4)*

**Site:** Stein described the Chalma-kazan site as lying 13 miles from Yotkan, being a ruined area about one and a half miles wide, between the west bank of the Yurung-kash River and the

foot of a low gravel ridge, flanking the debouchment of the river. The remains of a stupa at the centre of the site had already been disturbed by treasure-seekers. The site was now visited only by jade-diggers, and Stein was not able to ascertain any further information about the site.
**Acquisition/archaeological context:**
**AK.IV.a:** Presented by Wang Daloi, 23 Nov 1900.
**AK.IV.b:** Purchased as coming from Chalma-kazan.

***AK.V: COINS FROM DANDAN-UILIQ (AK: 283)***
**Site:** Dandan-Uiliq ('the houses with ivory'). Stein described the site as lying on high land between the Yurung-kash and Keriya rivers. Once a large site, it had been badly damaged by wind erosion. Stein found the remains of shrines and dwellings, and identified the Dandan-Uiliq site as being the Lixie mentioned in excavated documents (AK: 267). Documents found at Dandan-Uiliq included Brahmi manuscripts, Chinese manuscripts including many loan documents, dated AD 780s, referring to Chinese coins; and a letter of the early eighth century written by a Persian-speaking Jew from Tabaristan, relating to business affairs.
**Acquisition/archaeological context:** Stein and hired labour collected 17 Chinese coins at the site, but exact find-spots are not indicated in the text.
**AK.V.a:** Brought by Turdi, 17 Nov 1900.
**AK.V.b:** Found at site.

***AK.VI: COPPER COINS FOUND AT RAWAK BEYOND DANDAN-UILIQ (AK: 306)***
**Site:** Rawak ('high mansion'). Stein described the site as lying north of Dandan-Uiliq, and consisting of a small stupa, a small round building and dwellings. Much of the site was buried under sand dunes. Kharoshthi documents were found here.
**Acquisition/archaeological context:** 'The coins picked up near the ruins afford useful chronological guidance. Of the six coins found five were small copper pieces without legends, of the type current under both Han dynasties and probably for some time later, while the sixth bears the mark of the K'ai-yüan period (713–741 AD). From the absence of any later issues, such as turned up at Dandan-Uiliq, and from the predominance of pieces without legends, I am inclined to infer that the settlement represented by Rawak was probably deserted somewhat earlier than that of Dandan-Uiliq. For this we might account without difficulty by its outlying and hence more exposed position' (AK: 306).

***AK.VII: COPPER COINS FOUND AT NIYA SITE (AK: 369)***
**Site:** Settlement site, now in the desert, beyond the Niya River (AK: 316–416). Stupa at centre of site. Chinese and Kharoshthi documents were found at the site.
**N.v** was a small, detached structure that yielded many documents (records rather than correspondence).
**N.viii** was an ancient storeroom that yielded weapons and a small number of documents.
**Acquisition/archaeological context:** Stein and team found 16 coins at site. One coin was found en route from Imam Ja'far Sadiq (up to 24 miles south of the Niya site) and cannot be associated with the Niya site.
**AK.VII.a:** Found near stupa, 28 Jan 1901.
**AK.VII.b:** Found west of stupa, 30 Jan 1901.
**AK.VII.c:** Found near ruin N.v, 7–8 Feb 1901.
**AK.VII.d:** Brought by Turdi to camp near N.v, 8 Feb 1901.
**AK.VII.e:** Found near ruin N.viii, 11 Feb 1901.
**AK.VII.f:** Found by Hassan Akhun c. 3 miles north of stupa, 1 Feb 1901.

***AK.VIII: COPPER COINS FOUND AT ENDERE SITE (AK: 429)***
**Site:** The Endere site lies midway between Niya and Charchan. In 1901 Stein found a Tang dynasty fort with circular circumvallation and stupa, and determined from Chinese graffiti dated AD 719 and manuscript remains in Brahmi, Tibetan and Chinese that the fort was occupied by a Chinese garrison during the early eighth century, and probably abandoned during the Tibetan occupation in the late eighth century (S: 276). In 1906 Stein found evidence, notably Kharoshthi tablets, proving that there had been re-occupation of this site. The earlier site had a small stupa, tower and dwellings, which had been abandoned and then later reoccupied (S: 277). The earlier period of occupation is represented by ruins south of the circular fort, by debris below the fort, by the great stupa north of the fort, and the circumvallation near it, by the fortified post and the traces of ancient dwellings at the southern end of the site. This earlier period of occupation probably ended in the late third or early fourth century, when Niya was abandoned. The circular fort with its small temple and Tibetan graffiti belong to the early eighth century (S: 286).
**Acquisition/archaeological context:** Eight Chinese coins were found within or near the fort, precise details not given.
**AK.VIII.a:** Found inside Endere Fort, 22–25 Feb 1901.
**AK.VIII.b:** Found near Endere Fort, 21–23 Feb 1901.

***AK.IX: COPPER COINS FOUND AT KARA-DONG SITE (AK: 447)***
**Site:** Kara-dong ('black hillocks'). Desert site, 150 miles north of Keriya, halfway between the Tarim River and Khotan. The main ruin was a quadrangular building, which Stein suggested might have been a caravansarai. 'The resemblance in the construction of the houses and in the type of objects of daily use found there is sufficiently close to justify the attribution of the ruins approximately to the period when the Niya and Lou-lan sites were abandoned, i.e. the third–fourth centuries AD' (S: 1242).
**Acquisition/archaeological context:** 'It is important to note that of the five Chinese copper coins found among or near the débris of the rampart, all bearing marks of long circulation, two are wuzhu pieces, while the rest show no legend. I may conveniently mention here that, of the other nine coins picked up on eroded ground at some distance to the east and south of the ruin, one belongs to a wuzhu issue, the rest bearing no legend or being too defaced for identification' (AK: 447).
**AK.IX.a:** Found within ruined quadrangle, 13–15 Mar 1901.
**AK.IX.b:** Found near Kara-dong ruin, 15–17 Mar 1901.

***AK.X: COPPER COINS FOUND AT UZUN TATI SITE (AK: 461)***
**Site:** Uzun Tati ('the distant Tati'). Site consisted of several extensive patches of ground, covered with potsherds and other debris. Scanty remains of a few buildings, which were badly eroded and disturbed by treasure-seekers. Stein identified the site as Pimo, mentioned by Xuan Zang.
**Acquisition/archaeological context:** Stein found two copper coins here: one Chinese and one Islamic, both of the eleventh century.

### *AK.XI: COPPER COINS FROM HANGUYA SITE (AK: 469–71)*

**Site:** Hanguya was the easternmost of the ancient sites in the Khotan oasis, a Tati site covered in red potsherds. Remains of stupa damaged by erosion and treasure-seekers.

**Acquisition/archaeological context:** In November 1900 Stein had purchased in Khotan some coins said to have been found at Hanguya Tati. He noted 'if they [the Sino-Kharoshthi coins] were really found here they would prove great antiquity for the site, but the statement as to their origin could, as in most of such cases, not be depended upon with certainty' (AK: 469–71).

**AK.XI.a:** Found near Hanguya stupa ruin, 5 Apr 1901.

**AK.XI.b:** Said to have been brought from Hanguya Tati, purchased at Khotan, 18 Nov 1900.

### *AK.XII: COPPER COINS FROM TAM-ÖGHIL (AK: 472–3)*

**Site:** Stein described Tam-Öghil as a small site close to Ak-sipil, less than 3 miles from the right bank of the Yurung-kash River. 'Of the character of the settlement which once occupied the site marked by this layer of ancient rubbish accumulations, and of its extent southwards, nothing definite can be asserted' (AK: 472–3). (See also S.IV.D.)

**Acquisition/archaeological context:** Stein noted that the culture-strata at Tam-Öghil, which yielded leaf-gold, old coins and terracottas, had, since the 1880s, been worked under conditions exactly similar to those described at Yotkan. 'It is probable that the amount of leaf-gold washed out of the paying seam was declared to be less than at Yotkan, and the secondary products of antiques and occasional small finds of value are also, judging from general report, proportionately far rarer. However this may be, I succeeded, in spite of diligent inquiries both at the site and previously at Yurung-kash, in obtaining only a few specimens of antiques. The single coin obtained from a Tam-öghil villager was a small Chinese copper piece without legend, while among the other four purchased at Yurung-kash two are copper coins of the [Song dynasty] Yuanfeng period (1078–85)' (AK: 472–3). Clay moulds for casting small bronze objects were also found at Tam-Öghil (S: 100).

**AK.XII.a:** Purchased at site, 7 Apr 1901.

**AK.XII.b:** Said to have been obtained at Tam-Öghil, purchased at Yurung-kash, 4 Apr 1901.

### *AK.XIII: COPPER COINS FROM AK-SIPIL SITE (AK: 474–6)*

**Site:** Ak-sipil ('white wall'). Fort with circular or oval circumvallation. Remains of Buddhist shrine stand one and a half miles WSW of the fort.

**Acquisition/archaeological context:** Stein noted that 'Ak-sipil serves as a popular designation for the whole of the débris areas stretching north of the Yurung-kash and Hanguya. Hence the evidence of the coins and antiques sold to me at Khotan as coming from "Ak-sipil" would prove little or nothing for the age of this particular ruin, even if such statements could always be accepted with confidence' (AK: 476).

**AK.XIII.a:** Found on remains of Ak-sipil rampart, 8 Apr 1901.

**AK.XIII.b:** Said to have been found near Ak-sipil; purchased at Khotan, 17 Nov 1900.

**AK.XIII.c:** Said to have been brought from Ak-sipil Tati; purchased at Khotan, 19 Nov 1900.

### *AK.XIV: COPPER COINS FROM RAWAK STUPA AND VICINITY (AK: 500–1)*

**Site:** Rawak ('high mansion') Stupa/Vihara, not to be confused with the Rawak site, which is in a different location.

**Acquisition/archaeological context:** Stein wrote about coins found at the stupa: 'Sticking between the plaster of the base on its four sides and the decayed wood of the boarding, at heights varying from 1.5 to 2 ft, were found numerous copper coins, which, as far as they have not suffered too much from oxidization, can all be recognized as wuzhu pieces. On the south side twelve complete coins were recovered, with numerous fragments of others; on the east side fourteen, with some others which broke into fragments when I attempted to separate pieces which corrosion had stuck together. From the west came twenty-two, with more fragments (pl. LXXXIX, 19), while twelve were discovered on the north face. There could be no doubt that they had been slipped into the places where they were found, through small interstices of the boarding, manifestly as votive offerings, just like the pieces previously discovered in small cavities below images and underneath plaster mouldings.

'Most of the coins are in good preservation, apart from the oxidization they have undergone, and do not show any marks of long circulation previous to their deposition. Only current coins are likely to have been used for such humble votive gifts; and as no coin finds of a later type have come to my knowledge, we are justified in assuming that the latest known date of these coin-issues marks the lowest chronological limit for the abandonment of the shrine. This conclusion is supported by the evidence of eighteen coins picked up by my men between the dunes near the ruins, ten of which bear the legend wuzhu, while the rest are small square-holed coins without legend. The great find, previously mentioned, of a pot full of wuzhu coins at an eroded spot about one mile to the south-east also agrees with it.

'The wuzhu currency belongs properly to the period of the Former and Later Han dynasties. The rule of the second extended from 25 to 220 AD, but the issue of its coin types appears to have continued in China up to the close of the fourth century, if not to the advent of the Tangs. It is thus difficult to determine the date when the current use of wuzhu coins, whether imported from China or locally coined, is likely to have ceased in Khotan. There remain, however, two significant negative observations to guide us. On the one hand, the fact of the numerous coin finds of the Rawak Vihara not comprising a single later piece makes it probable that the date of these votive deposits could not have been removed by many centuries from the period of the Later Hans, when the wuzhu coinage was the recognized currency of the Chinese empire. On the other, the complete absence of Sino-Kharoshthi pieces seems to preclude the assumption that the shrine had existed in the first centuries of our era. The absence among the votive deposits of the earliest Chinese coin type, that without legend, points also in the same direction. Possibly the complete excavation of the Vihara may hereafter provide a more definite indication of date. But combining what evidence is at present available in the coins, the style of the sculptures, and such minor antiquarian indications as may be derived from the constructive plan and the materials of the ruins, we can scarcely assert more than that the extant shrine must have been abandoned at some period between the third and seventh centuries of our era.'

Stein heard of the discovery of a large pot of Chinese copper coins near the ruined stupa. The text (AK: 483) indicates that he purchased 78 wuzhu with few marks of wear, but only two groups (l–m) in the List of Coins correspond to that find. Perhaps Stein also included group (n) in his description here? The List of Coins indicates that he did not purchase the coins on the same day or in the same place.

**AK.XIV.a:** Found at southeast foot of stupa base, 13 Apr 1901.
**AK.XIV.b:** Found below relief R.xi, 12 Apr 1901.
**AK.XIV.c:** Found behind relief R.xxvii, 15 Apr 1901.
**AK.XIV.d:** Found in wall on north side of gateway, Rawak stupa court, 16 Apr 1901.
**AK.XIV.e:** Found at foot of statue R.lxix, 16 Apr 1901.
**AK.XIV.f:** Found on south side of small stupa base, 11 Apr 1901.
**AK.XIV.g:** Found on east side of small stupa base, 17 Apr 1901.
**AK.XIV.h:** Found on north side of small stupa base, 17 Apr 1901.
**AK.XIV.i:** Found on west side of small stupa base, 17 Apr 1901.
**AK.XIV.j:** Found between dunes near Rawak stupa, 11 Apr 1901.
**AK.XIV.k:** Found by labourers near Rawak camp, 15 Apr 1901.
**AK.XIV.l:** From large find made near Rawak stupa; purchased at Khotan, 30 Nov 1900.
**AK.XIV.m:** From large find made near Rawak stupa; purchased at Khotan, 6 Dec 1900.
**AKXIV.n:** Said to have been brought from Ak-sipil, Rawak and Jumbe-kum; purchased at Yurung-kash, 6 Apr 1901.

#### *AK.XV: COPPER COINS FOUND AT JUMBE-KUM SITE (AK: 502)*

**Site:** The Jumbe-kum site lies northeast of Khotan, c.4 miles northeast of Rawak: 'the site itself proved to be a débris-strewn Tati, with only the scantiest of structural remains'. Hard-stamped loess and remains of bricks indicated the remains of a structure, surrounded by potsherds at the surface. About two and a half miles to the northeast stood the remains of a small stupa.
**Acquisition/archaeological context:** Three small worn coins were picked up at the surface close to the brick remains, 14 Apr 1901.

#### *AK.XVI: COPPER COINS FOUND NEAR KARA-DÖBE (AK: 515)*

**Site:** Kara-döbe ('the black mound') was a tati site west of Kara-kash town, consisting of a stretch of eroded ground, covered in potsherds, covering about a mile north–south, with the remains of a stupa at the centre.
**Acquisition/archaeological context:** Found near Kara-döbe, 30 Apr 1901. 'Close by [to the decayed small mound of sun-dried bricks, known as the "tim" 8 ft square at its base] fragments of small Chinese copper coins, probably without legend, were picked up by my companions.'

#### *AK.XVII: COPPER COINS SAID TO COME FROM MAZAR-TAGH, NEAR LOWER YURUNG-KASH (AK: 314, 579)*

**Site:** The coins listed here did not come from the Mazar-tagh fort itself (see S.XXX) but from 'the small rocky hills, which as the last isolated remains of a completely decayed mountain range crop out of the desert near the courses of the Khotan and Yarkand rivers are everywhere known by the name of Mazar-tagh "the hill of the sacred shrine"' (AK: 314 n 12). 'My doubts about the provenance of the coin batch said to have come from Mazar-tagh and detailed in *Ancient Khotan* (p. 579) were fully justified' (S: 1279 n19).
**Acquisition/archaeological context:** Said to come from Mazar-tagh site, near lower Yurung-kash; purchased at Khotan, 18 Nov 1900.

#### *Kh.002: PURCHASED IN KHOTAN, 16 OCTOBER 1900 – NOT INCLUDED IN STEIN'S LIST OF COINS*

**Acquisition/archaeological context:** Purchased in Khotan, 16 October 1900.

### SERINDIA

#### *S.I: COINS OBTAINED AT YARKAND (S: 84)*

**Acquisition/archaeological context:** The Amban at Yarkand offered to Stein 'a representative set of ten specimens' (one Tang and nine Song dynasty coins) from a hoard of coins found near the official buildings of the District Magistrate, long before Stein's arrival. The Sino-Kharoshthi coin is not mentioned in the text.
**S.I.a:** Presented by Pên Da-rên, Amban of Yarkand, from a local find.
**S.I.b:** Purchased at Yarkand.

#### *S.II: COINS PURCHASED AT KARGHALIK*

**Acquisition/archaeological context:** The only reference to Stein's coin-purchasing at Karghalik is in *Ruins of Desert Cathay*, p. 141: 'An imposing posse of Hindu money-lenders which received me some three miles from the town showed that the business of these sharp Shikarpuris flourished more than ever. Since 1901 their community had increased by some thirty per cent of new arrivals . . . Among the Shikarpuris who subsequently in a solemn deputation came to pay their respects at my temporary quarters, there was one who had drifted to Karghalik from Bokhara some twenty years before. He was a queer-looking old man with the face of a harpy, more than a match for the cleverest of Turki debtors who may fall into his clutches. He had brought a good number of Bactrian, Arsacidian, and other Greek coins with him from Bokhara, – or had since been supplied with them by friends left behind there. Most of the silver pieces proved to be forgeries, and this, together with the big prices asked, prevented a business transaction.' The provenance of these coins is therefore unreliable.

#### *S.III: COINS COLLECTED FROM TOGUJAI, MOJI (S: 1312)*

**Site:** See AK.I.
**Acquisition/archaeological context:** ' The route [back to Khotan] was necessarily the same as I had first followed in 1900, and this enabled me to supplement the collection of small antiques from the old sites near Moji, already described in *Ancient Khotan*, by some additional specimens.' Although not specified, these finds were probably purchased.

#### *S.IV: COINS COLLECTED WITHIN KHOTAN OASIS (S: 101–2)*

**Acquisition/archaeological context:** Of these coins, Stein wrote: 'the value of the chronological evidence furnished by coins must obviously be much smaller in the case of Acquisitions by purchase than when coin finds can be authenticated at the site itself. At the time when these Acquisitions were made, my leisure did not suffice for more than a most cursory inspection . . . In order to obtain a safer basis for observations on this point I have thought it best here to leave aside the coins which I purchased at Khotan, but about the origin of which no information was available . . .

'The chronological range of the coins acquired from Yotkan, all copper, with the exception of a single piece in lead, agrees strikingly with that indicated by the collection which I obtained in 1900–1 and discussed in *Ancient Khotan* [p. 203] at some length. It extends from the Sino-Kharoshthi currency of Khotan, issued probably during the first few centuries of our era, down to pieces of the Song dynasty, the latest of these bearing the "nianhao" of AD 1078–86. In addition, the Indo-Scythian coinage is represented by two pieces of Kanishka (see pl. CXL, nos 9–10).

'While the total number of identified coins amounts to 337, the number of main issues represented is relatively small. Apart from the few non-Chinese pieces just mentioned, there are 47 coins of the local Sino-Kharoshthi type, bearing Chinese legends on the obverse and Indian Prakrit ones on the reverse (pl. CXL, nos 4, 6, 7). The early Chinese coinage, in the shape of wuzhu pieces such as were issued both under the Former and Later Han dynasties, takes up a large portion of the total with 113 specimens. It must, however, be noted that not less than 48 of these belong to a single hoard, the accidental discovery of which was bound to upset the usual proportion. To the Song and Sui dynasties of the fifth and sixth centuries AD Mr Allan ascribes three wuzhu pieces of a later type.

'Of the cash bearing the legend Kaiyuan tongbao (pl. CXL, no. 39), which was first introduced by Gaosu (AD 618–26) but was minted throughout the whole Tang period, there are only four specimens. On the other hand, the different issues showing the name of the Qianyuan period (AD 758–9) are represented by not less than 134 pieces. The last Tang nianhao which appears among these coins is that of Dali (AD 766–79), being found on twenty-eight pieces (pl. CXL, no. 47). (Song and Islamic coins)

'It is of some interest to compare the ratio in which the various issues are represented in this collection from Yotkan with that shown by the aggregate of the coin sets which were brought to me at Khotan avowedly from old sites beyond the north-eastern edge of the oasis, such as the "Tatis" of Ak-sipil and Hanguya. Here a total of 124 identified pieces comprises 1 coin of Wang Mang (AD 14–19; pl. CXL, no. 14), 9 Sino-Kharoshthi coins, 8 wuzhu coins of Han times, 26 clipped wuzhu probably of the fifth century AD, 17 Tang coins (mainly Qianyuan), 17 Song coins, and 46 coins of various early Islamic rulers. This analysis demonstrates a markedly greater proportion of late coins for these "Tati" sites. This is fully in keeping with what other antiquarian evidence indicates as to their time of abandonment. This fact, coupled with the close agreement shown between my present and former collections from Yotkan, must add weight to the numismatic evidence which even such chance Acquisitions afford for the history of the ancient capital.'

#### *S.IV.A: COINS PURCHASED AT OR FROM YOTKAN SITE (S: 97)*

**Site:** See AK.II and AK.III.

**Acquisition/archaeological context:** Stein wrote: 'All objects acquired by me either personally or through my trustworthy local factotum Badruddin Khan, the headman of the Indian and Afghan traders, as avowedly coming from Yotkan bear the distinguishing mark of *Yo.* in the descriptive list . . . But even in the case of these objects the evidence as to their provenance can obviously not claim the same value as if they were finds resulting from systematic exploration on the spot. As regards antiques acquired through other channels there is still greater need for caution before making any individual piece a basis for antiquarian argument.'

**S.IV.A.a:** Purchased 11 Aug 1906.
**S.IV.A.b:** Purchased 12 Sept 1906.
**S.IV.A.c:** Presented by Khuda-berdi, Yüz-bashi of Yotkan.
**S.IV.A.d:** Purchased 29 July 1906.
**S.IV.A.e:** From a hoard of copper coins found at Yotkan.

#### *S.IV.B: PURCHASED AT KHOTAN, MOST PROBABLY BROUGHT FROM YOTKAN*

**Site:** See AK.II and AK.III.

**Acquisition/archaeological context:** The group of coins S.IV.B.j.22 to S.IV.B.l.32 was acquired by Stein at Yotkan in July 1908 (S: 1319) but they were not included in the original inventories.

#### *S.IV.C: COINS OF MISCELLANEOUS ORIGIN PURCHASED AT KHOTAN (S: 1341–2)*

**Site:** Stein described Halal-bagh as a large collection of hamlets SE of Yotkan. Kum-bagh and Tar-bogaz are not mentioned in the text.

**Acquisition/archaeological context:** Of miscellaneous origin, purchased at Khotan: 36 wuzhu coins from Halal-bagh, a region associated in local legend with treasure seeking operations in the late fifteenth and early sixteenth centuries, which had yielded precious stones, gold and silver (AK: 226–7); 10 Qianyuan zhongbao coins allegedly from a hoard found at Kum-bagh, Tosalla canton; 36 Islamic coins allegedly found south of Tar-bogaz, Zawa canton.

**S.IV.C.g:** From Badruddin Khan.
**S.IV.C.h:** From find at Halal-bagh.
**S.IV.C.i:** From hoard found at Kum-bagh, Tosalla canton.
**S.IV.C.k:** Said to have been found south of Tar-bogaz, Zawa canton.

#### *S.IV.D: COPPER COINS BROUGHT TO KHOTAN FROM TATI SITES EAST OF YURUNG KASH (S: 102)*

**S.IV.D.a:** Collected by 'treasure-seekers' of Tam-Öghil (see AK.XII).

**S.IV.D.b:** Said to have been found north of Jiya and Suya. Stein described Jiya as a fertile canton northeast of Khotan, with Suya being one of the last villages before the desert, en route to the Rawak stupa (S: 127–31).

**S.IV.D.c:** From site south of Sampula. No further details of site given.

**S.IV.D.d:** Said to have been found at, or near, Kine-tokmak (S: 133). Other finds allegedly from Kine-tokmak include small bronze objects, terracotta monkeys and seals (see S.V.b).

**S.IV.D.e:** Said to have come from Tatis of Ak-terek (see S.VI).

### *S.V: COPPER COINS FOUND AT DESERT SITES NORTH OF JIYA (S: 129–31)*

**Sites:**

**Kök-kumarish** was the name given by fuel-collectors to a small tati site, with remains of stupa and shrine, about four miles southeast of Rawak (S: 129).

**Kine-tokmak** was a small tati site with remains of a stupa and dwellings, about four miles southeast of Rawak Vihara. North

of Kine-tokmak were the remains of timber and wattle walls: in one of the rooms was a row of circular holes in the plaster flooring, once occupied by large jars (S: 131).
**Acquisition/archaeological context:**
**S.V.a:** Found at Kök-kumarish. Found at Kök-kumarish. 'I also picked up several tiny Chinese coins, without legend and showing much clipped rims, which Mr J. Allan is inclined to ascribe to the fifth century AD' (S: 129).
**S.V.b:** Found at Kine-tokmak. 'It is noteworthy that the only coins among the day's "finds" at Kine-tokmak were both uninscribed Chinese pieces of a type ascribed to about the fifth century AD' (S: 131).

### *S.VI: COPPER COINS FOUND AT AK-TEREK SITE (S: 137, 140)*

**Site:** For tatis of Ak-terek see also S.IV.D.e. The Ak-terek site lies east of the Yurung-kash River. Stein found the remains of a Buddhist temple buried in sand, with evidence of much stucco relief, and gilded wall decoration. Siyelik was a flat debris-strewn area clear of dunes, with the outlines of a small Buddhist temple still visible, and evidence of stucco images (S: 139).
**Acquisition/archaeological context:** 'The only coin discovered in the [Ak-terek] ruin was a "cash" piece of the uninscribed type which was current both under the Former and Later Han dynasties. It was found close to the floor of the west passage, A.T.v, near the foot of the outer wall where it may have been originally deposited as a votive offering below the base of some image. The negative evidence which the absence within the ruin of any later coins furnishes, has some claim to attention; for it contrasts strikingly with the abundance of coins belonging to the Tang, Song and early Islamic issues which the surrounding "Tati" area yielded, and which conclusively proves that the ground itself continued to be occupied down to much later periods' (S: 137).

'It is probable that much of it [pottery debris] dates from early Islamic times, since among the coins which my guides had collected for me from the whole Ak-terek site, including Siyelik, specimens of local Islamic coinage as well as "cash" pieces of the Song dynasty were largely represented' (S: 140). 'Among 80 copper coins thus collected there were 28 of issues earlier than the Tang dynasty; 21 Chinese pieces of the Tang period (mainly Qianyuan and Dali) and 21 Song and Islamic coins. The only coin picked up in my presence was a Song "cash" bearing the nianhao of Baoyuan (AD 1038–40)' (S: 140 n13). These 80 coins include S.IV.D.e.
**S.VI.a:** Found between Ak-terek and Siyelik.
**S.VI.b:** Collected from tatis of Ak-terek.

### *S.VII: COPPER COINS FOUND AT KHADALIK AND NEIGHBOURING SITES (S: 159)*

#### *S.VII.a–c: KHADALIK*

**Site:** Khadalik ('the place with the sign stake'). The Khadalik site lies northeast of Domoko. Stein found the remains of a large temple (S: 155). When Stein returned to Khadalik in March 1908 he found that the area containing the ruined shrines had been brought under irrigation from the Domoko stream, thereby destroying the sites (S: 200).
**Kha.ii** refers to a ruined shrine, 25 × 24 ft on the inside, enclosed by a passage 8 ft wide on the north side, and 5 ft wide on the other sides (S: 157–9).
**Kha.vi** refers to the remains of a small shrine, where Brahmi votive manuscripts were found (S: 160).
**Acquisition/archaeological context:** Stein wrote: 'Votive deposits of far greater archaeological value came to light in the shape of Chinese copper coins, discovered deep down under the débris which filled the north-west corner of the enclosing passage (marked *a* in Plan) [of Kha.ii]. First there was found on the floor a scattered batch of thirteen "cash" pieces all belonging to the Tang period, and then, as if to satisfy my craving for exact chronological evidence, quite close to the foot of the wall two completely preserved rolls of coins, counting twenty and fifty-four pieces respectively, still held together by the original string which the last owner had passed through their square holes. Rapid examination showed me that these rolls were made up, apart from a few wuzhu pieces, of Tang coins only, the latest being issues of the Dali period (AD 766–79). Almost all of these coins were in very good preservation. The detached set comprised nine coins of Qianyuan (AD 758–60), three of Dali, and one wuzhu. In the smaller string Mr J. Allan found besides one wuzhu and one "cash" of the Kaiyuan issue, current from AD 618–27, sixteen Qianyuan and two Dali pieces. The second roll was made up of two wuzhu, two Kaiyuan, forty-two Qianyuan and eight Dali coins.

'Votive deposits of this kind must obviously belong to the period immediately preceding the abandonment of the shrine, and only current coins are likely to have been used for them. None of the Tang coins shows any marks of long circulation, so that it is safe to fix the date of abandonment for the whole Khadalik site, with its closely adjoining ruins and remains of identical type, at the close of the eighth century AD. In confirmation I may also note that of the sixteen Chinese coins, found by me elsewhere at the site and most of them close to the west of Kha.ii, all with the exception of one wuzhu piece belong to the Tang periods already noted, and that the four coins brought to me from the vicinity of the ruins none goes down later than the Jianzhong period.'
**S.VII.a:** Two strings of 'cash' pieces found in northwest corner of cella Kha.ii.
**S.VII.b:** Found outside western wall of cella Kha.ii.
**S.VII.c:** Found in shrine Kha.vii.

#### *S.VII.d: KIGHILLIK*

**Site:** Kighillik ('the dung-heap') lay half a mile east of Khadalik, with traces of rush-and-plaster walls marking the position of stables and cow-sheds (S: 197). Layers of dung had acted as protection against erosion.
**Acquisition/archaeological context:** Found at site, details not given.

#### *S.VII.e: KHADALIK*

**Site:** See S.VII.a–c.
**Acquisition/archaeological context:** Received from Mullah Khwaja as found near Khadalik.

#### *S.VII.f: BALAWASTE*

**Site:** Balawaste (= Ak-taz, AK: 453; S: 197) lay one and a half miles north of Khadalik. There was a patch of open ground, measuring 260 yd in diameter, and at the centre were remains of a rough rush-and-plaster dwelling 70 × 60 ft. About 8 yd west of the dwelling was a smaller building which yielded

Chinese wood slips (similar to those found at Mazar-Tagh). A line of cursive Brahmi writing below the Chinese characters indicated that the issuing office was of local character and not confined to a Chinese garrison. Another document had Chinese on one side, cursive Brahmi on the other (S: 197).
**Acquisition/archaeological context:** Found at Balawaste. 'Not far from this [larger] structure there was found on eroded ground a copper coin badly effaced in which Mr Allan believes he can recognize a late Wuzhu piece of the Liang dynasty' (S: 197).

### *S.VII.g: MAZAR-TOGHRAK*

**Site:** Mazar-toghrak ('wild poplar shrine') lies south of the Domoko oasis. About 150 yd to the west of the shrine was a small plateau (210 ft N–S, 135 ft E–W at widest point) covered in potsherds, which turned out to be an ancient rubbish heap. Remains of plastered floors were the structural traces. The site had been disturbed in the 1870s by villagers digging for saltpetre. The local name for this rubbish heap was Köne-ötang ('old postal station') (S: 205–6). Over fifty Chinese wood slips (similar to those found at Balawaste) were found by the western edge of the mound. A few of these are bilingual: Chinese and cursive Brahmi writing in the Iranian language of old Khotan. Small fragments of wooden tablets inscribed with cursive Brahmi characters (similar to those found at Niya); torn pieces of paper documents inscribed in cursive Brahmi, in the old language of Khotan; and two torn paper documents in Chinese (S: 205–6).
**Acquisition/archaeological context:** Found at Mazar-toghrak. 'It is curious to note that a copper coin, found on the eroded slope near the place where the heap of wooden documents had been thrown down, is taken by Mr J Allan to be "probably a late banliang cash, of the latter half of the second century BC"' (S: 206).

### *S.VIII: COPPER COINS FOUND AT NIYA SITE (S: 217, 227, 242)*

**Site:** See AK.VII.
**Acquisition/archaeological context:** Stein wrote: 'The ten copper coins found near the excavated ruins, or picked up from eroded ground elsewhere at the site, comprise only pieces which were current under the Later Han dynasty (AD 25–220) or immediately after its close. The analysis of the coin finds made on my former visit had yielded exactly the same result' (S: 242) 'The proportion between the various types represented was approximately the same as indicated [here] . . . but no huoquan were previously found' (S: 242 n8).
**N.XIV** was a large structure (56 × 41 ft) with massive pillars once supporting a roof, and to the east of the structure was a huge refuse heap (53 ft northeast to southwest, 50 ft wide). Over a dozen wood slips found in the refuse heap: eight in Chinese and in perfect condition, one slip and two fragments had Chinese writing, and the rest were blank. All were forwarding notes attached to gifts. Eight intact pieces were 'originally fastened to presents consisting of a jewel' (S: 218) and had 'dedicatory Chinese inscriptions to members of a local royal family' – Stein remarked that 'this proves on the one hand the correctness of the Chinese records which mention the separate existence of the small kingdom of Jingjue down to the middle of the third century AD [a Chinese document from N.XV was dated AD 269] in a position clearly corresponding to the tract watered by the Niya river. On the other hand, the same find illustrates again the important influence which Chinese administration and culture exercised here at that period' (S: 242). The presence of royal correspondence in the rubbish heap suggests that the large structure N.XIV was the residence of the local chief.
**N.XXIV** was a large ruined residence, perhaps two-storey, with living rooms at the centre and to the east, and outhouses and stables to the west (S: 225). Over fifty Kharoshthi documents on wood were found, some in perfect condition, mostly concerning accounts, lists and petty administration. A further 26 double rectangular tablets were found in a hidden archive below the floor (N.XXIV.viii): 18 of these still had the original fastening and were unopened. Many were deeds of sale. (S: 225–32). The coins were found near the ruin, no further details given. Stein noted that the seal impressions on some documents were similar to representations of the king on Kushan coins of Kujula Kadphises and Huvishka; also that many other impressions compared well with stone or metal seals found at Yotkan, and that the originals had probably been prepared in the Khotan region (S: 231–3).
**S.VIII.a:** Coins found near ruin N.XII (ruined dwelling).
**S.VIII.b:** Coins found near ruin N.XIV.
**S.VIII.c:** Coins found near ruin N.XXIV.
**S.VIII.d:** Coins found in northern portion of site. No details given.
**S.VIII.e:** Coins found near southeastern ruins of site. No details given.

### *S.IX: COPPER COINS FOUND AT ENDERE SITE (S: 282)*

**Site:** See AK.VIII.
**Acquisition/archaeological context:** Stein wrote: 'Chronologically special interest attaches to the coins, all Chinese and in copper. Of those picked up near the Tang fort or between it and the stupa most are of wuzhu types current from the Later Han dynasty onwards. Two among them are of the clipped variety which Chinese numismatists seem inclined to associate with the (Liu) Song dynasty of the fifth century AD, but which may equally well be debased specimens of earlier issues. From the "Tatis" near the stupa and northward come four wuzhu pieces and one uninscribed coin of a type which is known from the Earlier Han dynasty onwards. In range these finds completely agree with those made during my visit in 1901 (see AK list). The total absence of Tang coins shows that the period of resumed occupation which the circular fort attests could not have lasted very long' (S: 282).
**E.VII** was the ruin of a tower, measuring 25 ft square outside, with adjoining remains of a dwelling, about a quarter of a mile west of the Tang fort (S: 278). The site had suffered serious wind erosion. Fragments of two rectangular Kharoshthi tablets were found in the dwelling. ' About 40 yards to the west of E.VII I traced the floor of a large but completely eroded structure, but was rewarded by no finds apart from a clipped copper coin of the Wuzhu type and a piece of pottery showing a rich blue-green glaze' (S: 278).
**Tang fort** (see also AK.VIII). 'The havoc wrought here by far-advanced wind erosion obviously accounted for the scarcity of structural remains of the earlier period; for pottery débris of distinctly ancient appearance was visible in abundance on all patches of bare soil for nearly a mile south of the fort. Moreover, the copper coins which were picked up near the fort showed

Wuzhu type. Their fragmentary state also attested the force of erosion.' A Kharoshthi document on leather (similar to finds at Niya) was found here (S: 278).

**S.IX.a:** Coins found near stupa. 'From the "Tatis" near the stupa and northward come four wuzhu pieces and one uninscribed coin of a type which is known from the Earlier Han dynasty onwards' (S: 282).

**S.IX.b:** Coins found between stupa and Tang fort. 'Of those picked up near the Tang fort or between it and the stupa most are of wuzhu types current from the Later Han dynasty onwards' (S: 282).

**S.IX.c:** Found west of ruin E.VII.

**S.IX.d:** Found near Tang fort.

.

### *S.X: COPPER COINS COLLECTED AT VASH-SHAHRI SITE (S: 307–8)*

**Site:** The Vash-shahri site (Chinese: Washixia) was a ruined site crossed by the Charklik-Charchan route about six miles west of Vash-shahri. Open patches of eroded ground, or Tati, reached for about a mile both north and south of the route, with a total width of about half a mile. In the southern part of the site were the remains of about six dwellings, each with one or two rooms, an orchard, and the remains of circumvallation 180 yd in circumference (S: 307). Stein confirmed its identity with Xincheng ('New Town', = Nuzhi) which the Tang History describes as having been settled by Kang Yantian, a chief of Sogdian origin. Documents from Dunhuang indicate that Xincheng was founded in the mid seventh century (IA: 161).

**Acquisition/archaeological context:** Stein wrote: 'but they [various small finds] cannot afford such clear chronological indications as the stoneware. For the evidence of the latter full confirmation was furnished by the coins which were either picked up during our visit or else brought to me by Vash-shahri villagers accustomed to search these small "Tatis". Among the eight copper pieces thus obtained, three belong to Kaiyuan issues starting from AD 618–27, and continued during the first century of Tang rule; another probably dates also from that dynasty, while the remaining four show nianhaos of the Song dynasty extending from AD 1023–1101. Thus the occupation of the site, probably from Tang times, down to the twelfth century is conclusively proved.'

### *S.XI: COPPER COINS FOUND AT LOULAN SITES*

**Site:** Loulan (Chinese) = Kroraina (Kharoshthi).

**Acquisition/archaeological context:** 'In the course of my explorations of 1906 and of 1914 I recovered an aggregate of over five hundred copper coins from the whole Lou-lan area. Yet among this great array of coins there is not a single piece showing a type later than those issued during Han times and down to the Western Jin dynasty' (S: 426). '[The numismatic evidence from L.A.VI.ii] has its special interest on account of the certainty with which the numerous finds of dated Chinese documents allow us to attribute the accumulation of the refuse deposits between the structures of L.A.III, V, and VI in the main to the second half of the third and the early decades of the fourth century AD' (S: 385).

Jasvant Singh, the Surveyor's cook, and the labourers, also dug at the site and brought many small finds to Stein: 'The abundance of small objects in bronze at this site is very striking, and far greater than comparison with the contemporary Niya site might have led one to expect. I think that we may recognize in it, as well in the disproportionately greater number of coins found, an indication of the busy traffic which the great Chinese trade-route once brought to the ancient station' (S: 392).

### *S.XI.A: COINS FROM LOULAN STATION L.A. (S: 361–85)*

**Site:** L.A. refers to the principal group of ruins at Loulan. It was a small fortified station, garrisoned by Chinese troops and intended to guard the route from Dunhuang to the main line of oases north of the Tarim River, which was first opened *c.*110 BC and in use throughout the Han dynasty (S: 406–7).

**L.A.I** was a large dwelling, probably the residence of a local headman or representative of the local administration of Loulan. Kharoshthi paper documents, and Chinese wooden documents, were found on the debris-covered slopes by the ruin.

**L.A.II** was the main building of a group of structural remains southwest of the stupa, and occupying a terrace-like piece of land, up to 200 yd wide. It stood near the centre of a walled square enclosure marking the ancient Chinese station. These buildings were the remains of the Chinese administrative headquarters at Loulan. Predominantly Chinese documents were found at L.A.II. Hedin found 42 Chinese wood slips, dated AD 264–70, in L.A.II, and from the same refuse heap, Stein dug out Chinese and Kharoshthi documents on wood and paper. Chinese dated documents of AD 265–74 (S: 375–6). In 1910 Tachibana found a Chinese document here dated AD 324 (S: 377).

**L.A.III** belonged to the southwestern wing of the Chinese administrative headquarters. L.A.III.ii refers to the small and almost completely eroded apartment of L.A.II. Two fragments of Chinese wood slips were found in L.A.III.ii. A further 37 Chinese wood slips and two fragments of Kharoshthi on wood were found at surface level to the southwest of L.A.III.ii (= the easternmost edge of the huge refuse heap L.A.VI.ii) (S: 378).

**L.A.IV** was a large dwelling, about 100 yd west of the Chinese administrative headquarters (internal arrangement of rooms similar to buildings at Niya). The presence of Kharoshthi documents indicated it was the residence of a non-Chinese local official belonging to the indigenous administration of the territory (S: 380). Three rectangular wooden double-tablets with Kharoshthi writing, two of which were wrapped in rags, appeared to have fallen from a receptacle in the wall or above the door. From refuse heap near the western entrance of the central hall came a fragmentary wooden Kharoshthi document, and a complete Chinese document on paper, which recorded tribute of various pieces of silk offered by a barbarian (S: 378 '[The numismatic evidence from L.A.VI.ii] has its special interest on account of the certainty with which the numerous finds of dated Chinese documents allow us to attribute the accumulation of the refuse deposits between the structures of L.A.III, V, and VI in the main to the second half of the third and the early decades of the fourth century AD'). A further 11 Kharoshthi wood documents were found northwest of L.A.IV. The number of coins in the text (S: 385) does not match the number in the List of Coins.

**L.A.IV – VI** were dwellings (S: 381).

**L.A.V** was the ruin of a small dwelling, about 20 yd north of L.A.III. Three Kharoshthi documents on wood, also a Chinese

wooden seal and Chinese wood slip, were found in the southernmost room. In the refuse layer were found a Chinese wood slip, and two Kharoshthi wood documents (S: 380).
**L.A.VI** represents the remains of modest quarters, adjoining small rectangular fenced spaces for animals. One damaged rectangular covering-tablet was found here.
**L.A.VI.ii** was a vast refuse heap, covering an area 100 × 50 ft, reaching from the eastern edge of L.A.VI to the western edge of L.A.II and L.A.III. Over 170 Chinese records on wood (some dated, to AD 264–70), and 60 Chinese records on paper (one dated, to AD 312). Some of the wood slips had been used as firelighters. Far fewer Kharoshthi documents were found: four fragmentary tablets, three torn pieces of paper, one large paper document, and two lines of Kharoshthi of a strip of silk. There was also a small torn scrap of paper with early Sogdian writing (S: 381–3).
**L.A.VII** was a group of small dwellings, about 100 yd south of the Chinese headquarters, L.A.II–III. Stein found the remains of walls and adjoining fences (S: 385). One Kharoshthi document was found here.
**L.A.VIII** No details.
**L.A.IX** was once a substantial dwelling, now badly eroded, about 40 yd from the stupa. There was a small layer of refuse in the corner of room to the southwest. A large oblong tablet, with Kharoshthi writing on both sides, probably lists or accounts, was found here (S: 385–6).
**Acquisition/archaeological context:**
**S.XI.A.a:** Found 9 miles north of Camp 122. 'A fragmentary square-pierced Chinese copper coin, uninscribed, but unmistakably of a type associated with the Han period, was found close by [to potsherds], and furnished conclusive evidence that the pottery débris marked a site which must have been permanently occupied during the historical period' (S: 361).
**S.XI.A.b:** Picked up west of L.A. site. 'In its [the dry river-bed] vicinity at different points we then picked up glass beads, the fragment of a well-finished bronze ornament, and three Chinese coins belonging to Han types. These finds furnish additional and conclusive archaeological evidence that this old river-course passed here through a belt of ground occupied by settlements of some kind during the early centuries of our era' (S: 361).
**S.XI.A.c:** Collected from wind eroded ground near ruined station L.A. 'Three wuzhu coins of the Han type' were found on the approach to Loulan (S: 362); 'Chinese coins of the wuzhu and uninscribed types were picked up in numbers around it [remains of stupa northwest of the Loulan station], and finds of bronze arrow-heads and of other small objects in metal had by now become frequent' (S: 362).

'The abundance of small objects at this site is very striking, and far greater than comparison with the contemporary Niya Site might have led one to expect. I think that we may recognize in it, as well as in the disproportionately greater number of coins found, an indication of the busy traffic which the great Chinese trade-route brought to the ancient station' (S: 392).
**S.XI.A.d:** Found at ruin L.A.I. 'The careful search of the débris-covered slopes of L.A.I. resulted also in the recovery of seven Chinese coins [S.XI.A.d], mostly fragmentary. They all belong to the type marked by the legend wuzhu and assumed to have been first introduced by the Emperor Guangwudi, AD 26–57' (S: 375). In the vicinity of L.A.I were found a small bale of silk [L.A.I.002: 'Roll of yellow silk fabric, unused; very dry and brittle; broken in two; plain weave. Found on completely eroded ground, south of L.A. stupa and near L.A.I. Length complete 1 ft and 6¾ ins, diameter 2½ × 1 ins'] (S: 373, 432–3) and a 'string of small "goose-eye" coins, *c*.16, corroded into solid tube, *c*. quarter of an inch in diameter. Pl. XXIX. Found on eroded ground, 18 December 1906' (S: 432). These were not included in the List of Coins.
**S.XI.A.e:** Found within, or close to, ruin L.A.II.
**S.XI.A.f:** Found in ruin L.A.III.ii.
**S.XI.A.g:** Found within, or close to, ruins L.A.IV–VI. 'Among the nineteen Chinese copper coins found at L.A.V and L.A.VI there are seven wuzhu pieces of fragments of such, one huoquan coin and eleven much-clipped pieces of a type illustrated by nos. 29–34 in Plate CXL [these numbers do not match those in the group S.XI.A.g]. The proportion between the full wuzhu and these small pieces, clipped down often to quite diminutive sizes, is not materially altered if we include the coins found at L.A.III and IV, the totals being then raised to twelve and nineteen respectively. We have here clear archaeological evidence proving that such clipped pieces must already have been extensively in circulation during the latter half of the third century AD, and that the view which would attribute the introduction of these thin coins, known to Chinese numismatists under the graphic term of "goose's eyes", to the short-lived reign of Feidi, AD 465, and his successors of the Song dynasty, is misleading. There seems good reason to believe that Chinese numismatists, too, are cognizant of these much-clipped pieces going back at least to the reign of Xiandi, the last emperor of the Later Han dynasty, AD 189–220. In reality the process of constant debasement to which this quasi-subsidiary currency owes its origin is likely to have set in far earlier' (S: 385). The number of coins given in the text does not match the number in the List of Coins.
**S.XI.A.h:** Excavated from refuse heap L.A.VI.ii.
**S.XI.A.i:** Found at ruin L.A.VII. 'An almost completely destroyed structure, on a terrace rising about twenty-six feet above the adjoining eroded depression, yielded only three wuzhu coins [S.XI.A.i.2–4], a wooden comb, and a few miscellaneous fragments in lacquered wood and metal' (S: 385). A further 17 coins are presented in the List of Coins, but not mentioned in the text.
**S.XI.A.j:** Found near ruins L.A.VIII–IX. 'On the eroded ground between and near L.A.VIII and L.A.IX finds of coins and small objects in stone, metal and glass were particularly numerous, and it has since occurred to me that they might possibly have been due to the fact that the entrance through the north-eastern gate of the station passed over this ground' (S: 386).

### *S.XI.B: COINS FROM RUINED SITE L.B. (S: 393–451)*

**Site:** L.B. was described as the western group of ruins.
**L.B.I–III** was a small group of ruins, occupying the top of an island-like plateau, about 250 ft long and rising 250 ft above the wind-eroded depression below it.
**L.B.I** was a larger structure northeast of the shrine.
**L.B.II** was a small, square Buddhist shrine, badly eroded.
**L.B.III** was another large structure to the southwest of the shrine.
**L.B.IV–V** were two buildings in the western group of ruins.

**L.B.IV** was the larger of the two, and stood about one mile east-south-east of the small shrine L.B.II. It occupied the top of an isolated terrace, running 170 ft northeast to southwest, and rising 8–15 ft above surrounding eroded ground level. Four Kharoshthi tablets/documents in perfect condition were found in L.B.IV, along with three seal cases (similar to finds at Niya).

**L.B.V** had once been a large dwelling.

**Acquisition/archaeological context:**

**S.XI.B.a:** Found in the vicinity of L.B. Details not given.

**S.XI.B.b:** Found at, or near, ruins L.B.I–III. 'Besides some small miscellaneous objects of bronze and paste, a quantity of rags of fabrics in silk, wool and felt, and three Chinese copper coins of Han types, there were found here [L.B.III] a number of pieces belonging to a large wooden chest or cupboard' (S: 395).

**S.XI.B.c:** Found at ruins L.B.IV–V. No mention of coin-finds in text.

**S.XI.B.d:** Found 1 mile southwest of Camp 126. Stein had set out southwest of Loulan to reach the terminal course of the Tarim River across the unknown desert area separating it from the dried-up delta of the Kuruk-darya. 'That this riverine area was visited during the historical period of Lou-lan occupation, probably as jungle grazing, was proved by some of the finds made there' (S: 450–1). 'Thus, close to our Camp 126 a well-preserved wuzhu coin was picked up, and some nine miles beyond it the fragment of a Chinese mirror' (S: 451).

### *S.XII: COPPER COINS FOUND AT MERDEK-TIM SITE (S: 453)*

**Site:** Merdek-tim (tim = 'ancient mound or tower') was a small circular fort with a rampart built mainly of stamped clay and overgrown with luxuriant reeds. The diameter of the fort was 132 ft, with the entrance gate at the south (S: 452–3).

**Acquisition/archaeological context:** Found on rampart of ancient fort. 'In view of such close agreement [brickwork similar to that at Loulan], approximately contemporary origin necessarily suggested itself, and this conclusion was strikingly confirmed by a succession of finds of Chinese copper coins which were picked up in various places on the top of the rampart. All belong to types current during Later Han times; two bear the legend huoquan, first introduced by Wang Mang (AD 9–22), and the other four are wuzhu pieces in a clipped condition . . . The evidence secured already left no reasonable doubt that this small fortified post must have been occupied during the early centuries of our era and perhaps down to the same period as the Loulan site' (S: 453).

### *S.XIII: COPPER COINS FOUND AT MIRAN SITE (S: 474)*

**Site:** The Miran site consists of earlier remains of Buddhist shrines, contemporary with occupation of Loulan, *c.* third to fourth century, and abandoned when Loulan ceased to be occupied. The shrines showed influence of Gandharan art, and were similar to those at Rawak stupa (S: 492). The settlement Yuni (the 'Old Eastern Town' of Shanshan), mentioned in the Chinese historical records, must have been nearby (S: 538).

These Buddhist remains were already ruins by the time of the construction of the Tibetan fort M.I. For the Tibetans, the Miran site occupied a particularly strategic location, guarding the most direct routes from Tibet to the Tarim Basin, as well as the main routes from the southern Tarim Basin to Dunhuang. The most direct route from Tibet (still used by traders and pilgrims in 1907) went from Lhasa, over the Chimen-tagh, and down into the valley of the Jahan-sai River. The second major route from Tibet passed west of the Tsaidam Lake and abundant grazing ground, and at Bash-kurgan joined the hill-road from Dunhuang, before leading down to Achchik-bulak and Miran.

The Miran fort also guarded the direct route from Dunhuang and Gansu (in the east), through the southern oases of the Tarim Basin westwards to the borderlands of Iran and India. Two routes set out southwestwards from Dunhuang, one running along the southern shore of the dried Lop Nor salt-lake, the other along the northernmost range of the Altin-tagh, and these routes met up just east of Miran (S: 475–6).

**M.I** was the Miran fort, which comprised an irregular quadrangle, with the longer sides facing east-north-east and northwest (240 ft each), and shorter sides facing west-south-west (168 ft) and south-south-east (200 ft). There were projecting oblong bastions at the corners and in the central section of each wall, the southern one being noticeably the largest and probably once served as a keep. The fort was occupied during the period of Tibetan predominance in the Tarim Basin, late eighth and ninth centuries, and abandoned soon after Tibetan occupation ended (S: 456–74). Over a thousand Tibetan documents were found in the refuse layers, especially in rooms along the east wall, approximately 75 per cent on wood and 25 per cent on paper. There were also some Pothi Buddhist manuscripts (similar examples were found at the Tibetan Endere fort), which had probably been brought from Tibetan monasteries much further south. The forms of the documents were similar to those found at Mazar Tagh. The contents mostly relate to administrative affairs. There was one document in Turkish Runic script, probably *c.* AD 790, which was a passport for travelling on from Miran (S: 462–74).

**M.III** was the smallest in a group of ruined mounds, just east of the remains of an ancient canal, about one mile west-north-west of the Tibetan fort. It was a shrine, with square exterior and circular interior (unusual in Tarim Basin, more common in Gandhara and the Hellenized East), which had once been surmounted by a dome, and had a small stupa in the centre. The main base was almost 30 ft square. Paintings on the walls showed very distinct Gandharan and Hellenistic influence (S: 493–4). Kharoshthi votive inscriptions (writing similar to those from Niya and Loulan) on silk banners were found here. 'Each of these short inscriptions contains a prayer in Prakrit for the health of a certain person, some of them also for that of his family, and the phrase used in expressing it is identical with that regularly found in Indian epigraphic records of the Kushan period where they indicate the benefits hoped for by pious donors in return for their gifts' (S: 495).

**Acquisition/archaeological context:**

**S.XIII.a:** Found north of ruined shrine M.III. Coin not mentioned in text.

**S.XIII.b–c:** Found on eroded ground north of, and within, ruined fort M.I. 'Of the nine copper coins found at or near the fort all but two show the type with the legend Kaiyuan tongbao, introduced by the first Tang emperor Gaozu (AD 618–27) and continued by his successors for more than a century. Of the two remaining coins, one shows the nianhao Zhenghe (AD 1111–17) and the other the more modern regnal name Guangxu of the late Manchu emperor (1875–1900)' (S: 474).

***S.XIV: COPPER COINS FOUND OR COLLECTED AT NANHU (S: 616–27)***

**Site:** Nanhu was a small oasis west of Dunhuang (S: 492). A small ruined town, known locally as Nanhucheng ('the walled city of Nanhu'), lies within one mile to the east of the oasis, roughly rectangular, with the northern face measuring 400 yd. To the north and northeast of the ruined town is wind-eroded ground, or Tati, known locally as Gudongtan ('stretch of land with old things') covered with small debris of hard materials, such as stone, glass, metal, etc. About one mile northeast of the Tati stood a ruined watch-tower, its base 36 ft 4 in. square, and a small domed structure. The tower marked the end of an ancient embankment that marked the direction of the road to Dunhuang. Stein identified the ruined site as the ancient Yangguan ('Yang Barrier') of Han times. As the embankment was of different construction to the *limes* and walls at Dunhuang, and there were no watch-towers, Stein accepted the local tradition that the embankment served as a directional, rather than defence, line (S: 615–19).

**Acquisition/archaeological context:**

**S.XIV.a-c:** Excavated within, or near, ruined town, or on eroded site east or northeast of ruined town. 'A careful search, made by Naik Ram Singh along the exposed portions of the rampart, brought to light on the east face fragments of a Han coin of the wuzhu type and of an uninscribed clipped copper coin of the same period, besides two fragments which are likely to belong to Tang issues. They were all found some inches below the surface. Similar evidence of antiquity was given by coins which were picked up under my eyes on wind-eroded ground outside and close to the north and east walls. These include eight wuzhu pieces and three uninscribed coins, which may belong to the fourth–fifth century AD . . . With the chronological evidence derived from the small miscellaneous "finds" on the "Tati" the numismatic evidence obtained on the same ground agrees in a striking fashion. Among the coins which were picked up by Chiang Ssu-yeh in the course of a careful search, mainly to the east of the ruined town, and which can be recognized, there are, as shown in Appendix B, only a single Song period coin with the nianhao of AD 1038–40, nine coins with the legend Kaiyuan belonging to the Tang period, and no less than eleven which certainly belong to pre-Tang issues. It is interesting to note that these last, besides three pieces of Wang Mang's issue of AD 14–19 and three wuzhu coins, comprise a copper coin bearing the legend banliang ("half an ounce") which is of a type of the second century BC not otherwise represented in my collection' (S: 616–17).

**S.XIV.d:** Found at abandoned settlement of Kuan-tsou (S: 626–7). The site of Kuan-tsou (Guanzhou), north of Nanhu, had been abandoned *c.*1840 (S: 626–7). 'Near one of the farms there visited, I found some patches of ground that were not covered by sand, and among the small débris scattered over them modern-looking fragments of porcelain, bronze, etc. were soon picked up. Definite chronological evidence in support of the local tradition concerning the abandonment of this "site" was supplied by finds of copper coins, including two pieces of Qianlong (AD 1736–96), besides one of Kangxi (AD 1662–1723) and one of Xianping (AD 998–1004)' (S: 627).

***S.XV: COPPER COINS FOUND ALONG ANCIENT LIMES OF TUN-HUANG (S: 575, 592, 635, 687)***

**Site:** Tun-huang (Dunhang). The *limes* refer to the line of defence fortifications built during the Han dynasty from Dunhuang westwards towards Loulan.

**Acquisition/archaeological context:** 'I may here in passing call attention to the curiously small number of coins found along the whole of the Limes west of Dunhuang; apart from the deposit at T.XIV.v, they are eight in all. The difference from the great number of coins picked up at the Lou-lan site is striking. I am inclined to explain it by the fact that the surface conditions of the ground, far less affected by wind-erosion, do not make it so easy to find the coins which were lost by ancient wayfarers, etc' (S: 687 n6).

**T.IV.c** was a ruined watch-tower on the western edge and top of a steeply eroded clay ridge, rising about 120 ft above the surrounding depression. The base of the tower measured *c.*18–20 ft square (S: 635).

**T.VI.b** was a watch-tower with a base *c.*21 ft square, standing on a ridge, with dwelling quarters adjoining it on the south, and extensive refuse heaps surrounding the watch-tower (S: 645–6). Within the dwelling quarters were found eight Chinese records on wood, including one dated 10 May 68 BC. In the refuse heap northeast of the tower were found over 310 Chinese wood slips, some dated 65–56 BC, and a further 100 blanks, which had probably been thrown out from an office archive. Numerous documents suggest that this station was garrisoned by a military company dominated by indigenous people. Further wood slips and shavings were found northwest of the tower (S: 646).

**T.VI.c** was a watch-tower that stood 3 miles west of watch-tower T.VI.b, on the flat top of a small and completely isolated clay terrace (E–W 80 yd, maximum width 30 yd). Its square base measured 20 ft. There were quarters adjoining on the south and east. A wooden tablet with Early Sogdian script (as seen in the paper fragment from Loulan L.A.VI.ii) was found here and is probably associated with indigenous people recruited for guard work (S: 652).

**T.XI** was a watch-tower, rising conspicuously above the easternmost edge of a lake. Its base measured 24 ft. To the west was a small room *c.*21 × 12 ft. To the north, northeast and west were the remains of a later (Song dynasty or later?) enclosure.

**T.XI.iii** refers to the refuse heap south of the watch-tower (S: 666–8). Chinese documents on wood were found in the refuse heaps around the watch-tower, the latest dating to AD 153 (S: 667).

**T.XIV** was a fort, occupying a strategic location, situated on raised ground. Protected by impassable marshes to the northwest and southeast, it commanded and guarded the route. All the watch-towers from T.XI to T.XIX were visible from the fort. The interior of the fort measured 54 ft square. Stein identified T.XIV as the site of Yumenguan ('Jade Gate') (S: 683–91). Chinese wood slips and shavings were found in a shaft (probably used as prison) on the western slope of the hillock 70 yd north of the fort. Documents indicated that the fort was the site of Yumenguan. Over sixty documents were found, including dated documents of 96 BC to AD 19 (S: 685).

**T.XIV.v** was a small structure on the highest part of the hillock north of the fort. Buddhist documents revealed it to be a shrine, of the Tang dynasty. Ten fragments of Chinese Buddhist texts on

paper (similar to those at Dandan-Uiliq and Khadalik), probably of the eighth century, were found when clearing the floor. Below the floor were Chinese wood slips of the Han dynasty.
**T.XV** was a watch-tower. Although no coins were found here, a very important find was made among the refuse heaps here. It was a strip of silk found with a Chinese inscription: 'Roll of silk from Kangfu in the kingdom of Rencheng [modern day Jining in Shandong province]; width 2 feet 2 inches; length 40 feet; weight 25 ounces; value 618 pieces of money'. The kingdom of Rencheng was established in AD 84, and a passage in the *Houhanshu* ch. 72, records that during Xuandi's reign (AD 126–44) there were several rebellions by the Central Asian barbarians, and the king of Rencheng offered coins and silk to subsidize expenses at the frontier. Chinese documents found in the same refuse heap dated AD 97–137 lend support to the historical record (S: 700–1).

Another, earlier, refuse heap at T.XV yielded two strips of fine silk, with a Brahmi inscription (similar to early Kushan period writing in India), reading 'cloth 46 gisti', probably indicating to the Western buyer the length of the roll of silk (rolls were produced in China in standard widths). Chinese documents found in the same refuse heap are dated AD 53. Stein concluded from these finds that traders accustomed to using an Indian language and script (not Kharoshthi as is more commonly found, but Brahmi script, used to write Prakrit mixed with Sanskrit) came across the *limes* to get silk (S: 699–701).

Stein also suggested: 'possibly the record of an officer's salary paid in another and more substantial kind of currency is preserved in [Chavannes's] Doc.490, which mentions the captain of a certain company as having received "32 ft of silk fabric". From M. Chavannes' supplementary evidence (see above, p. 701), it is seen that according to a statement of the Later Han Annals a king of Rencheng in Shandong sent subsidies "in coins and pieces of silk" for the frontier expenses at a time (AD 126–44) when "the barbarians of Central Asia repeatedly revolted". Could the piece of silk received by that captain have been meant for payment in a kind of silk currency?

'It is true that the document No.490 probably belongs to the time of Wang Mang, as the Guangxin company seems to be named in it (see above, p. 670). But the use of silk as a sort of currency is likely to have been resorted to in China long before Later Han times. Silk is not among the local products of Western Gansu.'
**T.XVIII** was a military magazine, including granary, measuring 560 ft east–west, comprising three big halls adjoining lengthwise. There were also badly eroded remains of an outer enclosure, with walls or embankments 80 ft to the north of the structure, and 100 ft to the south. To the southeast of the inner enclosure was a small clay terrace with layers of refuse, beneath which were the foundations of a room (T.XVIII.iii) about 15 ft square (S: 715–16). Chinese wood slips and blanks were found. Those with inscriptions indicated that the structure had been a granary, including receipts for cartloads of grain delivered from Dunhuang, and dated wood slips of 52 BC (S: 714–16).
**T.XX** was a ruined watch-tower with four rooms, east of the military magazine (S: 719). It stood on a clay ridge, from where the *limes* wall was visible for over 50 yd towards the marshy foreshore of a lake about three miles long and one and a half miles wide. Over ten Chinese wooden documents were found on the slopes below the watch-tower.
**T.XXVI** was a watch-tower which had once had a small apartment, about 8 ft square, at its southeastern corner.
**T.XXVII** was a watch-tower which had a room (14 ft × 14 ft) on its western side. The tower stood southwest of watch-tower T.XXVI.
**T.XXVIII** was a watch-tower which stood one and a half miles southwest of T.XXVII. Its base measured 20 ft square. There were no structural remains other than the tower, but there was refuse on the southern slopes. Chinese wood slips were found in the room west of tower T.XXVII, including dated slips of AD 35–61. Over seventy Chinese wood slips, dated first century AD, were found in refuse on the southern slopes of watch-tower T.XXVIII. They were mostly made of poplar (the usual material in this region), but also in conifer-wood (the most likely source of which was Nanshan), bamboo (from further afield) and tamarisk-sticks (local material).
**T.XXXIV** was a watch-tower with a heap of debris about 20 ft east of the tower. Chinese wood slips were found in the debris.
**Acquisition/archaeological context:**
**S.XV.a:** Found at watch-tower T.IV.c. 'At the northern edge of the ridge, about forty yards off [from the tower], scanty traces of a hut survived, built with clay walls which had been faced or strengthened by vertical bundles of reeds. Here we recovered a much-clipped copper coin of the wuzhu type [S.XV.a.1] and small fragments of a woollen material and tanned leather' (S: 635).
**S.XV.b:** Found near watch-station T.VI.b. Coin not mentioned in text.
**S.XV.c:** Found on top of watch-tower T.VI.c. Coin not mentioned in text.
**S.XV.d:** Found at ruin T.XI.iii. Coin not mentioned in text.
**S.XV.e:** Found in refuse on slopes of T.XIV. 'Hasan Akhun, my experienced head camel-man, had carefully searched the ground at the ruin and picked up there two copper coins. They proved to be of the wuzhu type of the Han, and thus furnished the first distinct indication as to the antiquity of this site' (S: 575).
**S.XV.f:** Found in bowl below floor of ruined shrine T.XIV.v. 'Clearing disclosed a small wooden bowl embedded below the reed flooring and containing, besides two brazen hairpins, eighty Chinese copper coins. With two exceptions, which were wuzhu issues apparently of the first–second century AD, all bore the legend Kaiyuan, which we know to have been introduced in the first reign of the Tang dynasty (AD 618–27) and continued through a great portion of the Tang period. These Tang coins showed scarcely any wear resulting from circulation . . . the route to Lop had last been an important line of communication, before the Tibetan invasion of the Gansu marches, after the middle of the eighth century AD, closed it to direct intercourse between China and the Tarim Basin' (S: 687). 'It is of interest to note that the only two other coins found at T.XIV, which came from the refuse heaps of the hillock, are of a wuzhu type attributed to the first century AD' (S: 687 n6).
**S.XV.g:** Found at ruined magazine T.XVIII.iii. One wuzhu coin was found in T.XVIII.iii with two woven string shoes, a wooden die and a fragmentary wooden document dated 52 BC (S: 716).

**S.XV.h:** Found on slope below watch-tower T.XX. 'On the slope below the tower a wuzhu coin of an early type, assigned to the first century BC, was picked up' (S: 719).
**S.XV.i:** Found west of watch-tower T.XXVI. 'I gave a more grateful welcome to the chronological evidence supplied by two Han copper coins of the wuzhu type, much clipped and corroded, which were discovered adhering to each other at five yards' distance to the west of the tower, and about a foot below the surface. Yet obviously these coins could not by themselves suffice for the dating of a ruin which even at the present day is within reach of people from the Dunhuang oasis; for we know that this type must have continued to circulate right down to the beginning of the Tang period' (S: 592–3). Chinese wooden documents were found southeast of the watch-tower.
**S.XV.j:** Found between watch-towers T.XXVII and T.XXVIII. Coins not mentioned in text.
**S.XV.k:** Found in refuse heap of watch-tower T.XXVIII (see above, and S.XV.j).
**S.XV.l:** Found on eroded ground near watch-tower T.XXXIV (see above, and S.XV.m).
**S.XV.m:** Found near watch-tower T.XXXIV (see above, and S.XV.l). 'In the debris, and about 2 ft above the natural soil, there turned up a copper coin of the wuzhu type attributed to the first–second century AD' (S: 605).
**S.XV.n:** Found at grazier's hut near Camp 171. Within 2 miles south-south-west of Camp 171a was a low broad terrace, which had been used as a grazing station relatively recently before Stein arrived. Coin not mentioned in text.
**S.XV.o:** Not in List of Coins.

### *S.XVI: COPPER COINS FOUND AT SO-YANG-CH'ÊNG SITE (S: 1103–6)*

**Site:** So-yang-ch'êng (local name) was a walled city, within a wind-eroded site measuring 5 miles east–west, and 3 miles north–south. Two city walls face eastwards as protection from wind damage. Watch-tower at northwestern corner of city. Cemetery about 1,000 yd northwest of the walled town. The remains of a stupa (of a later style than usually found in the Tarim Basin) stood less than a mile east of the outer eastern wall of the city (S: 1101–6).
**Acquisition/archaeological context:** Within the walled quadrangle, 'only at relatively few points, where larger refuse heaps or mounds of clay, evidently formed by the débris of completely decayed buildings, rose above the drift-sand level, could fragments of pottery, including porcelain and glazed stoneware, and bronze coins of the Tang period be picked up on the surface' (S: 1103). 'The evidence of the coins, which is necessarily more definite [than pottery], fully agrees with this [occupation during Tang and Song times], but at the same time leaves the possibility open of occupation having started somewhat earlier . . . the total of 38 identifiable copper coins or fragments of such is made up of 25 pieces showing the legend Kaiyuan, first used under Gaozu, AD 618–27, but reproduced on coins through most of the Tang period: 1 of Qianyuan, AD 758–60; 2 of Song times; with the addition of 10 wuzhu pieces, of which one may be attributed to the Sui dynasty (AD 581–618), while the rest are evidently earlier' (S: 1106). 'The finds of coins stop short with a piece belonging to the regnal period of the Jin dynasty (AD 1156–61)' (S: 1103).

### *S.XVII: COPPER COIN FOUND AT HEI-SHUI-KUO SITE, WEST OF KAN-CHOU (S: 1133)*

**Site:** Hei-shui-kuo (local name) was a tati site *c.* 6 miles northwest of the main gate of Kan-chou (Ganzhou = Zhangye). The site covers 3 miles north–south and 2 miles east–west, and consists of a small fort and the remains of three large walled enclosures. Most structural remains were long since removed by people needing building materials. Remains of three circumvallations. Ceramic finds at the site indicate that it was abandoned during Ming dynasty. Finds made at the site were often taken to Ganzhou for collectors (S: 1132).
**Acquisition/archaeological context:** 'Close to its [circumvallation at the northern edge of the tati] west face a Tang coin with the legend Kaiyuan was picked up on wind-eroded ground. Taking into account Mr Li's statement that metal objects of Tang times have been found at Hei-shui-kuo, and the fact that among the decorated fragments of stoneware and porcelain I picked up there are some which Mr Hobson ascribes to the Song period, I am led to conclude that the site was already occupied at that time' (S: 1133).

### *S.XVIII: COPPER COIN FOUND EAST OF CHONG HASSAR, TURFAN (S: 1161–6)*

**Site:** Chong Hassar ('big castle', = Hassar-shahri) was the local name for a small oblong fort (200 × 150 ft on the outside), and an adjoining outer enclosure, not far from the eastern end of a marshy salt-lake bed. A massive 'keep-like structure' rose within the northeastern corner of the fort. Vaulted chambers filled most of the interior fort. Small Buddhist shrine on the southwestern wall of the fort. The keep was a good vantage point, and was well adapted for guarding routes from the northeast and southeast towards Gaochang. East of the site there passed a route from Lukhun to Singer, a strategically important oasis in the western Kuruk-tagh, from where there were tracks towards Loulan and Kara-shahr (S: 1160–3).
**Acquisition/archaeological context:** No mention of coin in text.

### *S.XIX: COPPER COINS FOUND AT YAR-KHOTO, TURFAN (S: 1168)*

**Site:** Yar-khoto (Chinese: Jiaohe, 'crossing rivers'). A city site stituated on plateau-island between two deep-cut ravines. It was the main city/capital of the region down to Tang times. Stein excavated at two 'modest ruins'.
**Y.K.i** was a 'small dwelling of which the basement storey, cut out of the clay soil, retained a deep layer of débris left undisturbed by diggers for manuring earth' (S: 1168).
**Y.K.iii** was a large room, near a partially excavated Buddhist shrine, which had escaped recent manure-digging operations by villagers. It lay less than 200 yd southwest of Y.K.i, close to where the northern end of the town area adjoined the western 'Yar' (ravine) (S: 1168).
**Acquisition/archaeological context:**
**S.XIX.a:** Found in ruined dwelling Y.K.i. 'Four copper coins of the Tang period, with the legend Kaiyuan, were picked up almost on the surface. Some feet lower down, but still 5 feet above the floor, there were found 96 more Chinese copper coins, lying close together. Out of these, 93 bear the legend Kaiyuan which, first introduced by the founder of the Tang

dynasty in AD 618–27, was continued in the mintage of his successor for more than a century. Two others are issues of the Qianyuan period (AD 758–60), while one is a wuzhu piece anterior to AD 600. From the way in which these coins turned up it seemed probable that they belonged to a small hoard of late Tang times that may have been placed in an upper-storey wall and had fallen down with it . . . Immediately adjoining this basement on the south-east were found the badly decayed walls of a diminutive shrine, about 4 feet square, with an enclosing passage only 1½ feet wide' (S: 1168).
**S.XIX.b:** Found in ruined shrine Y.K.iii. 'Of two Chinese copper coins found in the same place, one shows the nianhao Jianzhong (AD 780–4), the other being a Kaiyuan piece. The previously mentioned shrine to the south, iv, occupied a high terrace, cut as usual at this site out of the natural clay soil' (S: 1168).

### *S.XX: COPPER COIN FOUND ON RAMPART OF RUINED FORT NEAR USHAK-TAL, KARA-SHAHR (S: 1181)*

**Site:** Kara-shahr (Chinese: Yanqi) was, from AD 719, one of the Tang dynasty 'Four Garrisons of the Western Regions'. Chong-köl ('big lake'; Chinese: Dalaoba) was the ruined fort six miles southeast of Ushak-tal. Roughly rectangular circumvallation: southwestern face measured 270 yd long, southeastern face measured 308 yd. There were towers of stamped clay at irregular intervals. Stein concluded that although of pre-Islamic origin, it was likely to have been occupied intermittently since (S: 1181–2).
**Acquisition/archaeological context:**'On the south-west rampart a well-preserved copper coin with the nianhao Qianyuan (AD 758–60) was picked up from the surface' (S: 1181).

### *S.XXI: COPPER COIN FOUND AT BAGHDAD-SHAHRI SITE, KARA-SHAHR (S: 1182)*

**Site:** For Kara-shahr see S.XX. The remains at Baghdad-shahri indicate a large oblong circumvallation of an important town, its northwestern face 1,030 yd long, and southwestern face 935 yd long. No structural remains survived within the town walls: 'the whole of it is occupied by salt-encrusted low ridges and hillocks, with a large earth mound of the same shapeless appearance a short distance off the middle of the south-west face. Remains of a square wall, apparently of later date, were traceable on its top.' Stein identified Baghdad-shahri as the site of the Kara-shahr capital, in Tang times (S: 1182).
**Acquisition/archaeological context:** 'There was found on the surface a well-preserved coin with the nianhao Jianzhong (AD 780–4), together with plenty of coarse pottery on the slopes. Fragments of a Tang coin, apparently a Kaiyuan piece, were picked up on the top of the previously mentioned mound' (S: 1182).

### *S.XXII: COPPER COINS EXCAVATED AT MING-OI SITE, NORTH OF SHOR-CHUK (S: 1187, 1189, 1191, 1194)*

**Site:** The Ming-oi ('the thousand houses') site was four miles north of Shorchuk, and consisted of over a hundred Buddhist shrines of different sizes (from 4–6 ft square to 80 ft on one side) and of five different types: (1) simple cella, (2) cella with vaulted chamber allowing circumambulation, (3) larger, square cella with ante-chapel, enclosing passages decorated with wall-paintings, (4) sepulchral monuments in form of stupa, (5) pillar-like structures (S: 1185–7).
**Mi.i** was a narrow passage, adjoining a small cella at the southern end of a row of stupas that had been destroyed (S: 1189).
**Mi.x** was the 40 ft long hall of the temple in the northwestern part of the site. The hall gave access to the temple cella (20 ft 6 in.), which was enclosed by passages six ft wide (S: 1191).
**Mi.xi** was the temple cella adjacent to Mi.X, which Stein described as 'a rich mine of stucco relievo'. The absence of any remains of large statues or image bases suggests that the walls were covered with stucco and painted (S: 1191).
**Mi.xii** was a chamber behind the temple cella Mi.xi. Remains of stucco statues and small relievos that had fallen from the wall-frieze showed the strong influence of the Graeco-Buddhist sculpture of Gandhara (S: 1192–4).
**Mi.xiv** was a shrine. It was the northernmost of a small group of closely adjoining small cellas, with Buddhist wood carving, showing strong Graeco-Buddhist influence (S: 1197). A fragmentary *pothi*-leaf from a paper manuscript in Brahmi script, apparently Sanskrit, was found here.
**Mi.xvii** was a conspicuous shrine, consisting of a rectangular cella and built on a high walled terrace, northeast of the central group of temples. Inside it was filled with hard-burned debris. Remains of stucco reliefs. (S: 1198).
**Acquisition/archaeological context:** 'None of the numerous Chinese coins, found mostly in places where they must have been deposited as votive gifts at image bases, etc., are of issues later than the end of the eighth century' (S: 1187). 'Out of 33 coins from the site, 31 were discovered, as it were *in situ*, within shrines. Only 5 of them belong to pre-Tang issues (with the legends wuzhu or huoquan); 8 show the legend Kaiyuan, current throughout the Tang coinage; 6 are of the Dali period (AD 766–79), and not less than 14 bear the nianhao Jianzhong (AD 780–3). It is worth noting that the last nianhao is the latest found on Tang coins from Khotan sites as described in the list of *Ancient Khotan*' (S: 1187 n10). 'Since none of the numerous finds of Chinese copper coins, originally deposited as votive gifts, were later than the close of the eighth century AD, it seemed reasonable to connect this burning with the earliest Islamic invasions' (S: 366).
**S.XXII.a:** Found before the image base in shrine Mi.i. 'Before a small niche in (i) [the passage], retaining part of a lotus base in plaster, there were found embedded in the flooring four Tang coins, just as they had been deposited as a votive offering. Two bear the legend Kaiyuan, two the nianhao Dali (AD 766–79); all are in excellent preservation, showing practically no wear' (S: 1189).
**S.XXII.b:** Found in ante-chapel Mi.x. 'Fourteen Chinese copper coins were found in the débris at heights varying from 1 to 4 feet above the floor. Ten among them were Tang issues, and the rest much-worn wuzhu pieces. From the position in which they were found it may be concluded with much probability that they were originally deposited on the projecting ledges, which here, as in the other parts of this temple, carried relievo friezes' (S: 1191).
**S.XXII.c:** Found in temple cella Mi.xi. No mention of coin in text.
**S.XXII.d:** Found at image base in temple passage Mi.xii. 'So it is well to lay stress on the conclusive numismatic evidence we

possess as to the late date up to which the shrine adorned with these relievos was frequented. On the base bearing the statues of the north-east corner seven Chinese coins were found, tucked away behind the feet or otherwise placed securely. One among them bears, indeed, the legend huoquan, used on the coinage of Wang Mang and ascribed to the regnal period AD 14–19. But we know that Chinese coins were liable to be continued for centuries by recasting. On the other hand, three coins of the Dali (AD 766–9) and Jianzhong (AD 780–3) periods, besides one Kaiyuan piece, make it certain that these particular images continued to be objects of pious worship down to the end of the eighth century, if not later' (S: 1194–5).
**S.XXII.e:** Found in shrine Mi.xiv. No mention of coin in text.
**S.XXII.f:** Found before entrance to shrine Mi.xvii. 'A Kaiyuan coin was found close to the entrance' (S: 1198).
**S.XXII.g:** Found among southeastern group of ruins. No mention in text.

### *S.XXIII: COPPER COINS FOUND NEAR RUIN KA.I, KARADONG (S: 1242)*

**Site:** See AK.IX. Ka.I was a dwelling and the largest ruin Stein found at Karadong (S: 1242).
**Acquisition/archaeological context:** 'With this dating [third to fourth centuries AD] the two coins found close to Ka.I fully agree; they are both wuzhu pieces, apparently of the second–third century AD. The coins found on the occasion of my first visit, fourteen in all, were also either wuzhu pieces or else uninscribed' (S: 1242).

### *S.XXIV: COPPER COINS FOUND AT FARHAD-BEG-YAILAKI SITE (S: 1246–55)*

**Site:** Farhad-Beg-yailaki ('Farhad Beg's grazing ground', named after the local beg, who, in Yaqub Beg's time, looked for saltpetre in the neighbouring ruins [S: 1246]). The site lay north of Malak-alagan. The remains of the site were scattered over an area measuring 4½ miles southeast to northwest, which lay between two old flood beds. Stein identified this site with Song Yun's Mocheng (S: 1255). The remains of dwellings and shrines, were similar to those of Dandan-Uiliq and Khadalik (S: 1246). There was a stupa to the northwest of the tati area (S: 1250).
**Acquisition/archaeological context:** 'Apart from the wuzhu coin unearthed on the floor of temple cells F.III, eight other Chinese coins were found at the site, all on the surface of wind-eroded ground, four of them near the ruined house F.I, three near the monastic dwelling F.II, and one at the "Tati" of F.V. All these are wuzhu pieces probably of the Later Han or uninscribed and clipped coins ascribed to the same period. Not a single Tang coin was discovered at the site. In order to emphasize the significance of this fact it will suffice to point out that among the coins actually found in the course of my exploration at the Khadalik site site not less than 98 belonged to Tang issues and only 5 were wuzhu pieces. Thus the numismatic evidence as to the earlier date of the remains at Farhad-Beg-yailaki appears to me very strong' (S: 1254–5).
**F.I** was a ruined house, consisting of a series of small rooms, grouped in several courts around a square tank (S: 1247). It had a small domestic shrine (F.I.b). Outisde the house were the remains of fenced enclosures and an orchard. A wooden tablet bearing five lines of Sanskrit, in Brahmi script, was found here (S: 1247).
**F.II** was a monastery which stood about half a mile west of F.I (S: 1249). It comprised a shrine with dwelling quarters, an open hall or court, and temple cella (F.II.iii). The remains were similar to those at Rawak, Dandan-Uiliq and Niya. In room F.II.i a mass of ex-voto fabrics and Brahmi manuscript remains were found under the foot of the image. The wooden tablets found in room F.II.i had writing in Brahmi (Gupta-type), probably of the old Khotanese language.
**F.III** was a monastery which stood about a quarter of a mile northwest of F.I.
**F.III.i** was a temple, standing higher than the other remains (S: 1249). A fragment of a paper document in Brahmi was found in F.III.i. A large wooden tablet in Brahmi was found in the small room F.III.ii (S: 1249).
**F.V** refers to two detached rooms on the tati area, which yielded no finds.
**Acquisition/archaeological context:**
**S.XXIV.a:** Found near ruin F.I.
**S.XXIV.b:** Found near ruin F.II.
**S.XXIV.c:** Found in cella F.III.i. 'On its [F.III.i] floor a wuzhu coin. The chronological find of this coin find and of the evidence furnished by the other Chinese coins from the site, all pre-Tang issues, will be discussed below [See S: 1254–5]' (S: 1249).
**S.XXIV.d:** Found near ruin F.V. Coin not mentioned in text.

### *S.XXV: COPPER COIN FOUND IN RUINED SHRINE, KARA YANTAK (S: 1262)*

**Site:** The Kara Yantak site lay less than a mile and a half east of Mazar-toghrak (see S.VII.g), and consisted of the remains of a Buddhist shrine, which had been destroyed as a quarry for timber. There were similarities with the main temple at Khadalik (S: 1262).
**Acquisition/archaeological context:** 'The conclusion drawn from these scanty art remains as to the date of this shrine, and probably of its abandonment also, which is approximately the same as that determined for the Khadalik temples, received striking confirmation by the discovery on the floor of a well-preserved coin of the Qianyuan period (AD 758–9), showing no sign of wear' (S: 1262).

### *S.XXVI: WEST LACH*

These coins were not included in the List of Coins, but were mentioned in the text, see below.

### *S.XXVI: COPPER COINS FOUND AT, OR BROUGHT FROM, TATI SITES, NORTHWEST OF DOMOKO (S: 1263–4)*

**Sites:** Ulugh-mazar (= Ulugh-ziarat, 'the holy shrine') was a desert pilgrimage place with extensive debris areas to the north and surrounding it. Stein identified Ulugh-mazar with Xuan Zang's Pimo, Song Yun's Hanmo, and Marco Polo's Pein (S: 1263–4).
**Acquisition/archaeological context:** 'The fresh numismatic evidence now secured from these "Tatis" fully agrees with the conclusion arrived at on my former visit, and at the same time shows that the occupation of this area must have already been of old date when Song Yun visited Han-mo. While among the coins actually picked up there on my own visit or R. B. Lal Singh's preceding reconnaissance one is a Song dynasty piece of AD 1102–7 and another an Islamic coin ascribed to the fourteenth century, there were secured also some much-worn

wuzhu pieces and one coin which seems to be of the Sino-Kharoshthi class. These finds of early coins are of special interest because they bear out Song Yun's statement with regard to the antiquity of the shrine with the miracle-working Buddha statue which he visited 15 li to the south of Han-mo, ie at the site now marked by the pilgrimage place of Ulugh-mazar. He mentions that of the multitude of votive banners he saw there about half showed dates of the Wei dynasty (AD 386–534), while one was of the period AD 384–417' (S: 1263–4).

'I may add that of five coins which were given to me at Keriya as having been brought from the "Tatis" near Ulugh-mazar two are Tang pieces (Kaiyuan), while the rest are of Song dynasty issues, ranging from AD 1017–1107. Of nine more coins received from Domoko in 1906 five are wuzhu "cash", tentatively ascribed to the fifth century, three Tang pieces of AD 758–9, and one probably a medieval Islamic coin' (S: 1264 n5).
**S.XXVI.a:** Found at sites near Ulugh-mazar.
**S.XXVI.b:** Received as from sites northwest of Domoko.

### S.XXVII: COPPER COINS BROUGHT AS FROM CHALMA-KAZAN (S: 1267)

**Site:** For Chalma-kazan see AK.IV.
**Acquisition/archaeological context:** 'I may add here that among the seventeen coins which Muhammad Sharif brought me as having been found at Chalma-kazan in different places of newly cultivated ground, six are Sino-Kharoshthi and two wuzhu pieces, while the rest are of Tang issues down to the Dali period (AD 766–80)' (S: 1267).

### S.XXVIII: COPPER COIN FOUND AT KARA-SAI SITE (S: 1273)

**Site:** Temple site, north of Khotan. No structural remains, but plentiful small relievo fragments were found on eroded soil, which had come from two Buddhist shrines 160 yd apart (S: 1273).
**Acquisition/archaeological context:** No mention of coin in text.

### S.XXIX: COINS FOUND AT, OR NEAR, TARISHLAK SITE (S: 1279)

**Site:** Buddhist temple site, two miles from the left bank of the Yurung-kash River, north of Khotan. The Kine-tokmak ruins lie about 13 miles east on the other side of the Yurung-kash River. The Rawak Vihara lies three miles south of the Tarishlak temple. Ta.i refers to the remains of a passage enclosing a temple cella or shrine, with the remains of a colossal seated Buddha in the southern corner, and other life-size Buddhist statues (S: 1274–9). A Central Asian Brahmi (Sanskrit) inscription was found on the wall of Ta.i. A fragment of a Kharoshthi inscription on coloured wall-plaster was found in the sand.
**Acquisition/archaeological context:** 'At the foot of the wall behind this statue [life-size, of a richly dressed male figure intact to the waist, in Ta.i] there was found a wuzhu coin embedded in the plaster of the base' (S: 1277). 'The safest evidence [for dating the site] at present is that of the coins. The two found at the ruin itself are the wuzhu piece already mentioned and an uninscribed copper coin from the foot of the wall ii. In addition eight poorly preserved Chinese coins were picked up on a small and completely eroded "Tati" area to the south of the site. They are either much worn wuzhu pieces or else uninscribed. The collective evidence of the coins thus points to the site having been abandoned before Tang times' (S: 1279).
**S.XXIX.a:** Found within ruin Ta.i, ii.
**S.XXIX.b:** Collected from tati south of site.

### S.XXX: COPPER COINS FOUND AT, OR BROUGHT FROM, MAZAR-TAGH SITE (S: 1287)

**Site:** See AK.XVII and IA.II. Mazar-Tagh ('hill of the sacred shrine') is the name of a chain of hills, rising in the midst of the desert. The site, with its height and natural commanding position, probably served initially as a watch-station, guarding the route by the Khotan River, on the only practicable route northwards from Khotan. The structural remains are those of a fort, built on the hill ridges, inaccessible from the south and east, and protected by a massive tower (possibly of earlier date) which stood 60 yd from the western bastion of the fort. The inner court of the fort measured 50 ft square. Remains of a Buddhist shrine (M.Tagh.ii). Refuse heaps on the rock slopes on the eastern and northeastern sides (S: 1287–91).

Tibetan documents on wood (similar to those at Miran) and on paper were found within the fort and in the refuse heaps, and indicate that the site was occupied by a Tibetan garrison (S: 1287–8). Over seventy documents in Central Asian Brahmi script (cursive Gupta) and Khotanese language were found at Mazar-tagh, and indicate that Khotanese was the language used for local administration and personal communication in the Khotan region. There were some bilingual records, with Khotanese on one side and Chinese or Tibetan on the other. Also found in the refuse were Chinese documents on paper (one was dated AD 786, others were accounts for a monastery in the Khotan region), two fragments of paper in Uighur, a script apparently derived from Aramaic and early Sogdian, and a wooden fragment with Kharoshthi script (S: 1289–90).
**Acquisition/archaeological context:** 'Two large pottery jars (probably for storing water) were found embedded in the floor, within the main fort walls. The larger measured 2 feet 6 inches in height, greatest width 2 feet 4 inches, diameter of mouth 10 inches. Within the larger one there turned up two copper coins bearing the nianhao Qianyuan (AD 758–60), and a third coin of the same date was found near the other jar. And here I may conveniently mention that of the remaining six coins actually found by us on the ground in the immediate vicinity of the ruins, or embedded in the refuse-layers below the fort, not less than four were Qianyuan pieces, while one bore the nianhao Dali (AD 766–80) and another the legend Kaiyuan in use throughout the Tang period. The valuable chronological evidence thus supplied will be considered further on' (S: 1287).

'The Dali piece, together with a Qianyuan coin, was found stuck on a small stick [M.Tagh.c.005] (S: pl. LI]. In view of the very definite chronological evidence furnished by the coins actually found at the ruins, it is curious to note that of the twelve coins brought to me at Islamabad and said to have been obtained at Mazar-tagh eleven are much worn wuzhu or "goose-eye" pieces, while the twelfth, with an inscription not otherwise known to me (pl.CXL, no.35), is described by Mr J. Allan as a wuzhu coin of AD 581–604. Is it possible that these pieces come from some "Tati" above or near Mazar-tagh the existence I had heard mentioned in vague talk and also by my old guide Turdi, but which I could not verify? See also AK, I, p. 579' (S: 1287 n4).

'The numerous copper coins I acquired from them [a party of Kelpin men who had just searched extensive debris areas of the "Tati" type in the wide belt of absolute desert between the arid outer hill chain of Kelpin and Tumshuk on the Aksu-Kashgar road] ranged from Han to Tang times and left no doubt about the antiquity of the settlements once occupying the area they had searched . . . One of these coins, of Tang type, shows four non-Chinese characters which have not been read as yet' (S: 1306 n9).

**S.XXX.a:** Found within ruined fort.

**S.XXX.b:** Found on path leading to fort.

**S.XXX.c:** Found in refuse layers below fort.

**S.XXX.d:** Brought from Mazar-tagh site.

### *S.XXXI: COPPER COINS FOUND AT, OR BROUGHT FROM, DESERT SITES SOUTH OF KELPIN (S: 1306–8)*

**Sites:** The sites lay in the desert between the Kelpin oasis in the north and Tumshuk and Maral-bashi in the south (S: 1306). **Chong-tim** ('the big tower'). This site consisted of a fort, with the remains of a watch-tower (25 ft square), and a square circumvallation (110 yd long on each face) adjoining it on the western side. Extensive debris indicated that there was once a large settlement here. The site is positioned on the most direct route connecting Chilan (and the route to Aksu) and leading north of Maral-bashi then skirting the foothills to Kashgar (S: 1306–7).

'Smaller patches of débris-covered ground were also passed up to a distance of about 3 miles on the resumed march to the south-west of Chong-tim, and more traces of old canals cropped out between the dunes' (S: 1308).

**Acquisition/archaeological context:**

**S.XXXI.a.** Found at Chong-tim site (S: 1306–8). 'Just outside the north face of the enclosure there were picked up eleven much-worn wuzhu and "goose-eye" coins lying close together, evidently as they had dropped from a string. Among other Chinese coins found near the circumvallation three are wuzhu coins and one a Tang coin with the legend Kaiyuan. Their evidence, indicating occupation from an early period down to Tang times, was supported by that of the coins which were brought to me at Kelpin, avowedly as having been found at the Chong-tim site on the "treasure-seekers'" latest visit. Of these, twelve were Tang pieces, the latest bearing the nianhao Dali (AD 766–80), and one a huoquan coin of Wang Mang (AD 14–19).

'In view of the abundant and clear evidence proving the early abandonment of the site, I felt much puzzled when three Chinese copper coins of quite modern issues were picked up close together a short distance to the south-east of the ruined fort. Two were coins of the Emperor Qianlong with a mint-mark later than AD 1759, the other a piece of Jiaqing (AD 1796–1821). The archaeological riddle thus presented was solved only after my arrival at the village of Tumshuk, on the present high road, when the aged Karaul-bashi, in charge of the local police post, related how about 1876 a force of the pretender Hakim Tora had been routed by Yaqub Beg's son Hakaullah in a fight near Yaide, two marches further on by the road to Aksu. Many soldiers of the defeated party had sought escape by turning into the sandy desert northward, and had miserably perished there by thirst and exhaustion under the hot August sun. Kelpin people subsequently searched the desert for the money and the valuables of the dead fugitives and buried the corpses' (S: 1308).

**S.XXXI.** Found on tati south of Chong-tim. 'Finds of one wuzhu and four Kaiyuan pieces showed that this ground, too, was occupied about the same period as Chong-tim' further on; 'the finds of small coins soon showed that the area now reached must have continued in occupation considerably longer than Chong-tim, and well into the Islamic period. Besides two Tang pieces they comprised two Song dynasty coins of AD 1034–8 and 1068–78 respectively, as well as a small silver coin of the Golden Horde struck at Khwarizm in AH 743' (S: 1308–9).

**S.XXXI.c:** Purchased at Kelpin as brought from Chong-tim site.

**S.XXXI.d:** Purchased at Kelpin as brought from different sites, also from west of Kudughun.

### *S.XXXII: COPPER AND SILVER COINS FOUND ON TATIS NORTH OF TUMSHUK (S: 1309)*

**Site:** Tumshuk was a village by the high road. Extensive remains of Buddhist shrines (excavated by Pelliot in 1906) stood at the foot of the hill northwest of Tumshuk. Nearby was the ancient circumvallation of Topa-shahr, and on the left bank of the dry river bed Gore-akin were the scattered ruins of Tokuz-sarai (S: 1309).

**Acquisition/archaeological context:** 'Coins of Muhammad Arslan had been brought to me at Tumshuk as finds from Tokuz-sarai, and suggested that the abandonment of this site could not have taken place earlier than the fourteenth or fifteenth century. This dating has its special interest with reference to the previously noted "Tati" remains lower down the Gore-akin, and a rapid examination of the ruins confirmed the chronological evidence of the coins. A day's halt at Tumshuk allowed me to visit also the ruins to be found at both ends of the long-stretched ridge which continues the line of the previously mentioned hill to the south-east beyond the gap passed by the high road. Those at the southern end manifestly belong to a pre-Islamic stronghold and might have tempted exploration had it been possible for me to spare time for the protracted labours there needed' (S: 1309).

### *S.XXXIII: COPPER COINS BROUGHT FROM TOKUZ-SARAI RUINS, TUMSHUK (S: 1309)*

**Site:** For Tumshuk see S.XXXII.

## INNERMOST ASIA

### *IA.I: COINS FOUND AT OR BROUGHT FROM SITES BETWEEN KASHGAR AND MARAL-BASHI (IA: 68)*

**Sites:** The sites mentioned in the List of Coins are Khan-oi; Kurghan; Astin-artush; land between Besh-tam and Bogach-köl; the foothills between Astin-artush and Maral-bashi; route to Lal-tagh (IA: 988).

**Acquisition/archaeological context:** Coins not mentioned in text.

**IA.I.a:** Brought from Khan oi.

**IA.I.b:** Said to have been found at Kurghan, Astin-artush.

**IA.I.c:** Found between Besh-tam and Bogach-köl.

**IA.I.d:** Brought by Ulugh Akhun as from foot of hills between Astin-artush and Maral-bashi.

**IA.I.e:** From route to Lal-tagh site.

### *IA.II: COINS BROUGHT FROM MAZAR-TAGH SITE (IA: 92)*

**Site:** See S.XXX. Stein discovered evidence for prolonged excavation of the hill crest before the Tibetan fort was built, and the remains of a ruined Buddhist shrine (eighth to ninth

centuries, but subsequently turned into an Islamic place of worship) on the eastern side towards the river bank.
**Acquisition/archaeological context:** Coins are not mentioned in text, but were probably included in the following comments: 'The specimens of their ["treasure-seekers"'] finds which Kasim Akhun had brought me, and which the List below specifies, left me in no doubt that they were in general of same origin and date as those yielded by my clearings of 1908' (IA: 92). 'A few pieces of exactly similar character were subsequently received by me from Badruddin Khan, the Khotan Ak-sakal, who had acquired them from "treasure-seekers" (IA: 92 n7).

### *IA.III: COINS COLLECTED AT OR FROM KHOTAN*

**Acquisition/archaeological context:** 'I employed the six days' stay [at Khotan] to gather such antiques as my ever-willing old friend Badruddin Khan, the Ak-sakal of Indian and Afghan traders, and the "treasure-seekers" dispatched by him, had collected from Yotkan and from desert sites in the vicinity of the Khotan oasis. The sites named as the provenance of these antiques had almost all been visited by me on my former journeys, and the various classes of objects ascribed to them correspond in their character to the collections previously obtained . . . As regards their provenance a word of caution may well be repeated. Obviously objects brought for sale to Khotan town or obtained from "Taklamakanchis" cannot be assigned to particular sites with complete assurance. But their comparison with the proceeds of my own former search at the sites named supports the belief that the local distribution of the several series of objects shown in the List below may be accepted as correct on the whole' (IA: 98).

### *IA.III.A: COINS OF MISCELLANEOUS ORIGIN (IA: 99)*

**IA.III.A.a:** Among the group described as 'antiques acquired or presented at Khotan town' (IA: 109).
**IA.III.A.b:** Presented by Li Ssü-yeh (IA: 67). Li Ssü-yeh (Li Siye, where *siye* is an honorific), of Hunan province, was Stein's Chinese assistant (IA: 67). The provenance of these pieces is not known, and, as these types are not known from archaeological sites in Xinjiang, they can be regarded as collectors' pieces, rather than numismatic evidence.
**IA.III.A.c:** Presented by Mr Moldovack. 'Mr K. Moldovack, an Armenian gentleman settled at Khotan kindly added to this miscellaneous collection some metal seals, coins, and a colossal stucco head of Buddha probably brought from some site like that of Ak-terek' (IA: 99).
**IA.III.A.d:** Received as from Arka-kuduk and Kumat (IA: 99). Arka-kuduk not mentioned in text. Kumat is famous for its jade-pits (IA: 99 n5).
**IA.III.A.e:** Received as from Jigda-kuduk. Not mentioned in text.
**IA.III.A.f:** Brought as from Lachin-ata. Lachin-ata was the site of an Islamic mazar, near extensive tati of Ulugh-mazar (S: 1263).
**IA.III.A.g:** Brought as from Kalalik (IA: 99). 'The position of Kalalik is unknown to me' (IA: 99 n5).
**IA.III.A.h:** Brought as from Bash-kumat. Location of Bash-kumat not known, but Stein believed it to be near to jade-pits of Kumat.
**IA.III.A.i:** Brought as from Kizil-yar. Site near Khotan.
**IA.III.A.j:** Brought from Karim Akhun, who was 'the hunter from Islamabad on the Khotan river' (IA: 82).
**IA.III.A.k:** Brought by Abbas from Khotan tatis. Abbas was one of Stein's 'treasure-seeking' party of 1906–8' (IA: 100).
**IA.III.A.l:** Brought by Muhammad Sharif. Not mentioned in text.
**IA.III.A.m:** Brought as from Yotkan. For Yotkan see AK.II.
**IA.III.A.n:** Received from Muhammad Sharif as from Yotkan. For Yotkan see AK.II and IA.III.A.m. For Muhammad Sharif see IA.III.A.l.
**IA.III.A.o:** Brought by Tokhta Akhun from tatis near Hanguya, Arkalik. For Hanguya see AK.XI. Arkalik ('back lands') was a local name for the narrow strip of desert projecting from the Hanguya tati to the south, and dividing the cultivation of the Hanguya and Yurung-kash tracts (S: 134).
**IA.III.A.o:** Brought as from Chalma-kazan. For Chalma-kazan see AK.IV and S.XXVII.

### *IA.III.B: COINS PURCHASED FROM BADRUDDIN KHAN*

**Acquisition/archaeological context:** For Badruddin Khan see S.IV.A; IA.II and IA.III. 'The large and varied collection of Khotan antiques brought by Badruddin Khan in 1915 comprises some series of which he had noted the alleged provenance. But since none of these show any distinctive character and since, having received them at Kashgar, I was unable to test otherwise the correctness of that record, a brief indication below of the different places of alleged origin will suffice.' The numbers given in the text are for non-coin objects (IA: 99 n5) and the only indication of the coin provenances is in the List of Coins. 'Ak-tiken is known to me as an alternative name used by Taklamakanchis for the Kara-dong site. Toghrak-mazar is the small site, southeast of Kotaz-langar. Bash-kumat and Kalta-kumat are likely to be localities near the jade-pits of Kumat. The position of Kalalik and Yantak-kuduk is unknown to me' (IA: 99 n5).
**IA.III.B.a:** From Yotkan. The batch number (Badr.0147–64) indicates that these coins probably came from Yotkan. Although there is a gap in Stein's list 'Yotkan (Badr.0122–46, 0170–202)' (IA: 99 n5), these lists refer primarily to the Lists of Objects at the end of each chapter, and do not always include coins, which were listed in the Appendix.
**IA.III.B.b:** From Yotkan. The batch number (Badr.0199–201) indicates that these coins came from Yotkan (see IA.III.B.a).
**IA.III.B.c:** Said to come from Hanguya tatis. See AK.XI and S.IV.
**IA.III.B.d:** Said to come from Yotkan. But, according to Stein's text (IA: 99 n5), this batch (Badr.0246–7) came from Hanguya Tati.
**IA.III.B.e:** Said to come from Ak-tiken. Ak-tiken was another name, used by treasure-seekers in the Taklamakan, for the Kara-dong site (see IA: 99 n5). This batch number is not mentioned in Stein's text.
**IA.III.B.f:** This batch (Badr.0268–9) is not mentioned in Stein's text (IA: 99 n5).
**IA.III.B.g:** Said to come from Arkalik. This batch (Badr.0270–1) is not mentioned in Stein's text (IA: 99 n5).
**IA.III.B.h:** This batch (Badr.0434–45) is not mentioned in Stein's text (IA: 99 n5).

### *NOT IN LIST OF COINS*

Among the Lists of Objects (IA: 121) are the following references to coins:

'**Badr.0396:** lead coin-like disc, pierced with long hole. On each side of this, on obverse, are raised Chinese lapidary characters. Reverse blank. Diam. ⅞ in.'
'**Badr.0403:** mass of bronze fragments; coins, ornaments, spoon, wire nails, etc. All small and corroded.'
'**Badr.0424:** elliptical lead disc resembling Chinese coin, but hole oblong and imperfectly pierced. Raised device on one side suggesting manner of lettering on Chinese coins, but characters probably not Chinese, *cf.* Badr.0396. $\frac{14}{16}$ in. × $\frac{13}{16}$ in.'

### *IA.IV: COINS COLLECTED FROM OR NEAR DOMOKO (IA: 130 ff.)*

**Sites:** The Domoko oasis lay east of Khotan. The ruined sites near Domoko reached from Ulugh-ziarat in the west to Farhad-Beg-yailaki and Khadalik in the east (IA: 128–9). 'The area of ruined sites northeast of Domoko of which Khadalik marks the centre and Balawaste and Kuduk-köl the north and south ends, is likely to have been the source also of the series of miscellaneous relics marked D.K. in the List below' (IA: 130). Documents in batch D.K. included scraps of Tibetan, Chinese, and Brahmi on wood (similar to those from Khadalik). Remains of manuscripts and some wooden records in Sanskrit and Khotanese, also Tibetan, came from Khadalik (IA: 130).
**Acquisition/archaeological context:**
**IA.IV.a:** Obtained by Badruddin Khan (batch D.K.). 'The small objects in metal, stone and bone, D.K.01–8, were brought to me at Achma, where I stayed for the night after clearing the remains at Kuduk-köl. The rest, D.K.09–104, were acquired by Badruddin either at Domoko itself or received from there through Mullah Khawaja and other inhabitants . . .The small objects acquired through Badruddin Khan, and mainly stucco fragments, Kha.01–4, were said to have been brought from Khadalik itself' (IA: 130).

Also in batch D.K. was: ['D.K.052 a–c. Bronze fr[agment]s. on string. (a, b) Two Chin[ese] coins, corroded. (c) Bronze ferrule, broad at open end, which is trumpet shaped; then narrowing, and finally spreading slightly again to opposite end, which is closed by plate perforated with two holes. Diam. 1¼ in., h. ⅞ in.'] (IA: 134). These are the only two coins of this batch listed in the text; it is not known whether they were also included in the List of Coins.
**IA.IV.b:** Brought as from Uzun Tati, batch U.Z. For Uzun Tati see AK.X. 'Small antiques in metal, stone and wood acquired by me at Domoko and marked in the List with U.Z. were said to have been found in the great débris area that extends north and south of the sacred burial-place of Ulugh-mazar or Ulugh-ziarat in the desert to the north-west of Domoko' (which Stein had identified with Xuan Zang's Pimo, and Marco Polo's Pein) (IA: 130).
**IA.IV.c:** Bought at Achma as from Domoko Tatis. See IA.IV.a.

### *NOT IN LIST OF COINS*

Also included in batch D.K. were two small items in lead:
'**D.K.03**: lead rod, doubled into loop. Partly corroded. 1⅝ in. × ¼ in.'
'**D.K.04**: ball of lead of irregular surface. Diam. ⅝ in.'

### *IA.V: COPPER COINS FROM NIYA SITE, CHARCHAN AND VASH-SHAHRI*

#### *NIYA*

**Site:** See AK.VII and S.VIII.
**Acquisition/archaeological context:** Coin found near stupa. Listed among 'miscellaneous objects found at Niya site' (IA: 148).

#### *CHARCHAN*

**Site:** The western limit of the Charchan oasis approached a small ruin known as Tam, and its southern limit encroached upon the large tati area known as Kone-shahr, which marked the site of an earlier settlement (IA: 157–8). Stein noted that Charchan was also known for its illicit trade in gold (mined in Arka-tagh) and opium (IA: 158–9).
**Acquisition/archaeological context:** 'That this [Kone-shahr] was occupied also during the Islamic period was made probable by a Song copper coin with the nianhao Zhihe (AD 1054–6), which I purchased, and an Islamic silver coin shown to me at Charchan, both declared to have been found on the wind-eroded Tati near Yalghuz-dong-mazar' (IA: 158).

#### *VASH-SHAHRI*

**Site:** See S.X. Stein found the southeastern edge of the site covered with human remains, from a wind-eroded (non-Islamic) cemetery (IA: 161).
**Acquisition/archaeological context:** 'The only coin obtained from the [tati] site was a Chinese "cash" of the Chongning period (AD 1102–7). Its date confirms the conclusion I had drawn from numismatic evidence obtained on my former visit that the site was occupied down to the twelfth century AD' (IA: 161).

### *IA.VI: COPPER COINS FOUND AT LOP DESERT SITES A–F*

Stein was at the Lop desert sites from February to March 1914.

#### *IA.VI.A: COINS FROM RUINED SITES L.K. (RUINED FORT) AND L.M. (SETTLEMENT SITE SUPPORTING L.K. FORT) (IA: 184, 188, 196)*

**Sites:**
**L.K.** The remains of the L.K. fort stand about 30 miles from the L.A. site, almost one third of the distance from the L.A. site to Miran. It was intended to guard this route (IA: 189). The fort was an irregular oblong. the northeastern and southwestern faces measured 620 ft, and the northwestern and southeastern faces measured 330 ft. Stein found a gateway on the northeastern face (IA: 184–6). In construction, dimensions and arrangement, the L.K. fort is similar to the defensive quadrangle at the Karadong site and is contemporary with the Karadong, Niya and Loulan sites (IA: 186).
**L.M.** was an agricultural settlement close to, and supporting, the fort L.K. (IA: 189). Surface remains scattered on both sides of dry river-bed winding west to east. Stein examined remains of dwellings over an area measuring one mile northwest to southwest. Structural remains similar to those at Niya (IA: 193–6). Refuse heaps yielded Chinese paper fragments, Kharoshthi writing on wood and paper, bilingual paper document (Chinese on one side, Kharoshthi on the other), also fragments of paper with 'slanting Central Asian Brahmi script and apparently Kuchean language', and Early Sogdian script on

paper (as seen at Loulan L.A. and at Han watch-stations west of Dunhuang) (IA: 194–5).

**Acquisition/archaeological context:**

**IA.VI.A.a:** Found near L.K. fort. Tokhta Akhun's 'description of the site [L.K.], supported by miscellaneous small objects, including two Han coins, that he had picked up near the ruin [L.K.], left no doubt about its antiquity' (IA: 180). L.K.017–18 is part of a group titled 'miscellaneous objects brought by Tokhta Akhun from site of L.K.' (IA: 189–90).

'In close vicinity to the place where we had come upon the first stone remains [about two and a half miles from L.K.], there was picked up under my eyes an excellently preserved Chinese coin of the wuzhu type. It alone would have sufficed to prove the correctness of the conclusion I had already drawn in 1906 from the discovery of a single bronze arrow-head of Han type about four and a half miles from Camp 121, that this ground had been visited by man in the first centuries of our era' (IA: 184).

'Among miscellaneous small objects picked up from wind-eroded soil around the fort some Chinese coins may first be mentioned. Two of them are wuzhu pieces, like the fragmentary one which Tokhta Akhun had brought me from his reconnoitring visit, and which he said he had found within the walled enclosure; another is an uninscribed Han coin. Two more coins of the last-named type, as well as a fragment of a huoquan piece, were found close outside when I visited the fort. Numismatic evidence therefore clearly favoured attribution of the ruins to the period that had seen the Lou-lan sites in the north occupied and abandoned' (IA: 188).

'Small miscellaneous objects of the "Tati" type that could be picked up at the site practically within a single day and without such systematic search as a longer stay would have permitted. Among such finds six Chinese coins may be mentioned in the first place. They are all of the inscribed and large wuzhu type, which belongs to Han times and the immediately succeeding period. The numismatic evidence agrees therefore with the evidence furnished by the manuscript finds in Kharoshthi and Sogdian, in its bearing on the chronology of this site' (IA: 196).

**IA.VI.A.b:** Found at L.M.site. 'Among such [Tati] finds six Chinese coins may be mentioned in the first place. They are all of the inscribed and large wuzhu type, which belongs to Han times and the immediately succeeding period. The numismatic evidence agrees therefore with the evidence furnished by the manuscript finds in Kharoshthi and Sogdian, in its bearing on the chronology of this site' (IA: 196). L.M.0125–8 is part of a group titled 'miscellaneous objects found at L.M.' (IA: 199).

### *IA.VI.B: COINS FROM LOULAN STATION L.A. OR ITS VICINITY (IA: 208, 217)*

**Site:** For Loulan L.A. see S.XI. Documents found here included paper fragments with Chinese writing, also Early Sogdian script; Kharoshthi writing on wooden tablets; also fragments of Chinese writing on paper pasted together to form backing for some painted decoration (IA: 217).

**Camp C.xciii** [= L.M. camp C.xciii] was within one mile of an ancient river bed (probably of Kuruk-darya) (IA: 206).Going north from the site where the coins were found was a dry river bed, followed by 3 miles of tati finds. To the NNE rose the stupa at Loulan L.A. (IA: 208).

**Acquisition/archaeological context:**

**IA.VI.B.a:** Found 8½ miles beyond C.xciii. See S.XI. 'The ground was cut up into a maze of short Yardang trenches, reaching a depth of 10 feet or so, . . . about eight and a half miles marching distance from Camp xciii. Here three Chinese coins of the Han type were picked up in quick succession. One is an inscribed wuzhu piece; another a much-clipped specimen of the same; while the third, also clipped, still shows a trace of the legend huoquan, introduced by the usurper Wang Mang about the time of Christ' (IA: 208). [C.xciii.064–6]

**IA.VI.B.b:** Found at, or close to, walled station L.A. 'It is scarcely surprising that after the diligent search made during my previous stay the number of coins now collected from eroded ground at the site and around it was not so large as before. Yet, as the list . . . shows, their total amounts to 56. With the exception of three bearing the legend huoquan, all the rest are pieces of the wuzhu type. The majority of them, thirty-two in all, retain the inscription Wu-chu, though many are clipped; the rest are small uninscribed pieces of the "goose-eye" kind. The proportion between these varieties approximately corresponds to that noted among the coins recovered before at the ruins L.A.III–VI. It thus confirms the conclusion drawn in *Serindia* that the circulation of those much-clipped pieces as a quasi-subsidiary currency goes back farther than has been assumed by some numismatists (cf. S: 385, 1344)' (IA: 217).

### *NOT IN LIST OF COINS*

**L.A.012:** 'Bronze disc, in form of Chinese coin, but thinner and concavo-convex. Diam. ⅞ in.' (IA: 220).

**L.A.VI.ii.059:** 'Small silk bag, oblong, one end open; inscribed one side with 4 lines Kharoshthi, on other with 2 lines. Some holes, but writing clear and black. Silk natural-coloured; rather open weave. Bag 2¼ in. × 1¾ in.' (IA: 223). Boyer determined that the bag was intended to convey a small gift: the names of sender and recipient being inscribed on one side, the gift (a precious stone?) on the other side (IA: 216 n9).

**C.xciv:** 'Numerous Chinese coins of the wuzhu type were again found in numbers in its vicinity [ruined stupa NW of L.A.], besides plentiful small objects in bronze' (IA: 271).

### *IA.VI.C: COINS FROM CEMETERY L.C. AND ITS VICINITY (IA: 246)*

**Site:** The cemetery was on a conspicuous mesa-terrace rising 35 ft above surrounding ground, measuring 56 yd northeast to southwest, with maximum width of 32 yd. At this height, it had been little affected by wind-erosion. Although textiles were excellently preserved, the skeletons showed signs of weathering and corrosion, hence Stein's conclusion that these remains had been collected from older graves and placed on the terrace some time before the Chinese station of Loulan was abandoned. The grave-pits either followed the lengths of the stone terrace or were placed in the centre. All were roughly rectangular and cut 5–6 ft deep, but surface dimensions varied from 40 sq ft to 70 sq ft (IA: 226–8).

**Acquisition/archaeological context:**

**IA.VI.C.a:** Found in grave-pits. 'The finds in the grave-pits of L.C. also included two well-preserved coins of the wuzhu type, perhaps intended to symbolize financial provision for the dead' (IA: 246).

**IA.VI.C.b:** Found near L.C. and on way to L.E. See IA.VI.C.a and IA.VI.D. 'As we continued our tramp north-eastwards [from

L.C.] an uninscribed coin was picked up about a mile from the mesa' (IA: 259).

***NOT IN LIST OF COINS***

**L.C.022:**'Embossed gold-foil disc, on iron base. Pattern, incised ring. Iron badly corroded. Gold, ⅞ in. diam. Iron 1 in., thickness $\frac{5}{16}$ in.' Pl.XXIV. (IA: 248).

***IA.VI.D: COINS FROM L.E. CASTRUM AND MESA L.F. (IA: 263, 266)***

**Sites:**

**L.E.** was a ruined fort, rougly rectangular: its eastern and western faces measured 450 ft, its southern and northern faces 400 ft. Main gate, about 10 ft wide, in southern wall; smaller gate in northern wall. Similar in construction and date to Dunhuang *limes* (IA: 260–1). Chinese wood slips and paper documents found here (IA: 262).

**Mesa L.F.** was an imposing ridge of reddish clay, rising very steeply to over 100 ft, on bearing NE to SW. At top of mesa was a ridge, the centre of which was occupied by graves, some intact, some eroded. This small (non-Chinese) cemetery was separated from the northeastern end of the mesa by a 6-ft wide trench, on the other side of which was a stronghold. Stronghold was an irregular oblong, measuring 200 ft long, 80 ft at widest. Small knoll, of natural clay, in centre of stronghold, had probably served as look-out (IA: 263). 'The post lay moreover in the same NE direction which, as the position of L.C. and L.E. showed, the ancient Chinese route from the Loulan station obviously followed' (IA: 263). L.F.iii was a room to the left of the entrance passage to the stronghold. Kharoshthi wooden document, Chinese wood slips and paper documents were found (IA: 263).

**Acquisition/archaeological context:**

**IA.VI.D.a:** Found near circumvallation of L.E. 'Apart from these [Chinese] records and a Chinese coin of the wuzhu type the only finds from the site comprise two bronze arrow-heads and a few small stone implements' (IA: 262).

**IA.VI.D.b:** Found in room L.F.iii, and at foot of Mesa L.F. 'It [L.F.iii] contained nothing but an uninscribed Chinese coin of the wuzhu type and a small heap of oats and oat-straw' (IA: 263).

'Nine Chinese copper coins, all of the wuzhu type, among them several small much-clipped pieces, which were picked up close to the foot of the Mesa, make it appear very probable that the occupation of L.F. continued as long as the desert route towards Tun-huang remained in use' (IA: 266)

***IA.VI.E: COINS FROM MINOR SITES L.D., L.G., L.I., L.J., L.Q. (IA. 218 ff., 284, 290, 744)***

L.D.–L.G.05–09, 011–016

**Sites:**

**L.D.** was a farm-dwelling, about two and a half miles distant from Loulan L.A., and contemporary with L.A. (IA: 218). Wooden documents with Kharoshthi script (similar to those found at Loulan and Niya) were found here (IA: 218).

**L.G.** was a very badly eroded dwelling on a *yardang*, about three miles from Camp xciv.a. Stein did not visit L.G. but from the changes in geological features concluded that L.G. marked the eastern limit of the environment immediately surrounding Loulan L.A. He also traced near L.G. the easternmost extension of the Kuruk-darya delta, in the form of a dry river-bed (IA: 219).

**L.I.** was a group of three mesas, rising to height of 60ft, near Camp C.c. No structural remains, but refuse indicated that this had been a camping place for indigenous herdsmen, from neolithic times onwards. L.I. lay in a northeasterly direction in line with L.C., L.E., L.F. sites (IA: 285–7). Northeast of L.I. was the watch-tower L.J. (See IA.VI.d).

**L.J.** was a Chinese watch-tower (contemporary with *limes* towers) on same line to the northeast as sites from L.A. to L.E. and beyond (IA: 287). Dry river-bed to the west of L.J. (IA: 288).

**L.Q.** was a small watch-tower and burial ground (IA: 284–5).

**Acquisition/archaeological context:**

**IA.VI.E.a:** Found at ruin L.D. 'A find of distinct interest had been made by Afraz-gul on his preceding visit, in close vicinity to the ruin; this was a well-preserved Chinese bronze coin of peculiar type (pl.CXIX, no.3), showing different seal characters at either end and attributed to Yuanyan (12–8 BC). The chronological indication furnished by the effaced remains of Kharoshthi documents is fully confirmed by the fact that the twenty coins picked up near L.D. were all of the wuzhu type, about half of them being small clipped pieces' (IA: 218).

**IA.VI.E.b:** Found at, or near, ruin L.G. On his [Afraz-gul's] way there [to Camp C.xciva] and on his farther journey to the north-north-east, he had picked up some fragments of metal and stone . . . as well as a dozen Chinese coins; the latter include a huoquan piece, while the remainder are of the wuzhu type, some retaining their inscription but others much clipped' (IA: 219).

**IA.VI.E.c:** Found northeast of L.I. 'About half-way to it [L.J.] Afraz-gul's keen eyes lighted upon two wuzhu coins close to our track, still preserving their legend, though worn' (IA: 290).

**IA.VI.E.d:** Found east-north-east of L.J. on ancient route line. 'At a distance of less than a mile from L.J., Tursun Akhun, one of the camelmen, marching ahead with me, suddenly called my attention to some scattered coins within five yd or so of our track. I had given strict orders ever since our start from the Lou-lan station that any objects discovered on the march were to be brought to my notice, but left undisturbed until I could pick them up myself. I was thus able to satisfy myself that Chinese copper coins by the score strewed the sandy soil along a line parallel to the direction of our march for a distance of some thirty yd.

'Rapid but careful examination showed that these coins, two hundred and eleven in all, were lying in groups or small heaps over a strip of ground nowhere more than three or four feet across. The coins were all wuzhu coins of the large inscribed type (pl.CXIX) and, with the exception of a few which had suffered breaks, were in perfect condition. They were all of uniform size and cast, and showing neither wear nor clipping seemed as if fresh from a mint. Examination with the compass proved that the well-defined line along which they lay ran from north-east to south-west. It was clear that all these coins had dropped from a caravan moving in the very direction in which I had supposed the ancient route to lie. They must have got loose from the string which tied them and gradually dropped out unobserved through an opening in their bag or case. The swaying movement of the camel or cart in which this receptacle was probably carried sufficiently explains why the line marked by the scattered coins had the width above indicated.

'Any doubt as to the character of the convoy from which this "petty cash" had been lost was removed when Naik Shamsuddin, on arriving with the camels, for which he acted as rearguard, and searching the ground near by, came up on a scattered heap of bronze arrow-heads behind a small Yardang, at a point about fifty yd S.50°W. from where the line of coins ended. The arrow-heads, all in very fair preservation, lay close together through corrosion, which suggests that they had been originally closely packed together in the same bag or box . . . The fact that these finds were both made close together and on the same line makes it appear very probable that arrow-heads and coins were dropped by some convoy of Han times coming from the side of China and carrying stores for troops. The way in which the coins as well as the arrow-heads had been allowed to remain on the ground, without being picked up at the time or by subsequent wayfarers, might suggest that the convoy moving towards Lou-lan from which they fell had been travelling at night-time, and probably a little off the main track, but still in the right direction. If more sand covered the ground than the winds have left now, small objects would continue to remain hidden from view, even though traffic may have continued to pass close by for several centuries' (IA: 290–1).

**IA.VI.E.e:** Found north-north-east of L.Q. 'The bronze buckle L.Q.02 was picked up after three miles' march, and some two miles farther on a Chinese copper coin of the Han type. Near by small bits of ore seemed to indicate a smelting-place' (IA: 744).

#### *IA.VI.F: COINS FOUND ON LOP DESERT MARCHES*

**Site:** The Lop Desert marches were the salt-encrusted lands of the ancient dry sea-bed which lay between Loulan in the west and Dunhuang in the east.

**C.xcvi** = Camp.C.xvi.

**C.xcix** = Camp C.xcix.

**C.ci**= Camp C.ci.

**Mesa east of C.ci.** This mesa [about 5½ miles from IA.VI.F.c] rose 25 ft above the ground, and was a natural halting place on the route to and from Loulan (IA: 296).

**C.ciii** = Camp C.ciii.

**C.ccxlix**= Camp C.ccxlix, which was near a dry river-bed (IA: 747).

**Acquisition/archaeological context:**

**IA.VI.F.a:** Found near C.xvi. 'Several bronze arrow-heads and miscellaneous metal fragments, were also picked up on this ground [near camp C.xcvi] besides fragments of two inscribed wuzhu coins' (IA: 274).

**IA.VI.F.b:** Found south of C.xcix. South of this camp 'just before we came upon this [salt-impregnated clay] ground dead tamarisks were found in patches, and near one of them we picked up a wuzhu coin, evidence of the passage of man' (IA: 284).

**IA.VI.F.c:** Found ½ mile east of C.ci. 'We had scarcely covered half a mile when the discovery of a wuzhu coin picked up under my eyes gave welcome assurance that notwithstanding the altered direction we could not be far off the line which the ancient Chinese route had followed' (IA: 296).

**IA.VI.F.d:** Found on mesa, 6 miles east of C.ci. 'Here a strange discovery awaited us. I was just preparing to climb the Mesa to inspect the ground ahead, when one of my men noticed three wuzhu coins lying in line, about a yard or so from each other, close to the western foot of the ridge. I picked them up myself, and found that the impression left by them on the salty clay was quite clear.' Other small metal objects were also found there. 'Finally we recovered two more wuzhu coins, large inscribed pieces and well preserved, like the first finds, together with the fine pale-green glass bead, on the northern slope about eight feet above the ground level.

'The discovery of all these relics close together was a dramatic surprise. There could be no possible doubt that they dated from the period when the Chinese "route of the centre" leading to Loulan was frequented by traffic. The evidence of the coins is completely supported by that of the small iron skewer, which in shape and make exactly conforms to five other specimens excavated in 1907 at different watch-stations of the Han Limes west and north of Dunhuang' (IA: 296).

**IA.VI.F.e:** Found 13 and 14½ miles southeast of C.ciii. 'We had scarcely proceeded more than half a mile to the SSW of the above-mentioned low hillock when a Chinese copper coin of the large inscribed wuzhu type was picked up by one of the camelmen in my presence. On continuing our march in the same direction for only two furlongs Afraz-gul's keen eyes lit upon a spherical bead of translucent white glass, lying on the coarse sand which here lightly covered the soil. These two small objects picked up along the very line of our march raised a strong presumption that they had dropped from traffic following a route of identical or closely similar bearing. A second coin picked up within a mile and three-quarters of the first fully confirmed this conclusion; but the find was attended by a discovery which at the time was bound to exercise our minds even more [fresh human footprints] . . . On tracking them . . . I found an inscribed wuzhu coin of the large type firmly adhering to the soil within eight yards of the foot of the hillock. There could be no further doubt now that our first march east of the dried-up sea-bed had brought us back again to ground once traversed by the ancient Han route' (IA: 302–3).

**IA.VI.F.f:** Found northwest of C.ccxlix.a 'Here between 3 and 4 miles' distance from camp there were picked up in succession first fragments of a Chinese coin and then miscellaneous small stone implements and potsherds' (IA: 747).

**IA.VI.F.g:** Found southwest of Toghrak-bulak. Coin not mentioned in text.

#### IA.VII: COPPER COINS FOUND ALONG ANCIENT HAN *LIMES* *(IA: 345, 349, 351, 373, 376 ff., 382, 384, 391 ff., 400)*

**Site:** For Han *limes* see S.XV.

**T.XXII.d** was one of a series of watch-stations stretching eastwards along the southern shore of the Khara-nor lake. The lake and marshland here served as a natural line of defence, and there were no remains of the wall or *limes* here. Tower T.XXII.d (with base 16 feet sq) stood on an eroded clay ridge rising 80ft above marshy bay to the west, and stretching 300 yd east north east to west south west. Refuse heap immediately southwest of the tower (IA: 344–5). Over ten Chinese wood slips, fragmentary, some dated: AD 47, AD 64, and 10 BC or AD 115, were found in the refuse heap (IA: 345).

**T.XXIII.b** (base 16 ft sq.) stood on an eroded ridge of clay about 50 ft high, one of a group of watch-towers connected by *limes* remains, which stopped about 300 yd northwest of T.XXIII.b. (IA: 348–9).

**T.XXIII.f** was a tower (base 14 ft sq.) which stood at the summit of a narrow isolated clay ridge running east–west and about

100 yd long. About 6 ft from the eastern base of the tower, a well (3 ft wide) had been cut into the clay. Lots of refuse lay around the tower, and on the southern slope (IA: 351).

**T.XL.a** was a watch-station along the *limes* north of the Sule river (Shule He). The tower (base 20 ft sq.) stood just north of an agger, or man-made embankment, some 34 ft at the base and rising to a height of 8–9 ft (IA: 373).

**T.XLI.c** was 'a conspicuous clay terrace, which had been converted into a natural tower by roughly cutting down the sides'. The base of the tower measured 20 ft square. A 10 ft high agger passed round the eastern, northern and western faces of the mesa (IA: 376).

**T.XLI.d** was about one and a half miles from T.XLI.c. It was 'a conspicuous tower of stamped clay, rising within 30 yd of the river bank and facing the lower end of the village lands of Jiudaogou on the bank opposite' (IA: 376).

**T.XLI.e** was a watch-station about one and a half miles from T.XLI.d, which stood on a rocky ridge jutting out towards the river. 'The watch-post consisted of a small room placed in a commanding position' (IA: 377).

**T.XLI.f** was a large tower 'perched conspicuously on the top of a detached hillock, rising about 150 ft above the riverine flat' . . . 'commands a distant view along the river both to the east and west'. Its base measured 24 ft square. The southern slopes below the tower yielded a large quantity of ancient refuse. The refuse heap yielded Chinese wood slips, including blanks and effaced slips (IA: 377).

**T.XLI.g** was 'a small enclosure of stamped clay, standing at the foot of the hillock, had a much more recent appearance' (IA: 377).

**T.XLI.k.** 'Having covered [following the remains of an agger] about 4 miles from Jiaowancheng, we crossed the well-marked track by which the route from Hami reaches the right river bank in present times. Close to it a clay terrace, about 3 ft high and about 75 ft in diameter, thickly strewn with Han pottery fragments and stones, marked the spot once occupied by a watch-post, T.XLI.k (IA: 382).

**T.XLI.l.** The agger continued from T.XLI.k for about a mile to a couple of small stupas 'obviously of late construction' close to the line of the *limes* (IA: 382).

**T.XLI.r** was a ruined tower, with a small guard-room near by (IA: 384).

**T.XLIII.a** was a watch-tower now 'decayed into a mere gravel-covered mound of small dimensions' surrounded by ancient potsherds and a refuse heap to the south'. Three Chinese wood slips found in the refuse heap (IA: 391).

**T.XLIII.g** was a watch-tower. In the same line of watch-towers as T.XLIII.a, this tower stood on a low mound. Refuse layers were found on the western and southern slopes. More recently, a herdsman's shelter had been built into the eastern side of the mound. Four Chinese wood slips were found here (IA: 392).

**T.XLIII.h** was a small gravel covered hillock about 30 ft high, and diameter 50 ft, with the foundations of a wall 5 ft thick on the eastern slope, which served as a look-out platform. Refuse found below wall on the eastern slope. Stein concluded that T.XLIII.h was a kind of sectional headquarters. Chinese wood slips, some dated 39 BC and AD 13 found in the refuse layer (IA: 392–3).

**T.XLIII.i** were the 'much-decayed remains of a brick-built tower, occupying a natural small knoll to the south of the wall.'. Refuse found on slopes. Chinese wood slips and seal-case found here (IA: 393).

**T.XLIV.a** was the northernmost of a group of watch-towers, which stood apart from the *limes* but stretching towards it. Stein concluded that these towers were not contemporary with the occupation of the *limes*, but later. The base of the tower measured 32 ft square, with a small structure on the eastern side. Refuse layers. Chinese wood slips found (IA: 399–401).

**T.XLIV.c.** was a watch-tower. See IA.XLIV.a. It was 'a much-decayed post, consisting of the foundations of a clay-built tower, about 16 ft sq, and of a room closely adjoining to the north'. Refuse heap close by. Chinese wood slips found in refuse' (IA: 401).

**T.XLIV.d.** was a tower. See IA.XLIV.a. Its base was 16 ft square, and it had a guard room (IA: 401). Stein noted that this tower was clearly visible from the caravan route to Suzhou. Chinese wood slips were found in refuse. One, dated AD 64, referred to operations at an agricultural colony (IA: 401).

**Acqusition/archaeological context:**

**IA.VII.a:** Found at watch-tower T.XXII.d. 'A much-clipped wuzhu coin was also found here [in refuse heap]' (IA: 345).

**IA.VII.b:** Found in watch-station T.XXIII.b. 'A clipped wuzhu coin and the fragment of a Chinese record on wood were also found here' (IA: 349).

**IA.VII.c:** Found at watch-station T.XXVIII.f. 'By clearing this [refuse] a few fragmentary Chinese records on wood were recovered, besides a large wuzhu coin and a variety of miscellaneous objects, as described in the List' (IA: 351).

**IA.VII.d:** Found at watch-station T.XL.b. 'A well-preserved wuzhu coin of the large type was picked up close to the tower' (IA: 373).

**IA.VII.e:** Found at watch-station T.XLI.c. 'That it has been used as a watch-station and probably occupied for a long time was proved by the abundance of potsherds of the Han type that thickly covered the ground near by, especially to the south. Here, too, a broken wuzhu coin was found' (IA: 376).

**IA.VII.f:** Found at watch-tower T.XLI.d. 'The fragment of a wuzhu coin was picked up near by' (IA: 376).

**IA.VII.g:** Found at watch-station T.XLI.e. 'Among the miscellaneous refuse was found the wooden spindle, and just outside the fascines an inscribed wuzhu coin of the large type' (IA: 377).

**IA.VII.h:** Found below, or near, watch-tower T.XLI.f. 'A Chinese coin found here, bearing traces of the inscription huoquan, also attests occupation in Han times. Two copper coins of the Manchu period which were discovered near the tower had obviously been left by men who had kept guard there in recent times' (IA: 377).

**IA.VII.i:** Found at ruin T.XLI.g. 'The numerous fragments of glazed ware and of porcelain found within and near by were in harmony with this [recent appearance], and likewise a coin apparently of the Kangxi period' (IA: 377).

**IA.VII.j:** Found at watch-post T.XLI.k. 'A large wuzhu coin was found near it' (IA: 382).

**IA.VII.k:** Found at station T.XLI.l. Coin not mentioned in text.

**IA.VII.l:** Found at watch-tower T.XLI.r. 'Here a wuzhu coin of the large type was picked up on the surface' (IA: 384).

**IA.VII.m:** Found at watch-tower T.XLIII.a. 'Close to the mound a wuzhu coin was picked up on the surface' (IA: 391).
**IA.VII.n:** Found at watch-tower T.XLIII.g. 'A broken wuzhu coin was also picked up here [in refuse]' (IA: 392).
**IA.VII.o:** Found at station T.XLIII.h. 'Apart from a fragmentary coin, apparently an issue of Wang Mang, nothing was found here' (IA: 392). 'In view of the chronological indication afforded by these (Han dynasty finds] and by the coin previously mentioned, the find of a torn piece of paper, uninscribed, has its special interest [leading Stein to conclude that this was a kind of sectional headquarters]' (IA: 392–3).
**IA.VII.p:** Found at tower T.XLIII.i. Coin not mentioned in text.
**IA.VII.q:** Found at tower T.XLIV.a. 'Quite close to the SW foot of the tower were found the fragment of a wuzhu coin and a bronze arrow-head, such as is common along the Limes' (IA: 400).
**IA.VII.r:** Found at watch-tower T.XLIV.c. 'From a small refuse heap close by . . . a bronze arrow-head of the regulation type and a huoquan coin. Another arrow-head of the same [regulation] type and a wuzhu coin were picked up on bare gravel soil to the north of the post' (IA: 401).
**IA.VII.s:** Found near watch-tower T.XLIV.d. 'About 50 yards to the south of the tower was picked up a copper "cash" of Kangxi (AD 1661–1728), which had evidently been dropped by some late visitor to this ground' (IA: 401).

***NOT IN LIST OF COINS***
***COIN FOUND AT WATCH-TOWER T.XLII.B***

'For three-quarters of a mile the agger runs on towards another small rocky eminence, where a completely decayed clay mound about 12 ft high is all that remains of the tower T.XLII.b. Fragments of Han pottery indicate that it was occupied contemporaneously with the wall. From some refuse close to the mound we recovered a roughly carved piece of Toghrak wood, perhaps the lintel of a door, and the fragment of a wuzhu coin' (IA: 384).

***IA. VIII: COPPER COINS FOUND AT OR NEAR KHARAKHOTO***
***IA. VIII.A: COINS FROM RUINED TOWN OF KHARAKHOTO (IA: 441 ff.)***

**Site:** Kharakhoto (Chinese: Heicheng, 'the black town'). 'It was a striking sight, the most impressive perhaps that I had ever seen on true desert ground, this dead town, with massive walls and bastions for the most part still in fair preservation, rising above the bare gravel flat which stretches towards it from the river bank' (IA: 437). Enclosed area measures on northern side 466 yd, on western side 381 yd. Gates, 18 ft wide, on eastern and western walls. Stupas. Stein identified the site as Marco Polo's City of Etzina (IA: 456). Western portion of town mostly occupied by shrines (IA: 442). Chinese, Tibetan, Mongolian paper documents (IA: 440–61), Xi Xia texts (IA: 449), Persian manuscript leaf (IA: 444) found at site.
**K.K.I** refers to the remains of a large shrine in the western portion of the town, with a large cella (32 × 50 ft). There had once been a colossal Buddha image here (IA: 442).
**Acquisition/archaeological context:**
**IA.VIII.a.** Found below image base in shrine K.K.I. 'Close to the east of the place where it [colossal Buddha image] once stood, there was found a Chinese copper coin, with the nianhao Xining (AD 1068–78), which may be supposed to have been laid at the foot of the image base as a votive gift' (IA: 442).
**IA.VIII.b.** Found in northwest corner of walled area. Coin not mentioned in text.
**IA.VIII.c.** Found within, or outside, walled town. 'The dates supplied by the coins that we found at the site do not extend beyond the third quarter of the twelfth century. A reference to the list of these coins in Appendix B will show that out of seventeen Chinese copper coins found within the town or immediately outside it no less than thirteen bear nianhaos falling between the years AD 1008 and 1161, while three show the Tang legend Kaiyuan and one is a wuzhu piece. It deserves to be noticed that all these thirteen coins, with the exception of a piece showing the nianhao Zhenglong (AD 1156–61) of the Jin dynasty set up by the Nü-chen Tartars, belong to issues of the Song dynasty. The total absence of coins of the Xi Xia rulers, issues of which are known to have been made between the years 1075 and 1226, is certainly very curious. It may be explained, with some degree of probability, by the reflection that the circulation of the imperial coinage of the Song must, owing to the preponderance of trade with China proper, have always been greater than that of the local rulers, even within the limits of the Tangut kingdom' (IA: 441).

***NOT IN LIST OF COINS***

'The discovery noted below (p. 444), of what Dr Laufer has recognized as remains of a Chinese paper-note dated in the first regnal period, Zhongtong (1260–4), of the Emperor Kublai, in a room of the ruined sarai, K.K.I.viii, agrees with the chronological evidence of the documents just referred to [dated 1290–1366]' (IA: 441). 'Here, too, were found the much-decayed pieces, K.K.I.viii.01.a–d, of what Dr Laufer has recognized as a paper-note dated in the nianhao Zhongtong (AD 1260–4), the first regnal period of the Mongol dynasty. Dr Laufer believes "this may lay claim to be the oldest paper-note now in existence"' (IA: 444). The note has since been identified as a 500-cash Zhongtong yuanbao jiaochao, and is now in the British Library collection [BL: Or.12380.2286 & 2287].

***IA. VIII.B: COINS FROM RUINED SETTLEMENTS EAST OF KHARAKHOTO***

**Site:** The remains of dwellings and small finds indicated that these ruined settlements were contemporary with the ruined town. There were ruins of dwellings for about four miles eastwards (IA: 453–4).
**K.E.IX–X** were ruins of an agricultural settlement positioned on open ground, where the rectangular outlines of fields were still visible (IA: 454).
**Acquisition/archaeological context:** 'It only remains for me to mention that the coins picked up by us at different points of the once cultivated area fully bear out the numismatic evidence already noted in connexion with the dwellings IX and X. Out of a total of seventeen coins, eleven belong to Song issues, the nianhaos represented ranging from AD 1017–22 to AD 1086–94. Of the other Chinese pieces two bear the legend wuzhu and two that of Kaiyuan, while another is the modern "cash" previously mentioned. One non-Chinese copper coin has not so far been identified. The direct chronological conclusion to be drawn from the coins found at this settlement is thus practically the

same as that indicated by the coins found within or quite close to the ruined town' (IA: 456).

**IA.VIII.B.a:** Found at ruin K.E.VI. Coin not mentioned in text.

**IA.VIII.B.b:** Found at ruins K.E.IX–X. 'I should have found it difficult to believe that these fields and farms had been abandoned to the desert as many centuries ago as the ruins on eroded ground near by and as the ruins of Khara-khoto, had not the conclusion been forced on me by the discovery in all of them of potsherds of identical type, and also of a number of coins close to the dwellings IX and X' (IA: 455). Among these eight coins, four are Song pieces, while two bear the legend wuzhu, and one shows the Tang nianhao Kaiyuan. The fact that the eighth coin showed the nianhao Jiaqing of AD 1796–1821 might have puzzled me greatly, had I not subsequently learned by chance at Gaotai that cultivators of that oasis, which, though fertile enough, offers no chance of expansion to meet the pressure of increasing population, had formed a plan for bringing this abandoned land east of Khara-khoto (known to them as Heicheng "the black town") once more under irrigation . . . It is likely enough that the modern coin was left there by one of these prospectors, or else by other visitors whom the tradition of this old colony had brought to the site' (IA: 455)

**IA.VIII.B.c:** Found at ruins K.E.XIV–XIX. 'With the exception of two unidentified pieces, all the seven [now eight] coins found in this southernmost portion of the once occupied area belong to Song issues' (IA: 455).

### *IA.VIII.C: COINS FROM RUINED FORT OF ADUNA-KORA (IA: 346)*

**Site:** Aduna-kora was the Mongol name for a ruined fort close to Kharakhoto. The fort consisted of two walled enclosures, one inside the other, but not concentrically placed. The inner fort enclosed an area of 83 yd square, with the gate through the southern face. The outer fort enclosed a quadrangle measuring 220 yd east–west and 180 yd north–south, with the gate on the eastern face (IA: 436).

**Acquisition/archaeological context:** 'The only definite chronological evidence was supplied by five Chinese copper coins, which were picked up on ground close to the outer wall on the east. Four of these are Kaiyuan pieces, current throughout Tang times, while a fifth shows the nianhao Xianping, corresponding to AD 998–1004. This last coin makes it clear that the ruined fort must have been occupied, at least intermittently, down to Song times. From the absence of structural remains, taken in conjunction with the absence of potsherds, I was inclined to conclude that the circumvallation had primarily served as a place of refuge or halt for caravans, etc, moving by the Etsin-gol route' (IA: 436).

### *IA.IX: COPPER COINS OF MANCHU DYNASTY FOUND AT LUOTUOCHENG AND BEITING (IA: 509 ff.)*

**Sites:**

**Luotuocheng** was a ruined town on the right bank of the dry Ganzhou river-bed. There was a rectangular circumvallation approximately one mile east–west and 1,430 yd north–south. A cross-wall divided the enclosed area into two unequal portions communicating by a gate in the middle. Gates on the eastern and northern walls. In the southeastern corner was a small enclosure with the remains of a well 80 ft deep and some half-ruined structures (IA: 509).

**Beiting** (Turkic: Besh-balik). Seat of Chinese protectorate during Tang times, previously known during Han period as Jinman. The outer walls enclose a roughly rectangular area 2,160 yd north–south and 1,260 yd east–west. Local digging for soil within the enclosed area. About 250 yd southeast of the northwestern corner of outer circumvallation was a small Chinese temple, still occupied in the Ming dynasty or later (IA: 555–7).

**Acquisition/archaeological context:**

**IA.IX.a:** From Luotuocheng. 'It was probably within or near this small enclosed area that Lal Singh picked up the fourscore odd fragments of Chinese coins which he brought me. All of them have proved to be modern, the nianhaos as far as legible ranging from AD 1644–62 to AD 1851–62' (IA: 509).

**IA.IX.b:** From ruined temple, Beiting. 'A small much-worn Chinese coin which was picked up near the ruin [of the small Chinese temple] has not yet been identified . . . This rarity [of finds] is indicated by the fact that inquiries I made at Hupuzi produced only three Tang coins with the legend Kaiyuan, for each of which the ridiculous price of two taels [of silver] was demanded.' (IA: 557).

### *IA.X: COINS EXCAVATED OR PURCHASED AT KARA-KHOJA (IA: 590 ff.)*

**Site:** Kara-khoja was Stein's base for visiting sites in the Turfan region: the ruined city of Gaochang (known locally as Idikut-shahri 'town of the Idikut or Uighur ruler'), the cemetery sites near the villages of Kara-khoja and Astana, also the cave-shrines of Toyuk, and the ruined temples near by. Stein noted that 'Destruction [since Grünwedel had visited the site in 1902–3] had made unchecked progress ever since. It had, as already hinted above, been accelerated by the profit which, as the villagers soon realized, could be secured from the sale of antiques and manuscript remains to archaeological parties and others. The proximity of Urumqi made it a convenient market, and the Trans-Siberian Railway offered facilities even for direct trade with European centres' (IA: 588–9).

**Kao.I** (Gaochang) was a large complex of buildings around a central court, with remains of an important temple on the western side, suggesting an important monastery. Kao.I.ii was a large hall, approached from the central court. Uighur, Chinese and Sogdian manuscripts were found here (IA: 590). See IA.X.a.

**Kao.III** was a large, octagonal stupa (IA: 591–2). Chinese, Brahmi and Uighur writing on paper, and Uighur writing on wood slip were found here (IA: 592).

**Acquisition/archaeological context:**

**IA.X.a:** Found in ruin Kao.I. 'Among other finds made here [Kao.I.ii] . . . and five Chinese copper coins all with the legend Kaiyuan, current during the Tang period' (IA: 590).

**IA.X.b:** Found near ruin Kao.I. Coins not mentioned in text.

**IA.X.c:** Found in hoard of ruin Kao.III. 'The large and very interesting hoard of metal objects was discovered on the north-eastern side of the passage [around the circular wall of the stupa] close to the outer wall and on a level nearly five feet above the floor. This clearly proves that when it was deposited, the interior of the passage must have been already filled to this height with debris from the vaulting and walls. The character of the objects and in particular the heap of broken pieces of iron and bronze belonging to different vessels, implements, etc, that formed part of the cache, leave no doubt that the person who placed it in the ruined structure hidden under the debris was a metal-worker. As originally deposited, we found lying close together in the cache the four bronze cauldrons, placed nest-like inside one another; the bronze cooking pot, filled with a mass of copper coins, small objects in bronze, silver, etc, and covered over with the iron casque, two bronze mirrors, bronze bowls and iron(?) saucers, a spear-head, knives and a heap of miscellaneous metal objects and fragments, such as might have been hurriedly gathered up in a workshop to which they had been brought from repair, sale or simply as "old iron" . . .

'What invests this deposit with special antiquarian value is the fact that it comprises many objects of everyday use and that its date, owing to the large number of coins found with it, can be determined with approximate certainty . . . The clearness of the chronological evidence supplied by the coins deserves to be specially appreciated. Out of a total of 61 Chinese copper coins, many of them in very fair preservation, the list given in Appendix B shows that 39 belong to different Tang issues, while the rest bear nianhaos of the Song period, ranging from Shunhua (AD 990–5) to Chongning (AD 1102–7). As more than half of these Song coins have the latter nianhao but little worn, the numismatic evidence clearly points to this cache having been made about the first quarter of the twelfth century' (IA: 593).

**IA.X.d:** Purchased at Kara-khoja. See IA.X. 'There remain to be briefly mentioned the miscellaneous objects which I was able to acquire, during my successive stays at Kara-khoja, from local cultivators or from petty dealers who collected antiques from the former. There can be little doubt that the great majority of these objects had been found, as asserted by the sellers, by persons digging for earth – or treasure – among the ruins of Idikut-shahri. The character of the objects, most of which may safely be ascribed to Uighur times, supports this view. A few, however, may perhaps have been obtained from tombs recently rifled in the extensive graveyards of Astana to be described below. The reason why the supply of objects brought for sale was not more abundant may have been that the most active season of digging for manure had only just started when we left Turfan; to some extent also I may have been forestalled by agents collecting for purchasers in Europe' (IA: 594). [Kao.O refers to the group of 'miscellaneous objects purchased at Kara-khoja'.]

### *IA.XI: COPPER COINS PURCHASED AT TOYUK (IA: 614 ff.)*

**Site:** Toyuk comprises Buddhist cave-shrines and temples along both sides of a gorge for a distance of about a mile from its mouth.

**Acquisition/archaeological context:** 'A series of small objects which were acquired at Toyuk by purchase.' Stein was unsure about the provenance of two stucco figurines which were very similar to pieces found at Astana. 'The provenance of the coins purchased at Toyuk is also uncertain. Twelve of them are Tang issues, six show Song nianhaos ranging from AD 1008 to 1056, and the remaining fourteen belong to the Manchu period' (IA: 619).

### *IA.XII: COINS FROM TOMBS AT ASTANA (IA: 646 ff., 659)*

**Site:** About two and a half miles from the northwest corner of Idikut-shahri (Gaochang) and north of the village of Astana cemetery was a large area covered with ancient cemeteries. The Astana cemetery covered an area of 1 and a half miles east–west with a maximum width of ¾ mile. The distribution of the burial places in this area was irregular. 'The rectangular enclosures [from 10 to 150 yd square in size], each containing a series of tombs more or less aligned, lie closest together in the SE portion. Farther to the north the little mounds marking the position of individual tombs, whether detached or in small groups, are widely scattered without any discernible order'. Most tombs had been disturbed (IA: 642–3). Associated with tomb Ast.I.iv were found three inscribed bricks. One, dated AD 608, records the death of the widow (née Qu) of Zhang Shuping. Two others, dated AD 646, commemorate a lady of the same Qu family and her husband Zhang Yanheng. An inscribed brick from Ast.I.vi, is dated AD 632. Tomb Ast.I.iv yielded many Chinese paper documents (IA: 647).

**Ast.i.3** was one of six tombs in group Ast.i, which lay in the extreme northeast of the cemetery, and appeared to be a separate group. Tomb Ast.I.iii had been disturbed. It contained two bodies: one male (Ast.I.iii.a) and one female (Ast.I.iii.b) (IA: 645–6).

**Ast.i.5** was a tomb in the same group (see IA.XII.a). It contained three bodies: (*a* = male; *b* = female; *c* = young male) (IA: 647).

**Ast.i.6** was a tomb in the same group (See IA.XII.a). It contained 2 bodies: (a = male; b = female). Inscribed burial brick (in Chinese) gives name and date of the deceased male: 'the official Zhang, a native of Dunhuang, who served the Gaochang state in a military capacity, and died, at the age of 73, in the 9th year of the local Gaochang nianhao Yanshou, corresponding to AD 632' (IA: 648–9).

**Ast.iii.** was a group of nine tombs in the northwest of the cemetery. They were marked by a regular enclosure, and all had entrances on the southwestern side. Ast.iii.3 yielded Chinese paper documents, some dated AD 722 and AD 743.

**Ast.v.2** was a tomb containing two bodies.

**Acquisition/archaeological context:** 'It is perhaps, of some significance, that several of the bodies provided with [silver] spectacles have furnished us with illustrations of another interesting burial custom, that of placing coins of precious metal in the mouth of the dead. In i.a.3, 5.a, 6.b these were gold pieces, imitations of an issue of Justinian I (AD 527–65); in v.2 a Sasanian silver coin. The custom of putting gold and other precious articles in the mouth of the dead goes far back into Chinese antiquity. According to Professor De Groot it is connected with a belief that such substances protect the body against decay. But the analogy offered by the coined pieces of gold and silver in the mouths of the dead of Astana to the obolus of Charon is too striking to be left unnoticed. In fact, a Buddhist story extracted by M. Chavannes from the Chinese Tripitaka, to which that great departed scholar drew my attention in 1916, clearly supports this analogy; for it directly mentions a piece of gold having been put into the mouth of a dead man with the object "that by the means of this present he may be able to gain the good graces of the king of the Great Mountain (the king of hells)".

'We may reasonably attribute a similar purpose to the coins found in several of the Astana tombs, whether copper "cash" of the wuzhu type in i.3, 6 and Tang issues with the Kaiyuan legend in ix.2.b, or else substitutes. Among the latter the small silver discs from i.3, resembling Chinese copper coins with their square holes, are curious as possibly indications of a desire to replace the current coinage of the Empire by something more valuable. On the other hand the strings of paper "cash" from iii.4 and the small circular pieces of bark from ix.2 take us straight to the paper money still used in present-day Chinese worship of the Manes and attested by literary evidence since the third and fourth centuries AD. There is reason to believe that the principle of avoiding waste in funeral rites, which prompted the substitution of such counterfeits, did not altogether prevent the deposit, on occasion, of articles of some value with the dead of Gaochang. Small ornaments of silver and gold were, it is true, found by us only in i.3. But the systematic plundering of the tombs, which frequently included a minute examination of the bodies, would scarcely have been so extensive had it not occasionally met with rewards of some intrinsic value' (IA: 671).

**IA.XII.a:** Found in mouth of body, and over eyes of body, in Ast.i.3. 'The most curious and instructive discovery here made was the following. Mashik, our special cemetery assistant, whom long practice in searching the dead had relieved of all scruples, by breaking the jawbones of the skull recovered from the mouth cavity a gold coin which I was able at once to recognize as Byzantine (pl.CXX). It has since been identified by Mr R. B. Whitehead as an approximately contemporaneous imitation of a gold coin of the Emperor Justinian I (AD 527–65). This at once provided a *terminus a quo* for this particular group of tombs. The chronological evidence was confirmed by finds in two more tombs of the same group, Ast.i.5 and i.6, of thin pieces of gold (pl.CXX), similarly showing the type of Justinian I's gold coinage but struck only on the obverse. Mashik claimed the distinction of having been the first to learn by experience to look for coins of gold or silver placed in the mouths of the dead, though his search was but rarely rewarded. That early pillagers had not made the same discovery was proved by the fact that in none of the tombs which we explored, and which Mashik stated that he had not himself touched, had the skulls suffered the rude operation by which he was wont to ascertain whether they contained a coin.

'The fact that out of the four coins actually found by us in the mouths of Astana corpses three are Byzantine gold pieces or imitations of such pieces (Ast.i.3.023; 5.08; 6.03) and one a Sasanian silver coin (Ast.v.2.02) might naturally predispose us to connect this practice with the ancient Greek custom of placing a coin between the lips of the dead as the fare due to Charon, the ferryman of Hades. But the reference with which M. Chavannes kindly supplied me in 1916 to a Buddhist story in the Chinese Tripitaka suggests that the custom was not unknown in the Far East also. It must further be borne in mind that as China had never had a gold or silver coinage, those who at Turfan wished to provide their dead with an adequate obolus for the journey to the world beyond would necessarily have to use a coin of Western origin for their pious purpose, if they wished it to be of precious metal . . . all the three gold coins above mentioned were recovered from bodies in one and the same group of tombs, the approximate period of which . . . is determined by inscriptional records [of the seventh century]' (IA: 646).

'Over the eyes [of Ast.I.iii.b, the female] was placed a pair of silver "spectacles", closely corresponding in shape and make to the one already described from the head of body a [the male]. Below this and covering the eye sockets were found two Sasanian coins, which Mr Whitehead has identified as issues of either Khusrow I (Naurshiwan, AD 531–79) or Ohrmazd IV (AD 579–91)' (IA: 647).

'There may have been originally some objects of value deposited with these bodies; for mixed up with the layer of earth and decayed matting near them there were found the following small articles, which the first pillagers of the tomb had evidently overlooked when turning the bodies out of their coffins. The three small discs of silver, i.3.06, with square holes in the centre, were obviously made in imitation of Chinese copper coins. The seven thin plates of silver, i.3.012 (pl.LXXXIX), crescent- or pear-shaped, manifestly formed part of some ornament . . . thin strip of plain gold . . . glass beads . . . and a Chinese copper coin of the wuzhu type, with a legend in four characters, reading *changping wuzhu*' (IA: 647, 681).

**IA.XII.b:** Found in mouth of body, Ast.i.5. 'From the mouth of *a* [male] a thin gold coin (pl.CXX) was recovered, derived like the one in Ast.i.3 from a type of Justinian I, but struck only on one side and manifestly a more distant imitation . . . *c* [a young male] eye-holes were found covered with small circular pieces cut from thin wood or the side of a gourd' (IA: 648).

**IA.XII.c:** Found in mouth of body, Ast.i.6. 'The mouth of *b* [female] held a thin gold coin (pl.CXX), struck on one side only, showing the three-quarter face bust of Justinian I, as it appears on the Byzantine coins of which this and the gold pieces from Ast.i.3 and i.5 are undoubtedly imitations. Two wuzhu coins, in perfect condition, were found near the head of *b*' (IA: 649).

**IA.XII.d:**From Ast.iii.2. 'In clearing the approach trench [to tomb Ast.iii.2] there was found just outside the entrance a Kaiyuan coin, of the type current throughout the Tang period, showing little or no wear' (IA: 651).

**IA.XII.e:** Found in mouth of body, Ast.v.2. 'In the mouth of the woman's body was found a silver coin too much decayed for identification, but from its size and design recognizable with certainty as a Sasanian piece. In conjunction with the inscriptional record from the adjoining tomb, Ast.v.1, this coin contributes to prove that this group of tombs is approximately contemporaneous with the group Ast.i' (IA: 659).

### *NOT IN LIST OF COINS*

**Ast.i.3.06:** 'Three Chinese coin-shaped silver discs without inscription, but drilled with two holes in opposite edges for threading as ornaments' (IA: 681) These may have been gilded [cf. Ying-pan]; Ast.i.b.01 was a cloth covering the face of the female, and there were fragments of gold leaf and copper in the dust surrounding it (IA: 647; 682).

**Ast.iii.4.04 (pl.XCIII):** 'strings of paper "cash"' (IA: 654).

**Ast.ix.2.b.08:** found inside the coffin of the official Fan Yanshi (d.689) was a basket 'within is a sandal-wood comb, well made and still springy; two folded napkins of fine silk (perished); and six Chinese copper coins with legend Kaiyuan . . . pl.LXXXIX) (IA: 708); 'by the side of the head lay the small round basket of neatly woven cane, and placed in it a sandal-wood comb, two folded pieces of fine silk, and six Tang coins, with the legend, Kaiyuan, showing no signs of wear' (IA: 665). Placed over Fan's coffin was a sheet of cotton fabric which was stamped with the placename Xin'an, in Zhejiang. A similar piece of fabric was found covering coffin a in the same tomb, and its inscription and stamps indicated that it recorded 'the receipt of a roll of cloth from a taxpayer at Wuzhou, Lanqi xian, Ruishan xiang,

Zhejiang, on a day of the 8th moon of the 2nd year of Shenlong (AD 706)' (IA: 665).

### *IA.XIII: COPPER COINS FOUND AT YINGPAN SITE (IA: 751, 753)*

**Site:** Remains at Yingpan ('military encampment') consisted of a circular circumvallation (as at Merdek and Ak-sipil), enclosing an area 194 yd in diameter, with gates on the western and eastern faces. The only remains to have survived periodic flooding were those of a ruined shrine Ying.II, about 100 yd from the western gate. The shrine (similar to Miran M.II) had been disturbed, but remains indicated that the dome had a diameter of over 17 ft (IA: 753–4).

Northeast of the Yingpan circumvallation stood the ruins of nine stupas grouped around a central shrine [Ying.I]. 'The ruins [of the stupas] rise on a small isolated plateau which a branch channel of the great flood-bed of the Shindi river descending from the northeast has cut off from the continuous gravel terrace behind.' The plateau measured 150 yd × 50 yd at widest, and was eroded into a number of narrow ridges, on which the stupas were later built (IA: 750–1). The lands around had subsequently been used as Islamic burial grounds (IA: 753).

West of the of the 'stupa-plateau' was a terrace with ancient graves on it (Ying.III). Some graves had already been washed away by the Shindi River, and many had been disturbed. Stein examined four graves, and concluded that they were graves of local (non-Chinese) people, 'settled around the old Chinese station at a period when prolonged contact with Chinese civilization had considerably modified their habits' (IA: 755–6).

**Ying.I** was the main stupa, with the dome about 14 ft in diameter. Kharoshthi wood documents and shavings were found here (IA: 751).

**Ying.II** was a ruined shrine, about 100 yd from the western gate.

**Acquisition/archaeological context:** 'A wuzhu coin, which was found lying on the surface near the north-western corner of the court gave me the first definite indication of the early date of these ruins' (IA: 751).

**Ying.I.05**: 'A Chinese coin which was picked up on the "Tati" to the east of the circumvallation shows the legend wuzhu used during Han times' (IA: 753). From a group of 'objects found on Tati to the east and southwest of Ying.I' (IA: 759).

**Ying.II.018 and 04**: From a group of 'objects found on "Tati" near ruined circumvallation Ying.II' (IA: 759).

### *NOT IN LIST OF COINS*

**Ying.I.a:**'We also came upon evidence that the sacred locality had been visited down to late Buddhist times, in the shape of a Kaiyuan coin, a Tang issue, of which two fragments were picked up on the top of the refuse near the NE corner of the platform [of main stupa]' (IA: 751; 754).

**Ying.III.2**: a grave containing an intact wooden coffin, which enclosed two bodies (1 male and 1 female, both grey-haired). 'Bodies wrapped in white silk. Heads swathed in strips of white silk: 'these were secured by a crimson silk band, close on an inch wide, which was drawn over the forehead. Over this band there lay in a row three small metal discs, apparently gold, Ying.III.03–8, which had been sewn to the head-band by means of two small holes in each' (IA: 756).

**Ying.III.2.03–5:** 'Remains of three metal discs, from head-band of right body. Thin, very fragile, pierced with two holes through which passed thread sewing them to band. Gold or gilt (?). Scraps of silk adhere. Broken. For other, see Ying.III.2.06–8, 3.03–5. Greatest diameter when complete ⅝ in.' (IA: 760).

**Ying.III.2.06–8:** Three metal discs from head-band of L body; as preceding. Gold (?), very thin, 08 was double, and has split apart. Diam. (06 and 07) 5/8". (IA: 760).

**Ying.III.3:** the grave of a bearded man, again with body wrapped in white silk. The head was covered in silk as seen in Ying.II. 'A narrow crimson band passed across the forehead, and on it were fastened three small discs, III.3.03–5, either gold or gilt' (IA: 756). **Ying.III.3.03–5**: 'Three metal discs, apparently gold, from head-band, as Ying.III.2.03–8. Diam. ⅜ in. to ½ in.' (IA: 760).

### *IA.XIV: COPPER COIN FOUND AT WATCH-STATION Y.i (KURGHAN) (IA: 770)*

**Site:** The small ruined watch-station Y.i stood on the route, marked by watch-towers, between Yingpan and Korla. It had a massive tower (base 34 ft square, and still rising 29 ft high in 1915) at its centre, surrounded by a square enclosure (outer faces measured 76 ft each). Construction similar to Han dynasty watch-stations (IA: 768–9).

**Acquisition/archaeological context:** 'That this occupation belonged to a period much later than that of the original construction and defence of the station was made clear by fragments of a Tang coin, with the legend Kaiyuan, which was discovered near the surface of the refuse in the north-eastern corner of the enclosure . . . These relics, together with the coin, show that traffic had moved along this route down to Tang times, if not even later' (IA: 770).

### *IA.XV: COPPER COINS OBTAINED AT KUCHA (IA: 822)*

**Site:** Kucha, known from the Han to Tang dynasties as the kingdom of Qiuci, occupies one of the prime locations in the region. In Han times, the Protector-General of the Western Regions was stationed at Wu-lei, close to Kucha; during the Tang dynasty, Qiuci was selected as the military and political centre of the Four Garrisons. Close to the Kucha oasis, the Muz-art and Kucha-darya rivers debouch into the Tarim River, thus watering a large area of cultivable land. To the north of Kucha rise the fertile Tianshan mountains and high, narrow routes through the mountains, which are defendable, but which allow access to other fertile lands from late spring to autumn. The Tarim river, reaching east–west, acts as a natural defence against the desert-sands of the Taklamakan (IA: 803–5). 'In view of the extensive archaeological work undertaken by the numerous scholars who had preceded me in the area of Kucha [e.g. Grünwedel, le Coq, Pelliot, Berezovsky], there was but limited scope for further antiquarian investigation during my own short stay' (IA: 804). Local manuscripts indicated that the language used at Kucha was Indo-European, known as Tocharian B.

**Acquisition/archaeological context:**

**Kucha.o** nos were 'acquired at Kucha town' (IA: 826). 'Owing to lack of time, and the wide extent of the ground over which the old remains of Kucha are scattered beyond the present limits of the oasis, my visits to the sites described above were necessarily very rapid. Yet the observations I made sufficed to familiarize me to some degree with the conditions under which the miscellaneous antiques acquired during my stay in the oasis . . . were found. All these small objects correspond closely in type to the "Tati" finds familiar to us from the sites of ancient civilization around the Khotan oasis, which have been abandoned to the desert since Buddhist times. Since wind-erosion is at work outside the irrigated area of Kucha, though to a much smaller degree than south of the Taklamakan, we can believe the statements of Mir Sharif and Aziz Palwan, who supplied most of these finds, that they were picked up at "Tatis" of Dawan kum and similar localities to the west and south-west of the oasis . . . The presence of comparatively numerous Sino-Kharoshthi pieces among the coins collected is of interest' (IA: 821–2).

**Kucha.041:** 'Bronze disc or coin, with Kharoshthi(?) chars. on one side. Much corroded. Greatest measurement ⅞ in.' (IA: 827).

**Yul.o** nos were 'acquired as brought from Yulduz-Bagh sites' (IA: 824).

**IA.XV.b:** Received as from south of Yulduz-bagh.

**IA.XV.c:** Brought as from Yulduz-bagh sites.

**IA.XV.d:** Brought as from Dawan-kum tati sites.

***NOT IN LIST OF COINS***

From the undated burial-ground near the Sarai-tam mound 'gold coins were believed to have been found in these tombs, and this report, whether true or not, would have sufficed to stimulate the exploitation indicated by the [burrowed] hollows pointed out to me' (IA: 811).

***IA.XVI: COPPER COINS FOUND AT SITES WEST OF KUCHA (IA: 813, 816)***

**Sites:** Stein understood Tajik and Toghrak-akin to be the westernmost sites of Kucha which still had structural remains. Tajik comprised 'a much-dilapidated quadrangle [Taj.I] and the remains of a Buddhist sanctuary, situated on a natural clay terrace at the mouth of the [dry river] valley, and a group of small shrines [Taj.II] scattered over low ridges higher up' (IA: 812–13).

**Tajik.** See above. 'In the area iii, adjoining the shrine i, we discovered three small paper fragments with Kuchean writing' (IA: 813). A paper fragment with Brahmi writing was found in the shrine Taj.II.i, and a wooden tablet with Kuchean writing (IA: 813).

**Toghrak-akin** (the name of the mouth of a narrow winding gorge) is about two miles distant from Tajik, and the remains indicated wooden structures and shrines carved into the rock. The main ruin was the cave-shrine (T.A.I) on the slope of a small ridge facing towards the mouth of the gorge. It has a series of four terraces rising above it in steps, with niches cut into the rock to hold images. The shrine's cella measures 10 ft square, has a passage behind (4 ft wide], and both have vaulted ceilings (IA: 815).

**Cave T.A.IV** refers to two groups of small caves facing each other on a steep little spur south of a large enclosure on top of a very steep hillock (probably the chief monastic quarters) (IA: 816). See IA.XVI.b.

**Dawan-kum tati site. See IA.XV.d.**

**Acquisition/archaeological context:**

**IA.XVI.a:** Found at Tajik. 'A Chinese coin found in i [a small Buddhist shrine adjoining the quadrangle] could not be identified' (IA: 813). 'In room ii [in structural remains in the northern corner of quadrangle] we found a Chinese coin, apparently uninscribed' (IA: 813).

**IA.XVI.b:** Found at T.A.I, Toghrak-akin site. Coin not mentioned in text [incorrect numbering; T.A.I.02 refers to 'fragment of wooden baluster rail'; more likely to be T.A.02 (IA: 823).

**IA.XVI.c:** Found at Cave T.A.IV, Toghrak-akin site. 'On removing the loose earth which filled these cave-dwellings, we found in the one marked *a* two dozen Chinese coins, partly embedded in the flooring [of T.IV.i]. Of these, twenty-one are Tang issues and three are uninscribed, probably of earlier date. Thus the conclusion, already suggested by the style of the wall-paintings, that the site had continued to be occupied during the Tang period received definite confirmation before the end of our visit' (IA: 816).

The coins listed as T.A.IV.01–3, from their numbering, may not be part of this group, which would explain the three extra coins [in group IA.XVI.c].

**IA.XVI.d:** Found at Dawan-kum. Coin not mentioned in text.

***IA.XVII: COINS FOUND AT SISTAN SITES, PERSIA***

**P.i.R.01:** 'a silver coin of Queen Boran was picked up under my eyes at a distance of about 3 ft from the northern foot of the rotunda [of Pai-kash-i-Rustam]. It is in excellent preservation' (IA: 946).

**Machi.o** nos refer to 'objects found at or near Machi site' (IA: 959).

**K.G.o** nos refer to 'objects found at or near Kalat-i-gird site' (IA: 960, 948).

***NOT IN LIST OF COINS***

***IA.XVIII. MERDEK SHAHRI (KORLA) (IA: 787)***

'During my stay at Korla I acquired the small antiques described below from a local trader who stated that he had obtained them from a Loplik as found at the site of "Merdek-shahr". Whether their alleged find-place is identical with the site marked by the ancient fort of Merdek-tim which I examined in January, 1907, I was unable to ascertain. The small objects are all of a type such as might be picked up on a "Tati". But vague information received by me in Charklik in January, 1914, pointed to the discovery by Lop hunters of a site also designated as Merdek-shahr somewhere near the lower Tarim since my first visit in 1906. The description given of objects which were said to have been brought from there and sold to Mr Tachibana suggested the survival of structural remains. I therefore regretted that want of time before I moved into the Lop desert prevented me from making a search for the alleged site' (IA: 787).

***OTHER***

**Har.** usually refers to 'the collection of antiquities obtained from Badruddin Khan, of Khotan, by Mr H. I. Harding, HBM's late Vice-Consul, Kashgar, and kindly presented by him on his passage through Kashmir in September, 1923, for inclusion in the Indian Government's Museum of Central-Asian Antiquities, New Delhi. A number of interesting fresco panels, which were also presented by Mr Harding, have since been set up by Mr Andrews at the Museum, New Delhi, and will be separately catalogued with other mural paintings. No definite information is available as to the provenance of the antiques here described. But it appears probable that they were brought to Khotan as a result of digging which villagers carried on at some ruins in the desert area covered with tamarisk-cones NE of Domoko' (IA: 1052).

# Part 3 Concordance of Stein and British Museum numbers

This concordance includes only those coins, or groups of coins, for which the original Stein number is known. It is arranged alphabetically by the Stein number.

| Provenance | Stein no. | BM no. |
|---|---|---|
| Togujai, Moji | (T)M.001 | AK.I.a–g |
| Arkalik and Hanguya, tatis near | Ark.Han.068.a | IA.III.A.o.2 |
| Arkalik and Hanguya, tatis near | Ark.Han.068.b | IA.III.A.o.3 |
| Arkalik and Hanguya, tatis near | Ark.Han.068.c–d | IA.III.A.o.4–5 |
| Arkalik and Hanguya, tatis near | Ark.Han.068.e–h | IA.III.A.o.6–9 |
| Arkalik and Hanguya, tatis near | Ark.Han.068.i–j, p–r, t–x | IA.III.A.o.10–21 |
| Arkalik and Hanguya, tatis near | Ark.Han.068.k–o, u–v | IA.III.A.o.22–28 |
| Arkalik and Hanguya, tatis near | Ark.Han.068.s | IA.III.A.o.1 |
| Arkalik and Hanguya, tatis near | Ark.Han.068.w | IA.III.A.o.29 |
| Astana | Ast.? | IA.XII.a.1 |
| Astana | Ast.i.3.024 | IA.XII.a.4 |
| Astana | Ast.i.3.025–026 | IA.XII.a.2–3 |
| Astana | Ast.i.3.06.a–c | IA.XII.f.1–3 |
| Astana | Ast.i.5.08 | IA.XII.b.1 |
| Astana | Ast.i.6.03 | IA.XII.c.1 |
| Astana | Ast.i.6.04 | IA.XII.c.2–3 |
| Astana | Ast.iii.2052? | IA.XII.d.1 |
| Astana | Ast.v.2.02? | IA.XII.e.1 |
| Yotkan | B.D.001 | AK.III.k.16 |
| Badruddin Khan | Badr. 0164 | IA.III.B.a.2–4 |
| Badruddin Khan | Badr.0147–0148 | IA.III.B.a.15–18 |
| Badruddin Khan | Badr.0150 | IA.III.B.a.14 |
| Badruddin Khan | Badr.0151–0152 | IA.III.B.a.2–4 |
| Badruddin Khan | Badr.0153–0154 | IA.III.B.a.6–7 |
| Badruddin Khan | Badr.0155 | IA.III.B.a.8–9 |
| Badruddin Khan | Badr.0156 | IA.III.B.a.12–13 |
| Badruddin Khan | Badr.0157 | IA.III.B.a.10 |
| Badruddin Khan | Badr.0158 | IA.III.B.a.11 |
| Badruddin Khan | Badr.0160 | IA.III.B.a.5 |
| Badruddin Khan | Badr.0161 | IA.III.B.a.12–13 |
| Badruddin Khan | Badr.0162 | IA.III.B.a.1 |
| Badruddin Khan | Badr.0163 | IA.III.B.a.8–9 |
| Badruddin Khan | Badr.0198 | IA.III.B.b.4 |
| Badruddin Khan | Badr.0199 | IA.III.B.b.1 |
| Badruddin Khan | Badr.0200–0201 | IA.III.B.b.2–3 |
| Badruddin Khan (Hanguya tatis) | Badr.0202.a–b | IA.III.B.c.36–39 |
| Badruddin Khan (Hanguya tatis) | Badr.0202.c–d | IA.III.B.c.42–43 |
| Badruddin Khan (Hanguya tatis) | Badr.0202.e | IA.III.B.c.1–35 |
| Badruddin Khan (Hanguya tatis) | Badr.0238 | IA.III.B.c.46–63 |
| Badruddin Khan (Hanguya tatis) | Badr.0239.a, e | IA.III.B.c.64–68 |
| Badruddin Khan (Hanguya tatis) | Badr.0239.b | IA.III.B.c.36–39 |

| Provenance | Stein no. | BM no. |
|---|---|---|
| Badruddin Khan (Hanguya tatis) | Badr.0240 | IA.III.B.c.69–71 |
| Badruddin Khan (Hanguya tatis) | Badr.0241–0242 | IA.III.B.c.44–45 |
| Badruddin Khan (Hanguya tatis) | Badr.0243 | IA.III.B.c.36–39 |
| Badruddin Khan (Hanguya tatis) | Badr.0244 | IA.III.B.c.41 |
| Badruddin Khan (Hanguya tatis) | Badr.0245 | IA.III.B.c.40 |
| Badruddin Khan (Yotkan) | Badr.0246 | IA.III.B.d.51 |
| Badruddin Khan (Yotkan) | Badr.0246.b | IA.III.B.d.1–45 |
| Badruddin Khan (Yotkan) | Badr.0247.a | IA.III.B.d.46 |
| Badruddin Khan (Yotkan) | Badr.0247.b | IA.III.B.d.49 |
| Badruddin Khan (Yotkan) | Badr.0247.c | IA.III.B.d.48 |
| Badruddin Khan (Yotkan) | Badr.0247.d | IA.III.B.d.47 |
| Badruddin Khan (Yotkan) | Badr.0247.e | IA.III.B.d.50 |
| Badruddin Khan (Ak-tiken) | Badr.0262.a | IA.III.B.e.1–37 |
| Badruddin Khan (Ak-tiken) | Badr.0262.b, j | IA.III.B.e.41–44 |
| Badruddin Khan (Ak-tiken) | Badr.0262.c | IA.III.B.e.46 |
| Badruddin Khan (Ak-tiken) | Badr.0262.d | IA.III.B.e.47 |
| Badruddin Khan (Ak-tiken) | Badr.0262.e | IA.III.B.e.61 |
| Badruddin Khan (Ak-tiken) | Badr.0262.f | IA.III.B.e.57 |
| Badruddin Khan (Ak-tiken) | Badr.0262.f | IA.III.B.e.62 |
| Badruddin Khan (Ak-tiken) | Badr.0262.g | IA.III.B.e.49 |
| Badruddin Khan (Ak-tiken) | Badr.0262.h | IA.III.B.e.52–54 |
| Badruddin Khan (Ak-tiken) | Badr.0262.i | IA.III.B.e.48 |
| Badruddin Khan (Ak-tiken) | Badr.0262.k | IA.III.B.e.45 |
| Badruddin Khan (Ak-tiken) | Badr.0263.a | IA.III.B.e.41–44 |
| Badruddin Khan (Ak-tiken) | Badr.0263.b, e | IA.III.B.e.50–51 |
| Badruddin Khan (Ak-tiken) | Badr.0263.c | IA.III.B.e.55 |
| Badruddin Khan (Ak-tiken) | Badr.0263.d | IA.III.B.e.60 |
| Badruddin Khan (Ak-tiken) | Badr.0263.f–g | IA.III.B.e.52–54 |
| Badruddin Khan (Ak-tiken) | Badr.0263.h | IA.III.B.e.56 |
| Badruddin Khan (Ak-tiken) | Badr.0264 | IA.III.B.e.1–37 |
| Badruddin Khan (Ak-tiken) | Badr.0265 | IA.III.B.e.58–59 |
| Badruddin Khan (Ak-tiken) | Badr.0267 | IA.III.B.f.1–16 |
| Badruddin Khan (Ak-tiken) | Badr.0267 | IA.III.B.e.1–37 |
| Badruddin Khan (Ak-tiken) | Badr.0267.b | IA.III.B.e.38–40 |
| Badruddin Khan (Ak–tiken) | Badr.0267.c | IA.III.B.e.63–64 |
| Badruddin Khan | Badr.0268.a, e | IA.III.B.f.18–25 |
| Badruddin Khan | Badr.0268.b | IA.III.B.f.17 |
| Badruddin Khan | Badr.0268.c | IA.III.B.f.27 |
| Badruddin Khan | Badr.0268.d | IA.III.B.f.26 |
| Badruddin Khan | Badr.0268.f | IA.III.B.f.28–29 |
| Badruddin Khan (Arkalik) | Badr.0270.a | IA.III.B.g.1–35 |
| Badruddin Khan (Arkalik) | Badr.0270.b | IA.III.B.g.36 |
| Badruddin Khan (Arkalik) | Badr.0270.c | IA.III.B.g.37 |
| Badruddin Khan (Arkalik) | Badr.0270.d | IA.III.B.g.39 |
| Badruddin Khan (Arkalik) | Badr.0270.e | IA.III.B.g.38 |
| Badruddin Khan (Arkalik) | Badr.0271 | IA.III.B.g.1–35 |
| Badruddin Khan (Arkalik) | Badr.0271 | IA.III.B.g.40–44 |
| Badruddin Khan | Badr.0396 | IA.III.B.j.1–2 |
| Badruddin Khan | Badr.0424 | IA.III.B.j.1–2 |
| Badruddin Khan | Badr.0434.a | IA.III.B.h.143 |
| Badruddin Khan | Badr.0434.b, m | IA.III.B.h.64–85 |
| Badruddin Khan | Badr.0434.d–e, o | IA.III.B.h.86–116 |

| Provenance | Stein no. | BM no. |
|---|---|---|
| Badruddin Khan | Badr.0434.e | IA.III.B.h.117–123 |
| Badruddin Khan | Badr.0434.f | IA.III.B.h.124–125 |
| Badruddin Khan | Badr.0434.g | IA.III.B.h.126–128 |
| Badruddin Khan | Badr.0434.h | IA.III.B.h.129 |
| Badruddin Khan | Badr.0434.i | IA.III.B.h.134–138 |
| Badruddin Khan | Badr.0434.j–k | IA.III.B.h.130–133 |
| Badruddin Khan | Badr.0434.k | IA.III.B.h.134–138 |
| Badruddin Khan | Badr.0434.l | IA.III.B.h.140 |
| Badruddin Khan | Badr.0435.a, i | IA.III.B.h.1–50 |
| Badruddin Khan | Badr.0435.b | IA.III.B.h.54–55 |
| Badruddin Khan | Badr.0435.c–e, n | IA.III.B.h.86–116 |
| Badruddin Khan | Badr.0435.f | IA.III.B.h.117–123 |
| Badruddin Khan | Badr.0435.g | IA.III.B.h.62–63 |
| Badruddin Khan | Badr.0435.h | IA.III.B.h.59 |
| Badruddin Khan | Badr.0435.j | IA.III.B.h.57–58 |
| Badruddin Khan | Badr.0435.k | IA.III.B.h.56 |
| Badruddin Khan | Badr.0435.l | IA.III.B.h.60–61 |
| Badruddin Khan | Badr.0435.m | IA.III.B.h.64–85 |
| Badruddin Khan | Badr.0435.o | IA.III.B.h.141 |
| Badruddin Khan | Badr.0436–44 | IA.III.B.h.148 |
| Badruddin Khan | Badr.0445–0456 | IA.III.B.h.164–165 |
| Badruddin Khan | Badr.0446, p–q | IA.III.B.h.117–123 |
| Badruddin Khan | Badr.0446.a, i | IA.III.B.h.1–50 |
| Badruddin Khan | Badr.0446.b, j | IA.III.B.h.51–53 |
| Badruddin Khan | Badr.0446.c | IA.III.B.h.54–55 |
| Badruddin Khan | Badr.0446.e, g, k–m, r | IA.III.B.h.64–85 |
| Badruddin Khan | Badr.0446.f | IA.III.B.h.60–61 |
| Badruddin Khan | Badr.0446.h | IA.III.B.h.62–63 |
| Badruddin Khan | Badr.0446.n | IA.III.B.h.123 |
| Badruddin Khan | Badr.0446.o | IA.III.B.h.57–58 |
| Badruddin Khan | Badr.0446.s | IA.III.B.h.86–116 |
| Badruddin Khan | Badr.0446.u | IA.III.B.h.142 |
| Badruddin Khan | Badr.0447–0448 | IA.III.B.h.166–167 |
| Badruddin Khan | Badr.0449 | IA.III.B.h.139 |
| Badruddin Khan | Badr.0450–0454 | IA.III.B.h.148 |
| Badruddin Khan | Badr.0455–0457 | IA.III.B.h.146–147 |
| Badruddin Khan | Badr.0458–0459 | IA.III.B.h.144–145 |
| Badruddin Khan (purchased Khotan) | Badruddin.003 | S.IV.C.g.1 |
| Besh tam | Besh-tam 01–03 | IA.I.c.1–3 |
| Chalma-kazan | C.001 | AK.IV.b.1–10 |
| Chalma-kazan | C.003 | AK.IV.a.1–9 |
| Lop desert, camp | C.ccxlix.a.014–016 | IA.VI.F.f.1 |
| Lop desert, camp | C.ci.010–014 | IA.VI.F.d.1–2 |
| Lop desert, camp | C.ci.09 | IA.VI.F.c.1 |
| Lop desert, camp | C.ciii.03–04 | IA.VI.F.e.1–2 |
| Loulan, camp near | C.xciii.066 | IA.VI.B.a.3 |
| Loulan, camp near | C.xciii.064 | IA.VI.B.a.1 |
| Loulan, camp near | C.xciii.065 | IA.VI.B.a.2 |
| Lop desert, camp | C.xcix | IA.VI.F.b.1 |
| Lop desert, camp | C.xcv.01–03 | IA.VI.F.a.1–3 |
| Chalma-kazan | Chal.018 | IA.III.A.p.1–2 |
| Chalma-kazan | Chal.019 | IA.III.A.p.3 |
| Chalma-kazan | Chal.020 | IA.III.A.p.1–2 |

| Provenance | Stein no. | BM no. |
|---|---|---|
| Charchan | Char. 01 | IA.V.a.2 |
| Dandan-Uiliq | D.001 | AK.V.b.1–2, 18–20 |
| Domoko Tatis (purchased Achma) | D.K.0105–0117 | IA.IV.c.2–43 |
| Domoko Tatis (purchased Achma) | D.K.0118 | IA.IV.c.1 |
| Domoko | D.K.052.a–b | IA.IV.a.2–7 |
| Domoko | D.K.059–060 | IA.IV.a.9–14 |
| Domoko | D.K.061 | IA.IV.a.2–7 |
| Domoko | D.K.065 | IA.IV.a.9–14 |
| Domoko | D.K.066–068 | IA.IV.a.2–7 |
| Domoko | D.K.070 | IA.IV.a.25 |
| Domoko | D.K.075 | IA.IV.a.9–14 |
| Domoko | D.K.081–082 | IA.IV.a.9–14 |
| Domoko | D.K.083 | IA.IV.a.8 |
| Domoko | D.K.094 | IA.IV.a.1 |
| Domoko | D.O.018–023 | IA.IV.a.44–50 |
| Domoko | D.O.024–027 | IA.IV.a.40–43 |
| Domoko | D.O.028 | IA.IV.a.44–50 |
| Domoko | D.O.029 | IA.IV.a.51–56 |
| Domoko | D.O.030–036 | IA.IV.a.57–63 |
| Domoko | D.O.037–038 | IA.IV.a.51–56 |
| Domoko | D.O.044–046 | IA.IV.a.51–56 |
| Domoko | D.O.058 | IA.IV.a.21 |
| Domoko | D.O.062 | IA.IV.a.28–29 |
| Domoko | D.O.063 | IA.IV.a.30–34 |
| Domoko | D.O.064 | IA.IV.a.23–24 |
| Domoko | D.O.069 | IA.IV.a.28–29 |
| Domoko | D.O.071 | IA.IV.a.37–38 |
| Domoko | D.O.072 | IA.IV.a.22 |
| Domoko | D.O.073 | IA.IV.a.16 |
| Domoko | D.O.074 | IA.IV.a.23–24 |
| Domoko | D.O.076–078 | IA.IV.a.30–34 |
| Domoko | D.O.080 | IA.IV.a.26–27 |
| Domoko | D.O.084 | IA.IV.a.35 |
| Domoko | D.O.085 | IA.IV.a.30–34 |
| Domoko | D.O.086 | IA.IV.a.15 |
| Domoko | D.O.087 | IA.IV.a.20 |
| Domoko | D.O.088 | IA.IV.a.36 |
| Domoko | D.O.088–089 | IA.IV.a.18–19 |
| Domoko | D.O.090 | IA.IV.a.37–38 |
| Domoko | D.O.091 | IA.IV.a.26–27 |
| Domoko | D.O.092 | IA.IV.a.17 |
| Domoko | D.O.093 | IA.IV.a.39 |
| Domoko, sites southwest of | Do.0012–0016 | S.XXVI.b.1–14 |
| Farhad-Beg-Yailaki | F.i | S.XXIV.a.1–4 |
| Farhad-Beg-Yailaki | F.ii | S.XXIV.b.1–3 |
| Farhad-Beg-Yailaki | F.iii.i | S.XXIV.c.1 |
| Farhad-Beg-Yailaki | F.v | S.XXIV.d.1 |
| Harding, Mr H.I. | Har. | x.1–46 |
| Kharakhoto, ruined settlements east of | K.E.ix.06 | IA.VIII.B.b.8 |
| Kharakhoto, ruined settlements east of | K.E.ix.07 | IA.VIII.B.b.7 |
| Kharakhoto, ruined settlements east of | K.E.ix.08 | IA.VIII.B.b.1 |
| Kharakhoto, ruined settlements east of | K.E.vi.01 | IA.VIII.B.a.1 |
| Kharakhoto, ruined settlements east of | K.E.x.03–04 | IA.VIII.B.b.5–6 |

| Provenance | Stein no. | BM no. |
|---|---|---|
| Kharakhoto, ruined settlements east of | K.E.x.05 | IA.VIII.B.b.4 |
| Kharakhoto, ruined settlements east of | K.E.x.06 | IA.VIII.B.b.2 |
| Kharakhoto, ruined settlements east of | K.E.x.07 | IA.VIII.B.b.3 |
| Kharakhoto, ruined settlements east of | K.E.xiv.020 | IA.VIII.B.c.1 |
| Kharakhoto, ruined settlements east of | K.E.xix.01–02 | IA.VIII.B.c.2–3 |
| Kharakhoto, ruined settlements east of | K.E.xix.03 | IA.VIII.B.c.4 |
| Kharakhoto, ruined settlements east of | K.E.xv.04 | IA.VIII.B.c.5 |
| Kharakhoto, ruined settlements east of | K.E.xv.05 | IA.VIII.B.c.6–7 |
| Kharakhoto, ruined settlements east of | K.E.xvi.02 | IA.VIII.B.c.8 |
| Kharakhoto, ruined settlements east of | K.E.xvii.02 | IA.VIII.B.c.6–7 |
| Kalat-i-gird | K.G.0211–0217 | IA.XVII.c.3–13 |
| Kalat-i-gird | K.G.0301 | IA.XVII.c.2 |
| Kalat-i-gird | K.G.04–06 | IA.XVII.c.3–13 |
| Kharakhoto | K.K.0123 | IA.VIII.A.c.23 |
| Kharakhoto | K.K.0124 | IA.VIII.A.c.10 |
| Kharakhoto | K.K.0125 | IA.VIII.A.c.24 |
| Kharakhoto | K.K.0126 | IA.VIII.A.c.1 |
| Kharakhoto | K.K.0127–0128.d | IA.VIII.A.c.18–19 |
| Kharakhoto | K.K.0128.a–b | IA.VIII.A.c.12–14 |
| Kharakhoto | K.K.0128.c | IA.VIII.A.c.25 |
| Kharakhoto | K.K.0129 | IA.VIII.A.c.7–8 |
| Kharakhoto | K.K.0130 | IA.VIII.A.c.15–16 |
| Kharakhoto | K.K.0131 | IA.VIII.A.c.2–4 |
| Kharakhoto | K.K.0132 | IA.VIII.A.c.7–8 |
| Kharakhoto | K.K.0133 | IA.VIII.A.c.9 |
| Kharakhoto | K.K.0134 | IA.VIII.A.c.6 |
| Kharakhoto | K.K.0135 | IA.VIII.A.c.11 |
| Kharakhoto (Aduna-kora) | K.K.0136–0139 | IA.VIII.C.a.1–4 |
| Kharakhoto (Aduna-kora) | K.K.0140 | IA.VIII.C.a.5 |
| Kharakhoto | K.K.0141 | IA.VIII.A.c.21 |
| Kharakhoto | K.K.0142 | IA.VIII.A.b.1 |
| Kharakhoto | K.K.0143 | IA.VIII.A.c.2–4 |
| Kharakhoto | K.K.0145 | IA.VIII.A.c.5 |
| Kharakhoto | K.K.0146 | IA.VIII.A.c.17 |
| Kharakhoto | K.K.0147 | IA.VIII.A.c.20 |
| Kharakhoto | K.K.0148 | IA.VIII.A.c.22 |
| Kharakhoto | K.K.072 | IA.VIII.A.c.2–4 |
| Kharakhoto | K.K.073 | IA.VIII.A.c.12–14 |
| Kharakhoto | K.K.ii.b.07 | IA.VIII.A.a.1 |
| Karadong | KA.I | S.XXIII.a.1–2 |
| Kalat-i-gird | Kalat-i-gird | IA.VII.c.1 |
| Kara-khoja (Gaochang) | Kao.010 | IA.X.d.5–11 |
| Kara-khoja (Gaochang) | Kao.0117 | IA.X.b.3 |
| Kara-khoja (Gaochang) | Kao.0118 | IA.X.b.1 |
| Kara-khoja (Gaochang) | Kao.0119 | IA.X.b.2 |
| Kara-khoja (Gaochang) | Kao.014 | IA.X.d.1 |
| Kara-khoja (Gaochang) | Kao.021–022 | IA.X.d.2–3 |
| Kara-khoja (Gaochang) | Kao.033 | IA.X.d.4 |
| Kara-khoja (Gaochang) | Kao.I.ii.067–069 | IA.X.a.1–5 |
| Kara-khoja (Gaochang) | Kao.III.0201–0202 | IA.X.c.43–44 |
| Kara-khoja (Gaochang) | Kao.III.0203–0205 | IA.X.c.45–48 |
| Kara-khoja (Gaochang) | Kao.III.0206 | IA.X.c.42 |
| Kara-khoja (Gaochang) | Kao.III.0207 | IA.X.c.40 |

| Provenance | Stein no. | BM no. |
|---|---|---|
| Kara-khoja (Gaochang) | Kao.III.0208–0210 | IA.X.c.52–61 |
| Kara-khoja (Gaochang) | Kao.III.0211 | IA.X.c.33 |
| Kara-khoja (Gaochang) | Kao.III.0212 | IA.X.c.41 |
| Kara-khoja (Gaochang) | Kao.III.0213 | IA.X.c.45–48 |
| Kara-khoja (Gaochang) | Kao.III.0214–0218 | IA.X.c.1–27 |
| Kara-khoja (Gaochang) | Kao.III? | IA.X.c.28–32 |
| Kara-khoja (Gaochang) | Kao.III? | IA.X.c.34–39 |
| Khotan | Kh.002 | AK.III.e.12–15 |
| Khotan | Kh.002 | AK.III.f.1–6 |
| Khotan | Kh.004 | AK.III.d.1–8 |
| Khotan (Jigda-kuduk) | Kh.0100–0102 | IA.III.A.e.1–7 |
| Khotan (Jigda-kuduk) | Kh.0103 | IA.III.A.e.8–17 |
| Khotan (Jigda-kuduk) | Kh.0104–0107 | IA.III.A.e.1–7 |
| Khotan (Jigda-kuduk) | Kh.0108 | IA.III.A.e.8–17 |
| Khotan (Jigda-kuduk) | Kh.0109 | IA.III.A.e.20 |
| Khotan (Jigda-kuduk) | Kh.0110–0111 | IA.III.A.e.8–17 |
| Khotan (Jigda-kuduk) | Kh.0112 | IA.III.A.e.21 |
| Khotan (Jigda-kuduk) | Kh.0113 | IA.III.A.e.8–17 |
| Khotan (Jigda-kuduk) | Kh.0114 | IA.III.A.e.18 |
| Khotan (Jigda-kuduk) | Kh.0115–0116 | IA.III.A.e.8–17 |
| Khotan (Jigda-kuduk) | Kh.0117 | IA.III.A.e.22 |
| Khotan (Jigda-kuduk) | Kh.0118 | IA.III.A.e.19 |
| Khotan (Jigda-kuduk) | Kh.0119–0121 | IA.III.A.e.8–17 |
| Khotan (Lachin-ata) | Kh.0122–0124 | IA.III.A.f.10–12 |
| Khotan (Lachin-ata) | Kh.0125–0131 | IA.III.A.f.1–8 |
| Khotan (Lachin-ata) | Kh.0132 | IA.III.A.f.9 |
| Khotan (Lachin-ata) | Kh.0133 | IA.III.A.f.1–8 |
| Khotan (Kalalik) | Kh.0134 | IA.III.A.g.10 |
| Khotan (Kalalik) | Kh.0135–0142 | IA.III.A.g.1–8 |
| Khotan (Kalalik) | Kh.0143 | IA.III.A.g.9 |
| Khotan (Bash-kumat) | Kh.0144 | IA.III.A.h.13 |
| Khotan (Bash-kumat) | Kh.0145–0156 | IA.III.A.h.1–12 |
| Khotan (Bash-kumat) | Kh.0148–0150 | IA.III.A.h.1–12 |
| Khotan (Bash-kumat) | Kh.0151 | IA.III.A.h.14–24 |
| Khotan (Bash-kumat) | Kh.0152 | IA.III.A.h.1–12 |
| Khotan (Bash-kumat) | Kh.0153–0154 | IA.III.A.h.14–24 |
| Khotan (Bash-kumat) | Kh.0155 | IA.III.A.h.1–12 |
| Khotan (Bash-kumat) | Kh.0157–0161 | IA.III.A.h.1–12 |
| Khotan (Bash-kumat) | Kh.0162–0168 | IA.III.A.h.14–24 |
| Khotan (Kizil-yar) | Kh.0169–0172 | IA.III.A.i.2–9 |
| Khotan (Kizil-yar) | Kh.0173–0175 | IA.III.A.i.10–21 |
| Khotan (Kizil-yar) | Kh.0176–0180 | IA.III.A.i.10–21 |
| Khotan (Kizil-yar) | Kh.0181–0182 | IA.III.A.i.2–9 |
| Khotan (Kizil-yar) | Kh.0183–0186 | IA.III.A.i.10–21 |
| Khotan (Kizil-yar) | Kh.0187–0188 | IA.III.A.i.2–9 |
| Khotan | Kh.0202 | IA.III.A.j.7–24 |
| Khotan | Kh.0202.a | IA.III.A.j.6 |
| Khotan | Kh.0203–0204 | IA.III.A.j.4–5 |
| Khotan | Kh.0205–0206 | IA.III.A.j.1–3 |
| Khotan | Kh.0207–0209 | IA.III.A.j.7–24 |
| Khotan tatis | Kh.0210.a | IA.III.A.k.1–11 |
| Khotan tatis | Kh.0210.b | IA.III.A.k.12 |
| Khotan tatis | Kh.0211 | IA.III.A.k.1–11 |

| Provenance | Stein no. | BM no. |
|---|---|---|
| Khotan | Kh.0212–0242 | IA.III.A.l.1–31 |
| Khotan | Kh.0267.b | IA.III.A.l.55 |
| Khotan | Kh.0267.c | IA.III.A.l.32–54, 56–58 |
| Yotkan | Kh.0268.a | IA.III.A.m.1–300 |
| Yotkan | Kh.0268.b | IA.III.A.m.301 |
| Yotkan | Kh.0268.c | IA.III.A.m.302 |
| Khotan | Kh.040 | IA.III.A.a.8–9 |
| Khotan | Kh.041–044 | IA.III.A.a.3–6 |
| Khotan | Kh.045 | IA.III.A.a.1 |
| Khotan | Kh.046 | IA.III.A.a.7 |
| Khotan | Kh.047 | IA.III.A.a.2 |
| Khotan | Kh.047.b | IA.III.A.a.8–9 |
| Khotan | Kh.048 | IA.III.A.b.1 |
| Khotan (Mr Moldovack) | Kh.050 | IA.III.c.1–8 |
| Khotan (Mr Moldovack) | Kh.052–054 | IA.III.c.1–8 |
| Khotan (Mr Moldovack) | Kh.055? | IA.III.c.9 |
| Khotan (Mr Moldovack) | Kh.056–058.a | IA.III.c.1–8 |
| Khotan | Kh.057 | IA.III.A.c.10 |
| Khotan (Arka-kuduk and Kumat) | Kh.061–062 | IA.III.A.d.7–10 |
| Khotan (Arka-kuduk and Kumat) | Kh.063–064 | IA.III.A.d.1–6 |
| Khotan (Arka-kuduk and Kumat) | Kh.065–066 | IA.III.A.d.7–10 |
| Khotan (Arka-kuduk and Kumat) | Kh.067–069.a | IA.III.A.d.1–6 |
| Khotan/Yotkan | Kh/Y | K.Y.1–39 |
| Khadalik | Kha.ii | S.VII.a.1–88<br>S.VII.b.1–14 |
| Khadalik | Kha.vi | S.VII.c.1 |
| Khan-oi | Khan-oi 01–02 | IA.I.a.1–2 |
| Khotan, purchased at | Khotan .0098 | S.IV.C.f.1–5 |
| Khotan, purchased at | Khotan.001–002 | S.IV.C.c.1–5 |
| Khotan, purchased at | Khotan.0026, 0029–0031 | S.IV.C.d.1–27 |
| Khotan, purchased at | Khotan.0074, 0084 | S.IV.C.e.1–2 |
| Khotan, purchased at | Khotan.0097 | S.IV.C.k.1–38 |
| Khotan, purchased at | Khotan.01.y | S.IV.C.a.1–14 |
| Khotan (Yurung Kash, east of) | Khotan.01–0045 | S.IV.D.a.1–142 |
| Khotan, purchased at | Khotan.04.a | S.IV.C.b.1–24 |
| Kohmari | Kohmari 010 | IA.III.A.q.1 |
| Kohmari | Kohmari 011 | IA.III.A.q.2 |
| Kohmari | Kohmari 09 | IA.III.A.q.3 |
| Khotan, purchased at | Ku.a–i | S.IV.C.i.1–10 |
| Kucha | Kucha 0100 | IA.XV.a.23 |
| Kucha | Kucha 0127–0131 | IA.XV.b.1–5 |
| Kucha | Kucha 0138–0143 | IA.XV.a.1–7 |
| Kucha | Kucha 086 | IA.XV.16–18 |
| Kucha | Kucha 087 | IA.XV.a.13–15 |
| Kucha | Kucha 088 | IA.XV.16–18 |
| Kucha | Kucha 089 | IA.XV.a.13–15 |
| Kucha | Kucha 090 | IA.XV.16–18 |
| Kucha | Kucha 091–094 | IA.XV.a.9–12 |
| Kucha | Kucha 095 | IA.XV.a.24 |
| Kucha | Kucha 096–098 | IA.XV.a.20–22 |
| Kucha | Kucha 099 | IA.XV.a.19 |
| Kucha | Kucha? | IA.XV.a.8 |
| Kurgan | Kurgan 01–03 | IA.I.b.1–3 |

| Provenance | Stein no. | BM no. |
|---|---|---|
| Loulan L.A. | L.A. | S.XI.A.a.1<br>S.XI.A.b.1<br>S.XI.A.c.1–125<br>S.XI.A.d.1–7<br>S.XI.A.e.1–7<br>S.XI.A.f.1<br>S.XI.A.g.1–29<br>S.XI.A.h.1–3 |
| Loulan L.A. (walled station) | L.A.0130 | IA.VI.B.b.33–54 |
| Loulan L.A. (walled station) | L.A.0148–0150 | IA.VI.B.b.1–29 |
| Loulan L.A. (walled station) | L.A.0151–0154 | IA.VI.B.b.33–54 |
| Loulan L.A. (walled station) | L.A.038–063 | IA.VI.B.b.1–29 |
| Loulan L.A. | L.A.064–065, 0135 | IA.VI.B.b.55–57 |
| Loulan L.A. (walled station) | L.A.077–089 | IA.VI.B.b.33–54 |
| Loulan L.A. (walled station) | L.A.I.01 | IA.VI.B.b.30 |
| Loulan L.A. (walled station) | L.A.VI.ii.018–019 | IA.VI.B.b.31–32 |
| Loulan L.A. | L.A.vii | S.XI.A.i.1–21 |
| Loulan L.A. | L.A.viii–ix | S.XI.A.j.1–17 |
| Lop desert site L.B. | L.B. | S.XI.B.a.1–3<br>S.XI.B.d.1 |
| Lop desert site L.B. | L.B.i–iii | S.XI.B.b.1–6 |
| Lop desert site L.B. | L.B.iv–v | S.XI.B.c.1–5 |
| Lop desert site L.C. (cemetery) | L.C.? | IA.VI.C.a.1–2<br>IA.VI.c.b.1–5 |
| Lop desert site L.D. | L.D.? | IA.VI.E.a.1–21 |
| Lop desert site L.E. (castrum) | L.E.? | IA.VI.D.a.1 |
| Lop desert site L.F. (mesa) | L.F.? | IA.VI.D.b.1–10 |
| Lop desert site L.G. | L.G.? | IA.VI.E.b.9–15 |
| Lop desert site L.G. | L.G.010 | IA.VI.E.b.8 |
| Lop desert site L.G. | L.G.012–014 | IA.VI.E.b.1–7 |
| Lop desert site L.I. | L.I. 021–022 | IA.VI.E.c.1–2 |
| Lop desert site L.J. | L.J.012 | IA.VI.E.d.1–50 |
| Lop desert site L.K. | L.K.? | IA.VI.A.a.1–3 |
| Lop desert site L.K. | L.K.? | IA.VI.A.a.7 |
| Lop desert site L.K. | L.K.017–018 | IA.VI.A.a.4–6 |
| Lop desert site L.M. | L.M.0125–0128 | IA.VI.A.b.1–6 |
| Lop desert site L.Q. | L.Q.03 | IA.VI.E.e.1 |
| Lal-tagh | L.tagh 026 | IA.I.e.1 |
| Luotuocheng | Lo-t'o Cheng 07, 08, 010, 013–015 | IA.IX.a.1–85 |
| Maral-bashi | M.bashi 04–05 | IA.I.d.2–3 |
| Maral-bashi | M.bashi 06 | IA.I.d.1 |
| Maral-bashi | M.bashi 07–08 | IA.I.d.4–5 |
| Miran | M.i | S.XIII.c.1–2 |
| Mazar-tagh site | M.tagh 018 | IA.II.a.1 |
| Mazar-tagh site | M.tagh 019 | IA.II.a.2 |
| Machi (Sistan) | Machi 091 | IA.XVII.b.1 |
| Machi (Sistan) | Machi 092? | IA.XVII.b.2 |
| Merdek-shahri | Mer.011 | IA.XVIII.a.1 |
| Ming-oi (north of Shorchuk) | Mi | S.XXII.g.1–2 |
| Ming-oi (north of Shorchuk) | Mi.i | S.XXII.a.1–4 |
| Ming-oi (north of Shorchuk) | Mi.x | S.XXII.b.1–14 |
| Ming-oi (north of Shorchuk) | Mi.xi | S.XXII.c.1–3 |
| Ming-oi (north of Shorchuk) | Mi.xii | S.XXII.d.1–7 |
| Ming-oi (north of Shorchuk) | Mi.xiv | S.XXII.e.1–2 |

| Provenance | Stein no. | BM no. |
|---|---|---|
| Ming-oi (north of Shorchuk) | Mi.xvii | S.XXII.f.1 |
| Niya | N.xii | S.VIII.a.1–2 |
| Niya | N.xiv | S.VIII.b.1 |
| Niya | N.xxiv | SVIII.c.1–3 |
| Nanhu | Nanhu | S.XIV.a.1–4<br>S.XIV.b.1–21<br>S.XIV.c.1–16<br>S.XIV.d.1–6<br>S.XIV.e.1–12 |
| Niya | Niya 020 | IA.V.a.1 |
| Pai-kash-i-Rustam (Sistan) | P.i.R.01 | IA.XVII.a.1 |
| Beiting | Pei-t'ing | IA.IX.a.86 |
| Rawak | R.002 | AK.VI.a.1–5 |
| Rawak | R.004 | AK.VI.a.1–6 |
| Sule He, south of | Su-lo Ho 02 | IA.VI.F.g.1 |
| Toghrak-akin | T.A.I.02 | IA.XVI.b.1 |
| Toghrak-akin | T.A.IV.01 | IA.XVI.c.5–20 |
| Toghrak-akin | T.A.IV.02 | IA.XVI.c.21–27 |
| Toghrak-akin | T.A.IV.03 | IA.XVI.c.1 |
| Toghrak-akin | T.A.IV.i.01–02 | IA.XVI.c.5–20 |
| Toghrak-akin | T.A.IV.i.012–015 | IA.XVI.c.5–20 |
| Toghrak-akin | T.A.IV.i.016–018 | IA.XVI.c.21–27 |
| Toghrak-akin | T.A.IV.i.019–023 | IA.XVI.c.5–20 |
| Toghrak-akin | T.A.IV.i.024 | IA.XVI.c.3–4 |
| Toghrak-akin | T.A.IV.i.03 | IA.XVI.c.2 |
| Toghrak-akin | T.A.IV.i.04–07 | IA.XVI.c.5–20 |
| Toghrak-akin | T.A.IV.i.08 | IA.XVI.c.3–4 |
| Toghrak-akin | T.A.IV.i.09–11 | IA.XVI.c.21–27 |
| Tunhuang *limes*, watch-tower on | T.iv.c | S.XV.a.1 |
| Tunhuang *limes*, watch-station on | T.vi.b | S.XV.b.1 |
| Tunhuang *limes*, watch-tower on | T.vi.c | S.XV.c.1 |
| Tunhuang *limes*, ruin on | T.xl.iii | S.XV.d.1 |
| Tunhuang *limes* | T.xiv | S.XV.e.1–2 |
| Tunhuang *limes* | T.xiv.v | S.XV.f.1–2 |
| Tunhuang *limes*, watch-station on | T.xl.b.01 | IA.VII.d.1 |
| Tunhuang *limes*, watch-station on | T.xl.c.06 | IA.VII.e.1 |
| Tunhuang *limes*, watch-tower on | T.xli.d.01 | IA.VII.f.1 |
| Tunhuang *limes*, watch-station on | T.xli.e.01 | IA.VII.g.1 |
| Tunhuang *limes* | T.xli.f Chiao. 02, 05–06 | IA.VII.h.2–3 |
| Tunhuang *limes*, watch-tower on | T.xli.f.025 | IA.VII.h.1 |
| Tunhuang *limes*, ruin on | T.xli.g.034 | IA.VII.i.1 |
| Tunhuang *limes*, watch-post on | T.xli.k.02 | IA.VII.j.1 |
| Tunhuang *limes*, station on | T.xli.l.03 | IA.VII.k.1 |
| Tunhuang *limes*, watch-tower on | T.xli.r.01 | IA.VII.l.1 |
| Tunhuang *limes*, watch-tower on | T.xliii.a.07 | IA.VII.m.1 |
| Tunhuang *limes*, watch-tower on | T.xliii.g.016 | IA.VII.n.1 |
| Tunhuang *limes*, station on | T.xliii.h.01 | IA.VII.o.1 |
| Tunhuang *limes*, tower on | T.xliii.i.05 | IA.VII.p.1 |
| Tunhuang *limes*, tower on | T.xliv.a.014 | IA.VII.q.1 |
| Tunhuang *limes*, watch-tower on | T.xliv.c. 08 | IA.VII.s.1 |
| Tunhuang *limes*, watch-tower on | T.xliv.c.02, 06 | IA.VII.r.1–2 |
| Tunhuang *limes*, watch-tower on | T.xxii.d.026 | IA.VII.a.1 |
| Tunhuang *limes*, watch-station on | T.xxiii.b.09 | IA.VII.b.1–2 |

| Provenance | Stein no. | BM no. |
|---|---|---|
| Tunhuang *limes*, watch-station on | T.xxiii.f.017 | IA.VII.c.1 |
| Tarishlak | Ta.i, ii | S.XXIX.a.1 |
| Toghrak-akin? | Toj.02 | IA.XVI.a.1–3 |
| Toghrak-akin? | Toj.I.i.02 | IA.XVI.a.1–3 |
| Toghrak-akin? | Toj.I.ii.02 | IA.XVI.a.1–3 |
| Toyuk | Toy.? | IA.XI.a.16 |
| Toyuk | Toy.? | IA.XI.a.18 |
| Toyuk | Toy.010 | IA.XI.a.14–15 |
| Toyuk | Toy.014–027 | IA.XI.a.19–32 |
| Toyuk | Toy.028 | IA.XI.a.17 |
| Toyuk | Toy.05 | IA.XI.a.13 |
| Toyuk | Toy.08 | IA.XI.a.11–12 |
| Toyuk | Toy.IV.02, 029–035, 012–013 | IA.XI.a.1–10 |
| Uzun-tati | U.Z.010 | IA.IV.b.17 |
| Uzun-tati | U.Z.011–012 | IA.IV.b.18–21 |
| Uzun-tati | U.Z.013–014 | IA.IV.b.22–23 |
| Uzun-tati | U.Z.015 | IA.IV.b.18–21 |
| Uzun-tati | U.Z.023–033 | IA.IV.b.1–13 |
| Uzun-tati | U.Z.035–036 | IA.IV.b.14–15 |
| Uzun-tati | U.Z.037 | IA.IV.b.18–21 |
| Vash-shahri | V.S.025 | IA.V.a.3 |
| Yotkan | Y.001 | AK.III.a.1–3 |
| Yotkan | Y.0025 | AK.III.b.1–2 |
| Yotkan | Y.0026 | AK.III.c.1–2 |
| Yotkan | Y.0027 | AK.II.a.1–81 |
| Yotkan | Y.005 | AK.III.h.1–2 |
| Yotkan | Y.006 | AK.III.l.1–5 |
| Yotkan | Y.007 | AK.III.i.1–4 |
| Kurgan, watch-station | Y.i.016 | IA.XIV.a.1 |
| Yar-khoto, ruined dwelling at | Y.k.i | S.XIX.a.1–105 |
| Yar-khoto, ruined shrine at | Y.k.iii | S.XIX.b.1–2<br>S.XIX.c.1 |
| Yingpan | Ying.i.05 | IA.XIII.a.1 |
| Yingpan | Ying.ii.018 | IA.XIII.a.2 |
| Yingpan | Ying.ii.04 | IA.XIII.a.3 |
| Yotkan (purchased Khotan) | Yo.00097? | S.IV.B.k.1–2 |
| Yotkan (purchased Khotan) | Yo.00102–00103 | S.IV.B.f.1–7<br>S.IV.B.l.1–13 |
| Yotkan (purchased Khotan) | Yo.00106 | S.IV.B.g.1–32 |
| Yotkan (purchased Khotan) | Yo.00108, 00123,<br>00128 | S.IV.B.h.1–6 |
| Yotkan | Yo.00124 | S.IV.A.d.1–10 |
| Yotkan (purchased Khotan) | Yo.00131 | S.IV.B.i.1–46 |
| Yotkan (purchased Khotan) | Yo.00132, 00137, 00155 | S.IV.B.j.1–25 |
| Yotkan | Yo.00136 | S.IV.A.e.1–48 |
| Yotkan (purchased Khotan) | Yo.0080 | S.IV.B.d.1–23 |
| Yotkan (purchased Khotan) | Yo.0085–0086 | S.IV.B.e.1–8 |
| Yotkan (purchased Khotan) | Yo.0086–0087? | S.IV.B.e.9–16 |
| Yotkan | Yo.0095 | S.IV.A.c.1–5 |
| Yotkan | Yo.0095 | S.IV.A.c.5 |
| Yotkan (purchased Khotan) | Yo.010 | S.IV.B.c.1–54 |
| Yotkan | Yo.012.e | S.IV.A.b.1–6 |
| Yotkan | Yo.0157.a | IA.III.A.n.1–10 |
| Yotkan | Yo.0157.b, c, e | IA.III.A.n.11–13 |

| Provenance | Stein no. | BM no. |
|---|---|---|
| Yotkan | Yo.0157.d | IA.III.A.n.14 |
| Yotkan (purchased Khotan) | Yo.03–04 | S.IV.B.a.1–15 |
| Yotkan (purchased Khotan) | Yo.06.g | S.IV.B.b.1–10 |
| Yotkan | Yo.3.a, b | S.IV.A.a.1–78 |
| Yulduz-bagh | Yul.085 | IA.XV.c.4–12 |
| Yulduz-bagh | Yul.086 | IA.XV.c.16–24 |
| Yulduz-bagh | Yul.087–089 | IA.XV.c.1–3, a–b |
| Yulduz-bagh | Yul.090.a | IA.XV.c.4–12 |
| Yulduz-bagh | Yul.090.b | IA.XV.c.13–15 |

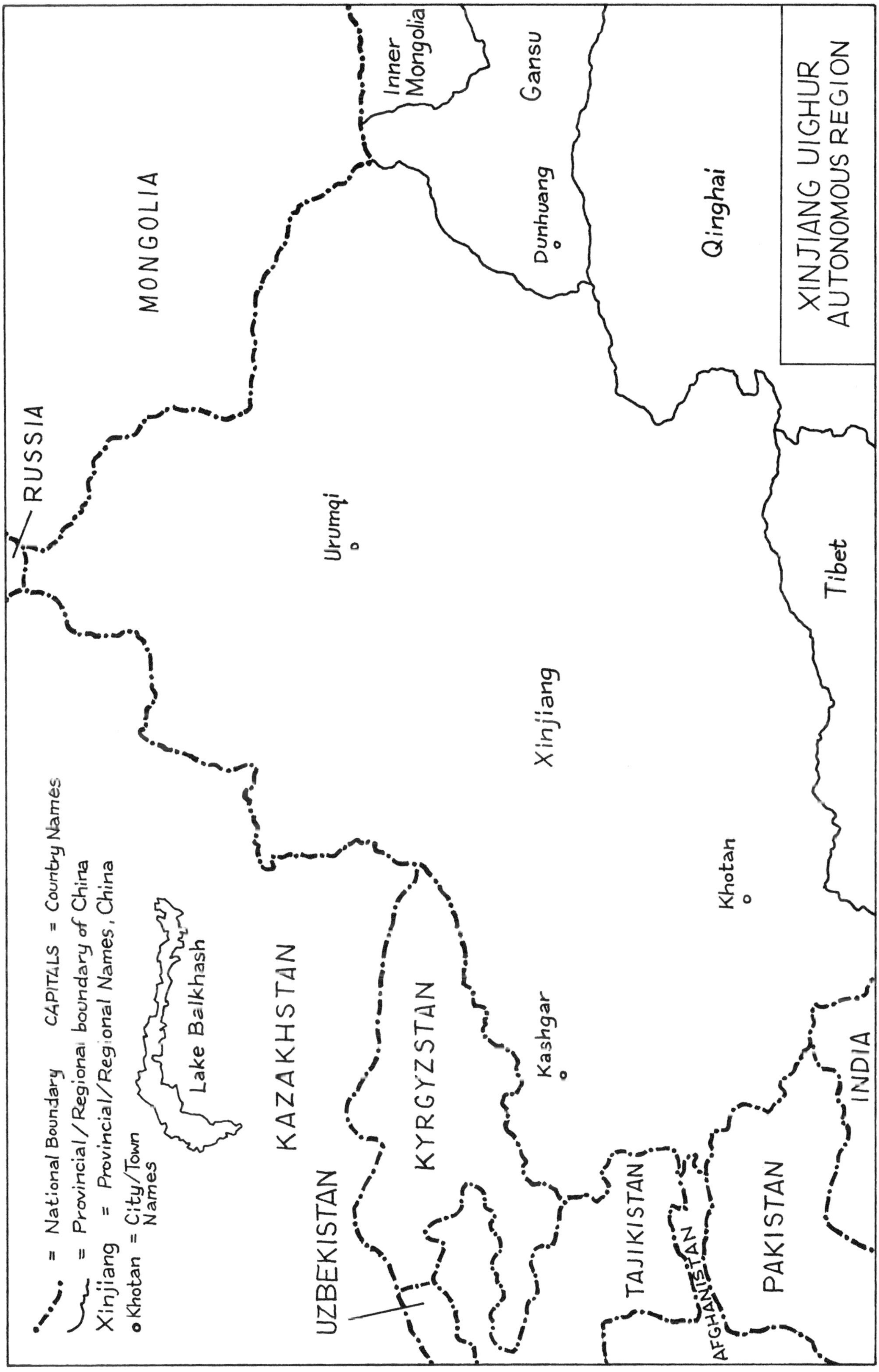
= National Boundary
CAPITALS = Country Names
= Provincial/Regional boundary of China
Xinjiang = Provincial/Regional Names, China
• Khotan = City/Town Names
XINJIANG UIGHUR AUTONOMOUS REGION
RUSSIA
MONGOLIA
Inner Mongolia
Gansu
Dunhuang
Qinghai
Urumqi
Xinjiang
Tibet
Khotan
Kashgar
Lake Balkhash
KAZAKHSTAN
KYRGYZSTAN
UZBEKISTAN
TAJIKISTAN
AFGHANISTAN
PAKISTAN
INDIA

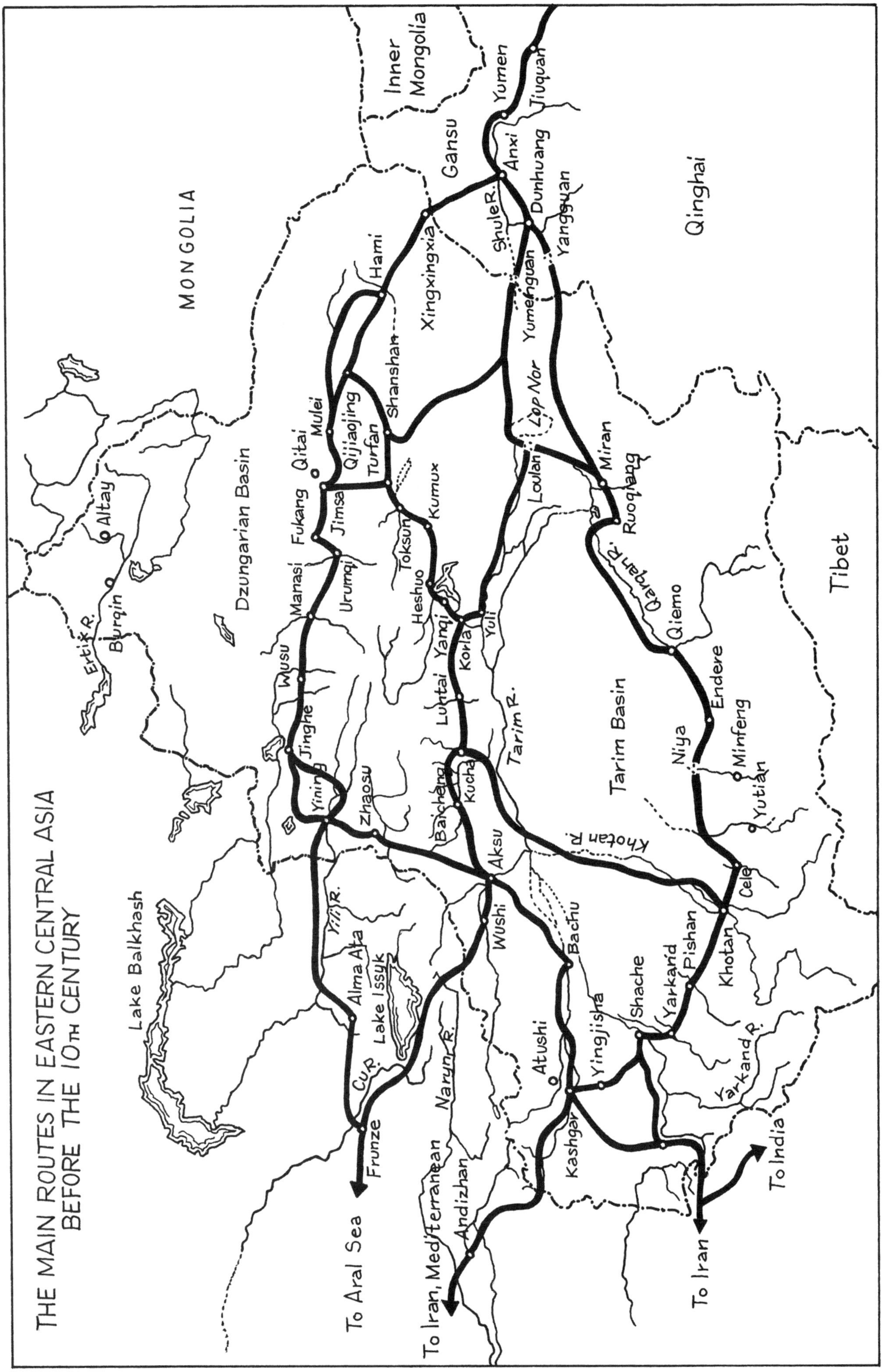
THE MAIN ROUTES IN EASTERN CENTRAL ASIA
BEFORE THE 10TH CENTURY
MONGOLIA
Inner Mongolia
Gansu
Qinghai
Tibet
Dzungarian Basin
Tarim Basin
Lake Balkhash
Lake Issyk
Ertix R.
Burqin
Altay
Qitai
Mulei
Hami
Xingxingxia
Anxi
Yumen
Jiuquan
Dunhuang
Shule R.
Yangguan
Yumenguan
Lop Nor
Loulan
Miran
Ruoqiang
Qarqan R.
Qiemo
Endere
Minfeng
Niya
Yutian
Cele
Khotan
Khotan R.
Pishan
Yarkand
Shache
Yarkand R.
Yingjisha
Kashgar
Atushi
Bachu
Wushi
Aksu
Baicheng
Kucha
Luntai
Tarim R.
Korla
Yanqi
Yuli
Heshuo
Toksun
Kumux
Turfan
Qijiaojing
Shanshan
Jimsa
Fukang
Urumqi
Manasi
Wusu
Jinghe
Yining
Zhaosu
Yili R.
Alma Ata
Cu R.
Frunze
Naryn R.
Andizhan
To Aral Sea
To Iran, Mediterranean
To Iran
To India

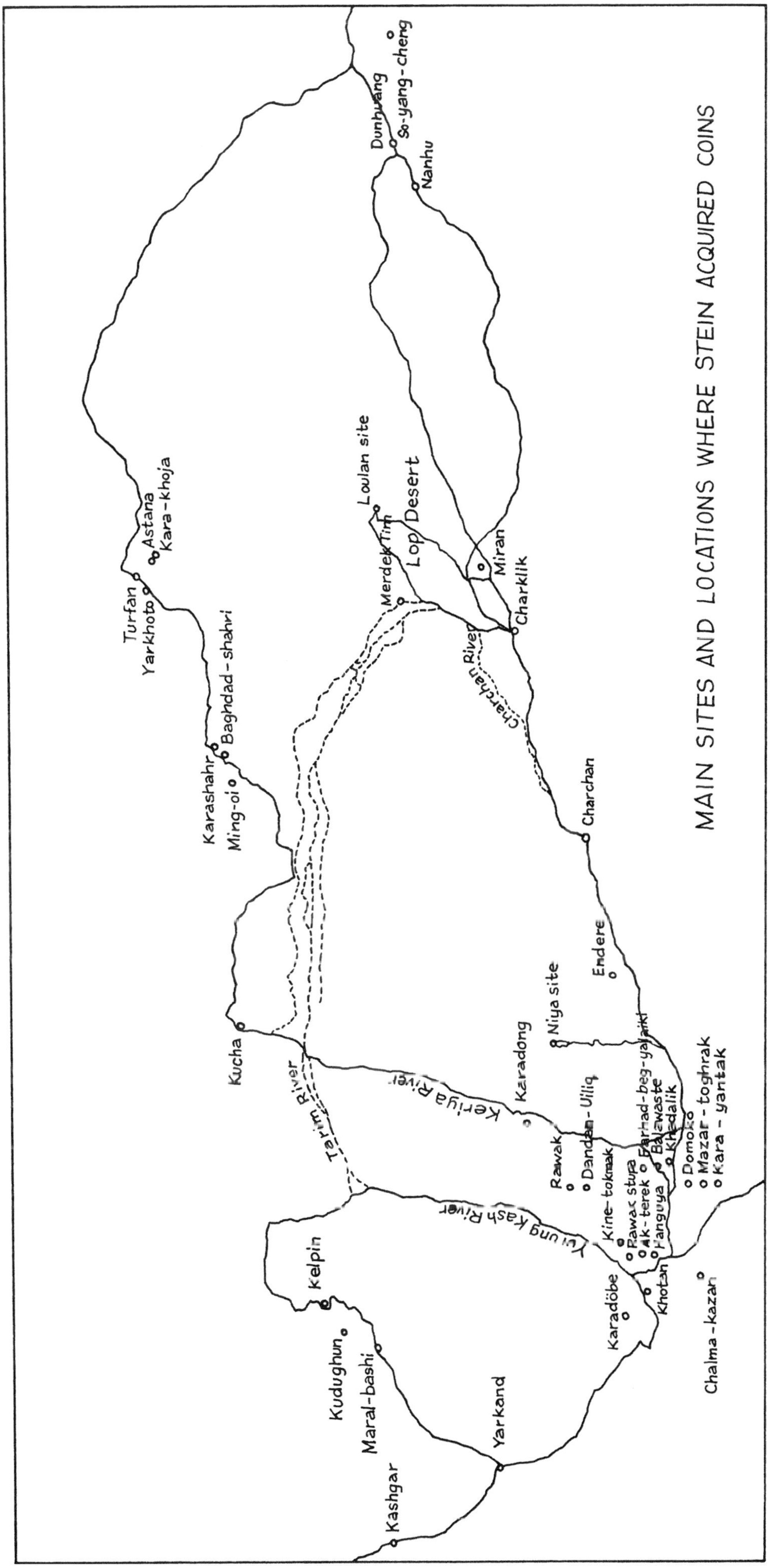
MAIN SITES AND LOCATIONS WHERE STEIN ACQUIRED COINS
Dunhuang
So-yang-cheng
Nanhu
Loulan site
Lop Desert
Merdek Tim
Miran
Charklik
Charchan River
Charchan
Turfan
Yarkhoto
Astana
Kara-khoja
Baghdad-shahri
Karashahr
Ming-oi
Endere
Niya site
Kucha
Karadong
Keriya River
Tarim River
Dandan-Uiliq
Rawak
Farhad-beg-yailaki
Balawaste
Khadalik
Domoko
Mazar-toghrak
Kara-yantak
Kine-tokmak
Rawak stupa
Ak-terek
Hanguya
Yurung Kash River
Kelpin
Karadöbe
Khotan
Chalma-kazan
Kudughun
Maral-bashi
Yarkand
Kashgar

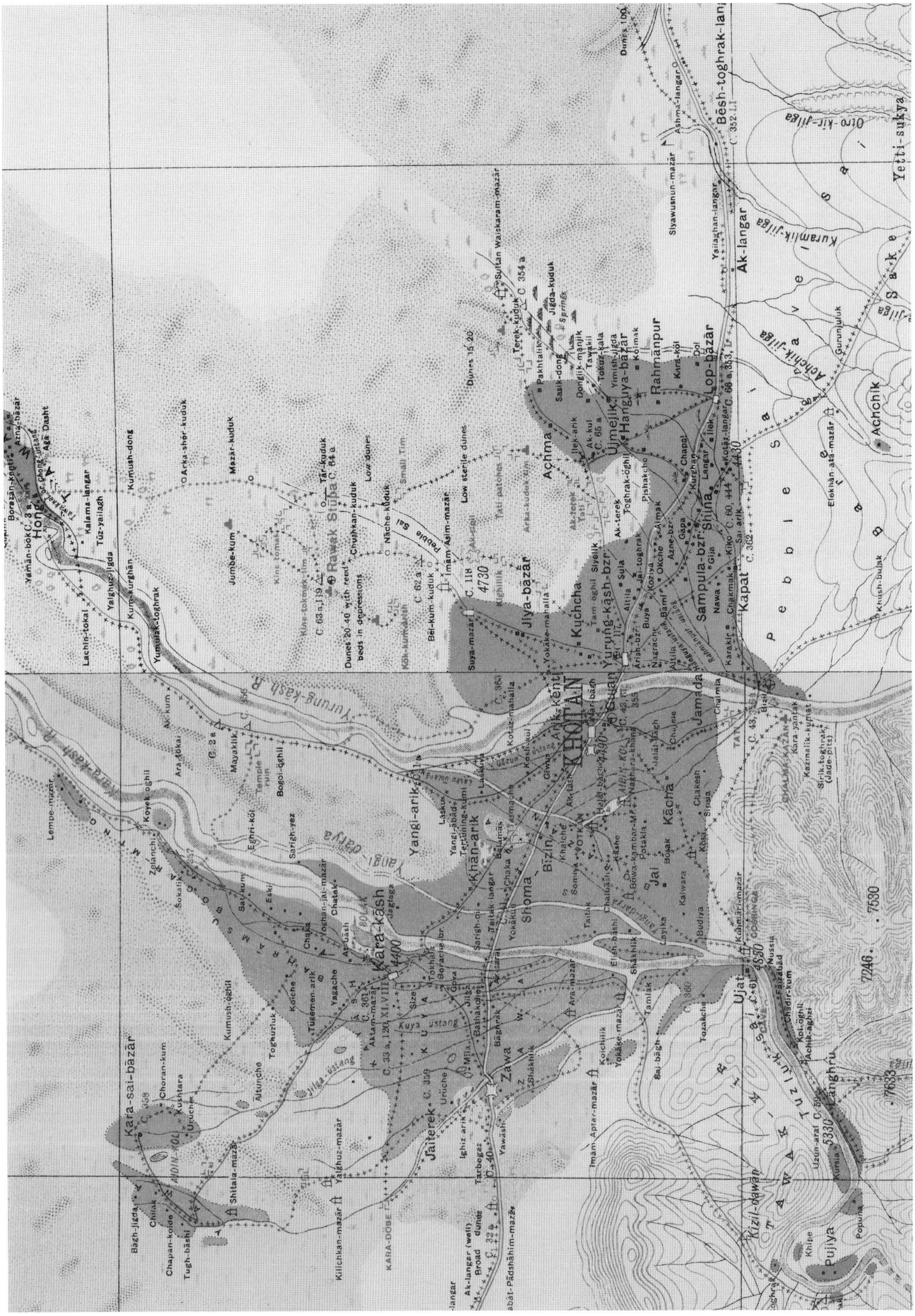
KHOTAN
Kara-kāsh
Yurung-kāsh-bzr
Jiya-bāzār
Kuchcha
Sampula-bzr
Lop-bāzār
Rahmanpur
Hanguya-bāzār
Achma
Ak-langar
Bēsh-toghrak-langar
Yangi-arik
Khān-arik
Shoma
Bizin
Jal
Kācha
Zawa
Jaiterek
Kara-sai-bāzār
Ujat
Pujiya
Achchik
Rawak Stupa
Yetti-sukya

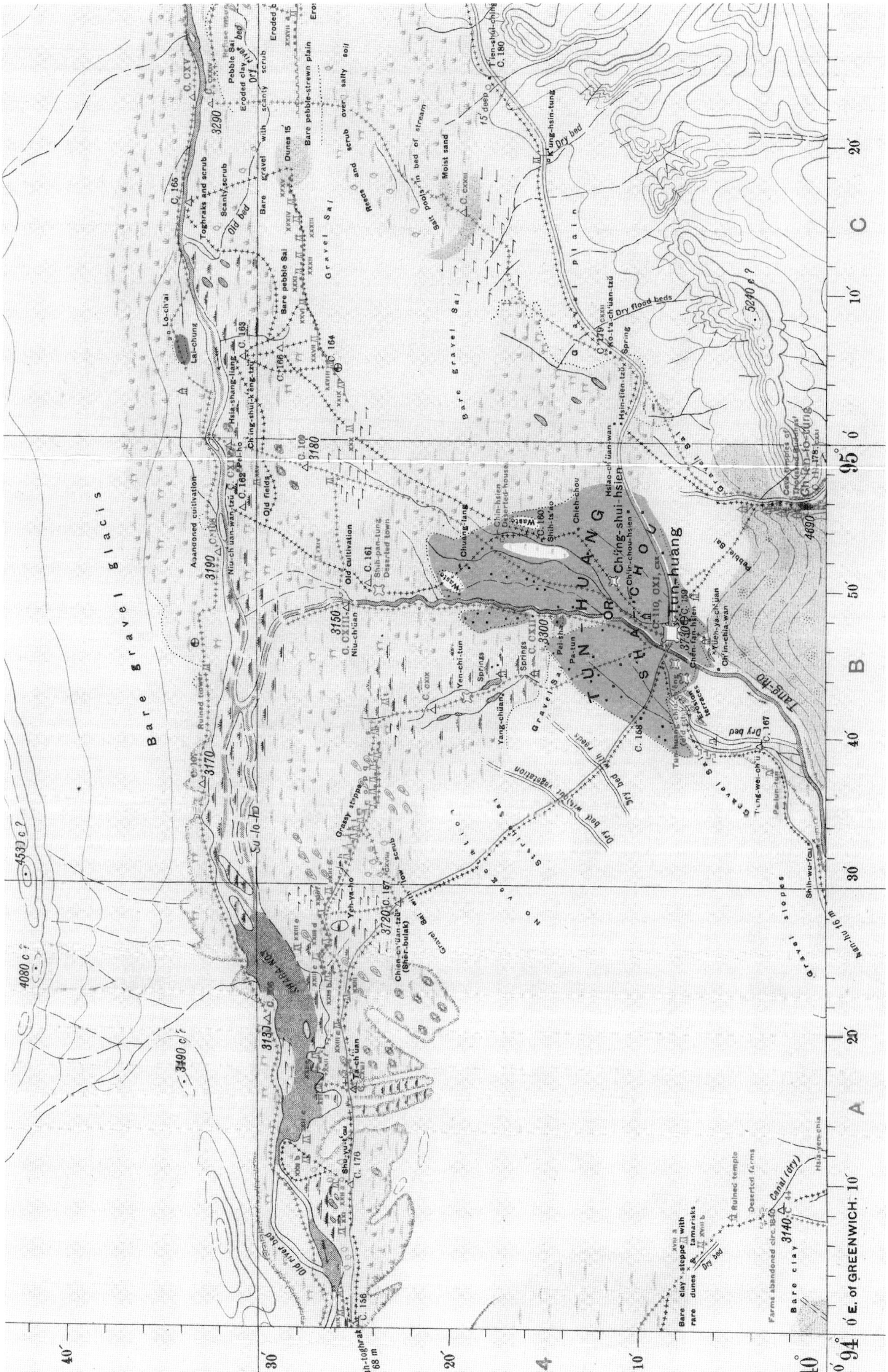
Bare gravel glacis
Su-lo-ho
Tun-huang
Ch'ing-shui-hsien
Ch'in-chou-hsien
Tang-ho
Yeh-ya-ho
Niu-ch'üan
Shih-pan-tung
Deserted town
Old cultivation
Abandoned cultivation
Ruined tower
Lai-chung
Lo-ch'ai
Hsia-shang-liang
Pei-ho
Toghraks and scrub
Scanty scrub
Old bed
Bare pebble Sai
Gravel Sai
Dunes 15
Bare pebble-strewn plain
Moist sand
Salt pools in bed of stream
Reeds and scrub
Dry bed
Dry flood beds
Spring
Springs
Yen-chi-tun
Yang-ch'üan
Grassy steppe
Chien-ch'üan-tzŭ
(Sher-bulak)
Shu-yu-tou
Bash-toghrak
68 m
Bare clay
Canal (dry)
Ruined temple
Deserted farms
Gravel slopes
Shih-wu-fou
Tung-wei-chu
Pa-tun
Pei-ta
Chuang-lang
Chieh-chou
Hsiao-ch'üan-wan
Hsin-tien-tzŭ
Ko-ta-ch'üan-tzŭ
K'ung-hsin-tung
Tien-shui-ching
Ch'ien-fo-tung
Cave temples of Thousand Buddhas
Yüeh-ya-ch'üan
Ch'in-chia-wan
Chen-fan-hsien
Pebble Sai
Terraces
Dry bed with reeds
Dry bed without vegetation
Bare gravel Sai
Eroded clay
Pebble Sai
Old river bed
Bare clay steppe with rare dunes & tamarisks
Farms abandoned circ. 1840
5240 c ?
4690
4533 c ?
4080 c ?
3490 c ?
3300
3290
3190
3180
3170
3150
3140
3133
3720
3730
40
40´
30´
20´
10´
10´
20´
30´
40´
50´
95°
94°
A
B
C
4
0´ E. of GREENWICH.

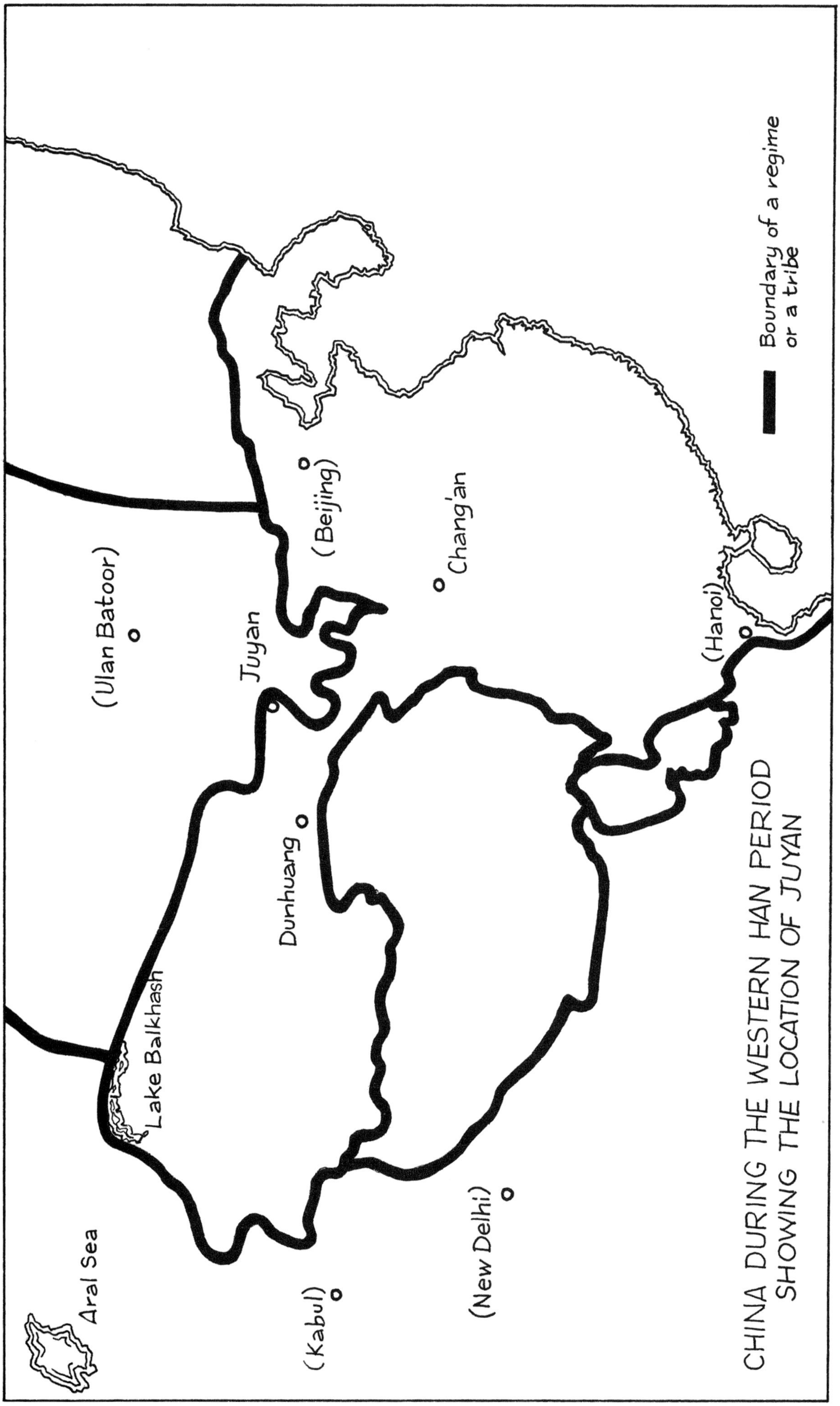
Boundary of a regime or a tribe
(Ulan Batoor)
Juyan
(Beijing)
Chang'an
(Hanoi)
Dunhuang
Lake Balkhash
Aral Sea
(Kabul)
(New Delhi)
CHINA DURING THE WESTERN HAN PERIOD
SHOWING THE LOCATION OF JUYAN

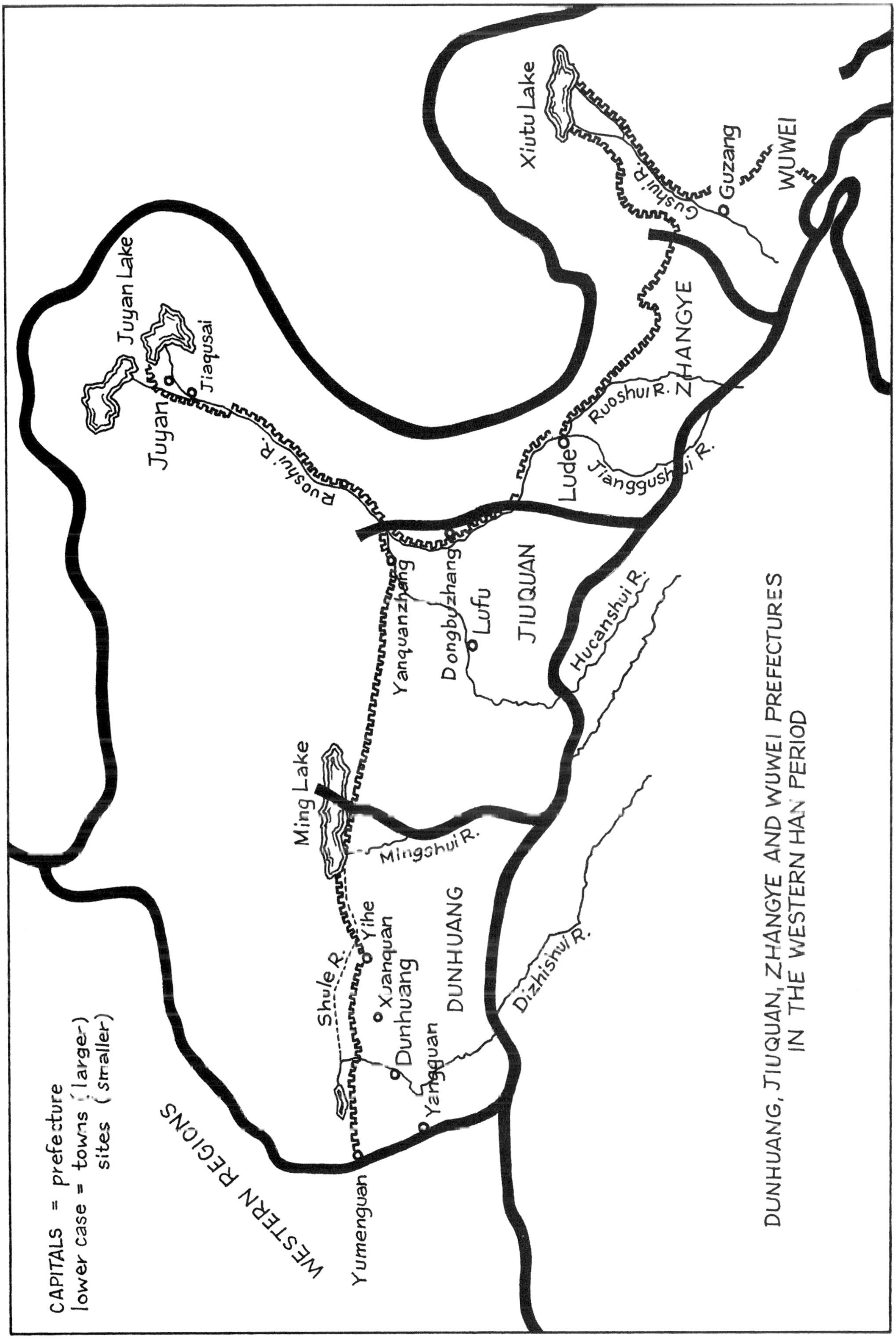


DUNHUANG, JIUQUAN, ZHANGYE AND WUWEI PREFECTURES IN THE WESTERN HAN PERIOD

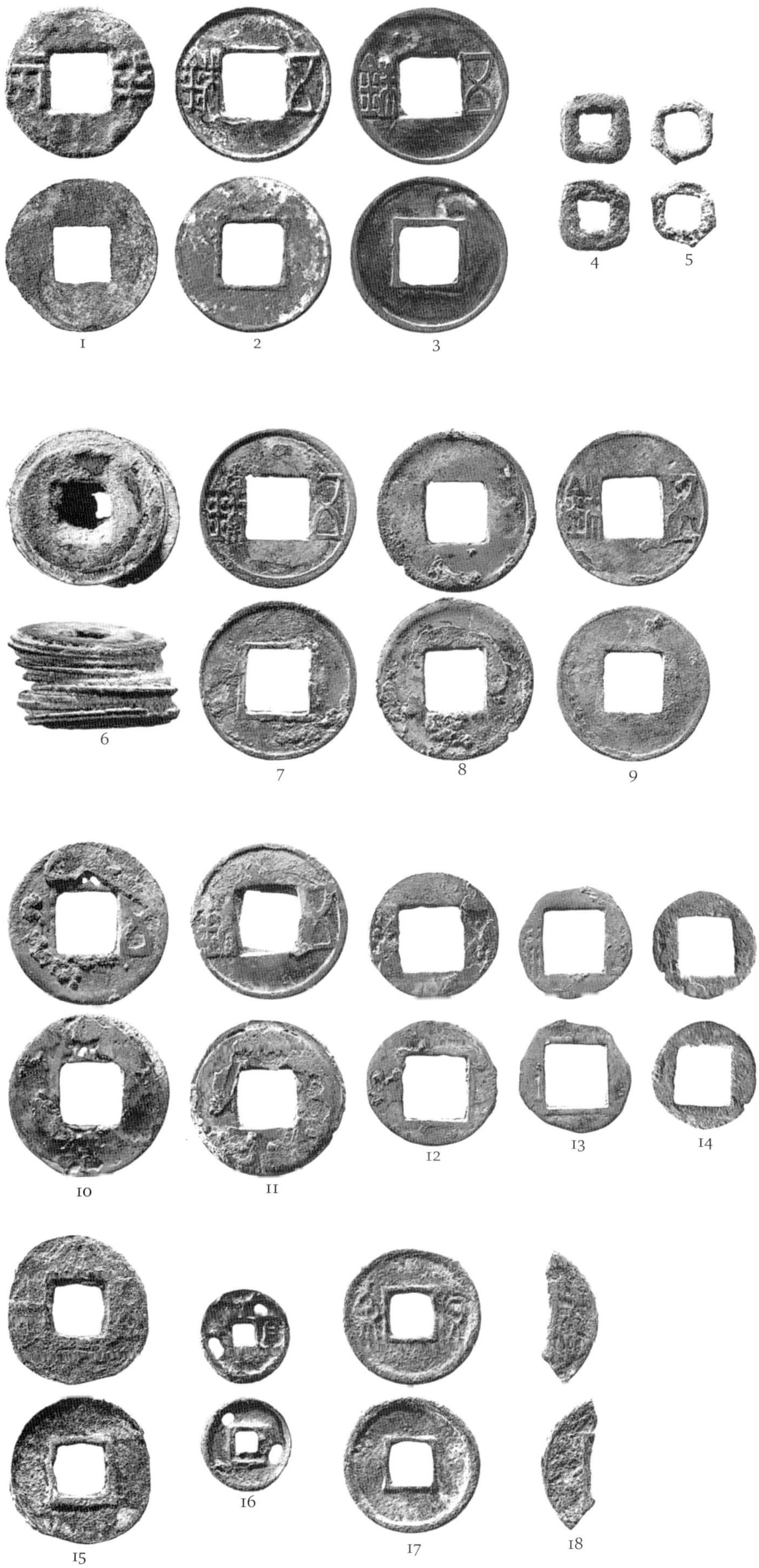
1
2
3
4
5
6
7
8
9
10
11
12
13
14
15
16
17
18

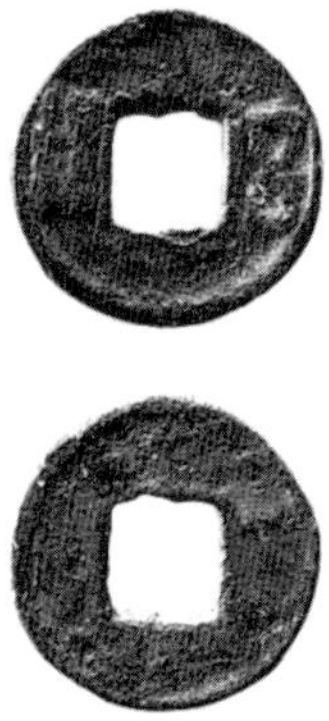

19

20

21

22

23

24

25

26

27

28

29

30

31

32

33

34

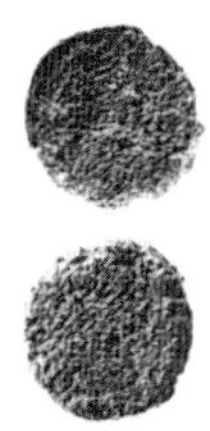
35

36

37

38

39

40

41

42

## PLATE 4

43

44

45

46

47

48

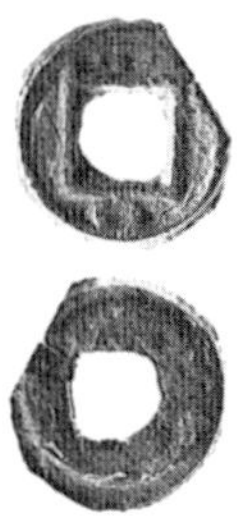
49

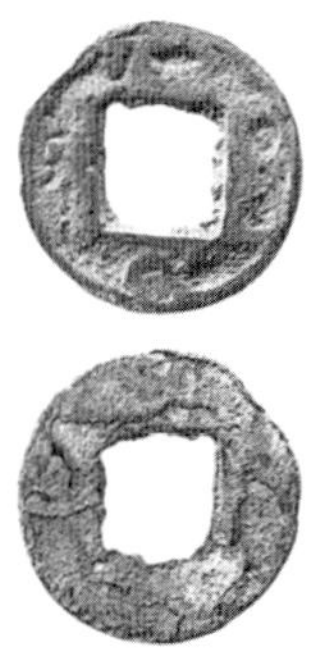
50

51

52

53

54

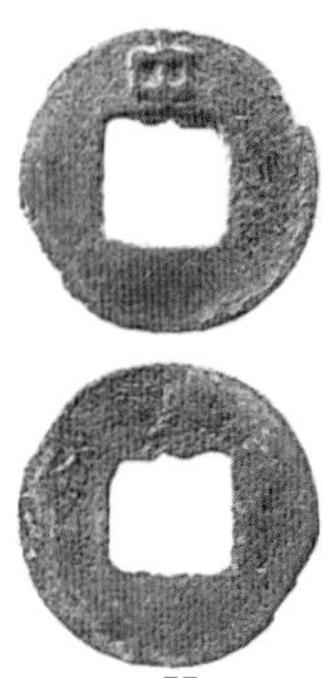
55

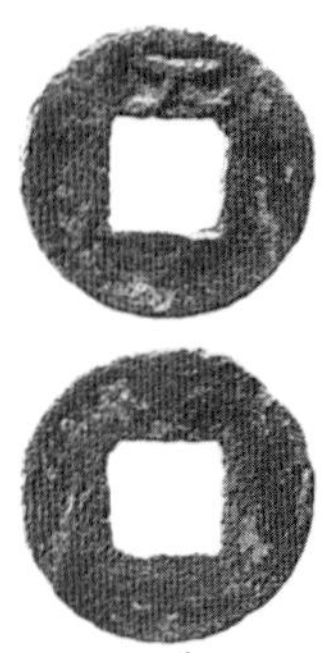
56

57

58

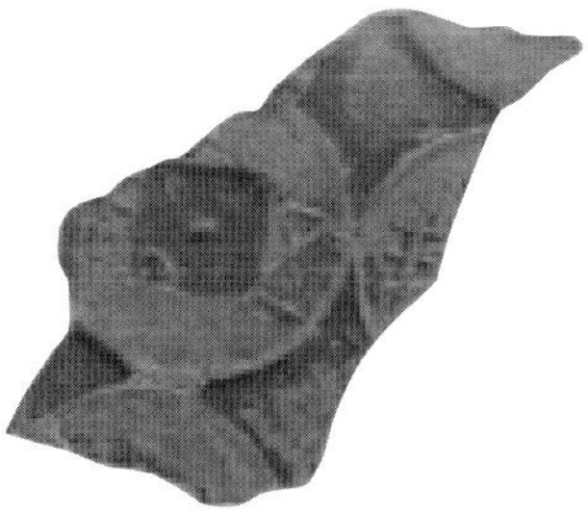

I

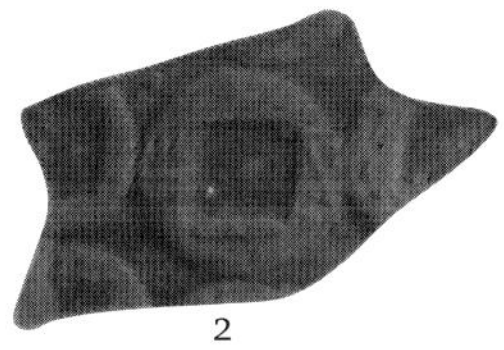

2

3

4

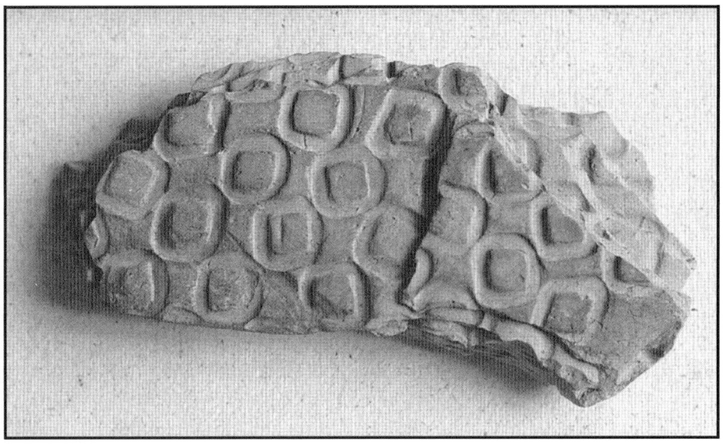

5

6

7

8

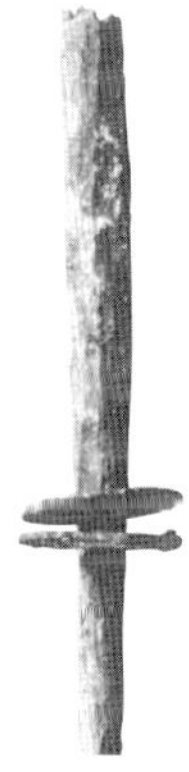

9

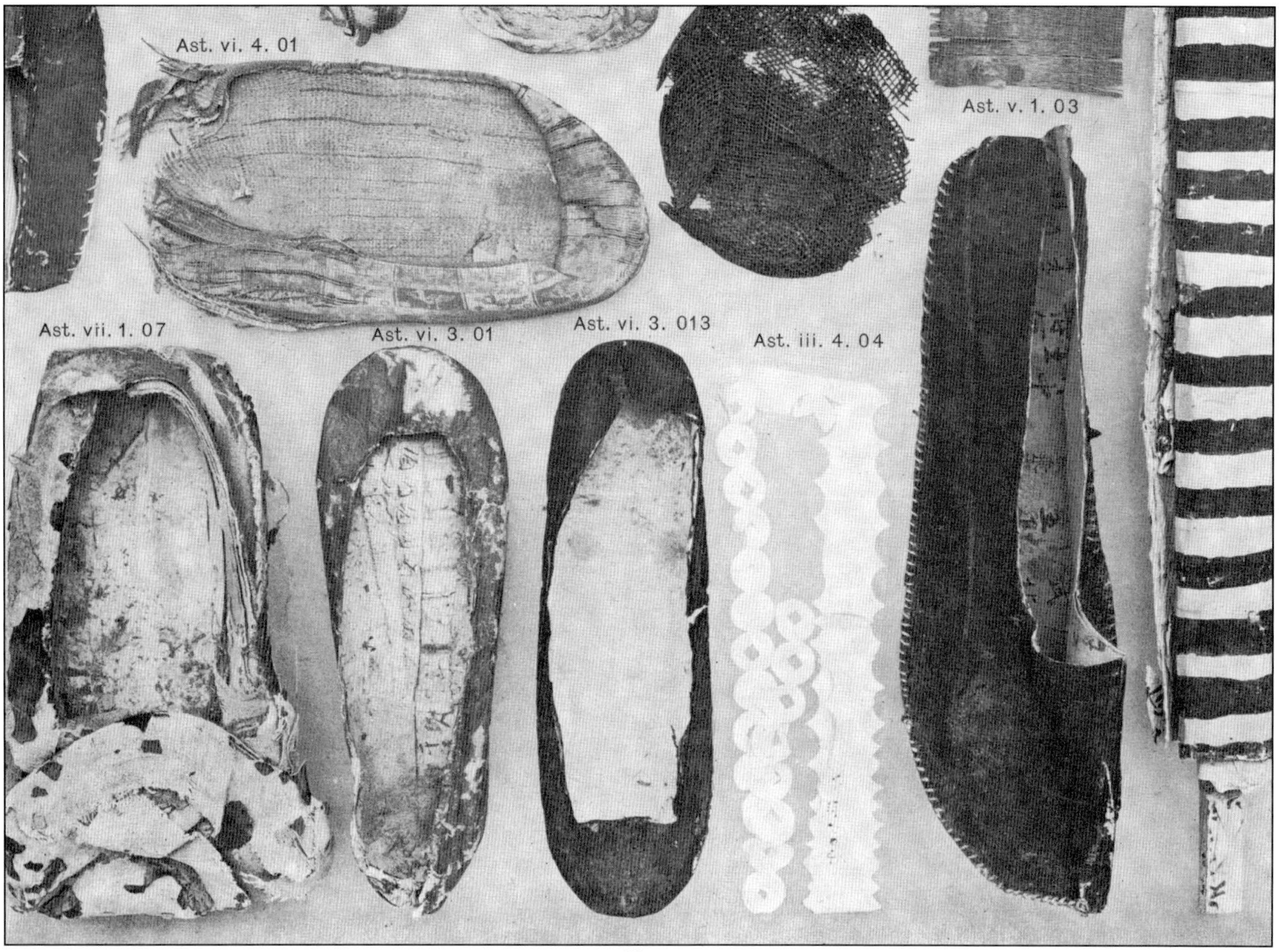
Ast. vi. 4. 01
Ast. v. 1. 03
Ast. vii. 1. 07
Ast. vi. 3. 01
Ast. vi. 3. 013
Ast. iii. 4. 04

10

# Index